Strategies for Teaching Students With

Special Needs

Methods and Techniques for Classroom Instruction

Kathleen M. McCoy
Arizona State University

LOVE PUBLISHING COMPANY®
Denver • London • Sydney

For my parents Vi and R. E. McCoy

and my family,

Tim, Elizabeth, and Patrick,

and

to all the master teachers in the schools.

Published by Love Publishing Company
P.O. Box 22353
Denver, Colorado 80222
www.lovepublishing.com

Library of Congress Catalog Card Number 2007933546

Copyright © 2009 by Love Publishing Company
Printed in the United States of America
ISBN 978-0-89108-328-3

Contents

12 Social Aspects of Inclusion: Preparing Students for Life   511

Tables

Figures

Preface

In a way, inclusion of all students in the general education setting is found in the lyrics of the song, "Everything old is new again!", but the newness of inclusive teaching and learning goes far beyond the one room school house. The advent of fresh teaching strategies and the use of technology have provided teachers with opportunities and time to differentiate instruction in a way our former teachers and mentors had never dreamed. *Strategies for Teaching Students with Special Needs* is intended to describe methods and techniques for differentiating instruction in the general education setting. Strategies presented in this text intentionally blur the distinction between and within categories of children with special needs and emphasize the act of learning for all children.

The types of strategies presented in this text are directed toward teachers, general and special, who provide educational services to children in the least restrictive setting. The strategies are simple, direct and in most cases able to be used at various levels for all children in the classroom with minor accommodations.

Strategies and methods presented in this text are centered on the general education curriculum. Teachers can use these strategies to help them assist their students to achieve their learning goals. *Strategies for Teaching Students with Special Needs* addresses more than academics. For children to be truly included in classroom activities, teachers need to facilitate their success in academic and social experiences in the schools and community. Although one chapter, "Social Aspects of Inclusion: Preparing Students for Life," is devoted entirely to the topic of social inclusion, many of the chapters have integrated the concept of social inclusion into academic instruction.

The author of this book has had extensive education and direct experience working in inclusive settings. The material in this text is reality based with direct links to research perspectives. The educational strategies and practices are real, with an emphasis on practical and efficient guidelines for what to do to meet the needs of 25 widely divergent students. The premise of this text is that teachers want to provide the best possible education for their students. This text provides simple and powerful descriptions of instructional activities which accommodate teachers' passion for instructing their students while simultaneously staving off teacher burnout. Strategies and techniques are designed with accommodations as integral aspects of instruction, not as add-ons or extras.

The text begins by providing a context for the inclusive movement and its impact on teachers and students. Next, the book proceeds to describe the evolution of categorization from attempts to classify learners in specific and discrete categories to the broader and more encompassing designations of high- and low-incidence disabilities, including the needs of children found on the Autism Spectrum Disorder. Just as definitions and categories have been refined, so have the practices and concepts in federally mandated IEPs. IDEA '04 has continued to erase the boundaries between general and special education teachers.

Because the target audience is teachers, the text provides many suggestions and examples of how to conduct meaningful assessment. Classroom based informal assessment guides teachers to make data based decisions supported with observational evaluation to provide each student with the most appropriate educational experiences based on curricular expectations. The chapter also directs teachers to assess social as well as academic needs of learners found in the general education classroom.

Specific informal evaluation techniques focusing on basic skill areas are also found in this text, for example, "Reading Evaluation in Inclusive Settings" and "Mathematics Evaluation in Inclusion Settings". Each of these chapters has a companion methods chapter, "Reading Methods in Inclusion Settings" and "Mathematics Instruction in Inclusion Settings." Throughout all chapters, but especially those dealing with evaluation and methods, runs the theme of the importance of language and how to accommodate for special communication skills of learners. The literacy/language relationship as well as the impact of communication is developed throughout the chapters in the text.

Informal assessment data is only useful if the teachers can manage to use the data. The chapter "Classroom Management: Building Schedules, Routines, and Instruction Formats" provides direction for the "how to" nuts and bolts needs of teachers who are responsible for educating 25–30 young minds. One of the major keys to successful inclusive classrooms is found in the organizational skills of teachers.

This text is designed for practicing teachers and for those teachers to be who will be working with the diverse population found in 21st century schools. Information in this text is founded on a solid theoretical framework that facilitates instructional delivery in an inclusive setting. The emphasis of this text is proactive in adapting the curriculum to meet the needs of students and to support teachers to provide the best possible education for their students.

Acknowledgments

The author acknowledges the role of Stephan Isaacson in the conceptualization of an earlier version of the literacy section of this book and to Virginia Usnick for her insights into the world of mathematics. Special thanks go to Carrie Watterson for untold hours of editing, and of course to Stan Love, a publisher without parallel, who has always supported my writing efforts. I am particularly indebted to Stan Dyer for his insights into technology. I am grateful to my coauthors Rebecca Gehrke, J'Anne Ellsworth, and Kathleen Danielson for their contributions to their chapters. Finally, special thanks to Jean Lee, a good friend and a great teacher.

CHAPTER

1

Mainstreaming and Inclusion Movements

KEY TERMS

- collaboration
- inclusion
- Individuals with Disabilities Education Act (IDEA)
- least restrictive environment (LRE)
- mainstream
- normalization
- regular education initiative (REI)
- trait theory

The social studies class in Ms. Rodriguez's class has been underway for about 20 minutes. George, Francesca, and Elizabeth are busy working on their class project. George is drawing a picture representing the main idea of today's lesson. Francesca is working with her partner, Elizabeth, as they dictate their responses on the computer. At another table, Mr. Samuels is assisting Amy and Roxanne in generating a story web for their social studies report. Which child has special needs? They all do. Which child needs to be served through special education? They all do. Which child needs to be in a general education setting? They all do.

Least Restrictive Environment

Scenes like this one occur every day in general education classrooms throughout the United States. Hundreds of children with special needs are returning to general education classrooms or are never leaving the general education setting at all. Hehir (1999) reported that between the 1987–88 and 1992–93 school years, the number of students with disabilities educated in general education classrooms for more than 80% of the school day increased from 1.3 million to more than 2.4 million. In the 1997–98 school year, the Twenty-Second Annual Report to Congress on Implementation of the Individuals with Disabilities Act reported that 46.97% of all students with disabilities between the ages of 3 and 21 were served in general education classes 80% or more of the day (Office of Special Education, 2000).

Officially, the exodus of many children with disabilities from special classes began on November 29, 1975, with passage of Public Law 94-142, the Education for All Handicapped Children Act. The Education for All Handicapped Children Act (EHA), now the Individuals with Disabilities Education Act (IDEA 1991), guarantees all students with disabilities a free appropriate public education and has continued mandating this promise with the successive amendments to P.L. 101-476 (1990; 1997; 2004). Through these acts, Congress declared that every child with a disability has an inalienable right to be educated in the educational setting most appropriate for that child. Furthermore, Congress specified that the most appropriate setting is one that can be described as the "least restrictive environment (LRE)."

Attempts to comply with this act form what is called the mainstreaming movement. General education classes in which children with disabilities participate are called mainstream rooms. A key feature of a mainstream room is that the group of children taught in the room is intentionally heterogeneous. Physical, emotional, and intellectual differences are recognized and respected but are neither diminished nor emphasized.

Prior to 1975, more than half of the children with disabilities in the United States either were institutionalized or did not receive appropriate educational services (Lance, 1976). Significant reforms in special education have resulted from EHA. Two of the most dominant reform trends have been directed toward achieving more social and, to a lesser extent, academic integration of students with severe disabilities and the education of students with milder disabilities in general education classrooms (Sailor, 1991). These two reforms reduce pull-out programs, such as self-contained settings and resource rooms, and emphasize settings that include children with mild and severe disabilities in the general education classroom. Over time, most children with disabilities will be integrated into general education classrooms, and these classrooms will become mainstream rooms or full-inclusion classes.

Congress periodically reviews IDEA as it does all mandated acts. In the mid-90s, Congress again demonstrated support for a national commitment to educating students with disabilities in the least restrictive environment. Thus, EHA and the 1997 amendment to IDEA both stipulate that children with special needs are to be provided with access to the general education curriculum (Morocco, 2001).

IDEA '97 is the signal that not only is the general education classroom the starting place for delivery of special services, but the general education curriculum must be accessible to children with special needs. Deviations from the general curriculum may not occur unless it is not meeting the needs of the child (O'Shea, Stoddard, & O'Shea, 2000). IDEA '97 also emphasizes the participation of students with disabilities in state and local assessments (Turnbull, Rainbolt, & Buchele-Ash, 1997).

Inclusion

Full inclusion, inclusion, inclusive schooling, inclusive education, and *progressive inclusion* are terms that have emerged from the mainstreaming movement. These terms are 1990s buzzwords referring to the increase in numbers and proportions of students who receive special services while attending general education classes (Reynolds, Wang, & Walberg, 1992). The changes required in the various federal revisions of EHA and IDEA continue to require that students with disabilities be educated in general education classes to the maximum extent possible, clearly making way for full inclusion.

The difference between mainstreaming and inclusion is sometimes confusing. The easiest way to separate inclusion from mainstreaming is to think about initial placement decisions. Mainstreaming takes students who are not functioning well in general education classes and places them in special settings until they are able to function academically and socially in such a setting. Inclusion, on the other hand, evaluates the school setting by placing students with special needs in general education classrooms as an initial placement (Bradely, King-Sears, &

Tessier-Switlick, 1997). If the initial placement turns out not to be in the best interest of the child, then consideration is given to placing the child in some type of special education setting for part or all of the day.

The rate at which children with disabilities are being included in general classrooms is the subject of much debate. Although the concept of inclusion has consistently been examined over the years, some fundamental problems persist. For example, preparing beginning and veteran teachers for the task of educating students with disabilities in the general classroom, that is, inclusion, has become a challenging goal (Shade & Stewart, 2001), and in some instances has been questioned as a viable practice for students with special needs (Zigmond, 2001). Inclusion is based on the following key principles:

- A "zero reject" model (i.e., no child is excluded).
- Students receive education at neighborhood schools with same-age peers.
- Children with disabilities are placed in general education at a rate equal to prevalence statistics.
- General educators assume primary responsibility with special education support.
- Classroom experiences are designed to develop relationships and social development. (Simpson, 1996, p. 205–206)

Changing Roles of Educators

Central to implementation of full inclusion are the teachers who are being asked to provide instruction to this broad range of students. General educators are teaching children who have a wider range of needs. Special educators are being asked to provide support to general educators in the general education classroom. Although legislation, judicial decrees, and advocacy pressure can place all children in the general education classroom, the success of educating the children there depends largely on the beliefs and behaviors of the children and teachers in those classrooms. Political and ideological support for inclusion is steadfast, but the reality of general education suggests that the essential attitudes and implementations of accommodations and adaptations for students with disabilities continue to need refinement (Kavale, 2002).

Since the mid-90s, educational inclusion of students with disabilities has been widely endorsed, resulting in an ever-growing number of students with disabilities receiving all or most of their educational services in general education classrooms (Mastropieri & Scruggs, 2000). Inclusion requires special education support services to be provided in the general education classroom setting (Idol, 1997). The general educators' willingness to include students with special needs in their classes is critical to the successful implementation of inclusive educational practices (Soodak, Podell, & Lehman, 1998). Although many general education teachers agree with inclusion on a philosophical level, they express reservations on a practical level, citing a lack of sufficient time, training, and resources (Scruggs & Mastropieri, 1996).

IDEA and its associated mandates require that students with disabilities be educated in the least restrictive environment. As a result, the instructional focus has been directed toward the inclusion of students with disabilities in general education classrooms with access to the general education curriculum (Treder, Morse, & Ferron, 2000).

Students with disabilities educated in the general education classroom will be exposed to the higher level thinking processes that are requisite for understanding the material found in the general education curriculum. In order to profit from the general education curriculum, students with disabilities will need to be exposed to authentic tasks, cognitive strategies, social mediation, and constructive conversation (Morocco, 2001).

Authentic Tasks

Students with disabilities will need to learn how to apply their prior knowledge to the content found in the general education setting. Students will need to learn how to ask questions appropriately, and learn how to gather, organize, interpret, and synthesize information they have found. To ensure genuine learning experiences, teachers will need to assist students in using higher level thinking processes as they engage in constructing knowledge from the general education curriculum.

Providing access to general education tasks will require, at minimum, format changes that accommodate identified special learning needs; for example, basic reading, writing, and arithmetic knowledge may be missing in the student's range of skills. Teachers will need to provide accommodations or modifications in the general education curriculum in order for some students to be able to access the content. Teachers will need to consider alternative modalities, such as supplementing or replacing written materials with films, photographs, or oral histories. They will need to consider teaching students how to use technology to access the general education curriculum (Zhao & Frank, 2003). Depending on the student's special needs, teachers will need to accommodate or change the instructional format in the general education setting for many students with disabilities.

Cognitive Strategies

Students with and without special needs must think and act when planning, completing, and evaluating performance on an assigned task. The generic term most often use to describe this process is *cognitive learning strategy*. Cognitive learning strategies are the students' ways of monitoring themselves as they apply techniques or rules that help them acquire, integrate, remember, and retrieve information across a variety of settings or situations. Cognitive learning strategies help students remember basic learning strategies such as those found in mnemonics or keywords for sequences. See chapter 2 for a discussion of mnemonic devices.

In the case of the order of operations for mathematics, a cognitive strategy would help students monitor their own memory. The popular mnemonic "Please Excuse My Dear Aunt Sally" reminds the budding mathematician to work the problems in parentheses first, then the exponents, followed in sequence by multiplication, division, addition, and, finally, subtraction. Students might ask themselves what word comes after aunt? or, have I included all the words in the sentence? Cognitive strategies teach more than study skills or memory tricks. Cognitive strategies are habits designed to promote self-monitoring. Teachers will need to teach students how to monitor their own learning strategies within the general education curriculum. Teachers will need to identify the strategies that are most related to success and also be able to teach them to their students in a meaningful way (Ellis & Lenz, 1996).

Social Mediation

If students with special needs are to be successful in the general education setting, teachers will need to guide the social interaction of some of their students. Teachers will need to design partnerships between and among students that encourage them to share their thought processes with each other when they are working on projects or activities.

Teachers will need to guide their students to learn how to build knowledge collaboratively to work on problems that call for a variety of viewpoints. If the students with and without disabilities are to share the ownership of an activity or project, they also must be encouraged to talk to one another or to make their thinking clear to one another, perhaps through talking or visual representations or materials or dramatic enactments (Morocco, 2001). Teachers will need to design strategies of instruction that can teach their students how to work with one another in the general education setting while taking into account the needs of special students.

Constructive Conversation

Collaborative work in the general education classroom typically requires communication exchanges involving conversation. Students with special needs must be able to ask and answer questions if they are to survive and flourish in the general education setting. Often initiating conversation or answering a question is seen as a high-risk activity. The answer may be incorrect or other students in the class may laugh at the question. Such risks are particularly challenging for students with disabilities, who may process information more slowly or not have the prior knowledge to respond correctly.

Creating a warm and nurturing environment is the first step that a teacher must take in order to encourage constructive conversation, but such an environment is not sufficient to encourage the kind of question asking and response demands found in the general education classroom. Constructive conversation skills will also have to be taught, reviewed, reinforced, and retaught (if necessary). Teachers will need to specify and prompt expected question and answer behaviors relative to the general education curriculum and classroom. Teachers will also need to provide practice times within the context of the general education setting and curriculum for some children with special needs to participate fully in the intellectual exchange of the general education classroom.

Successful inclusion can only occur when general and special education teachers share possession of the skills necessary to meet the needs of students with disabilities in the general education classroom (Klinger & Vaughn, 2002). In the best of all possible situations, both the special and the general teacher must be experts in teaching students with disabilities and at the same time understand the requirements of the general education curriculum and various teaching approaches. Access to the general education curriculum is perhaps the most important consideration in recent IDEA amendments (Council for Exceptional Children [CEC], 1998).

Teachers in inclusive settings face many challenges. Some of the most obvious challenges include (a) scheduling students and teachers, (b) finding mutual planning time for general and special educators, (c) personality compatibility between general and special education teachers, (d) compatibility between general and special education instructional methods and philosophies, and (e) sufficient administrative support.

Collaboration and Co-teaching

As more and more students with disabilities are educated in the general education classroom, the inclusion model that is most popular is *co-teaching* or *collaboration* between special education teachers and general education teachers (McLeskey, Henry, & Axelrod, 1999). Like collaboration, co-teaching is defined as a situation in which two or more teachers, usually one general educator and one special educator, share physical space in order to actively instruct a blended group of students consisting of children with special needs and children without special needs. Co-teaching holds the promise of making a wider range of instructional alternatives available than in classrooms where instruction is provided by only one teacher. In addition, co-teaching is based on the premise that the participation of students with disabilities as full classroom members is enhanced and that their performance improves as a result of participating in the general education classroom (Cook & Friend, 1996).

Research Evidence

In 1999, 40 articles were identified that discussed co-teaching or team teaching. Of these 40 articles, only 12 reported empirical research. The results of a review of these articles suggest that teachers were generally reporting favorable attitudes toward the various forms of teaming, but little information is available about whether or not students were performing academically and socially to their potential (Welch, Brownell, & Sheridan, 1999). The effects of co-teaching appear to be inconsistent and, in many cases, insufficiently documented (Weiss & Brigham, 2000). In fact, the research base for co-teaching is virtually nonexistent (Zigmond, 2001).

Issues Related to Inclusion Models

Teacher Preparation

Ensuring that educators are skilled to work with students with disabilities in general education classrooms and curricula is fundamental to the legal mandates and education reform movements of the last decade (McLaughlin, 1999).

Providing a free public education for all children and youth with disabilities in inclusive settings poses unique challenges to general education systems as well as to those who provide supportive services, such as special education and compensatory education programs. To complicate matters further are the increasing demands of federal legislation to raise the academic bar as well as related measurement issues, such as high-stakes testing and determining schools' accountability through student performance. Teachers are also faced with an increasing number of students identified as at risk who are being asked to change from segregated special education classes to more inclusive settings (Riggs & Mueller, 2001).

As a growing number of students with disabilities receive general education services, questions arise over whether educators working with these students have the necessary instructional qualifications. Thus, undergraduate preservice general educators and experienced general educators have voiced concerns about the appropriateness of the general education classroom for serving the needs of students with disabilities (Hobbs & Westling, 1998; O'Shea et al., 2000). Inclusion, while accepted on a theoretical basis, requires meaningful planning and cooperation between general and special educators. Care must be taken that inclusion becomes synonymous with the least restrictive environment; however, the least restrictive environment is not always the general education classroom.

Education

Studies suggest continuing resistance to educating students with disabilities in the general education classroom. Teachers who have completed coursework in special education as part of their training programs typically have more positive attitudes toward inclusion than teachers who have not taken such coursework (Chung, 1998). Without sufficient resources to implement appropriate educational services, attitudes, like silver without appropriate polishing, tarnish rapidly when faced with the realities of today's society. Individual teachers will most likely find the majority of support within the repertoire of strategies and techniques they have developed through preservice and inservice educational programs focusing on classroom-based instruction. Acceptance or resistance seems to be related to teachers' knowledge base and experiences. Teachers who are prepared to work with children with disabilities are more positive about including these children in their classrooms (Cook, Tankersley, Cook, & Landrum, 2000).

Professional preparation programs for general and special educators need to include a large knowledge base that focuses on the types of instructional and social issues teachers and their students face in the least restrictive environment. Instructional tools and strategies for addressing these issues may or may not include the support of or collaboration with special educators.

Preparing general education teachers to work with a diverse student body may solve part of the issue of successful inclusion, which incorporates accommodations and instructional options. Rather than focus on feelings and legislation related to the educational needs of children with disabilities, a stronger focus on individual planning, curriculum alignment, and cooperative learning must be a part of initial preparation or continuing professional development programs for general and special educators (Sabornie & deBettencourt, 2004). Differentiation of instruction in the general education classroom clearly needs to become an integral part of any general education preparation program.

In light of prevailing class sizes, teacher resources, and the special needs of students with disabilities, special education teacher preparation programs also need some reality-based adjustments to meet the challenge of inclusion. Typically, programs designed for special educators focus on teaching to the individual's needs through carefully tailored objectives based on research data. Although the content matter of the curriculum must be the same for students receiving special education services as that for all students, sometimes this curriculum must be presented in special ways using different texts, different examination techniques and pacing, as well as different grading standards (Zigmond, 2001).

Teacher education programs for special educators place a high priority on consultation with general educators, a theoretically promising practice. However, special education teachers and general education teachers are very busy people. Each has defined roles and responsibilities in providing services to a child with disabilities as defined by the individualized education program (IEP) team. What these educators do not appear to have is sufficient time, energy, and resources to allow for the type of consultation and collaboration that is needed if they are going to assume joint responsibility for a student with disabilities. Many special educators are discovering that they will spend less than two hours per week in individual instruction with their students (CEC, 2000). Provision of mini-lessons, simulations, or presentation of relatively short tasks designed specifically for practice in applying new skills, and providing students with special needs tasks that engage them in extended reading, talking, or writing are skills expected of special educators, but because of the limited amount of time special educators spend in a general education classroom, the techniques will most likely be delivered by the general educator. The intensity and goal-directed nature of special education training may not be the best preparation for working with students or consulting with the general education teacher, who is responsible for the education of a student with special needs for all or part of the day in the general education setting.

Inclusion models demand teacher education reform. The current models of consultation and collaboration need to be adapted to work with the expectations that are placed on general and special educators (Klinger & Vaughn, 2002). The notion of least restrictive environment must also be reassessed in light of another other important federal clause found in IDEA, which is to provide a free appropriate public education to students with disabilities.

Peer Acceptance and Social Skills

Placing children with disabilities in the general education classroom affects not only them and their teachers but other students in that setting as well. Peer contact plays a major role in school-aged children's understanding of self and others (Berk, 2002). Often, but not always, children with disabilities obtain lower social preference, are less likely to be popular, and tend to be socially neglected or rejected, even when initially accepted (Kuhne & Weiner, 2000). Some students with disabilities have limited knowledge of appropriate social skills. Some are not very adept at initiating and maintaining positive relationships with their peers or their teachers (Kerr & Nelson, 2002). They do not know how to contribute successfully in a classroom or how to cope effectively in social situations (Wood, 2002). Systematic encouragement is necessary to foster positive attitudes toward children with disabilities. Programs designed specifically to teach peers to accept classmates with disabilities have shown positive gains in student acceptance (Siperstein & Leffert, 1999).

Programs as varied as teaching social skills to students with disabilities, teaming low-achieving students with popular peers, and viewing films showing students integrating across settings have all been shown to increase acceptance among peers. To help breach attitudinal barriers, other programs have used role-playing to expose students to "disabilities," puppets to depict vignettes and lead discussions, and the wide spectrum of children's literature depicting children with disabilities (Hazel, Schumaker, Sherman, & Sheldon, 1995; Sargent, 1998).

When social skills issues are relatively mild, the general education teacher can be expected to provide techniques to help students develop appropriate social behavior (Friend & Bursuck, 2002). Instruction in social skills is appropriate for all students in the general education classroom, not just those with special education needs. Teaching common courtesy, respectful interactions, managing conflict, and generally exhibiting good will toward all class members are part of the general education teacher's role. By modeling appropriate behavior, establishing classroom rules, and incorporating problem-solving and self-monitoring techniques into the classroom, the general education teacher is teaching social skills that are beneficial to all students.

Another teaching approach used for developing social skills in the general education setting focuses on schoolwide application, rather than on individual classroom application. Schoolwide systems create a sense of consistency relative to behavioral expectations. Children are taught to identify and practice acceptable behaviors and to reduce unacceptable actions. Schoolwide programs often center on behavioral principles to produce socially and culturally acceptable behavior, and they can be perceived more as a disciplinary approach rather than a proactive instructional technique focusing on individual social skill needs of students (Gagnon & Leone, 2002).

If, on the other hand, the social skill level requires more formal intervention, most likely a special education teacher or counselor will provide social skill instruction in settings outside the general education classroom (Sabornie & deBettencourt, 2004). Many of these programs also focus on learning to get along with others. Success in developing social skills in such programs depends on the skill level of the teachers, degree of support needed by the student, and the time available for instruction.

Self-Concept

During the school years, children with and without disabilities begin to develop a self-concept through social comparisons. They begin to judge their appearance, abilities, and behavior in relation to their peers, with younger children comparing themselves to one other student whereas older children compare themselves to multiple peers (Butler, 1998). Self-esteem remains relatively high for students whose cognitive levels are similar to those of preschoolers, but students with normal or slightly below normal intelligence adjust to a more realistic level. During the first few years of elementary school, self-esteem declines as children become more aware of themselves as members of a group, but self-esteem begins to rise for most children as they achieve goals (Marsh, Craven, & Debus, 1998).

Strong relationships exist between everyday behavior and self-esteem. For example, academic self-esteem influences willingness to learn new tasks, athletic prowess encourages children to participate in physical activities, and high social self-esteem is related to popularity. Some students with disabilities, however, do not develop high self-esteem in one or more of these areas, or in any area, and even when successful they usually attribute their success to some external factor. Children with poor self-concept often do not feel pride associated with success because they attribute their success to some outside factor, such as luck (McInerney, 1999).

Children with disabilities also must come to terms with the social/emotional impact of having a disability. Many individuals with disabilities go through several stages when coming to terms with their issues:

a) Becoming aware of their *differentness* from their peers
b) Attempting to identify what is *wrong* or *different* with them
c) Acquiring an understanding of the limits imposed by their disability and seeking help or compensation
d) Adapting responses to minimize weakness and maximize strengths
e) Accepting the condition (Higgins, Raskind, Goldberg, & Herman, 2002)

The degree to and rate at which students deny or accept these stages will have a marked impact on how successful they will be in an inclusive setting.

Factors Contributing to the Inclusion Movement

Several factors have contributed to the current notion of inclusion. Impetus for the inclusion movement comes from the normalization principle, disillusionment with special class placement, special education reform efforts, administrative concerns, and dissatisfaction with the process by which children are identified and labeled. Each factor has made a unique contribution to the inclusion movement.

Normalization

The Scandinavian Experience

Historically, the roots of EHA and IDEA began in Scandinavia during the mid-1960s (Bank-Mikkelsen, 1969). A principle embodied in the term *normalization* emerged from the Scandinavian experience in providing services to people with mental retardation. The principle emphasized providing children and adults with retardation with experiences that approximate, as closely as possible, the experiences of typical society. Applications of the normalization principle include living in community-based homes rather than in large institutions; experiencing the normal rhythms of the year, complete with holidays, birthdays, and other special days of personal significance; and wearing age-appropriate clothing.

In the United States, proponents and some parent advocate groups have expanded the normalization principle to view a person's life satisfaction, worth, and personal competence as products of involvement with activities that are culturally normative. This position reflects a commitment to full inclusion. By the mid- to late-1980s, advocacy for, and in some places actual experimentation with, integration of students with severe and profound disabilities into general education classrooms began on a partial or full-time basis (Mesibov, 1990; Sailor, 1991; York, Vandercook, Macdonald, Heise-Neff, & Caughey, 1992).

Individual Experiences

Normalization is both culture- and person-specific. Even though the celebration of holidays is universal, many cultural differences are apparent in the manner in which the same holiday is observed. For example, in the United States the new year is met with confetti and paper hats, while in China the new year is met with much pageantry and dignity. The normalization principle asserts that people with disabilities should be allowed to celebrate the new year in the way that is common to the culture of their country or cultural group. Thus, a pupil in Akron, Ohio, should be granted a chance to blow horns and throw confetti, and a pupil in China should be allowed to observe the dragon miracle.

Goals of Normalization

The normalization principle also suggests that services and activities for people with disabilities should be as integrated as possible in the goals and methods of delivery (Wolfensberger, 1972). In addition, the principle suggests that, whenever possible, the social, vocational, and life goals of the person with disabilities should approximate the goals of the mainstream population. In general, they must be integrated into society as well as possible. The physical context in which a person with disabilities will receive services may be a sheltered workshop, a ward in a hospital, a public school classroom, or even the natural home. Choice of a setting is related to the nature and extent of the handicapping condition. Promising results of research indicate that including even students with severe disabilities in the general education classroom can be perceived positively by general and special educators, as well as by most of the children's classmates (York et al., 1992).

Normalization also implies social acceptance of the person with disabilities and stresses the value of human dignity for all persons, with or without disabilities. The soundness of the philosophical intent of the normalization principle is difficult to question. Normalization provides the catalyst for the least restrictive service alternatives in educational settings for children with disabilities.

In addition, normalization has an important and often overlooked component. Normalization means that persons with disabilities, whether mild, moderate, or severe, have a voice about issues that affect them. Controlling and patronizing behaviors of persons without disabilities toward those with disabilities flies directly in the face of normalization. Persons with disabilities have the right to make personal decisions. Therefore, children and adults with disabilities should not be marginalized or excluded from making personal choices relative to their life, liberty, and pursuit of happiness in their home, school, or community. They are the decision makers for their own destiny (Johnson, 1998).

Disillusionment with Special Class Placement

Having established that all children and youth with disabilities have the right to receive a free appropriate public school education, many students receive special education services for part or all of their school day in the general education classroom. However, the practice of inclusion and other kinds of classroom placements have yet to demonstrate conclusively the most appropriate service delivery for students with special learning needs or where it should take place (Horn & Tynan, 2001; LaMare & de la Ronde, 2000). Thus, no concrete evidence exists to establish that the academic and social needs of pupils with disabilities are better served in special education settings than in general education classes. Respected professionals in special education have questioned the large-scale placement of children with special needs in special education classes or pull-out classes as the primary educational environment over a decade (Bulgren & Carta, 1993; Ysseldyke, Algozzine, & Thurlow, 1992).

Special education class placement is extremely expensive. Yet, in the minds of many, special education placements seem to make no significant educational contribution to increasing graduation rates and may even contribute to unnecessary segregation practices with children of color (Lovitt & Cushing, 1999; Williams, 2001; Young, 2002). Meanwhile, legislation, such as the No Child Left Behind Act of 2001, has mandated the unreasonable expectation of grade-level academic achievement for many students receiving special education services, thus adding fuel to the fire of discontent with the effectiveness of special education programs.

Although academic performance is vital to school success, the quality of children's lives also is important. Opponents of inclusion have argued that quality of life will be enhanced if the child with a disability is separated from children without disabilities. Such arguments are based on the belief that the unique needs of many children with disabilities are not tolerable to the mainstream. Special classes are viewed as safe harbors or sanctuaries for children with disabilities. Theoretically, if a child with disabilities is given a supportive environment, which is supposed to be easier to provide in a segregated setting than in a general education setting, the child's self-concept will be more positive. It is argued that the more homogeneous the classroom, the better the child's self-concept. Thus, it is assumed that children with disabilities will develop a better self-concept if they are placed in special settings than if they are placed in general education class-rooms—but will they?

The one-size-fits-all metaphor for testing (i.e., individual differences are ignored) has been soundly shredded, maligned, and in many instances discarded entirely. The question arises then, why does this metaphor persist when discussing appropriate placement for students with disabilities? Full inclusion for many students with disabilities is the perfect fit. However, it does not work for all students.

Results of research suggest that some children prefer receiving special education services outside of the general education classroom. Many children have reported that they like going to special education classes, that services in those classes are beneficial, and that they enjoy having special assistance and the opportunity to work in the quieter setting provided through a special education placement (Klinger, Vaughn, Schumm, Cohen, & Forgan, 1998; Padeliadu & Zigmond, 1999; Vaughn, Elbaum, & Boardman, 2001). In one study, over half the students with mild disabilities preferred special class placements to general education settings, as they had experienced strong negative experiences in the general education setting, while slightly fewer than half of the students preferred the general education setting (Lovitt, Plavins, & Cushing, 1999). In another study some older students, who had severe disabilities, reported that they were more comfortable attending classes with friends who had similar abilities and interests (Palmer, Fuller, Arora, & Nelson, 2001). Respect for individual differences, the cornerstone of special education, must put its practice where its philosophy is, or more succinctly stated, support a full range of services. One placement model does not fit all when it comes to where students will participate in well-designed instruction.

Special Education Reform Efforts:
The Regular Education Initiative (REI)

In 1986 a proposal, radical for its time, was advanced suggesting that the education of children with disabilities become the shared responsibility of general and special educators. At that time, Madeline Will, assistant secretary for the U.S. Office of Special Education and Rehabilitative Services, stated that the "so-called pull-out approach to the educational difficulties of students with learning problems has failed in many instances to meet the educational needs of these students and has created, however unwittingly, barriers to their successful education" (Will, 1986, p. 412). With screams of delight by some and howls of rage by others, this proposal became known as the *regular education initiative* (REI).

REI targeted the general education classroom as the preferred learning environment for students with mild and moderate disabilities. Included in the REI were three other educational bullets (Davis & Maheady, 1991):

- Co-teaching, consultation, and building support teams would be service models in which general, special, and compensatory teachers would serve children with disabilities.

- All money, materials, and personnel from general, special, and compensatory programs would be pooled under the auspices of the building principal.
- Administrative policies would be developed to facilitate the placement of children with special learning needs in the general classroom.

Many of the key components of the REI proposal have been adopted for the current inclusion model, and many aspects of REI can be found in current educational practices to a greater or lesser extent in school districts across the country. Since the original REI proposal in 1986, a gradual progression of practices has been designed to integrate general and special education (Lerner, 2003). Prior to REI, a separate-but-equal notion was in place; students with disabilities typically were not in placements with their nondisabled counterparts. The *mainstreaming* movement, popular in the 1970s and early 1980s, took the next step of integrating students with disabilities in the general education setting for part or all of the day, if and when they possessed the skills that would allow them to achieve with their typical peers. REI took integration to the next level by recommending that children start placement in the LRE and then, if necessary, move to a more restrictive environment.

The basic tenets of REI can easily be seen in the 1997 Amendments to IDEA, which ensures access to the general education curriculum in the least restrictive environment for students with disabilities. IDEA '97 and its 1999 regulations recognize that individuals with disabilities need special education or related services but stress that services be provided in the LRE, the basis of the inclusion movement. LRE provisions mandate, to the extent appropriate, that students with disabilities have experiences in school with nondisabled students.

To promote normalization experiences, placement decisions must reflect the LRE for each student. The general education classroom, composed of the greatest number of students without disabilities, would be considered the least restrictive placement. Given appropriate accommodations, many students with disabilities would be placed initially in the general education setting.

Administrative Concerns:
Commitment to the General Education Class

Services delivered outside the general education classroom are costly. As the numbers of students receiving special education services has soared, so has the cost of providing a free appropriate public education. Federal aid was supposed to fund 40% above the cost of educating the average general education student, but the level of fiscal support promised by IDEA (P.L. 94-142) has never been authorized by Congress or requested by the executive branch. In fact, the average federal funding level has never risen above 12% (Chambers, Parrish, & Harr, 2002).

The expenses involved in providing special education services have become a significant part of the cost of providing public education for all students. Funding special education placements and services often requires substantial fiscal support from individual school districts. Providing appropriate services in the general education classroom is one potential way to reduce the costly expenditures associated with special education placements.

To quote Milofsky (1974), "Unavoidably, the first commitment of the public schools is to the vast majority of students attending regular classes. Special education is a marginal enterprise" (p. 439). He might have qualified his statement to read: "Special education *as a segregated and administratively isolated entity is a marginal enterprise.*" Public schools are committed to educating all youngsters. As in most markets, however, attention is paid to the largest consumer group. General education classrooms significantly outnumber special classrooms. As a result, more administrative attention is directed to general education classroom teachers and pupils than to special classrooms.

While administrators have always been concerned with the achievement levels of all their students, past assessment practices focused primarily on the performance of typical students. IDEA '97 redirected the attention of administrators, policymakers, and educators and held them publicly accountable for all students' performance in the general education curriculum. Furthermore, all students, even students with disabilities, are expected to be subject to challenging standards. Thus, students with disabilities are required to take part in state and local program standards based on the general education curriculum and evaluated using the same process that is used with their more typical peers (Spinelli, 2002).

With the advent of more recent federal and state legislation, administrators are facing even more pressure to ensure that all students, including students with disabilities, achieve at a prescribed grade level (Zigler, 2002). Districts, schools, administrators, teachers, and students who don't meet the appropriate level on statewide normative tests can suffer serious consequences (Fuchs & Fuchs, 2001; Ysseldyke, 2001).

To increase the odds that all students will achieve at the designated level, administrators have been investing in often costly scientifically based educational programs, retraining teachers, and providing supplementary services to all underachieving students. With tight budgets and additional expenditures, the practice of instructing students with disabilities in an inclusive setting has a certain fiscal appeal. Inclusive settings have the additional appeal of providing students with disabilities access to the general education curriculum, when provided with appropriate accommodations.

Providing high-quality programs for special students and satisfying the administrative concerns of general education classrooms can be complementary functions. The specialized teaching methods used in special education classes are often extensions and refinements of core teaching behaviors and skills (Friend & Bursuck, 2002). The old saying that "good teaching is good teaching" seems to be true. The decision of whether children with disabilities will receive this good teaching in special education classrooms or in the general education setting, is still undecided.

Collaboration bridges placement settings. Collaboration or collaborative consultation is an instructional model used to capitalize on the strengths of special and general education service models. In a collaborative consultation model problem definition, planning, provision of services, and evaluation of outcomes are shared responsibilities (U.S. Department of Education, 2001).

Collaboration can exist across various types of service models, but most often is associated with collaboration between special and general educators. General and special education teachers pool resources and expertise to implement appropriate educational services in the general education classroom for students with disabilities. The premise is that professionals with diverse backgrounds and educational experiences can create solutions to problems that their mutual students experience. Collaboration among classroom, bilingual, special, and remedial education teachers focuses mainly on children with disabilities and those who are not profiting from classroom experiences.

By making general education classrooms more flexible, public schools can ensure that many special needs students receive an appropriate education in general education classrooms. Inclusionary models produce more appropriate education for students with disabilities in the context of the general education classroom. In these collaborative inclusion classrooms, all children are encouraged to achieve and to value diversity. Flexibility can be increased by strengthening the factors that help reduce the size or number of special classrooms. Support for inservice education for the general education class teacher, purchase of appropriate materials, and provision of support services to the general education teacher (e.g., a specially trained consultant or master teacher) contribute to better instruction in the general education classroom.

Effective general and special educators share at least five common practices (Mastropieri & Scruggs, 2004):

- Identification and clarification of problems
- Direct observations
- Identification of instructional strategies and techniques
- Delivery and evaluation of strategies
- Development of teacher knowledge of coping strategies for challenging situations

Better instruction leads to fewer special classrooms. Reducing the number of special classrooms can encourage reallocation of instructional funds to support flexibility in general education classroom setting. This cycle is depicted in Figure 1.1 as an endless loop. No single point represents the beginning of the cycle. All parts are related, so a change in one component will produce a change in another. The more flexible the general education setting, the less need there will be for more special classes. The more funds that are allocated to the general education classroom, the more support the general education teacher will receive. The loop continues endlessly.

Section 504: Vocational Rehabilitation Act of 1973 (P.L. 93-112)

It took almost 20 years before Section 504 of the Vocational Rehabilitation Act made its debut as a key player in classroom service delivery. When that law was

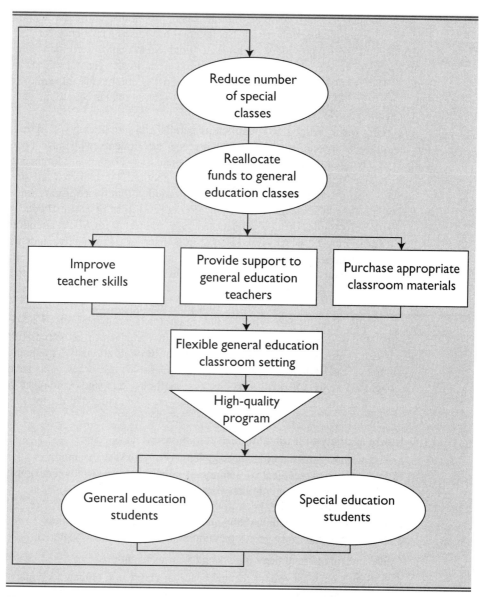

Figure 1.1   Administrative Support Cycle

first enacted, it was directed at providing physical access to buildings. People with physical disabilities would not be discriminated against because of architectural barriers. The law further extended civil rights for individuals with disabilities in education, employment, and housing.

More recently, Section 504 has been instrumental in providing all students a right to access the general education curriculum, participate in extracurricular activities in school, and receive appropriate instructional and curricular adaptations in the general education setting. Section 504 has raised a challenge for general education service providers. A child does not have to qualify for special education services to receive classroom accommodations in the general education setting. The general education staff, however, must accommodate all children who have been judged to need special assistance to have equal access to the general education curriculum.

In many ways, Section 504 regulations parallel the requirements of IDEA, but are more far-reaching. Section 504 protects all students who have been defined as having any physical or mental impairment that substantially limits one or more major life activities, including learning. Section 504 applies to all students who meet this definition, even if they do not fall within the eligibility categories of special education and even if they do not need to be in a special education program. Examples of these students include children with AIDS, attention deficit disorders (ADD or ADHD), or emotional disorders. Frequently, students who have transitioned out of special education receive Section 504 services. In fact, any child whose condition substantially limits functioning in the general education program is considered "handicapped" within the meaning of Section 504. The teachers of record are general education teachers.

Essentially, Section 504 requires the general education teacher to make accommodations that will enable each student in the class to be successful. Students can demonstrate mastery of class content through alternative methods. For example, some students may need extended time for testing, or tests may have to be concluded orally. Calculators, computers, spell-checkers, and other aids can be permitted during tests, daily work, or homework. Accommodations for students in the general education classroom are outlined as follows:

1. Utilize a variety of learning formats during instruction.
   a) Use gestures and natural expressions to convey further meaning.
   b) Present new or technical vocabulary visually (e.g., on a chalkboard) or use a handout that lists unfamiliar words.
   c) Use terms from the textbook in the context of the student's daily life.
   d) Give assignments both verbally and in writing to avoid confusion.
   e) Provide written study guides or sample questions for class material.

2. Guide students to help them understand your expectations.
   a) Tell students what your expectations are for classwork, homework, and in-class behavior. Provide your description in both written and oral form.
   b) Be specific about your grading criteria. Provide due dates and checklists.
   c) Begin each class with an advanced organizer (e.g., an outline of the material that will be covered). End each lesson with a summary of the key points.
   d) Raise student awareness of what constitutes an acceptable answer in class as well as on tests.
   e) Help students schedule and determine the amount of time required to complete assignments.

f) Teach students to stay on task by providing them with systematic instruction in attending behaviors.

Fortunately for all concerned, the accommodations for children who qualify under Section 504 are often similar or identical to the accommodations made for children who meet the eligibility criteria for special services and are receiving their education in the general education setting.

Typically, parents or teachers refer students for services under Section 504. Delivery of services is not automatic. If sufficient evidence exists that the child may need 504 services, then evaluation to determine eligibility and the type of services needed occurs. The evaluation is primarily based on professional judgment rather than test scores (Smith, 2001). Once eligibility has been determined, a written plan is designed to identify and accommodate the child's special needs in the general setting. The accommodations are usually based on sound and inexpensive teaching practices. Cost is a consideration because the law does not provide funding.

Classification, Labeling, and Disabilities

In order to receive special education services in any education setting, students must be classified according to strict criteria listed in federal guidelines. The federal and state governments have chosen to use a categorical approach to identify individuals needing special services (U.S. Department of Education, 1999). IDEA defines 13 disability categories:

- Autism
- Deaf-blindness
- Deafness
- Emotional disturbance
- Hearing impairment
- Mental retardation
- Multiple disabilities
- Orthopedic impairment
- Other health impairment
- Specific learning disability
- Speech and language impairment
- Traumatic brain injury
- Visual impairment

Each of these conditions exists on a continuum of severity; that is, the impact of the condition can range anywhere from minimal or mild to extreme or severe. In addition, an individual can exhibit more than one of these conditions simultaneously (e.g., a person can be deaf and also have a learning disability in reading). For eligibility purposes, at least one of the conditions must be present, but services can address needs based on more than one classification.

The prevalence of the 13 categories also varies. The high-incidence disabilities are speech or language impairments, learning disabilities, mental retardation (mild to moderate), and emotional disturbance. Thus, individuals in these groups comprise approximately 88%–90% of the total population of students with disabilities ages 6–21 (U.S. Department of Education, 2001). Students with high-incidence disabilities are those who are most commonly seen in schools.

Children and youth who have lower incidence disabilities typically are not found in inclusion settings as often as those with higher incidence disabilities. Low-incidence disabilities include visual impairments, hearing impairments, physical and other health impairments, severe and multiple disabilities (including severe mental retardation), and autism. These students represent a much smaller number, approximately 8–10% of the population receiving services through IDEA. Definitions, acronyms, and typical characteristics associated with these categories are presented in Table 1.1.

Special Education Categories

Classification and labeling is a complex process involving politics, ethics, fiscal considerations, and educational interests (Luckasson & Reeve, 2001). The political side of classification is typically influenced by groups of parents and professionals who are associated with a certain category. These people are stakeholders and ideally also advocates for the individuals represented in the category of interest. The stakeholders want to ensure that the definitions and criteria associated with the category are appropriate and inclusive. Ethical considerations for determining who fits and who does not fit a category have a significant impact on funding and subsequent provision of educational services. Although categorical labels are useful for funding purposes, an overemphasis on the labels or their acronyms can promote lowered or unrealistic expectations. First and foremost, we must focus on students as individuals with unique personal characteristics to bring to the world.

Fortunately, "descriptions" have moved away from an emphasis on the condition to an emphasis on the person. Prior to the late 1980s, the disability was mentioned first and the child second (e.g., a mentally retarded child or a learning disabled person). As public sensitivity has been raised, traditional labels, while still necessary, have become less visible when used to discuss individuals with disabilities. For example, the term *learning disabled person* has been replaced with a *person with learning disabilities.* Although this wording reversal may not seem like much more than a politically correct action, the distinction reflects a profound change in attitudes toward people with disabilities. The reversal in terms is personally correct. The individual is primary; the condition is secondary.

As in all classification schemes, the conceptual process of classifying exceptional students involves establishing categories to which children can be assigned. The number of categories changes constantly, expanding or shrinking as various experts or advocacy groups abstract or consolidate identified or assumed characteristics of children. Consider, for example, the "Do-It-Yourself

Table 1.1   Major Categories of Disability

Category	Acronym	Definition
Autism Spectrum Disorders	ASD	A developmental disability significantly affecting verbal and nonverbal communication and social interaction, generally evident before age 3, that adversely affects the child's performance. The term does not apply if the child's educational performance is adversely affected primarily because the child has a serious emotional disturbance. (U.S. Department of Education, 1999, p. 12421) Engagement in the addictive activities in stereotyped movements; resistance to environmental change or change in daily routines; unusual responses to sensory experiences
Deaf–Blindness		A disability wherein the individual has both vision and hearing problems but may not be both profoundly deaf and blind.
Deafness		Inability to perceive environmental sounds with or without hearing aid; inability to use hearing as a means to gain information.
Emotional Disturbance	ED	A condition characterized by disruptive or inappropriate behaviors that interferes with the student's learning, relationships with others, or personal satisfaction to such a degree that intervention is required.
Hearing Impairment	HI	Indicates a hearing loss that advresely affects access to educational, social, and performance areas.
Mental Retardation	MR	Characterized by cognitive impairments, limited adaptive behavior, and need for support; initial occurrence is before age 18.
Multiple Disabilities	MD	More than one disability in an individual.
Orthopedic Impairment	OI	Conditions related to a physical deformity or disability of the skeletal system and associated motor function.
Other Health Impairments	OHI	Chronic or acute health problems resulting in limited strength, vitality, or alertness; a category that includes attention deficit/hyperactivity disorder along with special health-care needs.
Specific Learning Disability	SLD	Disability in which the individual possesses average intelligence but is substantially delayed in academic achievement.
Speech and Language Impairments	SLI	Speech and language disorders are present when the interactive exchange of ideas is impaired.
Traumatic Brain Injury	TBI	As a result of head injury, the individual experiences reduced cognitive functioning, limited attention, and impulsivity.
Visual Impairment	VI	A condition in which corrective lenses must be supplemented with compensatory strategies for the student to gain access to learning.

Terminology Generator" developed by Edward Fry (see Figure 1.2). It is a facetious approach to labeling and classifying children with learning disabilities. According to Fry, an LD child can be "defined" by simply appending a qualifier, as in "minimal brain dysfunction," "mild brain dysfunction," or "minor brain dysfunction." This method will generate 1,000 terms. Although this estimate seems ridiculous, it is a fairly accurate representation of the process of term generation. In classifying children, we typically attempt to identify a problem, an area of involvement, and any relevant qualifier. Furthermore, since the development of this generator by Fry, many new terms have been coined that could be added to columns 1, 2, or 3.

Heterogeneous Grouping

The practice of labeling special populations grew out of the belief that certain characteristics identify homogeneous groups of exceptional children for instructional purposes. According to this belief, if we educate children whose needs are similar together, we can be more effective in our instruction. If children are the same, texts can be the same, assignments can be the same, and rate of learning may be the same. Educators have known for well over 30 years, however, that ability grouping is not particularly beneficial for students. Research (Kirp, 1974) examining the effects of ability grouping and special education revealed that classification, as typically used, does not promote individualized learning, does not

Directions: Select any word from Column 1. Add any word from Column 2. Then add any word from Column 3. If you don't like the result, try again. it will mean about the same thing.

1 Qualifier	2 Area of Involvement	3 Problem
Minimal	Brain	Dysfunction
Mild	Cerebral	Damage
Minor	Neurological	Disorder
Chronic	Neurologic	Dis-Synchronization
Diffuse	CNS (Central Nervous System)	Handicap
Specific	Language	Disability
Primary	Reading	Retardation
Disorganized	Perceptual	Impairment
Organic	Impulse	Pathology
Clumsy	Behavior	Syndrome

The above system will yield 1,000 terms, but if that is not enough, you could use *specific dyslexia, aphasoid, neurophrenia,* or *developmental lag.*

Source: From Edward Frye, Do-It-Yourself Terminology Generator. Used by permission of Edward Frye.

Figure 1.2   Do-It-Yourself Terminology Generator

promote more effective teaching to groups of students of similar ability, and does not accomplish any other goals classification is meant to achieve.

As classroom instruction becomes more skill-oriented, the need to label children with disabilities diminishes. Classroom demands become more focused on a child's specific skill needs and less on identification for the purpose of classification. Because the emphasis in inclusion classes is on the skills of individual children, they are multilevel; that is, all students are not expected to progress at the same rate or to need the same instruction. Appropriate education in inclusion settings relates to the success and willingness of the general classroom teacher to make adaptations that accommodate the extraordinarily diverse student populations characteristic of public schools (Schumm, Moody, & Vaughn, 2000).

Traditional Special Education Categories

The main purpose of labels and categorization of children is to provide information that can be used in education. The immediate practical purpose of diagnosis is to identify an educational problem so it can be corrected (Adelman, 1979). To diagnose Bobbi as a child with physical impairment has no practical value unless educational needs related to Bobbi's physical impairment are made explicit. If Bobbi's physical impairment causes her to tire easily, a modification in her educational program is warranted. She may need to take a short rest midmorning, midafternoon, or both. If Bobbi's physical impairment has no educational ramifications, her diagnosis as physically impaired is about as useful for instructional purposes as knowing that she has blue eyes and blond hair.

Problems of Labeling

The power of language to shape our behavior and attitudes is well established (Sapon-Shevin, 1979). A focus on the disability or performance deficit lodged in the label or category may create an expectation that centers on what the individual cannot do rather than what the individual can do or be. Teachers and peers, parents, and taxpayers can hold negative biases that cloud the view of the individual, resulting in assumptions and behaviors that may not be based in reality. An overemphasis on the category can have profound impact on the degree to which inclusion in the school and community can be successful. Therefore, the language we use in describing children is important. When labels with negative connotations are applied, prejudice toward and rejection of the child are likely to result.

To label Bonnie Sue "mentally retarded" conjures a more vivid set of expectations than does labeling her as "lagging two to three years behind in reading." Bonnie Sue's reading performance remains two to three years behind whether she is called mentally retarded, emotionally disturbed, gifted, or normal. The power of the label is to attribute a whole set of behaviors to Bonnie Sue. If she were called emotionally disturbed, characteristics stereotypic of emotionally disturbed children might be ascribed to her. A label of normal would evoke a different set of expectations. In each case her reading behavior might be explained as a function of the label. Bonnie Sue cannot read because she is mentally retarded. Bonnie Sue cannot read because she is emotionally disturbed. Bonnie Sue cannot read because she is lazy. (We can't say "Bonnie Sue cannot read because she is normal," so we have to substitute a behavior normal children often exhibit—in this case, laziness.)

Let's look at another illustration of the power of language. On a school playground a group of children are heatedly debating the coach's decision to call a penalty on one of the soccer players. Eric, whose team has the dubious honor of receiving the penalty, is thoroughly convinced the coach's decision is wrong. As Eric moves back onto the playing field, he can be heard muttering under his breath, "That coach! Oh, brother, what a retard!" Whether or not Eric is aware of his behavior, he is demonstrating the use of *trait theory*. In trait theory, behavior is explained in terms of traits thought to be relatively consistent across situations. Eric explained the coach's behavior in terms of traits often ascribed to people who are mentally retarded.

According to Polyson (1979), objections to trait theory as an explanation of an individual's behavior center on four major arguments. He stated:

> First, traits are not explanatory constructs and their use involves circular logic. Second, the way people define traits in others is influenced by stereotypic expectations related to sex, age, appearance, etc. Third, attitude and perception of the receivers prevent trait inference from being unbiased. And fourth, the assumption that people do in fact have stable and identifiable response dispositions across situations is challenged or in effect a skepticism that traits exist at all. (p. 34)

The influence of trait theory can be diluted by replacing labels that have negative connotations with descriptions of observable social or academic performance. Fortunately, attitudes can change. Inclusion activities based in the school and community can decrease bias. The more positive the interaction between the individual categorized in a certain way and significant others, like teachers, peers, and other members of the community, the more likely it is that the effects of label bias will diminish. Contact with and knowledge about children with disabilities can influence attitudes in a constructive way.

As people become personally involved with each other, empathy and identification increase. Getting to know someone and learning about his or her likes and dislikes help create a relationship based on all the beautiful and new things that can be learned about each other day by day. As the child becomes known on a personal level, the label fades and, gradually, the special kid becomes Michele or Patrick or Elizabeth, the kid who is the video game champion, the best violinist, or the one with the most pets.

Overlap Across Categories

Sometimes categorization of the student is a simple process, but at other times choosing the correct label or category becomes problematic. A brief inspection of the characteristics associated with various categories quickly reveals overlap. Overlapping traits or characteristics of children with mild disabilities but significant educational needs makes it difficult to determine which category is the best match for the needs of the student. Sometimes different labels are assigned to children who exhibit the same behaviors. Jorge and Marisol, for example, exhibit similar behaviors but are assigned different labels. Jorge is categorized as learning disabled, whereas Marisol is classified as mildly mentally retarded. This discrepancy is often the result of factors other than the child's school performance. The time of year of the diagnosis (early versus late in the school year), availability of a place in a special program, teacher preferences for working with specific types of children, and related factors, especially among children with high-incidence disabilities, may determine whether a child is labeled as mentally retarded, learning disabled, emotionally disturbed, or normal.

Overidentification and Labels

As the ranks of children with disabilities continue to swell, a serious look is being given to determine who is truly eligible to receive special education services. The number of students, aged 6–21 receiving special education services under the federal governments disability categories between the years 2000–2001 was approximately 5,762,935 (U.S. Department of Education, 2002). Although this percentage is small compared to the total number of students receiving a public education, the actual number of children is large. The question being raised is: Are more than 5 million children so different from the norm that they require an individualized program of special education and related services to fully benefit from education?

Two types of populations are being scrutinized very carefully in this respect. The first population consists of students who are classified under one or more of the 13 categories, but who are achieving well in the general education setting. These students appear to no longer need an individualized program of special education or related services as long as they have accommodations. They can access classroom information in an inclusive setting, as long as the general education instructor provides appropriate accommodations and do not need the support of special education services to be successful learners.

The second population is more problematic. This population consists of students whose opportunity to learn suggests a high probability of failure in a traditional public school setting. The majority of these students are poor and have not experienced the educational advantages associated with success in public school settings. Most of them would be considered for services under high-incidence disabilities. Some of the students are Caucasian, but a disproportionate number are African Americans, Mexican Americans or Latinos, and Native Americans (Daugherty, 2001). The challenge with these students is to separate those with true disabilities from those whose environmental conditions have created an educational need that mimics characteristics associated with federally defined special education categories. The decision to place children with disabilities who no longer need special services and to place children who are poor and appear to need individual or specialized educational programs in the general education setting underscores the complexity of the political and ethical issues surrounding classification.

Summary

With the passage of the Education for All Handicapped Children Act (EHA; P.L. 94-142), requthorized as the Individuals with Disabilities Education Act (IDEA), Congress declared that all children with disabilities have the right to education in the most appropriate educational setting, the "least restrictive environment." Attempts to comply with this mandate were initially referred to as the mainstreaming movement and subsequently became referred to as the inclusion movement. Factors contributing to the inclusion movement include the disillusionment with special class placement, special education reform efforts, administrative concerns, and dissatisfaction with the process by which children are identified and labeled.

The normalization principle emphasizes experiences for people with developmental disabilities that approximate, as closely as possible, experiences of nondisabled people. This principle suggests that, whenever possible, the social, vocational, and life goals of people with disabilities should approximate the goals of mainstream populations. Further, choice of placement is related to the nature and degree of the disabling condition.

Another factor contributing to the inclusion movement is the disillusionment with special class placement. The extent to which special class placements have positively affected both the social and academic growth of children with disabilities is not clear. Administrators concerned with the quality of educational programming for students with and without disabilities have sought to improve the educational flexibility of general education classrooms. This flexibility has allowed inclusion of many more children with disabilities within general education classrooms.

Classification and labeling practices reflect the type of placement and services students will receive. With the inclusion model, regardless of how students labeled, most will receive initial services in the general education setting. The political, ethical, and social complexities associated with labeling practices have created an ever-widening diversity of skill levels in the general education setting, which must be addressed by competent and well-trained educators.

References

Adelman, H. S. (1979). Diagnostic classification of LD: A practical necessity and a procedural problem. *Learning Disability Quarterly, 2,* 56–62.
Bank-Mikkelsen, N. E. (1969). A metropolitan area in Denmark: Copenhagen. In R. B. Kugel & W. Wolfensberger (Eds.), *Changing patterns in residential services for the mentally retarded* (pp. 227–254). Washington, DC: President's Committee on Mental Retardation.
Berk, L. E. (2002). *Infants, children, and adolescents.* Boston: Allyn and Bacon.

Bradely, D. F., King-Sears, M. E., & Tessier-Switlick, D. M. (1997). *Teaching students in inclusive settings, from theory to practice.* Boston: Allyn and Bacon.

Bulgren, J. A., & Carta, J. J. (1993). Examining the instructional contexts of students with learning disabilities. *Exceptional Children, 59*(3), 182–191.

Butler, R. (1998). Age trends in the use of social and temporal comparison for self-evaluation: Examination of a novel developmental hypothesis. *Child Development, 69,* 1054–1073.

Chambers, J. G., Parrish, T., & Harr, J. J. (2002, March). *What are we spending on special education services in United States, 1999-2000? Advance report No. 1.* Palo Alkto, CA: The American Institutes for Research. Retrieved June 22, 2007, from http://csef.air.org

Chung, S. (1998). *The compatibility of reform initiatives in inclusion and science education: Perceptions of science teachers.* Unpublished doctoral dissertation, Purdue University.

Cook, L., & Friend, M. (1996). Co-teaching: Guidelines for creating effective practices. *Focus on Exceptional Children, 28,* 1–16.

Cook, B. G., Tankersley, M., Cook, L., & Landrum, T. J. (2000). Teachers' attitudes toward their included students with disabilities. *Exceptional Children, 67,* 115–117.

Council for Exceptional Children. (1998). *IDEA 1997: Let's make it work.* Arlington, VA: Author.

Council for Exceptional Children. (2000). *Bright futures for exceptional learners.* Reston, VA: Author.

Daugherty, D. (2001). *IDEA '97 and disproportionate placement.* Retrieved July 22, 2005, from http://www. naspcenter.org/teachers/IDEA_disp.html

Davis, J. C., & Maheady, L. (1991). The regular education initiative: What do three groups of education professionals think? *Teacher Education & Special Education, 14*(4), 211–220.

Education of All Handicapped Children Act of 1975, 20 U.S.C. 33 § 1400 *et seq.*

Education of All Handicapped Children Act Amendments of 1990, 20 U.S.C. 33 § 1400 *et seq.*

Ellis, E. S., & Lenz, B. K. (1996). Learning disabilities in adolescents: A prospective. In D. D. Deshler, E. S. Ellis, & B. K. Lenz (Eds.), *Teaching adolescents with learning disabilities: Strategies and methods* (2nd ed., pp. 9–60). Denver, CO: Love Publishing Co.

Friend, M., & Bursuck, W. D. (2002). *Including students with special needs: A practical guide for classroom teachers* (3rd ed.). Boston: Allyn & Bacon.

Fuchs, L. S., & Fuchs, D. (2001). Using assessments to account for and promote strong outcomes for students with learning disabilities. In D. Hallahan & B. Keogh (Eds.), *Research on global perspectives in learning disabilities: Essays in honor of William M. Cruickshank* (pp. 93–110). Mahwah, NJ: Erlbaum.

Gagnon, J. C., & Leone, P. E. (2002). Alternative strategies for school violence prevention. In R. J. Skiba & G. G. Noam (Eds.), *Zero tolerance: Can suspension and expulsion keep schools safe?* (pp. 101–125). San Francisco: Jossey-Bass.

Hazel, J. S., Schumaker, J. B., Sherman, J. A., & Sheldon, J. (1995). *ASSET: A social skills program for adolescents.* Champaign, IL: Research Press.

Hehir, T. (1999). The changing roles of special education leadership in the next millennium: Thoughts and reflections. *Journal of Special Education Leadership, 12*(1), 3–8.

Higgins, E. L., Raskind, M. H., Goldberg, R. J., & Herman, K. J. (2002). Stages of acceptance of a learning disability: The impact of labeling. *Learning Disability Quarterly, 25*(1), 3–17.

Hobbs, T., & Westling, D. L. (1998). Promoting successful inclusion through collaborative problem solving. *Teaching Exceptional Children, 31*(2), 12–19.

Horn, W. F., & Tynan, D. (2001). Time to make special education "special" again. In C. E. Finn, Jr., A. J. Rotherham, & C. R. Hokanson, Jr., (Eds.), *Rethinking special education for a new century* (pp. 23–52). Washington, DC: Thomas B. Fordham Foundation and the Progressive Policy Institute.

Individuals With Disabilities Education Act Amendments of 1991, 20 U.S.C. 33 § 1400 *et seq.*

Individuals With Disabilities Education Act Amendments of 1997, 20 U.S.C. 33 § 1400 *et seq.*

Individuals With Disabilities Education Act Amendments of 2004, 20 U.S.C. 33 § 1400 *et seq.*

Idol, L. (1997). Key questions related to building collaborative and inclusive schools. *Journal of Learning Disabilities, 30,* 384–394.

Johnson, K. (1998). Deinstitutionalization: The management of rights. *The Disability & Society, 13,* 375–387.

Kavale, K. A. (2002). Mainstreaming to full inclusion: From orthogenesis to pathogenesis of an idea. *International Journal of Disability, Development, and Education, 49*(2), 201–214.

Kerr, M. M., & Nelson, C. M. (2002). *Strategies for addressing behavior problems in the classroom* (4th ed.). Upper Saddle River, NJ: Merrill/Prentice Hall.

Kirp, D. (1974). Student classification, public policy, and the courts. *Harvard Educational Review, 44,* 6–52.

Klinger, J. K., & Vaughn, S. (2002). The changing roles and responsibilities of an LD specialist. *Learning Disability Quarterly, 25*(1), 19–31.

Klinger, J. K., Vaughn, S., Schumm, J. S., Cohen, P., & Forgan, J. W. (1998). Inclusion or pull-out: Which do students prefer? *Journal of Learning Disabilities, 31,* 148–158.

Kuhne, M., & Weiner, J. (2000). Stability of social status of children with and without learning disabilities. *Learning Disability Quarterly, 23*(1), 64–75.

LaMare, L., & de la Ronde, M. (2000). Links among social status, service delivery mode, and service delivery preference in LD, low-achieving, and normally achieving elementary-aged children. *Learning Disability Quarterly, 23*(1), 52–62.

Lance, W. D. (1976). What you should know about PL 94-142. *Educational Communications & Technology, 21,* 14.

Lerner, J. (2003). *Learning disabilities: Theories, diagnosis, and teaching strategies* (9th ed.). Boston: Houghton Mifflin.

Lovitt, T. C., Plavins, M., & Cushing, S. (1999). What do pupils with disabilities have to say about their experience in high school? *Remedial and Special Education, 20,* 67–76, 83.

Luckasson, R., & Reeve, A. (2001). Naming, defining, and classifying in mental retardation. *Mental Retardation, 39,* 47–52.

Marsh, H. W., Craven, R., & Debus, R. (1998). Structure, stability, and development of young children's self-concepts: A multicohort-multioccasion study. *Child Development, 69,* 1030–1053.

Mastropieri, M. A., & Scruggs, T. E. (2000). *The inclusive classroom: Strategies for effective teaching.* Columbus, OH: Prentice Hall.

Mastropieri, M. A., & Scruggs, T. E. (2004). *The inclusive classroom: Strategies for effective teaching* (2nd ed.). Columbus, OH: Prentice Hall.

McInerney, D. M. (1999). What should teachers do to get children to want to read and write? Motivation for literacy acquisition. In A. J. Watson & L. R. Giorcelli (Eds.), *Accepting the literacy challenge* (pp. 95–115). Sydney, Australia: Scholastic.

McLaughlin, M. J. (1999). Access to the general education curriculum: Paperwork and procedures or redefining "special education." *Journal of Special Education Leadership, 12*(1), 9–14.

McLeskey, J., Henry, D., & Axelrod, M. I. (1999). Inclusion of students with learning disabilities: An examination of data from reports to Congress. *Exceptional Children, 66,* 55–66.

Mesibov, G. B. (1990). Normalization and its relevance today. *Journal of Autism & Developmental Disorders, 20,* 379–390.

Milofsky, C. D. (1974). What special education isn't special. *Harvard Educational Review, 44,* 437–458.

Morocco, C. C. (2001). Teaching for understanding with students with disabilities: New directions for research on access to the general education curriculum. *Learning Disability Quarterly, 24*(1), 5–13.

No Child Left Behind Act of 2001, 20 U.S.C. 70 § 6301 *et seq.*

Office of Special Education Programs. (2000). *To assure the free appropriate education of all children with disabilities. Twenty-second annual report to Congress on the implementation of the Individuals with Disabilities Act.* Washington, DC: Author.

O'Shea, L. J., Stoddard, K., & O'Shea, D. J. (2000). IDEA '97 and educator standards: Special educators' perceptions of their skills and those of general educators. *Teacher Education and Special Education, 23*(2), 125–141.

Padeliadu, S., & Zigmond, Z. (1999). Perspectives of students with learning disabilities about special education placement. *Learning Disabilities Research and Practice, 11,* 15–23.

Palmer, D. S., Fuller, K., Arora, T., & Nelson, M. (2001). Taking sides: Parent views on inclusion for their children with severe disabilities. *Exceptional Children, 67,* 467–484.

Polyson, J. A. (1979). Toward a better view of children's problem behavior. *Psychology, 16,* 33–37.

Reynolds, M. C., Wang, M. C., & Walberg, H. J. (1992). The knowledge bases for special and general education. *Remedial & Special Education, 13*(5), 6–10, 33.

Riggs, C. G., & Mueller, P. H. (2001). Employment and utilization of paraeducators in inclusive settings. *The Journal of Special Education, 35*(1), 54–62.

Sabornie, E. J., & deBettencourt, L. U. (2004). *Teaching students with mild and high incidence disabilities at the secondary level* (2nd ed.). Upper Saddle River, NJ: Pearson.

Sailor, W. (1991). Special education in the restructured school. *Remedial & Special Education, 12(6),* 8–22.

Sapon-Shevin, M. (1979). Mainstreaming: Implementing the spirit of the law. *Journal of Negro Education, 48,* 364–381.

Sargent, L. E. (Ed.). (1998). *Social skills for school and community: Systematic instruction for children and youth with cognitive delays.* Reston, VA: The Division of Mental Retardation of the Council for Exceptional Children.

Schumm, J. S., Moody, S. W., & Vaughn, S. (2000). Grouping for reading instruction: Does one size it all? *Journal of Learning Disabilities, 33,* 477–488.

Scruggs, T. E., & Mastropieri, M. A. (1996). Teacher perceptions of mainstreaming/inclusion, 1958–1995: A research synthesis. *Exceptional Children, 63,* 59–74.

Shade, R. A., & Stewart, R. (2001). General education and special education preservice teachers' attitudes toward inclusion. *Preventing School Failure, 46*(1), 37–41.

Simpson, R. L. (1996). *Working with parents and families of exceptional children and youth* (3rd ed.). Austin, TX: Pro-Ed.

Siperstein, G. N., & Leffert, S. J. (1999). Managing limited resources: Do children with learning problems share? *Exceptional Children, 65,* 187–199.

Smith, T. E. C. (2001). Section 504, the ADA, and public schools: What educators need to know. *Remedial and Special Education, 22,* 335–343.

Soodak, L. C., Podell, D. M., & Lehman, L. R. (1998). Teacher, student, and school attributes as predictors of teachers' responses to inclusion. *The Journal of Special Education, 31,* 480–497.

Spinelli, C. (2002). *Classroom assessment for students with special needs in inclusive settings.* Upper Saddle River, NJ: Pearson Education.

Treder, D. W., Morse, W. C., & Ferron, J. M. (2000). The relationship between teacher effectiveness and teacher attitudes toward issues related to inclusion. *Teacher Education and Special Education, 23*(3), 202–210.

Turnbull, R., Rainbolt, K., & Buchele-Ash, A. (1997, December; 1998, January). What does IDEA 97 say about evaluations, eligibility, IEPs and placements? *TASH Newsletter, 20–22,* 31–35.

Vaughn, S., Elbaum, B., & Boardman, A. G. (2001). The social function of students with learning disabilities: Implications for inclusion. *Exceptionality, 9,* 264–290.

Vocational Rehabilitation Act of 1973, Pub. L. No. 93-112, Section 504.

U.S. Department of Education. (1999). Assistance to states for the education of children with disabilities program and the early intervention program for infants and toddlers with disabilities: Final regulations. *The Federal Register, 34,* CRF Parts 300 and 303.

U.S. Department of Education. (2001). *Twenty-third annual report to Congress on the implementation of the Individuals with Disabilities Education Act.* Washington, DC: U.S. Government Printing Office.

U.S. Department of Education. (2002). *Twenty-fourth annual report to Congress on the implementation of the Individuals with Disabilities Education Act.* Washington, DC: Author.

Weiss, M. P., & Brigham, F. J. (2000). Co-teaching and the model of shared responsibility: What does the research support? In T. E. Scruggs & M. A. Mastropieri (Eds.), *Advances in learning and behavioral disabilities 25,* 217–245. Oxford: Elsevier Science.

Welch, M., Brownell, K., & Sheridan, S. (1999). What's the score and game plan on teaming in schools? *Remedial and Special Education, 20,* 36–49.

Will, M. (1986). Educating children with learning problems: A shared responsibility. *Exceptional Children, 52,* 411–415.

Williams, B. T. (2001). Ethical leadership in schools servicing African-American children and youth. *Teacher Education and Special Education, 24,* 38–47.

Wolfensberger, W. (1972). *The principle of normalization in human services.* Toronto, Canada: National Institute on Mental Retardation.

Wood, J. (2002). *Adapting instruction to accommodate students in inclusive settings* (4th ed.). Upper Saddle River, NJ: Prentice Hall.

York, J., Vandercook, T., Macdonald, C., Heise-Neff, C., & Caughey, E. (1992). Feedback about integrating middle-school students with severe disabilities in general education classes. *Exceptional Children, 58*(3), 244–258.

Young, B. A. (2002). *Public high school dropouts and completers from common core of data: School years 1998–99 to 1999–2000* (NCES Report 2002-328). Washington, DC: U.S. Department Of Education, OERI, NCES.

Ysseldyke, J. (2001). Reflections on a research career: Generalizations from 25 years of research on assessment and instructional decision-making. *Exceptional Children, 67,* 295–308.

Ysseldyke, J. E., Algozzine, B., & Thurlow, M. (1992). *Critical issues in special and remedial education* (2nd ed.). Boston: Houghton Mifflin.

Zhao, Y., & Frank, K. A. (2003). Factors affecting technology uses in schools: An ecological approach. *American Educational Research Journal, 40,* 807–840.

Zigler, D. (2002, April). *Reauthorization of the Elementary and Secondary Education Act: No Child Left Behind Act of 2001.* Arlington, VA: The Council for Exceptional Children, Public Policy Unit.

Zigmond, N. (2001). Special education at a crossroads. *Preventing School Failure, 45*(2), 70–74.

CHAPTER

2

Children With High-Incidence Disabilities

KEY TERMS

- ◆ brain injured
- ◆ generalization
- ◆ mental imagery
- ◆ mnemonic devices
- ◆ negative reinforcement
- ◆ reinforcement
- ◆ spaced reviews
- ◆ stimulus selection

For an hour and a half, six people crowded around a conference table had tried to determine eligibility for special services for one 11-year-old named Chad. Chad's social and educational disabilities were not so severe taken individually, but together they created challenges for accessing social and cognitive learning.

Chad did not have any usable phonics skills, but he could read whole words fluently with appropriate intonation patterns. Unfortunately, Chad could comprehend very little of what he read unless the information was related to the weather. In fact, Chad was so interested in anything related to weather that he had made an e-mail contact with a local meteorologist. Chad's ability to read climatological charts and graphs was little short of amazing. He would converse via e-mail with the meteorologist for hours on end, but when asked to use the word processor to produce information related to classroom topics, Chad became all fingers and was not able to create anything.

When Chad used concrete objects or realia, he appeared to understand classroom material more fully. Chad couldn't count to 20 unless he was using objects, such as pennies or matchsticks as placeholders, but with them he could count to 100 and beyond. When using concrete objects, Chad could complete simple addition, subtraction, and multiplication problems involving regrouping, but he could not recall addition, subtraction, multiplication, and division facts. He was a master with a hand-held calculator, but problem solving, unless related to weather, eluded him.

Chad's social behaviors also appeared mixed. He was polite and, in fact, charming when he was in the presence of an authority figure, like a teacher. Once the teacher's back was turned, however, Chad would begin taunting the other children. When confronted with his behavior, Chad would lie or place blame on the other children. He would claim that the other children had been making fun of him or calling him names when the truth was that he was the name caller.

Chad was also becoming something of a bully. His chosen targets were often children much weaker, smaller, or younger than himself. Occasionally, however, he would misjudge and find himself the victim with the scratches and bruises to testify to his error of judgment.

Chad is representative of individuals with multiple mild disabilities. Children like Chad often find themselves in the categories associated with high-incidence disabilities, such as, mental retardation, emotional disturbance, learning disabilities or Aspergers (a mild form of autism). The general education, or inclusion, teacher with some type of support most commonly serves children like Chad in the general education classroom for all or part of the day.

Although some characteristics may suggest one category versus another, many disabilities overlap. Prior to the inclusion movement, many students with high-incidence disabilities received educational services by a special education teacher in a cross-categorical classroom. Cross-categorical classes were typically composed of children representing a variety of disabilities who were instructed by special educators. Often these classrooms were self-contained (i.e., segregated from students in other classes).

A brief discussion of cross-categorical programming for students with high-incidence disabilities provides a historical perspective on the evolution of the inclusion movement. The major focus of this chapter, however, is devoted to how services are provided in an inclusive setting for students with disabilities that occur most frequently and are relatively mild. Special emphasis is placed on the service delivery model in which the general education teacher provides the majority of the educational services with varying degrees of support from the special education teacher.

Evolution of Cross-Categorical Programming

Historically, the first children with intellectual and emotional disabilities to be treated had extremely severe impairments. Treatment was based on medical, rather than educational, findings, so it was not unreasonable to find physicians initiating educational programs for these children, since many children with more severe disabilities have problems in physical development along with their intellectual or emotional problems.

Children with extremely low intellectual functioning were fairly easy to distinguish from children with highly abnormal emotional responses—or so it seemed. Even with some children who showed extremes of intellectual or emotional behavior, however, "the chicken-or-the-egg" problem arose. Were certain children severely disturbed because they were severely retarded, or were they severely retarded because they were severely disturbed? Did the child have a severe intellectual deficit or a severe emotional problem, or both?

During the late 1800s, awareness of people with severe disabilities in the community led to development of institutional programs for the "feeble-minded" or "mentally defective." For adults and children to qualify for such a program, a judgment was made to determine if the person was subnormal enough to warrant specialized care and training.

Intelligence Tests

With the development of the intelligence test in the early 1900s, an "objective" means of determining degree of subnormality became available. Traditionally, the intelligence test was administered by psychologists. It was given only once to each potential "defective." After the testing, the psychologists assumed a more clinical role. As clinicans, they were free to examine "leftover" behavior that could not be measured on an intelligence test. Often this leftover behavior was identified as pathological (Balthazar & Stevens, 1975). Based on the assumption that different "conditions," such as mental retardation and emotional disturbance, required different treatments, segregated institutions sprang forth. Institutions for the severely mentally handicapped coexisted with institutions for the "insane." A certain uneasy inertia set in for a short time.

"Traumatic Dements"

During this period, a psychologist, Goldstein, decided to investigate a group of people he labeled "traumatic dements." His subjects were brain-injured soldiers from World War I. Through careful clinical observation, Goldstein identified five behavioral characteristics in his patients: forced responsiveness to stimuli, figure-background confusion, hyperactivity, meticulosity, and catastrophic reaction (Goldstein, 1939). In brief, Goldstein found persons with traumatic dements to be distracted easily and to have problems focusing their attention. They also exhibited extreme motor activity and had such bizarre perceptions that they frequently lost contact with reality, ultimately leading to a total emotional breakdown (Hallahan & Kauffman, 1976). The institutional walls of the asylums for the mentally retarded and insane began to quiver. Goldstein's patients were demonstrating behavioral overlaps with the severely retarded and the emotionally disturbed.

Perhaps not much more would have happened if Adolf Hitler had not risen to power. Ironically, Hitler's actions set up the situation that led to the collaboration of Alfred Strauss, a neuropsychiatrist and associate professor at the University of Heidelberg, and Heinz Werner, a developmental psychologist and associate professor at the University of Hamburg. Strauss and Werner each fled Germany to emigrate to the United States.

Brain-Injured Children

Building on Goldstein's research, Strauss and Werner turned their attention to children who were mentally retarded and were presumed to be brain injured. Through a series of investigations, Strauss and Werner concluded that brain-injured children with mental retardation were similar behaviorally to Goldstein's brain-injured adults. They also found that non-brain-injured children with mental retardation were unlike either Goldstein's adults or brain-injured children with mental retardation.

Strauss and Werner's research methods were criticized. Yet the fact remained that all retardates did not behave identically. Individual differences did exist. As a consequence, within a relatively short time, the dawn of individual educational or psychological programming began to peek over the institutional horizon. As the first rays of individualization struck, asylum walls began to crumble. The era of learning disabilities had begun.

The learning disabilities movement produced two major results:

1. Acknowledgment of subgroups within the categories of mental retardation and emotional disturbance
2. Recognition that not all learning and emotional problems are medically based

The acknowledgment of subgroups resulted in new and more specific classification schemes. Although not comprehensive, Table 2.1 lists characteristics related to classification of children with mild disabilities and one of the following labels: mental retardation, emotional disturbance, or learning disabilities. Ultimately, the very specificity of these labels with their overlapping characteristics backfired to the point that classifications became far less important than identification of the skill needs of the individual child.

Distribution of the Population

The demographics of the high-incidence disabilities, that is, the disabilities where 90% of the children eligible for special education services are found, are further complicated by the cultural and racial diversity of the United States. Distinguishing the impact of a student's culture, values, and beliefs on academic and social achievement in the classroom from the existence of a true disability can be very difficult (Nieto, 2000). Socioeconomic status further compounds the difficulty of identification and service provision. Children who live in poverty typically do not receive good teaching and good programs or attend good schools. Most often, the success of students from impoverished areas, as measured by middle-class norms, is typically jeopardized, resulting in poor test scores and low academic achievement. The performance of students from low-income areas—whether whites, African-Americans, Hispanics, or Native Americans—looks remarkably similar to the achievement of many students in the high-incidence category.

In spite of countless attempts to carefully separate the truly disabled from the apparently disabled, a disproportionate number of culturally and ethnically diverse students are receiving special education services (Smith, 2001). Several reasons have contributed to the confusion surrounding the identification of students associated with cultural or linguistic diversity. First, learning problems may be social or dynamic in nature; that is, more a function of a cultural mismatch between middle-class expectations and life experiences than a neurological or physiological problem. Second, students coming from chronic poverty or unaddressed trauma find it difficult to place school as the primary priority, especially if they are hungry, sick, tired, or emotionally stressed. Third, most teachers do not have the shared life experiences of students who are raised in poverty, are culturally and/or racially dissimilar, and may not have a firm grasp of English. Teachers often find themselves at a loss in classrooms representing multiple types of diversity, including the diversity of the child with mild disabilities. As academic demands increase, the cumulative effects of these factors often become

Table 2.1　Deficit Characteristics Associated With Individuals Labeled as Having Mental Retardation, Learning Disabilities, or Emotional Disturbance

	Severe	Moderate	Mild
Educable Mental Retardation			
Time of Identification	■ Birth or an early age	■ Birth or an early age	■ Often not until school entrance
Social and Emotional	■ Dependent on others for social direction ■ Minimal speech	■ Outer-directed ■ Failure expectancy ■ Delayed social and emotional growth ■ Delayed speech	■ May withdraw from peers ■ May seek attention in inappropriate ways ■ Delayed speech development
Intellectual and Cognitive	■ Self-help skills (e.g., toileting and feeding) ■ Do not seem to profit from academic programs	■ Self-help skills with emphasis on daily living (e.g., simple food preparation or making change) ■ Heavy emphasis on vocational training	■ Problems may be specific to one subject or generalized to all subjects ■ Profit from academic programming
Physical and Health	■ Poor motor coordination ■ Dependent on others for physical care ■ Often have multiple handicaps	■ Distinct physical characteristics ■ May have more than one handicap	■ May sow slower development than normal ■ No one global trait at this level; no generalization is appropriate
Educational Experience	■ Institution or sheltered group home	■ Self-contained public school programs (usually referred to as EMH)	■ Public school in special classes, resource room, or general education classroom
Learning Disabilities			
Time of Identification	■ Birth or early age ■ After a stroke or tumor	■ Early childhood	■ Often not until school entrance
Social and Emotional	■ May be compulsive ■ Tend to be egocentric ■ May show inappropriate or excessive emotional response	■ Reduced social perception ■ Confusion in interpreting nonverbal language (e.g., facial expressions)	■ Socially immature behaviors more frequent than conduct disorders
Intellectual and Cognitive	■ Impairment in expressive and receptive language ■ Abnormal perceptual experiences ■ Perceptual distortion of time and space	■ Attention deficits ■ Specific developmental disorder (e.g., reading or math disorder) ■ Language disorders ■ Perceptual disorder (e.g., of time, space, vision)	■ Problems may be specific to one subject or generalized to all subjects ■ Profit from academic programming

(continued)

Table 2.1   *(continued)*

	Severe	Moderate	Mild
Physical and Health	■ May have multiple disabilities (e.g., cerebral palsy and LD) ■ Same as severe for ED with severe problems in eating, sleeping, and elimination	■ May be hyperactive or immovable ■ Perseveration behavior ■ Physical development seems normal	■ May show slower development than normal ■ No one global trait at this level; no generalization is appropriate ■ May be clumsy or awkward
Educational Experience	■ Institution ■ Special schools	■ Special schools ■ Self-contained classes in public schools	■ Public school in special class, resource room, or regular classroom

Emotional Disturbance

	Severe	Moderate	Mild
Time of Identification	■ Variable, though specific disorders can be age-linked (e.g., infantile autism)	■ Variable	■ Often not noticed until school entrance
Social and Emotional	■ May have peculiar speech patterns or elective mutism ■ May be self-destructive ■ May lack responsiveness to others or be extremely dependent	■ Intense anxiety ■ Personal discomfort ■ Inappropriate or ineffective coping ■ Depression	■ May be withdrawn from peers ■ May seek attention in inappropriate ways ■ Exhibit socially immature behaviors or conduct disorders
Intellectual and Cognitive	■ Abnormal perceptual experiences ■ Distorted space and time orientation	■ Attention deficit disorders ■ Specific developmental disorders (e.g., reading or arithmetic disorders) ■ Language disorders	■ Problems may be specific to one subject or generalized to all subjects ■ Profit from academic programming
Physical and Health	■ May be hyperactive or immovable ■ Perseveration behavior ■ Physical development seems normal ■ Severe problems in eating, sleeping, and elimination	■ May be hyperactive or immovable ■ Perseveration behavior ■ Physical development seems normal ■ Severe problems in eating, sleeping, and elimination	■ May show slower development than normal ■ No one global trait at this level; no generalization is appropriate
Educational Experience	■ Institution ■ Special schools	■ Special schools ■ Self-contained classes in public schools	■ Public school in special class, resource room, or general classroom

more and more difficult to separate from conditions not created by cultural mismatch, poverty, or linguistic differences.

Teaching curricula and American ethics have stressed equality (i.e., all people should be treated fairly regardless of race, color, creed, disability, age, gender or sexual preference). Many teachers, among others, have equated educational equality with providing everyone with the same services, products, or experiences. This interpretation of equality needs to be reassessed and interpreted in light of the multiple needs of the children receiving a public education. Rather than attempting to treat all students similarly, true equality means providing children and young adults with an education that addresses their individual needs. Rather than delivering a blanket instructional approach or a singular type of assessment (Thurlow & Liu, 2001), educational equality must address meeting individual needs, which may require quite different types of acknowledgments and learning styles. The task of the educator is complex, challenging, and sometimes incredibly difficult.

Legislation at the federal and state levels justifiably requires schools to educate an increasingly diverse population of students unlike any that has ever before been in the public schools. Federal legislation, such as No Child Left Behind, is straining school resources and requiring districts to be more accountable for student performance. The buck stops, both literally and figuratively, with the classroom teacher. Classroom teachers are held personally and professionally responsible for ensuring that their students achieve academically (Simplicio, 2004). Regardless of ethnic or class background, the majority of students who fall into the mildly handicapped high-incidence categories usually receive services for all or part of the day in the general education setting.

Who Are the Children in High-Incidence Categories?

Children with high-incidence disabilities are the kids down the street, the next-door neighbor, and the first-prize winner in the school coupon-drive contest. Most children with high-incidence disabilities look, act, feel, and talk just like anybody else. If no one had labeled them, they would be indistinguishable from most children labeled "normal." To be sure, some idiosyncrasies would pop up here and there, but who doesn't have an Aunt Bessie who is regarded affectionately as a "little spacey" or a cousin Harry who is great at math but cannot spell his name without a dictionary? Children with high-incidence disabilities are characterized accurately as being *mildly* disabled—just a little bit disabled.

Not all people with high-incidence disabilities are disabled in the same way. Some children have problems in a highly selected area (e.g., fine-motor skills that involve handwriting or cognitive skills that require matching shapes). Other children have multiple disabilities. Ayla, for example, cannot read or write well; she also has some minor problems expressing her thoughts clearly. When a child's primary high-incidence disability is focused on some academic or social behavior, the child becomes noted for that behavior and, as a consequence, receives a special education label. The most popular labels for children with academic and social problems are learning disabled (LD), emotionally disturbed (ED), and educable mentally handicapped (EMH).

Role of the School in Identification

Children with high-incidence disabilities are almost never identified until they reach school age. School, with its ever-present and rigidly adhered-to curricula, does not allow for much deviation. All first-grade children learn to read via the first-grade basal; all second-grade children read the second-grade basal; and third-grade children ... ad nauseam.

Socialization in the schools also has its prescriptions: Hands must be raised before speaking; affectionate jabs are reserved for the playground; lines must be silent, straight, and orderly. A label of high incidence disability awaits any child who violates the school norms with undue frequency.

Quality of Behavior

Norm violators (i.e., children with high-incidence disabilities) who remain in school may have some minor social and emotional problems. They may have brought these problems with them, or they may develop them as a result of inadequate school attendance. Some children with high-incidence disabilities withdraw from their peers, preferring either solitude or the companionship of much younger children. Other, but by no means all, children with high-incidence disabilities may need assistance in practicing the social skills that will enable them to be more acceptable to their peers. Still others may have difficulty making or maintaining friendships. Some children with high-incidence disabilities are in trouble with teachers, parents, or any other authority figure. Strained relationships with teachers and peers can be traced to many different and overlapping sources. Low self-esteem as a learner is often linked to having emotional or behavioral problems thant further impact academic success. Inclusive practices in and of themselves can be stressful in the regular school curriculum (Arman, 2002).

Being excluded or singled out for special services can add to a diminished sense of self and increase stress either from a sense of being different or from not receiving sufficient assistance to access classroom content. Further, excessive conflicts in school can self-perpetuate marginalization from peers, teachers, and school in general. Overriding all these potential sources of frustration is the impact of the disability itself. Toss in a mismatch between the culture of the school and the culture of the child, mix this with a little mutual mistrust between school personnel and the student, and the recipe for school failure is almost a guarantee. Korey represents a whole class of students for whom the system did not work well.

Korey, a fifth-grade boy whose father was white and whose mother was Mexican and Native American, developed an attitude almost as big as he was tall by the time he was 10 years old. Korey was the baby of the family. He had three siblings, two brothers and one sister. Korey had not seen his sister for two years;

she was a runaway. Korey's oldest brother was locked up for pushing drugs, and his other brother, 13-year-old Michael, was actively being recruited into a gang.

Korey was easily three years behind academically in reading and any math above third grade remained a mystery to him. Korey scraped by in school by copying from his neighbors and attempting to charm his teachers, but soon even the peer support was insufficient for passing grades. Korey received special help, but nothing was working.

Korey was not fond of school. He exhibited chronic absenteeism due to bouts with asthma, or he would claim he was too tired. Korey's grades were poor, and his meager skills were failing him fast. Worst of all, Korey began feeling stupid in school, but smart on the streets. Korey was becoming quick to anger and was expelled from school after threatening a teacher.

Five years later, 15-year-old Korey was under house arrest for attempted armed robbery and possession of narcotics. He wore a monitor when attending an alternative school, was still reading at about a third-grade level, and would be eligible for parole in about six months.

Korey, like some students with high-incidence disabilities, had developed a wall of resistance that got in the way of learning (Quiocho & Rios, 2000). Not all students with high-incidence disabilities have the same discouraging tale as Korey, but a great many become alienated from school (Osterman, 2000). School can be a painful reminder of a system that has failed them. The failure to learn effectively can easily contribute to the belief that they cannot compete in school; disenchantment and alienation are close companions for many students with mild high-incidence disabilities. Many children, like Korey, lack the emotional confidence to believe they can learn (Beers, 1999).

Strained Relationships with Peers

Some students with high-incidence disabilities have problems relating to their classmates. For a host of reasons, including an inability to appropriately judge social situations, low self-esteem, and academic stress, many children with high-incidence disabilities in inclusion settings become victims. Two types of profiles for victimization occur: the aggressive victim and the submissive victim. The overarching characteristic of both types of victims is low self-esteem (Egan & Perry, 1998; Perry, Hodges, & Egan, 2001).

Aggressive victims are students who bring on attacks by being disruptive, attention-seeking, or antisocial (Schwartz, Proctor, & Chien, 2001). They are sometimes characterized as being bullies, disrespectful, and unpleasant to be around. They may torment, frighten, or attempt to oppress other children and teachers. They engage in behaviors that get them in trouble, thus proving to them that the world is against them. Peers often avoid them or set them up to get in trouble.

Aaron, for example, likes to name call. He is not selective in giving out verbal abuse to parents, teachers, or peers. He is particularly fond of calling people retards or worse. Aaron struggles with schoolwork. He seems bright, but he is performing about two years behind expected grade level in reading, writing, and any area, like social studies or science, involving reading or writing. He is large for his age, loud, and aggressive. When his teachers threaten to send him to the principal's office or to call his parents, he typically responds with the phrase, "I don't care." When questioned about why he reacts the way he does, he simply shrugs his shoulders and says, "The teachers don't like me."

Behaviorally, however, the majority of victims are passive and submissive. Interaction with others is minimal if at all; passive victims appear ill at ease with their peers. Name-calling and other types of bullying behavior are frequent occurrences in the lives of passive victims. Such children are at increased risk for depression, anxiety, and emotional disturbance. Many passive victims are unable to ward off attacks. They often develop antisocial behaviors and low self-esteem. In addition, some have been characterized as being lonely, having few friends, and even exhibiting suicidal tendencies. They dislike and avoid school and have poor academic performance (Perry et al., 2001). Both aggressive and submissive children are vulnerable; many such children also have high-incidence disabilities.

For victims with high-incidence learning disabilities, it is difficult to determine which comes first, the sociocognitive disability or low academic self-esteem? The proverbial chicken-or-the-egg dilemma seems apropos; nonetheless, classroom teachers in inclusion settings must face the potential problem of victimization for all students, and especially for students with high-incidence disabilities. Teachers must be careful to accurately assess the emotional needs of their students as a contributing factor to classroom behavior. Children who refuse to participate in class discussion by acting out or withdrawing may not be demonstrating rebellious behavior, rather they may resist participation because of fear of being mocked by others in the class. Teachers need to avoid making value judgments about inappropriate conduct and instead look for alternate explanations for atypical behavior. In responding to students who passively opt out of learning opportunities or actively sabotage instruction, teachers must avoid reinforcing their student's past experiences of failure and approach the situation from a problem-solving stance. Instead of reacting or overreacting to a dysfunctional behavior, teachers and students can take a proactive approach to reducing the students' negative emotional issues. (Tschannen-Moran & Hoy, 2000).

Friendships are particularly important for children who are candidates for victimization. Because victims often have a difficult time establishing positive relationships, teachers must guide and shape experiences that provide opportunities for friendship development. Children learn socialization processes through and with their friends; friends serve a particularly unique function by socializing each other. Submissive or aggressive victims can benefit from having friends who are socially well adjusted (Browning, Cohen, & Warman, 2003). If, in fact, children learn social skills from each other or at least can be influenced by each other to develop appropriate social skills, victimization is likely to decrease when friendships are encouraged (Smith, Shu, & Madsen, 2001). The development of friendships cannot be left to chance for children who are potential candidates for victimization. Inclusion teachers must proactively create environments that encourage and nurture opportunities for developing friendships and interaction. Class activities that involve small groups designed to include high peer interaction is one example of how opportunities to provide socialization can be created in inclusion settings.

Risk-Taking

Another characteristic often associated with children with high-incidence disabilities is a need for security. Better to be safe than sorry or, rephrased, better to not try than to fail could be the motto of many children with high-incidence disabilities. Learning is a risky business. In the process of learning, many failures will occur. Effective students risk making mistakes in the learning process and appear to take more pleasure in what they have learned than being concerned about mistakes made along the road to knowledge.

Risk-taking is an important factor in school success. Children who take educational risks typically learn more easily than those who don't. Children who find learning overly uncomfortable typically avoid risking failure. Consequently, they avoid learning situations because they do not trust themselves to learn. Thus, the circle of failure begins. Lack of success increases risk, which leads to even greater discomfort in future learning situations, which leads to even further withdrawal. Once this cycle is established, beliefs that inhibit learning are difficult to modify (Hymes, 2000).

In reading and writing, for example, many children with high-incidence disabilities are painfully reminded of their failure to learn to read and write effectively and efficiently. Oral reading becomes a public humiliation, and spelling is another visual reminder of their disabilities. Because reading and writing are such large parts of the school experience, children with high-incidence disabilities in reading and writing become disenchanted and alienated from school. Without intervention, their participation in reading and writing activities is often marginal (Vacca, 2001).

Due to past experiences, children with high-incidence disabilities have negative attitudes toward learning, and, without appropriate teacher support, they are in danger of avoiding learning opportunities. The key is appropriate support. In well-meaning attempts to assist children with mild learning disabilities, some teachers have enabled them to become passive learners. Another term describing passive learners is *learned helplessness.*

Learned helplessness refers to students' beliefs about themselves as being academic victims who are unable to learn independently. Unless given direct help, they are unwilling to try to learn. They often become dependent on a teacher, classmate, or parent to learn for them. Most often they use the teacher to enable them to be passive learners. Rather than actively engage in learning activities, students with learned helplessness sit and wait for the teacher to do the task for them. When they come to a task that requires a certain amount of struggle to understand, they raise the white flag of surrender by either quitting, never starting the task, or uttering phrases like, "I don't get this"; "Show me how to …"; "This is too hard."

Because they perceive themselves as being unable to learn independently, children who have learned helplessness usually sabotage any effort to learn. Such sabotage is successful in that whatever limited repertoire of strategies they do have stays underdeveloped and sometimes lost altogether. Many children with high-incidence disabilities have learned helplessness. Aides, teachers, and peers can provide appropriate support to these students by encouraging them with prompts and cues for utilizing strategies of learning rather than giving them the answers directly. Inclusion teachers must pay attention to students' beliefs about themselves as learners, and incorporate instructional goals for developing a positive learning self-image (Henson & Gilles, 2003). Instructional plans will only be successful to the extent the learner is willing to engage in the act of learning.

Variability of Behavior

What is quite clear is that the academic and social behavior of children with high-incidence disabilities as a group demonstrates more variability than does the behavior of typical children. Within the category of high-incidence disabilities are greater differences in academic performance than within the category of typical. That is, children classified with high-incidence disabilities appear to be more of a "mixed bag" than children who are classified as normal. If, for example, 50 normal children take a spelling test for grade level, most of them will spell 45 to 50 words correctly, and a few will misspell more than 5. If a group of children with high-incidence disabilities were given the same spelling test, the range of scores would more likely be between 40 and 50, with a few children misspelling more than 10 words. Predicting the spelling score for a child with high-incidence disabilities is harder than predicting the spelling score for a normal child. The normal child has a small range of probable scores (i.e., 45 to 50), whereas the child with high-incidence disabilities has a range of scores twice as large (i.e., 40 to 50).

Another characteristic often associated with high-incidence disabilities is inconsistency of behavior, especially academic behaviors. After three days of successful schoolwork in addition of mixed fractions, the child suddenly may become confused by the process and revert to previous patterns of errors. Yet, on the following day, the entire process may return to the child as if computation of mixed fractions were the most natural event in her mathematical repertoire. No one knows why this variability of behavior occurs, but for children who have high-incidence disabilities, a good educational rule of thumb is to take each teaching day one day at a time. (This rule of thumb may be applied safely to children without disabilities as well.)

Experimental studies with children with high-incidence disabilities have shown that, on the average, they perform the same as normal children on some tasks and below normal on others (Prehm, 1976). The same statement can be made with respect to academic and social behaviors. These observations, taken together with the notion of variability, point strongly to the unique nature of the individuals within the category of high-incidence disability. Just like normal children, not all children with high-incidence disabilities have specific problem areas unique to the individual that need special attention from the teacher. Thus, just as for normal children, the assumption cannot be made that the child with high-incidence disabilities will have problems learning academic or social behaviors. What we can assume is that many children who have been labeled as having high-incidence disabilities will be self-conscious, easily embarrassed, and lacking in confidence in one or more areas of school life. Others may feel no hope for school success and thus will be afraid to try new classroom activities for fear of failure. Through instruction, problems will be uncovered and, through instruction, problems can be resolved.

Academic and social achievement are the major thrusts of inclusion classrooms for children with high-incidence disabilities. Therefore, fewer and fewer special materials and more and more regular materials are used in inclusion settings. More often than not, children with high-incidence disabilities are taught the same subtraction concept in inclusion settings, with or without support of a special education teacher. A significant question arises, however: Can children with high-incidence disabilities be provided with an education in inclusion settings that meets their needs in terms of rate of presentation, number of concepts introduced at one time, and amount of practice available to the student?

In most classrooms for children with high-incidence disabilities, instruction centers on observable academic or social behaviors (e.g., the rate at which a child produces short vowel sounds or the number of times a child uses appropriate question-asking techniques). The primary instructional emphasis is on areas that will lead the child to success in a general education classroom setting, regardless of the child's classification.

Theoretically, the practice of including students with high-incidence disabilities in the general education setting is an appealing one. Achievement differences no longer can be assumed by grade-level placement. The range of instructional levels in general education classrooms, on average, seems to be about 5.4 grade equivalents (Jenkins, Jewell, Leicester, Jenkins, & Troutner, 1991). Probably, in Mrs. Hiser's third-grade class, some children are performing at levels lower than Belinda, Jorge, and Randy, who have been labeled officially as having high-incidence disabilities.

Instructional Adaptations for Inclusive Settings

"Access to the general education curriculum" is the educational motto of the inclusion movement. Accessibility refers to making general education academic and social concepts available to students with disabilities. Access to the general education academic and social content is usually possible for children with high-incidence disabilities when appropriate adaptations are provided. The impact of the adaptations must be considered for instruction and the assessment. When students need adaptations in order to learn, they usually need the same adaptations when they are assessed. Adaptations are two types: accommodations and modifications.

Accommodations are provisions in how students access information and demonstrate learning. Accommodations do not change the instructional level, content, or performance criteria. *Modifications,* in contrast, refer to substantial changes in what the student is expected to learn and demonstrate. Modifications may change the instructional level, content, or performance criteria. Modifications are most often used with children with moderate to severe disabilities; accommodations are most often associated with children who exhibit high-incidence disabilities and who are typically educated in the general education classroom.

Accommodations and modifications must be determined for each student based on individual strengths, needs, and current goals. Students who require accommodations in some areas may need modification in other areas, and the more intensive the students' needs are, the more likely it is that the student will need adaptations. The type of adaptation needs to be described very clearly. Teachers must know exactly what adaptations are needed for the student to be successful in accessing educational and social content. Vague statements, such as "extended time for tests" or "modified assignments," are too broad to be very useful. Instead, statements such as "double the allotted time for test-taking" or "create assignments using font size 24" are much more precise and, therefore, more easily implemented.

Many accommodations do not look much different than best practices in educational delivery; that is, instruction that has proven successful for children without disabilities. Instructional practices that enable the typical learner access to content can also work for many at-risk or atypical learners in inclusion settings. Recent implications for instruction based on brain-based research, for example, provide a lot of ideas for how to give all students support in accessing content. A brief list of teaching suggestions founded on brain-based research is presented in Table 2.2. Accommodations, however, target individual students' specific identified needs. Accommodations can include changes in setting, presentation format, response mode, timing or scheduling.

Table 2.2 Synopsis of teaching practices derived from brain-based research

Brained-Based Principle	Application to Classroom
Present an overview of the whole assignment for projects and then move to the details.	Give the students the big picture first: • what they'll be learning • how it relates to what they've already learned • why it is important to learn • where this information will be used
Learning related to personally relevant information is highly motivating.	Determine if the topic is relevant to your students. If the topic is not relevant, plan activities that will make the content more significant to your students. Students are more motivated to study and learn information that is personally relevant.

(continued)

Table 2.2   *(continued)*

Brained-Based Principle	Application to Classroom
Identify patterns that connect learning to prior knowledge.	Brainstorm ideas with your students that focus on how the new topic is similar to what they've learned in other classes, times, subjects, or personal experiences. Teach students to use words that help them compare, for example, *like, similar to, same as,* etc.
Utilize as many senses as possible.	Incorporate as much as possible activities engaging sight, hearing, smelling, touching, and tasting. The more senses we use, the more we are likely to learn.
People use more than one kind of intelligence to learn.	Draw upon the multiple intelligences (a list is provided at the end of this chapter) to tap into students preferred learning style. Try to teach using as many different types of intelligence as you can in a lesson, but focus on each of them on a regular basis.
Provide the appropriate level of difficulty.	The tasks should be neither too difficult nor too easy. The tasks that are too difficult will cause the student to give up. The tasks that are too easy will create boredom.
Emotions provide another avenue for learning.	Learning should engage positive affect. Incorporate activities that will provide the students with the sense of fun, excitement, caring, or interest.
Choices in learning create motivation.	Provide your students with outlines or lists of choices for demonstrating or learning new information.
Novelty attracts attention.	Alter the who, what, why, where, how, and when of a lesson format (e.g., bring in a guest speaker, change the topic, rearrange the room, etc.).
Create a sense of stability.	Students like predictability of routine. Create classroom rituals, for example. When finished with the task, students can choose to listen to music or play a game. Another example of ritual is the highly anticipated popcorn party on Friday afternoon.
Provide formative feedback.	Teachers may provide learners with constructive feedback while they are designing and developing their projects. Students can modify and revise their work to end up with better results when subtle suggestions, cues, and prompts are provided prior to task completion.
Allow time for reflection.	Students need time to think about or consider what they are learning, strategies they used in learning, why the knowledge is important, and how they could learn more.

Source: Adapted from "Planning Your Lessons to Be Brain-Friendly by D. Wurst, 1998–99 (Winter), *The Mailbox Teacher, 27,* 12–17.

Setting Accommodations

Setting refers to where students receive instruction or assessment. Setting may be considered the room itself or the physical arrangement of furniture and materials in a classroom. The setting can also be considered according to group size; for example, one-on-one, small group, or large group. Andrew, who is highly distractible and has issues with attention, rarely comprehends task expectations when presented to the entire class. On the other hand, he is able to achieve on grade level if he is provided with one-on-one instruction for 5–6 minutes at the beginning of the independent work time. Melanie also needs accommodations if she is going to demonstrate her understanding of the social studies content. Melanie has problems integrating information. She cannot organize information to take notes or to produce answers to essay questions. In addition, she has fine-motor issues, which create fatigue in her hands when she must write for more than 2–3 minutes. An accommodation setting for Melanie might be to take written exams in another room with the special education teacher serving as a secretary or to use a voice synthesizer and dictation program to respond via computer rather than in manuscript or cursive. Melanie's organizational issues and note-taking challenges would need to be addressed with other types of accommodations.

Accommodations in Presentation Format

Presentation format refers to what the teacher does to material or delivery of content to allow a better match between the student's needs and access to content. For example, a student with visual perception problems may need textbooks with large print, less material on a page, or whatever change in material allows the student access to the content. For some students with severe reading disabilities, an accommodation in presentation format could be to provide the material via some type of auditory format, for example, books on tape. Written material, such as worksheets, quizzes, or handouts, can be scanned and put on a personal computer, which then transforms the print media into auditory output.

Accommodations in presentation format may also include highlighting key words or phrases, putting stop and start signs on answer forms, providing outline guides for essay questions, and, in the case of Melanie, a preprinted set of class notes. Many ideas for response mode accommodations can be derived from utilizing multiple-intelligence activities, as well as many of the principles found in brained-based research.

Response Mode Accommodations

Response mode accommodations focus on how the students demonstrate that they are able to access classroom knowledge. How can students within the high-incidence categories in inclusion settings show the teacher what they have learned? Can they bubble in answers or do they need to write the answer on a test book form and have them transcribed later? Can they physically manipulate a writing instrument or is a computer need for narrative response? How much fatigue does the required response mode create?

Fatigue from a variety of factors is a constant companion for Tyrone. Analysis of the responses on Tyrone's quizzes would suggest that three different children answered this test. The first third of the test is well done, organized, and legible. The second third of the test starts to show deterioration in Tyrone's responses, and by the time the third section of the test is reviewed, almost no responses are produced, and the ones that are completed make very little sense. Spelling, ideation, and organization go from excellent at the beginning of the test to almost nonexistent or very poor by the time Tyrone is finished. Many students with high-incidence disabilities, like Tyrone, understand general education information but have limited stamina or underdeveloped skills in reading and writing to demonstrate their actual knowledge level.

Timing or Scheduling Accommodations

Some students with high-incidence disabilities are overwhelmed by the amount of time a task may take. Many students do not know how to organize large bodies of time or tasks requiring more than one part. Paola, for example, would be unable to complete a social studies project involving more than one component and requiring about two weeks to complete. A typical "research a state" social studies project, including components like drawing a state tree, writing a one-page history, producing a state flag, and generating a brief biography of a famous person from a state, would be overwhelming to Paola. Even if the teacher attaches dates to the subprojects, Paola would be lost. A timing accommodation that would meet Paola's needs is a 2- to 3-minute daily progress review with her teacher. For Paola, the tasks within each project may need to be broken into even smaller units. Paola needs a sequence to follow for drawing the state tree. (Paola's sequenced direction sheet for drawing a state tree is presented in Table 2.3.) Not all students will need as detailed a list as Paola, but many students with organizational disabilities can profit from sequenced and detailed instructional directions for tasks requiring multiple steps.

Classroom tests or quizzes for children with high-incidence disabilities can be scheduled in a number of ways. The midterm and final exams commonly found at the middle school level may be overwhelming to these students. Rather than schedule the midterm exam or final on one day, the teacher may need to break up the exam over five days. The content and format being examined will be the same, but the scheduling or timing will be distributed rather than concentrated on one day.

Other types of scheduling accommodations include the need for routine with the easiest or warm-up tasks presented prior to more difficult or new information. In taking a classroom quiz, for example, some children will need to start with identification items like multiple-choice or true/false items and then proceed to essays. Coupled with the fatigue factor, however, other children may need to start with the essays and finish the test with the multiple-choice or true/false items.

Accommodations must fit the needs of the child to be assisted. A sample of various types of accommodations is presented in Table 2.4. The accommodations

Table 2.3 Paola's schedule for drawing a state tree

Follow these directions in order to figure out how to draw the state tree. Check off each step as it is completed.

Find out the name of the state tree of Arizona.

Step 1: Go to the computer.   _____
Step 2: Go to www.google.com.   _____
Step 3: Ask for name of the state tree of Arizona.   _____
Step 4: Write down the name of the tree.   _____

Find a picture of the state tree of Arizona.

Step 1: Go back to www.google.com.   _____
Step 2: Ask for a picture of the name of the tree.   _____
Step 3: Print a picture of the tree.   _____

Draw a picture of the state tree of Arizona.

Step 1: Look at the colors and shape of the tree.   _____
Step 2: Use ½ of the paper to draw the tree.   _____
Step 3: Use your crayons or markers to color the tree.   _____
Step 4: Label the tree.   _____
Step 5: Put your name on the drawing.   _____
Step 6: Put your drawing in your state portfolio.   _____

suggested are meant to serve as a prompt or beginning point for designing potential accommodations that are an appropriate fit between classroom expectations and accessibility issues faced by a particular child in the high-incidence disabilities category who is being served in the general education classroom.

As student diversity increases, the process of modifying the instructional environment in general classrooms becomes as reality-based as the 35 labeled and unlabeled majority and minority students who greet their teachers each school day. Fortunately, techniques exist that can ease the educational tug and pull of change. Ways to increase learning that teachers can use include (a) setting expectations, (b) providing instructional feedback, (c) assisting the child in organizing information, (d) furnishing practice time, and (e) delivering systematic incentives or consequences. These methods should serve as a kind of mental checklist when considering the mental operations for the learning task.

These five methods are by no means all the options that teachers can use to encourage learning. They do, however, contain the major areas of teacher influence. If these five methods are used effectively, many of the cognitive and social learning problems within our schools could be eliminated or reduced greatly. The extent to which teachers involve themselves with these factors is relative to the child's needs.

Table 2.4   Samples of various types of accommodations used in inclusion settings

Area of Instruction	Common Accommodation Strategies
Vocabulary	Modified vocabulary list: In English or any other disciplines that require vocabulary, a shortened vocabulary list can be helpful. Picture cards: Pictures that represent the terms can be used in place of or in addition to verbal descriptions
Organization of Assignments	Monitored assignment books: The teacher signs the student's assignment book or log of daily assignments, indicating that the assignment is written in the book correctly. Parents are notified if the assignment is not turned in on time. Copies of lesson plans: Teachers will give parents a copy of their lesson plans for the week so parents know ahead of time what major assignments are due and know when tests are scheduled.
Spelling	Word banks: Individualized spelling vocabulary based on the student's requests or most frequently used words. Audio spell-checkers: Many students with poor spelling skills need an audio presentation to accompany the visual list of choices.
Note Taking	Copy of lecture notes: Lecture notes may be provided to the students. Such notes may either be complete or partially completed with the expectation that the student will complete the notes. Peer note takers: Another student in the class can take notes using carbon paper and provide an additional copy to the student in need.
Oral Presentations	Pictures: Students may be allowed to have pictures on note cards in place of or in addition to narratives.
Reading Comprehension	Pre- and post-reading discussion: Highlight main ideas and significant details before and after reading a paragraph, a page, or two or three pages. Look-back strategies: Have students answer questions that require rereading or looking back at previously read paragraphs, sections, or units.

Setting Expectations

Role of Motivation

Intrinsic motivation is characterized by inspiration, drive, and enthusiasm generated by the learner. Intrinsic motivation could easily be called internal motivation because the motivation comes from within the learner's values and beliefs. For some students with high-incidence disabilities, motivation to learn has been dimmed. Repeated failure lowers the students' self-motivation while success raises competence and confidence (Alfassi, 2003). Teachers can create a classroom that will rekindle or start the fire of self-motivation for students having low academic self-concepts.

Teachers first may have to focus on activities that jump-start children who no longer believe in themselves as learners or the school system to teach them to learn. Jump-start techniques are typically related to external motivation. Since school is no longer motivating to many students in the high-incidence disabilities categories, teachers need to identify what is motivating while simultaneously removing situations that are not motivating (Hertzberg, 2003). Teachers need to create situations that not only remove or minimize factors that discourage students, but also encourage them through successful experiences.

External motivation means that the teacher is in charge of providing some sort of a reward or, in some cases, a punishment that will encourage a child minimally to go through the motions of learning. As children's extrinsic motivation is externally reinforced, for example, using incentives such as money, grades, free time, and so on, to begin or complete a task, teachers can also provide verbal information about the importance of the tasks. Once again, the teacher must be able to judge how much external reinforcement is enough to motivate a given child. If the teacher gives Roxanne external rewards as reinforcement for behavior that she already find inherently rewarding, the teacher may undermine Roxanne's interest in the tasks and also the quality of her work (Eisenberger, Pierce, & Cameron, 1999). Teachers need to be careful not to trivialize the learning tasks by rewarding minimal performance.

When children buy into appropriate incentives, the teacher has a better chance of securing attention and persistence from them as learners. As the students begin to develop more skills, they become more able to do the schoolwork. They begin to experience some successes that can lead to attributing some value to themselves as learners. The teacher can foster the beginning sense of motivation by ensuring that success is plentiful and frequent. Successful learners are typically calmer and often more motivated at least to attempt to work. The idea that the task is important and worth the effort to do without extrinsic motivation can build upon the child's success (Deci, Koestner, & Ryan, 1999; Dev, 1998). Success builds success. Success as an independent learner reduces learned helplessness and creates a sense of personal pride.

Teachers determine the child's success level. Therefore, teachers must systematically construct classroom practices that foster the growth of internal motivation. For children who have become disenchanted with themselves as learners, teachers cannot leave to chance the number and type of successes their students will experience. In other words, planned situations that create opportunities for success are critical when developing intrinsic motivation in all students, but especially so for students who have classified themselves as unsuccessful learners.

Take the case of Emmett. He was being devoured by fears of academic and social failure. Some days he seemed like a squirrel frantically running in an exercise wheel—lots of motion but getting nowhere. Other days he seemed like a puppet with all its strings removed. Emmett finally stopped doing his classwork and reduced his interactions with peers and teacher.

The classroom teacher realized she had a scared and lonely child in her room. She had to reduce Emmett's fear of failure, so she removed possible sources of failure. Out went formal written tests. In their place came informal teacher conferences and small-group discussion. Grades were the next to go. Much written and verbal praise made Emmett believe that his work was valued. Through encouragement and less pressure (internally and externally produced), Emmett began to develop a more positive view of himself. Through the continued use of teacher-assisted self-evaluation, Emmett began to assess both his strengths and his weaknesses more realistically. As the layers of academic and social learning problems eased, a bright and happy child emerged. By the end of the school year, Emmett was president of the math club at school and was reading everything available. Not all stories end quite as positively as Emmett's, but you can establish a classroom in which an expectancy of success is fostered for all children.

Role of Reinforcement

Reinforcement is any consequence of behavior that increases the probability of that behavior being repeated in the future (Meyen & Skrtic, 1995). Self-efficacy is the extent to which people expect that they can complete a behavior successfully. For example, if Margaret believes that paying attention in health class will result in a good grade, she is more likely to pay attention to her health instructor. Similarly, if Joel believes that he is going to receive a poor grade in health no matter how much he pays attention, he is not likely to pay attention and is very likely to receive a poor grade.

Both Margaret and Joel base their expectations for success and failure not only on their experiences in health class but also in their other classes. Margaret is used to experiencing success in academic work, and Joel knows only failure. Because of Margaret's previous successes, she sharpens her attending skills. Joel's lack of success has decreased his attending to the teacher. On the rare occasions when he attempts to attend, his knowledge base is so incomplete that he is lost. Saddled with unpracticed attending skills and a shaky knowledge base, Joel is well poised to fail again. If the teacher does not watch out, Joel can even be a triple loser. If he uses Margaret as the standard by which he judges his own worth, his self-concept is liable to take a meteoric plunge.

Cultural Differences

Reinforcers are not all equally reinforcing. Tangible reinforcements like stars, certificates, or other benefits of competition may be reinforcing to some students, but not to others. Achievement differences and reinforcing objects or events among students in cultural groups are found in the various goals that are valued (Dembo, 2004). For example, Michael, a white male student, wants good grades in school so that some day he can make a lot of money. Juan, a Latino student in the same class, said that he wanted to do well in school so that he would be able to help his brothers and sisters with their schoolwork. Both students wanted to succeed, but what motivates Michael is very different from what motivates Juan. Michael is more likely to be reinforced with stars, certificates, and other benefits of competition. Juan, on the other hand, may find very little use for stars, preferring instead grades that represent what he truly has learned in school. Reinforcement cannot be thought of as an absolute; it is relative to the needs of students. Such relativity means that students respond to their environments in terms of their experiences (Strand, Barnes-Holmes, & Barnes-Holmes, 2003), but they also make choices, weighing the benefit of one type of reinforcement against another.

Children, regardless of culture or disability, operate according to a kind of cost-benefit analysis principle. The cost-benefit analysis principle means that decisions are made based on the repercussions of some behaviors as weighed against the impact of alternate or competing behaviors (Rachlin, 2000). Reinforcement has to do with choice, but the choice is within the child more than the teacher.

Let's return to the example of Michael and Juan. For Michael, being first in his class represents his chance to be a big money maker later in life. He prefers to work hard so that he will be a success in the future. For Michael, failure to work hard is not compatible with his goal of financial remuneration. Juan also balances his need for success against the impact of school failure. If Juan fails in school, the future of his brothers and sisters is also in jeopardy. Both Juan and Michael look at the benefits of the effort that they must exert in order to arrive at their goals. Both Juan and Michael have decided that the effort in school is worth ultimately achieving their goals.

For students in the high-incidence disabilities categories, the principle is the same; that is, they must weigh their effort in learning against success or failure in school. If the effort is too great, as perceived by the child, then no amount of stars, certificates, or even success for the family is reinforcing. Reinforcement is a delicate balancing act. The one in charge of this act is the student who determines which behavior(s) will create the best personal benefits (Snyder, 2002). For example, Idella rarely finishes her classwork. Idella prefers to enjoy the company of her friends, to daydream, and to avoid classwork at all costs. No amount of tangible reinforcement or fear of retribution from her teachers or parents can convince Idella that completing her work is more beneficial to her than avoiding her work. In Idella's scheme of the world, not doing work is more beneficial than struggling through material that requires too much psychological or cognitive effort.

To help Idella choose a more constructive and ultimately more advantageous approach to choosing reinforcement, a more indirect method for changing her work completion behavior is needed. One such indirect technique is "Errorless Compliance Training" (Ducharme, Atkinson, & Poulton, 2000). Using this procedure, Idella's teachers and parents would refrain from generating or applying negative consequences whenever Idella did not complete her schoolwork. Instead, Idella would be asked to complete some aspect of her work that she is most likely to do. For example, she may initially be asked to write one or two sentences in place of a five-paragraph essay describing her current social studies topic. As Idella becomes successful with each phase of instruction (that is, completing the two sentences), her teachers will request increasingly, but not perceptually, more demanding aspects of the work. As the momentum for compliance is generated, Idella, at least in principle, will increase her capacity and willingness to finish her schoolwork under increasingly more complex conditions. In essence, Idella will find completion of a small portion of the task more personally reinforcing than the previously more reinforcing off-task behaviors.

Failure Mentality

Teachers of children with cognitive and social learning problems are concerned about the effect of student failure, for these students seem to have a high generalized expectancy for failure. A failure mentality causes too much energy to be directed at avoiding academic and social school behaviors. With continued failure on school tasks, the child can resort to noninvolvement, token observance of tasks, or reduction of the sense of failure by not competing (Peach, Cobb, Caudle, Craig, & Wilson, 1991).

Providing Instructional Feedback

After a child has given an answer, the teacher provides feedback on the correctness of the answer. Based on instructional feedback, the child can continue answering or adapt the response. For example, if Kevin's teacher tells him his penmanship is very good, Kevin knows to continue using that style of penmanship. If, on the other hand, Kevin's teacher tells him his handwriting bears a remarkable resemblance to chicken scratches, Kevin may choose to alter his penmanship style.

The way in which feedback is provided also can influence learning. Let's return to Kevin. Kevin's teacher can provide feedback in a number of ways. The technique his teacher uses will determine the effect of the feedback on Kevin's future performance in penmanship.

Nonfunctional Feedback

A partial list of rather useless but commonplace feedback techniques is as follows:

1. Appeal to the child's "thinking habits."
2. Appeal to the child's "work habits."
3. Appeal to the child's "sense of history."
4. Appeal to the child's "sense of fair play."

APPEAL TO THE CHILD'S "THINKING HABITS"   "Now Kevin, just think about how those letters should look!" Kevin may have been thinking about those letters, and he may have produced them the way he thought they should look. The teacher has given him two feedback messages. Feedback message number 1: Your penmanship is awful. Feedback message number 2: Your thinking skills aren't too sharp either! What Kevin's teacher has *not* provided is instructional information. Kevin could sit and think about penmanship all day, but unless he is given some focus, he may not know what to think about—though bike riding may be a rather pleasant option.

APPEAL TO THE CHILD'S "WORK HABITS"   "Kevin, don't be so lazy. Try harder!" Assuming Kevin is willing to "try harder," he is still left with a rather vague notion of what to try harder about in penmanship. Should he press his pencil harder, or should he hold his paper tighter?

APPEAL TO THE CHILD'S "SENSE OF HISTORY"   "Kevin, I've taught both your older brother and your older sister. They had excellent handwriting, and I expect the same from you!" Poor Kevin. Not only must he improve his handwriting without being given any instructional information, he also must follow in the penmanship steps of his brother and sister.

APPEAL TO THE CHILD'S "SENSE OF FAIR PLAY"   "Kevin, I've worked very hard to teach you to write. Now please show me that you can do better." Not only does Kevin have a penmanship problem, but he's also being drenched in guilt. Guilty or not, Kevin still does not have a clue about how to improve his handwriting.

Functional Feedback Techniques

The key to providing functional feedback is to give useful instructional information. Three techniques that provide useful information to the child are the following:

1. Provide rules.
2. Provide immediate feedback.
3. Provide correction of responses.

PROVIDE RULES   Not all instructional information is useful. Take the example of Kevin one more time. His handwriting is still not the model of perfection. His teacher has avoided all the "appeals" feedback techniques. She says, "Kevin, your handwriting is too large. You need to write a little smaller." At last Kevin has been given some instructional information but, alas, not quite enough. The next time Kevin shows his work his teacher exclaims, "Kevin, now your handwriting is too small! You need to write a little larger." What's the poor child to do? He needs a rule. In Kevin's case the sought-after rule is "the uppercase letters are a whole space high and lowercase letters are a half space high."

PROVIDE IMMEDIATE FEEDBACK   For all children, but especially children with social and cognitive learning problems, the more quickly feedback is given, the more willing the child is to proceed with the task. To avoid the fear-of-failure syndrome, the child must receive some sort of feedback signal that all is well. If all is not well, the teacher should provide feedback even more immediately to prevent the child from practicing incorrect work. In a class of 30 to 50 students, the teacher may not be willing or physically able to bound from desk to desk providing feedback. No problem—personal delivery of feedback is neither necessary nor recommended. Remember that feedback provides a rule; then any technique for presenting the rule should be acceptable.

Three alternatives for providing rules are group response, self-correction, and peer or cross-age tutors.

1. Group responses can be delivered orally or in writing. In a typical classroom, an example of a written group activity might center on a lesson in addition facts. The teacher calls out a fact: "3 + 7"; the students write their answer on a small chalkboard (a piece of scrap paper, a 3" x 5" index card, etc.) and hold up the answer for their teacher to see. The teacher is the only one who can see the answers (eliminating a potentially embarrassing situation) and with one quick scanning motion can see immediately who has the correct (or incorrect) response. The teacher then can provide the rule "3 + 7 = 10" and proceed to the next number fact.

Oral group responses can be a little more tricky. Although the teacher usually can pick out the child in the group who is saying the short *u* sound for the long *u* sound, so can everybody else. Most of the children will not be attending to anyone but themselves, but that in itself can become a problem for the child who expects failure. In a situation where a child is likely to become embarrassed, judicious use of group responses is recommended. The teacher may want to set up the child to answer correctly, especially if she has just erred. Consider the following example.

Mr. Alexander has just introduced the basic rule for adding –*ing* to words. He has written the following list on the chalkboard:

hum _____ humming
stop _____ stopping
set _____ setting
pet _____ petting

As he points to the word, he says, "Hum becomes _____" and waits for the children's responses. All goes well until the word *set*. From Cleo's tiny little voice comes the response "setter." Mr. Alexander needs to set Cleo up to answer correctly. He repeats the correct answer: "*Set* becomes *setting.* Everyone, what does *set* become?" We hope the word from Cleo is *setting.* To single Cleo out could have become a source of embarrassment to her. Instead, Mr. Alexander provided Cleo, along with the rest of the class, with the rule, feedback on her response, and a chance to try again, all within the context of a large-group setting.

2. Self-correction allows children to monitor themselves. If the teacher has provided correct responses, children can check their work against the responses. Checking can be immediate and not create a demand on the teacher. Self-monitoring also allows children to actively engage in their own learning.

Answer keys can come in various shapes and formats. How a teacher chooses to use an answer key depends on the purpose of the lesson. The rule for getting the correct answer should be available on the key. If the children are working on equations, the rule on the answer key should state clearly that if you change one side of the equation, you have to change the other side. An example of the rule is always helpful. If the answer lends itself to a step-by-step solution, the steps also can be shown.

What if the child simply copies down the work from the response key? At least the child is copying the correct response rather than copying a potentially incorrect response from a neighbor. Granted, no teacher wants the child copying every response every time, but occasional copying to complete assignments is preferred to no attempt or repeated incorrect attempts.

To lessen the chance that the children will think they have fooled the teacher or gotten something for nothing, the teacher can simply state that it is all right for students to copy answers they cannot solve and that they should indicate in some way when they have copied. Teachers also can control copying by providing answers and models for every other problem.

3. Peer or cross-age tutors constitute a third method of providing immediate feedback. When students from upper grades work as classroom aides or assistants, no one child is isolated for tutorial assistance. The cross-age tutor's main function is to answer questions and check seatwork.

Another technique for peer tutoring is to use the children in the classroom. Instead of working in isolation, children can work together on special projects. Most children are capable of completing their work if they get some help from one of their peers. Some authorities have suggested that children learn more from their peers than from adults. The point is not whether children will copy but, rather, to provide them with immediate and regular feedback.

PROVIDE CORRECTION OF RESPONSES   Correction is necessary and vital to teaching/learning. Children need to be told when their responses are incorrect as well as when their responses are correct. Unfortunately, some teachers suffer from the "Oh-dear-I'm-afraid-I'll-hurt-their-feelings" syndrome. Students are in much greater danger of being hurt if they build their knowledge base on faulty information.

Correction Procedures and Self-Image

Preserving the child's self-image is a critical part of the correction procedure. Engelmann (1969) provided an excellent correction technique:

1. Repeat the child's correct answers, perhaps adding "good."
2. Do not repeat the child's incorrect answers, but say "no," and then give the correct answer.

Suppose the teacher is trying to teach Clara how to identify parallel lines for a geometry lesson. Clara indicates that she thinks parallel lines mean perpendicular lines by pointing to a set of perpendicular lines and saying, "These lines are parallel." If Clara's teacher responds positively or doesn't respond at all, Clara will accept perpendicular lines for parallel ones.

Clara's teacher must let her know immediately. She could say, "No, Clara, these lines are not parallel," and then demonstrate the concept of parallel and perpendicular lines with two sets of pencils, pointing out how parallel lines never can touch. In a concrete manner, Clara's teacher has provided a corrected response, a rule for the correct response, and a model for getting the correct answer. The teacher's tone of voice and body language reassure Clara that she is valued even though her response was incorrect. Corrections frequently make up as much as 60%–70% of teacher responses. When this is the case, the task should be restructured. Not only are the children not learning the task, they also may be feeling like failures. The teacher should restructure the task, not the goal, so the children will succeed. As Engelmann (1969) suggested:

> Simplify the task, or distribute it over a number of teaching sessions, so that he will see your [the teacher's] yes and no responses in proper perspective—as sources of information and not as punishment or as proof that he is stupid. (p. 54)

Final Words Regarding Verbal Feedback

The type of verbal feedback that is provided to a child makes a difference in how the child will perform. Verbal feedback can shape the child's confidence and competence as a learner. The way praise is provided to children differentially influences their efforts (Watts Jr., Cashwell, & Schweiger, 2004). When, for example, Paloma is told that she is working very hard on her drawing, she is being given praise for her effort. Paloma can internalize this praise and begin to value working hard or persisting on the task. On the other hand, Paloma could be told that she is really good at drawing. With this message, Paloma can interpret that she has very good ability in drawing. Paloma can internalize this message as indicating that she has artistic skills. A third means of providing Paloma with praise could be to tell her that she has produced a beautiful drawing. Now the praise goes to the outcome or the product, not really to Paloma.

Teachers of children in the high-incidence disabilities categories must carefully think through the type of feedback or praise they provide. The influence of various types of feedback is complex; teachers of children in the high incidence disabilities must carefully craft the type of information they hope to have their students internalize. Does the child need to build a positive self-image? If so, feedback and praise need to focus on the student's competence. Does the child need to feel particular pride with a specific skill? If so, feedback and praise need to focus on a product created by the student.

Assisting the Child to Organize Information

Many students in the high-incidence disabilities categories have organizational issues so great that they are unable to benefit fully from instruction. Most of these children do not have an active organizational plan for selecting strategies for organizing material in such a way that they can manage classroom-related assignments. Their organizational issues range from overall self-management to organization for studying.

Mickey, a bright and socially confident child, is such a student. Mickey is constantly losing books and papers, missing assignment deadlines, and failing often to follow written directions. He lacks strategies for studying and often relies on classroom discussions as his primary source of information. Mickey's written responses appear to be more streams of consciousness than a logical sequence. His finished papers look like rough drafts with ideas often out of order or missing. Children like Mickey create daily challenges for inclusion teachers.

One important factor in student achievement is conscientiousness. Conscientious children tend to be organized, careful, and disciplined; they are the exact opposite of children like Mickey, who are often disorganized, careless, and impulsive (Brothen & Wambach, 2001). Conscientious students monitor and control their behaviors (Dembo, 2004), whereas disorganized students typically neither check nor manage their behaviors.

Disorganized students need teachers to teach them how to be more conscientious. Most children learn organizational skills indirectly or with minimal exposure. However, many students with high-incidence disabilities are either lacking or severely limited in organizational knowledge. Many of these students do not need major instructional assistance; they do need systematic guidance. Inclusion teachers need to prioritize the amount and degree of instructional assistance needed by their disorganized students.

The following sequence can be used as an instructional guide for teachers who are working with students who often exhibit disorganized behaviors in the classroom (McCoy, 2000). The activities are listed in order of use and delivery, with the first activity being the simplest and least time-consuming:

- Improve notebook organization
- Provide a study partner
- Monitor organizational progress

Improve Notebook Organization

Teaching students how to organize their notebooks is neither a complex nor difficult instructional task, but it must be taught for students who lose their papers, stuff material into their backpacks, and cram their desks to overflowing. Formal instruction in how to organize notebooks is very important for students like Mickey who lack organizational structure or order. The first level of order will be to address Mickey's binder; that is, if Mickey has a binder at all. Many disorganized students have no place to put their papers. As a result, papers can be found almost anywhere and in no particular order. The concept of categorizing materials by dates, content, or type is nonexistent. The lowly three-ring binder can become an all-powerful organizer for Mickey and his disorganized peers. Any kind of binder is better than no binder at all, but the best binder would be a zippered three-ring notebook, sometimes referred to as a trapper-keeper. Trapping would be the optimal term for Mickey's papers. A zippered binder is one safeguard for trapping papers that might otherwise fall out of the binder before being appropriately sorted.

The binder is divided into areas by class and separated by tabbed dividers and a pocket folder for class assignments and the final divider for announcements to go home. The tabbed dividers are placed according to the sequence of classes or subjects the student is taking and are used to provide the student with a sense of order, for sequence, time, and organization of material. The teacher can take nothing for granted and must assume that the student needs to be directly instructed in how the tabs reflect sequence, time, and organization of material. Return to Mickey. Mickey's teacher cannot assume that Mickey will understand that the tabs are directly related to the courses he takes during the day. His teacher must show him that Tab 1 relates directly to the first class of the day. Then Mickey's teacher must explain that the tabs are used to organize material by class content.

A pocket folder is also a vital part of the organizational system. A pocket folder is included in each instructional area. The purpose of the pocket folder is to hold only assignments that need to be returned to the teacher. Notes or papers for a particular class are placed behind the pocket folder. The pocket folder becomes the sole storage place for assignments. Students like Mickey will have one and only one place to collect work for each class.

Monitoring the Binder

The degree and amount of time the teacher will spend to monitor the notebook depends on the performance of the student. Most disorganized students will need daily monitoring until the notebook system becomes automatic. Monitoring entails a cycle of continued modeling, guided practice, and independent practice. As the student's organizational skills become more habitual, the teacher can gradually reduce the time spent in the monitoring cycle. Once the student no longer loses assignments or homework, little or no monitoring will be necessary.

The monitoring process can be done by a variety of persons, with the ultimate goal of the student doing self-monitoring. The initial step to teaching self-monitoring organization will entail some kind of check sheet that lists the steps needed to determine the success of the organization. Figure 2.1 represents a binder check sheet that can be used initially with the student and teacher and eventually by the student independently. The binder check sheet is like a metacognitive organizer, but in print form.

Providing a Study Partner

Sometimes notebooks and check sheets are not sufficient to keep a student organized or on track. Jesse, for example, kept her notebook organized, but she did not complete all assignments and homework. Jesse was not always certain about what the assignments were or when they were due. She needed support in focusing on the task demands and time management. Jesse was lucky because her teacher was very organized and a good manager. Instead of trying to check on Jesse every day, the teacher provided support through the formation of study partners.

Study partners are other students in the class who typically complete assignments consistently. In other words, at least one of the partners is characterized as conscientious with respect to classwork. More often than not, students can choose

Directions: Please use this form every day to check that your binder is organized. Place a Y in each box that is complete.

	Mon.	Tues.	Wed.	Thurs.	Fri.
All papers are filed in the correct sections.					
Completed assignments to give to teacher are in their pockets.					
Notes and extra papers are placed in the correct section behind the pockets.					
Announcements to take home are in the correct sections.					
This form is in the front of your binder.					

Monitored by: _____

Figure 2.1 Binder Check Sheet

their own study partners. The study partners do not actually study with each other, but rather serve as contacts who can be relied on to clarify assignments or due dates. Students can check with each other during class, after school, or in the evening at home to verify assignments.

Monitoring Daily Work

In order for some students to establish organizational skills necessary to access classroom content, instruction in the use of a daily planner becomes critical. Many schools provide planners for all the students, but usually the students who need them the most have no idea why they should be using a planner. Often the planners are checked for completion, and, more often than not, the student who is failing classes has not completed the planner in any conscientious manner. Ironically, these disorganized students find themselves week after week, month after month, receiving some sort of punitive recognition for not being conscientious enough to fill out the planner. Although many students can use planners appropriately, disorganized students need direct instruction and monitoring. Monitoring the daily planner entails the same cycle of continued modeling, guided practice, and independent practice as used to monitor the binder.

Sometimes the daily planner adopted by the school needs to have a more detailed supplementary sheet to provide the students additional structure. The purpose of the supplementary sheet is to provide specific lists of what has to be accomplished in each subject area or throughout the day, not to create additional work for the student. An example of a supplemental sheet is shown in Figure 2.2.

The supplemental sheet can be an adaptation of the standard progress forms used in the school. The behaviors in the first column are the same behaviors as those targeted for teacher evaluation. The numbers 0–4, ranging from unacceptable to outstanding, are also part of the school's progress forms. The teacher can transfer the information directly from the forms to grading sheets or use them to describe progress at parent–teacher conference meetings. To avoid losing sheets, the supplemental form can be stapled to the tabbed divider. A supplemental sheet would be created for each subject area.

Monitoring the supplemental sheets entails the same cycle of continued modeling, guided practice, and independent practice as used for monitoring the binder and daily planner. The supplemental sheets take the monitoring one step further. The supplemental sheets could be considered an informal contractual relationship between the student, the student's parents, and the teacher. Each will review the supplemental sheet and include a signature denoting inspection. Depending on the degree of disorganization shown by the child, monitoring with the teacher or with a study partner could occur at the end of each class or at the end of each day.

Subject: _____					
Daily information	**Monday**	**Tuesday**	**Wednesday**	**Thursday**	**Friday**
Assignments in class					
Homework					
Tests					
Attention in class					
Participation & cooperation					

Name: _____   Date: _____

4 = outstanding	2 = satisfactory	0 = unacceptable
3 = very good	1 = needs improvement	NA = not assigned

Figure 2.2   An Example of the Supplemental Sheet

The ultimate goal of using supplemental sheets is to instill a sense of organization and to reinforce school survival skills. Initially, the teacher may need to write in areas that the student has missed, but eventually the student is expected to write in assignments and due dates. At the end of each class or day, the student must make personal contact with the teacher, who, in turn, indicates progress by writing the appropriate number, 0 through 4, for the day's behavior in the corresponding row. If either the parent or the teacher wishes to communicate a particular idea, space is provided on the bottom of the form. This form, like the binder and study partner, is a means to instill organizational habits in otherwise disorganized learners.

Conscientiousness is just another term for good organizational practices. Conscientiousness is a learned behavior, and as such students can learn self-regulatory behaviors with direct instruction, thus enhancing their achievement and raising their opinion of themselves as learners (Boekaerts, Pintrich, & Zeidner, 2000).

Learning Strategies

Many students with high-incidence disabilities have organizational problems that extend to acquiring, maintaining, and retrieving classroom information within content areas. A variety of organizational strategies have been identified to help students learn classroom material. Students in the high-incidence categories in inclusion settings need to be taught the value and use of cognitive organizational strategies. Many students use cognitive strategies to solve problems and learn about the world in which they live, but some students need to be taught how to apply strategies for organizing, handling, and using knowledge (Lee & Das Gupta, 2001). Cognitive strategies require students to attend, remember, think, and use language (Sowell, 2000). Teachers need to explain why strategies are important, but the explanation must relate to the students' real world.

Ms. Fladeland, for example, when teaching her fifth-graders about problem solving wanted her students to understand why they use strategies to solve problems. She knew that she would need some way to relate the importance of using strategies to her students. She asked them if they had ever played the hot lava game, where you cannot touch the floor as that means you will step in hot lava. Many of her students said they still played this game. Ms. Fladeland had them imagine that they were playing hot lava right now. Next, she asked them to imagine themselves on a desk in the room, having to get to the next desk without stepping in the hot lava. She asked them how they would get from one desk to another. They came up with all kinds of answers. She told them that their plans were really strategies that would help them find a solution to their problem. The class then discussed the fact that many strategies could be used to get from one desk to the next; however, some were better and safer than others.

Ms. Fladeland used the hot lava game to help her students understand that they use strategies every day to solve problems. The students' real-world experience gave meaning to the problem-solving unit, and the students had great success. In order for many students within the high-incidence disabilities categories to use strategies, they must be able to relate them to their real-world experiences. Some of the more popular and generalizable organizational strategies include mnemonics, grouping, stimulus relevance, mental imagery, and distinctiveness.

Mnemonic Devices

Coding or categorizing techniques often are taught in the general education classroom. A mnemonic device popular among children is to create a word or a sentence by using the first letter or word of the series when learning important concepts or when reviewing or preparing for tests (Choate & Rakes, 2004).

Some commonly used mnemonic devices are attaching labels to pictures to be recalled, grouping long series of numbers or words, or forming associations to isolated or meaningless words. An example of attaching a label to a picture to be recalled would be to take a picture of a dog and label the picture "d-o-g." The next time the child sees a real dog, the letters d-o-g and the picture will come to mind. Grouping long series of numbers or words is used most often in the primary grades but is an appropriate strategy at any grade level. When children are learning numbers, they are taught to group by even numbers or odd numbers. Math problems that teach sets, such as sets of shapes, also teach children the basics of how to categorize. Most children eventually categorize new information seemingly automatically.

Children with social and academic learning problems may need direct assistance. Techniques for teaching children to form associations are well within the scope of the general education classroom. Memory hints such as "Your principal is your pal" help to teach the difference between *principle* and *principal.* Or "Your basic nine number fact quotients add up to nine." For example, 9 x 4 = 36; 36 is the quotient. In the quotient, 3 + 6 = 9. Another trick of mnemonic teaching is to use the first letters of a list of answers. Perhaps a child has been asked to memorize the five Great Lakes. A student might remember them as HOMES— *H*uron, *O*ntario, *M*ichigan, *E*rie, and *S*uperior.

Through mnemonic strategies, students have a systematic guide for recalling information. Students not only learn the content but also techniques that help them remember. The key to using this strategy is to be certain that the mnemonic is meaningful to the student. Fortunately, most students with mild disabilities can generate their own mnemonics and apply them to new learning situations (Mastropieri & Scruggs, 2002).

Grouping

Grouping, chunking, or clustering information into smaller pieces or parts to be learned is an effective organizational technique. Grouping also can be an intrinsically reinforcing activity for students who have not been successful learners. When assignments are broken into many discrete tasks, the completed task becomes reinforcing. Grouping, chunking, or clustering can increase discrete task completion and also increase the rates of reinforcement for learners (Billington & DiTommaso, 2003; Skinner, 2002).

Grouping is probably one of the easiest methods of organizing information, but many students with mild disabilities in high-incidence categories need to be taught how to group information found in the general education classroom. Students can be taught to group information at least four ways: spatially, temporally, perceptually, and categorically.

1. Spatially, by presenting different visual arrangements. An example of spatial grouping is a phone number (965-6198). Visual arrangements also can help children to group information. For example, in teaching the components of good nutrition or a well-balanced meal, all the pictures or labels of dairy products, proteins, produce, and grains could be grouped separately. The components of good nutrition are presented simultaneously but in four distinct visual clusters.
2. Temporally, by presenting the material with a pause or time lapse between items. For example, 3 plus 5 is—pause—8. In another variation of temporal spacing, information is related to rhythms or melodies, such as in the "alphabet song."
3. Perceptually, usually by enclosing certain information in a shape or configuration or highlighting it somehow. An example in reading might be to indicate the first letter of each printed word by drawing a circle around the letter (e.g., ⓡed ⓑall).
4. Categorically, by content or inherent commonality of items. As an example of category clustering, take the words *diamond, pearl,* and *emerald.* Although these words might appear at widely separated times in various contexts, they may be recalled together when the teacher asks questions or discusses content relevant to the general category "precious stones." The words *precious stones* serve as a cue for the child to recall these words together, as a group.

Other Operations

Other operations that can assist a child to learn are stimulus selection, relevance, mental imagery, and distinctiveness. Ability to use these processes develops as a result of the child's experience with language. As language experience develops, so does the ability to organize information for recall (Berk, 2002).

Often children with mild learning disabilities develop language atypically. For example, Jeremy seemed to have a lot of problems remembering the names of common objects such as hammers, pencils, and trikes. When attempting to recall their names, Jeremy would describe what each did, and then he could produce its name. He knew what each was used for, but his word retrieval was slow. Many children with mild disabilities need help with focusing on the world around them. Teachers often have to regulate attention and extract essential from nonessential information. Whenever possible, the teacher can model an organizational strategy to help the children recall information efficiently.

STIMULUS SELECTION   If the concept to be learned consists of a number of distinctive parts or stimuli, the teacher can help the child focus on important components or features through stimulus selection. Focusing on or choosing the feature on which to concentrate can be related to the position of that feature. In reading, for example, many poor readers focus on the beginning of a word but not on the middle or end. Hillary always got the first letter of words correct, but beyond that her responses to new words were unpredictable. She might say *bed* for *beautiful* or *relief* for *rat.* Hillary's teacher helped her to look beyond the first letter when identifying words. She showed Hillary how to see other important features of the word, such as length of word, middle sounds, and endings.

RELEVANCE   Relevance, or the meaning of material, also can help organize information. If you use the child's past experiences or current interests to build new experiences, the child is more likely to cluster or categorize the new information. Jed is enamored with minibikes. His teacher has capitalized on that interest by relating minibikes to the transportation systems of Indochina. As a result, Jed can explain why minibikes can and cannot be used in Indochina. Jed also can explain the economic and social impact of minibikes versus alternative forms of transportation used in Indochina. Jed's educational history suggested that his memory capacity was barely greater than a water bucket riddled by a shotgun blast. Thanks to Jed's creative teacher, that leaky water bucket image is quickly fading.

MENTAL IMAGERY   Pictures, referred to in psychological jargon as *visual illustrations,* have a positive effect on memory and attention by promoting learning and recall. Pictures help children whose language skills are atypical or deficient. Pictures make the abstract more concrete in such a way that learning becomes easier and teaching becomes more positive. While different, pictures that are seen by the eye are close cousins to imagery. Mental imagery, a picture seen by the mind's eye, is also an important nonverbal process that is used by learners to increase meaning of material. Meaningfulness is developed by relating information that is already in memory to new or incoming knowledge. Teachers can provide a powerful teaching environment when visuals such as pictures are combined with instructions for constructing mental pictures about the content to be learned.

Some students in the high-incidence disabilities categories have problems with mental imagery. Imagery is built upon experiences in combination with language. A lot of experiences are learned incidentally, or indirectly, without teacher assistance. However, some children in the high-incidence categories have missed many opportunities for incidental learning because they have not developed the language references needed to be able to relate words to the images they have encountered in their daily lives. Other children in the high-incidence disabilities categories may not have noticed or attended to salient characteristics of the images found in their environment.

In inclusion settings, teachers must be aware of the possibility that not all children in the high-incidence disabilities categories can use mental imagery to assist them in learning unless they are taught how to use their mind's eye to learn.

Angela and Levi are a case in point. They went to the zoo with their class. Each described the experience, but afterward the teacher wondered if they had both been on the same field trip. Levi said he saw a big tiger. When prompted for more information, he said he could not remember anything else about the tiger except that it was big. Angela, in contrast, also saw a very big tiger, but one with shiny black eyes and yellow teeth. She said the tiger smelled funny and made loud growling noises. She said the tiger's ears had white spots, and his paws were bigger than her dad's feet. Angela said the tiger was hard to see in the trees, and went on and on. When the teacher asked the students to imagine the tiger in the poem they were reading, who had the more powerful image, Angela or Levi? Levi has very little imagery to draw upon for future reference; Angela will be able to use her memories across a wide variety of learning situations.

For some children to use the powerful tool of imagery, teachers must create classrooms where relevant pictures, videos, television, CDs, and so on can be paired with the classroom concepts to be learned. More and more, educators are recognizing the powerful potential of including visual and electronic messages found in films, Websites, television programs, magazines, and newspapers as sources of text that communicate and carry meaning to learners (Hobbs, 2001).

Seeing is not enough for many children with underdeveloped imagery. Discussion focusing on similarities, differences, and prior knowledge can add to instructional lessons teaching children how to use mental imagery. Additionally, when a concrete visual image is not available, understanding that can ultimately be used to develop mental imagery can be attained through field trips, drama, and even music, with actions always coupled with a discussion of what was seen and how the image is related to content expected to be acquired. Accessing, analyzing, evaluating, and communicating about what an image conveys can provide the foundation for mental imagery as a learning tool for children, like Levi, receiving services in inclusion settings.

DISTINCTIVENESS   The distinctiveness of the material, too, can help the child organize and remember information. A well-known phenomenon is the confusion of *b* and *d*. Although some people view this confusion as a potential harbinger of brain damage, many others view it as a developmental problem. Young children (up to around age 7) commonly confuse *b* and *d*. By the time most children are 8 years old, this problem disappears.

In part, the problem has been created by the arbitrariness of our Arabic alphabet. If *b* were to look like @, few children would confuse @ for *d*. Unfortunately for our school children, *b* and *d* look identical except that one faces left and one faces right. To further complicate matters, *b* and *d* are close in the alphabet and often are taught consecutively.

Problems in teaching *b* and *d* could be reduced if *b* and *d* were distinctive from one another. Differentiating the letters *b* and *d* could extend beyond their shape. Changing the color of either *b* or *d* to red or underlining only the *b* or the *d* can make the two symbols more distinctive.

Furnishing Practice

Drill and Practice

Practice makes perfect, or at least should lead to expertise. Students are expected to acquire well-structured knowledge of classroom content through deliberate practice (Hatano & Oura, 2003). Drill and practice are used widely to influence student learning.

Drill is a technique in which the child repeats a series of tasks that all include the same components. An example of drill is to have children redo the addition of double-digit numbers with regrouping. Practice is an activity in which a child uses a skill to solve problems that may have other components. An example of practice is to regroup double-digit numbers for addition in balancing a checkbook. When carefully arranged and designed, validation of both drill and practice is found in the quality of work produced by students. Students can acquire knowledge, elaborate skills using this knowledge, and even develop a corresponding interest in classroom content through deliberate practice (Alexander, 2003). Caution: Make sure the student doing the learning perceives the worth of the drill and practice activities. Learners need to value the drill and practice activities in order to profit cognitively from them (Lajoie, 2003).

Teachers also must understand and value the function of drill and practice activities. Drill and practice have come under heavy attack from many educators—in part because the drill and practice activities have been used inappropriately, in part because they have long been associated with behaviorism. This attack has been directed at behaviorists (followers of B. F. Skinner). In highly behaviorally oriented teaching, instruction begins with small amounts of information. Then it is sequenced, with the easiest material presented first. As material is mastered, new information is introduced. Until students produce the desired response or the correct answer, they drill and practice. The behavioral approach to instruction has proven highly successful when working with children with social and academic problems.

Behaviorism has been attacked mainly because of the theory that it does not represent rather than the theory that it does represent. In other words, some forms of behaviorism do not take into account the complexity of learning and reduce cognition to an almost mindless act. Extreme behaviorism suggests that all learning is a kind of additive event and that all learning is observable. First a child learns one "thing." That "thing" allows the child to build to the next level of information. When dealing with basic discrete or concrete skills (e.g., sound–symbol relationships), the behavioral viewpoint has been effective. When dealing with more abstract notions such as reading or language comprehension, behavioral techniques have not been reviewed so favorably (Chomsky, 1959). Because behavioral theory cannot adequately explain the acquisition of a process such as language or thinking, some extremists have suggested eradicating behavioral theory and all associated techniques from the teaching world.

Often general education teachers find behaviorism distasteful because they feel that the use of this approach reduces children to little more than responders to stimuli. Misunderstandings of the nature of behavioral principles are unfortunate, because educational history repeatedly has demonstrated the successes of behaviorally based technologies, especially with children who qualify for special education (Strand et al., 2003). Reluctance to use drill and practice and other behaviorally based techniques has contributed to disillusionment and stresses between general and special educators (Maloney, 2002).

Drill and practice, only a part of the behavioral bag of teaching techniques, probably is among the most effective and powerful. As with any technique, behavioral techniques are highly appropriate for some types of lessons and questionable for others. If Norris is having creative writing problems, his teacher probably would use a combination of drill and practice and cognitive or child-centered techniques. Cognitive theories emphasize building the teaching instruction upon the child's prior knowledge and current interests.

To use Norris's previous knowledge and his immediate interests, the teacher might have him dictate or write a story from his own experience. His teacher then might choose sight vocabulary or spelling terms from Norris's own story. She might even examine his grammar and punctuation and initiate a language arts program. The teacher's techniques for teaching sight words, the mechanics of grammar, and spelling words probably will involve a lot of drill and, eventually, practice. Cognitive theorists would view this practice favorably.

Another, and probably more serious, reason for attacking drill-and-practice techniques has arisen from their inappropriate use. In some classrooms, teachers have misunderstood the purpose of drill and practice. This technique is used to strengthen or to help the child retain newly acquired information. By drilling and practicing with new information, the child's ability to use the information becomes less labored and more automatic. Consider how difficult manuscript writing is for a child just learning to write. Even printing the first and last name becomes a major event. After having written the name roughly 100 times (i.e., at least one time on every worksheet for the first two or three months of school, with proper feedback), most children can write their names without so much as a second thought.

The major problems with drill-and-practice activities lie in two mistakes: (a) failing to provide appropriate feedback, and (b) assigning inappropriate work levels. Appropriate feedback techniques (discussed earlier) apply to drill and practice exercises as they do to any other area.

Assigning appropriate work levels has special meaning for drill and practice activities. First to be considered is whether the child will be working independently or with someone else. A teacher who is drilling sounds with a child is in a position to provide immediate instruction. This means that the child's skills still may be in the acquisition stage, since the teacher is there to provide instructional assistance. When the child is acquiring new knowledge, drill and practice must never be done independently. Without instructional guidance during a new learning task, a child will not have a knowledge base for completing the exercises no matter how hard he or she tries. Asking a child to complete a drill exercise without the prerequisite knowledge is setting the child up to be classified as having a social or an academic learning problem.

Children must already know a basic concept before they can be given independent drill and practice activities. Drill and practice give the child additional opportunities to use previously gained knowledge. The activities become busy work only when they no longer are increasing the child's efficiency. A drill and practice exercise can reach a point of diminishing return. That judgment is based on intuition, the teacher's experience, and written recordkeeping.

Retention

Three techniques that can enhance retention of knowledge are (a) prompts and cues, (b) spaced reviews, and (c) overlearning.

PROMPTS AND CUES   Prompts and cues are instructional techniques designed to help students give the correct response. An example is saying the first sound of a word the child is having difficulty remembering. Prompts and cues can be physical, verbal, written, and imitative. They usually are used with specific drill-and-practice exercises in which the child is acquiring or has just acquired a skill.

Physical prompts consist of assisting a child to perform fine- or gross-motor acts. A fairly routine prompting technique is helping children learn to use a pencil. The teacher moves and holds the pencil but gradually reduces the hand pressure so the child can write independently.

Verbal prompts also help the child produce the correct answer. Voice inflections and verbalization (modeling) of the correct answer with a child are two commonly used verbal prompts. For example, the teacher could be leading a discussion about World War I and President Woodrow Wilson's beliefs about peace. He could be explaining Wilson's belief that the only way to prevent another war would be for all countries to join an organization in which worldwide discussions would be held. The teacher could write "League of Nations" on the board and say, "Wilson believed the League of Nations could help prevent future wars. What organization did Wilson believe could help prevent future wars?" Before the class can answer (correctly or incorrectly), the teacher gives the response "League of Nations." The teacher also can give verbal prompts such as, producing the sound of the letter *l* (for "League") or mouthing the phrase before the child responds.

Written prompts or cues are most likely to occur during drill-and-practice exercises when the child is strengthening previously learned behaviors. The prompts or cues are used as reminders. Let's look at Albert and his spelling words. His teacher has provided him with a model of each word on his spelling worksheet. Albert's practice is cued by having him look at the model, trace the first letter, fill in the spaces, and then write the word. Another example of a written prompt involves putting an arrow over math problems to show children where to start.

Building cues or prompts into instructional material is called *accenting* or *highlighting*. Common ways to highlight include making important features bigger, underlining them, or presenting them in a contrasting color or type. By the way in which they are organized, many texts prompt or cue students. For example, the phrase "I wish to make three points" contains no factual content, but it does signal that three important facts will follow. Cues and prompts, like signals, serve as reminders for using strategies to organize information, thereby increasing the likelihood of successful learning for students in the high-disabilities categories in inclusion settings.

Children themselves are perhaps the greatest users of *imitative prompts and cues.* Just picture their imitations of teachers and peers. Children model the tone, body movements, and personal idiosyncrasies of their teachers, sometimes with a precision that could win them an Oscar. Similarly, many social behaviors are learned through observing and imitating the teacher. Children often practice their learned social behaviors on other classmates. If the classroom climate is tense and structured, children tend to be tense. If the teacher is zestful and curious about life, the students are likely to show interest in the world around them.

Social behaviors and attitudes are not the only behaviors that are learned through imitation. Teachers often demonstrate work on the chalkboard and by overhead projection. Students then can use this work to model their own. Teachers routinely use modeling techniques when they take their students through a step-by-step process, such as diagramming a sentence, and have the students copy each step throughout the demonstration.

Phrases such as "Watch me" or "Do this with me" alert children to be ready to imitate the teacher and serve as handy openers for drill and practice. For example, a teacher trying to teach a child natural pauses in reading material may read a passage aloud. She then may ask the child to read the same passage aloud. Generally, imitation is used during guidance rather than independent instructional drill and practice.

SPACED REVIEWS   *Spaced reviews* require recall of information at reasonable intervals after initial learning. Teachers often provide practice of a newly learned concept immediately after instruction (and learning). If the practice is done immediately after the presentation, the value is somewhat limited, but recall or memory of the new concept is enhanced greatly when additional practice is spaced in time over days or weeks (Gagné, 1975).

Spacing practice may occur within a day for some children. Consider Joey. His teacher gave him flashcard practice every day for 5 minutes. Joey looked at the flashcards and checked his answers on the back of the card. After 5 minutes Joey's teacher, Mr. Hassett, gave him a 1-minute timed quiz. At the end of two weeks, Mr. Hassett noted that Joey's multiplication facts were unchanged from the day he started, so he initiated another plan. Five times throughout the day Joey pulled out his flashcards. Using a timer, Joey practiced for 1 minute only. Mr. Hassett continued recording Joey's 1-minute timed quizzes. By the end of the first week of Joey's new five-times-a-day practice schedule, correct multiplication facts were forthcoming. By spacing out the 5 minutes of practice each day, Joey was able to assimilate his multiplication facts.

Spacing practice for two or three children like Joey is possible in a general education classroom. The teacher has to be highly selective about the tasks to be spaced, in terms of the type and length. In Joey's case, two weeks on an intensive schedule worked. If Joey had required an intensive schedule like this for much more than two or three weeks, his instructional needs would be too great for the general education setting. The demands of such an intense schedule or spaced review would have to be shared by the general and the special education teachers. Again, depending on the degree and extent of the spaced review, the general education setting is the most appropriate for some children with social and academic learning problems.

A general education setting was not for Mike. He was removed from the classroom, where he not only was unable to complete any assignments but was rapidly developing some inappropriate classroom behaviors. Mike's special education teacher then provided him with tasks that lasted 5 minutes and occurred a minimum of 15 times each day, presented in a variety of formats. The special teacher gradually reduced Mike's spaced review from 15 times to once a day. When Mike had reached grade level and, more important, could recall and learn material with a spaced review of once a day, he was sent back to the general education setting. Mike had much less time to develop inappropriate social behaviors because now he could do a lot in the general education classroom.

Spaced reviews that seem most reasonable in a general education classroom are those that center on basic or foundational skills, as these are necessary for continued or advanced work. Three examples of foundational skills are reading, writing, and math. General education classroom teachers must be selective about the extent to which skills are presented in a spaced review. Reading, for example, might be spaced twice a day, once in the morning and once in the afternoon. New vocabulary could be introduced during the early reading period and reviewed later in the day. Teachers should not feel compelled to have one reading period a day and that it must last 60 minutes. If a teacher is tied to a number, that number could be split—45 minutes in the morning and a 15-minute afternoon review. Whatever works for the teacher should work for the students as well.

OVERLEARNING   Overlearning refers to repeated drill beyond the point at which acceptable learning has been achieved. Let's say, for example, that a teacher had set a goal of having a child read 10 new vocabulary terms at the end of three days. The child achieves this goal (i.e., she reads the 10 new words accurately at the end of three days). To ensure that she maintains those vocabulary terms, the teacher schedules at least two more drill and practice activities with these words. These two "extra" activities are examples of overlearning. Overlearning is the most commonly suggested technique for maintaining a skill (Travers, 1967).

Overlearning suggests that a child has learned a skill to some prespecified standard. Standards may be stated in terms of accuracy (e.g., Ted can define 18 of 19 world history terms). Standards also can be set in terms of fluency, or how quickly a task can be done: Mary Jo will accurately diagram 19 sentences in 15 minutes. Naturally, a fluency criterion would not be set until accuracy had been met.

In addition to fluency and accuracy, standards can include another component. Tied in with spaced review, this component has to do with length of time over which a criterion is met. For example, Aaron completes an independent practice exercise with 100% accuracy for three consecutive days. The "three consecutive days" is a length-of-time standard.

Setting a length-of-time standard is strongly recommended for children with learning problems in either academic or social areas. Length of time provides for overlearning or more opportunities to practice a desired skill or behavior. A common problem, linked to insufficient practice, is the seemingly inconsistent behavior of children with academic and social learning problems. Often teachers say, "I just taught Harold how to write his name. Yesterday, he could write his name perfectly. Today, he acts like he's never even seen a pencil and a piece of paper!" Harold may have given the appearance of being capable of writing his name, but he obviously needed more guided practice before he was ready to write on his own. Before Harold's teacher can decide that he has forgotten how to write his name, she should establish that he has truly learned to write his name. Setting a length-of-time standard can help determine whether a child actually has learned a task.

The question now becomes how long the length-of-time standard should be. The answer is that it must be determined by the needs of the individual student. For some students, only 2 or 3 days of overlearning is necessary. The basis for the answer lies within the class structure. The teacher must assess his or her organizational plan realistically to determine how it can accommodate overlearning. If no scheduled time is set aside for overlearning, the teacher needs some guidance in how to reorganize instructional time. If, on the other hand, time for overlearning has been incorporated into the teaching schedule, the teacher must examine the depth of the children's needs. If only one or two students require the length of practice to be a week or more per concept, meeting their needs in the general education setting may not be possible. If, on the other hand, more than four or five children need the length of practice per concept to be about a week, the needs of these children might be met easily in the general education classroom.

A cry of dismay has just been uttered from the harried classroom teacher: "Why should one or two children be sent from my room when I'm expected to work with five or six who have similar needs? Why can't I keep the one or two and send out the five or six?" The demands of a class of 30 students or more may make teaching more difficult if the teacher has only one or two children with special practice needs than if he or she has a small group. A small group with similar practice needs allows the teacher to provide the same practice materials for several children. The teacher may have to spend the same amount of time developing materials for one child as for five or six students.

Another consideration in setting the length of time for overlearning is that a child's practice needs will probably vary from one task to another, as well as within a task. Children rarely need the same degree of overlearning for all areas. Fred is a whiz in science. He can learn science concepts almost before the teacher has had a chance to decide what he wants to teach. But the same cannot be said for his ability to spell scientific terms. Although Fred needs no teacher-directed drill or practice for science concepts, he most definitely requires drill and practice to the point of overlearning so he can spell his science terms correctly.

Bradley provides an example of a student whose length-of-time standards changed within a task. When Bradley was first introduced to letter sounds, he needed at least three days of overlearning before he could proceed to the next sound. Without those three days of overlearning, he either forgot previously learned sounds within a week or confused learned sounds with each other. After Bradley had learned the first eight letter sounds, his teacher noticed that he was more involved with the task. She had the feeling that Bradley's learning had accelerated since the beginning of the year. To test her hunch, she reduced his overlearning practice to one day. Her hunch was correct. Bradley proceeded to learn the rest of his sounds with only one day's worth of overlearning. He had learned how to learn his letter sounds.

The technique of overlearning lends itself well to the general education classroom for both social and academic tasks. One student may need overlearning in asking questions and hand-raising. Another may need to overlearn how to clear off her desk. Any behavior, social or academic, that lends itself to drill and practice is suitable for overlearning.

Generalization

The goal of instruction and accompanying drill and practice is to help students apply skills to new problems, adapt to new situations, and successfully adjust to school, home, or community settings (Haring & Liberty, 1990). In a very pragmatic sense, knowledge is learned for two reasons: first, to be successful in school; and second, to be successful outside of instructional situations. If Patrick cannot apply his knowledge of money counting outside of the classroom, in spite of his 100% accuracy on timed drill sheets, the functional worth of drill and practice for this child on this skill is questionable. For some children, with and without mild disabilities, ample reason exists to question whether they automatically generalize to different settings.

Teachers in inclusion classrooms must have a systematic plan to help students in high-incidence disabilities categories maintain generalized knowledge and skills learned in the classroom (Alberto, Troutman, & Feagin, 2002). Teachers must not only provide opportunities for generalization of classroom knowledge, they must also model and provide both guided and independent practice for all students, but especially those with high-incidence disabilities.

To facilitate successful generalization, teachers first must be sure that the student has mastered the content/concept (attained somewhere between 65%–80% accuracy). Next, the teacher must identify situations that are relevant to the daily life and future of the student. Finally, the teacher must vary instructional techniques, materials, and expected responses from the child. Impossible? Impossible things are happening every day as long as the teacher is systematic.

Let's see some ways that Jorge's teacher can help him generalize his skills with long vowels. Jorge has mastered long vowels. He can identify 60 *cvvc* (e.g., *boat, peek*) words and *cvce* (e.g., *tape, kite*) words with 100% accuracy in 60 seconds from a dittoed sheet. Jorge's teacher has now reached a point where she must plan generalization strategies. While she might wish that Jorge will generalize for himself, she cannot count on her dreams coming true unless she consciously designs and implements a generalization teaching plan.

She has decided to help Jorge generalize by altering his response formats and the conditions surrounding his drill and practice. Jorge has been reading his long-vowel words aloud from a list of individual words. His teacher altered his response format by using multiple-choice or open-ended questions and game formats. To change the situation whereby Jorge has typically read long-vowel words, his teacher embedded targeted long-vowel words in larger projects such as his personal journal, a social studies notebook, and even a play he was writing with a friend.

Does Jorge's teacher know for sure that he can generalize reading long-vowel words in all new situations? No, but she has increased his odds by providing him with opportunities to apply his newfound skills in a variety of settings. As any gambling aficionado will tell you, the more the odds are increased, the higher the probability of success both in poker and academia.

Summary

Most children categorized as having a high-incidence disability are likely to be receiving educational services in the general education classroom for all or most of the school day. The actual label does little to distinguish the educational needs of children in one category from another. Many of the effective techniques and good teaching practices used with typical children are beneficial to students within the high-incidence disabilities categories, but often these approaches need to be adapted to individual learner needs and abilities. All children with high-incidence disabilities do have learning needs that require more instructional attention than the learning needs of their typical peers. Adaptations, in the form of accommodations, are often necessary for students with mild disabilities to access the general education curriculum. Further, many of these children need systematic instruction to learn how to learn in the general education classroom and learn how to learn general education content.

Teachers can assist children in increasing desirable behaviors and decreasing undesirable behaviors by providing them with early and frequent successful learning experiences. The environment for instruction that directs learning can be provided through the selective use of five teaching methods. The extent to which teachers must attend to the five teaching methods is directly proportional to the needs of the child with mild disabilities. Teachers in inclusion settings, who, by definition, are providing instruction for students eligible for special education services, must ensure that they are systematically setting expectancies, providing instructional feedback, and assisting their students to apply organizational skills. The purpose of inclusion is to provide appropriate educational experiences that allow access to the general education curriculum for students with disabilities. Most children with high-incidence disabilities receive their education in the general education classroom.

References

Alberto, P. A., Troutman, A. C., & Feagin, J. R. (2002). *Applied behavior analysis for teachers* (6th ed.). Upper Saddle River, NJ: Merrill/Prentice Hall.

Alexander, P. A. (2003). The development of expertise: The journey from acclimation to proficiency. *Educational Researcher, 32,* 10–14.

Alfassi, M. (2003). Promoting the will and skill of students at academic risk: An evaluation of an instructional design geared to foster achievement, self-efficacy and motivation. *Journal of Instructional Psychology, 30,* 28–40.

Arman, J. F. (2002). A brief group-counseling model to increase resiliency of students with mild disabilities. *Journal of Humanistic Counseling, Education, and Development, 41,* 120–128.

Balthazar, E. E., & Stevens, H. A. (1975). *The emotionally disturbed mentally retarded: A historical and contemporary perspective.* Englewood Cliffs, NJ: Prentice Hall.

Beers, K. (1999). Literature: Our way. *Voices from the Middle, 7,* 9–15.

Berk, L. E. (2002). *Infants, children, and adolescents* (4th ed.). Boston: Allyn & Bacon.

Billington, E., & DiTommaso, N. M. (2003). Demonstrations and applications of the matching law in education. *Journal of Behavioral Education, 12,* 91–104.

Boekaerts, M., Pintrich, P. R., & Zeidner, M. (Eds.). (2000). *Handbook of self-regulation.* San Diego, CA: Academic Press.

Brothen, T., & Wambach, C. (2001). The relationship of conscientiousness to metacognitive study strategy use by developmental students. *Research and Teaching in Developmental Education, 18,* 25–31.

Browning, C., Cohen, R., & Warman, D. M. (2003). Peer social competence and the stability of victimization. *Child Study Journal, 33,* 73–90.

Choate, J. S., & Rakes, T. A. (2004). Reading to construct meaning and to comprehend. In J. S. Choate (Ed.), *Successful inclusive teaching* (4th ed., pp. 86–128). Boston: Pearson Education, Inc.

Chomsky, N. (1959). A review of "Verbal Behavior," by B. F. Skinner. *Language, 35,* 26–58.

Deci, E. L., Koestner, R., & Ryan, R. M. (1999). The undermining effect is a reality after all: Extrinsic rewards, task interest, and self-determination: Reply to Eisenberger, Pierce, and Cameron (1999) and Lepper, Henderlong, and Gingras (1999). *Psychological Bulletin, 125,* 692–700.

Dembo, M. H. (2004). Don't lose sight of the students. *Principal Leadership, 4,* 37–42.

Dev, P. C. (1998). Intrinsic motivation and the student with learning disabilities. *Journal of Research and Development in Education, 31,* 98–108.

Ducharme, J. M., Atkinson, L., & Poulton, L. (2000). Success-based, noncoercive treatment of oppositional behavior in children from violent homes. *Journal of the American Academy of Child and Adolescent Psychiatry, 39,* 995–1004.

Egan, S. K., & Perry, D. G. (1998). Does low self-regard invite victimization? *Developmental Psychology, 34,* 299–309.

Eisenberger, R., Pierce, W. D., & Cameron, J. (1999). Effects of reward on intrinsic motivation: Negative, neutral, and positive: Comment on Deci, Koestner, and Ryan (1999), *Psychological Bulletin, 125,* 677–691.

Engelmann, S. (1969). *Preventing failure in the primary grades.* Chicago: Science Research Associates.

Gagné, E. E. (1975). Motivating the disabled learner. *Academic Therapy, 10,* 361–362.

Goldstein, K. (1939). *The organism: A holistic approach to biology derived from pathological data in man.* New York: American Book.

Hall, T. & Stegila, A. (2003). *Peer mediated instruction and intervention.* Wakefield, MA: National Center on Accessing the General Curriculum. Retrieved June 26, 2007 from http://www.cast.org/publications/ncac/ncac_peeermii.html

Hallahan, D. P., & Kauffman, J. M. (Eds.). (1976). *Teaching children with learning disabilities.* Columbus, OH: Charles E. Merrill.

Haring, N. G., & Liberty, K. A. (1990). Matching strategies with performance in facilitating generalization. *Focus on Exceptional Children, 22*(8), 1–16.

Hatano, G., & Oura, Y. (2003). Commentary: Reconceptualizing school learning using insight from expertise research. *Educational Researcher, 32,* 26–29.

Henson, J., & Gilles, C. (2003). Al's story: Overcoming beliefs that inhibit learning. *Language Arts, 80,* 259–267.

Hertzberg, F. (2003). *Who says elephants can't dance? Inside IBM's historic turnaround.* New York: HarperCollins Publishers.

Hobbs, R. (2001). Improving reading comprehension by using media literacy activities. *Voices from the Middle, 8,* 44–50.

Hymes, M. (2000). I read for facts: Reading nonfiction in a fictional world. *Language Arts, 77,* 485–495.

Jenkins, J. R., Jewell, M., Leicester, N., Jenkins, L., & Troutner, N. M. (1991). Development of a school building model for educating handicapped and at risk students in general education classrooms. *Journal of Learning Disabilities, 24*(5), 311–320.

Lajoie, S. P. (2003). Transitions and trajectories for studies of expertise. *Educational Researcher, 32,* 21–25.

Lee, V., & Das Gupta, P. (2001). *Children's cognitive and language development.* Oxford, UK: Blackwell.

Maloney, M. (2002). Why public schools don't change. *Living and Learning, 2,* 1–3.

Mastropieri, M., & Scruggs, T. E. (2002). *Effective instruction for special education* (3rd ed.). Austin, TX: Pro-Ed.

McCoy, K. M. (2000). Helping middle school students overcome common dysfunctional behaviors which impede academic success. *Middle School Journal, 31,* 42–46.

Meyen, E. L., & Skrtic, T. M. (1995). *Special education and student disability.* Denver, CO: Love.

Nieto, S. (2000). *Affirming diversity: The sociopolitical context of multicultural education* (3rd ed). New York: Addison Wesley Longman.

No Child Left Behind Act of 2001, 20 U.S.C. 70 § 6301 *et seq.*

Osterman, K. (2000). Student's need for belonging in the school community. *Review of Educational Research, 70,* 323–368.

Peach, W. J., Cobb, S. E., Caudle, A., Craig, K. E., & Wilson, V. (1991). A comparison of ratings of LD students with the ratings of BD students using the revised behavior problem check list. *Journal of Instructional Psychology, 18*(1), 73–75.

Perry, D., Hodges, E. V. E., & Egan, S. K. (2001). Determinants of chronic victimization by peers: A review of new model of family influence. In J. Juvonen & S. Graham (Eds.), *Peer harassment in school: The plight of the vulnerable and victimized* (pp. 73–104). New York: Guilford Press.

Prehm, H. J. (1976). Learning performance of handicapped students. *High School Journal, 59,* 275–281.

Quiocho, A., & Rios, F. (2000). The power of their presence: Minority group teachers and schooling. *Review of Educational Research, 70,* 485–528.

Rachlin, H. (2000). *The science of self-control.* Cambridge, MA: Harvard.

Schwartz, D., Proctor, L. J., & Chien, D. H. (2001). The aggressive victim of bullying: Emotional and behavioral dysregulation as a pathway to victimization by peers. In J.

Juvonen & K. Madsen (Eds.), *Peer harassment in school: The plight of the vulnerable and victimized* (pp. 147–174). New York: Guilford Press.

Simplicio, J.S.C. (2004). Today's teachers struggle to educate a generation of students unlike any that has ever been seen before. *Journal of Instructional Psychology, 31,* 71–74.

Skinner, C. H. (2002). An empirical analysis of interpersonal research evidence, implication, and applications of the discrete task completion hypothesis. *Journal of School Psychology, 30,* 1–22.

Smith, A. (2001). A faceless bureaucrat ponders special education, disabilities, and weight privilege. *Journal of the Association for Persons with Severe Handicaps, 26,* 180–188.

Smith, P. K., Shu, S., & Madsen, K. (2001). Characteristics of victims of school bullying: Developmental changes in coping strategies and skills. In J. Juvonen & S. Graham (Eds.), *Peer harassment in school: The plight of the vulnerable and victimized* (pp. 332–351). New York: Guilford Press.

Snyder, J. (2002). Reinforcement and coercion mechanisms in the development of antisocial behavior: Peer relationships. In J. B. Reid, G. R. Patterson, & J. Snyder (Eds.), *Antisocial behavior in children and adolescents: A developmental analysis and model for intervention* (pp. 101–122). New York: American Psychological Association.

Sowell, E. (2000). *Curriculum: An integrative introduction.* Upper Saddle River, NJ: Merrill Prentice Hall.

Strand, P. S., Barnes-Holmes, Y., & Barnes-Holmes, D. (2003). Educating the whole child: Implications of behaviorism as a science of meaning. *Journal of Behavioral Education, 12,* 105–117.

Thurlow, M., & Liu, K. (2001). *State and district assessments as an avenue to equity and excellence for English language learners with disabilities* (LEP Projects Report 2). Minneapolis: University of Minnesota, National Center on Educational Outcomes. http://education.umn.edu/NCEO/OnlinePubs/LEP2.html

Travers, R. M. W. (1967). *Essentials of learning: An overview of students of education.* New York: Macmillan.

Tschannen-Moran, M., & Hoy, W. (2000). A multidisciplinary analysis of the nature, meaning, and measurement of trust. *Review of Educational Research, 70,* 547–593.

Vacca, R. T. (2001). Thank you, Mrs. Bean: Seeking balance for students who struggle as readers. *Voices from the Middle, 8,* 8–14.

Watts, Jr., R. H., Cashwell, C. S., & Schweiger, W. K. (2004). Fostering intrinsic motivation in children: A humanistic counseling process. *Journal of Humanistic Counseling, Education and Development, 43,* 16–24.

Wurst, D. (Winter, 1998–99). Planning your lessons to be brain friendly. *The Mailbox Teacher, 27,* 12–17.

CHAPTER

3

Children With Low-Incidence Disabilities

KEY TERMS

- albinism
- anophthalmos
- blindisms
- cerebral palsy
- conductive hearing loss
- congenital
- degenerative
- epilepsy
- expressive language
- fine motor
- gross motor
- multiple sclerosis
- muscular dystrophy
- nystagmus
- photophobia
- receptive language
- sensorineural hearing loss
- spastic diplegia
- spina bifida
- visual acuity

George is an 11-year-old student who is legally blind and has a mild hearing loss, for which he wears hearing aids. George has limited functional use of his voice, and his poor fine-motor skills have interfered with developing sign language. George uses nonverbal communication techniques to express himself. He makes use of facial expressions and a variety of hand gestures, such as thumbs up or thumbs down to indicate responses to yes-or-no questions. George also employs augmented devices that are programmed to produce a variety of phrases, such as *I am hungry, I don't understand,* and *Please repeat.* George is receiving his education in Ms. Cheney's fifth-grade general education classroom.

George, who exhibits multiple disabilities, is among the many students who fall into the low-incidence disabilities categories. Low-incidence disabilities, in contrast to high-incidence disabilities, are far less common in individuals or in students in inclusion classrooms. Lower incidence disabilities, while relatively small in number, include a wide variety of conditions ranging from mild to severe and can include any disability, but are most often associated with physical, visual, auditory and moderate to severe cognitive and emotional issues.

Approximately 10% of the school-age population has low-incidence disabilities. Many children in the low-incidence disability categories have severe or multiple disabilities. Even though some of the disabilities are mild in nature—for example, a transitory hearing loss or chronic bronchitis, the greater the degree of impact on learning, the more severe the disability is within the school setting. Individuals with severe disabilities or multiple disabilities are often discriminated against (Rainforth, 2000). Some disability labels carry greater stigma than others, and the degree or level of involvement of disability is a huge factor in terms of acceptance in inclusive education.

Most general education classroom teachers have had limited, if any, firsthand experience interacting with children who have physical or sensory impairments. Watching some heartrending made-for-TV movie about a child with physical, visual, or hearing impairments may have left you with a strong sense of commitment to these children and a deep resolve to assist them in any possible way. The strength of this commitment, however, can be sorely tested when such a child becomes one of your students. At first you may feel a great deal of anxiety and have serious doubts about your ability to provide appropriate educational experiences for the child. These feelings are normal. Dealing with these feelings requires some insights into the nature of the physical or sensory problem and how current teaching strategies can be applied to the child.

Promoting full inclusion and participation of children in the low-incidence disabilities categories has been strongly supported by professional education organizations for more than a quarter of a century (Brown et al., 1977; TASH, 2004). Results of hundreds of rigorous studies have also demonstrated the effectiveness of integrating students with low-incidence severe disabilities. No evidence exists showing that segregated service delivery models provide a more effective education than integrated models for students with severe disabilities (Falvey, Blair, Dingle, & Franklin, 2000). Indeed, research evidence is strong in supporting an integrated inclusive service delivery model for students with severe disabilities (Hunt, Doering, & Hirose-Hatae, 2001; "National Study on Inclusive Education," 1995).

However, legal and policy decisions plus demonstrations of the appropriateness and effectiveness of inclusive practices for students with severe disabilities have not significantly reduced resistance for inclusive education. While progress has been made by many states toward educating students with disabilities in the general classroom, other states have made little advancement. However, legal and policy decisions plus demonstration of the appropriateness and effectiveness of inclusive practices for students with severe disabilities have not significantly reduced resistance for inclusive education. The wisdom of allocating significant amounts of time, money and human resources on the education of children who have such serious disabilities that they may never be able to function independently has been questioned. Some educators, law makers and citizens prefer to see resources spent on children with higher potential. When economic times are difficult, the quality of educational services for all children is threatened and the cry for shifting funds from children with severe disabilities is exacerbated (Heward, 2006).

Surprisingly, one of the greatest barriers to full inclusion for students with low-incidence disabilities has come indirectly from the field of special education. With the best of intentions, many professionals in special education adopted a continuum of services model. A continuum implies the level of involvement between the teacher and student based on student need. Often the type of service was housed in a particular kind of setting. Students with significant physical therapy needs, for example, were typically schooled together in order to consolidate financial and instructional resources. The greater the student need, the more restricted or segregated the environment. The most restrictive level was likely to be a self-contained school or residential placement, whereas the least restrictive environment would be the general education classroom.

An updated version of a cascade of integration options is presented in Table 3.1. Unfortunately, a continuum of services opens the possibility for pervasive segregation because the continuum helps legitimize grouping children by ability levels and disability categories. The continuum of services is very much alive and supported in many current interpretations of the law (Yell, 1995).

Nothing is inherently wrong with a continuum of services, but over the years this approach began to be identified with the place in which the services were delivered. That is, rather than services being viewed as a range of involvement

---

Table 3.1   Cascade of Integration Options

Unadapted participation in the general curriculum

Same activities, same objectives, same setting

- Can the student complete the activities as written for the general education classroom?
- Do one or more lesson objectives match the student's IEP?

Adaptations to the general curriculum

Same activities, different (related) objectives, same setting

- Can the student meet the lesson objectives with minor modifications (time, response mode)?

Embedded skills within the general curriculum

Similar activity, different (related) objectives, same setting

- Are there components of the activity that can be met by the student, even if not the central objective of the lesson, that match an IEP objective?

Functional curriculum in the general education classroom

Different activities, different (related) objectives, same setting

- Are the class activities greatly unrelated to the student's IEP? Are there IEP objectives that could be met in the same setting?

Functional curriculum outside general education classroom

Different activities, different (or related) objectives, different setting

- Are the class activities greatly unrelated to the student's IEP? Are IEP objectives better met in a different setting (required equipment, repetition, etc.)?

Source: From "Making Inclusion a Reality for Students With Severe Disabilities," by P. S. Wolfe and T. E. Hall, 2003, *Teaching Exceptional Children, 35,* p. 57. Reprinted by permission of the publisher.

---

between teacher and student, the places themselves became viewed as the continuum. In order to move from the more restrictive and segregated placements, students in effect had to earn the right to move to the next level or the next least restrictive environment. In other words, inclusion was seen as something to be earned, rather than a given right.

Confusion over the notion of a continuum of services and place of service delivery began as early as 1975, when the passage of the Education for All Handicapped Children Act (EHA) required schools to educate students in the least restrictive environment. Some interpreted this mandate as requiring a continuum of placements that routinely became more restricted for students with more severe disabilities. Since 1993, the courts, in cases such as *Oberti v. Clementon School District and the United States Department of Education* (1994 through the present), have consistently stated a strong preference for educating all children in general education settings with supplementary aids and services (Rainforth, 2000). Although a continuum of services was still required based on the needs of individual students, the starting point for educational services was to be in the general education setting. The continuum of services was not dead, but had been dealt a serious blow by the mandate that students with special needs should be served in the general education setting until this setting was no longer the most appropriate and least restrictive environment.

To underscore the desire for inclusive education for all students, the Individuals With Disabilities Act (IDEA) Amendments of 1997, while continuing to require availability of a continuum of placements, also calls for the following assurances:

1. Removal of children with disabilities from the regular education environment occurs only if … education in regular classes with the use of supplementary aids and services cannot be achieved satisfactorily.
2. The child with the disability is not removed for education in age-appropriate regular classroom solely because of needed modification in the general curriculum.

The 1997 amendments clarified the desire for all students, including those in the low-incidence categories and those with the most severe disabilities, to be included in the general education environment with age-appropriate peers. Educating these students with age-appropriate peers lessened the tendency of past practices to focus on developmental measures to determine their needs (Falvey, 2004). In other words, the chance of providing students with materials that were not age-appropriate or were designed for younger children was reduced. Students with low-incidence disabilities and significant educational needs could be educated with age-appropriate material in an inclusive setting. Providing all students with access to the general education curriculum strengthened attention to personal interests and other important age-appropriate needs and characteristics. Students were expected to have access to the general education curriculum in the general education setting with whatever adaptations were appropriate for their needs.

Ironically, one other source that engendered apprehension toward inclusion of students with severe disabilities in the low-incidence categories came from the most unlikely place, the Council for Exceptional Children (CEC). The CEC is one of the major and most highly esteemed professional organizations supporting individuals involved in educating persons with disabilities. In 1998, CEC created accreditation standards for noncategorical teacher education programs for preparing teachers of students with disabilities. The wording of the accreditation standards suggests that teachers who work with students with milder disabilities should be prepared to work within the general education curriculum. In the same accreditation standards, the CEC provided guidelines for preparing teachers of students with more severe disabilities to work within an individualized independence curriculum. The phrase *individualized independence curriculum* suggested that two different types of curricula existed: one for students with mild disabilities, another for students with severe disabilities. As a result, both general and special educators generally expressed anxiety when asked to provide inclusion activities with low-incidence students with severe disabilities. They were concerned that they were not prepared to provide inclusive education for students with severe disabilities (Rainforth, 2000).

Strategies for Acquisition of Knowledge

Regardless of the type of disability, many common educational strategies are appropriate. In fact, a number of the flexible and inexpensive strategies that are used with students in the high-incidence disabilities category are at times equally appropriate for students in the low-incidence disabilities category, such as individual daily schedules (Downing & Peckham-Hardin, 2001), active involvement in learning, time on task, and feedback. For example, effective interventions provide feedback. Feedback includes descriptive praise for correct response and constructive, sensitive error correction (Werts, Wolery, Holcombe, & Gast, 1995). Regardless of disability category, if Pearl, who is in the low-incidence disabilities category, or May, who is in the high-incidence disabilities category, or Mona, who is considered typical, reads the word *apple* correctly, the teacher may offer some kind of praise or may expand the praise to include more information. The teacher may say, "Good, apples grow on fruit trees." Or in the case of misreading, the teacher might say, "No, the word is *apple*." Or the teacher might add further instruction by saying, "No, the word is *apple*. Ap-ple. Now you say it." So, if many of the strategies or adaptations that are associated with best teaching practices work for all students, then why do problems with integration continue to exist for students with low-incidence disabilities?

Although many studies offer clear direction for defining and teaching skills to students in the low-incidence disabilities category, most do not address how to use these strategies in the general education setting (Browder & Cooper-Duffy, 2003). Furthermore, most intervention research has been conducted in self-contained special education classrooms or schools (Snell, 1997). Herein lies part of the inclusion problem. Teachers and researchers who have been working in relatively segregated settings have identified and implemented many positive techniques for providing students in the low-incidence categories with access to curricula. Thus, while these techniques have been validated in segregated settings, they have not been tested in the general education classroom. Although no doubt motivated by good intentions, the proponents of inclusion appear to have placed the cart before the horse, at least when addressing the needs of students in low-incidence disability categories in the general education setting.

Instructional Context

The great leap to inclusion was not without significant challenges when faced with implementation in instructional context. The phrase *instructional context* refers to the ecology of the classroom. More specifically, when looking at the context of the classroom a variety of factors must be considered. Interaction among teachers, students, and the type of instruction that occurs are all part of the ecology of the classroom. In addition, the amount of time teachers focus on particular students, the physical location of students, types of classroom activities, time spent in instructional activities, and level of student engagement are also critical components of the classroom environment (McDonnell, Thorson, & McQuivey, 2000).

The instructional context of a self-contained classroom is simply not the same as the instructional context of a general education setting. What kinds of adaptations take place in a general education setting? In 2004, Dymond and Russell decided to analyze the instructional contexts of six students with severe disabilities and six students with mild disabilities. In first and second grade, the children received instruction from and interacted with the special education teacher, but when the students reached the third, fourth, and fifth grades, almost all other special education support was delivered by paraprofessionals. In fact, the majority of students with severe disabilities, including all students in grades three to five, received two or fewer hours of instruction a day in general education settings. In contrast, the six students with mild disabilities continued to receive educational services in a general education setting for five to six hours per day.

To add insult to inclusion injury, in terms of individualized curriculum adaptations, even students in the high-incidence disability category appeared to receive adaptations that worked for the whole group, but may or may not have been appropriate for their specific needs. One study, for example, focusing on inclusive classrooms containing children with specific learning disabilities, discovered that, in this instructional context, most teachers adapted their instructional strategy for the whole class rather than making individualized adaptations (Baker & Zigmond, 1995). Such a discovery bodes poorly for students with low-incidence or severe disabilities, because the likelihood of a general education teacher implementing specific instructional strategies for unique needs in the general education context appears low.

Another interesting finding by Dymond and Russell (2004) initially appears to contradict the observation that students with severe disabilities in the general education classroom are not receiving appropriate adaptations. In fact, these researchers reported that students with severe disabilities received substantially more adaptations than students with mild disabilities. Students with severe disabilities were receiving curriculum adaptations for more than 50% of the intervals during which they were observed, as compared to 1% of the intervals involving students with mild disabilities. What's wrong with this picture?

Several aspects of this picture are inconsistent with the ideology of inclusion. Besides the fact that students with mild disabilities were not receiving a significant number of adaptations, students with severe disabilities, who needed more specialized instruction, were not receiving lessons from the inclusion teacher. Most often the students were instructed by a paraprofessional. Two significant questions must be asked at this point. How can students who present the greatest educational challenges be taught in inclusive settings by paraprofessionals who have had the least amount of training (Giangreco, Broer, & Edelman, 1999)? Second, if the students are being taught by the paraprofessionals, how can they be truly included with their peers when, in reality, they are being isolated within the classroom?

While moving along the trail of broken promises, how about adding one more piece to the quandary of inclusion for children in the low-incidence disability categories? General education teachers appear to feel responsible for students who are included full time; they view special education teachers as responsible for students who are included part time (Dymond, 2000). Many students in the low-incidence categories who exhibit severe disabilities find themselves as part-time students in the general education setting. Even when students with severe disabilities are participating in the general education classes on a frequent basis, few efforts appear to be made to provide them with access to the general education curriculum. Such practices are not as shocking as they should be considering the results of one study, which suggested that many general education teachers do not believe that access to the general curriculum is appropriate for students with severe disabilities or that these students should be held to the same performance standards (Agran, Alper, & Wehmeyer, 2002).

Table 3.2 describes how teachers feel about access to the general curriculum for students with significant disabilities. Implementing the philosophical values of inclusive education for students with high- and low-incidence disabilities takes a lot of hard work. General education placement alone is insufficient to guarantee that students with severe disabilities will gain access to an educational and socially appropriate learning environment (Wolfe & Hall, 2003).

Taking the *Special* out of Special Methods

Because of the need to cover content with a large group of students and the increasing pressure to be accountable for students meeting national and state standards, general educators typically rely on curriculum-focused strategies rather than individualized student-focused strategies (McDonnell, 1998). In spite of the fact that most experts have recommended using systematic instruction in inclusive school contexts (Jackson, Ryndak, & Billingsley, 2000), general education teachers may find such strategies difficult to implement.

Methodologies and instructional techniques typically used by special educators in self-contained or pull-out programs must be evaluated within the context of general education settings and practice. The usefulness of specialized techniques must be established within the context of the general education setting (Jackson et al., 2000). No matter how powerful or how often research has prescribed a particular technique for working with children in either the high- or low-incidence disabilities areas, the technique is useless if it does not fit well into the general education classroom. For inclusion techniques to be implemented, they must not be considered adjuncts to the methodologies that are present in general education classes, but as an integral part of daily instruction.

Table 3.2   Teachers' Attitudes Toward Access

Statement	Strongly Disagree	Disagree	Agree	Strongly Agree
Students with moderate to severe disabilities should be held to the same performance standards as nondisabled students.	4%	8%	48%	40%
Access to the general curriculum is more important for students with mild disabilities than those with severe disabilities.	24%	39%	25%	12%
The emphasis on access will promote inclusion of functional skills into the general curriculum.	18%	56%	25%	1%
It is important to have alternate assessment procedures for students with severe disabilities.	60%	36%	2%	2%
Ensuring students' access to the general curriculum will help increase educational expectations for students with moderate to severe disabilities.	21%	54%	19%	6%
My school district has a clear plan to involve students with moderate to severe disabilities in the general education curriculum.	12%	35%	29%	24%

Source: From "Access to the General Curriculum for Students With Significant Disabilities: What It Means to Teachers," by M. Agren, S. Alper, and M. Wehmeyer, in *Education and Training in Mental Retardation and Developmental Disabilities, 37,* p. 123–133. Copyright © 2002.

Teachers are more likely to implement many of the available inclusion practices when they see significant changes these techniques can have on the instructional level of all their students. Educators need to take the *special* out of special techniques and ensure that all teachers, not just special education teachers, understand the continuum of approaches, ranging from large-group to individualized instruction, that are appropriate in the general education classroom. Most important, inclusion teachers must feel ownership over this continuum of strategies and understand how these strategies can be applied to any of the students in their classrooms. Separation of instructional methods is likely to lead to segregation of students.

Active involvement in learning and the amount of time students are on task are two of the most critical variables contributing to academic achievement regardless of setting. The use of activities that allow for multiple methods of response and small-group instruction appear to be important for enhancing the active engagement of students with developmental disabilities in inclusive classrooms (Katz, Mirenda, & Auerbach, 2003). However, these techniques need not be reserved for students with disabilities. They are applicable to all students and fit well into the context of the general education setting.

Expanding the Instructional Methods Continuum

Differentiated Instruction

Large-group instruction and independent seatwork have been the cornerstones of the general education classroom since the beginning of the public school system, and variations of these two instructional methodologies are alive and well in 21st century schools. The intent of the approaches is to maintain attention over extended periods. To accomplish this goal, instructional methodologies have gone from discouraging passive learning to encouraging a more active approach to acquiring or maintaining information. In the most progressive schools, the practice of differentiated instruction is creating opportunities for all students to be actively involved in learning tasks to the greatest meaningful extent possible (Wehmeyer, Lance, & Bashinski, 2002).

Differentiated instruction replaces the one-method-fits-all approach. Students who have difficulty understanding verbal communication can learn through imitation or be given opportunities to touch, handle, or examine to develop comprehension. Students who need more time to process auditory information or who expend too much energy and become overly fatigued when decoding or writing can be provided with appropriate assistive technology.

Differentiated instruction impacts the degree to which students can access the curriculum. Accordingly, teachers can use an assortment of instructional formats, such as, lecture, small group discussion, one-on-one conferencing, in the general education setting. In a similar vein, students can demonstrate their understanding of the content using a variety of formats for classroom tasks, homework, or tests. The general education curriculum may or may not be modified, even when considering students with significant disabilities (Castagnera, Fisher, Rodifer, & Sax, 1998). Differentiating instruction seems surprisingly like creating adaptations, previously thought to be the sole property of students eligible for special education, and has a good fit in the context of the general education classroom.

Classroom instructional strategies that been found to effectively improve the acquisition of skills set out in the IEPs of students with severe disabilities who have been placed in general education classrooms include cooperative learning in math, peer-mediated instructional strategies, self-management, practicing how to ask questions, and following teacher directions (Copeland, Hughes, Agran, Wehmeyer, & Fowler, 2002; Gilberts, Agran, Hughes, & Wehmeyer, 2001; Hunt, Staub, Alwell, & Goetz, 1994). All of these strategies are perfectly appropriate for use with students, typical and atypical, in the general education setting.

Universal Design

Adaptations and differentiated instruction are siblings in the family of universal design. Universal design promotes access to instruction through a myriad of techniques designed to assist all students on a schoolwide basis. Universal design is appropriately named because the universe being addressed is the entire school, not just the small world of special education. Universal design is a giant step forward in conceptualizing inclusion by addressing the needs of all students, not just a few.

Initially, universal design concepts addressed architecture and architectural barriers. Advances in architectural design and technology laid the seminal groundwork for universal design concepts by promoting the idea that everyone can live and work better in attractive and accommodating facilities (Leibrock & Terry, 1999). When considering the needs of all students architecturally and the advances in technology, many details such as lighting, vision panels on doors, spaces for storage, traffic patterns, access to switches and handles, and even colors are taken into account. While many of the elements of universal design are directed toward architectural construction, others include ideas that teachers can use. For students with all types of mobility issues, area rugs or mats need to be permanently installed. Loose rugs can immobilize wheelchairs and create tripping hazards for students with perceptual issues. Using paneling on the ceilings and walls can absorb extraneous noise and increase students' sound and speech perception. Appropriate height for workstations and shelves plus stable and sturdy desks and stations can be provided for students. Equally important is that students be able to have a clear view of all instructional events. Many more architectural areas could be addressed, such as bathroom stalls, stairways, chalkboards, and so forth, but most notably, the point of universal design is accessibility for all students.

In recent years, universal design concepts have expanded to include instructional delivery. Universal design incorporates visual or graphic organizers to accompany oral presentations and employs the use of models, demonstrations, or role-playing. Teacher presentation cues, whether gestural, visual, or verbal, are used to emphasize key points. Universal design models can also incorporate scaffolding key concepts, promoting active learning, and providing appropriate pupil response techniques (e.g., thumbs up/thumbs down or lecture response cards). Manipulatives also can be used under universal design models (Janney & Snell, 2000). Universal design concepts fit well in the general education classroom. A list of principles for use in examining the degree to which instructional materials utilize principles of universal design is found in Table 3.3.

The principles of universal design should be applied to standard setting, curriculum design and planning, and instruction to ensure that all students are able to access and benefit from the curriculum (Wehmeyer et al., 2002). The elegance of the principles of universal design is that they promote one set of instructional principles creating accessibility to classroom content for all students. Specialized techniques are replaced by planning that addresses a continuum of practices appropriate to the general education setting. De facto segregation is either reduced or eliminated, promoting a realistic approach to inclusion and a higher quality of life for one and for all.

Table 3.3   Principles of Universal Design Applied to Instructional Materials

Principle	Explanation
Equitable Use	Standards, curriculum, instructional interventions, and educational materials are designed to be used by students with diverse abilities, including typical learners.
Flexible Use	Appeals to a wide range of user preferences and abilities (i.e., access to materials in various modalities and levels of complexity).
Simple and Intuitive	Materials and interventions are designed so that directions are explicit and easily understood, with steps for success clearly communicated in discrete, manageable chunks.
Perceptible Information	Directions for students, regardless of sensory disability, must be presented in a way that the students can use the material independently and that the essential information is highlighted and redundant to ensure complete understanding.
Tolerance for Error	Students can make mistakes and still complete the activity and achieve success (i.e., students have enough time to respond, receive feedback, redo previous responses, monitor progress, and practice).
Low Physical and Cognitive Effort	Can be used by people who have limits to physical stamina or capacity or poor visual spatial skills.
Size and Space for Approach and Use	Appropriate and accessible space is available so that students can physically access materials and learning activities.

Source: From *Universal Design Checklist* by G. D. Lance and M. L. Wehmeyer, 2001, Lawrence: University of Kansas, Beach Center on Disability; and "Promoting Access to the General Curriculum for Students With Mental Retardation: A Multi-Level Model," by M. L. Wehmeyer, G. D. Lance, and S. Bashinski, 2002, *Education and Training in Mental Retardation and Developmental Disabilities, 37,* pp. 223–234.

Developing Classroom Membership

If students with low-incidence disabilities are to receive a meaningful education in inclusive settings, two essential components must be present: (a) IEP goals based on the general education curriculum and (b) a sense of classroom membership. At least four types of instructional connections between students with severe disabilities and their classmates have been identified (Ohtake, 2003):

- Thematic
- Social
- Contributing
- Distinctive

Thematic connections refer to parallel activities, but with no interactions. In essence, the student with severe disabilities makes no contribution to classmates' learning. Realistically speaking, when given parallel activities, students are no more a presence in the classroom than if they were left in a segregated self-contained setting. Trudy, for example, has severe cognitive limitations. Although she is doing a writing assignment during the same time as the other students in a class, she is not expected to nor required to address the same concepts as her peers.

Social connections allow students to practice IEP skills by sharing their activities with their classmates. Clearly, social connections are a step up on the classroom membership ladder from thematic connections, but still place the student with severe disabilities in a somewhat passive role. Peer tutoring may encourage social relationships, but usually such relationships are not reciprocal. The student with severe disabilities is seen as the one needing assistance, but not as a class member who can contribute meaningfully to others. Social relationships built on peer tutoring may encourage a friendship between the peer and the student being tutored, but, in general, peer-tutoring relationships usually do not enhance class membership status. Sometimes students with severe disabilities assume the role of a buddy and may not be viewed as an equal.

Contributing connections refer to the direct contribution by the student with severe disabilities to classmates' learning. In this way the tutoring situation may be altered. For example, Jordan, who is a very good mathematician, works with Woody. Woody is a student with multiple disabilities. Jordan's teacher explains to her how to conduct a math activity being sensitive to Woody's needs. Woody, too, has a responsibility in his relationship with Jordan. Woody's role is to provide Jordan with feedback on the effectiveness of her instruction. In the case of Woody and Jordan, they both assume the roles of tutored and tutor. The relationship is more balanced. Woody is supporting and contributing to Jordan's learning and progress as a mathematics instructor. Woody's status as a member of the class is a more active one, at least in relationship to Jordan, and his input is valued.

Distinctive connections refer to unique contributions that the student with severe disabilities can make in the general education setting. In this type of connection, a child with severe disabilities can share his knowledge with classmates. Nigel, for example, uses a voice synthesizing system utilizing a laptop computer. His unique contribution can be to provide the other students in the room with the opportunity to understand how his assistive technology system works. Nigel can assume a valued and important contributing role in his classroom, thereby increasing his visibility and interaction with class members.

Factors Inhibiting Inclusion

Sometimes the concept of inclusion is mistakenly identified with the practice of placing students with disabilities in the general education setting. Literally placing students in the general education setting does not guarantee that they become members of the class. Several obstacles stand in the way of truly including a child with severe disabilities as a contributing and positive member of the class. Such obstacles often can be found in educational practices originally designed to create a means by which children with severe disabilities could be educated in the same setting as their more typical peers. Some educators, for example, strongly believe that opportunities for teaching functional and life skills curricula can be created through multilevel curriculum (Giangreco, Cloninger, & Iverson, 1998). No doubt, these educators are correct that multilevel curriculum can be successfully promoted in the general education setting, but the curriculum must be reflecting the same content as the curriculum that all general education students are receiving. If the curricula are not the same, inadvertently the students have become segregated.

Another practice, which at face value seems appropriate in inclusion settings, is one-on-one instruction or instruction delivered primarily by an aide. Once again, the student with severe disabilities is isolated. Opportunities for interaction with classmates are limited or entirely missing when the educational delivery system is overly personalized. By redefining IEP goals to include maximizing classroom membership, emphasis on one-on-one instruction is likely to decrease. The roles of the teachers and aides who assist children with low-incidence disabilities in the general education setting will also be modified.

Developing Social Relationships

Emphasizing the responsibility of teachers and aides to include development of classroom membership can be incredibly helpful in assisting children with low-incidence disabilities to interact with classmates. Teachers and aides can work with each other to design and deliver the appropriate adaptations to create opportunities for students to develop helpful and significant personal connections. For example, teachers can design multiple methods of response, which can be supported by guidance from an aide. Small-group instruction, designed by the teacher, can be used to facilitate active engagement and interaction between class members. Collaboration, cooperative learning, direct instruction of social interaction skills, and peer tutoring have all been identified as effective strategies for enhancing social relationships (Jackson et al., 2000).

Systematic strategies for building social relationships in and out of the classroom are critical to successful inclusion. One of the most important factors contributing to the development of positive relationships and social acceptance, regardless of age, gender, or ethnicity, is the opportunity to be helpful to peers (Coie, Dodge, & Kupersmidt, 1990). Inclusion teachers who observe and interact with students with low-incidence disabilities are more able to determine the effect that the disabilities create for social networking and the degree to which the student can be helpful to classmates. Based on such information, teachers can implement classroom practices that enable students in low-incidence disabilities categories to be helpful to and interact with their peers (Cox & Dykes, 2001). Only when students in the low-incidence disabilities categories are granted full acceptance as contributing members of the class will the goals of inclusion be fully realized.

Specialized Strategies for Specific Low-Incidence Needs

In addition to the common types of issues and challenges faced by children in low-incidence categories, specialized strategies have been developed to address the unique nature of individual physical, cognitive, or emotional conditions. Children with physical disabilities, for example, have no need for instruction in Braille. Similarly, children with visual disabilities typically have no need for learning sign language. Children with severe cognitive issues may or may not have a need for specialized medications or equipment. Children with multiple disabilities, however, are often found in the low-incidence disability category. These children may require any combination of common adaptations, as well as modifications that are specific to their various physical, cognitive, or social needs.

In addition to the more typical types of adaptations, which could be used with all class members, some adaptations have been designed specifically for children with physical disabilities and health impairments, visual impairments, hearing impairments, and significant cognitive disabilities. The adaptations are often difficult to separate from specialized curriculum, especially for students with visual, auditory, or significant disabilities. In addition to general education content, the curriculum for students with visual, auditory or significant cognitive disabilities also includes specialized knowledge such as Braille, American Sign Language, or functional life skills.

Children With Physical Disabilities and Health Impairments

Children with physical disabilities and health impairments represent a diverse group of students who are grouped together because they are not typical in physical or health ability. These categories include children with disorders of the nervous system, musculoskeletal problems, and congenital malformations. (Oddly, it also includes pregnant school-age girls.) Examples of disorders of the nervous system include cerebral palsy, epilepsy, other convulsive disorders, and multiple sclerosis. Musculoskeletal problems include conditions such as clubfoot, rheumatoid arthritis, and muscular dystrophy. Examples of congenital malformations are dislocation of the hips, spina bifida, and malformations of the heart. Many other disorders, such as cancer, diabetes, acquired immune deficiency syndrome (AIDS), and limb malformations, may also be included. The list grows and shrinks as new health disorders are discovered and old ones are conquered. These categories represent approximately 6% of all school-aged children receiving special education services (Sexton & Dingle, 2001). This percentage, however, may be somewhat low because many physical and health impairments occur in combination with other disabilities.

As with all conditions, the ramifications of physical and health-related disabilities are important to understand in order to create appropriate adaptations, but they also can produce unique circumstances. Special health care routines such as taking prescribed medications, using a ventilator, or managing nutrition or dietary needs are examples of adaptations needed for children with physical disabilities or health impairments. Additionally, the nature of some physical and health impairments may lead to emergency medical situations. A student could undergo a seizure—that is, experience a dysfunction in the electrical chemical activity of the brain that causes a temporary loss of consciousness and control of muscles. Another example of a potentially hazardous situation requiring immediate intervention could be encountered in a child with diabetes. Students and teachers must be aware of dietary restrictions, as well as what to do in case of insulin shock. Information related to any physical disability or health impairment that affects access to typical classroom activities should be prominently placed in the student's IEP.

Information regarding physical and health impairments that can affect children as well as their teachers and classmates, must be discussed and understood thoroughly by all concerned parties. Teachers and students, as well as the student with the disability, need to know the appropriate course of action to take to maintain a healthy and safe environment or to respond to an urgent situation. A well-thought-out emergency plan delineating the roles of the teacher and students in the class can make all the difference between chaos and order. Education can dispel fears and encourage proactive behavior for children with physical or health impairments. Quick thinking and immediate intervention can mean the difference between life and death.

Academic Provisions

The teacher's best bet in understanding the educational and social needs of children classified as having physical disabilities or health impairments is to question parents, medical specialists, and special educators who have worked with them. Teachers can gain the most useful information by asking questions that are educationally relevant. The answers can be helpful in developing an educational program for the student.

Table 3.4 presents a format for sorting information about selected motor impairments. Eight basic questions may be asked:

1. What is the expected intelligence range?
2. What kind of speech communication should be expected?
3. How does the condition affect hearing?
4. How does the condition affect vision?
5. Where is the site of the condition, or how does the condition manifest itself?
6. What is the prognosis while the student is in an educational setting?
7. What kind of mobility does the child have?
8. What general classroom considerations should be anticipated?

With this background information, the teacher is better prepared to design or modify the classroom to fit the academic and social needs of all children with physical disabilities and health impairments, other class members, and the teacher.

Due to advances in biomedical science, pediatric oncology, and medical technology, many children are returning to school after receiving treatments on an outpatient basis. As a result, many students with physical or health issues come back to school in compromised physical states, which may limit their physical

Table 3.4   Selected Physical Disabilities and Health Impairments

	Intelligence	Speech	Hearing	Site	Vision	Prognosis	Mobility	General Classroom Consideration
Cerebral Palsy								
Spastic diplegia	Normal range	Normal	Normal	Major involvement of lower limbs; minor involvement of upper limbs	Crossed eyes	Static, non-progressive malfunction of the brain	Restricted	Walk unaided but can fall backward easily
Spastic hemiplegia	Some mental retardation	Normal	Normal	Involves one arm and one leg on the same side	Normal	Static, non-progressive malfunction of the brain	Restricted	Involved hand lacks sensation; should not force use
Total body involved	Normal or above normal	Non-existent or nonintelligible	Normal	Involuntary motions of all limbs, trunk, and often the head	Normal	Static, non-progressive malfunction of the brain	Restricted	Usually cannot walk, and may lack sitting balance; compensating devices such as wheelchairs and special typewriters will be necessary
Muscular Dystrophy	Normal	Soft but normal	Normal	Progressively weakened muscles	Normal	Irreversible; progressive weakness of all muscles; death in early 20s	Restricted	Wheelchair and occasional use of an electric typewriter

(continued)

Table 3.4 *(continued)*

	Intelligence	Speech	Hearing	Site	Vision	Prognosis	Mobility	General Classroom Consideration
Spina Bifida (Meningomyecele)	Normal range	Normal	Normal	Lower limbs paralyzed according to line of spinal cord disruption	Normal	Static, non-progressive	Restricted	Braces or wheelchairs; toileting involves use of a catheter or bag fixed to an abdominal wall opening
Juvenile Rheumatoid Arthritis	Normal	Normal	Normal	Involvement of joints	Normal	Progressive	Restricted to site	Adaptive equipment for writing
Osteogenesis Imperfecta	Normal	Normal	Normal	Bones	Normal	Progressive	Normal	Limited playground participation; may use wheelchair or braces

activities or require nursing intervention. For example, students will fatigue more quickly after they have received chemotherapy, radiation, or other treatments. Some physical conditions have multiple effects, such as cardiac problems, fatigue, compromised organ functioning discomfort and pain, limb amputation, and so forth (Spinelli, 2004). Awareness and understanding of the child's physical or health condition plays a major part in developing appropriate adaptations.

Suppose you have just been informed that Jen, a child diagnosed as having osteogenesis imperfecta, is earmarked to enter your classroom. You might seek answers to the eight questions above. You learn that Jen has normal intelligence, speech, hearing, and vision, but that her bones break easily and her condition will deteriorate over time. A major implication for the classroom is to ensure that Jen does not participate in activities that may cause damage to her bones. You may have to restrict physical activities such as running and hanging from monkey bars. Equipped with this basic information, you should prepare the other children in your class for Jen's special physical needs. No other special modifications are needed in classroom materials or teaching techniques. You have no need for further assistance in developing a program and can proceed as you would for any other child.

What about a child with physical disabilities or health impairments whose disabilities have more serious educational implications than Jen's? Suppose Hugh, a child with cerebral palsy (specifically, spastic diplegia), is enrolled in your class. In obtaining answers to the eight questions, you learn that Hugh's intelligence, speech, and hearing are normal, but that he may have vision problems. Hugh's mobility is restricted; his legs are affected seriously by the cerebral palsy, and his arms are affected slightly. While Hugh can walk, he has trouble maintaining his balance. His condition is stable, so no major changes are expected during the time he is in your classroom.

If you have not had much experience with children who have problems like Hugh's, you will need assistance. At this point you can ask specific questions: Can he hold a pencil, or should he be taught to use a typewriter to complete his classwork? Figure 3.1 provides a set of checkpoints that can help teachers ask specific classroom questions. They are divided into four basic categories: (a) physical condition, (b) visual systems, (c) auditory systems, and (d) other communication. Information concerning these categories has immediate and direct consequences for educational planning. A list of checkpoints completed for Hugh is presented in Figure 3.2. Using Hugh as an example, we consider implications of knowledge about each category.

First, Hugh's physical condition, though it is serious, merely requires a desk that does not open from the top; his weakened arms would not be strong enough to lift a heavy desktop. You can solve this problem by providing Hugh with a desk that opens from the front or a table with drawers. Second, the condition of his visual system (slightly crossed eyes) is corrected with glasses but drains his energy. Therefore, you may want to decrease the amount of reading or close work that you require of Hugh. Third, no special modifications or adaptations are needed for Hugh in work that requires use of his auditory system. Finally, Hugh's communication skills, in both speech and writing, require no special

Name of Student_____   Date _____

Physical Condition	Visual Systems	Auditory Systems	Other Communication
___ No special considerations	___ No special considerations	___ No special considerations	___ No special considerations
___ Special desk	___ Cannot use any visual materials	___ Cannot use any auditory materials	___ Cannot produce intelligible speech
___ Rest area	___ Problems with chalkboard	___ Special equipment (e.g., hearing aid)	___ Cannot use writing tools
___ Mobility assistance	___ Special reading materials	___ Sign language	___ Modified writing tools (e.g., typewriter)
___ Special toileting	___ Talking books	___ Lip reading	___ Other
___ Special equipment to use in manipulating text	___ Large-print books	___ Special adaptations by speaker (e.g., speaks more slowly or loudly)	
___ Medication	___ Glasses	___ Other	
___ Cannot manipulate textbooks	___ Visual aids (e.g., magnifying glass)		
___ Other	___ Other		

Remarks: Remarks: Remarks: Remarks:

Contact Person(s)   Contact Person(s)   Contact Person(s)   Contact Person(s)

_____   _____   _____   _____

Phone_____   Phone_____   Phone_____   Phone_____

Times Available   Times Available   Times Available   Times Available

Agency_____   Agency_____   Agency_____   Agency_____

Figure 3.1   Checkpoints for General Education Classroom Participation

Physical Condition	Visual Systems	Auditory Systems	Other Communication
Name of Student _Hugh_		Date _September_	

Physical Condition	Visual Systems	Auditory Systems	Other Communication
___ No special considerations	___ No special considerations	_X_ No special considerations	_X_ No special considerations
_X_ Special desk	___ Cannot use any visual materials	___ Cannot use any auditory materials	___ Cannot produce intelligible speech
___ Rest area	___ Problems with chalkboard	___ Special equipment (e.g., hearing aid)	___ Cannot use writing tools
___ Mobility assistance	___ Special reading materials	___ Sign language	___ Modified writing tools (e.g., typewriter)
___ Special toileting	___ Talking books	___ Lip reading	___ Other
___ Special equipment to use in manipulating text	___ Large-print books	___ Special adaptations by speaker (e.g., speaks more slowly or loudly)	
___ Medication	___ Glasses	___ Other	
___ Cannot manipulate textbooks	___ Visual aids (e.g., magnifying glass)		
___ Other	_X_ Other		
Remarks: *Can't lift heavy desktop*	Remarks: *Fatigues easily— decrease dose of sight work*	Remarks:	Remarks:
Contact Person(s) *Janitor*	Contact Person(s)	Contact Person(s)	Contact Person(s)
Phone	Phone	Phone	Phone
Times Available	Times Available	Times Available	Times Available
Agency	Agency	Agency	Agency

Figure 3.2   Completed Checkpoints for Hugh

materials or teaching methods, but you may have to judge the amount and quality of Hugh's handwriting using less stringent standards than those applied to the writing of children who have no muscular problems. Once established, the standards set for Hugh should be adhered to, just as the other children must adhere to their standards.

Continuing to work with experts may be necessary. Their job is to assist you in providing the most appropriate setting for each child. Sometimes, keeping a record of interactions with the expert or contact person can be useful. Especially important is a list of times when the contact person is available. Making phone calls repeatedly and receiving no response is frustrating. You also may want to give the contact person a list of times when you can be reached.

Social Adjustment

Just as no single physical characteristic applies to all children with physical disabilities or health impairments, no gross generalization applies to psychosocial interactions and development. Personalities of some children with physical disabilities are not affected by their disability, whereas the personalities of other children with physical disabilities are affected in some way.

Some experts have suggested that the greater the disability, the more involved the related psychological problems will be. We do know that some disorders or diseases, such as cancer, sickle cell anemia, and arthritis, create varying degrees of pain (McGrath & McAlpine, 1993). As teachers, we must take into account the child's understanding of pain and resultant coping strategies. The way the child communicates about pain may not always take the form of detailed verbal description. Some children may act out, whereas others withdraw. Children who are "on the go," such as those with type A personalities, tend to be less involved with their pain than those who are more easygoing (Leikin, Firestone, & McGrath, 1988).

Self-Care

Some children with physical disabilities, and to a lesser degree some children with health impairments, need adaptations in the area of self-care. Self-care can be divided roughly into the areas of moving or mobility, eating, toileting, and medicating. These four areas go beyond academic growth. Careful planning in these areas allows a child with physical disabilities to experience a more simplified and efficient work routine.

Mobility

The term *mobility* refers to a child's ability to move. In the classroom, space for wheelchairs or other equipment may be needed. Modifications of doorways and walkways may be necessary. Building structures that cause a person with physical disabilities to depend on other individuals are called architectural barriers. A checklist of architectural barriers is provided in Figure 3.3.

Use this brief checklist to find out if your school is free from architectural barriers and accessible to students with physical and health disabilities.

Sidewalks
- ☐ Do curb cuts exist to provide access?
- ☐ Is the width at least 48"?
- ☐ Are sidewalks level, without irregular surfaces?
- ☐ If the door swings in, is there a level area of 5' by 5'?

Ramps
- ☐ Are handrails present (32" high)?
- ☐ Is the grade of the ramp less than a 1' rise in every 12' length?
- ☐ Does the ramp have a nonslip surface in all types of weather?

Doors (including elevator)
- ☐ Is there an opening of at least 32" when door is open?
- ☐ Are floors level for 5' in both directions of the door?
- ☐ Are the thresholds navigable (½")?

Floor
- ☐ Do hallways, stairs, and class areas have carpeting or some other nonslip surface?

Toilets
- ☐ Is one stall 3' wide by 4'8" deep with handrails 33" high?
- ☐ Is the toilet seat 20" high and urinals 19" from floor?
- ☐ Are sinks, towel dispensers, mirrors, etc., 36"–40" from floor?

Water fountains
- ☐ Are the controls hand-operated?
- ☐ Is the spout in the front of the unit?
- ☐ Are fountains mounted 26"–30" from the floor?

Source: From "Environmental Alternatives for the Physically Handicapped," by B. B. Greer, J. Allsop, and J. G. Greer, in *Implementing Learning in the Least Restrictive Environment* (pp. 128–129) by J. W. Schifani, R. M. Anderson, & S. J. Odle (Eds.), 1980, Baltimore: University Park Press. Copyright © 1980 by University Park Press. Reprinted by permission.

Figure 3.3   Checking the School for Accessibility

Ideally, no architectural barriers should exist. Legislation requires that all new buildings constructed with federal funds must provide for the needs of people with physical disabilities. But suppose Penny, a child with muscular dystrophy, shows up at your school—a school that fully intends to comply with the legislation but has not yet made some of the necessary modifications. What are you to do? In a word, "improvise." If a light switch is too high, Penny might be given an "arm extension," a bent coat hanger, to pull and push the switch. If the classroom desks are too low, they may be placed on cement blocks for extra height. If the floors are too slick, self-adhering bathtub grips can be affixed. The janitor may not appreciate sweeping over little frogs and fish, but the student will be more likely to remain upright. Eliciting help from the school custodian may yield a wealth of ideas and a veritable warehouse of materials to be used. Classroom modifications are limited only by imagination and the school principal.

Eating

Eating may be difficult for a child who has coordination problems, head and trunk control problems, or problems related directly to the shoulder, arm, hand, or mouth. Adaptations may be useful in helping children with physical disabilities eat independently. Many adaptations involve silverware (e.g., changes in the size and type of handle). Contoured handles often are made of clay or sponge rubber. Any special modifications and equipment must be available to the child during eating periods. The teacher's responsibility may simply entail inspecting the child's lunchbox to see if it contains the necessary equipment, or providing enough cafeteria space to enable the child to eat comfortably. The height of serving lines may have to be considered as well.

Specific eating or drinking problems are unique to each person. One of the child's parents or a specialist, preferably one who has worked with the child, is the best source for this type of information. Occasionally, dietary restrictions apply. Although you are not expected to determine the child's diet, you may be expected to monitor the food eaten (or not eaten).

Any modification of eating utensils or equipment tends to draw attention to itself. Other students should be prepared for these modifications, perhaps through discussion or examination of utensils. The preparation should not be excessive or embarrass the child. Role-playing a child with physical disabilities eating with modified utensils is an example of overkill. Good judgment concerning the extent of classroom preparation is called for.

Toileting

Bowel and bladder care is a major component of physical independence. Some children with physical disabilities require special consideration in this area. Before children enter a general education class, most have learned toileting self-care. General education teachers are not likely to have to teach a toileting program but may need to monitor or assist in a program already developed.

Consider Richard, a child with spina bifida. Because of the location of damage to Richard's spinal column, he is unable to control his bladder. To allow him normal freedom of motion and to reduce embarrassment associated with a bladder accident, Richard wears an external device that collects urine. The device is emptied at appropriate times. Richard may have to be helped in establishing a routine to avoid accidents and to be maximally comfortable. The teacher also may have to assist him in the case of an emergency leakage. Help may be available by consulting with parents, the school therapist, and perhaps an interastomal therapist.

Special fixtures may be needed for some children with physical disabilities. Handrails can help a child maintain balance, for example. The size and shape of a toilet stall also determine usefulness for children with physical disabilities. Some young children may need help transferring from a wheelchair to a toilet seat. Most older children can transfer themselves.

Medicating

Some children with disabilities, children with physical disabilities included, need to take medication. The classroom teacher may be asked to monitor a child's behavior on or off medication. The importance of monitoring a child's behavior cannot be overstressed. Thanks to the alertness of Jen's classroom teacher, Ms. Smith, Jen was given prompt and necessary medical attention. Ms. Smith had noticed that Jen was dropping her pencil more often than usual. Some days Jen dropped her pencil eight or nine times. For 2 weeks, Ms. Smith counted the number of times Jen dropped her pencil each day. Ms. Smith discovered that she had underestimated the frequency; Jen actually was dropping her pencil an average of 25 times a day. Ms. Smith conferred with Jen's parents, and as a consequence of a thorough medical examination, Jen was discovered to be epileptic. Given proper medication, she was able to lead a normal and full school life in the general education classroom.

When a teacher is given monitoring responsibility, teachers or parents may be misled into thinking the teacher is a doctor. The job of the classroom teacher is to teach. Teachers are not doctors, and their job is not to prescribe medication. Whether they administer medication or not is determined by local policy; in most states only authorized medical personnel can administer medication. If the district has no policy concerning medication, written parental and medical permission should be obtained if the teacher is asked to administer medication. Many children medicate themselves and require only a reminder from the teacher. The ideal arrangement is one in which the child is able to self-medicate.

Communication

Communication is a two-way street between sender and receiver. Without a sender, no one gives information. Without a receiver, no one gets information. The receiving function in communication is referred to as *receptive language*. Children with physical disabilities in the general education classroom rarely have extreme difficulties with receptive language. Most language problems for children with physical disabilities in a general education classroom are difficulties of *expressive language*.

Among children with physical disabilities who have expressive communication problems, the type of problem depends on the physical area that has been affected by the child's condition. Involvement of the throat, mouth, or vocal cords will affect the ability to produce sounds. Speech may be garbled or difficult to understand. Some physical disabilities affect the fine-motor muscles in the hands, the gross-motor muscles of the arms and shoulders, or both. Children affected in these areas may have difficulty writing.

Working With a Child Who Has Difficulty Speaking

When working with a child whose disability results in an expressive language problem manifested in difficult speech, the following tips may be helpful:

1. Use signals, especially for common words or phrases such as "yes," "no," "I don't know," and "maybe."

2. Allow time for the child to produce a response.
3. Recognize frustration or deadlocks.
4. Encourage the use of assistive technology.
5. Teach the other children what works.

Each of these tips will be discussed separately.

Use Signals

Signals are nonverbal signs used to communicate. The key to effective use of signals is to be sure the sender and receiver share a common understanding of the signals. For example, if a lowered head means yes to the sender but not to the receiver, confusion and misinterpretation will result.

The simplest way to determine the need for signals is to work with the child. The simpler the system, the more likely it will be useful. Some systems use pictures, some use printed words, and others use bodily movement. The system should be the one that works best for the student and the teacher.

ALLOW TIME FOR SOUND PRODUCTION   Some children need more time to express their ideas than others. Motor movements may be difficult, or a child may need time to recall which motor movements to use. Some children with cerebral palsy have major problems in producing intelligible sounds. A slow response does not mean no response. Similarly, slowness of response is not to be equated with slowness of thought. After a teacher has worked with a child for a while, he or she will be able to judge the appropriate response time. Each child will have a unique response time, just like children without motor problems.

RECOGNIZE FRUSTRATIONS OR DEADLOCKS   Sometimes communication is blocked. Identifying frustration in children with physical disabilities who have oral communication problems entails the same process used with nondisabled children, that is, identifying behaviors that interfere with communication. The blocked behaviors fall roughly into two categories, withdrawal from the conversation which ends in silence or inappropriate acting out behaviors such as angry verbal or physical expressions.

Deadlocked conversations can impede communication. A typical example of reaching a premature conclusion in a deadlocked conversation is as follows:

Alice, a young girl with cerebral palsy, described a field trip to the circus, the animals, the activities, and the performers. The teacher checked all the details and said, "Alice, you must have enjoyed your time at the circus."

Alice:	No.
Teacher:	You didn't?
Alice:	No.
Teacher:	But you told me all about it. Did something bad happen?
Alice:	No.
Teacher:	But didn't you enjoy your visit to the circus?

Alice:	No.
Teacher:	Well, you did go, didn't you?
Alice:	No.
Teacher:	You didn't! Were you somewhere else?
Alice:	No.
Teacher:	Were you ill?
Alice:	No.
Teacher:	I don't get it then.

The problem was that Alice was trying to tell about a field trip that her class was planning to take next week. The teacher assumed that the field trip had already occurred.

ENCOURAGE THE USE OF ASSISTIVE TECHNOLOGY   Assistive technology has opened doors of communication that were previously locked for some students with physical disabilities or health impairments. For many children with physical disabilities and health impairments, a simple flip of the assistive technology switch helps translate inclusion philosophy into reality. Assistive technology includes a wide variety of tools that allow children with physical impairment and special health needs to communicate with others (Bryant & Bryant, 2003). Adaptations associated with assistive technology can be either high or low technology. Computerized synthetic speech programs, like Dragon Naturally Speaking, that read written material aloud for students who cannot access print, or translate speech into type for students who cannot communicate through manuscript or cursive, are examples of high-tech applications. Examples of low-tech devices include communication boards, picture communication books, or pencil grips.

High-Tech   Operational adaptations designed for students with severe physical disabilities are remarkable in their ingenuity. For example, computers can be controlled by voice, movement of an eye, a mouth stick, a sip-and-puff breath stick, a single finger, a toe, a head wand, or any other method appropriate to the child's abilities. Additionally, special keyboards are available for people with limited dexterity or hand strength (Lahm & Everington, 2002). Rachel uses a wireless keyboard when she is working on a group project. She and her classmates can gather around a small table instead of being crowded at the computer station. Her classmate Aaron, who is frequently in and out of the hospital due to his radiation treatments, keeps in touch with his teacher and classmates via e-mail and instant messaging.

Students with multiple disabilities have higher rates of illness and hospitalization than other children (Surgeon General, 2001). Students with physical disabilities, health impairments, and multiple disabilities may require hospitalization for weeks or even months during the academic year (Kennedy & Thompson, 2000). High-tech programs can keep communication between the general education setting and the hospitalized child flowing almost seamlessly, thus avoiding skill regression and decreases in academic and social functioning often associated with extended absences. In fact, IDEA '97 requires that explicit support strategies be developed for students who have IEPs and are hospitalized (Borgioli & Kennedy, 2003).

High-tech programs can also be arranged to provide adaptations for students with multiple disabilities. Children who have multiple disabilities involving health issues and several senses may access the general education curriculum by using a combination of software programs. Communication for children previously unable to speak, hear, see, or move is possible in the 21st century, thanks to dramatic advances in technology. However, advances in technology must be accompanied by advances in education. Teachers and support personnel need to learn about the types of assistive technology devices that fit the needs of the child to access the general education curriculum.

The characteristics of the child, the potential assistive technology device, and the costs associated with implementation must be considered (Best, Reed, & Bigge, 2005). Two more key players contributing to the success of the assistive technology adopted are the general education teacher and the classroom aide. Their willingness to develop the knowledge and expertise needed to support and encourage the child's use of the assistive technology will be the deciding factor in either bringing the system to the forefront as an instructional tool or leaving it as a very expensive dust collector.

Low-Tech   Many children with physical disabilities who have difficulty in writing require a lower level of assistive technology and other types of adaptations. Writing is difficult for some children with physical disabilities, especially those who have difficulty controlling their shoulders, arms, hands, or fingers. Some children with gross-motor coordination problems can use pencils and pens but may need more time to write or copy information. Writing may be labored and cause the child to tire easily.

Special equipment to accommodate motor problems is available. The equipment can range from a piece of clay wrapped around a pencil to a computer system complete with speakers and a visual display of what is typed. Each child's need for equipment relates to his or her physical problem. A quick consultation with the child's physical therapist or occupational therapist should clarify classroom considerations.

The child's writing progress should be monitored. If progress seems too slow, the teacher may want to see what other equipment is available for the student. In the case of Richard, a child with poor gross-motor and fine-motor control, his classroom teacher was the first to notice problems in writing. Richard had been using a laptop for his classwork. During the first part of the school year, the laptop seemed appropriate. As the school year progressed, however, the teacher observed that Richard was becoming reluctant to use the computer. She also noticed him carrying pencils and pens in his pockets. After a short talk with him, the teacher discovered that Richard was embarrassed to use his laptop. Richard wanted to be more like the other kids.

Consulting with Richard's physical therapist, the teacher discovered that Richard had more fine-motor control than previously thought. Even though his fine-motor control was minimal, he could grasp a specially modified pencil. Richard's teacher constructed a 1/8" grooved template of Richard's name (see Figure 3.4) and taught him how to use it. Richard and his teacher reached a compromise. Richard would be allowed to write his name on the top of every paper written. The teacher was pleased because Richard was completing his assignments. Richard was pleased because he could write his name in the same way as everybody else.

TEACH THE OTHER CHILDREN WHAT WORKS   Ironically, when utilizing high-tech equipment, your students will often be teaching you how to run the equipment. Your best friends in the high-tech world may turn out to be your own students; 21st-century children are often technologically savvy and curious about high-tech applications. Both the student who uses the high-tech equipment and the students who are naturally drawn to this type of equipment can raise their status in a class by demonstrating their competence to others.

More than likely, most children in your classroom will pick up ways to communicate with the child with physical disabilities. Teachers can shorten the learning time by teaching the other children any signals or codes that have been established. Teachers also should inform the other children about wait time, that is, allowing students sufficient time to produce their verbal responses or contributions. Depending upon the age of your students, a quick lesson in empathy might be appropriate.

Children With Visual Impairments

About 73% of blind and low-vision students attend either general education or resource room programs in their local public schools (U.S. Department of

Figure 3.4   1/8" Grooved Template

Education, 2001). Even though they are among the most integrated of all students with disabilities, the level of disability varies greatly from child to child. In order to succeed in a general education setting, some students with visual disabilities need substantial accommodations, while others need only minor adaptations. Categorical definitions of children with visual impairment offer no clues to successful classroom programming. Individuals with visual impairment form a highly heterogeneous group whose one common characteristic is some degree of visual loss. About 2 out of every 1,000 schoolchildren have visual disabilities and receive special services under IDEA (U.S. Department of Education, 2002). Approximately 14,000 children between the ages of 6 and 17 receive special education because of low vision or blindness, with about one third of this group categorized as legally blind (Tuttle & Ferrell, 1995). Almost 50% of children with visual disabilities have more than one disability (e.g., deaf–blindness) and are typically included in the multiple disabilities category (Dote-Kwan, Chen, & Hughes, 2001).

Some children with visual impairment are totally blind. Others are able to distinguish between light and dark. Some can even see several feet away. Others, with tunnel vision, have good sight for distance but are handicapped by a narrow visual field. Some children have such a high degree of sensitivity to light (*photophobia*) that even with minor visual impairment they are restricted in many activities. All of these children have some kind of visual impairment, but they function differently from one another in their school and home environments, and therefore need different accommodations.

Children with visual impairments have different experiences with sight than their normally seeing peers (Kingsley, 1997). Students' ability to use vision as well as how much they use their other senses for learning are important descriptors when discussing students who are referred to as low vision, functionally blind, or blind (Cox & Dykes, 2001; Turnbull, Turnbull, Shank, Smith, & Leal, 2002). Some children with visual impairment may not be able to see a complete image, so the brain may receive a fuzzy or nonmeaningful picture. Visual identification of objects or the ability to define form and detail can be affected in a variety of ways. Even the standard "20/20 vision" can be misleading because the numbers do not predict how well the child interprets visual information. Take the example of Danielle. She has "perfect" acuity (20/20 vision), but she has limited ability to control her eyes. Danielle's condition often causes blurred and distorted images similar to double exposures on photographs. She must use an enormous amount of energy directing the motor components of her vision, leaving little energy for cognitive processing of the images she sees.

Functional ability and need plus capability of benefiting from service form the practical basis for describing the types of adaptations needed by children with low vision. The degree of usable vision directly impacts the type of service the student with low vision needs in order to access the general education curriculum. The child visual efficiency, that is, how the child learns best and what accommodations are needed to enhance visual, tactile, or auditory channels for learning are also important instructional factors. Organizational issues based on universal design plus specific needs related to low vision include placement of furniture, ease of mobility, types of additional equipment needed, such as Braille letters or personal computers, or need for adapted materials, such as texts with large print.

Two additional factors that can have a major impact on the abilities and needs of a child with visual impairment are age of onset of the impairment and manner of occurrence (Ashcroft & Zambone-Ashley, 1980; Spungin, 2002). A child who has been blind from birth will have a set of visual experiences that are very different from those of a child who became blind at a later age. Joey and Tanya are both classified as blind. Joey, who was born without true eyeballs has been blind since birth. Tanya was blinded in an automobile accident when she was 5 years old. Tanya has a set of visual experiences that Joey can never have. Thus, their abilities and needs are quite different. To teach Joey about "the soft, fluffy white clouds" will require a set of techniques different from those required for teaching Tanya the same thing. The terms *white* and *clouds* are already within her repertoire of experiences. For Joey, however, these terms will have to be related to something for which he has meaning.

The manner of occurrence of visual impairment has profound psychological implications. A child who gradually loses sight because of a degenerative condition may be prepared psychologically over time. In contrast, a child who has lost sight from trauma such as an automobile accident may have a major personality shift. Interpersonal relations, self-concept, body image, and other aspects of personality may be altered temporarily or permanently (Hanninen, 1975). In some cases, counseling for the child, parents, and teachers is strongly encouraged.

Whatever the cause, low vision is unique to each child. The characteristics, consequences, and implications are child-specific. Low vision is just one characteristic of the child.

Academic Provisions

Generally speaking, the most appropriate curriculum for a child with visual impairment enrolled in a general education classroom is the curriculum used for all the other children. Adaptations usually do not involve content but, rather, special equipment or textbooks. Adapting educational materials is not the responsibility of the general education teacher. If a child needs large-print or Braille materials, a special vision teacher will make the modifications.

Vision Teachers

Usually, special teachers for children with visual impairment are referred to as itinerant or resource vision teachers. The itinerant teacher often plays an active role in the education of a child with visual impairment by providing supplementary instruction. A specialist trained in meeting the instructional needs of children with visual impairments, the itinerant teacher also may show the child how to use special visual aids such as the loupe (a hand reading glass), spectacle magnifiers (ordinary glasses fitted to give a closer focus), and litescopic aids (appliances that can clip over the lenses of ordinary glasses).

The itinerant teacher supports general education classroom instruction. For this reason, the general education and itinerant teacher must have open, clear lines of communication. If the classroom teacher lets the itinerant teacher know what content he or she is going to teach, the itinerant teacher can provide appropriate materials for the child with visual impairment. In addition, he or she can provide tutorial time for the child.

If the classroom has a child with visual impairment, a vision teacher probably should be in the classroom to ensure that the child is completing work appropriately and using special materials or equipment efficiently. Furthermore, having the vision teacher in the room will vastly reduce note exchanges between the two teachers. Consider the situation in which the classroom teacher puts weekly spelling words on the chalkboard. Instead of handing a list of words to the vision teacher, he or she simply can copy the words in Braille (if necessary) or modify them on the spot for the child. In any event, the content of classroom instruction will be determined by the classroom teacher. The vision teacher will assist to the extent that special services are required.

Key Questions for the Inclusion Teacher

Even though an itinerant teacher will assist, the inclusion teacher spends most of the school day with the child and therefore has the primary responsibility for teaching the child. Because approximately 80% of all children who are visually impaired have some remaining sight, the inclusion teacher might have questions related to the use of vision in the classroom. The answers to the following four questions can help the classroom teacher make decisions concerning a child's education:

1. How does the child use any remaining vision?
2. If the child is partially sighted, what should the viewing distance be?
3. How much illumination should the child have?
4. What medium for reading should the child use?

Several children with visual impairment may have the same acuity rating or classification but need very different educational provisions. Consider Santina and Conrad. They both have low vision and cannot see without some sort of optical aid. Santina has a condition known as *albinism*. One result of albinism is a reduction in visual acuity to about 20/200, compared with normal acuity of 20/20. In addition, albinism often is associated with nystagmus, an involuntary, rapid movement of the eyeball. Finally, albinism often causes acute light sensitivity, or photophobia. Conrad's situation is quite different. He has a condition known as open-angle glaucoma. He has lost all of his peripheral vision and is left with a narrow visual field.

Educational provisions for Santina and Conrad will be quite different. Santina cannot tolerate light, whereas Conrad needs high-intensity lighting. Santina need books with large print, whereas Conrad can read regular type as long as he uses a hand magnifying glass. The inclusion teacher cannot be expected to diagnose Santina's or Conrad's educational needs but is expected to accommodate whatever needs have been diagnosed. No special training is required to seat Santina away from direct sunlight. Similarly, no special training is needed to remind Conrad to use his hand magnifier.

By analyzing the needs of Santina and Conrad, the teacher may realize that no single answer prescribes the way all children with visual impairment or blindness should be taught. All children with visual impairment or blindness cannot be limited to a single medium or piece of equipment.

Adjustment Factors

Whatever the medium or equipment selected, helping the child learn with the greatest efficiency and effectiveness is a major objective of the educational program. Consideration of the following areas may increase the rate at which a child with visual impairment or blindness adjusts to the educational program.

1. *Introducing the child to the setting.* Because a child with visual impairment or blindness is limited in the visual environment of the general education classroom, the teacher has to orient the child. The child will need to know the location of the work spaces (desks, teacher desk, tables, learning centers). In addition, the child will have to be shown where to find common classroom materials such as the pencil sharpener and wastebaskets. Orientation will proceed more smoothly if the teacher introduces places sequentially, perhaps adding one or two new locations a day. Another means for assisting a child with visual impairment to learn locations is by applying the "All Roads Lead to Rome" technique (providing a focal point or pivotal spot from which all locations may be found) once the child has a permanent reference point. More than likely, the child's own desk will be the most appropriate pivotal point. The child with visual impairment has to be told, of course, of any rearrangements of furniture or additions of equipment.

2. *Presenting learning material appropriately.* The clarity of verbal directions can be crucial for a child who sees poorly or not at all. Other than tone of voice, the child may be unable to read the teacher's nonverbal communication. For the child to know what is expected, a verbal signal may be needed. The start of a lesson, for example, can be signaled with the word *listen* or the phrase *get ready*. In addition, the instructional purpose should be stated clearly at the beginning of the new lesson and repeated at the end of the lesson. The beginning or ending of a lesson should be vocalized so that the child has time to gather or put away any required materials.

3. *Allowing adequate time for work.* Children with low vision need more time to complete classwork, especially if it entails reading. Children with low vision read isolated words as well as words in context more slowly than most of their sighted peers; they need about 1½ to 2 times the amount of time as do sighted children (Bosman, Gompel, & Vervleod, 2006; Gompel, Janssen, van Bon, & Schreuder, 2003). If the child with low vision needs more time and energy to decode words, he or she also has proportionately less time available for processing capacity and working memory—that is, rate of

decoding can affect comprehension. When classroom teachers give children with low vision enough time to read, study, or do classwork, comprehending material in print is usually no longer a problem (Gompel, Janssen van Bon, & Schreuder, 2004).

4. *Modulating quality of voice.* The teacher may need to listen to a recording of her own voice and analyze it. A grating, monotonous, or unpleasant voice may cause the child with visual impairment to stop listening. Loudness of the voice and competing sounds also must be considered in relation to the child's auditory needs.

5. *Accommodating classroom for special equipment.* Children with low vision can gain access to the general education curriculum through a number of specialized devices and learning tools. Low-tech examples that might be helpful for some children include magnifying glasses that can slide across print or a monocular that magnifies like binoculars but is used with just one eye. Putting printed material into an appropriate font size, maybe 14 to 18 points depending on the students' needs, is easily accomplished through the use of most word processing programs.

On the technology continuum, many children with low vision use Braille writers and specialized computer programs that allow screen reading of print and speech synthesizers that enable the student to listen to the information presented on the screen. For taking notes, some students use Braille; specialized equipment for brailling includes Braille writers, a slate and stylus, or portable note takers.

Space may have to be created to house these materials. If the child's desk is not an appropriate place for storing materials, a small table or stand next to the desk may be helpful. A rubber pad will soften the sound of a Braille-writer or typewriter. Earphones can be used with a tape recorder or computer. Other accommodations include Optacons, a tool that scans and transforms printed material electronically into vibrating letter configurations, talking calculators, and Kurzweil reading machines, computer-based instruments that convert print into synthesized speech.

6. *Providing opportunities for reinforcement.* Sighted children are presented with multiple incidental learning experiences that assist them in the classroom. A sighted child may learn the word *street* in school. On the way home, the child may see the word *street* again on a street sign or billboard. In contrast, a child who has visual impairment has limited chances to have formal learning reinforced by incidental learning. A partial solution to this problem is for teachers to provide multiple experiences in a variety of situations for whatever concept is being presented.

7. *Encouraging independence.* For the child with visual impairment, like all other children, self-sufficiency is a major goal. Helping the child to be aware of his own responsibilities is one step on the road to independence. Other steps include the development of orderly work habits with regard to storage and retrieval of equipment and working materials. As much as possible, a child with visual impairment should be increasingly responsible for getting

out books and work. To help the child function actively in the classroom, desks, shelves, and other work areas can be labeled in large print or Braille.

Overall, working with a child with visual impairment should be a positive experience for both the teacher and the child. We have known for a long time that educationally advantaged children with visual impairment usually function at a normal level by school age or shortly after (Fraiberg, 1959). When low-vision children are given special training in visual development in kindergarten, they are able to perform as competently in the general education classroom as their sighted peers (Hull, 1973).

Social Adjustment

Children with visual impairment exhibit a wide range of personality characteristics and social adjustment. Because they are quite dependent upon the people in their primary social environment at first, these people intensely shape personality and social adjustment. If a child is reared in the natural home, the primary influence will come from the family. If a child is reared in an institution, the primary influence will come from the institutional environment and personnel. As for any child, variables such as education, intelligence, residual vision, and social class also influence these individuals' feelings of worth and independence.

The process for developing social interactions for sighted children typically begins in infancy and continues to develop throughout childhood. Social skills are in part developed through visual information. Facial expressions and body language provide the foundation for refining and developing appropriate social skills. Children with vision problems do not have access to visual information and thus may have difficulty maintaining friendships, attracting and directing the attention of peers, playing, and resolving conflicts. Many children with low vision, unless given specific instruction, do not understand the social behavior of their peers and sometimes engage in inappropriate social exchanges (Buhrow, Hartshorne, & Bradley-Johnson, 1998). As a result, social skills may need to be taught directly to children with low vision (Baird, Mayfield, & Baker, 1997).

Realistic Dependency

Like most people with disabilities, children with visual impairment risk being dependent and passive. A delicate balance exists between realistic dependency and overdependency. Sometimes students with vision smother their classmate with low vision by going overboard in their desire to help. Classmates of the child with low vision need to be informed about the impact of the visual impairment and the appropriate types of behaviors expected of them (Peavey & Leff, 2002). The inclusion teacher can model an appropriate level of assistance.

Teachers should encourage the child to do as much as possible independently. The most serious problem may not be a child's unwillingness to cooperate but, rather, the oversolicitousness the teacher and other students feel. Although empathy is to be encouraged, sympathy must be discouraged. An empathetic teacher understands the need for independence; a sympathetic teacher is likely to create dependency. The vision teacher can provide insight into how the child works in other school or home environments. Indeed, the inclusion teacher may want to observe the child in other environments.

Ana, a child with low vision, presents the classic "shrinking violet" pose in the classroom. She sits quietly waiting for the world (her teacher) to come to her doorstep, making no attempt to finish assignments or even to begin them. However, on the playground a miracle occurs. The violet blossoms into a wonderfully interesting bouquet. She laughs, tells stories, and finds friends at every turn of a corner. Ana is not socially maladjusted. If anything, she has learned the system too well. If Ana can be a trailblazer on the playground, she is capable of showing the same initiative in the classroom.

STEREOTYPIC BEHAVIORS   One problem of concern is the management of stereotypic behavior, or *blindisms*. These are repetitive behaviors that are age inappropriate and excessive. Common stereotypic behaviors include body rocking, light gazing, and hand flapping. Not all children with visual disabilities exhibit stereotypic behaviors, and no one is sure why these behaviors develop. However, such behaviors are distracting and draw attention to the person emitting them. If a child with visual disabilities exhibits blindisms, the behavior probably can be arrested by providing the child with an activity that is incompatible with the blindism. For example, if Josh is flapping his hands, he could be given an activity that requires use of his hands. If Kevin is light gazing, he might be directed to media for reading. In general, the frequency of stereotypic behaviors can be reduced by keeping a child interested in classroom activities.

Any attempt to shame or punish the child is likely to increase the undesirable behaviors. If the behaviors interfere with standard classroom routine, a vision specialist can be consulted and an appropriate management program developed jointly.

Self-Care

Mobility

For children with visual disabilities, the aspect of self-care most often discussed is mobility. Mobility refers to both locomotion and independent travel. Common mobility aids for people with visual disabilities are the seeing-eye dog and the white cane (Hill & Snook-Hill, 1996). In many states, use of a white cane has been restricted to those who are legally blind. In addition to providing guidance to the person who is using it, the cane is a signal for traffic to yield the right of way. Various electronic devices have been developed to assist in mobility, but only a few are available commercially.

Mobility training is the responsibility of the vision teacher. One of the first things taught in mobility training is body image. Awareness of body parts helps children with visual impairment conceptualize themselves and their relationship to the environment, which is vital to successful travel and movement.

In the early grades, the general education curriculum includes activities centering on left–right discrimination and naming body parts. Classroom teachers can reinforce the vision teacher's instruction through the general education curriculum. In addition to learning body parts and "what is connected to what," children with visual impairment (like most children) need to learn position terms such as *up, down, forward,* and *backward*. Most children with visual impairment are given instruction in position terms relative to their bodies (e.g., *shoulder level* or *feet together*); this instruction can be beneficial to normal children, too. Working on these activities as a total class allows the child with visual impairment to share experiences with everyone in the classroom. Teaching body parts and left–right discrimination, however, may not be grade-appropriate activities. Support activities in the general education classroom are intended to integrate children with visual impairment, not segregate them from other children or make them stand out as different.

Perhaps the greatest disability a child with visual impairment experiences in mobility is the overconcern of others. Other children in the room should be encouraged to allow the child with visual impairment to experience movements for himself or herself. To help sighted students understand the mobility needs of the student with visual impairment, some form of presentation by the vision teacher and the student with visual impairment might be given, such as an information exchange in which preconceptions are dispelled and new information is conveyed.

Eating, Toileting, Medicating

Eating, toileting, and possibly medicating are everyday occurrences for children with visual impairment. The primary responsibility of the inclusion teacher is to expect the child with visual impairment to participate in these activities just like the other children. Again, it may be necessary to discourage other students from "killing with kindness." Students with visual impairment are capable of preparing their own food trays and walking through a serving line. The vision teacher will teach the child the physical arrangement of the cafeteria. The inclusion teacher may want to reinforce cafeteria procedures and be certain that the child is made aware of any changes—either physical, such as rearrangement of lunch tables, or procedural.

To assist a child with visual impairment in achieving independence in toileting, the child has to be taught the location and room layout of the bathrooms. Beyond this, little instruction is necessary.

Medication should not be administered without appropriate medical authority. The inclusion teacher can be alert to problem signs, however, and report any peculiarities to the vision teacher or the child's parents. If an emergency occurs, teachers should do the best they can to protect the child from injury, just as they would any other child.

Communication

Children with visual impairment in the general education classroom rarely have problems with expressive language per se. However, some receptive language problems can influence expressive language. For example, if Jonathan has never seen a volcanic mountain, he probably will have conceptual difficulties with the eruption of Mt. St. Helens. Unless Jonathan is given specific instruction compensating for his visual impairment, the next time he speaks about mountains or eruptions, he is likely to misuse the terms. The message receiver may or may not notice the misuse of terms. A major language problem of children with visual impairment is that receivers or listeners often do not share the same conceptual basis as the child with visual impairment. The following tips may be helpful when working with a child with visual impairment who has receptive language problems:

1. *Verbal references.* When using verbal references to objects or actions, relate them to references that the child knows or has experienced. Clarification of references may mean presenting information by touch as well as verbally. Consider the term *mountain.* You can verbally describe a mountain and also present an embossed referent sheet that depicts in scale a mountain, a hill, and flat ground. Given sufficient notification, a vision teacher usually can provide the materials. If you need an immediate referent, you can use some glue, a ball of string, and a tiny bit of ingenuity to create raised surfaces on ordinary paper for tactile discrimination.

2. *Anticipatory sets.* Establish an anticipatory set. This goes beyond providing a child with a signal for attending. An anticipatory set focuses a child's auditory attention by setting up anticipation for what is going to be heard and then comparing what was expected with what actually is heard. Normally, children with visual impairment and other children must be taught to establish an anticipatory set. This can occur any time during the school day when you want the children to attend to auditory information. If, for example, you are teaching a lesson on frogs, you might use the following format:

   Signal: Okay, everyone, I've got something to tell you.
   Anticipation: I've got something in this box that's green and hops and swims in a pond.
   Expectation: What do you think is in this box? (Allow time for children's responses.)
   Comparison: (Open the box and show the children a frog.) Look, I've got a frog. What made you think I had something else?

   By establishing some kind of format, you will train the children to develop the habit of using an anticipatory set.

3. *Tactile presentations.* Many students with low vision need to have instruction which involves tactile formats. When demonstrating or modeling, which typically requires visual attention, encourage the students to touch or feel the objects involved in the demonstration. Tactile information requires individual physical contact and therefore takes more time than presenting pictures

or providing verbal explanations. Allow extra time when presenting information where students have an opportunity to touch, handle, examine, and synthesize information (Downing & Demchak, 2002).

Tactile format presentations are not for all students. Some children have a very low sensory threshold and are hyper-responsive to certain types of sensory stimulation (Williamson & Anzalone, 2001). Some students react negatively to tactile information. Such reactions, often referred to as tactile defensiveness, can vary from child to child or type of material. No child should be forced to touch, be touched, or feel material that creates tactile defensiveness, even if learning through touch would be the most direct route for conceptual understanding.

4. *Braille literacy.* The literature strongly supports teaching children who are blind how to read and write using Braille (Johnson, 1996). In addition to technological advances such as talking computers and speech-recognition devices, a vital component for effective participation in a literate society is the ability to use written language. The written language most associated with children with low vision is Braille.

Most special and general education teachers do not have the skills nor are they expected to teach children how to use Braille for reading or writing. However, some children have difficulty acquiring Braille, and that difficulty may be related to their spoken language abilities, particularly phonological awareness (Gillon & Young, 2002). Regardless of the reading or writing system used, teachers are expected to instruct children with low vision or who are blind how to use their language system in order to build knowledge for any reading or writing system, including Braille. Specifically, the child with low vision, including blindness, needs access to the general education curriculum in the areas of reading and writing, and the inclusion teacher is the teacher who teaches reading and writing. The vision specialist builds on the child's knowledge of reading and writing to extend the information to a Braille system.

Notes are an important source of visual information for children with normal vision. Children with visual impairment often are capable of taking their own class notes. However, transferring information from auditory to visual media is time consuming. Children with visual impairment often use cassette tape recorders to record verbal information and later transfer it into another form. Some children with visual impairment use a slate and stylus to take notes, yet others take handwritten notes. In either case, note taking is slower for children with visual impairment than for children with normal vision. Teachers may have to repeat key points several times or allow for longer pauses between critical ideas. Note taking for a child with visual impairment may require extra concentration and be very fatiguing. To account for the fatigue factor some children with visual impairments experience, perhaps the vision teacher might be able to transcribe the notes.

Teachers in a general education program that includes students with visual disabilities must take into account how the visual disability affects the child cognitively, emotionally, and socially. Teachers with real or vicarious experience with students with low vision or blindness appear to have a more positive attitude toward inclusion than teachers without such experiences. As experience with students who have low vision or are blind increases, teachers tend to have more confidence in their own abilities to work with the students and to be more positive toward inclusion of such students (Wall, 2002).

Familiarity with the implications of the particular visual disability experienced by a particular child is the key to providing an appropriate education in the general education setting. As with all areas of inclusion, collaboration is an important element in determining the quality and effectiveness of educational programming for students who are visually impaired. The special nature of many types of visual impairments creates a true need for collaboration requiring contact and financial sharing between local school districts and specialized private schools or agencies addressing the needs of children with low vision (Zebehazy & Whitten, 2003). In a general education classroom, observations made by the inclusion teacher and a vision specialist can be transformed into systematic instructional adaptations that will lead to successful academic and social experiences.

Children With Hearing Impairments

Impact of Hearing Loss

Children who have hearing disabilities usually are referred to as deaf or hard of hearing. In both conditions, something has altered normal auditory reception, interfering with the ability to hear and understand speech sounds. The degree of hearing loss ranges from slight, mild, moderate, severe, to profound, depending on the ability to use hearing to understand speech. The descriptions are misleading, however, because even a minimal hearing loss can have a negative effect on the student's educational performance, as well as on psychosocial development.

Hearing and listening are complementary processes. Hearing relates to the ability to detect the presence of sound, whereas listening refers to paying attention to the sound in order to comprehend meaning (Gordon-Langbein, 2001). Children may be able to hear sounds or some of the sounds of speech, but the actual words or sounds may be unintelligible. Some children with hearing loss experience frustration, anxiety, stress, and fatigue when they are trying to understand the speech of others (Bess, Dodd-Murphy, & Parker, 1998).

In inclusion settings, a more functional definition focuses on the child's ability to use hearing to understand and learn language and the effects of the hearing loss on educational performance. Only about an estimated 1.2% of all school-age students receiving special education services have significant hearing issues and are receiving their education in an inclusion setting. Another 0.11% of the population with hearing issues continues to be educated in segregated settings (U.S. Department of Education, 2002). Interestingly enough, when compared with previous decades, more children with hearing loss are being identified with mild or moderate hearing loss, and a high incidence of hearing loss in the slight and mild levels is found in the Cuban American and Puerto Rican American populations of the United States (Nelson, 2001).

In spite of such small numbers, students who qualify for special education services due to a hearing loss are an extremely heterogeneous group (Easterbrooks, 1999). Like many other disabilities, deafness can coexist with other conditions (e.g., mental retardation, cerebral palsy, deaf-blind). Almost a quarter of the students who are hard of hearing—that is, who can gain meaning from speech by using a hearing aid—also have associated disabilities (e.g., learning disabilities, 9%; mental retardation, 8%; vision problems, 4%; and emotional or behavioral disorders, 4%) (Holden-Pitt & Diaz, 1998; Karchmer & Allen, 1999).

The age at which the auditory system is impaired is a critical variable. Children who are born deaf or become deaf before 2 or 3 years of age do not have a chance to acquire normal speech and language. Children who have relatively normal hearing up to about 2 or 3 years of age can build upon their language with more facility. Generally, the ease with which children acquire language varies inversely with the severity of the hearing loss. As with all generalizations, however, exceptions occur. Hearing disabilities are a highly individualized problem. For example, Lindy may be able to perceive some sounds well, but she still may be considered deaf if she cannot hear and understand connected speech even with a hearing aid. Other factors that contribute to the individual nature of a hearing impairment are the cause and type of hearing impairment.

As shown in Figure 3.5, the ear has three major parts: (a) outer (external), (b) middle, and (c) inner. Hearing loss has been classified into two major types, conductive and sensorineural, according to which part of the ear is affected.

Conductive Hearing Losses

A *conductive hearing loss* is caused by some problem in the outer or middle ear, like a bean lodged in the ear canal. Wax build-up also can cause conductive loss. Another common condition leading to conductive loss is interference with movement of the bones in the middle ear. Up to about the age of 5 or 6, many children get middle-ear infections called *otitis media.* This can impair the movement of the middle-ear bones and produce a conductive loss.

Children who have a conductive hearing loss usually hear lower- and middle-frequency tones (*m, n, ng,* and vowels) as muffled or faint. They may show severe articulation errors of substitution or omission. The overall speech signal is depressed. A child with a conductive hearing loss must expend a great deal of effort to hear. Some children may appear to be lazy or inattentive when the reality is that they simply do not have enough energy to make sense of an auditory kaleidoscope of muffled sounds.

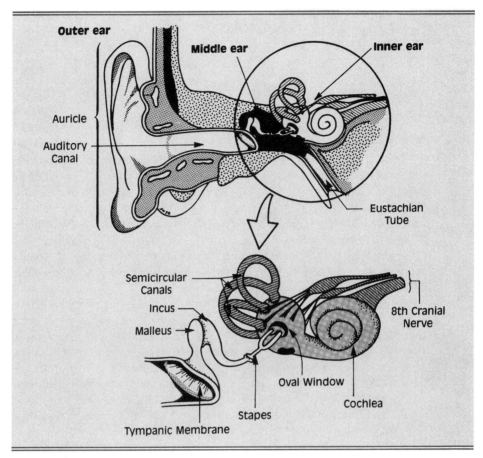

Figure 3.5   The Ear

Children with a conductive hearing loss may speak softly or quietly. They also may seem to have a syntax problem, which often turns out to be an articulation error of omission rather than a syntax error. Nickie often leaves out plurals and the word *is*, as in "The five boy went home." Nickie understands the plural concept of five boys, but she has difficulty hearing and thus producing the plural ending.

Sensorineural Hearing Losses

The other type of hearing loss, *sensorineural hearing loss*, results from a problem in the inner ear, the acoustic nerves, or both. Sensorineural losses vary in severity, but usually are more serious than conductive losses. In a sensorineural loss, sounds may be both muffled and distorted. High-pitched sounds such as *th, f, ch,* and *t* present problems for many children with sensorineural losses. If any sounds are heard at all, they are so distorted that the child has a difficult, if not impossible, time matching his or her speech sounds with the sounds of others. As a result, communication can be frustrating.

Lipreading is a viable communication tool for many children with a sensorineural loss. To read lips, a child must be able to see the communicator's lips. Classroom teachers may have to be sensitive to their facial position in relation to the child's line of vision. The glare or light from a window behind the teacher may make his lips hard to see.

Another potential problem in the general education classroom is background noise. Typical background noise in a classroom can interfere with whatever hearing a deaf or hard-of-hearing child has. Distance from the communicator is a critical factor in this regard. The optimal distance from the speaker's mouth to the child's ear depends on the type of hearing loss. For some children, the correct distance is a matter of inches; for others, distance is irrelevant. Teachers in inclusion settings where children need a very small distance between themselves and the teacher or other speakers can maintain that distance when standing still. Classroom teachers tend to walk around the room as they lecture, though, so they may want to spend less time traveling during group instruction and circulate more during individual or practice instruction.

Because sensorineural disabilities affect sound processing to a great extent, care must be taken to ensure that a child truly understands the concepts being communicated. Jane is a classic example of a deaf child who seems to understand classroom concepts but actually has no idea what she is supposed to be learning. She is agreeable; whenever her teacher asks if she understands, Jane smiles and nods her head. She completes all of her assignments on time, usually with accuracy. Jane has learned an excellent survival tactic: She can imitate. She looks around the classroom and gets cues as to what she is to do from the other kids or from directions in the text. The trap is that Jane is doing busy work rather than the conceptualization that the material is supposed to engender. On the surface, she seems to be developing vocabulary and participating in class activities like her classmates who hear normally. Digging a little deeper, though, one discovers that she is lacking in basic information. Inclusion teachers are in an excellent position to guard against the "imitation syndrome." Together with a hearing specialist, they can devise a classroom strategy that is most comfortable and likely to help children like Jane truly conceptualize information.

Academic Provisions

Other Professionals

Educating children with hearing impairments in a general education classroom is a team responsibility. The inclusion teacher and other professionals must develop open lines of communication to ensure that appropriate help for the child is available. Two professionals with whom the inclusion teacher might work closely are the teacher of children with hearing disabilities and the speech–language clinician.

The teacher of children with hearing disabilities can work directly with the child and also serve as a resource person. He or she can develop strategies for teaching concepts from the general education curriculum. These strategies revolve around the child's level of language development. This special teacher also will be able to use various special communication modes such as signing or total communication. Keeping a list of new vocabulary words or key concepts in the weekly lesson book and providing access to the lesson book can greatly facilitate communication of classroom materials.

A speech–language clinician primarily deals with speech and language problems, working directly with the child but not necessarily instructing on curriculum subject matter. The clinician can provide suggestions for use in the classroom, and the inclusion teacher may be able to describe areas in which the child needs help from the speech–language clinician. A common practice is to keep a daily notebook of the kinds of errors the child makes. The notebook need not be exhaustive, nor does the teacher have to be compulsive about recording observations. A rough picture of the typical classroom performance of the child with a hearing impairment will do. An example of entries in a weekly notebook for Joel is presented in Figure 3.6.

Armed with notes from the general education classroom, the speech clinician can institute remedial work with the final *s* sound, science vocabulary, or whatever else is an apparent problem for the child. Evaluating Joel's progress in speech and language in the general education classroom allows the speech clinician not only to determine areas for remedial work but also to determine how effective Joel's instruction has been.

General Guidelines

Although responsibility for educating a child with a hearing impairment will be shared, the inclusion teacher spends most of the school day with the child. Some general guidelines related to the use of hearing in the classroom are discussed next.

1. *Use whatever hearing capacity the child has.* Many children with hearing impairments have some residual hearing. The amount and utility of this residual hearing vary with each individual. Try to capitalize on residual hearing by having the child use hearing whenever possible. Encourage the child to listen as well as look when information is presented. If students are to listen to a tape of reading material and follow the words in a book, the child with hearing impairment also should "listen" to the tape and follow along in the book.

   Encouraging a child to use residual hearing is called *auditory training*. Auditory training for children with hearing impairments is much like auditory training given to children with normal hearing. Training may begin with identification of selected environmental sounds (such as a lunch bell), localization of sound sources, and distance listening. Training may lead gradually to word discrimination on the basis of vowel or consonant differences. With

	Speech	Language
Teacher *Ms. Jones*		
Student *Joel*		
Date *9/18 – 9/22*		
Monday	*Dropped "s" off words* *Left out verb "is"*	
Tuesday	*Problems with "s"*	*Confused about "beside" and "around"*
Wednesday		
Thursday	*Final "s" problem* *Leaving out words like "the" and "a"*	
Friday	*Still final "s" and omission of "the" and "a"*	*Confused about science vocabulary*

Figure 3.6   A Weekly Speech and Language Notebook

a child with hearing impairment, the inclusion teacher can capitalize on auditory events throughout the day to provide reinforcement for specific auditory training content. A quick check with a hearing or language teacher can be useful in determining the level of expectation the inclusion teacher can demand from the child with hearing impairment in the general education classroom.

Residual hearing also can be enhanced through amplification provided by a hearing aid. First and foremost, be sure the aid is working. The child probably will not be able to recognize a malfunction in the hearing aid. As the power of the battery diminishes, so does the aid's effectiveness. Set up a frequent and thorough periodic check system.

Four key points are as follows:

■ Amplification raises the level of sound, but it does not decrease distortion in sound. Distortions, like all other sounds, will be louder.

- Most children using amplification use a monaural or one-receiver system. Therefore, the child should be placed so the "good" ear is toward the most important source of sound.
- The teacher's voice may become lost in other sound signals.
- A child with amplification hears whatever sound source is closest.

2. *Provide visual access to classroom information.* One of the most obvious ways to convey information to a child with hearing impairment is through the visual system. A child with hearing impairment learns a lot by seeing things. Therefore, the classroom teacher must take special care to provide visual aids when teaching. Fortunately, visual media that are appropriate for a child with hearing impairment can also be used with students who hear normally. Transparencies, films, filmstrips, closed-captioned TV, and pictures can be valuable teaching aids. Providing printed words to accompany these visual aids enhances their teaching value. By furnishing outlines of lectures or films prior to delivery, teachers can maximize input for a child with hearing impairment. Displaying classroom directions and directions for assignments is another technique for clarifying classroom expectancies.

Jeremiah was a lucky child. When he first entered the general education classroom, he seemed inattentive. He appeared disoriented and rarely completed assignments. His teacher, Ms. Rhoton, sensed an impending crisis and began to analyze the problem. She noticed that Jeremiah, rather than being obstinate, seemed not to know what he was supposed to do. Because Ms. Rhoton did not want to embarrass Jeremiah or single him out from the rest of the class, she began to write directions for assignments on the chalkboard. Jeremiah's problem disappeared. By eliminating a major source of frustration for Jeremiah, Ms. Rhoton also eliminated the possibility that Jeremiah might be placed incorrectly in a class for children with emotional disturbance. Finally, based on her observations, Ms. Rhoton referred Jeremiah for evaluation of his hearing ability.

3. *Provide classroom work on the basis of subject-matter performance.* The critical determiner of subject-matter placement for a child with hearing impairment, as with all children, is the entry-level skill brought to the learning program. Consultation with the speech–language clinician or the teacher of children with hearing impairments should provide a solid estimate of a child's skills. Based on the child's skills, the inclusion teacher will be able to design a program that fits the child's needs.

Degree and severity of a hearing disability relate to the success of classroom performance. Placement within a classroom or within content matter would seem to be indicated according to the severity of the disability. At face value this logic seems fine, but closer inspection reveals glaring fallacies. Morgan, who suffered a sensorineural loss at age 9, presents a far different skill level than Tommy, whose hearing loss occurred during infancy. Tommy did not have many of the auditory experiences that Morgan did. Both children share the label of sensorineural loss, and both now are enrolled in the fifth grade. Morgan, whose loss of hearing was relatively recent, grasps subject matter typical of her age and grade. Tommy, on the other hand, continues to have many problems in language comprehension. Although Tommy is capable of critical and analytical thought, the written style of fifth-grade subject matter must be altered so information is presented using less complex syntax. Sentences must be simplified, and Tommy will need many concrete examples of the fifth-grade vocabulary terms. Tommy and Morgan are not likely to learn at the same rate; Tommy's progress will probably be slower. As a result, subject-matter placement should be different for Tommy and Morgan.

Expectations for children with hearing impairments are the same as those for children with normal hearing. That is, one can expect basically normal performance from children with hearing impairment who have normal entry skills. Although adaptation of materials may be necessary, content need not be diluted or altered from content taught to other students in the class. A child with hearing impairment who enters the classroom with slightly lower than normal entry skills may require modification of content, however. Modifications for a low-achieving child who has hearing problems are basically the same as modifications for a low-achieving child with normal hearing. The key to successful programming in subject matter for children with hearing impairment is to find a good match between entry-level skills and expected classroom curriculum.

4. *Establish opportunities for incidental learning.* Incidental learning is learning that occurs without planning or formal instruction. In a classroom, incidental learning usually takes place as a result of some related learning experience that *is* planned. For example, if a teacher is talking about fire engines, he or she might play a tape of a fire engine siren or ask the children to tell what a fire engine siren sounds like. Thus far, the lesson has been planned. But the discussion of fire engine sirens may lead to a general discussion of other warning systems—other sirens, chimes, bells, buzzers, and so forth. The discussion of other warning systems was not planned, but the students are able to relate or generalize from past experiences. The students even may identify additional warning systems as they walk home from school that afternoon. When children "pick up" information without formal instruction, incidental learning has transpired.

Hearing is used to communicate and convey information and plays a significant role in acquiring incidental learning. Vocabulary is an essential element in providing a label for concepts being experienced. Many studies have shown that school-aged children with hearing impairments often have smaller vocabularies than children with normal hearing (American Speech-Language-Hearing Association [ASHA], 2001). Knowledge gained by a child with normal hearing through common, everyday auditory activities is often unavailable to a hearing-impaired child. A child with hearing impairment walking home from school may not hear the sound of a passing siren. Thus, this chance for reinforcement of school information is not available to the child with hearing impairment. Similarly, much incidental learning occurs from watching television, listening to a radio, and participating in everyday conversation. Children with hearing impairments may not be able to participate fully in these activities.

Classroom teachers can provide opportunities for incidental learning. Materials in the room that are suitable for use with a child with hearing impairment may be usd with all students to informally teach new concepts or reinforce concepts presented formally. These materials should be visual or audiovisual in nature. Specially captioned films and television programs usually can be obtained through the school district. Time must be set aside to allow children with hearing impairments and other children to use the materials.

5. *Establish opportunities for regular feedback.* Feedback lets children know whether their behavior matches expected behavior, thus enabling them to measure their performance against a chosen standard. A child with normal hearing has many opportunities for auditory feedback. These opportunities, much like opportunities for incidental learning, are part of the normal everyday environment. For example, a student may overhear a classroom conversation about an assignment or may hear the teacher explain a task to another student. A child with hearing impairment may be unable to use this kind of feedback. Students with hearing loss often have problems with academic assignments, not because they cannot do the task but, rather, because they have not understood the vocabulary used in the written or verbal directions provided. Inclusion teachers must be sure to provide systematic and regular feedback to the child with hearing impairment. You cannot depend on environmental feedback.

When providing feedback to children with hearing impairments, teachers must be more thorough than when providing feedback to students who hear normally. A smiling face on a paper may not be enough to let a child know what aspect of the performance merited the feedback. It may have to be more specific. William's teacher usually takes a few minutes to write out feedback, which might include a smiling face accompanied by phrases such as "Your penmanship was very legible" or "You solved these math problems just right." By writing out phrases, the teacher not only informs William that he has done good work but also helps him understand what the good work was about. William may or may not be imitating the work of others around him, but at least he is aware of the purpose of the activity.

When chosen carefully, self-instructional materials provide an opportunity for immediate feedback. When using self-instructional materials, the child with hearing impairment must understand the vocabulary and concepts presented in the programmed materials. A tendency to fill in the blank without really grasping the concepts is always a danger in programmed texts. This danger exists for children with normal hearing as well as for children with hearing impairments.

Immediate and *frequent* are two key terms to keep in mind when providing feedback to a child with hearing impairment. The newer the concept, the more critical the immediate feedback becomes. When a child with hearing impairment is struggling to acquire new knowledge, frequent feedback is necessary. As the child practices or rehearses prior learning, the need for immediate and frequent feedback decreases.

Social Adjustment

Informed Classmates

To help a child with hearing impairment become integrated socially into the class, the teacher and the other students should be well-informed about the implications of a hearing loss. Jack wanted to be treated just like everyone else, so he kept his hearing problem a secret. He used his ability to read speech to understand others. Soon he was accused of being a snob. When other kids in the room talked to Jack, they did not understand that he needed to see their lips to understand that he was being addressed. When he did not respond to a typical hallway greeting or a passing remark, the other kids thought he was ignoring them. A vicious cycle developed. The other kids began to ignore Jack, and he became upset and withdrawn. Finally, Jack actually did begin to ignore the others.

A somewhat belated but quick classroom solution was instituted. Jack's teacher initiated a science program covering the five senses, beginning with a unit on hearing. Through the course of this unit, Jack related some of his personal needs and explained that he was a speech reader. A classroom discussion ensued in which feelings were aired and misunderstandings corrected. Children in Jack's class now are more sensitive to his hearing needs. Jack learned that he need not hide his condition and that people are much more accepting than he had thought previously.

Age-Appropriate Behavior

One adjective frequently attached to children with hearing impairment is *immature*. Many children with hearing impairment function at a developmentally younger stage than their normally hearing peers. Some of this behavior may be attributed to less sensitivity to subtle social nuances. Tone of voice conveys much social information. A phrase such as "the teacher is gone" can elicit fear or excitement, depending on tonal quality. Frequently, children with hearing impairments are unable to discriminate tonal differences. Although tonal differences usually are accompanied by body language, which would seem to compensate for an inability to hear, children with hearing impairments take longer than others to learn to read body language because a critical cue in reading body language comes from hearing an accompanying vocal tone.

Inclusion teachers can help children with hearing impairments act in ways that are appropriate for their age. They can work within the context of the classroom, just as they would with any immature child. For a child with hearing impairment who is immature, standard teaching techniques are fine, with accommodations geared to hearing needs.

Other Social Skills

Social goals for a child with hearing impairment are the same as for typical children and children with other disabilities. Inclusion teachers already have the skills to help children reach these social goals. If lack of knowledge about the hearing impairment causes uncertainty about teaching methods, discuss the issue with the teacher for students with hearing disabilities. This two-way communication will be beneficial for both teachers and the child.

Self-Care

Classroom Rules

By the time a child with hearing impairment enters the public school system, self-care skills in mobility, eating, and toileting usually are well-developed. Generally, the most severe problem in self-care of children with hearing impairments is an unclear or vague understanding of classroom or school rules.

When 6-year-old Lee Ann first entered a general education classroom, all seemed well. She appeared to be happy, well-adjusted, and enthusiastic about her new school environment. About 2 weeks later, however, a terrible event occurred. Lee Ann had an "accident"; she wet her pants. The child hid her accident from everyone. Five days later, another accident took place. This time it wasn't easy to conceal. Lee Ann's teacher helped downplay the incident, and life continued. Unfortunately, so did the accidents. Lee Ann's teacher became concerned, but rather than panic, she decided to see what she could do for Lee Ann. With gentle questioning the teacher discovered that Lee Ann didn't know how to ask to be excused. Lee Ann's teacher had explained the rules to her the first day of school, but in all the excitement, Lee Ann had forgotten. Because of her hearing impairment, she could not hear the other children ask to be excused, so she had no way of knowing what to do. What could have been some severe psychological problem turned out to be a small but significant communication problem.

The inclusion teacher can help a student with a hearing disability avoid embarrassing situations by not leaving knowledge of rules to chance. If a child can read, the child should receive the self-help rules in writing. The behavior of the child with a hearing disability should be noted at least three times after the rule or direction is first given to ensure comprehension.

Communication

If inclusion teachers could choose only one area for helping a child with hearing impairment integrate successfully into a general education classroom, communication should be the choice. Communication forms the basis for all classroom activities. A great deal of our communication is transmitted through speech and language, but avenues of speech and language are restricted for children with hearing impairments.

To send a communication, a sender must have a set of speech sounds that the receiver can understand. Most people learn speech sounds by modeling and practicing the sounds others emit. A child with a hearing disability again is at a disadvantage because he or she has less exposure to speech sounds in the environment than does a child who hears normally. Because modeling and practice are limited, children with a hearing disability often have problems with speech and language. Thus, they often encounter a double communication problem—limited ability to both receive and send information.

Expressive Language

Expressive language problems of children with hearing impairments are most noticeable in speech production. A child with a hearing impairment may distort sounds, as in the phrase "wed wabbit" for "red rabbit." Some of the sound distortions are acceptable (and even normal in certain parts of the country) and do not interfere with communication unless the distortions embarrass the child or disrupt classroom communication. When distortions are cause for concern, a speech–language clinician can help. The inclusion teacher usually does not design a program dealing with a child's speech problems but may be able to reinforce the clinician's program. The speech–language clinician may be able to provide information about the child's personal speech code (e.g., "Mac substitutes l's for r's and leaves off –ed endings").

Depending on the severity of the hearing loss and its impact on language production and reception, a variety of special techniques or adaptations may be used. Most general and special education teachers do not have the training in, nor are they expected to use, these very specialized approaches. Some of these approaches include signing, finger spelling, and manual communication.

Regardless of the system used by the student, the teacher and other children in the classroom need to understand the basics of how the system works. An alternate form of communication will be necessary for the students with hearing impairments to communicate with their hearing teacher and classmates. An inclusion teacher needs to think of a student with hearing impairment as being bilingual. All the techniques used to communicate with non-English-speaking students need to be reviewed for application with students with hearing disabilities.

Fortunately, most children are fascinated by alternate language systems and are likely to welcome at least a cursory introduction to the language used by the child with hearing disabilities. Even though most hearing children will not become proficient with the new system, this language method can be acknowledged and respected in many of the same ways that other linguistic systems are. In signing, for example, a simple and nonintrusive idea is to place both the signed alphabet and a traditional print or cursive alphabet in the classroom. The teacher might also invite a person who uses an alternate form of communication from standard English to teach a song using that approach. These types of activities communicate a message to children with and without hearing disabilities that all can hear loudly and clearly.

Expressive communication problems also may affect the child's ability to participate in group discussions. Producing speech is a slow and laborious process for some children with hearing impairments. Not only can the speech activity be emotionally draining for the struggling speaker, it can also be draining for the listeners. They must take care not to finish or anticipate the finish of a child's word or phrase. They also must be careful not to rush the child to complete the communication. Rushing the child will lead to more frustration. On the other hand, a child with a hearing impairment may become extremely isolated if not given chances to participate actively in social groups (Haller & Montgomery, 2004). The physical integration of students with hearing losses does not guarantee socialization (Cambra, 2002). Systematic instruction in teaching students with and without hearing loss in how to interact with each other may be necessary to ensure true classroom inclusion.

Inclusion teachers have to deal with their own feelings and encourage empathy in the other students. At times, children with hearing impairments who have speech problems are treated cruelly simply because ignoring difficult or slowly produced speech is much easier than allowing for breaks in the conversation or conversation that is irregularly paced.

Depending on the type of hearing disability involved, some children may also have difficulty producing appropriate words. Because of limited interactions involving language, vocabularies of some children with hearing impairments are not as large as those of their peers who hear normally. Restricted ability to hear language also may affect the order in which words are put together. Problems with expressive word order, or *syntax,* need not be a major cause for concern. As in problems with speech sounds, if a syntax disorder does not interfere significantly with communication, the inclusion teacher may opt to reinforce the speech–language clinician's program rather than developing a different one.

Receptive Language

Problems in *receptive language*, or in the ability to receive information through sounds, often challenge the child with a hearing impairment. Because the child may not always hear all the sounds clearly, communication may be strained. What the child hears (aside from disorder) depends in part upon the child's position in relation to the source of the sound. When Carrie Ann sits away from her teacher, she just sits. She's not being obstinate; she just doesn't know what is going on. Resolving Carrie Ann's problem is simple: Seat her close to the teacher.

Some children with hearing impairments face a more formidable challenge. For some children hearing is intermittent. One day, Matthew can sit close to his teacher and follow communication very well. On the next day, Matthew can have the identical physical relationship to his teacher's voice and not understand a word said.

Conferring with the teacher for hearing disabilities may provide insight concerning the receptive skills of a child with hearing impairment. Hearing ability may change frequently, however. Thus, a written report on a child may not reflect anything more than the child's ability on the date of the report. Fluctuations in hearing ability need not raise undue alarm.

A trained teacher can easily determine if a child is not completing assignments, is not following oral directions correctly, or is not attending as the teacher speaks. If bringing the child closer does not alleviate any of these problems, consistently or intermittently, the teacher may have to alter the communication format.

All oral information can be paired with visual information. If a child can read, the teacher has a solution, as putting information on paper is simple and effective. If the child cannot read, symbols can be substituted for words or instructions can be modeled directly.

Repetition, paraphrasing, or both are techniques that a teacher can use to ensure the child with the hearing disability is receiving the correct information. Thus, information may have to be repeated, paraphrased, or both. Sometimes a child with a hearing impairment may not have a visual or experiential referent for a specific word or phrase. By altering the wording slightly, the teacher may present more complete information that is better understood. Body language, especially facial expressions, and the pace at which information is delivered are additional factors to consider when delivering instructional content.

A child with a hearing disability may require a little more time to process auditory information than a child with normal hearing. Patience on the teacher's part will produce the best results. Slowness in processing does not necessarily mean slowness in intellectual functioning. For some children with hearing impairment, sorting out distorted sounds is difficult, especially when the child is trying to learn or recall a new concept. Inclusion teachers can reduce receptive language problems by controlling the length and complexity of oral delivery or instructions. By using short, succinct instructions, the teacher can reduce both the memory load and the number of potential distortions.

Receptive Language and Technology

Increasing the Ability to Use Sound

Every day technology is used to increase people's ability to use auditory channels, creating substantial and positive advances in accessing speech and language for children with hearing losses. But even technology has its limitations, which are determined by the degree, configuration, and type of hearing loss.

Many factors contribute to positive listening situations for children with hearing losses, and the inclusion teacher can control a lot of these dynamics. Whatever type of technology or amplification system is used, teachers must take into account the child's developmental age and language skills and the complexity of the message. Short simple sentences are always easier to understand than long complex sentences with embedded ideas. Classroom lighting also must be sufficient for the child with hearing loss to be able to see the speaker's facial expressions and lips.

Visual Components

The addition of a visual component to instruction also improves accuracy for many children with hearing loss and even for some without hearing loss, especially in classrooms with poor acoustics (Steinfeld, 2001). Text-based supplementary devices like speech-to-text translation, real-time voice-to-text translation (RTC), and television captioning are additional technologies that increase students' access to meaningful language by providing visual images and associated printed captions. Text-based supplementary devices put less demand on a child's working memory resources. When Helen uses a text-based supplementary device, she does not need to use as much energy to guess about meaning derived from reading her teacher's and peers' lips. As a result, she can focus more of her energy on thinking about the topic of the lecture or discussion. Text-based supplementary devices have freed Helen from juggling all the auditory, thinking, and guessing receptive language balls needed to access the general education curriculum. A welcome bonus Helen gets from using text-based supplementary devices is less stress and fatigue and more openness to learning.

Transient hearing loss affects many children. Numerous children, especially in the primary grades and those who experience chronic respiratory infections, are plagued by middle-ear infections, colds, and allergies. Their potential for learning is greatly increased when they can use a text-based supplementary device to refer to classroom information. The impact of fluctuating auditory ability is greatly reduced when text-based supplementary devices are available.

A very low-tech but successful technique used by many experienced teachers to attract attention is to flip the classroom lights on and off a couple of times. The instruction can follow the light flicks using a verbal strategy of "Stop. Look. Listen." Directions can also be accompanied by finger signals (e.g., the number of fingers shown indicates the number of minutes the child has left to finish an activity) (Inkson, 2002).

Another tried-and-true low-tech approach is to write the student's daily schedule in a prominent place in the classroom. Couple the daily schedule with a consistent and organized classroom routine and students with and without hearing losses will not need to spend time listening for new instructions or learning new routines. Predictability is a major player in the world of successful inclusion.

Increasing Sound Level

One of the most important factors teachers can control in delivering speech is a favorable signal-to-noise ratio (SNR); that is, the words and sounds need to be at a sufficiently loud level if the sender's message is to be understood clearly. Under the best classroom situations, the distance between the speaker and the listener should not be more than 6–8 feet, and the teacher or classroom peers should speak about 6–8 inches from the child's ear or speak through a microphone (Bess, 2000). Inclusion teachers can design activities that take into account the SNR between themselves and their students, as well as the distance between the child with a hearing loss and children with normal hearing abilities. Teachers can also encourage other class members to use the microphone to paraphrase classroom directions, assignments, or activities.

Hearing aids have come a long way from the original amplification of all sounds, wanted or unwanted, to the more modern hearing aids, which can be individualized to each child's specific pattern of hearing loss (Niklaus, 2007). Hearing aids are probably the most commonly used assistive device, allowing many children to hear within the normal range and receive education in inclusion settings. In addition to hearing aids, technology has created powerful new tools to assist children with hearing disabilities access the auditory world. Part of the trick to using any of these technologies successfully is at least a superficial understanding of how they work. Inclusion teachers probably need multiple spares of every commonly replaceable part of the device (e.g., batteries for hearing aids as well as a technology assistance center hotline number).

A variety of listening tools are available. A fairly common device is the personal frequency modulation (FM) amplification system. FM systems, like the Desktop Sound Pak, use a radio link between the teacher and the child with the hearing loss. The teacher wears a small microphone and the child with the disability wears a receiver that doubles as a personal hearing aid (Crandell & Smaldino, 2001). Figure 3.2 depicts an example of an FM system. FM systems reduce background noise and allow a clearer presentation of sound. One drawback, however, is that the child does not have the same access to classroom communication with peers as with the teacher.

A variation of the personal FM amplification system is the sound-field FM system. The sound-field system delivers the teacher's voice by using one or more carefully placed loudspeakers. In addition, the field application FM systems are designed to benefit all children in a class, not just one. Field application systems do not improve the SNR as much as a personal FM system, but they are extremely cost effective (Crandell & Smaldino, 2001).

A technological advancement becoming more commonly used is the cochlear implant (CI). A CI uses a surgically inserted prosthetic device that directly links with the cochlea and provides electrical stimulation to the auditory nerve, thus restoring or providing access to the auditory channel for those who never experienced or had previously lost hearing (Lachs, Weiss, & Pisoni, 2002). Federal guidelines have allowed implantation of CIs in children with profound deafness as young as 12 months and in children with severe to profound hearing loss at ages 2 and older. Early implantation appears to minimize initial language delays and promotes the development of age-appropriate receptive and expressive language skills (Kirk, Miyamoto, Ying, Perdew, & Zuganelis, 2002; Svirsky, Chute, Green, Bollard, & Miyamoto, 2002).

A CI is not a miracle cure for all children. Children who have lost their hearing at a very young age and then learned spoken language while using a CI show different degrees of proficiency in the speech and language skills they acquire. Some children develop excellent auditory listening skills and highly intelligible speech; other children with similar medical histories do not demonstrate the same level of ability (Cleary, Pisoni, & Kirk, 2002). The child's ability will be a major factor in the type of adaptations that will be provided in the general education setting.

Impact of Noise on Communication

NOISE LEVEL   The degree to which both expressive and receptive language can be functional in an inclusion classroom is highly influenced by the noise level inside and outside the walls. Background noise that would either be ignored or tuned out by children with intact auditory systems can have dire consequences for children with even slight hearing losses. Even the most sophisticated hearing assistive technology can be rendered useless without appropriate modification of the classroom (Crandell & Smaldino, 2001).

Ambient noise and reverberation are two of the leading contributors to interference with auditory input for students with even slight hearing losses. Ambient noise typically refers to sounds that are commonly found in the environment—for example, the soft persistent sounds of the heating or cooling system, small crackles associated with faulty lighting fixtures, movement of desks and chairs, and even the gentle tapping of a typewriter or keyboard. Reverberation can be compared to the echo level of the classroom. Classrooms with high ceilings and hard walls and floors create persistence and reflection of sound. Ambient noise and reverberation can impact auditory systems and can create even more significant problems in understanding speech and language for children with hearing loss.

TECHNIQUES FOR IMPROVING ACOUSTICS   Most classrooms today are likely to be active, multicenter places that encourage active communication and hands-on activities. In many newer school buildings, the notion of four walls per classroom has been thrown out in favor of creating more open learning spaces. Small groupings of classes within a large open space may create special hearing problems for students who have issues understanding speech and language. In order for students with hearing loss to access knowledge in such lively and non-defined environments, improved acoustics are critical.

Using absorptive surfaces, such as carpeting, draperies, and acoustical ceiling tiles, can reduce noise levels. Ceiling tiles can be attached to particularly noisy walls, both inside and outside the room (e.g., walls located next to a music room, gym, or cafeteria). Even if you do have the best acoustical situation, some of the following suggestions can further reduce classroom noise:

- Place a small rubber pad or carpet remnant on a table or desk to reduce reverberations created through hands-on activities, hard plastic manipulatives, and keyboard noises.
- Replace noise-making manipulatives, such as poker chips or dice, with softer rubber or soft plastic material.
- Use soft absorbent fabric, like corduroy or flannel, as a background cover for bulletin boards.

Reducing classroom reverberation and noise can positively affect access to speech, reading, spelling ability, attention, and concentration. By reducing the noise level of the classroom, the adaptations provided through personal assistive devices will be able to maximize the child's contact with the auditory world.

Summary

Children classified as having a low-incidence disability are similar in many ways to students in the high-incidence categories. A major distinguishing factor is that their numbers are much smaller. Children in the low-incidence categories are most often associated with disabilities affecting physical, health, or sensory issues. Children categorized with physical and health impairments, visual impairments, and hearing disabilities are typically considered in the low-incidence categories. Children with multiple disabilities, such as deaf–blind, also fall into the low-incidence categories. Many of the strategies used with typical learners and students in the high-incidence categories are appropriate for children in the low-incidence categories. Moreover, strategies used within one category are often appropriate for use with children in other categories. Some strategies are specific to physical, health, or sensory issues presented by the disability. Many strategies that have proven to be successful with children with low-incidence disabilities in self-contained settings are currently being tried in general education environments.

References

Agran, M., Alper, S., & Wehmeyer, M. (2002). Access to the general curriculum for students with significant disabilities: What it means to teachers. *Education and Training in Mental Retardation and Developmental Disabilities, 37,* 123–133.

American Speech-Language-Hearing Association (ASHA). (2001). *Language and literacy development.* Washington, DC: U.S. Department of Education and American Speech Language Hearing Association.

Ashcroft, S. C., & Zambone-Ashley, A. M. (1980). Mainstreaming children with visual impairments. *Journal of Research & Development in Education, 13*(4), 22–36.

Baird, S. M., Mayfield, P., & Baker, P. (1997). Mothers' interpretations of the behavior of their infants with visual and other impairments during interactions. *Journal of Visual Impairment and Blindness, 91,* 467–483.

Baker, J. M., & Zigmond, N. (1995). The meaning and practice of inclusion for students with learning disabilities: themes and implications from the five cases. *The Journal of Special Education*, 29, 163–180.

Bess F. (2000). Classroom acoustics: an overview. *Volta Review. 101,* 1–14.

Bess, F. H., Dodd-Murphy, J., & Parker, R. A. (1998). Children with minimal sensorineural hearing loss: Prevalence, educational performance and functional status. *Ear and Training, 5,* 339–354.

Best, S. J., Reed, P., & Bigge, J. L. (2005). Assistive technology. In S. J. Best, I. W. Heller, & J. L. Bigge, *Teaching individuals with physical or multiple disabilities* (5th ed.), (pp. 179–226). Upper Saddle River, NJ: Merrill/Prentice Hall.

Bigge, J. L., Best, S. J., & Heller, K.W. (2001). *Teaching individuals with physical, health, or multiple disabilities* (4th ed.). NJ: Prentice Hall.

Borgioli, J. A., & Kennedy, C. H. (2003). Transitions between school and hospital for students with multiple disabilities: A survey of causes, educational continuity, and parental perceptions. *Research & Practice for Persons with Severe Disabilities, 28,* 1–6.

Bosman, A. M. T., Gompel, M., & Vervleod, M. (2006). Low vision affects the reading process quantitatively but not qualitatively. *The Journal of Special Eduation, 39,* 208–219.

Browder, D. M., & Cooper-Duffy, K. (2003). Evidence-based practices for students with severe disabilities and the requirement for accountability in "No Child Left Behind." *The Journal of Special Education, 37,* 157–163.

Brown, L., Wilcox, B., Sontag, E., Vincent, B., Dodd, N., & Gruenewald, L. (1977). Toward the realization of the least restrictive educational environments for severely handicapped students. *The Journal of Research & Practice for Persons with Severe Disabilities, 2004, 29*(1), 2–8. (Reprinted from *The American Association for the Education of the Severely/Profoundly Handicapped Review, 2*(4), December, 195–201.)

Bryant, D., & Bryant, B. (2003). *Assistive technology for people with disabilities.* Boston: Allyn and Bacon.

Buhrow, M. M., Hartshorne, T. S., & Bradley-Johnson, S. (1998). Parents' and teachers' ratings of the social skills of elementary-age students who are blind. *Journal of Visual Impairment and Blindness, 92,* 503–511.

Cambra, C. (2002). Acceptance of deaf students by hearing students in regular classrooms. *American Annals of the Deaf, 147,* 38–45.

Castagnera, E., Fisher, D., Rodifer, K., & Sax, C. (1998). *Deciding what to teach and how to teach it: Connecting students through curriculum and instruction.* Colorado Springs, CO: PEAK Parent Center.

Cleary, M., Pisoni, D. B., & Kirk, K. I. (2002). Working memory spans as predictors of spoken word recognition and receptive vocabulary in children with cochlear implants. *The Volta Review, 102* (monograph), 259–280.

Coie, J. D., Dodge, K. A., & Kupersmidt, J. B. (1990). Peer group behavior and social status. In S. R. Asher & J. D. Coie (Eds.), *Peer rejection in childhood.* New York: Cambridge University Press.

Copeland, S. R., Hughes, C., Agran, M., Wehmeyer, M. L., & Fowler, S. E. (2002). An intervention package to support high school students with mental retardation in general education classrooms. *American Journal on Mental Retardation, 107,* 32–45.

Cox, P. R., & Dykes, M. K. (2001). Effective classroom adaptations for students with visual impairments. *Teaching Exceptional Children, 33,* 68–74.

Crandell, C. C., & Smaldino, J. J. (2001). Improving classroom acoustics: Utilizing hearing assistive technology and communication strategies in the educational setting. *The Volta Review, 101*(5), 47–64.

Dote-Kwan, J., Chen, D., & Hughes, M. (2001, June). A national survey of service providers who work with young children with visual impairments. *Journal of Visual Impairment and Blindness, 95,* 325–337.

Downing, J. E., & Demchak, M. A. (2002). First steps: Determining individual abilities and how best to support students. In J. E. Downing, J. Eichinger, & M. A. Demchak (Eds.), *Including students with severe and multiple disabilities in typical classrooms: Practical strategies for teachers* (2nd ed., pp. 37–70). Baltimore: Paul H. Brookes.

Downing, J. E., & Peckham-Hardin, K. D. (2001). Daily schedules: A helpful learning tool. *Teaching Exceptional Children, 33,* 62–68.

Dymond, S. K. (2000). *A participatory research approach to evaluating an inclusive school program.* Unpublished doctoral dissertation, Virginia Commonwealth University, Richmond.

Dymond, S., & Russell, D. L. (2004). Impact of grade and disability on the instructional context of inclusive classrooms. *Education and Training in Developmental Disabilities, 39,* 127–140.

Easterbrooks, S. (1999). Improving practices for students with hearing impairments. *Exceptional Children, 65,* 537–554.

Education of All Handicapped Children Act of 1975, 20 U.S.C. 33 Section 1400 *et seq.*

Falvey, M. E. (2004). Toward realizing the influence of "Toward realization of the Least Restrictive Educational Environments for severely handicapped students." *Research & Practice for Persons with Severe Disabilities, 29,* 9–10.

Falvey, M. A., Blair, M., Dingle, M., & Franklin, N. (2000). Creating a community of learners with varied needs. In R. Villa & J. Thousand (Eds.), *Restructuring for caring and effective education.* Baltimore: Paul H. Brookes.

Fraiberg, S. (1959). *The magic years: Understanding and handling the problems of early childhood.* New York: Charles Scribner.

Giangreco, M. F., Broer, S. M., & Edelman, S. W. (1999). The tip of the iceberg: Determining whether paraprofessional support is needed for students with disabilities in general education settings. *Journal of the Association for Persons with Severe Handicaps, 24,* 281–291.

Giangreco, M. F., Cloninger, C. J., & Iverson, V. S. (1998). *Choosing outcomes and accommodations for children: A guide to educational planning for students with disabilities* (2nd ed.). Baltimore: Paul H. Brookes.

Gilberts, G. H., Agran, M., Hughes, C., & Wehmeyer, M. (2001). The effects of peer delivered self-monitoring strategies on the participation of students with severe mental retardation in general education classrooms. *Journal of the Association for Persons with Severe Handicaps, 26,* 25–36.

Gillon, G. T., & Young, A. A. (2002). The phonological-awareness skills of children who are blind. *Journal of Visual Impairment & Blindness, 96,* 38–49.

Gompel, M., Janssen, M. A., van Bon, W., & Schreuder, R. (2003). Visual input and orthographic knowledge in word reading of children with low vision. *Journal of Visual Impairment & Blindness, 97,* 273–284.

Gompel, M., Janssen, M. A., van Bon, W., & Schreuder, R. (2004). Reading by children with low vision. *Journal of Visual Impairment & Blindness, 98,* 77–89.

Gordon-Langbein, A. (2001). 9 things to know about listening and learning in today's classrooms. *Volta Voices, 8,* 23–27.

Haller, A. K., & Montgomery, J. K. (2004). Noise-induced hearing loss in children: What educators need to know. *Teaching Exceptional Children, 36,* 22–27.

Hanninen, K. A. (1975). *Teaching the visually handicapped.* Columbus, OH: Charles E. Merrill.

Heward, W. L. (2006). Exceptional Children (8th ed.). Upper Saddle River, NJ: Pearson.

Hill, E. W., & Snook-Hill, M. (1996). Orientation and mobility. In M. C. Holbrook (Ed.), *Children with visual impairments: A parents' guide* (pp. 260–286). Bethesda, MD: Woodbine House.

Holden-Pitt, L., & Diaz, J. (1998). Thirty years of the annual survey of deaf and hard of hearing children and youth: A glance over the decades. *American Annals of the Deaf, 142*(2), 72–76.

Hull, R. H. (1973). Group vs. individual screening in public school audiometry. *Colorado Journal of Educational Research, 13,* 6–9.

Hunt, P., Doering, K., & Hirose-Hatae, A. (2001). Across program collaboration to support students with and without disabilities in general education classrooms. *Journal of the Association for Persons with Severe Handicaps, 26,* 240–256.

Hunt, P., Staub, D., Alwell, M., & Goetz, L. (1994). Achievement by all students within the context of cooperative learning groups. *Journal of the Association for Persons with Severe Handicaps, 19,* 290–301.

Individuals with Disabilities Education Act Amendments of 1997, 20 U.S.C. 33 Section 1400 *et. seq.*

Inkson, D. (2002). Reflections on succeeding with a child with hearing loss as a public school teacher. *Volta Voices, 9,* 23–25

Jackson, L., Ryndak, D. L., & Billingsley, F. (2000). Useful practices in inclusive education: A preliminary view of what experts in moderate to severe disabilities are saying. *Journal of the Association for Person With Severe Handicaps, 25,* 129–141.

Janney, R., & Snell, M. E. (2000). *Teachers' guides to inclusive practices: Modifying schoolwork.* Baltimore: Paul H. Brookes.

Johnson, L. (1996). The Braille literacy crisis for children, *Journal of Visual Impairment & Blindness, 90,* 276–278.

Karchmer, M. A., & Allen, T. E. (1999). The functional assessment of deaf and hard of hearing students. *American Annals of the Deaf, 144,* 68–77.

Katz, J., Mirenda, P., & Auerbach, S. (2002). Instructional strategies and educational outcomes for students with developmental disabilities in inclusive "multiple intelligences" and typical inclusive classrooms. *Research & Practice for Persons with Severe Disabilities, 27,* 227–238.

Kennedy, C. H., & Thompson, T. (2000). Health conditions contributing to problem behavior among people with mental retardation and developmental disabilities. In M. Wehmeyer & J. Patten (Eds.), *Mental retardation in the 21st century* (pp. 21–231). Austin, TX: Pro-Ed.

Kingsley, M. (1997). The effects of visual loss. In H. Mason & S. McCall (Eds.). *Visual impairment: Access to education for children and young people* (pp. 23–29). London: Fulton.

Kirk, K. I., Miyamoto, R. T., Ying, E. A., Perdew, A. E., & Zuganelis, H. (2002). Cochlear implantation in young children: Effects of age at implantation and communication mode. *The Volta Review, 102,* 127–144.

Koenen, M., Bosman, A. M. T., & Gompel, M. (2000). Kijk eens hoe ik lees; Een onderzoek naar het leesgedrag van slechtziende en normaalziende kinderen [Watch me reading: a study of the reading behavior of children with low vision and of sighted children]. *Tijdschrift voor Orthopedagogiek, 39,* 95–106.

Lachs, L., Weiss, J. W., & Pisoni, D. B. (2002). Use of partial information by cochlear implant users and listeners with normal hearing in identifying spoken works: Some preliminary analyses. *The Volta Review, 102,* 303–320.

Lahm, E. A., & Everington, C. (2002). Communication in technology supports. In L. Hamill & C. Everington (Eds.), *Teaching students with moderate to severe disabilities: An applied approach for inclusive environments* (pp. 51–79). Upper Saddle River, NJ: Merrill/Prentice Hall.

Lance, G. D., & Wehmeyer, M. L. (2001). *Universal design checklist.* Lawrence: University of Kansas, Beach Center on Disability.

Leibrock, C. A., & Terry, J. E. (1999). *Beautiful universal design.* New York: Wiley.

Leikin, L., Firestone, P. J., & McGrath, P. J. (1988). Physical symptom reporting in type A and B children. *Journal of Consulting Clinical Psychology, 56,* 721–726.

McDonnell, J. (1998). Instruction for students with severe disabilities in general education settings. *Education and Training in Mental Retardation, 33,* 199–215.

McDonnell, J., Thorson, N., & McQuivey, C. (2000). Brief report: Comparison of the instructional contexts of students with severe disabilities and their peers in general education classes. *Journal of the Association for Persons with Severe Handicaps, 25,* 54–58.

McGrath, P. J., & McAlpine, T. (1993). Psychologic perspectives on pediatric pain. *Journal of Pediatrics, 122*(5) (Suppl.) S2–S8.

McGregor, G., & Vogelsberg, R. T. (1998). *Inclusive schooling practices: Pedagogical and research foundations.* Baltimore: Paul H. Brookes.

McLeskey, J., & Henry, D. (1999). Inclusion: What progress is being made across states? *Teaching Exceptional Children, 31,* 56–62.

McLeskey, J., Henry, D., & Hodges, D. (1999). Inclusion: What progress is being made across disability categories? *Teaching Exceptional Children, 31,* 60–64.

National study on inclusive education: Overview and summary report. (1995). *National Center of Educational Restructuring Inclusion, 2*(2), 1–8.

Nelson, P. (2001). The changing demand for improved acoustics in our schools. *The Volta Review, 101,* 23–31.

Niklaus, M. (2007). Flexible DSP circuits have put advances in hearing aid technology on a fast track. *The Hearing Journal, 60*, 22- 24.

Ohtake, Y. (2003). Increasing class membership of students with severe disabilities through contribution to classmates' learning. *Research & Practice for Persons with Severe Disabilities, 28*, 228–231.

Peavey, K. O., & Leff, D. (2002). Social acceptance of adolescent mainstreamed students with visual impairments. *Journal of Visual Impairment & Blindness, 96*, 808–811.

Rainforth, B. (2000). Preparing teachers to educate students with severe disabilities in inclusive settings despite contextual constraints. *Journal for the Association for Persons with Severe Handicaps, 25*, 83–91.

Sexton, S. B., & Dingle, A. D. (2001). Medical disorders. In F. M. Kline, L. B. Silver, & S. C. Russell (Eds.), *The educator's guide to medical issues in the classroom* (pp. 29–48). Baltimore: Brookes.

Snell, M. E. (1997). Teaching children and young adults with mental retardation: School programs: Current research. *Behavior Change, 14*, 1–33.

Spinelli, C. G. (2004). Dealing with cancer in the classroom: The teacher's role and responsibilities. *Teaching Exceptional Children, 36*, 14–21.

Spungin, S. (Ed.). (2002). *When you have a visually impaired students in your classroom: A guide for teachers.* New York: American Foundation for the Blind.

Steinfeld, A. (2001). The case for realtime captioning in the classroom. *Volta Voices, 8*, 6–8.

Svirsky, M. A., Chute, P. M., Green, J., Bollard, P., & Miyamoto, R. T. (2002). Language development in children who are prelingually deaf who have used the SPEAK or CIS stimulation strategies since initial stimulation. *The Volta Review, 102* (monograph), 199–213.

Surgeon General. (2001). *National meeting on health and health care needs of individuals with mental retardation.* Washington, DC: Surgeon General's Office.

TASH. (2004). *What is TASH?* Retrieved February 5, 2004, from http://tash.org/misc/index.htm

Turnbull, A., Turnbull, R., Shank, M., Smith, S., & Leal, D. (2002). *Exceptional lives: Special education in today's schools* (3rd ed.). Upper Saddle River, NJ: Merrill.

Tuttle, D. W., & Ferrell, K. A. (1995). Visually impaired. In E. L. Meyen & T. M. Skrtic (Eds.), *Exceptional children and youth: An introduction* (4th ed., pp. 487–532). Denver, CO: Love.

U.S. Department of Education. (2001). *Twenty-third annual report to Congress on the implementation of the Individuals with Disabilities Education Act.* Washington, DC: U.S. Government Printing Office.

U.S. Department of Education. (2002). *Twenty-fourth annual report to Congress on the implication of the Individuals with Disabilities Education Act.* Washington, DC: Author.

Wall, R. (2002). Teachers' exposure to people with visual impairments and the effect on attitudes toward inclusion. *RE:view, 34*, 111–119.

Wehmeyer, M. L., Lance, G. D., & Bashinski, S. (2002). Promoting access to the general curriculum for students with mental retardation: A multi-level model. *Education and Training in Mental Retardation and Developmental Disabilities, 37*, 223–234

Werts, M. G., Wolery, M., Holcombe, A., & Gast, D. L. (1995). Instructive feedback: Review of parameters and effects. *Journal of Behavioral Education, 5*, 55–75.

Williamson, G. G., & Anzalone, M. (2001). *Sensory integration and self-regulation in infants and toddlers: Helping very young children interact with their environment.* Washington, DC: Zero to Three. (ERIC Document Reproduction Service No. ED 466 317)

Wolfe, P. S., & Hall, T. E. (2003). Making inclusion a reality for students with severe disabilities. *Teaching Exceptional Children, 35*, 56–61.

Yell, M. L. (1995). Least restrictive environment, inclusion, and students with disabilities: A legal analysis. *Journal of Special Education, 28*, 389–404.

Zebehazy, K., & Whitten, E. (2003). Collaboration between special schools and local education agencies: A progress report. *Journal of Visual Impairment & Blindness, 97*, 73–84.

CHAPTER

4

Individualized
Education Program:
Fact or Fiction?

KEY TERMS

◆ achievement tests
◆ ad hoc teams
◆ attention-deficit hyperactivity disorder (ADHD)
◆ audiogram
◆ authentic assessments
◆ behavior intervention plan (BIP)
◆ collaboration
◆ criterion-referenced tests
◆ grade equivalents
◆ individual family service plan (IFSP)
◆ individualized education program (IEP)
◆ IQ
◆ mean
◆ normal curve
◆ norm-referenced tests
◆ percentile scores
◆ perceptual-motor performance
◆ portfolio
◆ present level of educational performance (PLEP)
◆ screening test
◆ sensory acuity
◆ standard deviation
◆ standard scores
◆ standardization group
◆ stanines
◆ task analysis

Ms. Huffacker and several of her colleagues have gathered after school to discuss how to provide an appropriate education for Susie. Susie is not doing well academically or socially in her fourth-grade classroom. As Ms. Huffacker looks at the faces of her colleagues, Susie's parents, and Susie, she is struck by the question, "What is a team?" Ms. Huffacker's reflections lead her to the thought that a team is a group of persons associated in some joint action that requires teamwork. Teamwork, in turn, is the coordination of effort with collective efficiency.

This small group of people is Susie's team. Their task is to coordinate their efforts with collective efficiency to ensure that Susie receives an appropriate educational experience. Ms. Huffacker has been on too many IEP teams to remember, but she never knows going into the meeting how the team will function. Will the team be coordinated in focusing on the child's needs or will some arbitrary factor upset the intent of the meeting? Sometimes the "team" concept is lost when players grandstand, refuse to contribute, or are unprepared. At other times the players move with grace and competence toward producing an individualized program that meets the needs of all team members. Each member of the team has unique contributions to make. Susie's parents have one perspective; her teacher another. Susie, of course, has her own view of her educational experiences. The school psychologist, the principal, and the occupational therapist have yet other contributions to make. Ms. Huffacker fervently hopes the team is skilled and used to working in a coordinated manner so that the end result for Susie will be a successful placement with a useful individualized education plan for learning in the least restrictive environment.

Components of the IEP

For more than a quarter of a century, since the passage of the Education for All Handicapped Children Act (EHA) in 1975, P.L. 94-142, the cornerstone of inclusion has been the individualized education program (IEP). An IEP is a written plan that describes the educational program most appropriate for a child with disabilities, whether the child is in a general education classroom for all, some, or none of the day. In fact, the IEP is federal mandated by P.L. 94-142. The IEP is not intended to specify how a teacher should instruct, but the IEP must account for the content of the general education curriculum.

Neither the IEP process nor the IEP product is perfect in and of itself. Often the content of the IEP is entirely academic, even if many children with disabilities need direct instruction in daily living skills and social/emotional areas (Landrum, 2000; Wehmeyer, Martin, & Sands, 1998). Implementation of the IEP in educational systems differs, not only between states, but also within cities in the same state (Leyser & Kirk, 2004). The IEP is the basis for outlining the appropriate education for students with disabilities (Torgerson, Miner, & Shen, 2004). As such, it is a collaborative tool, not written by a single individual but during a multidisciplinary meeting with team members (Clark, 2000).

The IEP process is an attempt to provide children with disabilities with thoughtful educational programs. The quality of any IEP is a reflection of its writers and, as such, may never be perfect. But all IEPs, it is hoped, will mirror the ideals of their original proponents.

The format of an IEP can vary from state to state and from district to district. The content of an IEP, however, is constant:

1. An IEP must state the child's present levels of educational performance, including how the disability affects involvement and progress in the general curriculum.
2. An IEP must propose measurable annual goals. These include benchmarks for short-term instructional objectives to meet the educational needs resulting from the child's disability and to enable the child to access and progress through the general curriculum.
3. An IEP must describe the special education and related services to be provided. It must detail the program modifications and supports that will enable the child to attain the annual goals and to participate in the general curriculum.
4. An IEP must include an explanation of the extent, if any, to which the child will not participate with nondisabled children in the general education class and related activities.
5. An IEP must outline individual modifications in the administration of state- or districtwide assessments.
6. An IEP must give the projected date for initiation of services and the anticipated duration of services. Beginning at age 14, a statement of transition service must include the following: a statement of (a) how the child's progress toward the annual goals will be measured, (b) how the child's parents will be regularly informed of their child's progress, and (c) the extent to which the progress is sufficient to enable the child to achieve the goals by the end of the year. (adapted from J. Venn, 2004, pp. 122)

Types of IEPs

Various types of IEPs exist. Some are related to specific ages or behaviors. Individual family service plans (IFSPs), transition IEPs, and behavior intervention plans (BIPs) are all variations of the IEP. The IFSP is for children younger than age 3. It addresses the unique needs of very young children with disabilities and their families. The transition IEP is designed for youth at age 14 with an emphasis on guiding them as they enter postsecondary education. Finally, BIPs are used to describe interventions for students with disabilities with challenging or difficult behavior and social skills.

IEPs focus on appropriate educational delivery, but the name of the IEP may vary depending on the purpose and state and local school districts' idiosyncrasies. In Arizona, for example, four basic categories of IEPs have been listed as

- initial
- annual
- amendment
- interim

Regardless of the name, IEPs must follow federal, state, and district guidelines.

The *initial IEP* is the first IEP written after the IEP team has determined that a student falls into one of the federally defined categories of disability. A student must be eligible under one of the many categories of special education in order to receive an IEP. However, even students who are categorized under one of the special education areas may not be eligible for an IEP if the student is receiving an appropriate education. To be eligible for an IEP, a student must meet the criteria defined by federal and state laws. Eligibility requires the use of formal and informal assessments prescribed by state and federal laws, but local districts may also require additional documentation. Just as the word *initial* would suggest, this IEP is the first formal documentation for the student developed by the team.

An *annual IEP* is used for the purpose of review and revision, if appropriate. Recent changes to IDEA, however, no longer require that all students receive an annual IEP to continue receiving services. Typically, children with severe physical, sensory, cognitive, or emotional disabilities whose condition is unlikely to have changed throughout the year might only need to be evaluated in a formal IEP meeting every three years.

An *amended IEP* is called if additions and/or changes are needed on the annual IEP. The entire team must make an amendment or change; no one individual can make changes. The duration of the change typically runs from the date of the amendment to the end of the current IEP. Amendment IEPs are particularly helpful when class demands have changed or when instructors need additional district support to provide a particular accommodation or modification.

Interim IEPs are completed for IDEA-eligible students before an annual IEP can be completed. An interim IEP may be permitted when

- temporarily placing a student in a program as part of the evaluation process, or
- the student with the disability, who is already receiving services, moves into a new district before the previous evaluation is received or a new one is completed.

For students eligible for special education services, each change of schools requires orchestration between the members of the current IEP team with the members of the next IEP team. Sometimes the student arrives before the IEP information, so an interim IEP is established until the previous IEP can be taken into account.

IEP Teams

Given an evaluation of a child's performance, a team develops, reviews, and revises an IEP. Members of the IEP team include a representative of the school district, the child's teacher, one or both parents, and a person who is knowledgeable about the evaluation procedures used and how to interpret those results. This person usually is a school psychologist or a special education teacher. When feasible, the student also is included in the team.

The concept of including a general educator in team planning for determining educational services for children with disabilities is no longer a radical idea. Although the level of team involvement varies, the classroom teacher must be involved, and when serving as part of an IEP team, his or her observations carry the same weight and responsibility as the observations of any other team member. If an inclusion teacher is referring a child from his or her room to special services, he or she will have valuable insight into the child's day-to-day performance. If an IEP in which an inclusion teacher has not been involved prescribes the return of a child to the inclusion classroom, that teacher should participate in the review and revision of the child's IEP (Yell, 1998). No one is more knowledgeable than the inclusion teacher about the performance requirements of that classroom.

Being a member of an IEP team may be intimidating at first. The psychologist and the special education teacher may use terms that are not familiar to other members of the team. Because no one likes to appear uninformed, discretion may seem to be the better part of valor. The inclusion teacher may not ask questions that he or she needs to have answered. Sometimes the psychologist or special educator will be unable to answer the teacher's questions. Although these communication problems may reflect gaps in training, they more likely reflect the psychologist's or special educator's inexperience in translating terms for people who do not share their educational and experiential background. In any event, whenever a concept, term, or decision is unclear, an explanation should be elicited. Much more than one's pride is on the line. IEP team members are making plans that affect the educational program and life of a child with a disability. Silence may be interpreted as tacit approval rather than reluctance to question and discuss.

Advance preparation is one of the most effective techniques for avoiding the "sounds of silence" in an IEP preconference, staffing, or review. Being prepared means that the inclusion teacher has examined the child's file, can discuss its contents, and has prepared a short list of topics related to the child for discussion. This list is essentially a set of notes or ideas that will help in making a more informed contribution to the IEP. The inclusion teacher, after all, is the person who has tried various specific remedial instruction approaches prior to the IEP meeting. Therefore, this teacher is in the best position to evaluate the child's skills in the education general classroom. Being prepared also means having a thorough understanding of each component of the IEP. The focus of this chapter is to describe each component of an IEP and examine the contributions of each member of the team.

Present Educational Performance Level

A description of the child's present educational level is simply a report of the child's current behavioral and academic performance. A child's present educational performance level is a composite of the contributions of the various members of the team. To get a truly accurate description of a child's present level of educational performance (PLEP) requires examining the results of a variety of evaluation measures used across an assortment of times and settings as viewed through the perceptions of each team member.

Initial evaluations differ from subsequent evaluations, but all evaluations using a team approach must, to the best extent possible, identify how or to what degree of proficiency the child is performing in the area(s) of concern.

Establishing a Meaningful PLEP

Many types of evaluation tools are available for establishing a PLEP. Different members of the team typically provide information from different types of assessment tools. The school psychologist often presents information from specialized and individually administered psychological or educational tests. Depending on the district's policy, the special educator may also supply information from individually administered educational tests or from classroom-based measures. The general educator typically makes available information from classroom-based measures and observations of classroom behaviors. Parents provide information related to their observations of the child's social or academic progress in school. Other members of the team who can contribute to a full understanding of the child's skills also bring their unique measurement tools and observations. For example, an occupational therapist or physical therapist could provide information related to the child's fine- and gross-motor skills as they affect access to the general education curriculum. A specialist in assistive technology could provide assessment information related to the child's ability to use particular assistive devices, such as toggles, keyboards, and voice-synthesizing programs.

The most important function of assessment is that the testing, observation, or any other appropriate method used provides the information needed to establish and document that educational decisions and services are appropriate for the student. Not all evaluation tools are equally useful in determining the child's PLEP. The value of the evaluation tools may vary from time to time and from purpose to purpose. For example, the school psychologist typically administers an individual intelligence quotient (IQ) test. An IQ test compares the child's current level of information relative to other children of similar age, grade, sex, socioeconomic level, and cultural heritage. The purpose of intelligence testing, along with several other measures, is to identify children who qualify for special education services. In order to determine whether Gary is eligible for special education services, he takes an IQ test. Based on the results of Gary's IQ test, in combination with several other measures of his performance, the IEP team determines that he is eligible. In this instance, administration of an IQ test added information to Gary's PLEP. However, since the results of IQ tests typically do not vary a great deal over time, continued assessment using an IQ measure is most likely unnecessary and inappropriate.

In contrast, suppose the IEP team, using information derived from informal classroom measures and observations, focused on Gary's ability to acquire math skills in the general education curriculum. The assessment tools must be capable of measuring instructional objectives and Gary's progress in the mathematics general education curriculum. Whatever tools the team identifies to measure Gary's progress most likely will need to be administered repeatedly as Gary proceeds through the math curriculum. In fact, Gary's daily progress in mathematics relative to identified objectives of the IEP must be documented. Since the IEP has identified areas in which Gary should be making progress, continuous assessment is necessary and appropriate.

Testing Traps

Getting a balanced picture of the child's skills should be a simple process, but many hidden agendas can create a less-than-perfect profile. Overtesting and undertesting are all too common when attempting to establish the PLEP. Children with suspected or identified learning problems often are subjected to repeated, repetitive, and decontextualized testing. Mario, who is 9 years old, has received educational services in a general education classroom and a special education setting for two years. During this time he has received no fewer than 21 hours of formal testing as compared to his friend Marisol, who does not qualify for special services and who has received 3 hours of testing.

Mario has an aversion to testing. The "special" tests do not reflect the content or method of what he is learning. While Mario learns about the rainforest, his special tests assess his basic skills in reading, writing, and spelling. Granted, reading, writing, and spelling are important skills, but, when measured out of context as isolated skills, Mario may not see the purpose of the test, causing him to become suspicious and cynical. In addition, his reaction is clouded by a history, albeit short, of poor test performance. Testing for Mario and others like him is no fun. When faced with formal testing, patterns of flight or fright may arrive disguised as anxiety, resistance, or learned helplessness, thus failing to provide a picture of Mario's true PLEP. Unless handled delicately, Mario, like many students, may try halfheartedly (Hacker, Bol, Horgan, & Rakon, 2000) or become anxious when taking formal tests, thereby undermining the validity of the test scores (Eccles, Barber, Jozefowiez, Malenchuk, & Vida, 1999; Hancock, 2001).

Mario's teachers and parents can save him and others like him from overtesting by providing clear and well-documented descriptions of the child's PLEP in the general education curriculum. Not only could Mario's reading, writing, and spelling performance be assessed relative to the rainforest or any other unit of instruction, but his approach to critical thinking and problem solving also could be described. The way that Mario arrives at answers or explanations, as well as his performance relative to that of other students in the class, is part of the important assessment information that teachers and parents can provide. In this way, Mario's classroom skills can be identified in the context of classroom material as a part of daily class activities. The type of assessment information teachers and parents provide is the most relevant knowledge about the success of providing services for Mario in the general education curriculum.

Responsibilities of Teachers and Parents in Establishing the PLEP

With the passage of the No Child Left Behind Act (NCLB), the child's PLEP is all about progress in the general education curriculum. The contributions of parents and teachers in establishing the PLEP, for all practical purposes, constitute the framework for establishing the goals and objectives found on the IEP. As established by NCLB, children receiving special education services are expected to achieve adequate yearly performance in the general education curriculum.

The responsibilities of teachers and parents as equal members of the IEP team in determining progress in the general education curriculum cannot be overstressed. Their contributions provide meaningful data directly related to curricular areas. Teachers and parents need to come prepared with documentation related to the type and occurrence of problems experienced by the child in basic skill or content areas. If accommodations or modifications have already been established, the impact on adequate yearly progress must be taken into account as part of the PLEP.

In addition, teachers and parents must provide their data relative to the child's school survival skills. School survival skills include using appropriate organizational strategies, attendance, appropriate question-asking techniques, completing tasks, and self-monitoring (Sabornie & deBettencourt, 2004). These skills, and similar behaviors, are necessary tools for students to be able to move successfully through the general education curriculum, but developing expertise in survival skills is not always formally taught.

For some students with special needs, lack of survival skills has overreaching consequences, impacting acquisition of information in basic skills and content areas. Issues related to survival skills can also impact social behavior. Carol, for example, has poor organizational skills. Students like Carol easily become frustrated with school when they are constantly failing to hand in assignments they have completed or don't even realize that assignments are due. Not surprising is Carol's lack of school attendance, either physically or mentally, which leads to even more frustration, leaves her precariously perched on the edge of the black hole of school failure.

Teachers and parents need to describe the type of survival skill problems the student exhibits. They also need to report what kind of accommodation or modification they have used with the student to increase appropriate survival skills. Documentation of the kind of problem the student is exhibiting, either academic or survival, must be compiled prior to the IEP meeting. Observations should be bulleted and take no more than one page of writing. By being concise, teachers and parents can focus on specific issues related to the child's PLEP.

Teachers and parents must be specific about the problematic behaviors. For example, to report that Jonathan is doing very poorly in reading is only helpful if that statement is followed up with specific behavioral descriptors; for example, "Jonathan is reading words with only one syllable fluently, but he has serious problems analyzing words consisting of two or more syllables." Another specific example of how Jonathan is doing poorly in reading could be that "Jonathan remembers very little of what he has read, recalling only one or two initial ideas in passages longer than three to four paragraphs."

Evaluation Tools Used to Establish PLEP

Many types of evaluation measures may be used to establish or to confirm a student's PLEP. Tools can be formal or informal, commercial or teacher-made. The purpose of the tool is to provide a clear picture of the skills the child has or needs in order to be able to access an appropriate public education.

Establishing the PLEP usually requires information from a variety of evaluation measures. No one measure is sufficient to describe the student's PLEP. Measurement tools may be categorized into several areas, the most common of which are general performance and academic achievement.

Measures or tests of general performance typically are norm-referenced and given individually to the student by a psychometrist, a professional evaluator trained to use to the the specific directions associated with the test. *Norm-referenced tests* are used to compare the performance of a child with the performance of other students of similar age and background.

On an IEP, two types of norm-referenced tests are typically used to describe the child's PLEP. One type measures academic achievement; the other measures intelligence. Most academic achievement tests measure past learning, or what a student has learned up to and including the time of testing. Academic achievement testing usually focuses on the three Rs, reading, writing, and arithmetic, and all their various subareas (e.g., spelling, grammar, fractions, or any other aspect of the general education curriculum). Intelligence testing is a type of achievement measure that describes what an individual knows but may or may not have been taught directly, like the formal subjects in the general education curriculum.

Results of academic achievement tests usually are indicated on an IEP as scores. Intelligence test scores generally are not put on IEPs because of confidentiality issues, although some districts do include them. These scores are designed to help interpret standardized test scores on IEP forms.

Achievement Tests

Achievement tests yield standard scores. A standard score is one in which the *raw score,* the actual number of items a student answered correctly, is transformed so the set of scores always has the same mean and the same standard deviation (refer to the Appendix on p. 557 for more detailed explanations of the general characteristics of norm-referenced tests). Two commonly reported scores are grade equivalents and percentiles.

Grade equivalents always are stated in years and months. Thus, a grade equivalency of 2.3 is read as "second grade, third month," and a grade equivalency of 7.9 is read as "seventh grade, ninth month." Grade equivalents seem easy to interpret and comfortable to use because they appear so straightforward. However, they can be deceptive. What appears may not be an accurate picture of the student's performance.

What the grade equivalent of 2.3 means in a technical sense is that the student scored as well as the average student who is placed at the 2.3 level, *not* that the student is working at the second grade, third month level. Suppose Joanna, a third-grader, earns a score of 2.3 in reading. Should an alarm be sounded? After all, she is almost a year behind the average student who is in the third grade. What does this mean? Interpretation of the 2.3 is all relative to the "average" student. The "average" student may be reading at the third-grade level or at the first-grade level relative to the school's curriculum. For example, in schools that stress early acquisition of letter and word recognition, Joanna's reading skills could be overestimated by the grade equivalency. In contrast, if Joanna has attended a school emphasizing language development in the early grades, her grade equivalency probably underestimates her skills in relationship to those of her peers. The "average" student's score is not a reflection of a student working at the second grade, third month. So much for straightforward interpretations.

Grade equivalents are not particularly useful, with or without correct interpretation, for specific instructional programming. Identical grade equivalents of 4.5 for two children actually may represent differences in specific knowledge. Tests that are scored by simply counting the number of questions a child answers correctly can give two children identical scores when they have correctly answered totally different questions.

Consider the following: Cody and Melinda each scored 1.7 on the spelling section of a norm-referenced test. Cody correctly spelled the words *dog, run, sheep,* and *salad* but misspelled all the words Melinda spelled correctly. Melinda correctly spelled the words *noise, go, yellow,* and *pineapple,* but she misspelled all the words Cody spelled correctly. Because both students spelled four words correctly, they received identical grade-equivalency scores even though they did not spell any of the same words correctly.

The spelling test in this example is a screening test that provided some general information about the spelling skills of the two students. The advantage of a survey or screening test is that it can tell you, within 10 or 15 minutes, who is going to need help in what. The more quickly general problem areas are identified, the more quickly performance on specific areas within a subject can be evaluated. Before administering the spelling test to Melinda and Cody, the teacher knew nothing specific about their level of spelling performance. If these two children are fifth-graders, their test scores suggest that they both need special instruction in spelling.

Percentile scores constitute another commonly reported standard score. Percentiles are based on a scale ranging from 0 to 100. A student's percentile score indicates the percentage of students who had scores equal to or lower than that student. Thus, if Stacey had a raw score of 72 and a percentile score of 55, this would mean that 55% of the students who took the same test had scores of 72 or lower. The students who took the same test are not the students in her class, however. Rather, the group of students against whom Stacey is compared is the standardization group, or normative group. Children in this standardization group should include those of the same socioeconomic background, culture, age, and sex as Stacey. If the aim of the test is to compare her performance with that of other children, her scores should be compared with scores of a normative group of children who have experiential backgrounds similar to hers.

Both grade-equivalency scores and percentile scores are obtained by comparing the performance of an individual with the performance of a normative group on the same test. All tests that provide a comparison between a score earned by an individual and scores of a normative group are called norm-referenced or normative tests.

Intelligence Measures

Perhaps the most confusing of all norm-referenced tests is the intelligence test. As in any normed test, scores on an intelligence test represent the amount of information of a particular kind that a child has demonstrated, relative to other children of similar age, grade, sex, socioeconomic level, and cultural heritage. The score is a numerical score that often measures many of the tasks a child must perform on a general achievement test (Salvia & Ysseldyke, 2001). Intelligence tests are designed either for group administration or for individual administration.

GROUP-ADMINISTERED TESTS   Intelligence tests that are group-administered are given most often by a classroom teacher. Group intelligence tests have been developed to provide a quick estimate of scores for a large number of children. Often group intelligence tests consist of a series of multiple-choice questions divided into timed subsets.

Most group intelligence tests intended for use with children in the fourth grade and up require reading ability. As a result, poor readers often produce relatively low scores on these tests, and it is difficult to determine whether a low score reflects poor reading skills, lack of familiarity with the concepts tested, or both. Thus, scores on group intelligence tests can be misleading for children who are poor readers. One of the most widely used group intelligence tests—the Otis-Lennon School Ability Test (Otis & Lennon, 1996)—has high reading demands.

Results of a group intelligence test must be interpreted carefully. These group tests have been designed as screening instruments and are thought to be useful in identifying children who are at the extreme ends of a normal distribution of intelligence. Generally, children are considered average if their scores fall within the range of scores of 68% of the normative population (within the interval from one standard deviation below the mean to one standard deviation above the mean). Children whose scores fall outside this interval possibly should be referred for more specific intelligence testing.

No definitive statement can be made about a student's performance on the basis of group IQ scores. If the standard error of measurement is large for a group measure, a student's score can vary considerably. For example, if Jose earns an IQ score of 100 on a test with a standard error of 15, his true IQ might be as low as 85 or as high as 115.

Results of group intelligence tests sometimes fail to identify children who need special services. Conversely, sometimes the results of group IQ tests identify children as needing special services when they really don't need them at all. In reality, the teacher is a much better "screener" than the group intelligence test is. When deciding whether to refer the child for evaluation, one must consider the child's daily class performance as well as test scores.

INDIVIDUALLY ADMINISTERED TESTS   When additional evaluation seems necessary for determining the most appropriate educational setting for a child, such an evaluation probably will include an intelligence test administered individually. Generally, classroom teachers are not trained to administer and interpret individual intelligence tests. Rather, such instruments usually are administered by a person certified as a psychometrician or psychologist, often a school psychologist. Special education teachers can give IQ tests only if they also are educated as psychometrists. Interpretation of IQ tests may be made only by persons trained as psychologists.

The two most commonly administered individual intelligence tests are the Wechsler Intelligence Scale for Children-III (WISC-III) (Wechsler, 1991) and the Stanford-Binet Intelligence Scale IV (Thorndike, Hagen, & Sattler, 1986). Each test is administered individually in a setting that is relatively free of distractions. Administration time varies from about 45 to 90 minutes, depending on the examiner's skills and the child's skills. Both the WISC-III and the Stanford-Binet IV require verbal responses. The WISC-III includes both a verbal section and a performance section. In the performance section, a child is required to do some manipulation tasks, such as putting puzzles together.

Administration of the Stanford-Binet IV results in four general cognitive ability scores and a composite score. The four cognitive areas are verbal reasoning, abstract/visual reasoning, quantitative reasoning, and short-term memory. Administration of the WISC-III results in three IQ scores: a verbal IQ score, a performance IQ score, and a total IQ score representing both verbal and performance scores. Each WISC-III subtest is scored individually and may reflect different skill levels within a child's repertoire.

Discussion of the results of IQ tests and individual subtests brings us back to the utility of test results in the classroom. Classroom teachers' instruction is modified directly by a child's performance in class; IQ scores probably make little difference in how they teach. If Sally Ann is having problems adding 2 + 2, you are likely to find the results of tests directly assessing her math performance more useful than tests that provide you with an IQ score of 100, 85, or 115. Depending on the intelligence test administered, the examiner's skill, and Sally Ann's experiential background, she may exhibit any one of these IQ scores, but no matter what her IQ score, she still will need to learn how to add 2 + 2. Information concerning how to teach her this math skill will more likely be found in a math methods text than in a manual for an intelligence test.

For teaching, therefore, an IQ score is functionally useless. For placement for special services, however, results of intelligence tests are frequently required to determine eligibility, depending on the disability category. Traditionally, a normal IQ, as measured by an individual intelligence test, was likely to influence a placement decision toward a general education class setting, an LD setting, or an EH setting. An IQ two standard deviations below the mean was likely to influence placement decisions toward an EMH setting. A child with an IQ two standard deviations above the mean was likely to be placed in a program for gifted and talented students.

Specialized Normative Tests

Normative or group-referenced tests have been developed for special populations. One example is the Leiter International Performance Scale (Leiter, 1979). This test was designed to assess the intelligence of children who have problems taking verbal tests, such as children who are deaf, hard of hearing, or speech impaired. A second example of a specialized normative test is the Blind Learning Aptitude Test (BLAT) (Newland, 1971). The BLAT was designed to evaluate the learning aptitudes of blind children.

The main reason for developing tests for special populations is to ensure fairness in testing. If a child cannot see, to ask the child to respond to questions presented in a traditional print format would be absurd. Another major consideration in developing specialized normative tests is the standardization population. Jane, a deaf child, has had a different acculturation or set of life experiences than Jim, who hears normally. Thus, comparing children with such vastly different life experiences defeats the purpose of group comparison.

Many special tests have been developed to assess the intelligence of children with disabilities. For a classroom teacher, the results of a specially adapted IQ test serve the same purpose as results of a traditional IQ measure. IQ measures do not provide much information that is directly useful in teaching, whether the IQ measures are modified or not.

Other Types of Normative Tests

Other types of normative tests that may appear in students' files may focus on sensory development or motor deficit areas. The Test of Language Development-Primary: Third Edition (TOLD-P:3) (Newcomer & Hammill, 1997) is a test designed to provide information about a young child's language proficiency. The Snellen Wall Chart or the Snellen E Test is commonly used to screen problems in visual acuity. A child with a middle-ear disorder might be tested with an audiogram.

Information from tests that describe developmental or physical and sensory deficits often can be used to help develop classroom objectives. Although the tests are normative, classroom provisions for individual children can be influenced by such test results. For example, if Kurt has an audiogram in his file, the classroom teacher has a responsibility to find out what the results mean to the instructional program. The subsequent development of services demands a clear understanding of the child's sensory skills.

Translating the results of tests of sensory acuity into meaningful classroom information is fairly straightforward. Based on results of Lou Ann's Snellen test, she might be moved to the front of the classroom. Kurt's audiogram may indicate that classroom noise must be kept at a minimum or that he be placed to the right or left of the teacher, depending on whether he has a unilateral hearing loss. Interpreting tests scores based on the five senses is clean, quick, and direct.

Informal Measures Used to Establish the PLEP

Complementary measures used to establish the PLEP are usually much less formal and often based on direct measures of the general education curriculum. The informality of these measures provides a different perspective on the child's performance. Sometimes the informal measures are more accurate descriptions of the child's true PLEP than formal measures. Taken together, formal and informal measures provide a fairly good picture of the child's PLEP.

Informal measures include teacher-made tests and quizzes, student performance on assignments, portfolio assessment, and observations by parents and teachers. Most informal measures of performance are based on how well a student performs on expected classroom tasks. For example, Al, Ann, and Katie are students in Mr. Lauer's general education classroom. They are expected to meet the writing standards established for Mr. Lauer's grade. Mr. Lauer measures their performance by giving them classroom assignments, tests, and quizzes. Mr. Lauer has noticed that Al and Ann appear to be progressing well. They do most of their work correctly, get reasonable test scores, and perform well on quizzes. In addition, Al and Ann work well with others in the class and generally demonstrate a positive attitude.

In contrast, Mr. Lauer has noticed that Katie is withdrawing more and more from her friends. She is passive in group activities and rarely completes tasks on time, if at all. She does not seem to understand what she is expected to do, nor does she demonstrate an understanding of classwork on quizzes or tests. Mr. Lauer is concerned about Katie's progress, and at a recent parent conference meeting discussed Katie's performance with her parents. Katie's parents are also worried about their daughter's progress. They have mentioned that she rarely reads a book and only does homework when threatened with being grounded or losing phone privileges.

Katie's teacher and her parents did not need formal evaluation measures to know that this child is having difficulty in school. If, however, Katie is to be considered for eligibility for special education, results of well-documented informal measures will be necessary to pinpoint specific instructional needs to provide a complement to more formal measures.

Measures of Authentic Assessment

Authentic assessment approaches focus on documenting the student's understanding of classroom instruction. That is, the student's performance is described in direct relationship to what has been taught in the classroom curriculum. Other names for authentic assessment include curriculum-based assessment, alternative assessment, and portfolio assessment. When a standard or level of expectation is attached to any type of authentic assessment, a criterion for acceptable performance is established. Typical authentic measures with established criteria for success are called *criterion-referenced tests* or *criterion-referenced measures*.

Let's return to Mr. Lauer's class. He has determined that the criteria for "progressing well" in writing can be translated directly to classroom scores of 80% or better on class tests, homework assignments, and class work. For all practical purposes, Mr. Lauer is engaging in authentic assessment practices that reflect a predetermined criterion. Since Katie is not progressing well according to Mr. Lauer's standards, she must be earning scores of less than 80% in writing. By examining Katie's scores, Mr. Lauer can determine if Katie is falling below 80% in only one area (e.g., class tests, homework assignments) or class work or in all the areas.

ACADEMIC   Criterion-referenced tests commonly are used to identify specific instructional needs. Other names for criterion-referenced tests (CRT) include classroom-based measures (CBM), classroom-based assessment (CBA), performance measures, objectives-based measures, and objective-referenced measures. Strictly speaking, a criterion-referenced interpretation describes the specific performance of a particular student, in this case Al. For example, Al produced five complete sentences in 20 minutes without error. Many of the current standards-based assessments are aligned with specific content standards (Linn & Gronlund, 2000). For better or worse, NCLB requires states to develop standards-based assessments that are aligned with the general education curriculum.

INTERPRETATION   Suppose you have three students in your class, Aaron, Wendy, and Ashley, and you want to see whether they can do basic arithmetic problems. You set your criterion at 100% (i.e., an answer to a problem is either correct or it is not) with no partial credit granted. More important, you arrange the test problems sequentially so the problems start at the lowest or simplest level of basic addition (e.g., 2 + 2) and extend to a complex level (37,890 + 20,359). Each child is given the same sequentially arranged test. Scores earned by Aaron, Wendy, and Ashley will reflect the degree of learning each has in basic arithmetic. Also, analysis of the errors will enable you to identify a clearly defined area that is related directly to instructional objectives.

Suppose analysis of Aaron's performance shows that the only concept he has mastered is the addition of two single-digit numbers. Wendy, on the other hand, has mastered all the basic concepts of addition. Ashley's performance is erratic. Each student's performance is analyzed relative to the problems on the test; no regard is given to a student's performance relative to the performance of another student. Testing that is criterion-referenced is designed to guide instruction as directly as possible.

Scores on criterion-referenced tests are based on a scale of 0 to 100% correct; expected criteria can be described in terms of the percentage of test items a student must answer correctly. The prescribed level of acceptable performance is arbitrary and is determined by the chooser's values. Criterion levels for acceptable performance, however, should vary with the content being evaluated. For example, by their nature, fundamental skills such as letter sounds and sight words demand a higher level of proficiency than do content or supplemental areas of instruction such as alliteration and metaphors.

RELATIONSHIP TO CLASSROOM OBJECTIVES In criterion measures, each test item can be reworded as a specific behavioral objective. The criterion test that will provide the most useful evaluation information is a test that measures the material in the curriculum. Ideally, this test also tests skills in the sequence in which they are taught and in the format of the classroom materials.

Results from a criterion-referenced test can provide information concerning where a child can succeed in a sequence of skills and whether the child can use that material and format. If a child can succeed at step 16 of a 225-step sequence of skills, the classroom teacher must decide how to accommodate that child. If the child with the next lowest skills in the room is on step 75 of the 225-step sequence, the teacher may need special assistance to work with the first child.

Authentic assessments that measure complex, long-term instructional goals are sometimes referred to as performance assessments. Performance assessments are also directly related to the classroom curriculum. Examples of complex performance tasks are written essays, laboratory experiments in science, creation of poetry, dramatic presentations, and projects, and typically reflect problem solving of some nature.

Establishing the PLEP in complex and long-term tasks requires clear and consistent documentation. Rubrics are typically developed to measure complex tasks. In any type of rubric, the scoring criterion is defined for any number of possible responses and focuses on the quality or characteristic expected for different levels of expertise. Rubrics can be commercially made or teachers can develop their own. The most critical piece of information in any rubric is that the performance, for example, the dramatic presentation or science project, is clearly and measurably defined.

Rubrics can also be used when teachers are using portfolios to collect and compare a student's work throughout a unit or semester. Rubrics provide guidance for the student relative to the type of content to be collected and the criteria for developing the portfolio. The teacher does not need to spend a lot of time organizing and collecting information for the portfolio. Instead the teacher can have the students become more responsible for their own work. Figure 4.1 is an example of a rubric teachers can use to have students become more engaged with their portfolio for language arts. Notice that the teacher provides feedback to the students about how well they are progressing. Not all students will need feedback to the same degree. The way the teacher provides feedback and the amount of time spent per pupil will vary with the needs of the child. The major point, however, is that students can use a rubric to help them learn how to collect and organize their classwork.

Portfolios can take a variety of forms and can be as simple or complex as the teacher desires. Although portfolios can serve a variety of purposes, to establish a PLEP the portfolio content must contain a purposeful collection of student work. On its simplest level, the portfolio can contain work sequenced by date and organized by topic. Organized collections of working folders must be able to be related directly to the objectives for the classroom curriculum. Since portfolios contain records of the student's work in the classroom curriculum, the content provides documentation of student progress by way of concrete examples of work and can be an important source for analysis of progress.

Name: _____   Teacher: _____

Beginning date: _____   Ending date: _____

Important information: We will be collecting school work to show to your parents.

Please:
- use this rubric as a guide to help you remember how to file your work in your portfolio.
- keep this rubric in the front of your portfolio
- keep your portfolio in your cubbie.

Thank-you!

(continued)

Figure 4.1   Class Portfolio: Language Arts

Content	Superior	Very Good	Good	Needs improvement	Review dates
Samples of Story writing	**One or more** stories per week included	**One story** or more per week included	**One story** included per week	Missing more than two week's of stories	
	Name on all stories	**Name** on all but one story	**Name** on all stories	Name missing on **3** or more stories	
	All stories are **dated**	All but one story **dated**	All but two stories **dated**	Date missing on **3** or more stories	
	All stories are **sequenced** by date	All but one story is **sequenced** by date	All but two stories are **sequenced** by date	Three or more stories are out of dated sequence	
Spelling Quizzes	Include each weekly spelling quiz	Include each weekly spelling quiz	Include each weekly spelling quiz	Missing each weekly spelling quiz	
	Name on all quizzes	Name on all quizzes	Name on all quizzes	Name missing from more than two quizzes	
	All quizzes dated	All quizzes dated	All but one quiz dated	Date missing from more than two quizzes	
	All quizzes are sequenced by date	All but one quiz are sequenced by date	All but two quizzes are sequenced by date	More than two quizzes are out of sequence.	
Reading record for each Trade Book	Name of book	Name of book	Name of book	Missing any of the information below: Name of book	
	Starting page indicated	Starting page indicated	Starting page indicated	Starting page indicated	
	Ending page indicated	Ending page indicated	Ending page indicated	Ending page indicated	
	Three most important ideas listed	Two most important idea listed	Most important idea listed	Most important idea listed	
	Three new words listed	Two new words listed	One new word listed	One new word listed	
	New words used in sentence	Words used in sentence	New word used in sentence	New word used in sentence	
	All days dated	All days dated	All days dated	All days dated	

Figure 4.1   Class Portfolio: Language Arts *(continued)*

Using the PLEP to Develop the IEP

The results of the child's PLEP evaluation should be presented in an IEP staffing. Such information can help the inclusion teacher and the rest of the team decide what content will be taught, who will teach which content, and when or in what setting the content will be delivered. Information gathered from normative tests will also help the inclusion teacher plan a specific program. Information from both normative and criterion-referenced measures is instrumental in determining exit from or entrance into the general education classroom.

Functional Behavioral Assessment

Children who are eligible for services under IDEA may have a wide range of inappropriate social or emotional behaviors as their primary need. The degree, the type, and the frequency of the behavior as it affects access to the general education classroom and curriculum determine whether or not the child needs a specific type of intervention offered through special education services. In other words, if the behavior is interfering to such a degree that the child no longer can have access to the general education curriculum, assessment must occur to determine the most fitting educational services.

In light of increasingly violent acts by some students in the public schools, Congress recognized the need for assessing behaviors and providing interventions. The 1997 amendments to IDEA mandate that functional behavior assessment (FBA) be used to develop positive behavioral interventions for children with certain types of problem behavior (Peterson, 2002). IDEA stipulates that the schools must begin an FBA when drugs or weapons have been involved, potentially violent behaviors exist, or when the student's misconduct hinders the learning of the student and other students. Students who have been suspended or whose educational placement has been changed due to behavior difficulties are required to receive an FBA. IDEA '97 spells out when and what the state and local school districts must do in response to challenging behaviors of children and youth (Yell & Shriner, 1997). In response to certain disciplinary actions, the IEP team has 10 days to meet to formulate an FBA plan and to collect data for developing or modifying an intervention plan (BIP) (Gable et al., 2003).

Broadly defined, FBA is "a systematic process of identifying problem behaviors and events that (a) reliably predicted occurrences of those behaviors and (b) maintain those behaviors across time" (Sugai et al., 2000 p. 137). Put another way, an FBA tries to identify the current problem, what is creating or aggravating the problem, and how to establish a proactive or positive intervention to eliminate the behavioral problem.

Let's take an example using Robbie. Robbie's behavior is interfering with his ability to learn new ideas as well as creating issues in learning for his classmates. His classmates are afraid of him. He bullies other students in and outside of class, threatens his teachers, and refuses to do classwork. He has already been removed from the general education classroom for part of the day and placed in a more restrictive setting during the afternoon. Robbie's problem has been identified, but now school personnel need to figure out what is creating the problem and how to establish some sort of positive intervention to eliminate or reduce his inappropriate behaviors.

Congress did not specify which techniques or strategies to use to address Robbie's problematic behavior. Consequently, the assessment format can vary considerably from state to state and school district to school district (Asmus, Vollmer, & Borrero, 2002). After interviewing Robbie's teachers and conducting several direct observations of Robbie in the general education setting, the FBA process has arrived at a hypothesis for why Robbie behaves the way he does. This phase of FBA is referred to as hypothesis testing or, to use educational jargon, *functional analysis*. The FBA discovered that whenever Robbie did not get his way, he engaged in one or more inappropriate behaviors. Robbie likes to be in control. Now the IEP team needs to identify strategies and supports that can be implemented in the classroom to address Robbie's control issues so that they no longer interfere with his ability to learn or the ability of his peers to learn (Quinn, Gable, Rutherford, Nelson, & Howell, 1998).

In the multistep world of FBA, after the identification of the problem and the development of a hypothesis, the implementation of the intervention (also known as hypothesis testing) must be evaluated. The more the FBA is based on data-driven evidence, the easier it is to determine how and if the intervention is successful. If the first intervention determined by the team does not decrease Robbie's behaviors, another intervention must be tried.

The majority of studies reporting the usefulness of FBA have been conducted in highly controlled settings, such as state residential facilities and inpatient clinical settings, raising questions about the utility of FBA in more typical inclusion settings (Peterson, 2002). Perhaps when the mandated use of FBA becomes more widely used in inclusion settings, standardization of the process with students who have mild disabilities will become more widespread (Sasso, Conroy, Stichter, & Fox, 2001). Some classroom teachers can use FBA in inclusion settings, but the elegance of the theoretical FBA becomes modified with realities of day-to-day classroom demands. Remembering to collect data every day may be the most difficult step to implement. However, although daily assessments may be ideal, they may not be a necessary component of conducting a valuable FBA. Substantial decreases in problem behaviors have been noted in at least one classroom where an inclusion teacher worked with two students with mild disabilities and did not maintain stringent daily data collection (Maag & Larsen, 2004).

Assessment Accommodations

According to the guidelines provided by the 1997 Amendments of IDEA, any accommodation or modification listed in the IEP as necessary for access to the general education curriculum or used to demonstrate knowledge of the general education curriculum can also be used as accommodations or modifications during assessment. The assessment accommodations must be clearly stated and documented in the IEP. For example, if Georgia is allowed to use a calculator with math problems involving number facts for homework or classwork, as long as Georgia's IEP team states that the use of a calculator is critical in demonstrating Georgia's ability to problem solve on assessments, she is also entitled to use this accommodation for any type of assessment measure, including state and national assessments.

Until 2001, no real issue existed when determining what kind of adaptation a student might use during instruction or assessment. The type of accommodation was the IEP team's decision. However, in 2001, the adaptation waters became muddy with the passage of NCLB. Inclusion now became paired with the accountability requirements established by the 1997 amendments to IDEA and the adequate yearly performance standards (AYP) outlined in NCLB. In other words, IDEA '97 requires that the curriculum for students eligible for special services must be the general education curriculum. NCLB stipulates that all children must meet AYP standards in the general education curriculum. The results of the assessment tool chosen by the state would demonstrate the degree to which students are making progress in the general education curriculum, thus providing federal, state, and local stakeholders with data to make policy and allocate public funds (Albrecht & Joles, 2003).

At face value, linking the general education curriculum with a measure of performance seems logical and praiseworthy. Unfortunately, alignment between curriculum and a measure that demonstrates progress within that curriculum has complicated the use of testing accommodations. However, in a memo dated January 21, 2001, the United States Department of Education continued to hold the position that assessment accommodations should be chosen on the basis of the individual students' needs and should generally be consistent with the accommodations provided during instruction. In this same memo, the U.S. Department of Education also gave state educational agencies and school districts the authority to determine how test scores are reported and used.

Despite IDEA intention for the IEP to identify appropriate individual accommodations and modifications for students with disabilities, state educational agencies and school districts are allowed to limit the use of test scores if certain accommodations or modifications are involved (Ideapractices, 2002). Loosely translated, the state or school district could ban certain accommodations or modifications during the yearly testing required by NCLB. If the child uses unacceptable accommodations or modifications, the results of the test would be considered invalid. If the percentage of students failing to meet AYP exceeds the limit established by NCLB, the threat of withholding funds or labeling schools as underperforming looms over states and school districts like the proverbial sword of Damocles. Students with disabilities can be forced to fend for themselves during high-stakes testing without access to the individual accommodations and modifications prescribed for them by the IEP team.

The tug-of-war between the requirements of NCLB and the rights of students with disabilities as outlined by Section 504 and IDEA has no defined winners, only defined losers. The first group of losers is children and youth who are unable to demonstrate their PLEP because they are denied accommodations or adaptations. The second group of losers is the stakeholders and policymakers who are getting invalid information about students' true level of educational performance.

This bizarre situation has come about in part because of a disparity in the use of accommodations across ability groups in districts and states. For students who cannot use vision or hearing to access content, accommodations and modifications are routinely accepted and change very little within and across states. On the other hand, for students who have vision but who process print ineffectively or not at all, the question of how much, how little, or what type of accommodation is not so clear. Variations in accommodations make comparisons of student performance within districts and across states difficult (Albrecht & Joles, 2003). The question of accommodation and modifications for students with sensory disabilities generally does not create a problem. For students with cognitive or behavioral problems, however, failure to provide appropriate accommodations or modifications has far-reaching consequences for the high-stakes testing required by NCLB. To confuse matters even more, few policies related to testing accommodations have been based on research findings (Thurlow, 2001). Accommodations, which have been deemed critical for students to have access to content, may not be allowed for use with instruments chosen by some states to demonstrate AYP. The proverbial legislative drawing board still has a long way to go in resolving the intention of two powerful but seemingly opposing federal attempts at educational reform.

Developing the IEP

Data from the evaluation of a child's PLEP will help the teacher set long-term goals and objectives. Goals refer to general areas and usually are written for the course of a year's instruction. Goals may be written for social as well as academic behaviors. An example of a goal in reading is: "By the end of the year, Caitlin will employ strategies to comprehend informational reading material."

Information provided from each evaluation measure should be related directly to the goals and objectives chosen for a student. The teacher and the IEP team should not simply abandon test information because they cannot decide how to meet the needs identified by the test any more than they should develop goals and objectives that are not based on evaluative data. For example, if spelling is an important curricular area, the team must be able to provide information about the student's current level of functioning in spelling before they write a spelling goal.

Objectives

Objectives are aligned with goals. Objectives are the measurable components of the goal. PLEP is established by measuring a student's performance on objectives. Growth on objectives determines the degree of mastery of the goal. In order to determine if Caitlin has successfully employed strategies for reading comprehension with textbooks, aligned objectives are designed. Three objectives that could be used to determine if Caitlin is mastering comprehension strategies are as follows:

- Caitlin will orally describe the topic of expository text, heard or read, without prompts.
- Caitlin will answer questions (who, what, where, when, why, how) about expository text, heard or read.
- Caitlin will identify organizational features (e.g., title, table of contents, heading, bold print) of expository text.

Instructional objectives are at the heart of the IEP. Objectives are personal in two ways. Objectives focus on the specific needs of a specific child. Objectives also provide adaptations appropriate to the cognitive, physical, or social needs of the specific child. Instructional objectives are typically written in one sentence containing four important components:

- Behavior: what the student needs to do
- Content: basic skill or subject matter area
- Criteria: the degree to which the student must demonstrate mastery
- Condition: the circumstances under which the child will work

The *behavior* Caitlin is expected to complete must be accountable or observable. In Caitlin's first objective, for example, she must orally describe the topic of expository text, heard or read. The verb is *describe*. Given the verb *describe,* Caitlin is to explain orally the *contents* of the objective. In this case the content is the topic of expository text. The number of times Caitlin correctly explains the topic is an indication of her PLEP.

The *criterion* specifies the degree to which Caitlin is expected to master or describe the topic of expository text. Typically, a criterion is specified with a percentage or an assumed percentage. In Caitlin's case, since no criterion has been stated, the assumed accuracy is 100%, or every time. Other ways of indicating criteria that are more informative include specifying the exact numbers; for example, describing the topic correctly for 8 out of 10 texts or identifying the topic within a prespecified time limit. Caitlin, for example, must orally describe the topic of the expository text she has read within 2 minutes.

Finally, *conditions* include the circumstances under which the child will work. As such, conditions define the type of modifications or accommodations that the student needs in order to have access to the general education curriculum. Some conditions include the type of method, level of independence (e.g., with or without a buddy), and assistive technology devices.

Establishing Priorities

Establishing priorities is important. The team must decide which goals and objectives to stress first. This decision-making process must focus on the needs of the child and take into consideration the requirements of the general education curriculum. A systematic approach to establishing general education curriculum priorities can be developed from state and local standards. The IEP team can determine what kind of adaptations or modifications will be most beneficial in providing the child access to the general education curriculum. Four guidelines that can help the IEP team find a common basis for decision-making are as follows:

1. Identify the student's PLEP in the general education curriculum.
2. Identify areas in need of intervention.
3. Determine which area each team member thinks has the highest priority for successful inclusion.
4. Identify the prerequisite skills for the instructional setting.

When setting goals, the team needs to keep both basic skill areas and content areas in mind. A grid that combines curricular areas with the four guidelines for establishing priorities can provide the team with a basis for planning goals and communicating about a student's needs. An example is presented in Figure 4.2.

A grid of this sort can reduce time spent shuffling papers and help the team zero in on the instructional areas that are critically related to goal development. By using a curriculum grid, team members can communicate with a shared vocabulary, making the task of defining the elements of curriculum areas relatively straightforward. More important, the demands of each curricular task can be stated in behavioral terms, which then can be translated directly into classroom demands. An inclusion teacher must clarify how classroom demands can interact with the curricular skills of the mainstreamed student.

General Education Classroom Development

Consider the case of Natalie. She is currently enrolled in a fifth-grade general education classroom for most of the school day. Natalie is instructed in all academic subjects, except mathematics, in the general education classroom. Her special education teacher believes Natalie may be ready to receive math instruction in the general education classroom. According to the results of normative tests, Natalie is operating at a fifth-grade level in math. Closer examination, however, reveals discrepancies between her current skills and the type of arithmetic skills she will need in a fifth-grade room. While Natalie can do the computations required in the general education classroom, she is hampered by a slow rate of recall for the number facts required.

In developing goals and objectives for Natalie, an IEP team must consider the environment of the general education classroom and what type of intervention, if any, would be necessary for Natalie to be successful. The team member most likely to understand the demands of the general education classroom is the inclusion teacher. The inclusion teacher is also in the best position to evaluate the success of implementing an intervention. By defining classroom demands in behavioral terms, the inclusion teacher and the rest of the IEP team can make realistic and functional comparisons between goals and behavioral objectives proposed for the student in inclusion settings. Employing a curricular grid as described here, a team can directly analyze Natalie's needs in arithmetic as they relate to the demands of the general classroom.

Curricular area	Present Level of Performance	Intervention Areas	Priority Areas	Demands of Setting	Other
Reading skills					
Word recognition					
Word analysis					
Oral reading					
Comprehension					
Language arts					
Spelling					
Grammar					
Expressive writing					
Handwriting					
Arithmetic					
Facts					
Computation					
Application					
Social interaction					
Peers.					
Teacher					
Other					

Code: **Present level of performance:** Fill in grade equivalency
Intervention areas: Fill in with check (✔)
Priority areas: Rank by number for main heading and number and letter for subarea
Demands of setting: List prerequisite skills
Other: Pertinent comments

Figure 4.2   Planning Grid

Figure 4.3 presents a grid that has been completed for Natalie for the curricular area of arithmetic. Her PLEP has been filled in. The checkmark indicates that her skills are inadequate in the area of number facts. However, the classroom teacher has not ranked number facts as the highest priority in her arithmetic curriculum. Rather, the ranking suggests that the teacher places a higher value on basic computation processes. Natalie's processing time for number fact retrieval is very slow. In fact, her reachable rate is so slow that she loses her thought process when attempting to solve algorithms or word problems. Computation drill for addition, subtraction, multiplication, and division facts has been tried for

Child: *Natalie*		Team member: *Classroom Teacher*		Date: *11/25/05*	
Curricular area	**Present Level of Performance**	**Intervention Areas**	**Priority Areas**	**Demands of Setting**	**Other**
Reading skills					
Word recognition					
Word analysis					
Oral reading					
Comprehension					
Language arts					
Spelling					
Grammar					
Expressive writing					
Handwriting					
Arithmetic	*WJ-III: 5.4*		*1*		
Facts	*10 facts /60 sec.*	*✔*	*1.b*	*55 facts/60 sec./2 errors*	*calculator*
Computation	*knows process*		*1.a*		
Application	*slow*		*1.c*		
Social interaction					
Peers.					
Teacher					
Other					

Code: **Present level of performance:** Fill in grade equivalency
Intervention areas: Fill in with check (✔)
Priority areas: Rank by number for main heading and number and letter for subarea
Demands of setting: List prerequisite skills
Other: Pertinent comments

Figure 4.3   Planning Grid for Natalie

the past four years, but no real progress has been gained. Natalie's number fact work is not at the same level as the demands of the classroom. As a result, the IEP team has recommended that Natalie be allowed to use a calculator when computing math problems. The classroom teacher also believes that the use of a calculator as an adaptation in mathematics is realistic in the general education setting and already has provided calculators for several other students.

Assuming that the other members of the IEP team have filled out their curricular grids similarly, decisions can now be made. One decision will pertain to a goal statement for Natalie in the area of arithmetic. If the team decision is to work with Natalie in number facts, her goal statement might be: "With the use of a calculator, Natalie will be on grade level in mathematics by the end of the year."

Most short-term objectives can be taken directly from district-level curriculum guides. Frequently, short-term objectives can be found in the teacher's manual for classroom texts. Ideally, the inclusion teacher can draw short-term objectives directly from a criterion-referenced test developed from the texts used in the classroom.

Whether or not short-term objectives are written at an IEP meeting depends on policies of the district and state. Placement can be determined only after goals and objectives have been developed.

Task Analysis

Short-term objectives often are written on an individual implementation plan (IIP), which consists of weekly or daily lesson plans. In writing an IIP, a team examines each short-term objective relating to an original goal on the IEP and breaks it into even smaller, more discrete objectives. The process of breaking goals and objectives into subobjectives or tasks is called *task analysis*. Task analysis is simply a way of breaking the essential parts of a larger task into subtasks and then sequencing these subtasks. As students learn each subtask, completion of the larger task becomes easier.

SPECIFICITY   One major difference between instruction in a general education class and instruction in a special class is the specificity (and therefore number) of subtasks included in a task analysis. When a child is placed in a general education class, it is assumed that tasks will not be broken down as much as they are in a special setting.

ESSENTIAL SUBTASKS   In writing a task analysis for either a general education or a special setting, only essential subtasks should be included. For example, when teaching reading, many texts have the following objective: "The student will be able to name the letters of the alphabet." This objective has some merit for spelling tasks because a person cannot spell aloud without names for the letters. However, this objective has no relevance to a reading task because children are not required to say the names of letters while reading. Actually, learning letter names is sometimes confusing in the early stages of learning to read. Children often confuse the name of a letter with its sound. Teachers often have to tell beginning readers, "No, *a* is the name of the letter. Please give me the short sound of *a*."

Determining essential subtasks is usually a matter of common sense. Essential subtasks are those that assist the child in learning a larger task. To use the previous reading example, if a child can learn to decode and recognize words without learning the names of letters, learning the names of letters is not essential to the task of decoding or word recognition.

SEQUENCING   Another consideration in task analysis is sequencing. Once the essential subtasks have been identified, they should be taught in a prescribed order. The first rule of thumb in sequencing tasks is to determine whether the tasks have a natural order. In math, for example, an obvious progression is that the sequence of instruction or tasks presented will deal first with regrouping into units, next into tens, then hundreds, thousands, and so on.

Not all subject areas are sequenced so obviously. Subtasks in a sequence are not always dependent upon acquisition of a preceding subtask. In many cases, several subtasks are at the same level of difficulty but are interdependent because knowledge of all the subtasks is necessary before the child can learn the objective successfully. When faced with interdependent subtasks, the teacher can choose a sequence arbitrarily. Generally, the most efficient sequence is one that parallels the classroom texts. However, interdependent objectives or subtasks have no single correct order.

Final Comments on Goals and Short-Term Objectives

Goals are documented in an IEP. Specific short-term objectives related to annual goals and objectives usually are described in an IIP. Goals and objectives as stated in the IEP and IIP are essentially educational plans for the child with disabilities. They are not binding contracts. However, the IEP team should make every attempt to help the child achieve the goals and objectives. The child's educational and social development will be influenced directly by the degree to which the team makes a good-faith effort. The good-faith effort is also driven by the NCLB provision of AYP.

In establishing annual goals and objectives for a student, task hierarchy becomes apparent. Broadly stated, goals are divided into more specific objectives. In turn, these objectives are divided into subobjectives or subtasks. The specificity of the subtasks will influence the degree of special education and the extent to which the child with a disability will be able to participate in the general education classroom.

Because goals and objectives on the IEP are expected to be taught, teachers have to be careful to guard against the "I wrote it; therefore, I will teach it" school of thought. Just because Song's IEP states that he needs to learn the short *a* sound in one month does not mean that this goal is engraved on his desk. The point of IEP objectives is to meet student needs, not bureaucratic needs. If Song's teacher finds that the short *a* sound is not an appropriate objective or that a month of unsuccessful drill on short *a* has elapsed, Song's teacher is at liberty to change his goal. A good practice is to ensure that the team agrees with the change in the goal. An amended IEP meeting would bring the team into the final decision-making phase for changing a goal. Because Song's goal has been changed, his teacher must inform his parents that a different goal has been substituted. Even though Song's teacher can be flexible in instruction, his parents have to be told about any changes on his IEP.

IEPs are good instructional guesses based on information about the student relative to yearly instruction. An objective or goal that made sense in September may not make sense in January. What does make good instructional sense is to seize the teachable moment. Seizing the teachable moment is a basic tenet of instruction, and not all teachable moments can be predicted on the IEP. The IEP is designed to support, not dominate, the teaching process. Teachers should feel free to modify or correct goals and objectives according to the child's skills.

Related Services for Students With Disabilities

Another important but sometimes overlooked area prescribed on the IEP by IDEA is related services. Related services are an important component in establishing a free and appropriate public education (FAPE) for many students with disabilities. IDEA provides a general description of related services:

> The term "related services" means transportation, and such developmental, corrective, and other supportive services (including speech/language pathology and audiology services, psychological services, physical and occupational therapy, recreation, including therapeutic recreation, social work services, counseling services, including rehabilitation counseling, orientation and mobility services, and medical services, except that such medical services shall be for diagnostic and evaluation purposes only) as may be required to assist the child with the disability to benefit from special education, and includes the early identification and assessment of disabling conditions in children. (IDEA, 20 U.S.C. § 1401(a)(17))

Related services include, but are not limited to:

- Assistive technology
- Audiology and speech pathology services
- Counseling and psychological services
- Occupational, physical, and recreational therapy
- Art, music, and dance therapy

Any other developmental, corrective, or supportive services like artistic and cultural programs may be included under related services if they assist the child with the disability in having access to FAPE (Downing, 2004). The IDEA regulations require that related services needs must be decided on an individual basis by the IEP team after a thorough assessment of all areas of concern. In addition, the evaluation must include all of the child needs, even though they may not be commonly associated with the student's special education classification. For example, Sophie is a student eligible for services under the category of learning disabilities. Sophie also has articulation problems and should be evaluated to determine the need for speech/language therapy as a related service.

Assistive Technology

IDEA '97 requires that assistive technology (AT) devices and services be considered for all students during IEP development. AT, as defined in IDEA '97, is

> any item, piece of equipment, or product system, whether acquired commercially off-the-shelf, modified, or customized, that is used to increase, maintain, or improve functional capabilities of a child with a disability. (20 U.S.C. § 1401(1))

AT devices can be as simple as pencil grips and as sophisticated as voice-recognition software. AT devices include text markers, talking texts, and simple communication boards—any type of object or device that facilitates the learning of students with disabilities. Examples of selected AT devices and services are as follows (Day & Huefner, 2003):

- Positioning systems that allow access to educational activities
- Daily living aids and products, such as specialized items for eating, toileting, and grooming
- Augmentative and alternative communication systems, including symbols, communication devices, electronic communications systems, and speech synthesizers
- Switches and controls for access to equipment
- Assistive listening devices, including hearing aids, personal FM units, telecommunications devices for the deaf (TDD), and closed captioning
- Visual aids such as contrast enhancement, enlargement/magnification of materials, technology hardware and software, refreshable Braille, electronic note-taking devices, and eyeglasses
- Tactile materials
- Auditory materials, including voice output devices and audiotape recorders
- Motor aids such as walkers, wheelchairs, and powered vehicles
- Recreational/leisure devices, including computer software, adaptive switches, and access devices (swimming pool lifts, adaptive sports equipment)
- Computer access, including switches, modified hardware, accessible software, and Internet access

In the early 1970s when federal legislation first intervened to support students with disabilities, most of today's AT did not exist, and what did exist was not yet developed for widespread use in public schools (Hagger, 1999). By the mid-1990s AT had come a long way and potential was turning into reality for students with disabilities. As a result, Congress passed several acts stressing the benefits of using AT devices along with special education program services and techniques as a means to help students with disabilities gain access to a FAPE in the least restrictive environment with a preference for inclusion settings (Day & Huefner, 2003).

Since the 1990s, AT devices such as personal computers, communication devices, specialized keyboards, and other devices have influenced teaching strategies and students' participation in the general education curriculum (Blackhurst, 1997; Blackhurst & Edyburn, 2001). Students like John, who do not have the capability to respond verbally to class questions or activities, such as circle time, can now utilize communication devices to produce a verbal response. And Monica, a child with the visual impairment, has gained independence because she is able to produce print assignments without the assistance of the Braille transcriber by using computers that print the assignment in Braille and manuscript.

In order to get the maximum benefit from AT devices, IDEA '97 also specifies services associated with AT devices in a broad manner: "any service that directly assists a child with a disability in the selection, acquisition, and use of an AT device" (20 U.S.C. § 1401(2)). Included in the services are the following:

- Evaluation of the student's needs, including evaluation in the student's customary environment
- Purchase, lease, selection, design, fitting, customization, and adaptation of devices
- Maintenance, repair, or replacement of devices
- Coordination of services and devices used with other therapies and interventions
- Training or technical assistance for teachers, staff, family members, and students (Day & Huefner, 2003, p. 24)

In spite of the advanced level of sophistication and affordability of AT devices and services and the mandate from IDEA '97, some studies have found that attitudinal barriers such as a negative image of technology or fear of technology are thwarting the use of AT in inclusion settings (King, 1999; Scherer, 2000). Couple these attitudinal issues with a significant lack of providers who are trained to use assistive technology devices (McGregor & Pachuski, 1996) and a dark cloud of ignorance covers the brilliant potential of AT devices and accompanying services. Finally, funding problems, time available, and equipment reliability (Lahm & Sizemore, 2002) are further challenges compounding attempts to integrate AT devices or services in public school settings. With parental permission, however, public school systems can request funds from the student's private insurance company to purchase AT devices or services (Hagger, 1999).

The good news is that technology in the 21st century is ubiquitous. Cell phones and personal computers are becoming commonplace. As more parents, teachers, and students become aware of the value of AT, they are becoming more insistent on using AT as an option for increasing access to the curriculum and fostering independence when facing environmental demands. Members of IEP teams can also request specific training for teachers, family members, and students so that the maximum benefits of the AT devices can be gained.

Audiology and Speech Pathology Services

Services provided through audiology and speech pathology relate to the identification, assessment, and delivery of appropriate assistance for students with hearing loss and or associated communication problems. Some children may qualify for speech and language services as their primary disability, but others whose disabilities fall into other categories may also qualify for speech and language assistance as a related service. Sometimes children like Cheyenne, for example, are classified as having a primary disability of mental retardation but also have secondary needs in the production of language and speech.

Identifying the related services required to provide appropriate assistance for children with hearing loss is typically done by professionals in the field and is rarely challenged as an appropriate service. If the hearing loss accompanies the primary disability and the loss is affecting access to a FAPE, the student can also qualify for audiological services.

Establishing speech and language services for children with milder disabilities, however, is not always so simple. IEP teams sometimes fail to consider the child's needs in language development if his expressive language appears appropriate. Often the student's primary disability overshadows the secondary disabilities. As a result, related services that may be necessary for the student to receive an appropriate educational program may be overlooked.

Counseling and Psychological Services

Counseling and psychological services are provided by qualified social workers, psychologists, guidance and rehabilitation counselors, or any other personnel with the relevant educational background. Related services include administration and interpretation of specific cognitive and behavioral measures, observations and interviews, writing diagnostic summaries, and designing positive behavioral interventions. Counseling activities can focus on career development, independence, and integration in the workplace and community. In addition, counseling the child individually or working in partnership with parents and others to improve or eliminate problems in the child's home, school, or community are also services provided in this category. Responsibility for developing positive behavioral interventions may also be found in this related service area.

Occupational, Physical, and Recreational Therapy

The goal of physical, occupational, and recreational therapy is to provide educationally relevant services that will assist students with disabilities in benefitting from special education. These therapies are designed to facilitate the development of the skills necessary for academic and vocational learning within the child's present and future educational settings.

Depending on the individual's needs, instruction may include improving gross- and fine-motor skills, sensory processing, coordination/balance, and adapting to the physical environment. In addition, teaching students to adapt to the physical environment, organize and use materials appropriately, develop time management skills, improve social/peer interaction, and acquire dressing or feeding skills appropriate to the school environment fall under the instructional range of professionals providing services in these areas (Neal, Bigby, & Nicholson, 2004). In the not-so-distant past, referrals for occupational and physical therapy were based primarily on a medical model or conditions that might be affecting the child's performance in school. At this time, however, referrals generally are the result of a member of the IEP team identifying educational activities that the student is having problems performing. Evaluation by an occupational or physical therapist can contribute significantly to determining whether a student is eligible for special education services.

For students with severe physical and cognitive disabilities, occupational, physical, and recreational therapists play important roles in helping team members understand the impact of sensory and motor deficits on classroom performance. Intervention focuses on increasing participation in educational activities, which will enable the child to actively participate in the school day.

Therapy is no longer provided in an isolated room but integrated into the inclusion setting. With Henry, for example, instead of focusing on strengthening his upper body in a prescriptive but isolated task, the team identifies functional classroom tasks that can meet the same objective. So the team, in conjunction with the specialist, tries to determine which classroom activities will help Henry to functionally use his head or hand in an art activity or what types of adaptive equipment he might need to access a computer or communication device or work on small-group projects with his peers.

For students with milder disabilities, like sixth-grade Dyanne, the focus is on the components of the academic tasks that are within her grasp and how she might be able to participate in these tasks. For instance, Dyanne has significant limitations in reading as well as problems with fine-motor skills. Dyanne wants to participate in a buddy reading program with kindergartners. Since Dyanne has problems turning pages as well as reading material, the specialists might select a switch that Dyanne could use to access a book on tape.

In contrast to physical therapy and occupational therapy, adapted physical education is a mandated service; however, recreational therapy (also referred to as therapeutic recreation) and traditional recreation are thought of as related services under IDEA. Physical activity is not a mere add-on. Appropriate physical activity experiences improve the ability to learn and regulate the balance of neurotransmitters and hormones that facilitate learning (Howard, 2000; Mears, 2003). Additionally, physical activity lessens the need for drug or chemical intervention for many individuals with attention disorder, depression, and various other personality/mental and behavioral disorders (Jensen, 2000).

Recreational therapists work closely with school personnel, including physical education teachers. Recreational therapists provide many interventions related to leisure resources in schools or the community. Accordingly, recreational therapists can be called upon in a wide variety of areas, including, but not restricted to, adaptive sports, adventure therapy and team building, anger management, animal assistive therapy, assertiveness training, assisted devices or modification, AT support, community integration, family leisure planning, and horticulture. Recreational therapists may also help students participate in recreation activities that require reading and math, such as, keeping score or playing board games (Etzel-Wise & Mears, 2004).

Art, Music, and Dance Therapy

Often creative arts provide entry and more direct access than words to uncomfortable feelings, memories, and ideas. The purpose of using the arts as therapy with children and youth with disabilities is not so much to develop art, music, or dance skills, but to provide services that will support and strengthen learning goals as indicated on the IEP.

Art therapy is a means by which students who are nonverbal or who have difficulty expressing their feelings or emotions can release tension or gain insight into their life situation through any number of art media. Music therapy uses musical responses to assess emotional well-being, physical health, social functioning, communication abilities, and cognitive skills. Activities are designed for individuals and groups based on client need using music improvisation, receptive music listening, song writing, lyric discussion, music and imagery, music performance, and learning through music. Dance therapy uses the power of movement in a therapeutic setting to facilitate expression of emotions, tell stories, treat illness, celebrate important events, and establish or maintain bonds with others. Children and youth with mental health needs, developmental and learning disabilities, brain injuries, physical disabilities, and acute and chronic pain are potential prospects for art, music, or dance therapy.

Both the physical act of creating art, music, or dance plus the image/content/dance of the work can express and heal trauma and visualize desired outcomes. Jeremy was school phobic, always nervous and tense when in the proximity of a teacher. In order to reduce some of his tension and to enable Jeremy to feel more in control of his environment, an art therapist began to work with him once a week. During this time Jeremy engaged in a variety of art activities, each activity generally guided by the therapist to help him to express his feelings toward teachers. After about the fifth session, the therapist asked Jeremy to draw picture of one feature from his teacher's face. Jeremy drew a mouth that was wide open displaying jagged teeth. Next, the therapist asked Jeremy to add another image to this drawing. Jeremy drew a picture of a giant fish eating the mouth. For the first time, Jeremy was able to express his sense of empowerment. He was the fish who destroyed the frightening teacher. From that point forward, Jeremy was more relaxed in school, and by the end of the year, he was no longer fearful of teachers. Jeremy was now free to approach academic tasks in a more relaxed and open manner. Art, music, and dance therapy can reduce stress and develop a sense of empowerment that is necessary for accessing school curricula.

Need for Related Services

IEP teams need to consider the value of related services for all students eligible for special education. Many IEP teams do not reflect on the need for related services or, when considering related services, often hold discussions in a token manner (Yell, 2004). IDEA clearly states that related services should be provided to assist children in benefiting from their specialized programs. When related services are not considered but could help students benefit from their educational program, the IEP teams are in danger of developing an inappropriate program that is neither meaningful nor legally correct.

Placement of Children With Disabilities

The school district should provide a continuum of placement options to meet the needs of children with disabilities. Such a continuum should include instruction in general classes, special classes, special schools, the home, as well as hospitals and institutions. Supplementary services, such as resource room or itinerant instruction, may also be provided in conjunction with general education placement.

Skills of the Inclusion Teacher

Teachers have to make an honest appraisal of their ability to meet the academic and management needs of a child eligible for special services. If, for example, Oscar needs special assistance with reading comprehension, his teachers must assess the adequacy of their expertise in meeting his learning goals. To complicate matters further, Oscar may also be categorized as autistic.

Most general education teachers have not been given much direct instruction in how to manage the needs of a child like Oscar. The teacher may be capable of working with Oscar's reading needs, but not quite sure of how to deal with his interpersonal characteristics. Similarly, a teacher may be capable of working with a child who acts out but not sure of how to deal with a shy or withdrawn student.

Teachers can write into the IEP an educational plan that increases their proficiency in working with children like Oscar, or any other children they have not been adequately prepared to instruct. Teachers working in inclusion settings have the legal right to ask for and receive instructional assistance in both classroom management and academic management. Teachers also must consider their classroom management skills relative to the needs of students with disabilities.

The demands of the classroom influence placement options for students with disabilities. The classroom format, materials, and curriculum may require minor modifications. The type and degree of modification needed will vary with the needs of each student. Once again, the teacher has the right to request assistance in making these modifications.

Availability of Special Services

Three levels of support can be identified: full time, part time, and outside. Full-time support means that a designated person in the building has primary responsibility for assisting inclusion teachers. This full-time person, most often called a consultant, works directly with teachers and indirectly with students. Part-time support usually involves a resource teacher or an itinerant teacher. Resource or itinerant teachers divide their responsibilities between direct involvement with inclusion teachers and direct involvement with students. They may share responsibilities with the inclusion teacher for the education of many mainstreamed children. Finally, with outside support, the classroom teacher may draw upon the resources of district-level consultants. Multiple variations of the three levels exist. Thorough knowledge of these variations can help an inclusion teacher choose an appropriate placement efficiently.

Placement Options

Placement options for children with disabilities fall on a continuum ranging from general education class placement with no assistance to residential or boarding school. Because the classroom teacher is part of the IEP team, general knowledge of this service continuum is appropriate. Figure 4.4 presents the original special education cascade (Reynolds, 1978).

In the special education cascade, consideration was given to five placement options involving the general education classroom:

1. General education classroom
2. General education classroom with consultative assistance
3. General education classroom with assistance by itinerant specialist
4. General education classroom with resource room help
5. General education classroom plus part-time special class

The inclusion teacher is expected to have primary responsibility for the education of a child with disabilities in these five settings (Culatta, Tompkins, & Werts, 2002). The teacher's input regarding placement in a general education setting is likely to be the most critical.

As the IEP team works to determine the most appropriate general education option for the child with disabilities, the decisions should be based on the relationship between the three general education classroom factors described earlier (teacher skills, demands of the classroom, and level of support) and the type of placement option. Figure 4.5 presents a grid that illustrates the inclusion teacher's needs in relation to an individual child. Assessments and objectives for the child have been determined. The inclusion teacher now must consider what, if any, needs she will have in order to meet the objectives.

As shown in Figure 4.5, the teacher indicated that she would like consultative assistance in the skill area of social behaviors (2/A.2). She also indicated that she will need consultation to assist in instructional formatting (2/B.1) relative to social behavior. The inclusion teacher is requesting materials (3/B.2), presumably

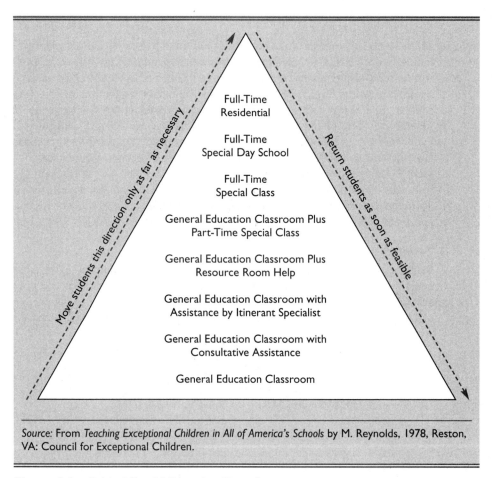

Source: From *Teaching Exceptional Children in All of America's Schools* by M. Reynolds, 1978, Reston, VA: Council for Exceptional Children.

Figure 4.4   Original Special Education Cascade

related to social behavior and formatting. She further sees a need for part-time support (4/C.2). By examining the teacher's needs relative to the child's needs, the team can focus more clearly on instructional placement and the amount of time the child will spend in the general education classroom.

Placement options vary with the needs of the student with disabilities. Traditionally, placement options have included either general education or special education, but this distinction is no longer clear. The either/or placement philosophy clouded the decision-making processes. In the past, placement decisions involved choosing between distinct places. Now, however, placement options no longer are primarily places. Rather, placement decisions involve choosing between processes. These processes are not mutually exclusive, so a child can receive the benefit of several processes simultaneously. The nature and degree of a child's needs determine the extent and type of processes most appropriate.

Student's Name _____

Teacher _____

Date _____

Continuum of Placement Options in the Classroom

General Education Class Factors	No Assistance Needed (1)	Consultative Assistance from Special Education (2)	Consultation Plus Special Materials from Special Education (3)	Resource Room Teacher Service from Special Education (4)	General Education Class and Special Class (5)
A. Teacher Skills					
1. Academic					
2. Social		*need*			
B. Demands of Classroom					
1. Instructional Format		*need*			
2. Materials			*need*		
3. Curriculum					
C. Level of Support					
1. Full Time					
2. Part Time				*need*	
3. Outside					

Figure 4.5   Grid for Determining an Inclusion Teacher's Needs for a Placement Option in the General Education Setting

Initiation and Duration of Special Services

When planning an IEP for an individual child, the IEP team must indicate timelines for the anticipated beginning and duration of service. Typically, timelines are written in terms of years. The degree and nature of the required services will direct the estimated duration of the special services. For a child who has mild disabilities in only one academic area, for example, special services may be needed for only 5 or 6 months. On the other hand, a child with severe disabilities in a sensory area (e.g., a child with visual impairment) may need special services for his or her entire school career.

Review of Services

Anticipated duration of services is typically more than one year for eligible students. One of the original provisions of IDEA was to review services annually with complete IEP teams. However, because of its repetitive nature, on the recommendation of the Council for Exceptional Children, the annual review is no longer required. In 2004, the reauthorization of IDEA no longer required schools to conduct annual IEPs for students with disabilities. Review of IEP goals may occur every three years or may coincide with the natural transition points, for example, moving from middle school to high school. Roughly translated, the reauthorization of IDEA in 2004 implies that schools are allowed to develop three-year IEPs rather than yearly IEPs.

The purpose of the review is to assess the degree to which the IEP is meeting the student's needs. The conferences are held to adjust the IEP in light of the student's projected needs. A projected timeline for meeting the student's goals is outlined during the conference and is compared with the student's actual performance. Discrepancies between real and anticipated performance result in changes to IEP goals.

Key IEP Team Players

All members of the IEP team have important roles to play in designing the most appropriate education for the student in question. When creating full inclusion or general education classroom options, some players, however, may have more critical pieces of the puzzle than others. Perhaps establishing successful inclusion is most strongly influenced by the contributions of the parents, the student, and the inclusion teacher(s).

Role of Parents

Parents and students are the only members of the IEP team who remain constant across all school settings and levels. Their unique role is not to suggest that they assume instructional responsibilities. Rather, parents become involved in the communication process with teachers from their perspectives as educational historians. The success of students with disabilities is dependent on the proactive assistance provided by parents to help inclusion teachers meet the social and academic needs of their child. Information provided by parents at transition times, such as moving from middle school to secondary school, are especially critical to the successful development of an IEP. Before meaningful IEP meetings can take place, the inclusion teaching staff needs a basis for making decisions. To get to know the student and how he or she performs in the classroom settings, teachers need to know who the student is and what behaviors to expect.

The special education teacher is expected to notify each of the inclusion teachers when a student with special needs will be enrolling in their class. In times of transitions, however, like the beginning of the first semester or quarter in a new school, the special education teacher knows the student as described in previous IEPs. Thus, only a partial image of the student is available. Parents in many cases can help to complete the educational and social picture.

The first step in giving inclusion teachers appropriate and timely information is to provide an introductory letter. The letter can be provided by the parents or by the student's previous inclusion teacher. It should be a page or less. Teachers have limited time for all they must do, and most teachers do not have the luxury to read and digest lengthy detailed missives no matter how well written. The content of the letter should briefly explain in understandable language the behavioral symptoms of the student's academic issues. Many teachers have only a cursory familiarity with special education vocabulary. In order to be sure the teachers do not under- or overestimate the impact of the disability on the student's performance, issues and interventions can be presented in a short introductory letter. Figure 4.6 is an example of a letter written by Fernando's mother as he transitions from elementary to middle school.

By having specific classroom activities identified, inclusion teachers are less likely to be overwhelmed as they develop strategies to provide the accommodations within their instructional expertise. Inclusion teachers are also given an

---

September 7, 2006

Dear Ms. Usnick,

Certain instructional accommodations have been necessary for my son, Fernando, to be successful in school. These accommodations have been defined in Fernando's IEP. Fernando has no cognitive or emotional problems. Fernando does have fine-motor issues with eye-hand coordination, near- and far-point vision, manuscript, and visual motor memory. In essence he cannot write, copy from a board or a book, or read for more than a few minutes without undue fatigue. When Fernando is overly fatigued, his concentration is lessened and he sometimes misses class requirements.

At this time, the following accommodations have been used successfully with Fernando:

- Providing extra time during essay tests, in-class writing, and reading assignments
- Allowing highlighting rather than copying important information
- Allowing the use of a tape recorder when possible
- Using homework logs on a daily basis to keep track of assignments.

In the next few weeks, you will be contacted to determine Fernando's success in your classroom. Please observe his behavior until an official IEP meeting can be arranged to discuss his goals. In addition, I will be contacting you toward the end of the first week of classes to discuss the content of this letter.

Thank you for your time, and I look forward to meeting you soon.

Sincerely,
Mrs. Lamas

Figure 4.6   Letter From Fernando's Mother

opportunity to observe the student and the success of the accommodation in their particular classroom setting. Further, the teacher can determine what, if any, additional professional training is needed in order to provide these accommodations.

A follow-up phone call by the parent or previous inclusion teacher to the current teachers ensures that the teacher has received the introductory letter and provides an opportunity to set up a brief meeting, if needed, during the first or second week of instruction. Meeting times are arranged around each teacher's schedule and should be no longer than 10–15 minutes. The primary purpose of the meeting is to ensure that the teachers have read and understood the content of the introductory letter, to inform them that an IEP meeting is forthcoming, and to initiate a homework log. If teachers have been trying out accommodations, and the parents and teachers have been in frequent contact, discussion at IEP meetings can focus on concrete rather than theoretical examples of appropriate instructional delivery (McCoy, 2000).

Students as Self-Advocates

The passage of the 1997 amendments to IDEA meant that students with disabilities are expected to be included in the development of their IEPs. Since the students are the recipients of the IEP, they should also have major input into developing or monitoring the success of the program (Barrie & McDonald, 2002).

Many students are able to communicate their strengths, needs, and goals to the team members (Hammer, 2004). Some students have a clear picture of themselves as learners; others do not have the same insights. However, not all students are excited about nor know how to participate in the development of their IEP. In spite of the fact that most students know what they need to be successful, they sometimes lack confidence and communication skills when dealing with adults. Take, for example, Jack and Karen. Jack understands his disability. He knows what kind of teaching helps him be successful in the classroom. He also knows what kind of teaching assignments he will have difficulty with or not be able to do at all. Karen, on the other hand, is like a leaf floating along a stream; she is totally subject to the flow of the classroom environment. Karen has no idea why she receives special services or that she has choices in how to complete her assignments. She never asks her teacher to clarify tasks, nor does she question her poor classroom achievement. Students like Jack can participate meaningfully in the IEP process; students like Karen need to be taught how to participate in the IEP process and how to advocate for themselves.

Students need to be taught how to take an active role in the IEP process. Providing direct instruction in teaching students how to be involved in their IEP meetings is relatively new and unexplored territory (Hammer, 2004). Teachers, as well as students, may need assistance in learning how to encourage students to participate in their IEP meetings. Teachers and parents who wish to involve their students in IEP meetings will also need some kind of strategy for encouraging student participation. Teachers, parents, and students need to be taught how to develop self-advocacy in students.

In order for students to understand their rights and responsibilities, they will need instruction not only in the legal arena, but also in how to present their case. To stand up for their rights and to make choices as independent members of the IEP team, students must learn how to articulate the following:

- The types of accommodations that have worked well
- The types of accommodations that have not been useful
- Areas in which they need no accommodations
- Areas in which they need accommodations, but are not sure what type would be most useful

Additionally, students need to learn how to ask questions in a way that is positive and proactive. The same principles apply to responding to questions. Sometimes when the student is the center of attention, the spotlight turns into the hot seat. Students can become very uncomfortable when a roomful of people, however well-intentioned, is discussing their personal academic and social issues. The natural inclination in such an uncomfortable situation is to resort to fight or flight, which results in various manifestations of verbal shutdown or confrontation.

Developing the skills needed for efficient communication as either a member or the leader of an IEP team does not need to occur overnight. For many children, the process of becoming articulate and knowledgeable may need to occur in successive approximations. Students need not attend IEP meetings in order for their voices to be heard. Some students may feel more comfortable filling out forms that indicate their learning styles, preferred accommodations, and overall goals and concerns. Some students would feel very uncomfortable being present at the IEP meeting, so another member of the team can present information from these forms in the IEP meeting.

The ultimate goal of training, however, is to enable the student to either lead or become a significant and contributing member of the IEP team. In fact, self-directed IEP meetings (meetings led by the student with the disability) are good forums for providing opportunities for students with disabilities to participate meaningfully in issues of equal access to the school or workplace (McGahee, Mason, Wallace, & Jones, 2001; Torgerson et al., 2004). Self-directed IEP meetings empower students and give them an opportunity to use the skills they need when communicating with inclusion teachers or potential employers. The student-led IEP meeting provides practice developing skills needed for being a self-advocate in the present and the future.

Contributions of the Inclusion Teacher

The inclusion teacher will recognize an obvious need for clarification of the special education services to be delivered. To present classroom information, the teacher has to help decide what services will be provided, when and for how long the services will be given, and who is responsible for providing services. Given the constraints of the school district, some service decisions may be preferred over others. Predetermined services are illegal, and strong judicial precedents have established that all levels must be considered. The IEP team will have to coordinate the service schedule. A format that can be used to simplify and coordinate instructional activities is presented in Figure 4.7.

Although a student may spend all or part of the day in an inclusion setting, the inclusion teacher shares time with other specialists. In most schools, scheduling must account for time with music, art, and physical education teachers. Also, special library times are usually a part of the general education classroom experience.

Name *Lee*   Date *October 25*

	Monday	Tuesday	Wednesday	Thursday	Friday
8:00–9:00	*Opening Reading* 8:30-9:00	→			→
9:00–10:00	*Reading* 9:00-9:30 *Math* 9:30-10:00	→ *1*		*1*	→ →
10:00–11:00	*Math* 10:00-10:30 *Music* 10:30-11:00	P.E. 10:00-10:30 *Lang. Arts* 10:30-11:00	*Math* 10:00-10:30 *Music* 10:30-11:00	P.E. 10:00-10:30 *Lang. Arts* 10:30-11:00	*Math* 10:00-10:30 *Lang. Arts* 10:30-11:00
11:00–12:00	*Lang. Arts* 11:00-11:30	→			→
12:00–1:00	*2*	*1*	*2*	*2*	*1*
1:00–2:00					*Library* 1:30-2:00
2:00–3:00					

Code

Services to be given	Hours per week	Duration
1. Language Therapy	5	November–May
2. Reading Resource	3	November–May
All other services in general education classroom	22	November–May

Figure 4.7   General Schedule for Service Delivery

Careful analysis of a child's social and emotional needs can help shape decisions about service priorities. If a child is having reading problems, decisions about scheduling must include consideration of where the child's reading needs are best met as well as the child's need for positive self-regard. One child may benefit from spending reading time in the general education classroom as well as in the resource setting. An intensified reading schedule may mean that this child misses art. If the child's main source of positive self-esteem stems from artwork, keeping him in art may be more important than giving him additional reading instruction. If, on the other hand, art has no major impact on the child's life, additional reading instruction during the art period is easily justifiable. Each decision must be based on the individual child in question and on state guidelines.

No one ever said scheduling would be easy. The child's and the teacher's program will have to be adjusted. During this phase of IEP planning, the inclusion teacher can save time and energy by bringing copies of his or her class schedule to the meeting. Once the child's schedule has been determined, teaching can begin.

Evaluation of the Plan

The IEP itself must be evaluated to determine the effectiveness of the instructional program and the child's progress. The last component on the IEP is the technique or evaluation plan to be used to determine the appropriateness of the IEP. The evaluation plan must describe evaluation procedures that will be used for evaluating the child's progress toward specified goals. Designing the plan is fairly simple, but implementation may require additional meetings outside of the IEP staffing. The impact of NCLB is very evident in the IEP evaluation process. Reauthorization of IDEA in 2004 eliminated short-term objectives from the IEP (except for students with the most significant cognitive disabilities) effective July 1, 2005. The paradigm presented in NCLB moved away from IDEA and individualized education toward yearly standardized tests in reading and math. IEP effectiveness is evaluated relative to the AYP in reading and math components as prescribed by NCLB.

More time may be required to develop evaluation tools, record-keeping systems, and procedures for sharing reviews. The teacher involved in instructing the child has to ensure that the evaluation tools and recording systems are compatible with other classroom responsibilities. Any evaluation tool used in an inclusion setting should be similar, with only minor modifications, to the tools used with any other student in the class. Examples of minor differences include size of the print, number of items per page, or use of special aids, such as a calculator or number line in math.

Record Keeping

Record keeping for students with disabilities should be similar to record keeping for other students. The records need not be extensive but should include the following:

1. Criteria for acceptable performance
2. Description of special methods or materials that helped achieve criteria

3. Description of any coordination of teaching between the inclusion teacher and another teacher

Examples of modified materials or methods can be dated and placed in the student's folder or portfolio. Notes about conferences with other teachers involved with the child can be dated and placed in the child's portfolio, too. An example of a completed record is presented in Figure 4.8.

The record-keeping system should be one that can be completed quickly. Long, involved records are too cumbersome and time consuming to be useful. Essentially, the system should enable the teacher to objectively evaluate a child's performance. These records will help determine the extent to which the child has achieved the goals as specified on the IEP.

Summary

An IEP is a written document that provides information about a student's academic and social skills and needs, program goals and timelines, the nature of services to be provided for the child, and a plan for evaluating IEP implementation. The IEP is at the heart of the process by which students with disabilities are provided an appropriate education in the least restrictive environment. The least restrictive environment, unless otherwise noted, begins in the general education classroom.

Student Name	Skill 1 Criterion 100% 2 days in a row	Skill 2 Criterion 100% 3 days in a row	Review Skills 1 & 2 90% or 9/10 correct	Skill 3 Criterion 100% 4 days in a row	Skill 4 Criterion 100% 3 days in a row	Review Skills 3 & 4 90% or 9/10 correct	Skill 5 Criterion 100% 2 days in a row
Tim	9/15 / 9/20	9/20 / 10/1a	10/3 / 10/3	10/6 / 10/15	10/15		
Laura	9/15 / 10/16	10/3 / 10/10	10/10 / 10/12	10/12			
Raymundo	9/15 / 9/20	9/20 / 10/1	10/3 / 10/3	10/6			
Mandy	9/15 / 9/25c	9/25 / 10/1	10/3 / 10/6	10/7 / 10/15	10/15		
Luis	9/15 / 10/1	10/1 / 10/14	10/15 / 10/15				

Code   a. Modified materials   b. Modified method   c. Coordinated teaching

Figure 4.8   Example of Class Record Keeping

Congress has concluded that the achievements of students with disabilities must reflect high expectations in the general education curriculum, and with the reauthorization of IDEA in 2004, the goals of NCLB and IDEA have become more integrated. Conscientious implementation of the IEP should guarantee that all children with disabilities will receive the educational and related services they need and are entitled to.

References

Albrecht, S. F., & Joles, C. (2003). Accountability and access to opportunity: Mutually exclusive tenets under a high-stakes testing mandate. *Preventing School Failure, 47,* 86–91.

Asmus, J. M., Vollmer, T. R., & Borrero, J. C. (2002). Functional behavioral assessment: A school-based model. *Education and Treatment of Children, 25,* 67–90.

Barrie, W., & McDonald, J. (2002). Administrative support for student-led individualized education programs. *Remedial and Special Education, 23,* 116–122.

Blackhurst, A. E. (1997). Perspectives on technology in special education. *Teaching Exceptional Children, 29,* 41–48.

Blackhurst, A. E., & Edyburn, D. C. (2001). A brief history of special education technology. *Special Education Technology Practice, 2,* 21–36.

Clark, S. (2000). The IEP process as a tool for collaboration. *Teaching Exceptional Children, 33,* 56–66.

Culatta, R., Tompkins, J. R., & Werts, M. G. (2002). *Fundamentals of special education: What every teacher needs to know.* Upper Saddle River, NJ: Merrill/Prentice Hall.

Day, J. N., & Huefner, D. S. (2003). Assistive technology: Legal issues for students with disabilities and their schools. *Journal of Special Education Technology, 18,* 23–34.

Downing, J. A. (2004). Related services for students with disabilities: Introduction to the special issue. *Intervention in School and Clinic, 39,* 195–208.

Eccles, J., Barber, B., Jozefowiez, D., Malenchuk, O., & Vida, M. (1999). Self-evaluations of competence, task values, and self-esteem. In N. Johnson, M. Roberts, & J. Worrell (Eds.), *Beyond appearances: A new look at adolescent girls* (pp. 53–84). Washington, DC: APA Press.

Education of All Handicapped Children Act of 1975, 20 U.S.C. 33 § 1400 et seq.

Etzel-Wise, D., & Mears, B. (2004). Adapted physical education and therapeutic recreation in schools. *Intervention in School and Clinic, 39,* 223–232.

Gable, R. A., Butler, C.. J., Walker-Bolton, I., Tonelson, S. W., Quinn, M. M., & Fox, J. J. (2003). Safe and effective schooling for all students: Putting into practice the disciplinary provision of the 1997 IDEA. *Preventing School Failure, 47,* 74–78.

Hacker, D. J., Bol, L., Horgan, D., & Rakow, E. (2000). Test prediction and performance in a classroom context. *Journal of Educational Psychology, 92,* 160–170.

Hagger, R. M. (1999). Funding of assistive technology. Retrieved February 1, 2001, from http://www.nls.org/specedat.htm

Hammer, M. R. (2004). Using the self-advocacy strategy to increase student participation in IEP conferences. *Intervention in School and Clinic, 39,* 295–300.

Hancock, D. R. (2001). Effects of test anxiety and evaluative threat on student achievement and motivation. *The Journal of Educational Research, 94,* 284–290.

Howard, P. J. (2000). *The owner's manual for the brain* (2nd ed.). Marietta, GA: Bard Press.

Ideapractices. (2002). *Questions and answers about federal policies and guidance on including students with disabilities in assessment programs* (family-friendly version). Washington, DC: Council for Exceptional Children and the U.S. Department of Education, Office of Special Education Programs. Retrieved October 12, 2002, from http://www.ideapractices. org/qanda.htm

Individuals with Disabilities Education Act, 20 U.S.C.§ 1401 *et seq.*

Individuals with Disabilities Education Act Regulations, 34, C.F.R. § 300.5 *et seq.*

Jensen, E. (2000). *Learning with the body in mind: The scientific basis for energizers, movement, play, games and physical education.* San Diego, CA: The Brain Store.

King, T.W. (1999). *Assistive technology: Essential human factors.* Boston: Allyn and Bacon.

Lahm, E. A., & Sizemore, L. (2002). Factors that influence assistive technology decision making. *Journal of Special Education Technology, 17,* 15–26.

Landrum, T. J. (2000). Assessment for eligibility: Issues in identifying students with emotional or behavioral disorders. *Assessment for Effective Intervention, 26,* 41–49.

Leiter, R. G. (1979). *Leiter International Performance Scale* (rev. ed.). Wood Dale, IL: Stoetling.

Leyser, Y., & Kirk, R. (2004). Evaluating inclusion: An examination of parent views and factors influencing their perspectives. *International Journal of Disability, Development and Education, 51,* 272–285.

Linn, R. L., & Gronlund, N. E. (2000). *Measurement and assessment in teaching* (8th ed.). Upper Saddle River, NJ: Merrill.

Maag, J. W., & Larsen, P. J. (2004). Training a general education teacher to apply functional assessment. *Education and Treatment of Children, 27,* 26–36.

McGahee, M., Mason, C., Wallace, T., & Jones, B. (2001). *Student-led IEPs: A guide for student involvement.* Arlington, VA: Council for Exceptional Children.

McCoy, K. M. (2000, June). A proactive room for parents in IEPs. *Exceptional Parent Magazine,* 62–68.

McGregor, G., & Pachuski, P. (1996). Assistive technology in schools: Are teachers ready, able and supported? *Journal of Special Education Technology, 13,* 4–15.

Mears, B. (2003). The effects of combined reading and physical education skill instruction on the development of local motor and reading skills. *Missouri Journal of Health, Physical Education, Recreation and Dance, 13,* 1–13.

Neal, J., Bigby, L., & Nicholson, R. (2004). Occupational therapy, physical therapy, and orientation and mobility services in public schools. *Intervention in School and Clinic, 39,* 218–222.

Newcomer, P. L., & Hammill, D. D. (1997). *Test of Language Development–Primary: 3rd edition.* Austin, TX: Pro-Ed.

Newland, E. T. (1971). *Blind Learning Aptitude Test.* Champaign: University of Illinois Press.

No Child Left Behind Act of 2001, 20 U.S.C. 70 § 6301 *et seq.*

Otis, A. S., & Lennon, R. T. (1996). *Otis-Lennon School Ability Test* (7th ed.). San Antonio, TX: Psychological Corp.

Peterson, S. M. P. (2002). Functional behaviour assessment in natural settings. *Education and Treatment of Children, 25,* 1–4.

Sabornie, E. J., & deBettencourt, L. U. (2004). *Teaching students with mild and high incidence disabilities and the secondary level* (2nd ed). Upper Saddle River, NJ: Pearson.

Salvia, J., & Ysseldyke, J. E. (2001). *Assessment* (8th ed.). Boston: Houghton Mifflin.

Sasso, G. M., Conroy, M. A., Stichter, J. P., & Fox, J. J. (2001). Slowing down the bandwagon: The misapplication of functional assessment for students with emotional or behavioral disorders. *Behavioral Disorders, 26,* 282–296.

Sugai, G., Horner, R. H., Dunlap, G., Hieneman, M., Lewis, T. J., Nelson, C. M., Scott, T., Liaupsin, C., Sailor, W., Turnbull, A. P., Turnbull, H. R. III, Wickham, D., Ruef, M., & Wilcox, B. (2000). Applying positive behavior support and functional behavioral assessment in schools. *Journal of Positive Behavioral Interventions, 2,* 131–143.

Thorndike, R. L., Hagen, E. P., & Sattler, J. M. (1986). *Stanford-Binet Intelligence Scale* (4th ed.). Chicago: Riverside Publishing.

Thurlow, M. (2001). A focus on high-stakes assessment: Current practice alerts. *Division of Learning Disabilities and Division of Research of the Council of Exceptional Children, 4,* 1–4.

Torgerson, C. W., Miner, C. A., & Shen, H. (2004). Developing student competence in self-directed IEPs. *Intervention in School and Clinic, 39,* 162–167.

Venn, J. J. (2004). *Assessing students with special needs* (3rd ed.). Upper Saddle River, NJ: Pearson Education.

Wechsler, D. (1991). *The Wechsler Intelligence Scale for Children—Revised.* New York: Psychological Group.

Wehmeyer, M. L., Martin, J. E., & Sands, D. J. (1998). Self-determination for children and youth with developmental disabilities. In A. Hjilton & Ringlaben (Eds.), *Best and promising practices in developmental disabilities* (pp. 191–203). Austin, TX: Pro-Ed.

Yell, M. (1998). *The law and special education.* Upper Saddle River, NJ: Merrill/Prentice Hall.

Yell, M., & Shriner, J. (1997). The IDEA amendments of 1997: Implications for special and general education teachers and administrators. *Focus on Exceptional Children, 30,* 1–30.

Yell, M. (2004). Mitchell Yell: IDEA and related services. In T. L. Earles-Vollrath (interviewer), An interview with … *Intervention in School and Clinic, 39,* 236–239.

Informal
Assessment

Kathleen McCoy and J'Anne Ellsworth

KEY TERMS

- anecdotal record
- assessment
- authentic assessment
- classroom-based measures
- critical reflection
- event sampling
- formative assessment
- global tests
- informal assessment
- informal tests
- normative or standardized testing
- PEPSI model
- performance measures
- portfolio assessment
- student-centered portfolio assessment
- teacher-centered portfolio assessment
- testing
- time sampling
- work product assessment

Ms. Debra Tanori, a fifth grade teacher, sits at her desk with a pensive look. Her attention is directed to the latest scores of her class on the state recognized instrument used to determine annual academic performance ratings. Content of the test instrument has been coded to the state standards. Ms. Tanori taught to the standards and even supplemented with additional complementary information. Ms. Tanori is both pleased and perplexed at the ranking of her students. Most of her students have placed at or above expected standards, yet a small number fell below expected standards. She thought everyone was making excellent progress, but the scores say otherwise. Ms. Tanori pauses for a few minutes to recall how she had determined that progress was satisfactory. Hmmm…maybe the weekly quizzes and end of unit project evaluations were not specific enough. Were her evaluations able to identify which students were not only learning the new information, but also remembering this knowledge over time? What would happen if the evaluation was more frequent and also included information previously learned? Ms. Tanori knew she would not create addition formal evaluations, but instead would rely on gathering information from daily classwork. But would she have the time and energy to collect more information on all the students? No, she thought with a resounding mental hand slap, but did she need to keep such detailed data on all her students for every behavior? No, of course not, she thought as her mood lightened. For the majority of her students, her current system worked quite well. Ms. Tanori realized that only a small group of students would need the intense kind of classroom evaluation to ensure that progress was continuous and learning maintained. With the thought of even more learning accompanying higher scores dancing in her head, Ms. Tanori began the task of developing some simple additional record keeping sheets to be used only with those children who seemed to be at the low end of performance in her class. Bring on the state evaluation tool, thought Ms. Tanori, and I'll show you some children whose performance will glow like a guiding light reflecting understanding of classroom curriculum.

Analysis of a student's daily performance is the best source of information for identifying the content each student needs to profit socially and academically in school. Linking evaluation of the student's performance with various teaching strategies can provide the evidence needed to determine the effectiveness of instruction in inclusion settings.

The purpose of this chapter is to analyze the meaning of informal assessment and to illustrate how such assessments guide teachers to provide the most appropriate education for children with special needs in inclusion settings. It is important to demystify informal assessment. Informal assessment occurs in every interaction in subtle ways, most often unconsciously. Some informal tests are more formalized, more intentional, and very specific.

Instructional materials and methods found in books on teaching the basic skills in reading, writing, and arithmetic, as well as content areas like social studies and science, stretch out like cyberspace highway maps. Which road should a teacher take? Can all of us fit into one mode of transportation and successfully arrive at the same destination? Do all of us need to be in the same educational place at the same time?

When taking a road trip, all along the journey we see and evaluate the countryside, the rest stops, highway markers, scenery, other cars, and people. Based on our focus, we pay closer attention to some things and give little note to others. Informal assessment is like that. Inclusion teachers need the skills to monitor, to see events in passing, and to be able to stop and scrutinize a situation or a youngster very closely.

Inclusion teachers need to move from a wide-angle view of all students in the United States to a microscopic view of each individual child in their classroom. Formal or normative tests (i.e. those based on the bell curve) give an overview—that full U.S. roadmap—and show how one state fits into the picture. Informal testing provides the detailed directions to reach the individual student.

All students have overlapping as well as unique strengths and needs—children classified as eligible for special education included. 100 students can be at 100 different places in learning. We place these students into clusters and groups: students who are gifted, students who are average in height, and so forth. We cluster or classify groups for ease of discussion and measurement.

The emphasis in normative testing is on group description. Group data are only meaningful as a starting or screening point for developing instruction. They give a general idea about skill strengths compared to the population of students who took the formal measure. Formal testing informs us about groups, about programs, about trends. When it is important to understand a classroom or a specific child, we turn to informal assessment. So when designing programs of instruction (i.e., an IEP), we want to go back into those clusters and get a much closer look at the scores of a particular student. The score taken from a normative measure gives us a starting point for more specific evaluation. In other words, formal testing gives us a reference point.

Personal decisions about instruction in the general education classroom and the learning objectives for a specific student come through informal assessment. The best source of evaluation always involves "asking" the student through informal assessment. Informal assessment asks the student to provide information for educational and social learning in a variety of ways. Informal assessment is colored by teacher and student experiences, emotions, momentary needs, level of fatigue, and a combination of current personal needs.

As an example, Mark acts up as soon as his teacher asks his students to get out reading material. Mr. Randal, the teacher, wonders if Mark cannot settle down because reading is held after recess. He tries several interventions with limited success. Mr. Randal watches the young man and finally develops a question: Is it possible that Mark is experiencing difficulty in reading?

The student records do not specify that Mark has difficulty reading, but his standardized scores are quite low. Standardized scores are global and give general information, so Mark's teacher feels it is important to do some individual observing and screening to determine reading and comprehension level. Mr. Randal begins with a reading interest inventory, asking Mark if he likes to read, what books he reads, and how often he chooses to read without a prompt. The responses to the reading inventory are specific, individual-driven information.

The global tests provide general information about performance. For example, they indicate information about average intelligence, note a short attention span, raise questions about short-term memory, and identify math and reading scores that are at least three levels lower than expected. Thus, global information begins to paint a picture of a child's performance, but only in large, sweeping terms.

The global information provided by many normative tests is only one piece of the educational picture. Informal assessment completes the picture. Formal tests are given only once or twice during the academic year. Informal tests, on the other hand, are teacher-made assessments and may occur any time during the day, week, month, and school year, as deemed appropriate and feasible.

Informal assessments may include, but are not limited to, paper-and-pencil tests, observation of work products under various situations, and insights gathered through dialogues between student and teacher. Informal assessment requires getting to know the youngster, building rapport, observing, gathering work samples, and collecting anecdotal behaviors to accumulate meaningful data for making instructional decisions.

Most often, informal assessment means giving the student specific assignments and watching his or her response and rate of success. Facts gathered from such information lead to hunches. That is, the teacher looks at all the accumulated facts and begins to develop a picture of how instruction is working for a specific student.

Informal assessments help the teacher work objectively at the same time that instruction and information gathering are personalized. Those two pieces, the objectivity of looking at what the student can do and is doing mixed with the subjectivity of how the student is acting and seems to be feeling, provide a wide array of information that allows the teacher to be more accurate in meeting student needs and developing instructional programs. Some of the information will be discrete, or countable, but other sources of information will be impressions, fuzzy places where two facts don't quite add up to the scores of the student's performance.

Ms. Patrick, for example, notices that Van does not always follow instructions. She watches Van and notices that he likes to be cooperative and spends a lot of time watching her and paying close attention to instruction. What could be going on with Van? As Ms. Patrick observes more closely, she begins to wonder if Van might have a hearing loss and talks to the speech–language pathologist at the school. The specialist tells Ms. Patrick that Van has a history of inner-ear infections that explain the times when he does not seem to hear sounds and words. Ms. Patrick's impressions were key in helping to provide accommodations for Van.

Informal assessment occurs daily and requires monitoring and adjusting. Mr. Lindam is working in the junior high for the first time. Before Jake comes to class, the best information Mr. Lindam has on him is that he is a 13-year-old male with difficulty reading. Once Jake is in the class, however, informal assessment— day-to-day involvement, talking with the student and trying different ways of introducing information and learning—provides a rich sense of who Jake is and what he can learn. Such informal assessment also helps Mr. Lindam become excited about the challenge of getting Jake more involved in learning.

Mr. Lindam starts a unit on transportation and finds that Jake is deeply involved in motocross. He gives him the option of focusing his reading on this favorite topic. Mr. Lindam asks students to read an article on the Internet. Jake surfs the Net instead. Mr. Lindam realizes that Jake is having difficulty reading the screen, so he gives him a processing program that reads the screen for him. Mr. Lindam also notices that Jake has difficulty with spelling and grammar, so he provides a word program with a spell-checker and grammar-checker.

As Jake begins to work independently and achieves some success, both Mr. Lindam and Jake experience a sense of accomplishment. Mr. Lindam's high expectations and willingness to monitor Jake's progress, adjusting tasks and tools as needed, meant formal and informal assessment made a difference for Jake.

Assessing Student Progress

Inclusion teachers use many methods to find out what students are doing in the classroom. *Testing* and *assessment* are two of the terms that are useful when talking about evaluation. Testing determines student ability to complete certain tasks or demonstrate mastery of skills or content knowledge (Overton, 2005). Assessment is the collection of information to identify what does and does not work so teachers can make effective educational decisions (Salvia & Ysseldyke, 2001). Assessment happens every day, all day long. An inclusion teacher watches students as they work on assignments. The teacher can see levels of concentration, times work stops, the ease of work, or the errors occurring as students complete their material.

Testing is usually more formal than day-to-day informal assessment. On a regular basis, the inclusion teacher probes for students' level of knowledge to be certain an acceptable level of competence is reached. Testing is often established as part of the process of teaching. Goals are set, and objectives are established. The objectives list times and ways to establish successful completion before going on to new objectives. Checking for success becomes equated with testing.

A well-written formalized objective includes how well the concepts will be learned and evaluated. This is a typical pattern for a goal and objective. The goal for Ms. Patrick, for example, is to teach the concepts in using fractions. When learning fractions, it is important to be able to identify proper fractions from improper fractions. The objective might be: "Given a quiz with ten fractions,

Lucy will be able to successfully identify all improper fractions." In this quiz, the teacher determines Lucy's ability to distinguish fractions.

Goal: Teach the concepts in using fractions
Objective: When given a quiz with 10 fractions, students will be able to successfully identify all improper fractions
Test: Quiz with 10 fractions, some improper, some proper

What if the teacher wants to find out how a student is doing before the quiz on Friday? This is a great time for informal assessment. One way to do that is to look at how students are working. Ms. Patrick can observe students who are off task or not enthusiastic about the assignment. These are observations or impressions suggesting that the task and student ability may not match. However, the behavior can also mean that the student does not have a pencil, that the work is a repeat of ideas the student already comprehends or that the student has a headache.

Ms. Patrick can walk to Brock and ask him to share his reasoning process. Student self-talk can tell the teacher a lot about how a student is thinking about the math problem and working for a solution. This kind of information is easy to gather as teachers walk around the classroom, asking students to share their ideas and thoughts. It is also a *formative* type of assessment. Such information helps inclusion teachers formulate teaching expertise for individual students.

Informal assessment includes the practice of walking around during seatwork. Mr. Lindam can spot-check daily work as it is occurring. If Jake is getting something wrong, more of the same work is not likely to meet his instructional needs. The informal assessment pinpoints the glitch in how Jake is using the information or the focusing process. By identifying the misconception, the teacher can adjust the assignment or find a different way to teach the missing concept and send Jake forward, succeeding at the task.

Informal Assessment

So what is informal assessment? Why do teachers do it? Informal assessment is monitoring classwork in progress. It can be a checklist, it may include the use of a rubric to articulate and catch data, or it may be as simple as watching who is on task at 5-minute intervals. This "with-it-ness" is an integral part of successful instruction. That makes it an essential part of teacher program evaluation (i.e., checking to see that concepts are being learned).

Informal assessment can be a systematic gathering of data or sporadic and frequent probes. Informal assessment may include error analysis, checklists, samples of work, or student self-report. Effective teachers use continuous assessment of every sort while teaching (Arends, 2004; Messick, 1984).

Informal assessment is crucial to matching student needs with content. When it is integrated into the flow of the instructional work, informal assessment can accomplish the following:

- *Identify aspects of a lesson that need to be retaught.* Yesterday Ms. Jones introduced writing dialogue to her class. She planned to have students write dialogue today. She explained the project of using two characters to talk to one another. In her example, she used Miss Kitty and Mr. Mouse. Then she divided the students into groups and gave them time to work on dialogues. Immediately, the noise level escalated. Frustrated, Ms. Jones started to call the class back to attention, but, instead, she decided to move around the room and find out what the chatter was about. By the third group, she knew that the students did not understand dialogue yet.

She called the class together and let them make finger puppets. Then, using the puppets, she helped students take turns coming up with things for the puppets to say while another partner recorded the words. In this case, informal assessment helped Ms. Jones recognize what was not working in her lesson strategies. Once she taught the missing pieces, the lesson was a great success.

- *Provide information about how fast to move forward.* Mr. Lantz started a unit on classifying animals. He had lesson plans laid out for three weeks of instruction. After giving his introduction, he asked the students to help him compare and contrast mammals and birds. The whole class enthusiastically joined in, and it was clear these fourth-graders knew how to use a Venn diagram and had studied animal classification before. In one session, nearly half the material had been presented with great success. Mr. Lantz realized he would need to add depth and speed to his plans.

- *Direct teachers to what kinds of added instruction might be necessary for students to succeed.* Mr. Lawrence was introducing long division to his class. He made the presentation, then began walking through the room as students tried the sample problems. They were not so simple for some youngsters. He realized quickly that about a third of his class did not know multiplication facts well enough to work effectively with even the simplest division problems. Before he could go into more complex steps in division, he would have to review subtraction and multiplication.

Informal assessment is also a great way to individualize instruction. The time spent with students helps the teacher meet individual needs and helps the class move forward with content. Informal assessment is an essential part of successful inclusion in the classroom (Wood, 2005).

Ms. Hayworth, for example, decided to introduce keyboard skills to her class. As she planned the unit, she thought about the developmental strengths and needs of her 8-year-olds. She knew that several students showed difficulty with small-muscle tasks. It would be helpful for them to have practice activities that strengthened hand–eye coordination. She smiled as she thought about Sophie. Her ability to compose stories had improved so much this year that her fingers could not keep pace with her thoughts. Keyboarding could help Sophie reduce the stress of using her awkward pencil grip and focus more on keeping her ideas flowing. Max and Jake would only try this if she could find an engaging game. She would need at least three different kinds of typing programs for the class.

In this example, informal assessment is reflective and is part of planning the lesson. It is important to gather these information bits so lessons can be successful from the beginning. Some might argue that the Internet is full of good lesson plans, so all a teacher needs to do is copy them and put them in place.

Ms. Hayworth knows better than to do that. She will have great success with her lesson in keyboarding because she matches the material she wants to teach with the abilities of her students. She realizes the great strength that comes from informal assessment, and she uses it to plan and implement her lessons and to evaluate her performance as a teacher and the learning in her classroom.

Informal assessment meets the following teaching objectives:

- Illuminates connection points so the teacher can monitor learning and adjust instruction to match student readiness to learn
- Finds or develop successful strategies for teaching each youth
- Serves the whole child
- Meets ethical obligations to the profession
- Individualizes student programs of study
- Fulfills the law

Informal assessment is a student's and a teacher's best academic friend.

Standardized Testing

Normative or standardized testing is also crucial. It provides the standard for comparing students. Most states mandate that students be tested and that scores be provided to parents, the state, and the federal government. These mandates form a significant part of Goals 2000 and the No Child Left Behind (NCLB) legislation and serve to provide general information about how a specific student compares with other students. But it is not the ultimate purpose of this testing. The testing provides summative information about school programs. It alerts districts, states, and the federal education department about general trends and weaknesses in the way we educate youth. It also provides a database for making informed guesses about poverty, levels of education, at-risk factors, and the relationships between funding and privatization of education, as well as new reading, writing, and math standards and processes.

Some of these uses are appropriate. When the scores are used in broad ways and give insights into programs, promising practices, and correlations between scoring success and the indicators being monitored the use is important and valuable.

Teachers need to understand this. Tests do not need to be demonized or testing practices halted. The cost of developing standardized tests is substantial. Representative samples of many populations of students, including varied demographic groups and special groups of students, must participate in the test to establish accurate norms for comparison. To get age or grade norms, thousands of youngsters must be tested with rigorous care, the scores compiled, and the information evaluated. This entire process must be completed before the test can be used correctly to give an accurate assessment score.

In summary, normed or standardized tests can help educators and parents make informed decisions about how a school is performing, how much children are learning, and how well a community is educating its children. They provide important indicators of how one student is doing when compared to peers who took the same test under similar conditions. However, the scores and indicators must be used properly, applied for the appropriate purposes, and explained thoroughly to parents.

Several words about testing help clarify what tests tell us.

Reliability	Validity	Standardized
Criterion-referenced test	Benchmark	National norms
Standard scores	IQ test	Achievement test
NCE – National curve equivalent	Percentiles	

The meaning of each of these terms will be presented in context rather than as a specific definition.

Classroom Standards

Each standardized test is developed to measure specific content or behaviors. If it is a good test, it is constructed so it does a good job of measuring. This is also true of informal evaluation. A good math test must do a good job of measuring a student's ability to do math. If it does, we say it is a *valid* test.

School grades stand for how much students have learned and how well they have met the teacher's expectations. Some grades represent what they know in a fair way, and some do not. Some teachers are good at grading and measuring progress. Other teachers are not very good at setting up a grading system, so the grades may not tell students, parents, or teachers very much. Here is an example.

Lucy's music teacher gives everyone an **S** or a **U**. Everyone gets an **S** unless the teacher becomes distressed with behavior problems. An **S** in music means Lucy is behaving. It does not mean that she can sing or that she likes music. Bernard's teacher appreciates music and is clear about what he wants students to gain in his class. This teacher also gives an **S** for satisfactory and **U** for unsatisfactory. But for this teacher, music represents a lot of skills and information. To get an **S**, Bernard must: (a) attend class, (b) sing during group chorus, (c) turn in a paper on a composer, and (d) successfully complete 10 lessons on music theory.

This provides a good example of grading. We are measuring and reporting student progress. Lucy and Bernard both get an S in music. It is the same mark or grade, but it does not mean the same thing.

	Lucy	Bernard
Grade	S	S
Grade meaning	I am good during music.	I attend class regularly.
		I sing in chorus.
		I wrote a paper.
		I learned music theory.

A grade or a score most often reflects what a teacher decides to measure or an entity decides to report. It is crucial to be certain that the test is valid and that the use of the scores is also valid. When a teacher gets a report, it is vital to determine its value, usefulness, and ability to measure what it reports.

Grades or normative data are often idealized. Teachers, parents, and children sometimes decide they mean something and then act as though they measure what they want them to measure. It does not make it true, but it gives people a sense of reassurance. Some of the debate about national tests involves this unwarranted idealization. Nevertheless, standardized tests are useful when utilized and interpreted correctly.

Anecdotal Records

An *anecdotal record* is "a written record kept in a positive tone of a child's progress based on milestones particular to that child's social, emotional, physical, aesthetic, and cognitive development," notes the American Association of School Administrators (1992, p. 21). The teacher observes and records a student's behaviors and actions as they occur. An anecdotal record is usually written as soon as possible after witnessing or hearing about an incident so that all important details can be included.

The notes are informal and based on vignettes of specific occurrences or a checklist with space for writing comments. An anecdotal record most often consists of the following (see Figure 5.1):

- A string of single anecdotes, each limited to a single incident
- A description of the situation in which the incident occurs so that the meaning of the behavior can be understood
- Factual, noninferential descriptions of the observed or reported incidents
- A separate section for describing one's interpretation of or feelings about the anecdote

Parent Conferences

Parents are a great source of information for getting to know a child. Many educators and administrators believe that an adversarial relationship exists between parents and education. A few parents are antagonistic toward their children's schools, but most are motivated by a wish to see their child succeed and a desire

```
DATE:


PLACE:


TIME:


NAME OF OBSERVER:


DESCRIPTION OF THE INCIDENT:


INTERPRETATION:
```

Figure 5.1   Sample Anecdotal Record Form

to look competent and caring. Here are some tips for getting the most out of a discussion with parents:

- Establish a friendly, open rapport
- Project respect and honor for the parent
- Ask good questions
- Listen carefully while parents talk
- Listen for patterns of thought
- Probe the parent for an explanation of what the child is doing
- Find the real story
- Ask for reflection (e.g., What do you make of that?)
- Give parents a chance to share how they view the child
- Move toward long-term goals or dreams for the child

Student Conferences

At the beginning of the conference, it is vital to assess the student's developmental level and to frame the interview so that age-appropriate interview techniques are used. Teachers should not confuse chronological age with normal developmental stages. A child's developmental age may not match her chronological age.

Integrate knowledge of child development with the child's sense of time, temperament, and language abilities. Some of this information may be obtained through interviews with the parents, questionnaires completed by the parents, consultations with previous teachers, or personal observations.

What the child says and does can best be interpreted by understanding the child's developing cognitive abilities and emotional state of mind. When formulating questions to ask a youngster, it is important that the questions be appropriate for his or her developmental level.

The teacher-led questioning may develop into a dialogue and then a true conference if deep listening occurs on the part of the teacher. It is vital to be ready to "hear" what the child is saying and to share control of the discussion as the student warms up and the rapport increases.

Steps in Good Conferencing

1. Begin the conference by establishing rapport and giving students time to talk about their attitudes toward school or their feelings about their personal level of competence. Teachers should not correct shared feelings; it is like telling a person he or she is wrong about a choice of a favorite color or food.
2. Give the student a forum for sharing current successes—"strut their stuff" time.
3. Ask the student to provide the next challenge. If the student is uncertain about the next step, offer a problem that dovetails with the current success and a challenging new skill.
4. Allow the student to attempt to solve the new challenge using personal skills, and make note of the strategies used and any verbalization of the issues involved in solving the challenge.
5. Jointly set a goal that moves the student into new challenges, and offer guidance on strategies to be employed in learning new skills.
6. Jointly develop an assessment plan.

As possible, allow students to work together in pairs to conference and build new goals, and, eventually, provide a weekly time for these strategy sessions to take place. Once a week, briefly review student progress; reviews can be done in about 60 seconds while students are setting goals or working independently.

Observation as an Informal Assessment Skill

Observations of children are tools for adjusting the curriculum and planning learning opportunities to meet children's individual needs. Observations also help teachers understand the different levels of mastery: what the student *has learned,* is *ready now* to learn, will be *ready soon* to learn, and will be *ready later* to learn. This information becomes the child's individual learning path, or education plan.

It is vital to observe and record students on a continuous basis. Observing is natural and enjoyable. Observation is also the key for deciding which learning activities will most benefit children. Observation of children can occur at any time and in any place. Children can be observed throughout the day as a natural part of what a teacher does. Children are always doing and learning.

Know what to look for: A teacher should have a good sense of the progression of capabilities for each area of development to be observed. When observers know what comes before and what comes next in development, they have an accurate focus.

Children often display capabilities in one setting that may not be readily observed in another. For example, a child may be highly verbal at home and talk very little at school. Insights provided by parents and other teachers and gained during library time, lunch, and recess can assist in adjusting curriculum to more closely meet the needs of individual students.

Teachers can take advantage of moments to observe by having a clear focus. Having a clear focus includes knowing what capabilities need to be observed, which children will be observed, and where observation will occur. Good questions to help with focus include: "What do I want to observe?" "Which children will I be observing?" "Where will I observe?" "What strategy or method will I use to remember what I observed?"

To get the most out of observation, define the purposes served by observations. Purposes may be to develop a weekly activity plan, determine how to individualize, or to revise an activity. Things to consider include, "What do I hope to learn from my observations?" and "How will I use the information I have learned?"

Use narratives or anecdotal notes to help describe what children do and how they do it. These methods are also very useful for recording concerns, goals, plans, and successes. When using narratives/anecdotes, remember to be accurate and objective.

As the student moves about in the learning community, use time and event sampling. There are occasions when knowledge of the frequency of a behavior is important (e.g., how often the same child is on task, chatting, or sharing). Such information can be useful for planning interventions to increase or decrease particular behaviors.

Use *time sampling* to record behavior over a short period of time.

- Decide which behaviors to observe.
- Decide how often to record the behavior, and stick with the time period. It may be necessary to get a substitute for a day to do this well.
- Observe and record the behaviors using tally marks.

Use *event sampling* to record social interactions.

- Decide which interactions to observe.
- When the event occurs, describe it.
- Include what is occurring, what happened before, and what happened after.
- Record how long the event lasted and anything that was said.

Advice from professionals:

- Increase your patience in order to slow down and watch.
- Pay close attention to your physical surroundings: who, what, when, where, and how.
- Be aware of people's reactions, emotions, and motivations.
- Ask questions that can be answered through observing.
- Be yourself.
- Observe with an optimistic curiosity.
- Be ethical.

Reflection

The ability to reflect critically about experience and observations is an acquired set of skills. Reflection involves integrating knowledge gained from experience with knowledge gained by watching. Critical reflection includes identifying the assumptions governing others' actions, questioning the meaning of such assumptions, and developing a series of ideas about what is part of the underlying reason for the actions. Part of the critical reflective process is to challenge the first and easiest idea that comes to mind and to look empathically at what needs a child may be working to meet.

As Maslow (1968) noted, student actions are motivated by needs and drives, culturally learned behaviors, and learned or modeled actions. Through the process of critical reflection, teachers come to interpret and create understanding of actions from observing and openly seeking to understand and empathize. Critical reflection blends learning through experience with theoretical and technical learning to form new knowledge constructions and new behaviors or insights.

Understanding Students

Informal assessment is based on a philosophy. This next section provides an opportunity to think about the strengths of informal assessment when the focus of the classroom includes student interests and needs. Students are people first, young and inexperienced at learning in a school setting. People begin to learn, to think, to make connections, and to change their actions to get their needs met in their earliest moments. People also love to learn. By the time a child comes to school, he or she has learned to walk, to talk, to control body functions, and to perform as a human being.

Children are already well-versed in learning when they enter school. It is useful to think of school as a place for them to formalize learning. At the same time, the child has a need to be understood, feel wanted, and experience a sense of safety. When that is ignored, children can be resilient and find a way to learn, but it is not the optimal process for achieving the highest level of education.

Students also have unique ways of learning and remembering information. The idea of an average youngster is a construction. No one wants to be average or feel unimportant all day every day. Many practices in schools assume that mass instruction is an effective and efficient way to pass on information, based on the idea of an average youngster. Because of class size and the high number of students to each teacher, the practice is widespread.

Still, to be fully successful, teachers and students must work together to recognize what is needed for each student to be successful at learning.

Beginning teachers should remember the following:

1. Most philosophies and the newest gene studies suggest that students have abilities, strengths, and needs that are hard-wired.
2. All students have a variety of ways to learn and acquire information.
3. All students have some ways of learning that are not effective for them. Lecture, presentations, and writing on the board while students take notes are some of the most frequently used and least effective learning techniques for youngsters.
4. All students already have internal dialogues, worldviews, and self-views that affect how they learn and what they learn.
5. IDEA (2005) identifies a large number of specific characteristics that can put a child's learning at risk if he or she is not provided extra services. Schools have a mandate to determine student need and provide necessary extra services.
6. Students may need help adapting their abilities to the expectations of the educational system.
7. All students have special needs. It is important to remember that every student benefits from an educational process that helps students make adaptations in areas where they have the least potential and expertise.
8. Students are ready to learn concepts at different times. Being 6 or 8 years old does not signal readiness to learn to read or write. Instead, it is the time when most teachers provide strong instruction and have high expectations for success. Many of those expectations are underscored by formal testing.
9. Students become ready to learn by reaching certain developmental milestones and through appropriate, well-timed introduction of concepts.

In summary, assessment is a critical piece of successful teaching. Wise utilization of results means finding out how a youngster learns and then doing what it takes for that youth to learn. Assessment means ongoing monitoring for every student in every class all day, every day of the school year. Informal assessment is hard work and takes energy and determination. Informal assessment requires insight, dedication, and a desire to know what the student knows, even when it means redesigning the teacher's work with the child.

Connections Between Learning and Teaching

Students have many ways of learning. Common sense and research tell us that we do not all learn in the same way, find interest in the same things, or approach teaching in the same way.

At present, our system of education sends out two conflicting messages:

- The individual really matters.
  and
- We teach subjects, not students.

These two incongruities are heightened with standardized testing. By the time a student gets into high school, the gap between what an individual student is able to learn and what that student had better be learning can be quite a chasm. The situation is made more difficult by pressures to use one set of scores to decide who is teaching and learning and the pressure for everyone to have a diploma to be considered for employment. For a student who does not learn in the typical way, trying to access knowledge can feel like being a piece of chum tossed to a pack of hungry sharks.

Since the educational climate is not likely to change, we need to be the professionals who find a way to serve our students. We cannot coax students to jump off the cliff without giving them the skills to succeed. At the same time, we cannot leave them teetering on the edge, unable to dive in and find success. Every student is precious, so it makes no sense to take a "survival of the fittest" stance. The cost of failure is high—high for the student, the family, the community, and our own sense of hopelessness and inadequacy.

So what can we do?

When inclusion teachers find something a student cannot do, they must regard it as a challenge rather than a disability. They must support students while preparing them. If a student has difficulty learning to read, educators teach coping, shortcuts, and memory tricks, and find pleasant ways to maintain interest while helping the student move through the steps that will make meaning of the symbols. They devise and instruct students in using available support systems and search for advances in assistive technology that help the student feel successful.

It may take several months of patience, tiny steps forward, careful nurturing, and support. After all, literacy skills are very complex. Some children intuitively combine those steps and are able to read or perform writing processes with little support. Teachers' real value lies in their ability to make meaningful progress with those who are not intuitive learners, who need just the right tiny step at just the right moment, repeated until the student is ready for the next "just right" step.

If a student is not able to learn math, inclusion teachers must utilize calculators, computers, peers, manipulatives, and daily tasks that include logic, patterns, and numeration until the child gains a sense of comfort. They then combine those comfortable operations with the conceptual framework that allows the student to have that flash of insight.

Short attention span? Inclusion teachers must help the student find ways to focus more efficiently. Watch for the time in the day when the child is most able to focus and then use that time to lengthen attention from a couple of minutes to

3. Then teach the youngster to focus for those 3 minutes, repeated by off-task for 3 minutes, and then 3 minutes of sustained attention again. Suddenly, instead of a child with a 2-minute focus, there is a youngster who can intentionally recognize and deal with loss of focus. As the child strings 3-minute segments together, a student with very little focus becomes a student who is focused half the time. That is a meaningful change that will support learning.

If a student has difficulty learning as most teachers teach, if entrance exams will be failed and doors closed because the student does not know how to learn, educators must teach the student how to find and use power tools. That is the ultimate message of NCLB or P.L. 107-110. Expedite learning for students who have previously been thwarted, thus utilizing the true gift of teaching.

Informal testing and screening provide essential information to the teacher. The skills emerge with time and attention to students. The ability to care about, to notice, and to ask questions about students and why they are learning or not learning opens the way for successful informal assessment.

There are many fine assessments available as well. They are accessible on the Internet and in methods texts, and often can be purchased with accompanying software to make it easier to score and record findings.

It takes time to acquire proficiency in screening, and it can take a year or two for a new teacher to become organized enough to consistently and methodically make use of informal assessment. It is a skill that emerges and strengthens over time. It is invaluable because it supports and builds relationship between teachers and students. It focuses the attention on student success and progress. It also informs the teacher of special ways to help students find success. Screening and informal assessment are crucial to successful teaching.

Forms of Informal Assessment

Informal assessment takes many forms. For some authors (Salvia & Ysseldyke, 2007) informal assessment closely resembles qualitative and mastery-based evaluations of student work. An example of this is the portfolio. Work product assessment can include samples of student assignments, skill tests, projects, and original artwork. A number of recent assessment alternatives supplement objective scores with more personalized assessments. These include Meyer's Authentic Assessment (1992), Lidz's Dynamic Assessment (1991), judgment-based assessment (Bagnato & Neisworth, 1990), and curriculum-based assessment (Salvia & Hughes, 1990). Informal assessment can be used to evaluate student progress and capture evidence with respect to student quality of work.

Informal assessment can also provide evidence that helps teachers get to know the student and how learning takes place. Informal assessment can help a teacher see learning stress points, recognize motivational and behavioral patterns, and get a sense of student ability level. Informal assessment can be as simple as watching the way a student turns on a computer and as complex as systematically observing a youngster.

Informal assessment is ideal for picking up social cues and socialization patterns. Informal assessment is a critical part of building relationships with youngsters. Watching youngsters play and noting interaction patterns can be an effective tool for recognizing friction points and boundary issues that get in the way of appropriate classroom actions. The dedicated teacher makes good use of careful, thoughtful, well-developed assessment and intelligent reflection. The process of informal assessment can also help the teacher and student build and strengthen mutual regard as it informs both of necessary steps to enhance learning.

Developing the Whole Student

Part of the special education mandate asks teachers to understand what normal child development looks like so they can accurately recognize developmental delays. Understanding normal development is a positive and proactive way to assess youngsters, see strengths and patterns, and support growth sequentially. It is surprising how much of a child's behavior can be understood by learning about the different ages and stages of normal development. For ease of presentation and to provide a mnemonic for sorting through and accommodating the vast wealth of developmental concepts, the material has evolved into a *PEPSI* model (see Table 5.1). The letters stand for *physical, emotional, philosophical, social* and *intellectual* development.

PEPSI refers to the five areas of progressive and continuous changes in the human essence that make up a developmental perspective of growth. These five distinct areas of development form a "hands-on" device for understanding youth and recognizing patterns that contribute to actions and behavior. They provide a frame of reference for looking at an individual and a sense of continuity about normal and predictable changes in children over time.

Table 5.1   PEPSI: A mnemonic for developmental concepts

Area of Development	Authority Cited
P - Physical	Gessell, Ilg, Ames
E - Emotional	Erik Erikson, ego psychology
P - Philosophical or moral	Kohlberg, Piaget
S - Social	Kagan, Langer, Moss, Mussen, social psychology
I - Intellectual or cognitive	Piaget, Inhelder, Vygotsky

The following example shows the value of informal assessment of a youth's developmental stages.

The teacher, Mr. Clark, talks with Mr. and Mrs. Albin, who have come in to ask for help with their 13-year-old son, Jason. The parents are concerned about a number of changes in their son's behavior patterns that seem to have started "overnight." They feel that Jason is not doing well in school and that he overreacts to almost every situation. They have talked with a neighbor, who suggested that they follow up on these worries by seeking help from a child therapist. The parents were upset at this suggestion and decided to find out how the teacher perceives Jason.

Mr. Clark talks with the parents about his perception of the lies, whining, lethargy, and obstinacy. The teacher points out that the behaviors are not that uncommon among the rest of the middle school students. Mr. Clark tells Mr. and Mrs. Albin that Jason has a very special gift in cartooning, but his behaviors are not always accepted by agemates in his class. The parents have begun to worry about drugs and suicide. They express a belief that their son fits the classic symptom list flashed on television, and they want to be reassured that their son's music listening habits are not indicative of such problems.

They add that their son has become moody and taciturn and seems to be having bad dreams at night. They inquire about occurrences at school that might be causing these things. Mr. Clark begins to see that many of these concerns fit the typical developmental profile for early adolescents. The parents then explain the event that precipitated the search for answers about Jason. It occurred a week earlier, when he burst out that he hated their rules, hated being told what to do, and thought he must be adopted because the whole family was mean to him. He threatened to run away from home.

The teacher's first step is to seek additional information from the parents. During the interview, which could be conducted with or without Jason, Mr. Clark will get a list of the concerns and also ask for instances of positive behavior. He will work to get a sense of how radical the differences are between the acceptable earlier behaviors and the current concerns. It is important to rule out illnesses or any catastrophic changes in the family. It is surprising how often a parent sees an event as unimportant, while a child finds it devastating.

In such a situation, it may be helpful to

- ask for a family history,
- inquire if either parent feels that the student is behaving as he or she did as an early adolescent,
- determine if some of the frustration is being fueled by significant others (in this case other teachers in the middle school) voicing new disapproval of the teen, and
- talk with the youngster and discuss pertinent issues.

As a next step, the teacher compares the list of behaviors to the age charts and the stage charts for normal development. It is usually easiest to lay out the charts for the student's chronological age and the levels on either side. Thus, initially, Mr. Clark pulls out the charts (three of them in this example) for ages 12, early adolescence, and late adolescence. As comparisons are made, it becomes clear that many areas are uncertain or unknown.

It is impossible in an interview and an informal observation session to gather enough information to make a definite decision. Teachers do not conduct a PEPSI to form a diagnosis or label. There may be an opportunity to call the parents and discuss some of the questions that arise. The same questions might also be broached with a previous teacher.

This is an initial screening. It is a time to look for impressions, establish a starting point, and become familiar with a youngster rather than looking for a label or diagnosis.

Because Mr. Clark is a caring professional, he will assist the parents in their quest for answers. As the teacher of 90 students, Mr. Clark could not do this extensive work-up on every child in the middle school. However, by giving the parents support and getting to know Jason better, he is developing trust and a relationship. Mr. Clark will continue to learn about each student in the class over time. Although he will not do a PEPSI for each youth, he will work toward accomplishing a PEPSI on students who seem to be having difficulty.

As Mr. Clark gathers data about Jason, he gets a sense that many of the concerns can be addressed by assisting the parents in recognizing a positive developmental occurrence. As Brazelton (1983) noted, typically a disorganization or disequilibrium occurs in children just as they begin to take on a new level of behaviors.

This often confuses and upsets adults. After several months of coping with behavior sets, the parents or teacher feels the problems are stabilized. They know what to expect, and the child has become equilibrated with the last set of new behaviors. As a new growth spurt begins, there is a typical destabilization. There may be a sense of futility from caregivers: "Last year we worked on lying and getting homework done on time. We made great progress and he had completely stopped lying. Now, all of a sudden we're back to lying, but now he's sneaky and deceptive about it. And that's not all. He gets nasty and belligerent when he's caught. We're further behind than when we started."

In moving into the new developmental stage, many of the consolidated skills are disrupted, almost like a regression. However, this disorganization is actually a step forward, signaling that a new array of skills is on the way. But the immediate evidence does not reassure parents, and the behaviors may feel like the last straw for a teacher who has been investing so much in helping a youth. Often the time right after winter break is very difficult in the classroom because many of the students moved to a different developmental level through emotional growth that occurred during the break.

Another pointer that suggests advancing development is the sudden onset of change in behavior patterns with no other precipitating factors. As the charting for

Jason is laid out, many of the offending behaviors show up on the chart of the early adolescent. This is inconclusive. The PEPSI model was developed and is best used to assist in sorting through those things that are normal and those that are more anomalous.

Intervention may still be advisable. After all, the family is expressing a sense of frustration and pain. However, it can be approached from a belief that health is building, a "person is becoming ..." perspective. The milieu allows for more optimism, a little humor. "It came to pass, it didn't come to stay" can be asserted in amusement, "Well, Mr. and Mrs. Albini, unfortunately, your son Jason is acting his age."

It is possible, as well as desirable, to teach parents and caregivers positive ways to optimize the student's growth. It also alleviates a great deal of concern, grief, and guilt, freeing up energy for better coping, if the parents can be reassured that what is happening is normal and that a child's growth often signals that the parents are providing a good environment, since stability and security are vital links in allowing the child to move to new stages. It is helpful for the youngster, too, if the parents feel they can understand the normalcy in what the youngster does. This advice applies to educators as well. Sometimes teachers, too, need to step back and consolidate successes and see growth as fragmented and messy when they feel discouraged because their efforts and energy do not create the hoped for changes immediately, or bad days are mixed in liberally with baby steps forward.

It is possible, even likely, that the PEPSI charting will show areas where the youth is advanced or has strengths, as well as areas with apparent delays. These can be developed as part of the educational plan. In this sense, it might be possible for the parent to come to the teacher for help with the child's lying, and after the developmental charting, for the lying to become secondary and the family interaction to become the main area for work. If the PEPSI screening turns up a need for the parents to focus on improvement of relationship and communications in the family system, the teacher wisely refers the parents to appropriate community counseling and family services.

For Jason's parents, looking at their son's schoolwork and report card were not good clues to the real issues or cognitive capability, and that is frequently the case when a youth is viewed as being at risk. From Mr. Clark's perspective, Jason was no more disruptive or out of control than most 13-year-old students. By helping the family see that Jason was moving along a developmental continuum, Mr. Clark made a difference in Jason's family life and probably averted esteem issues for Jason.

Most youths who create disturbances in the classroom are manifesting developmental delays that create a sense of frustration for the teacher and for other students. By developing PEPSI charts, it is possible to begin to see common patterns. Seeing these patterns in turn helps the teacher to work with the student more effectively rather than seeing the student as dysfunctional.

Students who are unusually bright, advanced in cognitive and moral reasoning ability, frequently show social and emotional delays. Having learned to work with adults, they may be lacking in effective social skills with other adolescents. In other cases, having thought alone and kept to themselves, they may be missing trust or interest in peers, which looks very much like emotional immaturity.

Understanding the potential for different types of advanced or delayed development assists the teacher in making sense of many student behaviors that previously were viewed with alarm. Recognizing and being able to explain unusual behavior patterns makes it easier to understand, accept, and then move the student forward in areas of delay. No one area of delay becomes overemphasized. More gifts are valued.

Some students have permanent developmental blocks. For instance, youngsters with severe cognitive disabilities are not just delayed; there are areas where they will never completely reach maturity. By understanding the pattern of intellectual delay that is paired with normal physical development, the teacher can work with the student at the appropriate intellectual level, fully understanding the futility of expecting the 15-year-old girl with Down syndrome, who is really more of a 4-year-old, to behave as a teen, while also recognizing how adult the child looks.

Looking at a diagram of a typical developmental array for a teen with Down syndrome clarifies how agemates might misunderstand the mature woman body who skips down the street expressing delight, wonderment, and excitement about Dorothy and the Wizard of Oz. It provides a frame of reference as teachers work with her in mixed chorus when she cannot remember the lyrics. It builds better understanding and acceptance for peers who sit next to her at lunch while she giggles about her Twinkies and milk.

The PEPSI screening process can be learned in a brief period of time. The information base is well-established, reasonably objective, and well-researched. Use of the information is more subjective. As the educator practices the model, reliability will increase. The ability to recognize behavior patterns will become sharper with increased familiarity with the factors and dimensions of development. The PEPSI screening tool can be useful, even during the learning process. It is vital to appropriate utilization to recognize the basic assumptions inherent in the tool.

Philosophical Understandings About Developmental Screening

1. The PEPSI assessment model is based on a humanistic philosophy, a belief in health and positive growth and maintains a human-centered focus.
2. It derives basic concepts from the research in developmental literature.
3. The screening procedure is informal, partially intuitive, and instructive, with outcome viewed as a starting point for assisting in recognizing patterns of behavior and general levels of human growth.
4. The PEPSI model is not intended as a set of criteria for labeling or diagnosing in any setting or with any student.
5. The PEPSI model is intended to be a flexible tool that can be adjusted to meet individual teacher needs.

6. Viewing the student through a PEPSI model may provide adult awareness of areas that can be strengthened and nourished in the youth.

7. Once a PEPSI is constructed for a student, a visible image of strengths, weaknesses, and areas of developmental progress may emerge that can assist in producing an individual growth plan that may be included in a student's portfolio.

8. PEPSI can be a self-help tool when taught to adolescent students to assist them in developing self-awareness.

In reading developmental charts, it is essential to remember that human development is nearly always sequential but it is not necessarily age-specific to any individual. Thus, the "norm" or general guidelines for 12-year-olds will be accurate for approximately 68% of children who are 12. The other 32% of the class will be beyond those guidelines or will not have reached them. Theoretically, with a class of 30 students and five differing areas of development, one or two students would be developmentally appropriate or "normal" across all levels and the other 28 students would probably fall above or below the guidelines in at least one area. Given this understanding of youngsters and their growth, the teacher, rather than labeling the student as abnormal, might set the goal for progress in the slower area and guide the youth to enjoy areas of strength. Safety, high expectations, and relationship are keys to optimal growth.

Once the teacher recognizes a developmental disparity, a goal can be generated to address growth. In addition, the teacher will be able to facilitate student

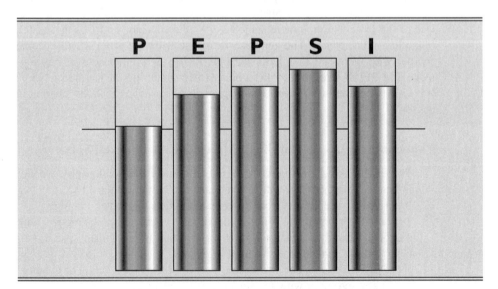

Figure 5.2 Sample PEPSI for Gifted

progress through increasing safety and structure in the classroom environment when a youngster is working to improve skills or increase levels of development. Showing pleasure in strengths as well as focusing on concerns can enhance student energy. It is also useful to provide practice in missing skills, which would be likely to come next, according to the indications from the charting. Finally, the teacher who rewards close approximations rather than focusing on errors will assist the young person in developing at an optimal level.

The Whole Person and Informal Assessment

Teachers are preparing youth for life, for entrance into society, for personhood, and must teach the whole person. The effective teacher does so by first recognizing the component parts of personhood, then learning the developmentally appropriate sequencing of the human growth. At that point teachers are in an excellent position to assist in optimizing the environment and energizing the youngster to take on the vital processes for enhancing individual development.

Assisting Student Development

By ascertaining a student's PEPSI, the teacher is able to see the child is pursuing a life journey that is developmental. Many times adults respond to childish antics with, "Act your age." Generally, the child is acting in an appropriate manner for the age and stage in which he or she is currently performing. The discomfort is due to the adult's lack of understanding that the child's behavior is most often purposive and not intentionally disruptive.

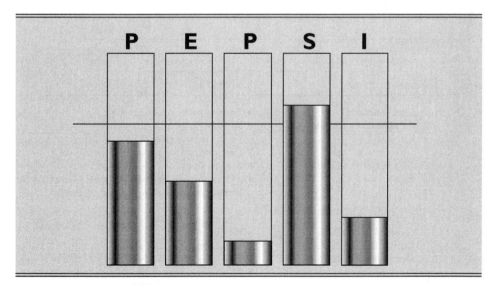

Figure 5.3   Sample PEPSI for Moderate MR

Recognizing the student's developmental steps and adult responses and behaviors facilitates development and fosters better understanding. The chart in Table 5.2 provides an overview of developmental tasks for children and the adult responses that facilitate completion of the developmental work.

Teachers need to add knowledge of other human factors as well to properly work with students: The nature and personality of children, social background, biological and psychological needs, levels of development, and capacity to learn contribute to better understanding.

The teacher looks to the whole person and works to synchronize the growth energy inherent in the student, as well as his or her special gifts, talents, traits, and abilities. The teacher assists the youngster in capitalizing on those parts of the course of study that harmonize with the developmental tasks at hand and the idiosyncratic potentials of each student. As the expert teacher combines understanding of the student's needs, developmental strengths and weaknesses, level of autonomous or heteronymous response, and learning needs and abilities, there is a deepening of ability to move the student forward, to attend to the youth as a loved one, to help the child accept personal responsibility to move forward.

Instead of engaging in power struggles or fruitless battles to get tasks accomplished, learning takes on a power of its own. The student, feeling understood, given a safe and secure environment, and empowered to fully utilize intrinsic motivation, accomplishes each day what cannot be done by push and shove in a year.

The teacher who gets to know each student will continue to learn about the nature of children and the human condition and will acquire excellent skills for building youth. The power implicit in democratic management should not be

Table 5.2   Developmental Work

Age	Student's Task	Adult's Task
K– Third	1. Social relations 2. Carry ideas to completion 3. Initiative 4. Small-muscle coordination 5. Concept of good and bad 6. Fair "to me"	■ Teach about respect, kindness ■ Assist with focus and structure ■ Foster independence ■ Provide creative outlets with detail work ■ Accept skills ■ Honor need for fairness but treat all with respect and provide for individual needs
4–6th	1. Peer relationships 2. Sense of competition 3. Desire to help others 4. Strong sense of self 5. Rules, privacy, and responsibility 6. Success as a friend 7. Reciprocity	■ Encourage self-worth through hobbies group memberships ■ Use consistency and praise ■ Show genuine generosity toward others ■ Make allowances for need for wanting "fairness" ■ Enhance active involvement ■ Use natural consequences, logic

underestimated. It can and will put joy back into the art of teaching and excitement and energy into the minds and hearts of youngsters allowed to work in those conditions.

The effective educator places emphasis on understanding each individual student and recognizing individual patterns of growth, and designs ways to reflect on the nature of people. By combining an awareness of human development patterns and specific patterns of individual students, the teacher can be alert to ways of implementing best practice in the classroom. Teachers use time-valued roles to energize the student to take on the processes for enhancing individual development and acceptance of special gifts and strengths as well as weaknesses. Teachers do that best when they believe in that vision and have built enough relationship with the student that he or she captures the magic in the vision and truly celebrates self.

Informal inventories like the PEPSI provide insights into student growth and learning patterns that lets teachers know what a youngster can do and areas of optimal growth. This may also illuminate some of the ploys and deterrents the student uses as barriers in settling into work.

Poor grades and low scores are markers that let a teacher know that a student did not accomplish a specific set of tasks. They may signal learning problems or missed skills, but they may also tell us that the student is not ready to process that information. They may let us know that math or reading is not a strength based on the patterns shown, but they do not inform teachers about specific skills or concepts that are missing.

There are specific steps a teacher can use. An excellent informal assessment can be made during a test, for example. Near the desk, ask a student who has difficulty in a subject to sit down and talk through the decisions being made on a test. It can be a spelling test, a math quiz, or a multiple-choice or short-answer quiz. As the student explains, look for cues about the depth of ideas, the missing concepts, and erroneous connections.

Low scores do not tell us much. They let us know that a student did not do well on the test, but they do not tell us what the student knows. Do high scores tell us more? Do we know that the student has the information we desire? Think of the situations that might make the score a false representation. The student has a cheat sheet. The student copied another person's answers. The student studied the right concepts, but will not remember the material if the test comes again in two weeks. The student made great guesses.

Instead of low and high scores on papers, teachers learn the most by observation and interaction with each student. The key to effective instruction is to look at what is working for students. By observing the things students can do and like to do, teachers can catch students' attention and interest and find learning abilities. Sometimes teachers even discover a student's passion. Using the subject that is a passion enhances the motivation and energy the student directs toward tasks.

Teachers also learn from the tasks a student cannot do, puts off, refuses to work on or complete, or finds frustrating and confusing. These task failures are often marked with acting-out and off-task maneuvers. Anger, abusive language, stalling, arguing, and getting off topic are examples of behaviors students who cannot work often choose instead. With observation and reflection, teachers can recognize these ploys and add them to their informal data. Very bright and capable students may also engage in these activities for attention and stimulation, but the energy and body language is quite different when it is a whimsical use of time rather than a countermeasure to save face.

Some student actions provide instant clarity that the work is not possible for them to do. When a student tries to write and her handwriting is illegible, the spelling inventive, and the words do not make a sentence, it is clear that the student is not able to write an essay, no matter how much effort is expended.

If teachers wish to teach students instead of subjects, they should listen to these openings for informal assessment:

- When a student says "No," find out why.
- When a student says "I can't," believe him or her and back up to the place where success can occur.
- When a student expresses discouragement, go beyond encouraging and listen to the student's true message.
- If a skill eludes a student, try the following:
  - Link math instruction to the student's current conceptual understanding.
  - Give students problems that pertain to their own lives.
  - Teach word problems as games and have students develop their own problems rather than solving preset ones.
  - Concentrate on success and what is going well.
  - Allow students to find personal methods for solving math problems and then get them to teach it to others.
  - Encourage students to use manipulatives, calculators, and computer games to enhance depth and rate of learning.
  - Find ways to generalize math operations to current, every day use of skills.

Presently, the testing programs in schools focus on intellectual strengths. It is not hard to understand why teachers work assiduously to prepare students to be successful academically and that the pressure for success includes being able to pass national and state tests. High-stakes testing focuses attention on the importance of reading, writing, and math. These are important skills, and students need to use them fluently to be literate and move ahead in higher education. Teachers are responsible for finding a way for the assessment to take place. The fact that there is no testing for other factors can cloud a teacher's vision, however. A whole child comes into the classroom. To be effective in educating that youngster, a teacher must address much more than those three R's.

Typical Classroom Assessments

Inclusion teachers need to have some way to determine if their students are learning basic classroom content and that their IEP goals are being met. Assessing classroom achievement includes all the various methods for determining the degree to which students are achieving the planned learning products or outcomes of instruction (Gronlund, 2006). Classroom-based assessments measure instructional objectives of the class.

Accordingly, inclusion teachers create and use a variety of assessment approaches, called classroom-based measures, when analyzing their students' work. Classroom-based measures are usually developed to coordinate with curriculum that has been taught in the class. As such, they can take place as formal or informal tests and quizzes. Other commonly used classroom assessments include performance and portfolio assessments.

Classroom assessments are useful when they provide information that informs the teacher and the students about how well students have learned and what they may still need to learn about the content they have been studying. Results of assessments also give teachers information about the effectiveness of lessons and classroom delivery. When classroom-based measures provide consistent information about the children's knowledge level of the material covered in class, the measure may be valid and reliable. The "may be valid and reliable" phrase means that even the most thoughtfully designed measure may be invalid and unreliable if the task demands and student ability to respond have not been taken into account.

Alignment Between Formats of Instruction and Testing

The format of the evaluation measure must mirror accommodations students use in their daily class activities. Larry, for example, uses a calculator when completing math assignments in class. To be valid, any measure of Larry's math skills should include access to a calculator. Karl has a reference card listing the steps for creating a five-paragraph essay, and he is allowed to use this card under any classroom condition, including quizzes and tests.

Any number of accommodations can be created that take into account the relationship between the task demands and student ability to respond (e.g., font size, response mode, time permitted, use of assistive technology). Table 5.3 includes additional suggestions for students needing adaptations in testing and assessment. Accommodations for certain types of evaluation measures must be listed on the student's IEP.

Need for Multiple Measures

To get a complete picture of students' skills or knowledge, information from multiple measures over a variety of classroom situations are most valid. Students in inclusion settings participate in a variety of classroom assessments (e.g., quizzes,

Table 5.3   Suggestions for Students Needing Adaptations in Testing/Assessment

Physical Adaptations of Material
- Provide test copies that are easy to read and uncluttered: typed, clear language, double-spaced and with ample margins
- Underline or highlight directions or key words
- Match font size to students' visual needs
- Eliminate or minimize copying activities by providing information on the test rather than from another source, like the board or a book

Format Adaptations
- Provide a word bank to select from for fill-in-the-blank questions
- Allow students to verbally supplement or orally complete a quiz or test
- Encourage students to use an assistive technology to support writing or organizing task demands

Time and Environmental Adaptations
- Allow extended time for completing the test
- Administer parts of the test on successive days rather than at one time
- Reduce the number of test items
- Reduce distractibility by using carrels or giving tests when no other students are around (e.g., after school)
- Administer the test in another setting (e.g., library or resource room)

tests, performance measures, and portfolio assessment). Quizzes and tests usually tap into individual students' long- and short-term memory. Performance measures often allow students to demonstrate their understanding through projects and activities, singly or with others, and portfolios provide a forum for examining and analyzing knowledge over a set of work.

Daily Classroom Formative Feedback

As an inclusion teacher, Ms. Brenes has accounted for learning styles and made appropriate accommodations for daily classwork. She is currently teaching a science unit on photosynthesis. The format of her evaluation tools mirrors the format of classroom task demands. Ms. Brenes uses a potpourri of classroom-based evaluation measures, including daily feedback, weekly quizzes, a formal summative test, a student-selected performance measure, and portfolio assessment. Since Ms. Brenes must give parents and students feedback for the science grade on report cards, and in some cases IEP reports, points are assigned to each of the measures and grades calculated on total points accrued.

Every day, Ms. Brenes provides her students with formative feedback about their work. The daily feedback serves an important function as the children move forward in their quest for knowledge about photosynthesis. By giving the students pointers while their work is in process, she is reducing occasions for frustration and increasing opportunities for praising student performance.

In Ms. Brenes' educational view, daily feedback consists of at least two kinds. Students get feedback about their understanding of their work as well as the quality of their work. Ms. Brenes focuses on two types of accuracy—accuracy for ideas and accuracy for following directions. When students are unclear about either content or directions, she guides them in the right direction based on level of need and learning style. Ms. Brenes' feedback for accuracy is typically verbal and, if needed, includes modeling; no points or scoring systems are involved with this type of daily feedback.

Ms. Brenes purposely does not give points for quality of daily work. She wants her students to welcome feedback and find her comments to be positive experiences that lead to increased understanding. She also wants to reduce the anxiety that some children feel when they pressure themselves to create *perfect* work. In addition, she takes into account accuracy of understanding the concepts required to complete learning tasks. Ms. Brenes has several children who need personalized explanations in order to understand what is expected, and in spite of being with a friend or within a group still need her assistance to completely comprehend the class assignment.

Ms. Brenes is a strong advocate for self-accountability. Accordingly, she expects some tangible product for the day's work from each student. She is a firm believer in recording progress and for the current unit requires each student to keep a photosynthesis log. At the end of each science period, all the children enter a brief summary of what they have accomplished for the day. Content and type of entries are flexible and reflect personal styles and skills of students.

Information can include descriptions of products; material found in books, journals, or the Internet; or two- to three-sentence descriptions of ideas discussed within a group or with a partner. Sketches may be used in place of written descriptions. When students have worked in groups or with partners, descriptions can be generated by the group, but each member must have a log entry, even if the documentation is identical to that of the other members of the group.

Ms. Brenes gives one point for the log entry and no points if no entry has been made. Points are recorded so students can earn 5 points a week for journal entries. Ms. Brenes believes that self-evaluation is an important aspect of learning, and, given the photosynthesis log assignment, one that all students can do. Thus, all students can be awarded points.

Weekly Quizzes and Unit Exams

Most daily work represents active learning principles and, accordingly, a lot of partner- and small-group work. But Ms. Brenes also wants to know how much each student has learned independent of the group as well as the quality of each student's understanding of photosynthesis. Ms. Brenes includes quizzes and end-of-unit exams as part of her evaluation approach. Prior to giving quizzes that count toward a grade, Ms. Brenes makes test preparation strategies part of the daily lesson.

Some of the strategies Ms. Brenes uses for test preparation include the following:

- Providing students with an example of the type of test questions they might be asked to complete
- Administering one or two items and then providing feedback the next day on both the content and the way the students responded
- Teaching the students strategies and skills for taking a variety of tests
- Practicing various types of testing formats

These strategies not only provide test preparation for students, but also give Ms. Brenes insight into her students' test-taking competencies.

For example, Ms. Brenes uses many types of classroom assessments to determine how well her students are learning and also uses many different types of test items to assess knowledge. She has organized the 4-week unit on photosynthesis by first creating the content grid shown in Table 5.4. From this grid, with a little label tweaking, Ms. Brenes can develop an outline that can be used for multiple purposes (see Table 5.5). She can use the same grid to develop weekly quizzes, a unit test, and a record-keeping sheet for the class as a whole and each of the students (Linn & Gronlund, 2000).

A quick glance at Table 5.6 shows that Ms. Brenes can create a 12-item quiz on basic terms by intersecting the first column with each of the words on the first row. In this quiz, Ms. Brenes is gathering information about her students' understanding of basic terms for photosynthesis. She is asking her students to demonstrate their knowledge of photosynthesis by

- identifying four basic terms,
- describing four basic terms, and
- constructing four basic terms.

Table 5.4 General Grid Template

	Identify	Name	Describe	Construct	Demonstrate	Total
Basic Terms						
Symbols						
Specific Facts						
Real-World Applications						
Total						

Table 5.5   Content Outline for a Four-Week Unit on Photosynthesis

The students will understand:

1. Basic terms
   1.1 matches term to definition
   1.2 matches term to picture of photosynthesis elements
   1.3 identifies correct and incorrect use of the term

2. Symbols for photosynthesis
   2.1 Matches symbol with the photosynthesis element
   2.2 Draws the symbol for a specific photosynthesis element
   2.3 Identifies the meaning of each symbol

3. Specific facts
   3.1 Identifies the three elements required for photosynthesis
   3.2 Distinguishes between correct and incorrect photosynthesis processes
   3.3 Explains how the meaning of the word *photosynthesis* is related to the process
   3.4 Explains how plants store energy through photosynthesis

4. Applying factual knowledge to real-world situations
   4.1 Identifies what happens to plants without sunlight
   4.2 Describes how to make unhealthy plants healthy
   4.3 Describes what happens to plants in different types of light

5. The effect of variables on real plants
   5.1 Observes the effect of light and dark on plants
   5.2 Infers the effect of various degrees of sunlight and darkness on plants
   5.3 Produces an explanation based on observations about how sunlight affected the plants

Table 5.6   Grid Template Used to Design 12-Team Quiz

	Identify	Name	Describe	Construct	Demonstrate	Total
Basic Terms	4	0	4	4	0	12
Symbols		4	4	4	2	14
Specific Facts	5	4	2	3	1	15
Real-World Applications	5	0	5	1	0	11
Total	14	8	15	12	3	42

Rather than generating an entirely new grid and creating more work for herself, Ms. Brenes can also produce a 42-item test over the entire unit using the same framework. The grid template allows Ms. Brenes to get an overview of the type and number of questions she is sampling, as well as saving herself time by not duplicating her efforts.

Ms. Brenes uses broad categorical terms like *identify, name, describe,* and so on, in her grid template to represent specific categories of behavior that are associated with particular types of test questions. Table 5.7 describes common synonyms and test items for the generic verbs used by Ms. Brenes in row 1 of the grid template.

Significance of Test Items

The type of test items used has particular significance for teachers in inclusion settings. Not all students will learn the same content at the same rate, nor will all students be able to produce the same type of responses. Test items that fall under the identification heading (e.g., matching, multiple choice, true–false) require students to pick the correct answer from a set of answers. Students with very slow processing rates or those who have difficulty retrieving information from memory are more likely to demonstrate their true knowledge of content on identification questions than if asked to produce information. All other item types found in

Table 5.7   Common Synonyms and Test Items for the Generic Verbs
(adapted from an a wise but unknown scholar)

Generic Verb	Sample Synonyms	Type of Test Question
Identify	Select, discriminate, point out, mark, match, recognize	■ Multiple-choice ■ True–False ■ Matching
Name	Label, list, multiply, compute	■ Completions ■ Fill-in-the-blanks
Describe	Define, explain, tell, state	■ Essay ■ Short-answer
Order	Arrange, alphabetize, rank, list in sequence	Ordering of ■ Objects ■ Events ■ Procedures
Construct	Prepare, draw, make, build, create, compose	Teacher gives a direction to produce a product. A checklist or rubric is provided.
Demonstrate (must be used with another verb that describes the action to be observed)	Deliver, catch, type, play, drive, march, throw, sing	Teacher gives a direction to demonstrate a skill that does not result in a product. A checklist or rubric is used as the demonstration progresses.

Table 5.7 require students to produce information in some form or another. As teachers move down the list of generic verbs, the type of test items become more complex and require higher skill levels.

Ms. Brenes can test all her students on basic terms of photosynthesis, but she can individualize the quiz by taking into account the skill strengths of her students. She can align test items with the cognitive, physical, and emotional levels of her students and can provide accommodations in her quizzes and tests by matching the task demands of the test items with her students' skills. Not all students need the same test items, but all students need to demonstrate their knowledge independent of the group.

Linus, Gavin, and Leigh are three of Ms. Brenes' students who need accommodations to demonstrate their knowledge of basic terms related to photosynthesis. Linus is cognitively low functioning compared to his class peers and has significant difficulty with fine-motor skills. He can read a few direction words, but, in general, reading is not comfortable for Linus. Linus wants to be part of his class group and does not appreciate being singled out for most activities, including quizzes and tests. Ms. Brenes has created a test for Linus that focuses on matching basic photosynthesis terms with pictures. In order for Linus' test to look length appropriate, i.e., not so obviously shorter than the tests his classmates are completing, Ms. Brenes asks Linus to answer four multiple-choice, four true–false, and four matching items, all involving pictures representing the vocabulary of photosynthesis that the class has been learning. To account for fine-motor difficulty, Linus uses a highlighter to indicate responses.

Gavin is a very bright student who has difficulty organizing information. Gavin does not need to have a quiz that asks identification questions. He needs a quiz that allows him to produce very short answers. Completions and fill-in-the-blank items best showcase Gavin's understanding of vocabulary associated with photosynthesis. With a prompt card for writing definitions, Gavin can also produce definitions with an example. Gavin's prompt card says:

1. Write the term.
2. Tell as many ideas as you can about the term.
3. Give one example.

Gavin's prompt card helps him organize, but does not provide any content information about basic vocabulary.

Leigh has a lot of ideas, but has difficulty expressing herself in writing and orally. Leigh is also deathly afraid of any sight, sound, or suggestion of quizzes or tests. Nonetheless, she has to be able to demonstrate her higher level thoughts. Ms. Brenes has found drawing to be the most valid accommodation for Leigh. Ms. Brenes has adapted Leigh's test responses by asking her to draw a semantic map for each of the vocabulary words accompanied by stick-figure drawings representing various applications of the terms. As Leigh's classmates are taking a quiz, Leigh has been excused from the exercise to create semantic maps. Both Leigh and Ms. Brenes are happy with this alternative to quizzes and exams.

Technology as a Time Saver

Before most inclusion teachers run from the room with the fear of multiple-test development, technology and flexibility of the organizational grid must be considered as ways to save teacher preparation time. Technology is a good friend for inclusion teachers. Through the use of personal computers, Ms. Brenes and her counterparts can create folders, files, and test items. Although Ms. Brenes does not always know who will be in her classes from year to year or what new content she will include in her units, she does know that she will be teaching photosynthesis.

The first year Ms. Brenes created the photosynthesis unit, she used the grid to guide test development. Even before she met her students, Ms. Brenes generated items to fit in the categories on the grid. Then she created a file for the items generated. As she got to know her students, she began to create additional files reflecting accommodations for specific needs (e.g., large print to accommodate Melissa's visual impairment). Throughout the years, Ms. Brenes has created files from which she can draw items that reflect the content, the type of knowledge tested, and accommodations that increased access for children with disabilities to demonstrate their knowledge. The files were put into folders by content (e.g., in this case, the photosynthesis file). Evidence of student and class achievement was also developed from grid categories.

Documentation of Class Test Data

Teachers like Ms. Brenes also use the grids to document progress. Because the items on the grid represent measurable behaviors, student progress on the number of correct and incorrect responses can easily be documented. Instead of creating mounds of paper, Ms. Brenes can document the progress of the entire class or an individual student within the class. Comparisons between an individual's progress and class progress can partially show success or lack of success for a particular subject in an inclusion setting. A comparison of whole-class documentation for quiz on basic terminology for photosynthesis with Jeremy's individual achievement is found in Table 5.8.

Ms. Brenes can get a lot of information about how well all the students are accessing basic terminology by recording how many children correctly answered particular sections of the quiz. She can see at a glance that something has going awry with descriptions of basic terms. Even though 19 students correctly understood concepts related to description of basic terms, 9 did not. Ms. Brenes sees a need for intervention; the intervention may be focused on content, instructional delivery, or maybe test format. When Ms. Brenes documents individual students' responses, she can begin to make comparisons for one student with the class as a whole. For example, Jeremy's total score was 9 test items correct out of a possible 12, or 75%. His overall score is low, but also misleading. When compared to the rest of the class, Jeremy had problems only in the area of describing basic terms. His errors were the same as those made by a small but substantial number of his classmates. By examining Jeremy's grid Ms. Brenes could also determine that, overall, Jeremy had a good grasp of basic terminology for photosynthesis.

Table 5.8   Comparison of Whole-Class Documentation for Quiz on Basic Terminology for Photosynthesis With an Individual Student's Achievement

Whole Class	Identify	Name	Describe	Construct	Demonstrate	Total
Basic Terms	23 + 5 -	NA 9-	19 + 4-	24+	NA	NA

Jeremy's Achievement	Identify	Name	Describe	Construct	Demonstrate	Total
Basic Terms	4/4 +	NA	1/4 +	4/4 +	NA	9/12+

Legend:
- numbers in whole class represent how many of Ms. Brenes' 28 students responded
- + means correct
- - means incorrect
- numbers in Jeremy's chart represent how many questions he got correct out of the numbers of questions asked

Based on an interpretation of student scores, Ms. Brenes can document progress and make data-based educational decisions. Some of her decisions may result in changes to her instructional approach, determination of grades, and a basis for parent conferences.

IEP Goals and Documentation

Items on a test should be aligned with the students' IEP goals. Test performance relative to instructional objectives or benchmarks aligned with the IEP goals represents important information for developing future goals and instructional accommodations or modifications. In Jeremy's case, the ability to describe content information is an IEP goal. Ms. Brenes can ask to have goals reassessed by the IEP team if

1. Jeremy continues to have problems describing symbols and specific and real-world applications of photosynthesis after one or more interventions have been implemented; and
2. an inability to describe the content of photosynthesis is negatively impacting Jeremy's ability to access information from the unit.

Fortunately for Jeremy, Ms. Brenes uses multiple types of assessments in addition to quizzes and tests to evaluate his progress.

Performance Assessments

Performance assessments usually reflect student ability to carry out an action or behavior according to a prescribed set of expectations. Performance assessments also go by the names *alternative assessments, direct assessment,* and *authentic assessment.* The prearranged expectations are often in the form of checklists, rubrics, or rating scales. The purpose of a checklist, rubric, or rating scale is to provide guidance about what kind of product is expected in the assignment and, when points are attached, the grading criteria. All three formats basically list activities or expectations for the project but with slight variations. Checklists, rubrics, or rating scales are equally acceptable for conducting performance assessments.

Performance assessment, or in more common parlance *authentic assessment,* is a means to evaluate the accomplishments of students engaged in personally meaningful problem solving. Performance assessment requires students to construct or perform a particular task or activity. The empowering aspect of performance assessment is that no single answer is the best; a variety of responses can be considered excellent. Performance assessments can be designed around IEP goals and are also one more piece of documentation of the inclusion process.

In Ms. Brenes' class, the children have been learning about photosynthesis. Ms. Brenes developed a number of ways to measure their understanding of photosynthesis through performance assessment of class projects. Two of the class projects included designing a poster and conducting a science experiment. In order to ensure that the students understand the expectations for their projects, Ms. Brenes and the class developed a rubric for creating a poster. To account for individual preferences when describing the science experiment, Ms. Brenes created three formats—a checklist, rubric, and rating scale—for following the guidelines.

Designing Assessments

Checklists, rubrics, and rating scales are often designed by the teacher and students together. The very act of designing a given set of expectations is yet another way to engage students in developing their own learning. The more precise the expectations are, the easier it is to determine proficiency levels. Clarity of expectations is a vital aspect of performance assessments.

Precision does not tell the student what answers are expected but supplies guidelines. The students can then determine how to fulfill the expectations. A rubric for developing a poster is presented in Table 5.9. The smiley faces are used to rate each requirement, but points may also be assigned based on the students' ages and the purpose for which the rubric is intended.

The rubric for developing a poster can be applied to any topic or any skill level. When Ms. Brenes decided to have her class create a poster, she could have labeled the topic "photosynthesis," but instead she let the students determine specific topics within the category of photosynthesis. Stefania's poster, for example,

Table 5.9 A Rubric for Developing a Poster

Performance Task Assessment List Poster

Element	Possible Points	Earned Assessment	
		Self	Teacher
Focus The topic is very clear when you first look at it.			
Main Ideas The main ideas are appropriate to the topic and are presented correctly.			
Supporting Details Appropriate and accurate details support each main idea.			
Purpose The purpose of the poster is clearly accomplished.			
Drawings and Illustrations All illustrations, photographs, and drawings add to the purpose and interest of the poster.			
Mechanics (C-U-P-S) There are no errors in capitalization, usage, punctuation, or spelling.			
Layout and Design The overall organization, design, use of color and space help to make the poster interesting and to communicate the message.			
Creativity The poster is highly original and creative.			
Neat and Presentable The poster is very neat and presentable.			
	Total:		

Did I do my best work?

😊TERRIFIC   😐OK   ☹NEEDS WORK

Source: Adapted from materials developed by Pomperaug Regional School District, Middlebury, CT.

depicted the effect of different degrees of light on the growth of her favorite flower, the daisy. Addison chose to use a *Star Wars* theme when he generated a poster depicting how light energy is trapped by chlorophyll. Personal interests do not alter the guidelines of the rubric.

Equally important, Ms. Brenes could take into account the skill levels of individual students. She could lengthen or shorten the expectations found on the checklist, rubric, or rating scale. For example, Wesley has difficulty producing and organizing ideas in print and is not a very good artist. After a discussion of various formats that could fulfill the assignment to create a poster, Wesley, with a little help from a computer-generated graphic organizer, decided to create a poster in the form of a semantic map. He met the requirement of drawings and illustrations by downloading pictures from the Internet and placing them in his map.

Wesley's classmate Merriam, who has significant cognitive deficits, created a poster with a different type of accommodation. Ms. Brenes made a poster template and developed a set of black-and-white line drawings related to photosynthesis. Merriam's task was to paste the drawings above the appropriate labels on the poster board. Merriam had choices within this task. Merriam could have mounted the pictures on construction paper, colored them, added glitter, or created any esthetic touch that she wished. Merriam chose to use markers scented with the essence of chocolate, cinnamon, and "very berry" to color in the drawings; she also artfully arranged spring flower stickers throughout the poster.

For the poster on photosynthesis, Ms. Brenes provided the children with performance criteria via a rubric, but for other topics she has found checklists and rating scales equally beneficial as a means of conducting performance assessment. In fact, sometimes Ms. Brenes provides her students with a choice of following a checklist, a rubric, or a rating scale when working on projects. Some children understand or feel more comfortable with different types of guidelines, even when the performance expectations are the same. The value of performance measures is that they allow another insight into children's knowledge base. The assessments can be adapted to match children's interests as well as cognitive, affective, and physical skills. As a result, all children can be included meaningfully in performance measures, and another source of data can be used to make educational decisions.

Portfolio Assessment

Portfolio assessment is another technique that can be used for evaluation purposes. Portfolio assessment is an ongoing process that can capture the many activities and accomplishments of individual students or can showcase the work of a class on a particular unit or project (Venn, 2004). Portfolios are collections of samples of student work and, depending on the purpose, can include results of systematic observations of student behavior. Most portfolios also include student reflection and self-evaluation components. Material in the portfolio is usually organized by chronological order and category. When portfolios are ordered, student achievement is more easily analyzed and development can be viewed over time. Ms. Brenes, like many inclusion teachers, uses two types of portfolio assessments: student-centered portfolios and teacher-centered portfolios.

Philosophical Orientation in Portfolio Assessment

The type of samples kept for portfolio assessment depends on the philosophy of the teacher and the school. Some portfolios are used to showcase the students' best work; other portfolios house random samples of assignments and tasks. In any event, portfolio assessment is used to review a child's work in a way that is beneficial to the teacher, student, or parent.

Student-centered portfolio assessment can target a broad array of skills or target student performance related to particular themes or instructional units (e.g., photosynthesis) and includes actual samples of student work.

Teacher-centered portfolio assessments include actual samples of student work and add records of systematic observations of the student's integration into the general education classroom. Teacher-centered portfolio assessment also provides information regarding skills, disposition, and work habits.

Both of these types of portfolio assessments are valuable approaches to reinforcing learning and making formative decisions about students' knowledge and growth (Wilkerson & Lang, 2003). General guidelines for selecting content for portfolios are found in Table 5.10. All content placed in any type of portfolio used for assessment is valuable when selection is based on established content and performance standards.

Student-Centered Portfolio Assessment

Student-centered portfolio assessment can include any aspect of a student's performance: writing samples, pictures of projects, examples of how the student solved mathematical problems, results of scientific experiments, artwork, songs. Any achievement that represents the child's work that can be documented in some way

---

Table 5.10 General Guidelines for Selection of Portfolio Materials

Entries should be:

- in harmony with the goals of instruction and the use to be made of the portfolio (e.g., to improve learning, for use in parent–teacher conferences, as part of a schoolwide assessment),
- provide a variety of types of evidence (e.g., written, oral, exhibits, projects),
- selected in terms of criteria to be used in judging them,
- selected by students, or at least they should be involved in the process,
- complex enough to allow for students' self-evaluations and their reflections on the learning that resulted,
- started early in the instructional program to better show growth in learning, and
- evaluated by using the criteria and standards established for the performance tasks.

Source: From "Assessment of Student Achievement," (p. 161), by N. L. Gronlund, 2006, Boston: Allyn & Bacon.

can be kept in a file or folder as a portfolio. Student-centered portfolios usually contain material selected by students (e.g., work samples, writing samples, drawings, performance tasks, projects, and assessment results from quizzes and tests).

Students must be taught how to choose material for their portfolios. A secondary benefit of portfolio assessment is to help them develop an awareness of the quality of their classwork. Most students can use the following questions to guide their selection of material (Gronlund, 2006):

- Why did you choose this entry?
- What did you need to do to complete this assignment or quiz?
- What have you learned from the entry selected?
- What, if anything, would you do to improve the work quality?

Some children, especially those with low cognitive or language skills or those who lack reflective experience, may need additional assistance before they can independently and meaningfully use questions to guide their material selection. An instructional approach of model–lead–test is applicable for teaching children how to make judgments about their work. Students and teachers can brainstorm the type of ideas that are important to think about when selecting material for portfolio inclusion and assess their product and process. First, the teacher can provide a model of what type of work is expected and how to place the material in the portfolio. Then, together, the teacher and students can discuss and demonstrate why they have chosen the work and where to place it in their individual portfolios. Through instruction and practice, most students will develop self-assessment and judgment-making skills for choosing which material to put in their portfolios.

Portfolio assessments involve students in the assessment process by encouraging them to think about their performance and evaluate their progress (McMillan, 2004). Reflection feedback forms can be developed to move children from dependence on the teacher to independence in self-assessment and to provide them with a system for choosing portfolio content.

Reflection feedback forms provide triggers or scaffolds for helping students develop a way to think about their work. These triggers or scaffolds are simple statements elaborating on the overall guiding questions. The larger question is: "Why did I choose this project?" The student picks the responses that are most applicable. An example of a generic reflection feedback form that students can use when assessing their product is found in Table 5.11.

The generic nature of the questions and responses allows the feedback form to be used with any type of project. It may be modified to reflect inclusion of test or quiz materials. Reflection feedback forms can be more basic or more complex depending on students' needs.

Teacher-Centered Portfolio Assessment

Teacher-centered portfolios may, but do not have to, include student selection. Teacher-centered portfolio assessments include content that is selected for very

---

Table 5.11   Example of a Reflection Feedback Form in Self-Assessment for a Project

---

Circle the statements that apply to you and the project included in your portfolio.

■ Why did I choose this project?
  I got a good grade.
  I liked the way I completed the answers.
  The topic was interesting.

■ What did you need to do to complete this assignment or quiz?
  I worked with my friend.
  I looked up information on the Internet.
  I read some books.
  I learned how to organize my information in a log.
  I made a poster.

■ What have you learned from the entry selected?
  I learned a lot, a little, or not too much about _____.

Please add your ideas about work quality

■ What, if anything, would you do to improve the work quality?
  I would do nothing more; the project is good.
  I would change the following because:
  a.
  b.
  c.

---

specific purposes. Some teachers keep formal and informal tests in the assessment portfolio. The teacher-centered assessment portfolio content exceeds work products by including an observation section. The choice of the type of observation tool is left to the teacher's discretion.

Analysis of the observations adds one more level of understanding of students' strengths and needs. Most children in inclusion settings do not need a teacher-centered portfolio. However, for children who do not seem to be progressing or for whom placement in the general education classroom is questioned, teacher-centered portfolio assessment provides vital data for decision making.

Observation tools used in teacher-centered portfolio assessment may include checklists, inventories, descriptions of student behavior, rating scales, and anecdotal records. Systematic observations allow teachers to examine students' behavior under different settings, time frames, and accommodations. The purpose of any type of observation tool is to describe a child's progress from the beginning to the end of a class, project, or unit using relatively unbiased techniques.

Portfolio Assessments as a Means of Communication

Student- and teacher-centered portfolios provide a basis for discussing class progress. The student-centered portfolio is child-friendly and can be used as the basis for classroom conferences. Student-centered portfolio assessments can also give students a sense of empowerment and accountability for their work. In a very real sense, a collection of student products can be an objective way for students to get a large picture of their classroom growth, including areas that need to be strengthened.

When portfolio assessments are used formatively, students can examine their work products as they are being completed. They can identify assignments that have been completed, which ones need to be finished, as well as overall achievement trends. Conferencing using a portfolio assessment can be particularly helpful for students who have a difficult time organizing information, managing time, or remembering what they had done and what they are expected to do, because the concrete evidence of progress is the actual work and not some abstract notion.

Ms. Brenes uses portfolio assessments both formatively and summatively for specific projects. She individualizes her portfolio conferences. Based on need, she confers with three of her students daily and one student every other day. Conferences with the remaining students in her class are rotated; Ms. Brenes usually sees each of these students every 4 or 5 days. In the formative conferences, Ms. Brenes asks students to explain the contents of their portfolios. She asks them questions and clarifies any needed dimension (i.e., content, expectations, or quality). Portfolio assessment conferences also give Ms. Brenes additional opportunities for praising student work. Ms. Brenes does not give grades when using the portfolio assessments formatively. Grades based on portfolio assessment are given at the end of the unit.

Portfolio assessment can also provide an excellent basis for discussion among adults involved in a child's educational life. The contents of the portfolio diminish miscommunication and increase understanding of a child's progress. Information taken from a teacher-centered portfolio can be used to help the teacher make education decisions and to bring documentation to parent conferences and IEP meetings.

Summary

Assessment is the collection of information to identify what does and what does not provide students with access to the general education curriculum. Inclusion teachers need to have techniques for determining the effectiveness of educational programming with a special emphasis on student progress toward IEP goals. Analysis of students' daily performance is the best source of information for identifying student achievement in the general education curriculum.

Informal assessments can include, but are not limited to, quizzes and exams. Performance and portfolio assessments are also important sources of academic achievement. Many aspects of informal assessment occur daily and require monitoring and adjusting of instructional delivery.

Assessment takes into account the physical, emotional, philosophical, social, and intellectual developmental level of the student. By combining awareness of human development patterns and the specific patterns of individual students, teachers can implement the most appropriate educational practices in inclusion settings. Through informal assessment, teachers and students work together to recognize what is needed to become successful learners.

References

American Association of School Administrators. (1992). *The nongraded primary: Making schools fit children.* Arlington, VA: Author.

Arends, R. I. (2004). *Learning to teach* (6th ed.). New York: McGraw-Hill.

Bagnato, S., & Neisworth, J. (1990). *System to plan early childhood services.* Circle Pines, MN: American Guidance Service.

Brazelton, T. B. (1983). *Infants and mothers: Differences in development.* New York: Delta/Seymour Lawrence.

Gronlund, N. E. (2006). *Assessment of student achievement* (8th ed.). Boston: Allyn and Bacon.

Lidz, C. (1991). *Practitioner's guide to dynamic assessment.* New York: Guilford.

Linn, R., & Gronlund, N. E. (2000). *Measurement and assessment in teaching* (8th ed.). Upper Saddle River, NJ: Merrill.

Maslow, A. H. (1968). *Toward a psychology of being.* New York: Van Nostrand.

McMillan, J. H. (2004). *Classroom assessment: Principles and practices for effective instruction* (3rd ed.). Boston: Pearson.

Messick, S. (1984). Assessment in context: Appraising student performance in relation to instructional quality. *Educational Researcher, 13,* 3–8.

Meyer, C. (1992). What's the difference between authentic and performance assessment? *Educational Leadership, 49*(8), 39–40.

No Child Left Behind Act of 2001, 20 U.S.C. 70 § 6301 *et seq.*

Overton, T. (2005). *Assessment in special education: An applied approach* (4th ed.). Englewood Cliffs, NJ: Prentice-Hall, Inc.

Salvia, J., & Hughes, C. (1990). *Curriculum based assessment: Testing what is taught.* New York: Macmillan.

Salvia, J., & Ysseldyke, J. (2001). *Assessment* (8th ed.). Boston: Houghton-Mifflin.

Salvia, J., & Ysseldyke, J. E. (2007). *Assessment: In special and inclusive education* (10th Edition). Boston: Houghton-Mifflin.

Venn, J. J. (2004). *Assessing students with special needs* (3rd ed.). Upper Saddle River, NJ: Pearson.

Wilkerson, J. R., & Lang, W. S. (2003, December 3). Portfolios, the Pied Piper of teacher certification assessments: Legal and psychometric issues. *Education Policy Analysis Archives, 11*(45). Retrieved July 1, 2005, from http://epaa.asu.edu/epaa/v11n45/

Wood, J. W. (2005). *Adapting instruction to accommodate students in inclusive settings* (5th ed.). Upper Saddle River, NJ: Pearson.

Classroom Management: Building Schedules, Routines, and Instruction Formats

KEY TERMS

◆ buddy system
◆ daily log
◆ materials inventory
◆ peer tutoring
◆ time management
◆ transition time

Ms. Roberts has returned from a meeting with the special education teacher. She has been informed that several of students with disabilities are being included in her general education classroom. One of the students, Jean, has mild learning disabilities in reading and writing. Nathaniel is labeled as having at emotional disturbances with mild retardation. Rebecca has a hearing problem, and Amy uses a wheelchair. Ms. Roberts is not too concerned. She has been teaching for more than 15 years and has discovered that working with kids with disabilities is not a lot different from working with kids who are not labeled.

Ms. Roberts knows that she needs a management plan that will reduce the extraneous, consolidate when possible, and manage time as efficiently as the clock and schedule will permit. Ms. Roberts realizes that her plan for managing her students with disabilities will also benefit many of her students who need similar services but do not qualify for either special education or 504 eligibility: the two students with attention deficit disorder, the five emergent English-speaking students, and the 10 students who are struggling to meet grade-level expectations. Ms. Roberts understands that academic and social achievement is related to effective and efficient management for all her students.

Reducing the Extraneous

Classroom Management and Principles of Good Instruction

Classroom management systems are the flip side of principles of good instruction. Classroom management is much like management in any organization. Teachers have to build schedules, establish routines, and develop instructional formats that support good teaching principles. At least six principles of good instruction (Astleitner, 2000) must be considered when setting up a classroom to meet the diverse needs of the students:

1. Opportunities for reflexive learning
2. Support for the learners' many different types of cognitive, motivational, and emotional characteristics
3. Consideration of the learners' strengths
4. Support for self-regulated learning

Opportunities for Reflexive Learning

As teachers, we know that instruction has to be systematic. Systematic instruction intentionally follows a sequence of skills in which one skill is the steppingstone to understanding the next. Systematic instruction also offers opportunities for students to think about what they are learning. Classroom management involves building in systematic opportunities for students to actively think about what they have been learning. When they do so, they expand prior knowledge and link it to new information.

The teacher can set up a classroom to enable students to actively engage in the exchange of ideas. Active engagement means that the structure of the classroom will have to be more student-centered with teacher direction than the more traditional teacher-centered approach. Interaction with other class members is one way to provide opportunities for reflexive learning. Students who have been used to the more traditional worksheet approach to managing instruction often lack the reflexive skills needed to expand their knowledge. As teachers, we can help them learn to be more reflexive by having him engage in conversations or activities with other class members.

Support for Learners' Cognitive, Motivational, and Emotional Characteristics

Instructional formats can be tailored to learners' many different cognitive, motivational, and emotional characteristics. Classroom management in these areas could include setting routines to activate prior knowledge or guiding and evaluating the learning process through feedback. All in-class assignments, for example, can be delivered orally while simultaneously being presented on an overhead or on the board. Students who cannot process auditorily and who have attention issues can count on finding the assignment posted.

The power of predictable routines for beginning, doing, and completing in-class work will meet the needs of many students on a variety of cognitive and emotional dimensions. Routines can also motivate previously confused and disorganized learners. If they can predict what they are expected to do, the tasks will become less confusing and more welcoming.

Consideration of Learners' Strengths

A well managed classroom allows students to use a variety of structures and formats to demonstrate knowledge, as well as to learn. Some learners have more confidence in their ability to create a visual representation of information, while others might feel more comfortable with verbal descriptions. Students can develop their strengths when they have opportunities to use them. Teachers who are good managers know how to capitalize on their students' strengths. These teachers also know how to have students complement each others' strengths.

Sometimes students with special needs benefit from systematic instruction showing them how they can use their strengths. Nancy, for example, is an excellent cartoonist. She doodles and draws and creates all sorts of whimsical characters, but she has no idea how to capitalize on this talent when she is studying her science text. Morgan, one of Nancy classmates, is an excellent writer, facile with spelling, grammar, and sentence structure. Their teacher capitalized on their strengths by creating an assignment in science that required the students to create an illustrated booklet on the lifecycle of the butterfly. Nancy could have created it by herself, and Morgan could have done it by himself. Together, however, the teacher set up a situation that would combine their strengths.

Support for Self-Regulated Learning

Self-regulated learning, ironically, is a skill that must be taught to most learners, labeled or not. Many students need to be taught how to remember and how to structure their activities. They also need to learn how to manage their time and how to relate new knowledge to all knowledge. Teachers can help students develop self-regulated learning by using checklists or the equivalent when they are working on tasks or managing time or material.

CHECKLISTS / RUBRICS   Initially, teachers can provide a checklist or have the class develop checklists to determine when an activity is complete or what parts must be developed to complete the task. From this simple beginning, and with the teacher's assistance, students can begin to develop rubrics for classwork. The rubrics provide a memory guide for what has to be done and also the extent to which the product shows excellence.

The first step in developing a checklist or rubric is to do a task analysis—to identify all the components of the expected activity. To engage the students in developing the task, any number of brainstorming configurations can be introduced—for example, whole class, small group, or partners. Once the brainstorming is complete, students can create the steps needed to complete the task or activity. The steps can then become part of the classroom routine for similar activities.

EXAMPLE   Let's take an example from Ms. Strickland's classroom. She is combining a literature and creative writing class to teach her students how to self-regulate the creative writing activity she has designed. She begins by reminding the students of the story they had just read. Next she wants the students to relate to the hero of the tale, a big yellow dog, by writing about an imaginary adventure they could take with the dog. Ms. Strickland could simply ask the students to write a story about themselves and their adventure with the big yellow dog. Her instructions could produce the desired stories, but she can take this lesson one step further.

First Ms. Strickland could work with the students to develop a system (a checklist) for how to create a new story. Together the class could brainstorm the sequence—beginning, middle, and end. Next, with some prompting from Ms. Strickland, the students could indicate mechanical areas such as spelling, punctuation, and capitalization. Ms. Strickland might also encourage them to use colorful adjectives, adverbs, comparisons, and so on.

When the students have finished generating their ideas, Ms. Strickland can create a temporary checklist on the board, followed later with a more permanent checklist, which can be attached to similar assignments or posted for all to see. The benefit of a class-created checklist or rubric is that the teacher can refer to the students' prior experiences with the checklist and relate it to the next project. In addition, through repeated use of the checklist or rubric, the students may eventually internalize or automatize the system.

Teacher Judgment

Teachers must also manage the content they wish the students to learn. Most states have developed minimum standards, which typically include a broad-based set of goals accompanied by performance objectives. Table 6.1 shows a sample page related to reading from the Arizona State Standards. The broad-based goals and performance objectives are typically used to measure achievement on state-level tests. Results of these tests are often used to determine the rate at which the students are learning or making annual yearly progress, as defined by the No Child Left Behind Act.

Many districts have chosen to expand the performance objectives into related instructional objectives. Goals and performance objectives typically apply to all students, whereas instructional objectives are more personalized and relate to specific needs of specific students as shown in Figure 6.1.

Table 6.1   Strand 1: Reading Process (Grades 1–3)

Reading Process consists of the five critical components of reading, which are Phonemic Awareness, Phonics, Fluency, Vocabulary and Comprehension of connected text. These elements support each other and are woven together to build a solid foundation of linguistic understanding for the reader.

Concept 1: Print Concepts	Grade One	Grade Two	Grade Three
Demonstrate understanding of print concepts.	PO 1. Alphabetize a series of words to the first letter.	PO 1. Alphabetize a series of words to the second letter.	PO 1. Alphabetize a series of words to the third letter.
	PO 2. Distinguish between uppercase and lowercase letters.	PO2. Recognize the distinguishing features of a sentence (e.g., capitalization of the first word, internal punctuation, ending punctuation, quotation marks).	PO2. Recognize the distinguishing features of a paragraph (e.g., indentation of first word, topic sentence, supporting sentences, concluding sentences).
	PO 3. Recognize the distinguishing features of a sentence (e.g., capitalization, ending punctuation).		
	PO 4. Identify the title, author, and table of contents of a book.		

Source: From "Reading Strand One—Reading Process," by Standards and Assessment Division, Arizona Academic Standards, 2003. Retrieved January 30, 2008 from http://ade.az.gov/standards/language=/arts/RdgStrand1FINAL.pdf

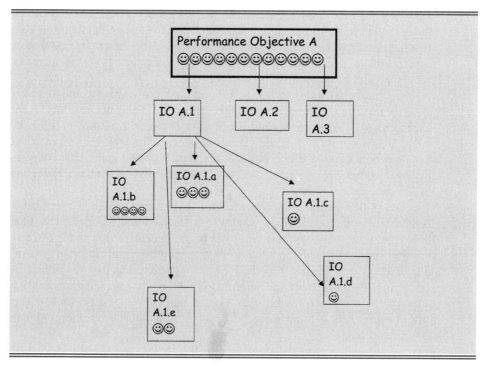

Figure 6.1   Personalizing Performance Objectives (POs)

States and districts have done a lot of work organizing, sequencing, and identifying the minimum standards of knowledge expected of learners at different grade levels. State-developed standards, goals, and performance objectives provide a base from which the teacher can reduce the extraneous content and streamline objectives, materials, methods, and evaluation. "Reducing the extraneous" means that the general education teacher must have a clear and definite vision of what the student needs to be able to access the general education curriculum and associated standards.

The teacher as classroom manager can capitalize on the work the state has done by creating and aligning personalized instructional objectives that can be found on the IEP, 504 Plan, or from years of familiarity with teaching. Experienced classroom teachers have a great deal of flexibility in designing and delivering the curricula and materials. States or districts have determined the minimum essential content, and teacher judgment determines the depth of coverage and how to convey the curriculum.

Depth of Coverage

If the district curriculum in social studies includes "an understanding of the need for cooperative effort in the family," the teacher determines the extent to which individual students within the classroom will learn that concept. You may decide that all students must learn certain aspects of the cooperative family effort concept (i.e., minimum competency will be established for the entire class), and other concepts related to cooperative family effort may be extraneous and not a prerequisite for learning the next major concept.

Key vocabulary terms such as *family* and *cooperative* are essential to understand the need for cooperative effort in the family. What may not be critical is for all students to be aware of cooperative efforts in 40 different cultures, or in 20 different families, or in 13 different periods of history. Although that sort of information is broadening and certainly can contribute to better understand cooperative family effort, not all students will be able to assimilate that much information in the same amount of time.

The skilled classroom teacher knows the students' limits—limits being determined by the number of concepts to be learned and the amount of time devoted to learn those concepts. For some of the students, reducing the extraneous may mean understanding the concept of cooperative family effort in the context of one or two families from the student's own culture in the present historical period. By identifying the information that is vital to understanding the concept, the classroom teacher may expand the knowledge base for students whose experiences warrant more information by building from the minimum competency base.

Individual Differences

"But wait!" cries the concerned educator. "Doesn't the principle of reducing the extraneous translate to 'the rich get richer and the poor get poorer?'" The answer is that the rich get richer and the poor get rich. In any general education classroom, the goal is to encourage students to reach their highest intellectual potential. The more effective the classroom teacher, the greater the individual differences between students will be. Students who have difficulty learning, for whatever reason, are taught basic concepts. In most curricula the basic concepts are few, but this doesn't imply that these few concepts are not rich in knowledge. Rather than attempting to rush all the students into learning essential and nonessential information, the wise classroom teacher teaches a few select concepts wisely. All students leave with a strong basic understanding of key concepts. No one is impoverished, and everyone learns.

Essential Information

The key to reducing the extraneous lies in decision making. Perhaps in collaboration with a curriculum specialist, the general education teacher must distinguish essential from nonessential information. Essential information is information that must be acquired to learn new information. It is the foundation upon which new knowledge can grow. In basic skill areas such as reading and math, essential information is generally easy to identify. A child receiving reading instruction, for example, need not learn the names of the letters to be able to sound-out words, as naming the letters is not essential to sounding-out in reading. Naming the letters, however, is essential to spelling tasks.

Guidelines

Content areas such as science, health, and social studies provide more opportunities to make subjective choices. In choosing essential terms, concepts, or units in content areas, consider the following three questions:

1. Is the term or concept one that will recur throughout the curriculum, or is it isolated within a specific unit?
2. Is the term, concept, or unit one that will recur in other grade-level curricula?
3. Is the term, concept, or unit one that will recur in more advanced curricula?

If the term or concept is isolated to one unit, chances are that it is not essential. The teacher must be careful, however, to become familiar with more advanced curricula to be sure that the isolated term or concept or unit does not become a major emphasis at a higher grade level. If it does, the teacher has to decide how much instructional time to allot to teaching the concept now. That decision will be based primarily on the individual makeup of the classroom.

Student Characteristics

If most of the students in a class are motivated, have a positive learning history, and learn at a rate that allows for the introduction of nonessential information, the teacher can probably teach an isolated term, concept, or unit. For students who have some learning problems, the teacher will be able to adapt or modify instruction to meet their needs as well. If, however, the class has a low motivational level, a history of negative learning experiences, and tends to need a lot of time to learn new concepts, the teacher probably cannot spend much instructional time in teaching nonessential information. But the critical information that is conveyed for students who are less than thrilled at being in a school setting can be managed more easily through active learning and brain-based principles (e.g., student-centered small-group formats). The premise behind small-group instruction is that peers working with each other are more capable of solving problems than individuals trying to solve the same problems independently (Vygotsky, 1978).

Establishing priorities for curricular goals and objectives is essential to reducing the extraneous. Priority setting takes into account the students' characteristics. Not all information warrants the same emphasis. The teacher should not be afraid to eliminate unnecessary information or to provide different amounts of information to the different students in the class.

Consolidating Students

Consolidation includes grouping students together, reducing and organizing materials, and carefully managing time. Each form of consolidation is important to effectiveness and success.

Basic Skills

By consolidating students when possible and individualizing when necessary, the classroom plan will include large-group, small-group, and individualized instruction. A standard instructional approach for many classroom teachers at all levels is to group students to learn and work together. As with reducing the extraneous, the teacher again is called upon to be a decision maker. The decision this time involves which subjects can be taught best under which conditions (lecture, small group, or one-to-one). These decisions must take into account the needs of individual students in the room.

Take the example of Augie and Raymond. Augie has been classified as having a mild learning disability. Raymond has been characterized as being average to quick in completing his schoolwork. Augie and Raymond are enrolled in the same classroom, and their teacher is expected to instruct them both in basically the same subject areas. When reading time begins, Augie often can be found in a small group, being instructed in basic reading concepts. Sometimes Augie will be found in a one-to-one story-writing session. During reading time, Raymond also will be found in a small group, but Raymond's group will be receiving more advanced instruction than Augie's group. Raymond, too, will be found in a one-to-one writing session. Both Augie and Raymond listen to their teacher during story-reading time.

Augie's and Raymond's teacher has consolidated her basic skills instruction wherever possible. She chose one-to-one story writing as a means to meet individual needs, and she chose small-group instruction as a means to bring together students of similar skill levels. Finally, Augie and Raymond's teacher chose large-group or total class participation when reading to the entire group. In this way, each child can learn from the story, reading at his or her own level and in accordance with his or her own background experiences.

Content Areas

Most teachers have more to teach than basic skills. They have to apply the consolidation principle to curricular content areas as well. Returning to Augie and Raymond, we find them in their respective science classes. The day before, the teacher had shown a film called *Insects Are Our Friends* to the entire class. Then the teacher solicited ideas that struck the students as being particularly interesting or relevant to the topic of insects. The following day, the teacher suggested several projects related to the students' interests and asked them to pick a project on which they wanted to work. The students worked in small groups in the area of their choice.

Augie and Raymond found themselves and three other classmates in a group that wanted to study ants. As a group, Augie, Raymond, and the other three students (with a little guidance from their teacher) designed, developed, and presented the results of their project. Each child within the group participated, but at different levels. Augie chose to collect or draw pictures of ants at work. Raymond and one other group member built an ant farm. Working within the framework of a small group, each child contributed at his or her own level.

Whole Class

In consolidating students in a content area, a teacher may begin by presenting the basic information to the entire class. A key to presenting information to the entire group is to present only one major concept per lesson. Information is presented such that all students understand the critical concept being conveyed. That critical concept is reviewed, followed by class discussion. The need for class discussion is twofold:

1. In listening to the students discuss a concept, the teacher has the opportunity to identify areas of weakness or misunderstanding. He or she can then re-teach or review concepts while conducting the discussion.
2. The students are given an opportunity to add new information related to the topic. Through guided class discussion the teacher can work with the entire class at one time.

Small Groups

As individual interests emerge from the discussion, the teacher can form small groups composed of students whose interests are similar. The students themselves can determine the breadth, depth, and organization of the group. With a little trust, the teacher can teach cooperative skills as well as subject-matter content. Assuming that the students are interested in their chosen topic, they may need only minimal direction. The teacher is then free to circulate among groups or spend time in any one group, as necessary.

Within groups, students can divide tasks among themselves. The use of small-group instruction in the classroom seems to positively affect academic achievement and student self-concept (Box & Little, 2003). Students, like adults, usually choose to do the kinds of tasks in which they have been successful previously. While each child does his or her own thing, the dynamics of a small group also can allow for a great deal of productive sharing and exchange of ideas. The group artist may receive a few ideas from the group bookworm; the group bookworm in turn might pick up a few fine points related to the artist's interpretation of the topic.

Management and consolidation take into account group and individual needs. By creating active learning environments involving large-group, small-group, and tutorial flexibility, teachers can accommodate the needs of all students successfully—those with and without disabilities.

Cooperative Learning, Collaboration, and Tutoring

Cooperative learning, collaboration, and tutoring are active learning approaches often used to describe situations in which students work together to solve problems, learn new concepts or practice gaining fluency with prior knowledge. These approaches have been consistently shown to be beneficial for various ages and cognitive levels (Berliner & Casanova, 1998; Johnson, Johnson, & Stanne, 2002; Slavin, 1995).

1. *Cooperative learning* transfers the responsibility for active learning from the teacher to the students. Through social interaction in classroom tasks, students actively create knowledge. Cooperative learning is powerful when it is well structured and organized by the teacher (Vermette, Harper & DiMillo, 2004).
2. *Collaboration* is a variation of cooperative learning wherein partners of approximately equal skills work together on the same problem rather than on different components of the problem (Brandon & Hollingshead, 1999).
3. *Tutoring* typically refers to two students learning together—one taking the role of the teacher, and the other, the role of the student.

Variations of groupings in which students engage actively with each other are as plentiful as the teacher's imagination. Literature circles and jigsaw formats are two common examples. Literature circles consist of a group of five to seven readers who are reading the same piece about the same topic. The students select their own reading from books that the teacher has selected previously. The students then decide how many pages to read and take turns leading a discussion about the topic. The leader of the discussion also prepares notes to guide the conversation (Stringer, Reynolds, & Simpson, 2003). Variations of the literature circle can be used with any content area. Content found in social studies, science, and even mathematics lend themselves to this format.

In the jigsaw approach (Box & Little, 2003), the students are assigned to a small home group. The home group is responsible for completing an assignment, which consists of a number of sub-parts or sub-concepts. Each student in the home group is assigned a concept and then moves to a concept group. That concept group becomes knowledgeable about that concept only, and students in each concept group become experts in that concept.

After the experts are relatively secure in their knowledge, they return to the home group. The home group is now filled with experts who pool their collective knowledge and complete the task. The jigsaw approach is most commonly used when the task is complex and is often applied in the areas of social studies and science, but easily lends itself to literature, creative writing, music, and art.

In spite of the many positive aspects of collaboration and cooperative learning approaches, what you see is not always what you get, like the tip of the iceberg. Teachers as classroom managers understand that they have to create groups and select members according to criteria that will maximize diverse learning styles and achievement. (Mitchell, Reilly, Branwell, Solonosky, & Lilly, 2004). In inclusion settings, teachers as managers must take into account the extent to which the students have learned to communicate appropriately, interact cooperatively, and provide resources to the group.

How the teacher manages group composition is critical in determining the effectiveness of the group activity or learning. Often, when students are allowed to select their own teams, they choose their friends or classmates who are like themselves. Low-achieving students are frequently left out or are accepted reluctantly. The positive nature of group activity can actually be undermined when low-achieving students have lower rates of interaction and do not take advantage of leadership opportunities (Evans, 1996).

The teacher as classroom manager cannot afford to leave to chance that students with or without disabilities truly understand how to create the most effective learning environments in a small-group setting. The teacher as manager will have to provide systematic modeling, guided practice, and corrective feedback to teach students how to learn effectively from and with each other. Time spent previously on conveying content information must shift to time teaching students how to work together effectively.

Group Composition

Before teachers set up various small-group formats, they must take into account how to best utilize the effects of the characteristics of their students. The development of students' helping behavior and learning in peer-directed small groups cannot be left to luck, and a systematic approach to teaching small-group skills must be incorporated as part of the classroom curriculum.

HETEROGENEOUS VERSUS HOMOGENEOUS GROUPS   Contrary to overwhelming agreement that heterogeneous groups are preferable to homogeneous groups, no real research exists to support this position. In fact, the results of several studies suggest that great care must be taken in considering the composition of the small group. The nature of questions that students ask each other, for example, has an important effect on the knowledge that will be exchanged. More skilled or older students usually ask more questions that allow them to master the content and fewer questions that elicit direct answers than younger and less capable peers do. Students who are more motivated to truly understand the content make more explicit requests for help than students who just want to finish the task. Students who have little knowledge and students who have a lot of knowledge ask fewer questions than average students do. Students with little knowledge ask more questions from their peers than high-knowledge students do (Paradis & Peverly, 2003).

When grouping students, then, the teacher as manager may not always want to set up entirely heterogeneous groups. More opportunities for reflection and interaction may be available for average students when they are working in groups composed of low and average students than in groups composed of high and average students.

QUESTION ASKING AND RESPONDING   Clear, precise, and direct questions are more likely than indirect questions to bring forth explanations (Webb & Mastergeorge, 2003). Some students have to be taught how to ask questions. Molly, an academically low-skilled student, prefers to sit back in the group. She is passive and is more than willing to let her friends take charge and lead the discussions. Molly has two issues. The first, and perhaps most significant, is learned helplessness. She has learned that someone in the group will always give her the answer or help her finish her work. Molly does not attempt to use the help received except when that help means that someone has done her work for her. Molly's second challenge, ironically, is that she does not know how to ask for appropriate help. She will ask general questions that do not refer to any specific part of the task at hand that will help her with the next step, or she will ask for the answers.

Molly's teacher realizes that she and Molly have some work to do to learn appropriate question-asking strategies. Rather than isolate Molly and potentially embarrass her, Molly's teacher might have all the students in her class role-play appropriate question-and-answer strategies for small-group settings. The class can routinely role-play asking questions and giving answers prior to the class breaking into active-learning small groups. The types of questions asked will vary with the content being learned. Consistent and systematic modeling of asking and responding to questions can be a powerful form of instruction for students like Molly. Teachers must systematically teach their students how to ask questions and answers in small-group settings to avoid negating the power of small-group interactions.

Sometimes, reluctance to ask questions is influenced by the fear of being labeled incompetent. Students may avoid seeking help because they feel personally, socially, and academically threatened (Ryan, Hicks & Midgley, 1997). The way teachers communicate expectations about help-giving and help-seeking behavior can either encourage or discourage students in their approach to asking questions in small-group settings. Role-playing appropriate help-giving and help-seeking questions such as explaining one's interpretation of the task and not directly giving out the answer will do much to clarify teacher expectations. In addition, teachers can use feedback routinely with the whole class, small group, and individuals that encourages taking risks and permits making mistakes (Palinscsar & Herrenkohl, 1999).

Small-group work promotes active learning in many specific ways. Students can give and receive help, and they can share knowledge by building on each others' ideas. Small-group participation also provides a forum for observing each others' learning strategies and internalizing problem-solving techniques used by individual peers and the group as a whole. Small-group work is successful to the extent that teachers as managers systematically teach their students how to interact effectively while taking into account learning styles and knowledge levels.

Cross-age or Peer Tutoring

When students work together as partners—that is, in sets of two—a variety of instructional arrangements can be managed. Students of equal skill level can work together. Students of different ages can work together. Students can work together on complementary tasks. The combination of tutors depends on the makeup of the class, access to students from other classes, and their level of content knowledge. As long as the tutors are knowledgeable about the content, learners can benefit from being tutored even when the tutors are inexperienced or when the tutor doesn't know what the tutored student does and does not know (Chi, Siler, & Jeong, 2004; Chi, Siler, Jeong, Yamauchi, & Hausmann, 2001).

No one knows for sure why tutoring works so well. Preliminary research does suggest that tutors are effective because tutorial explanations prompt those being tutored to think harder with the knowledge they already possess. In addition, when tutors follow the "ask more and tell less," advice, the tutored student learns more (VanLehn, Siler, Murray, Yamauchi, & Baggett, 2003). If this is true, what the tutor says or even whether the tutor understands the explanation, may not be as critical as the mere fact that the student being tutored is talking and thinking about the content of the task. The discussion serves as a way to motivate and engage the student being tutored to draw upon prior knowledge and apply it to the new learning situation.

In inclusion classes, tutors typically have one or both of two types of tasks: those that (1) help the tutored child acquire a new skill or (2) help the tutored child practice fluency with an acquired skill. In either event, to be effective, the tutor must have a solid knowledge base of the content. From a humanistic viewpoint, tutors should also be given some systematic training in how to provide feedback, praise, and reinforcement effectively. The same is true for the student being tutored.

Tutor–tutee etiquette is similar to the etiquette in small-group activities. Teachers must teach their students how to give help and how to seek help from each others through methodically and carefully sequenced instructional activities. Without instruction in tutorial etiquette, an unacceptable and unhealthy codependency can slip silently into the relationship. If Martha always plays the role of "teacher" for Sarup, Sarup may become overly dependent and take on a thinly disguised learned-helplessness role.

Three of the many ways by which teachers as managers can encourage independence in learning when students are paired are (a) to change tutorial pairs, (b) to exchange the roles from tutee to tutor, and (c) to initiate cross-age tutoring. Students in inclusion settings, who typically are the tutored in the classroom, can gain academic and positive self-esteem as learners by tutoring younger students (Davenport, Arnold, & Lassmann, 2004).

In most elementary grades, students enjoy one-on-one contact, whether that contact is with another student or with a care professional or an adult volunteer such as a room mother. Student-to-student teaching can occur on several levels. It can be formal one-to-one tutoring, usually referred to as peer tutoring or cross-age tutoring. Cross-age or peer tutoring also might consist of one student tutoring a small group of students. Another type of tutoring is much less formal. For want of a better term, this type of tutoring can be called the *buddy system* or "love-thy-neighbor" system.

In cross-age tutoring, one child, usually the tutor, is older than the other child. In contrast, peer tutoring refers to a teaching system in which both the tutor and the tutee are approximately the same age. Typically, peer or cross-age tutoring refers to a fairly formal one-to-one relationship in which one child is assisting another in an academic area (Burden & Byrd, 2003). For more than three decades, numerous articles have reported the effectiveness of cross-age and peer tutoring across written expression, spelling, arithmetic, and reading.

Academic tutoring can be in any area in which the student needs either remedial help or extensive practice.

Beneficial experiences are not born by chance but are made by teacher design. To arrange a successful peer or cross-age formal tutoring experience, the teacher should consider the following:

- selection of tutors,
- selection of tutees,
- amount of tutor training,
- extent of supervision, and
- spatial and material resources.

SELECTION OF TUTORS   In a formal cross-age or peer tutoring program, the roles are firmly delineated. The tutor acts as a representative of the teacher, and the tutee is expected to be the student. Because of this formal arrangement, tutors must be selected carefully. On the one hand, students who are well behaved and who excel in their schoolwork often make good tutors. On the other hand, students who have some academic weakness may be more empathetic and, thus, effective tutors. No formula exists for discriminating potentially good tutors from poor tutors. Selecting tutors who either volunteer or show some interest in the task is a good idea.

SELECTION OF TUTEES   The easiest (but fairly elusive) guideline to follow in selecting the tutee is to pick students who wish to be tutored. Capitalizing on a student's desire for a tutor saves the teacher and the student from a potentially unpleasant teaching situation. Enthusiasm of the student aside, the teacher should consider the student's personality. Does the student have enough internal control to work in a one-to-one relationship? Some students can work well in a tutorial situation, and others cannot. The match between the tutor's and the tutee's personality is critical. If the student is highly manipulative, he or she may have to be matched with a tutor who is relatively sophisticated in social perception.

Selection of tutees also can be viewed from the teacher's perspective. Instead of asking students to volunteer for tutoring, the teacher might simply make tutoring a part of the normal class presentation. If tutoring sessions are a routine part of the class procedure, almost all the students in the class are tutored in some area. Providing tutors for all can avoid inadvertently segregating members of the class. If only learners with low skills receive tutors, everyone soon figures out that the tutored students are in the "turkey" learning group and everyone else is an "eagle." Being tutored can easily become stigmatizing.

Consolidating Material and Spatial Resources

Physical arrangement of the classroom can make or break the success of active learning instruction in large-group, small-group, tutorial, or individual activities.

Room size, number of students, effect of disability, furnishings, instructional materials and equipment, plus the number of closets and cabinets and amount of open shelving are variables that must be managed so the students can have easy access to each other and to materials.

Consolidating Materials

Consolidation also applies to the ways in which instructional materials are used. A general education classroom teacher, responsible for teaching both general education and special populations, does not need the added aggravation and hassle of spending a lot of time developing materials to use with the students. Although teachers may have to develop some materials to accommodate the specific skill levels of certain students, typically they will have more than enough material at their disposal already. Nine times in ten, the problem with materials does not result from too few but, rather, too many!

Materials Inventory

To consolidate materials, a materials inventory is the first step. Teachers often spend years gathering dittos, worksheets, and miscellaneous teaching tools, scavenging book fairs and acquiring materials from the stockpiles of friends who have retired. Inventorying your materials allows you to throw away materials. Your files should be consolidated systematically. Many organizational systems are available, some better than others. Filing alphabetically sells a lot of file dividers—and buries material. Filing by coursework taken in college classes is almost as effective as random filing, but not quite as useful. Because you are operating under the consolidation principle already, you may want to reduce the extraneous. The reducing-the-extraneous principle asks that you identify and prioritize key curricular content, so throwing out and retaining can be done fairly easily.

Filing

FILING BY OBJECTIVES   Filing can be done by subject matter and, within the larger category, by objectives. New teachers, teachers with new content, and teachers who want to clean house have a couple of choices in how to file. Traditionalists alphabetize files and place them in a file cabinet. The more ecologically conscious teachers keep files within the memory of a personal computer. Regardless of the system chosen, the operative concept is quick access to the content.

Books change, but objectives remain basically the same. Throughout the years, intermediate grades have studied South America, North America, and Europe. Students still learn the basics about the geography, culture, and economies of these countries. Although some of the teaching content varies over time (e.g., the role of social equality in Third World countries), the basic facts about democratic forms of government remain stable.

Teaching aids such as worksheets and textbook passages can be placed in a folder and filed by objective number. In general mathematics, for example, all material related to the student's ability to perform long-division problems can be placed in a coded file. Material for each objective can be coded and filed sequentially according to your teaching priorities. Students who enter with different skills, of course, will be using materials commensurate with their skill levels.

FILING ACCORDING TO SPECIAL NEEDS   Setting up files sequentially and prioritizing them by objectives allows the teacher to match the child's skill level with the material (coded by objective) that matches the child's level or special need. Take the case of Fran, who is hard of hearing. As with many students with hearing impairment, her understanding of idioms is poor. Suppose Fran is learning how to read maps. An expression such as "follow the map" is sure to cause her some confusion. Special care must be taken to ensure that the material Fran reads either is idiom-free or has an immediately available explanation for the idiom.

The teacher can file a dictionary of idiomatic terms that are likely to occur with each objective. In addition, special materials, as idiom-free as possible, can be filed along with other nonspecialized materials that cover the objective. An example of a file sequenced by prioritized objectives that accounts for special needs is presented as Figure 6. 2. Not all files would have the headings shown in the figure. If you were working with a child like Fran, you probably would gather a great deal of information useful to students with hearing impairment rather than information that could be used with students who have visual or physical disabilities. Materials are gathered as the need arises.

General education teachers do not necessarily have to be the ones who develop the special materials. They just ought to have the material on file. Highly specialized material is typically developed by a special education resource teacher or consultant. To help that specialist provide materials, the general education teacher must be specific. Much time can be saved by presenting the resource teacher with a list of objectives and showing him or her a matched-to-objectives filing system. Then, instead of having innumerable conferences, the resource teacher can simply go to the general education teacher's files to select materials.

Saving Time

Systematizing files by objectives may seem time-consuming at first. In the long run, however, this system is time-saving. Once the major objective headings and file headings have been set up, an aide, a volunteer, or even a student can manage the process with little supervision. Further, the teacher need not gather all material for every subject before initiating a file-by-objectives system. In the first year, objective headings can be listed for each subject. During the year, the teacher can reorganize along the way, gathering and filing materials as the students progress through the program. By the end of the school year, the teacher may not have the total file but will have made a good start. Some subjects will be more complete than others, but at least some material will be organized and available.

An additional bonus to filing materials by objectives is that these can be used with future students. Once materials covering a broad range of skills within an objective are collected and organized, teachers can spend more time on

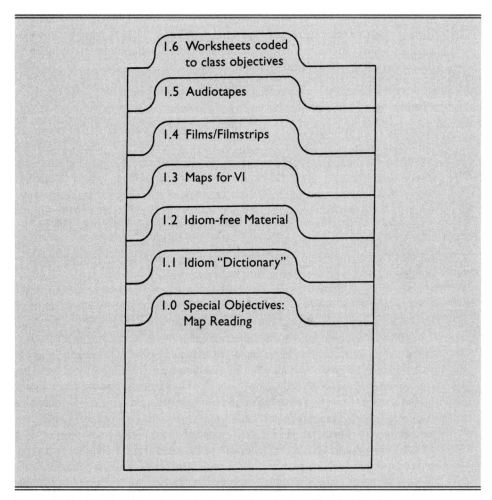

Figure 6.2   File Sequenced by Prioritized Objective for Special Needs

instruction. They will have more time to work with students and spend less time searching for teaching tools.

If you teach at each child's rate, organizing materials by objectives is also practical. Because the material is sequenced, students with lower skills are able to use materials that already have been gathered for more advanced students. You really collect only one set of materials, but the rate at which the students move through the materials can be based on small-group or individual needs.

In many ways, the general education classroom teacher becomes an educational manager or engineer. He or she identifies the objective to teach; matches the objective with the student's academic, social, and sensory needs; pulls the materials from the file; and provides the students with a successful learning experience. A teacher can also add codes related to state standards to the filing system. These codes, however, are often subject to adjustments as changes emerge in the curriculum. State standards probably should not be in the major or primary heading of the filing system.

Managing Physical Space

Although not too much can be done about the actual physical size of the room, the arrangement of furnishings can increase workspace. Unnecessary aisles should be eliminated. Desks and students's work tables can be pushed together to accommodate small groups. This may free up some corner space for work tables. If any student uses a wheelchair, the teacher must make sure that the student's workspace allows for ease of movement. Rather than seating that student in the center of a group of desks, he or she should be seated on an outside aisle.

Freeing corner space allows for a private tutorial space. For tutoring situations that require concentration, this is a good option. If space for tables is limited, the floor can be used for seating or for working.

Not all students need isolated tutorial space. Most can work at their desks with a tutor. To avoid overcrowding, tutors can be scheduled to come into the classroom at different times. This offers a reasonable way to use space.

The teacher's work area should be such that the teacher can see all the students and tutorial teams at all times. As the teacher works with a small group or an individual, he or she should scan the class constantly. In this way, the teacher can provide supervisory feedback to tutors and work groups, as well as monitor progress, work flow, and other classroom events. Physical space needs may also be influenced by contingencies associated with certain types of disabilities. Miscellaneous considerations for various disabling conditions will appear when working with the tutorial teams. Students with visual disabilities should be able to see both the teacher's face and the tutor's face. Students with behavior problems may benefit from sitting closer to the teacher during tutorial sessions. Students who tend to be distracted easily may be better off sitting in a screened-off area or facing a wall. Regardless of where the child or group of students is working, the teacher must organize the room in such a way that all students can be seen at all times.

Body posture and movement can reveal a lot about what is happening within a group or a tutorial partnership. The comfortable couch, sometimes found in classrooms, may be placed with its back against a wall, thereby avoiding areas where the teacher loses direct visual contact with students.

Managing Instructional Materials

Managing instructional materials is another pivotal factor in successful inclusion settings. Students should know where to find materials and where to put material once they have completed a task. Students will have to be taught where to put their completed work. In either an activity-based or a traditional classroom, teachers may want to set up individual files for students to keep their work. Files can be kept in any number of places, but an alphabetized accordion file or small plastic tub has spatial and physical advantages. Color-coding files is helpful for students with reading disabilities. For students with motor problems, files and lightweight tubs are easily transported.

To instill organizational habits and self-management skills, students can be taught how to use a simple three-ring binder. The subdivisions can be ordered according to the sequence of class content. For example, if reading is the first activity of the day, the first tab or divider is the one for reading. Within each subdivision, several small pockets can be inserted—Work to Do, Work Completed, Homework, and any other pocket that makes sense for the class material (McCoy, 2000).

The key to teaching self-management using files, tubs, or three-ring binders is systematic modeling, guided practice, and independent work with feedback. Students who need to learn self-management skills will benefit from teachers who follow through and help them establish new habits. The effective teacher as manager provides appropriate monitoring, individualized in keeping with the child's needs in any academic area.

Modeling

Modeling is one of the most powerful forms of instruction. Teachers are models of organization and management of materials for their students. Where can materials be stored so their location is predictable? Most general education classrooms offer several possible locations, including filing cabinets, shelves, closet space, and the pupils' own desk.

The classroom can be organized into various areas. For example, three shelves on the far west wall might contain reading books sequenced by level of difficulty, and the bottom shelves might contain CDs. If the materials are kept in the same place all year, students should be able to find them without seeking teacher assistance.

Special materials can provide accommodations for students with various disabilities so they will not have to resort to teacher direction. Students who have difficulty with fine-motor skills may have to use special pencil grips, and those with visual disabilities may require large-print books. Other students may need specially constructed worksheets developed by the special teacher. Materials can be kept at the teacher's desk; however, a specially designated space would free the teacher and allow the students more self-determination. This special space must be easily accessible and relatively permanent.

Grouping Work Items That Are Similar

Combining Basic Skills with Content Matter

Grouping similar work items allows the teacher to stretch the teaching dollar further by doubling up. Consider the area of reading instruction. The teacher usually teaches students how to recognize words, sound-out words, or gain meaning from a word or a group of words. In educational jargon we refer to these areas as *word analysis, word recognition, oral reading,* and *reading comprehension.* Normally, teachers use a basal reader and an occasional phonics workbook to teach reading skills. Basal readers are convenient, and the teaching steps are usually laid out well.

These same teaching steps can be used with subject-matter books. Instead of introducing the controlled vocabulary list from the sixth-grade basal reader during reading time, the teacher can introduce the critical vocabulary terms from the social studies text. That same text can be used for practice in oral reading and comprehension. Free reading time can be used to learn some aspect of the social studies content from a library book, and language experience stories in social studies can build on the students' own vocabulary. Thus, social studies and reading are intertwined. Time can be saved or gained by (a) reducing preparation time (e.g., preparing only one combined reading and social studies class rather than two classes, one in reading and one in social studies); (b) reducing the number of class periods by one; and (c) providing more opportunities to work with students who are having reading problems.

The student with reading problems will not be penalized for being unable to read the social studies material, because the teacher will be directly teaching those materials along with reading skills. By combining content and reading instruction, the teacher also will be able to reduce some of the behavior disturbances that students exhibit when they are asked to complete work using materials they cannot fully understand.

Combining Related Skills

In some cases, because of either a school board dictum or a personal belief system, teachers may not feel comfortable combining content material with basic skill areas in reading or math. They may feel more at ease working with obviously related areas such as the skills involved in language arts. Language arts skills center on aspects of reading, spelling, writing, and handwriting. Instead of scheduling a separate instructional period for each language arts area, they can be combined. Table 6.2 shows various combinations of activities.

Let's look at the example presented in the first column. Activities in oral reading, word recognition, spelling sight words, and handwriting have been combined. Using Sadie's work as an example, her teacher first identified key words for Sadie to learn. These words were taken in part from the basal series and in part from words Sadie had used in her experience stories in the past. Sadie's teacher has her practice the words through a flashcard exercise. Sadie is part of a small group working on the key vocabulary terms from the basal along with six special or personal terms.

The students in Sadie's group use the basal and special terms for spelling. Their teacher has them practice spelling and reading the words with each other. In handwriting activities Sadie's teacher has a ready-made list of practice words. Finally, after Sadie's teacher is convinced that the time is right (i.e., the students in the group have learned all the words at the acquisition level), she is ready to

Table 6.2 Instructional Relationships Between Language Arts Subjects

Activities	1	2	3	4	5	6	7	8	9	10	11	12	13	14	15	16	17	18	19	20
Reading																				
Oral reading	x	x	x		x	x	x	x												
Word recognition	x		x			x	x	x												
Word analysis			x	x					x	x	x									
Comprehension		x	x									x	x							
Spelling																				
Sight words	x		x		x		x	x					x	x	x					
Phonetically regular words			x						x	x	x				x	x				
Writing																				
Creative			x						x	x		x			x	x		x		
Guided/Topical				x	x			x						x			x		x	x
Handwriting																				
Isolated letters				x					x						x	x		x		
Words	x	x	x			x		x				x	x	x		x	x	x		

hear them read from the basal reader. The students have achieved proficiency, and success is ensured.

The way that Sadie's teacher, or any other teacher, chooses to present information is a matter of personal style. Some teachers may choose to present four short lessons during an hour's time (mini-lessons in oral reading, word recognition, spelling, and handwriting). Other teachers opt for one or two longer lessons each day in only one or two areas.

The advantage of presenting work in combinations is that the students are shown new concepts or ideas in a variety of ways. They may do an oral drill-and-practice activity with a set of words, spell those words in a worksheet activity, and write those same words for manuscript practice. Thus, students are reviewing continually and, as a result, spending more time with concepts. The review and reinforcement will aid students with learning problems to perform successfully in a general education classroom environment (Smith, 1981).

Managing Time

Determining Teaching Time

Managing time assumes that the teacher knows what he or she wants to accomplish in the time available for teaching. At face value, managing time looks like a piece of cake, but looks can be deceiving. So before you dig in for a mouthwatering bite, put down your instructional fork and inspect the ingredients a little more closely. How much time do you have? Surprisingly enough. A typical class day consists of approximately 8 hours. Roughly 6 of those hours are spent with students, and 2 hours are used for planning and personal needs. During the time without students, planning implies organization in areas such as providing feedback through correcting papers, preparing the next day's lessons, and attending professional meetings. Personal needs consist of eating lunch, drinking the 11th cup of coffee, and solving world problems with colleagues. In the time spent with students, each curriculum area has time management needs of its own.

Time as measured by clocks and calendars has a certain permanence that smacks of iron-clad limitations. Trying to fit all the activities deemed necessary into the boundaries of measurable time might not be the most efficient or effective use of the day (Hargreaves, 1991). Perhaps, then, the ingredient to look at is not time as constrained by clocks and calendars but, rather, time as defined by values and goals (Lippit, 1969).

The school system has imposed some restrictions on physical time as well as educational goals. Within the system, however, teachers have flexibility and can make choices. Instead of being overly concerned with covering all the material, they may want to reconsider and become more concerned with appropriate coverage of some material. Productivity is important, and the teacher's role is to teach students basic information. Counterproductive to this role is racing to reach the end of the book at the expense of leaving half the class behind. The way that teaching time is parceled out should reflect the teacher's personality and experiences. In finding your own time-management system, you can assess your values and goals relative to your students' needs and your school's demands.

Value Systems

The first step in assessing one's value system relative to students' needs and school's demands is to learn to focus on the essential. Ask yourself the following questions:

- What academic and social skills do I believe are essential for my students' present situation?
- What academic and social skills do I believe are essential for my students' future situation?
- How do my beliefs correspond to my students' expectations?
- How do my beliefs correspond to my district's expectations?

A Personal Time Management System

Answers to the questions just posed can help the teacher define a personal time management plan for the classroom. Mixing clock time with value time offers a basic framework within which to work. Considerations in managing school time include the following:

1. *Teaching purpose:* achieving the most student benefits with the most effective use of teacher time.
2. *Goals:* all the realistic expectations.

3. *Clock and calendar time:* the actual countable minutes, days, weeks, and months of the school year.
4. *Plan:* matching the current time management system from where it is to where the teacher wants to be.

Daily Activities

Accomplishing the initial planning steps leads quickly to the everyday routine. The time available for instruction is roughly the same for every teacher. Given that timeframe, some teachers are able to accomplish much more than others. The first questions to ask are:

What do I do with my time?
Am I instructing, or am I running frantically from one raised hand to the next?
Do I find myself disciplining more than teaching?

The second set of questions is:

With whom am I working?
Am I spending a lot of time with the student who always says "please" and "thank you?"
Do I carefully avoid dealing with the students who need three or four explanations before even understanding the directions for the task?
Do I interact more with some students than with others?

Daily Log

The best bet for identifying "what and who with" is to keep a daily log. The log should be based on roughly 15- to 30-minute time increments and maintained for 1 to 2 weeks. A fairly quick analysis of that log should provide major insights into time use and abuse. The sample log presented in Figure 6.3 is just one of many ways to check use and abuse of time. Once the teacher has figured out what activities he or she can do and with whom, that teacher ought to have a fairly clear idea of where classroom time is spent.

Organizing Teaching Time

Having determined where the time is being spent, the next task is to examine how the time is organized.

1. Delegate all possible tasks.
2. Group work items that are similar.
3. Keep starts and stops to a minimum.
4. Have an established schedule.

Delegating

Delegating is the art of appointing, assigning, or entrusting responsibility or authority to another. Delegation is an art because you must balance what is

---

Sample: Reading Period

Time	Student	Activity
9:15–9:30	*John*	*Small-group instruction* (a)
	Sally	
	Erik	
9:20	*Tom*	*Corrected for daydreaming*
9:20–9:30	*Rosa*	*Small-group instruction* (a)
	Barry	
	Elena	
	Will	
9:25	*Tom & Erik*	*Corrected for talking out*
9:30–9:50	*Jeff*	*Small-group instruction : L.E. Story*
	Michael	
	Beth	
	Michelle	
9:35	*Tom*	*Corrected for talking out*
9:40	*Tom*	*Corrected for daydreaming*

Figure 6.3   File Sequenced by Prioritized Objective for Special Needs

reasonable to expect from another person against what you can reasonably expect from yourself. In the classroom, this means overcoming the "I can do it better myself" fallacy. A certain amount of trust, guided by good judgment, will be bestowed, of necessity, on colleagues and subordinates. Whether working with a peer or a subordinate, delegation will be successful only if the task is explained thoroughly and expectations are stated clearly. Another major consideration is the relative task importance. Some tasks simply do not carry the same life-weight as others. Given your resources, you can delegate less critical objectives to other persons.

The ultimate accountability still lies with the person who does the delegating. Freedom from responsibility simply does not exist. Assigning duties to others, however, helps teachers complete duties more efficiently. By delegating some authority, teachers can become more result-oriented and less activity-oriented.

In active-learning inclusion settings, one major source of delegation is the students. Through teacher facilitation, the learners become responsible for helping each other gain knowledge through small-group and tutorial activities. Other obvious sources of delegation are formal and informal volunteers such as parents and grandparents, interns from local colleges and universities, and the list goes on. Volunteers, while welcome, are relatively transitory. They cannot be expected to be in a classroom for more than a short time, and perhaps not even at regularly scheduled times. A vital question remains to be answered: Whom does the general education classroom teacher call upon when he or she wishes to delegate? The teacher has two major sources of people power: colleagues and kids. And colleagues and technology represent sources for delegation.

Collegial Delegation

Collegial delegation turns out to be more of a trade-off than a straight request. The basic line is: "If you do this for me, here's what I can do for you." The general education teacher and the special education teacher can share teaching responsibilities and acquisition of materials. The two can work collaboratively on mutually chosen objectives and determine where the primary instruction occurs and how to reinforce that instruction.

Working with other classroom teachers requires the same collaborative effort but on a grander scale. Three or four students in a grouping might be exchanged for their unique skills, to cut down the number of groups taught. Or the teacher may wish to limit the exchange to materials, and sharing materials can cut down considerably on time demands. For example, one teacher can teach the science classes while the other teacher develops materials for those units. How teachers decide to share teaching responsibilities is limited only by their imagination, their fear of trying something they've never done before, and school policy.

Technological Delegation

As technology continues to advance, educators have unlimited opportunities to apply powerful technological tools to manage the way students of all capabilities are learning. One of the most commonly used technological tools is the personal computer. Managing the classroom and students's learning experiences can create active learning environments and simultaneously provide the teacher with opportunities for time to work with students who need special attention. Students' knowledge is enhanced greatly by the appropriate use of computer technology. Computers can enable students to complete missed assignments, strengthen skills, accelerate learning, and explore many worlds inside and outside of the classroom. Specific accommodations can be made for specific disabilities.

In the past, computers were used primarily in solitary activities. Times have changed, and with these changes the computer has become a medium for collaboration. Project-based learning via computer mediation provides ample resources for allowing new forms of knowledge to be expanded through collaboration (Laffey, Tupper, Musser, & Wedman, 1998). Some research suggests that the quality of interaction between learners in a computer-mediated environment may be even better than interaction in a face-to-face environment (Uribe, Klein, & Sullivan, 2003). In a meta-analysis of 122 studies examining small-group and individual learning with technology, small groups were found to be more effective for learning than when individuals worked in isolation (Lou, Abrami, & d'Apollonia, 2001).

An example of how to encourage social interaction and collaboration is story writing using the computer. The students take turns composing sentences for their joint story. Adding computer graphics to the story provides another dimension and opportunity for social interaction and collaboration.

Thus, the language arts center might include a writing center where Dante, Tamara, and Sonia can discuss and plan stories. This center might include a computer for use by the three students to write and edit stories. Access to the Internet provides the students with a worldwide library center. Given the appropriate software, they can read print along with the computer audiotext. In this center, Dante, Tamara, and Sonia can make 3-D models of their main characters or create a PowerPoint presentation complete with illustrations as a rendition of their stories.

Computer-based teaching and learning have had positive effects in the classroom. Students seem to be motivated to learn though the computer. Students react positively to media responses and practices offered through various computer programs. Even struggling readers can practice skills without becoming embarrassed or exposed to classroom situations that call attention to their poor reading performance. Most students are motivated and show a positive attitude toward learning when they use computers for classroom activities (Forcier, 1999).

To use computers effectively as instructional tools and as a means to delegate aspects of instruction, teachers must have basic instructional and classroom management strategies for implementing small-group or individualized work within any learning environment (Moore, Laffey, Espinosa, & Lodree, 2002). Many of the same issues that apply to small-group instruction apply to working with a computer in small groups. Teachers must determine group membership and provide instruction in the etiquette of computer use. Among other issues that have emerged that are unique to using the computer as a management tool are availability and scheduling of computers and the cognitive and the mechanical effects of a disability when using a computer.

AVAILABILITY AND SCHEDULING   Many classrooms have access to no more than one or two computers outside of the computer lab. Naturally, then, not all students can work on the computer simultaneously. When students are working in groups, one or two students from each group can be assigned to work on the computer at a specified time, or if the groups are small enough, groups can be delegated to work on the computer at designated hours during the day.

Students can also be encouraged to gather material ahead of time for use during their computer time. To eliminate the chaos of students waiting impatiently for their turn, all students in the class must have access to the computer at a designated time. Once in front of the computer, members of a group will have to take turns using it (Mandell, Sorge, & Russell, 2002).

EFFECTS OF DISABILITY   First and foremost, students must be instructed in how to use the programs or the hardware. Although many students are more computer-savvy than most of their teachers, teachers cannot take for granted that students understand or have already learned how to navigate computers.

Cognitive level encompasses more than IQ. Relevant to using the computer is the student's problem-solving ability. Questions that are helpful in determining how to accommodate the student's needs are related directly to how a child approaches tasks:

How does the student gather information?
What type of assumptions does the student make in solving problems?

The developmental level of students should be the determining factor in selecting computer activities.

Sometimes students have fine-motor or gross-motor disabilities that interfere with typical computer operation. Alternative methods are available for these students. Given the appropriate software, students do not have to know how to type very well, or even have to type at all, to be able to use a computer in classroom projects or activities.

For example, software programs allow students to control computer commands through voice activation. For students with serious coordination problems and those who cannot use speech production to control computer commands, devices known as key guards can be effective. These guards consist of plastic sheets with holes corresponding to the key positions, mounted over the standard keyboard, to help students control key strikes. Other devices for individuals with poor hand coordination are the hand stylus and the joystick. The admonishment, "Use your head," can have literal meaning for students with restricted movement. The head wand using eye or head movement is another accommodation for students with special needs. Head wands are pointers affixed to a band around the head. The pointer can act as an extension of the fingers when the fingers are not capable of movement. And in another accommodation, "deep eye movement" enables the student can use eye movement to control a computer.

Often, students with physical disabilities can use the same physical accommodations to control movements as they use to control their daily environment. Familiar accommodations permit the student to expand known techniques to other situations.

Social Interaction

Of particular note is the need for communication in classroom social interaction. All work and no play makes for extreme isolation. Communication for students who are nonvocal is essential for social interaction is and also necessary to dispel the stigma that easily can become associated with their disability. Sometimes peers, teachers, or other school personnel attribute a wide range of imperfection simply because the child is not vocal. Uneducated people tend to think of non-speakers as cognitively impaired. When students are nonvocal, social communication can be available through an increasing number of augmentative and alternate communication (AAC) systems. These devices have increased more rapidly than the ability of many educational programs to incorporate these new tools into teaching and learning experiences.

The role of general educators and the special education teachers alike is to ensure a constant flow of communication with the technology specialist in their school or district. Some of the most advanced technological equipment and up-to-date knowledge can be accessed for use with students who are blind or who have severe physical disabilities such as those with cerebral palsy. Assistive technology specialists working in centers for the blind or working out of hospital settings are excellent sources of current information in technology. Although classroom teachers are not expected to set up AAC systems, they can assist the specialist by identifying terms or phrases that would be helpful in the classroom or on the playground. Predicting all the situations that might arise is impossible, of course, but key phrases could be prioritized. Other class members might even generate a *phrase bank* for use by the classmate. Peers of students with severe vocal disabilities are in the best position to provide age-appropriate words and phrases, including the most current slang. The phrase bank can be organized categorically to reflect the purpose of conversational communication for social purposes in the areas of, for example (Light, Roberts, Dimarco, & Greiner, 1998):

- communicating needs,
- transferring information,
- keeping social closeness, and
- social etiquette.

When done sensitively, assisting another classmate to communicate can create a true sense of inclusion in the classroom community.

When adaptations are introduced, all students, or at least the interested ones, should have the opportunity to try out the accommodations or modifications. By encouraging other students in the class to learn about or use some of the specialized computer adaptations, a common ground can be established between the student with physical restrictions and those who are not so restricted. Classroom teachers should also try to use the devices to gain insight into planning lessons for that child or for understanding how that child can work with others in a group.

Teacher Proficiency

Without doubt, continuing advancements in technology have changed the way in which classroom teachers and their students relate prior knowledge to new information. Unfortunately, the consensus among business leaders, parents, and educators is that current educational practices cannot prepare students sufficiently for our ever-changing technological society. In part, the problem resides with classroom teachers. Teachers still report limited computer use for classroom instructional purposes, as well as limited proficiency in their own computer skills (Wilson, Notar, & Yunker, 2003). Even though teacher skills in working with technology are increasing, nearly two-thirds of all teachers feel unprepared or only somewhat prepared to use technology in teaching (Pianfetti, 2001).

Computers and related systems may be the light at the end of the educational tunnel for teachers in the 21st century. Computers present opportunities to profit from technology in ways that can accommodate the instructional needs of an increasingly diverse population of students. Identifying the most appropriate hardware and software for students of the 21st century in inclusion settings is essential if teachers are to provide appropriate public education for their charges. Clearly, a lab outside the classroom is not an acceptable alternative when considering the daily needs of teachers and students with and without disabilities.

Summary

Classroom management systems and effective teaching practices are complementary aspects of inclusion settings. Classroom management is much like management in any organization. Teachers build schedules, establish routines, and develop instruction formats that support good teaching principles. States and districts have lessened teachers' workloads by organizing, sequencing, and identifying the minimum standards of knowledge expected of learners. Based on broad goals and performance objectives identified by the state or district, teachers can streamline instructional objectives, materials, methods, and evaluation to meet the needs of their students. Teachers can present these instructional objectives utilizing techniques based on active learning and brain-based research.

Inclusion teachers as managers often utilize the active learning approaches found in cooperative learning, collaboration, and tutoring, which have been consistently shown to be beneficial for various ages and cognitive levels. To manage active learning approaches, teachers must take into account group dynamics, individual strengths and weaknesses, and time for teaching students appropriate learning etiquette. Managing instructional materials is a pivotal factor in successful inclusion settings. Inclusion teachers teach their students how to self-manage. In addition, the teacher's classroom becomes a model of management in terms of scheduling, instructional format, and physical arrangement of classroom centers and furniture.

Teachers also are making greater use of technology for individual, small-group, and project-oriented activities. To use computers effectively as instructional tools and as a means to delegate aspects of instruction, teachers must use instructional and classroom management strategies. Many of the same issues that apply to active learning formats also apply to using computers in classroom situations. The questions of how to determine group membership and how to provide instruction in the etiquette of computer use must be practiced and monitored.

References

Astleitner, H. (2000). Designing Emotionally Sound Instruction: The FEASP-Approach. *Instructional Science, 28,* 169–198.

Berliner, D., & Casanova, U. (1998). Peer tutoring: A new look at a popular practice. *Instructor, 97,* 14–15.

Box, J. A., & Little, D. C. (2003). Cooperative small-group instruction combined with advanced organizers and their relationship to self-concept and social studies achievement of elementary school students. *Journal of Instructional Psychology, 30.*

Brandon, D. P., & Hollingshead, A. B. (1999). Collaborative learning and computer-supported groups. *Communication Education, 48,* 109–126.

Burden, P. R. & Byrd, D. M. (2003). *Methods for Effective Teaching.* Boston: Allyn and Bacon.

Chi, M. T. H., Siler, S., & Jeong, H. (2004). Can tutors monitor students' understanding accurately? *Cognition and Instruction, 22,* 363–387.

Chi, M. T. H., Siler, S., Jeong, H., Yamauchi, T., & Hausmann, R. G. (2001). Learning from human tutoring. *Cognitive Science, 25,* 471–533.

Davenport, S. V., Arnold, M., & Lassmann, M. (2004, Spring). The impact of cross-age tutoring on reading attitudes and reading achievement. *Reading Improvement, 41,* 3–13.

Evans, J. L. (1996) SLI subgroups: Interaction between discourse constraints and morpho-syntactic deficits. *Journal of Speech and Hearing Research. 39,* 655–660.

Forcier, R. C. (1999). *The Computer as an Educational Tool: Productivity and Problem Solving.* New York: Prentice Hall.

Hargreaves, A. (1991, April). *Prepare to meet thy mood? Teacher preparation time and the intensification thesis.* Paper presented at annual meeting of the American Educational Research Association, Chicago.

Johnson, D. W, Johnson, R. T. & Stanne, M. B. (2002). Cooperative Learning Methods: a Meta-Analysis. *Advances Physiology Education, 2,* 72–84.

Laffey, J., Tupper, T., Musser, D., & Wedman, J. (1998). A computer-mediated support system for projectbased learning. *Educational Technology Research and Development, 46,* 73–86.

Light J. C.; Roberts, B., Dimarco R., Greiner, N. (1998). Augmentative and alternative communication to support receptive and expressive communication for people with autism — An introduction. *Journal of Communication Disorders, 31,* 153–180.

Lippit, G. (1969). Looking at our use of time. *Training & Development Journal, 23,* 3–6.

Lou, Y., Abrami, P. C., & d'Apollonia, S. (2001). Small group and individual learning with technology: A meta-analysis. *Review of Educational Research, 71,* 449–521.

Mandell, S., Sorge, D. H., & Russell, J. D. (2002). TIPs for Technology Integration. *TechTrends, 46,* 39–43.

McCoy, K. M. (2000). A proactive role for parents in IEPs. *Exceptional Parent, 30,* 62–68.

Mitchell, S., Reilly, R., Bramwell, G., Slonosky, A., & Lilly, F. (2004). Friendship and choosing groupmates: Preferences for teacher-selected vs. student-selected groupings in high school science classes. *Journal of Instructional Psychology, 31,* 20–32.

Moore, J., Laffey, J., Espinosa, L. & Lodree, A. (2002). Bridging the digital divide for at-risk students: Lessons learned. *Tech Trends, 46,* 5–9.

Palinscsar, A. S., & Herrenkohl, L. R. (2002). Designing collaborative learning contexts. *Theory into Practice, 41,* 26–32.

Paradis, L. M., & Peverly, S. T. (2003). The effects of knowledge and task on students' peer-directed questions in modified cooperative learning groups. *The Child Study Journal, 33,* 117–139.

Pianfetti, E.S. (2001). Teachers and technology: Digital literacy through professional development. *Language Arts, 78,* 255–262.

Ryan, A. M., Hicks, L., & Midgley, C. (1997). Social goals, academic goals, and avoiding seeking help in the classroom. *Journal of Early Adolescence, 17,* 152–171.

Slavin, R. E. (1995). Enhancing intergroup relations in schools: Cooperative learning and other strategies. In W. D. Hawley & A. W. Wells, (Eds), *Toward a commondestiny: Improving race and ethnic relations in America* (pp. 291–314). San Francisco: Jossey-Bass.

Smith, D. D. (1981). *Teaching the learning disabled.* Englewood Cliffs, NJ: Prentice Hall.

Stringer, S. J., Reynolds, G. P., & Simpson, F. M. (2003). Collaboration between classroom teachers and a school counselor through literature circles: Building self-esteem. *Journal of*

Instructional Psychology, 30(1). Retrieved January 11, 2008 from http://findarticles.com/p/articles/mi_m0FCG/is_1_30/ai_99983048

Uribe, D, Klein, J.D., & Sullivan, H. (2003). The effect of computer-mediated collaborative learning on solving Ill-defined problems. *Educational Technology, 51,* 5–19.

VanLehn, K., Siler, S. A., Murray, C., Yamauchi, T., & Baggett, W. B. (2003). Why do only some events cause learning during human tutoring? *Cognition and Instruction, 21,* 209–249.

Vermette, P., Harper, L, & DiMillo, S. (2004). Cooperative & collaborative learning ... with 4-8 year olds: how does research support teachers' practice? *Journal of Instructional Psychology.* Retrieved November 15, 2007 from http://findarticles.com/p/articles/mi_m0FCG/is_2_31/ai_n6130124/pg_1

Vygotsky, L. S. (1978). *Mind in society: The development of higher psychological processes.* Cambridge, MA: Harvard University Press.

Webb, N. & Mastergeorge, A. (2003). Promoting effective helping behaviour in peer directed groups. *International Journal of Educational Research, 39,* 73–97.

Wilson, J. D., Notar, C. C., Yunker, B. (2003). Elementary in-service teacher's use of computers in the elementary classroom. *Journal of Instructional Psychology, 30.* Retrieved January 11, 2008 from http://findarticles.com/p/articles/mi_m0FCG/is_4_30/ai_112686159

Reading Evaluation
in Inclusive Settings

KEY TERMS

- ◆ basal reader
- ◆ comprehension
- ◆ DIBELS®
- ◆ linguistic approach
- ◆ phonics
- ◆ skills-based instruction
- ◆ whole-language instruction
- ◆ whole-word method
- ◆ word analysis
- ◆ word recognition

George started kindergarten just like every other child his age. Excited about going to school, George discovered the world of reading. Every day his teacher would read stories about interesting people, places, and events. George had always been aware of letters, but he was beginning to understand that letters had sounds and meaning.

By the beginning of first grade, George could read his name, the words *red, yellow, green,* and *blue,* and he knew the names of all the letters of the alphabet. His first-grade teacher, Ms. Rice, continued reading wonderful stories that captured George's imagination and desire to learn more. By second grade, George had memorized around 50 words and could read special books provided by his teacher, but sounds were becoming confusing. Luckily for George, Mr. Powell, his second-grade teacher, continued to read marvelous fictional stories as well as nonfiction accounts of the world in which George lived. By third grade, George was hopelessly lost in the tangle of letters, words, sounds, and meaning from print. Even though decoding print eluded George, he continued to develop his knowledge about the world from stories, fiction and nonfiction, read by his teacher and gathered from videos and CDs.

George is a bright boy who cannot freely enter the world of print. The reading door is locked, and the odds are high that George will never find a key. What will happen to George? Will he be doomed to failure and relegated to minimum-wage employment, or will he thrive and graduate from an Ivy League college? George's future depends a great deal on how his teachers address his reading issues.

The good news–bad news for children like George is that at no other time in history have the political, sociological, and educational spotlights been focused so strongly on children's ability to read, write, and calculate. Spurred by the enactment of the No Child Left Behind Act of 2001 (NCLB) and the Individuals with Disabilities Education Improvement Act of 2004 (IDEA), educators, for better or worse, are forced to examine classroom practices and student outcomes. The overriding goal of NCLB is to ensure that all children, including the approximately 5.3 million school-aged children served by special education programs and services, will reach or exceed a minimum level of proficiency in reading and language arts by 2014. This goal is piggybacked with a need to examine classroom practices and subsequent student outcomes (Inman, Marlow, & Barron, 2004; Turnbull & Turnbull, 2007).

George and his classmates must be able to read a text accurately and quickly in order to understand what they are reading. Reading fluency allows children to acquire new vocabulary, which in turn assists them in becoming more fluent and developing comprehension when using print. One of the most frightening and disturbing ideas set forth by research is the notion that children who are not fluent in reading by second grade will never catch up to other students (Murphy, 2004). If the idea that literacy is the key to competence in all other subjects (Marsh, 1999) is valid, it is no wonder that legislators, educators, and parents are deeply concerned about school practices in reading.

Student performance in reading must be measured in order to determine the effectiveness of teaching practices. A federal priority has been to provide annual reading assessment beginning in third grade. Formal achievement measures, such as those found on state and national standardized reading tests, are one of the ways to determine reading proficiency (Mindes, 2003). Low performance on these measures can have serious ramifications at the state and local level, not to mention the effect on the emerging readers. In order for many children to obtain adequate yearly progress (AYP) on standardized measures, they must be provided with appropriate reading instruction.

To determine the appropriateness of the reading instruction, or the students' ability to comprehend meaningfully from text, requires more than an annual measure of accountability. When daily reading performance is being monitored, then and only then, can teachers determine the effectiveness or the appropriateness of the reading instruction.

The most sensible and pragmatic concern of inclusion teachers is how to monitor day-to-day individualized reading of all their students and to check that the instructional activities are facilitating reading improvement (Papalewis, 2004; Topping & Fisher, 2003).

While teachers and policymakers continue to debate the most effective and ethical methods of standardized testing, what remains uncontroversial is that students must demonstrate reading skill development. For primary-level students, the focus of reading instruction and evaluation typically is directed toward basic skill acquisition directly related in various proportions, depending on the method of instruction, to word recognition, phonics, and comprehension. Somewhere around third grade, the instructional emphasis on these basic skills shifts to proficiency or fluency through application to content areas such as history, science, and any other reading-based academic area. Thus, not only must George be fluent with sounds, whole words, and comprehension skills, he must also use the skills as tools for reading literature, social studies, health, science, and even mathematics.

Despite the complexity of designing assessments, the outcome of appropriate individual reading instruction is obvious to both the sophisticated and the not-so-sophisticated evaluator. Children who easily comprehend material presented through oral or silent reading are said to be good readers. Poor readers are those students who are often defined by low scores on reading comprehension tasks on standardized tests and difficulty with everyday reading experiences. Regardless of the score earned on the standardized test, if students cannot read meaningfully, their educational experience must be altered.

Analysis of children's reading skills, under a variety of situations, is the first step in trying to develop an appropriate reading environment. The level of the students' motivation, stress, or general cognitive skills, however, can also influence reading comprehension. To identify and develop appropriate reading programs, inclusion teachers have to isolate the factors that make up the child's complete reading experience (Guron & Lundberg, 2003).

Whole-Word Versus Phonics Controversy

Look-Say Method

For years, the great debate in the area of reading instruction has centered on whether to teach the whole-word method (often referred to as the look-say method) or to teach phonics. The whole-word method advocates that reading instruction first focus on meaning. To teach children to read for meaning (whole words instead of isolated sounds), only a limited sight vocabulary is taught. With the basal reader the child is able to recognize a limited set of words as wholes. These words are arranged into sentences and stories about topics of interest, as in the archetypal "Spot, Spot. See Spot go. Go, Spot. Go, go." Vocabulary was not all that was restricted. Reading instruction with the basal series was firmly based in the folkways of school reading practices. Then along came Dale Chall.

Phonics Approach

In 1967 Chall researched phonics teaching versus the whole-word approach and found that initial intensive and systematic phonics teaching was superior not only in developing word recognition but also in developing reading comprehension. Chall was not alone. Research demonstrating the need for phonics instruction as a base for teaching nonreaders to recognize words deluged the educational community. The ability to decode words enables children to analyze the visual structure of a word and assists with meaning when the context alone is insufficient to support word identification. Knowledge of letter–sound relationships provides a tool for minimizing uncertainty, ultimately allowing the child to transform an unknown word into a sight word (Koriat, Greenberg, & Kreimer, 2002; National Institute of Child Health and Human Development, 2000).

With this plethora of evidence, one might wonder if the basals should be rewritten, and in place of "Go, Spot. Go, go," read, "Go, Spot. Went, gone." Instead, a new wave of antiphonics persuasion swept across the reading instruction landscape. Some theorists suggest that the development of reading skills or literacy is innate. They contend that children begin to read only when the written symbol is meaningful, contextualized, and social (Halliday, 1969). Many 3- and 4-year-olds score 100% with words such as "McDonald's," "Pepsi," and "ice cream." More sophisticated toddlers are even able to read foreign print (e.g., "Häagen-Dazs"). Beginning reading is viewed as a communication system, and the way children find significance in written language may even be cultural (Clay, 1976).

Goodman and Burke (1973) reached the conclusion that nonproficient readers tend to get bogged down in their preoccupation with letters, and, as a result, words lose meaning for them. Goodman and Goodman (1979) went so far as to say that creating curricula based on artificial skill sequences and hierarchies is a serious mistake.

The notion that it is a serious mistake to create curricula based on isolated skills has merit, but the whole-language position of the extremists on phonics is misguided. Students do not create their own sound systems or develop a systematic approach to phonics without instruction (Heymsfeld, 1992).

Young or poor readers tend to overuse content, and too many inappropriate substitutions in context lead to word guessing. Some whole-language theorists have suggested that good readers engage in sampling print, skipping what they do not know, and guessing the rest from context and experience, but in reality only poor readers "read" this way (Liberman & Liberman, 1990).

When a child has limited knowledge of sounds, both spelling and reading strategies become inefficient. When sound patterns are accurate and well-established, on the other hand, young and poor readers can translate sound–symbol systems into speech sounds. With accurate translation, children have yet another tool to help them recognize words they have never seen before but have heard (Adams, 1990).

In spite of this research-based information, the whole-language views of the Goodmans and their disciples continue to be revisited. In the 1970s, 1980s, and 1990s, advocates made statements asserting that phonics is a trivial skill in learning to read or a peripheral concern for the child who is learning to read.

Although basals were not ruled out entirely, the emphasis on meaning became stronger than ever. Whole-language philosophers pushed basals to the back of the bookcase and moved "Big Books" to the front. Big Books typically have a controlled vocabulary and build from sentence or phrase repetition. (Oddly enough, despite the inventive stories and beautiful illustrations, Big Books strikingly resemble their not-too-distant cousins, the basals.) Suffering an inordinate amount of verbal pummeling in the first decade of the 21st century, basals nonetheless continue to be used either as the basic reading program or in conjunction with other reading approaches in most classrooms in North America.

Bridging the Phonics Versus Word Recognition Chasm

Linguists attempted to bridge the gap between the phonics and whole-word approaches. In the linguistic approach a restricted vocabulary, based on phonetically regular words, was to be the chain that reunited the two camps. Early attempts, such as "Fan the tan man," proved to be a weak link at best. The linguists moved on and seemed to meld into one or the other of the two reading camps. Some of the linguists and many reading teachers continued to wonder whether problems in reading are in the visual stage, i.e., phonics or sound–symbol association, or in a linguistic stage, i.e., problems understanding the meaning of the language (Liberman & Shankweiler, 1985). While the linguists continued to ponder, teachers continued to teach. Some inclusion teachers dealt with basals only, some with phonics only, but many more felt a little guilty and began to deal with both.

While many teachers were incorporating both whole-word and phonics instruction into the reading program, researchers began to make some distinctions between practiced and beginning readers. New jargon began to evolve. Skilled readers use a top-down reading process; developing readers use a bottom-up reading process (Weaver & Resnick, 1979). Top-down by any other name is still a meaning-based approach (Fredericksen, 1979; Smith, 1971), and a bottom-up process clearly refers to phonics (Perfetti & Hogaboam, 1975). When gearing reading instruction to primary-level children, emphasis in reading skills might focus on phonics. If, on the other hand, reading instruction is geared to intermediate or more advanced readers, the classroom method tends to draw heavily upon experience or meaning.

Fortunately for some reading theorists, later reading research discovered what guilty and effective teachers have known for a long time. Top-down and bottom-up processing should be occurring at all levels of reading at the same time (Adams & Collins, 1977; Rummelhart, 1989). Instruction in reading must take into account both phonics skills (or decoding) and word recognition. The goal for sound recognition and word recognition is automatic recognition that enables the reader to focus attention on reading for meaning (Adams, 1990; Mason & Au, 1990). The question of how to help children achieve automaticity becomes the issue of debate. Developing automaticity is especially crucial for at-risk and beginning readers (Sinatra, 1992). The only cloudy issue in this silver-lining view of reading instruction is the extent to which emphasis is placed on teaching phonics skills and meaning-based instruction.

Using Skill Level in Instruction

Verifiable research data tell us that skilled and novice readers perform differently. New readers, as well as readers who have reading problems, tend to read slowly. They may even attend to isolated letters or words instead of phrases or clause units. New readers sometimes get lost on the page and skip whole lines or ignore punctuation. Skilled readers, in contrast, tend to read smoothly and in phrases. Reading is automatic, quick, and accurate, with little conscious attention or effort. Expression for skilled readers is typically appropriate, and they generally read relatively comfortably. Although the terms used to describe skilled and novice readers are not measurable, differences in their oral reading performance are distinguishable.

The passage from novice to skilled reader is a mysterious one. Even though research has shown a number of the processes involved in skilled reading, we still are not sure when or in what manner reading behavior evolves from inefficient to proficient and automatic (Naslund & Samuels, 1992). In contrast, we do know that success in reading for children who are at risk is achieved when these students are participating actively in a carefully structured program based on their individual needs and are taught by those who firmly contend that students at risk can and will succeed (Bowers, 1990).

This information could guide the format of a reading program. For the new or unskilled reader, emphasis on word recognition and instruction in phonics should go hand-in-hand. Because both types of instruction have obvious merit, both methods can be used simultaneously and accorded instructional time on a per-child-as-needed basis.

Components of Reading

Because reading is a complex act, teachers as evaluators need to analyze the total picture of how a child reads under a mixture of circumstances (e.g., when reading a storybook, a textbook, directions on the board, reading aloud or silently). In order to capture the reading big picture, teacher–evaluators must identify the relationship between the child's skills in the many related components of reading and how they impact day-to-day comprehension. Reading consists of many related and overlapping components, sounds, letter shapes, word order, and meaning, among others, that all interact with word recognition and comprehension for single words, phrases, sentences, and passages consisting of one or many paragraphs. Although not a perfect solution, perhaps the easiest way to determine the effectiveness of a reading program is to examine the reader's skills for basic reading components.

Although the act of reading can be divided in many ways, one suggested approach is to consider evaluation in four areas: word analysis, word recognition, oral reading, and comprehension. In common parlance, *word analysis* can refer to decoding, word attack, phonics, or any other activity that requires a student to analyze sounds or combination of sounds. Word analysis requires the reader to recognize that words are made of sounds and that these sounds carry meaning. *Word recognition* refers to the ability to read or recognize whole words instantly— orally, vocally, or neurologically—which are meaningful to the reader and have been stored in memory. *Oral reading* skills typically combine word recognition and word analysis skills with oral language development and often include evaluation of fluency. Reading fluency is the ease with which the reader pronounces words and sentences. Finally, *comprehension* implies the ability to grasp meaning associated with the sounds of a word or group of words or passages.

To evaluate, and ultimately determine, appropriate instruction for readers, inclusion teachers need to identify the skill level of their students in each of the four areas as well as the impact of each skill on the other in influencing the child's total reading achievement. Language development is also key for children learning to read. Accordingly, language development and experiences with language (i.e., receptive and expressive interactions with others) must be evaluated along with the mechanics of reading. Finally, the visual system can also impact reading from print and must be taken into account when evaluating reading.

Word analysis, word recognition, oral reading, and comprehension interact with each other and are also influenced by the students' knowledge base. The students' knowledge base is heavily influenced by familiarity with the world around them. Identifying the meaning of the word *ocean* is different for Ravi, whose home is on the coast of Southern California, than for Mary Jane, who comes from Nebraska and has never seen the ocean. Yet, both children successfully produce the correct pronunciation and comprehend the meaning *ocean* relative to their life experiences. Life experiences also develop from the cognitive, affective, and sensory skills of the reader. Angela is blind, and her understanding of the term *ocean* is very different from that of either Ravi or Mary Jane.

Given that reading is a complex act composed of a variety of components and influenced by cognitive, sensory, and affective skills, the stereotype notion of *poor reader* must be discarded. Students with reading disabilities, whether eligible for special education services or not, are a heterogeneous group. No evidence supports one factor or characteristic that applies to all children who have reading issues. Children can have difficulties in learning any, all, or combinations of the four major reading skill areas.

William, Louise, Roberto, and Cindy are all children with reading disabilities, reading issues so severe that comprehension from print is seriously affected. William has problems with decoding. Louise cannot remember anything she has ever read. Roberto can tell you everything he has read verbatim, but when asked to paraphrase he has no comprehension of the material. Although Cindy has excellent comprehension for the first few paragraphs in a story, she typically takes a turn with her imagination, embellishing the story to such a degree that by the time she has finished telling it a new plot with imaginary characters has emerged. Moreover, unless directly told the pronunciation for a new word, Cindy cannot figure out how the sounds work together to form words.

Identification of Skill Level

Identifying appropriate instructional programs for children begins with surveying or screening their present level of educational performance (PLEP). Two major questions must be addressed at the screening level. The first question asks, "What is the child's previous reading history?" The second question is, "What are the child's reading scores like when compared to other students in the same grade in the same school?" We can begin to answer both questions by using formal and informal evaluation resources.

Screening Tests

The child's reading history can be obtained from various sources. Normative or standardized tests help to pinpoint an approximate grade level. In Ms. Tanner's third-grade class, most of her students' scores on normative tests, like those of Alyssa, Julia, and Lauren, fall into the third-grade range. If Ms. Tanner took these grade-equivalency scores at face value, she might inadvertently present material that is too difficult for the children to read. Grade-equivalency scores are simply signals suggesting that all might be well in the third-grade reading world. However, Ms. Tanner has had enough experience with grade-equivalency scores to understand the need for more direct evaluation with classroom material. Ms. Tanner, like all experienced reading evaluators, recognizes that normative reading tests have limited value when assessing an individual's strengths and weaknesses (Moseley, 2004).

Depending on the specificity of the tests, the inclusion teacher either receives a general reading score or scores for specific subareas. Many of the tests used to determine yearly growth are based on the reading curriculum used in the state or district. Annual tests, regardless of the source, can give the teacher the first introduction to the skill levels of her students. The skillful teacher–evaluator understands that annual tests can mask the true reading ability of some students. Scores of children with test anxiety, children with good guessing skills, and children who borrow answers from their neighbors typically do not reveal true reading ability. Even accounting for appropriate adaptations, by the very design of the standardized tests, some children, like Barbara, appear to have a reading disability when in fact none exists. Other children, like Melody, may actually have reading problems, but not be identified by the measure used. Barbara's score would be called a *false positive,* and Melody's score would be called a *false negative* (Kauffman & Hallahan, 2005). Teachers understand that annual reading test scores are just one type of evaluation material and not the only means of identifying skilled and unskilled readers.

Anecdotal Records

Anecdotal records are another good screening technique. Anecdotal records are informal collections of the memories of people who have been involved with child-rearing or nurturing situations that require reading. A family member, such as a grandparent or mother, babysitters, and former teachers are good sources for screening a child's reading history. Jack's mother, for example, works with Jack on his homework five days a week. Jack's mother has many insights into Jack's reading skills. She may not use educational jargon, but her descriptions of Jack's reading behavior are right on target. Jack's mother knows when her son is struggling with words and does not truly understand the directions or how to complete assigned classwork. The teacher-evaluator can translate Jack's mother's descriptions into more professional terms and locate additional evaluation material if needed.

In order for inclusion teachers to tap into anecdotal knowledge about their students' reading, a simple survey, not longer than one page, can either be sent home or be administered during parent conferences. The simpler the survey, the more likely it is that the information will be returned. Jack's teacher, Ms.

Petronila, prefers to gather descriptions at parent conferences. Ms. Petronila sometimes contacts parent over the phone or via e-mail. The results of her conversations give Ms. Petronila insights into Jack's reading skills as well as the level of home involvement. When possible, Ms. Petronila also checks with Jack's former teachers. Information gathered from previous teachers often helps Ms. Petronila save time in designing more specific reading evaluation plans.

Informal Student Interviews

Without a doubt, students themselves are in a good position to give their teachers insights into their personal world of reading. Depending on the age or maturity level of the students, teachers can design opportunities for students to describe their experiences with reading. Screening tools can be as sophisticated as asking the children to write a brief essay about their experiences and feelings toward reading or as simple as having them underline one of several circle faces representing answers to questions raised by the teacher about reading.

An example of one of the circle-face questions Ms. Petrolina uses with her students is presented in Figure 7.1. Ms. Petronila asks the whole class a question, and each student underlines the face that most represents their thoughts. Ms. Petronila does not need a sophisticated statistical tool or a lot of time to figure out which of her students have serious issues related to reading. A quick glance at the facial expressions underlined by her students lets her know which students have had positive experiences with reading and which have not. Most likely those children, like Hector, who have underlined many negative faces will need closer diagnostic attention than those children, like Oscar, who have consistently chosen happy faces to the questions asked by Ms. Petronila.

Curriculum-Based Assessments

Curriculum-based assessments are another rich source of information for identifying children's individual strengths and weaknesses in reading. Curriculum-based assessments are created from the materials used daily in the classroom. Curriculum-based assessments are usually more informative than norm-referenced measures (Moseley, 2004) and can be used diagnostically to determine which skills the student has or needs. Curriculum-based measures in reading can

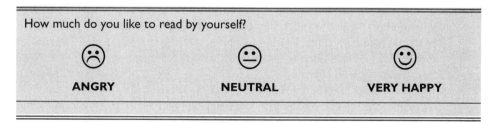

Figure 7.1   Sample Question From Ms. Petronila's Reading Survey

be administered individually or in groups, depending on the questions the teacher is attempting to answer.

Regardless of the test scores found on the annual reading evaluation measures, the teacher has to determine where the child is reading relative to the class materials and curricula. Alyssa, Lauren, and Julia, students in Ms. Tanner's third-grade class, have already been screened. The results of their tests indicate that they are reading at grade level, but Ms. Tanner knows that test results can be misleading. In class Alyssa completes all assignments accurately and appropriately within the given time constraints. Based on Alyssa's performance, Ms. Tanner felt no need for further reading evaluation. In contrast, when Julia tries to read from the social studies text, she cannot finish her assignments. Julia seems to be unable to find the main idea of the passages. Lauren, too, seems unable to complete her work for similar reasons. Ms. Tanner realizes that these possible comprehension problems could stem from many sources.

Instead of using commercial or more formally designed classroom-based assessments, Ms. Tanner began the process of identifying Julia's problem by asking her to read a passage from her social studies book aloud. Julia could barely identify 80% of the words. Ms. Tanner had her read two more texts used in the classroom. Julia could easily read the words in the math book, but struggled with words in the classroom reading series. Ms. Tanner had Julia read two more texts written at lower levels from the reading series until she found one where Julia could read with 95% accuracy. Once Ms. Tanner had established a reading level at which Julia could read accurately, Julia's comprehension problems disappeared.

By using the classroom texts as evaluation tools, Ms. Tanner realized that Julia did not have a comprehension problem when the material was written at a level that matched her mechanical skills. Additionally, Ms. Tanner was able to identify areas where Julia would need accommodations when using the social studies text, although she would not need accommodations when using the math text. Ms. Tanner also noted that Julia would need assistance in developing her word analysis skills. Further testing specific to word analysis would clarify Julia's needs in that area.

Lauren's story was somewhat different. The special education teacher was giving Lauren services related to language development. The teacher learned that Lauren had a language problem that interfered with her comprehension of written material. Lauren had difficulty processing orally presented information. She processed information very slowly and, as a consequence, missed about 50% of what was said around her. As a result, Lauren's vocabulary was very small. She also comprehended only literal information, missing more subtle aspects of the spoken or written word. Lauren's word recognition and word analysis skills were grade-appropriate, but she had comprehension problems based on language issues. Instead of further testing, Lauren needed special assistance in learning how to access the content found in the third-grade textbooks. Ms. Tanner would need to provide Lauren with accommodations in order for her to access material from all of her texts.

Although the same normative screening test was used for Alyssa, Julia, and Lauren, three different evaluation decisions became apparent through class participation. Julia needed additional evaluation to determine the match between her skills and basic classroom materials. Lauren did not need further testing, but she would need accommodating. Alyssa did not need more evaluation or special instruction. Most children in the general education classroom are like Alyssa, but for the students like Julia and Lauren, if no special teacher can provide insight, additional testing in classroom materials is necessary before identifying and designing appropriate adaptations. To be most effective, results of reading evaluations need to report reading behavior, which occurs in the naturalistic setting of the classroom (Ross, 2004).

Informal testing based on class material can also pinpoint specific reading problems in word analysis, word recognition, and comprehension. In Julia's case, more information needs to be gathered about her word analysis and word recognition skills. Ms. Tanner, like all teachers, does not have a lot of time to separate evaluation from instruction. Without appropriate identification of skill needs, however, valuable time spent in teaching may be lost. Although hundreds of tests are available for reading diagnosis and many of these tests are teacher friendly (The Southwest Educational Laboratory, www.SEDL.org), unless the information can be embedded in classroom instruction, evaluation and intervention is unlikely to occur. Ms. Tanner, like all inclusion teachers, needs a "twofer"—an evaluation that is directly related to classroom curriculum.

Commercial Classroom-Based Reading Assessments

Basal reading series, reading kits, and commercially designed reading programs are found in most inclusion settings. Often these reading materials provide placement tests or evaluation tools, which can be used to measure how well the student is reading the content. Additionally, many of the evaluation tools associated with commercial classroom material use computerized learning information systems (LIS), a sophisticated phrase for machine-scored tests.

An LIS is designed to provide the teacher with immediate feedback on the appropriateness of the reading material for given students. The positive side of using any LIS is that many children's scores can be viewed very quickly. The negative side is that the information provided about a child's reading is only as good as the tests. In other words, test scores derived from commercial classroom reading materials, just like normative reading tests, can be misleading. Most LIS are designed to measure only one or two components of reading and under only one condition (i.e., the parameters of the commercial classroom material).

One of the most popular reading programs using LIS is known as the Accelerated Reader (AR) created by Advantage Learning Systems. The appeal of this program is that it provides individualized assessment of comprehension of real books (i.e., freestanding books that can be found in most libraries or bookstores). Readers can choose from thousands of texts for which AR quizzes have been designed. In addition, since the books are readily available from many sources, the children can read at their own pace at home or in school.

Once the book has been finished, the child uses a computer to take a multiple-choice AR comprehension test. Results of the test provide immediate feedback to the student and the teacher and also forms a basis for discussion about the book (Topping & Fisher, 2003). Each book has been rated according to length and difficulty. The AR comprehension test provides a score based on the number of correct answers to 20 primarily literal comprehension items. From the test, the teacher can get an automatically updated analysis of scores for individuals, the whole class, or subgroups within the class. (More specific details of how AR works are available online at www.readingonline.org/critical/topping).

At first glance, the AR system appears to be a diagnostic dream come true for the harried inclusion classroom teacher. Like most dreams, however, the harsh reality of consciousness suggests, once again, that the most important factor in determining reading skill is the teacher–evaluator. Let's look at Ms. Paulsen's inclusion classroom and her students, who represent a potpourri of cultures, development, and reading expertise. Casey, Fabiola, and Alma, like all the other students in Ms. Paulsen's room, are using the AR program.

Casey has visual processing and hand–eye coordination issues. She reads her books very slowly. Rate of reading is no problem for the self-paced aspect of AR. But when Casey sits in front of the computer to take her test, the glare from the screen hurts her eyes. Casey needs a modification for the computer screen. She also sometimes accidentally chooses the incorrect response by losing her place on the screen. Casey's scores suggest that she does not comprehend as well as she really does. The testing format does not work very well for Casey.

Fabiola is from Columbia. Although her conversational skills are very good, Fabiola is still developing vocabulary in English, and most of her life experiences are based on the customs and culture of her native Columbia. Fabiola, however, is very clever, and she is a very good guesser. Fabiola's scores should be awarded for logical deduction rather than for reading comprehension. Ms. Paulsen needs to identify ways other than multiple-choice items to determine Fabiola's comprehension skills and needs.

Alma has yet to develop sufficient mechanical reading skills to access any of the thousands of books coded to the AR system. Ms. Paulson cannot use AR to identify Alma's reading needs without making some format changes. Ms. Paulsen could modify the system by reading to Alma and then asking for a story retell as well as responses to the 20 multiple-choice items for the book.

AR and similar systems have a place in inclusion settings, but they are only a part of the diagnostic menu. Systems such as LIS are quick and simple to use and provide information of a specific type. As children with multiple skill levels and needs enter the classroom and as teachers and districts are more accountable for demonstrating proficiency in reading, LIS can be one of many sources of evaluation directly related to classroom curricula.

Classroom Reading Kits

Reading kits have been developed to account for the multiple levels of reading skills found in any one classroom. Reading kits are typically composed of placement tests, graded reading material, and student record books. The function of a reading kit is to provide the teacher with sources of graded reading material that can be used to develop one or more reading skills. Most kits provide reading passages of two or three pages accompanied by quizzes that measure targeted reading skills. Reading kits can be targeted at a range of grades (e.g., kindergarten to third grade) or for the intermediate and secondary levels where reading skills are more diverse. Skills can range from primary through 12th grade. Some reading kits contain recommendations for remediation based on students' performance.

Science Research Associates (SRA) has produced some of the most enduring and versatile classroom reading kits. The most popular are the SRA Reading Laboratories and Open Court Reading. The SRA kits have multiple levels and address word analysis, word meaning, comprehension, and writing skills. They also produce a Spanish edition focusing on culture as well as reading skills.

The typical procedure when using SRA kits is to have the children read a graded one- to two-page passage silently. Immediately after reading the passage they answer 5–10 multiple-choice comprehension questions along a variety of comprehension dimensions (for example, the vocabulary meaning, main idea, detail, and inference). The children then work on an activity related to vocabulary development or word analysis skills. Once they have completed a passage and related evaluation items, they can check the answers from an answer key independently or with the teacher. Scores are charted according to specific skills, making interpretation quickly accessible for teacher decision-making. Open Court Reading stresses phonemic awareness, phonics, comprehension, and vocabulary development in combination with writing. Open Court Reading also uses literature selections for instruction. Thematic learning units are developed by grade.

Kits may be used as supplements or complements to the basic reading program. If the teacher is choosing a classroom reading kit, the decision must be based on the ease and value of the kit's evaluation system and the skills of the children involved. The evaluation system assists the teacher in making instructional decisions in the various areas of reading. Many reading kits emphasizing a wide spectrum of skills and evaluation approaches are available. Cost must be taken into consideration when deciding to adopt a kit.

Another important aspect of using classroom kits for evaluation purposes is taking into account the skills of the children in the class. In the SRA kits, for example, children must be able to keep their eyes on the line being read, circle a response in a multiple-choice item, comprehend directions without significant teacher assistance, and learn how to record time on task. Children with significant visual, motor, attention, or cognition problems would need accommodations in order to use most classroom reading kits. Accommodations may include using the material with a teacher-led, small-group format or reading the material orally to the child to develop reading comprehension skills, even when mechanical skills are missing or nonfunctional.

Skill Categories in Reading

Regardless of the type of reading assessment the inclusion teacher uses, teacher-made or commercial, interpretation of the results provides direction for program development in the inclusion classroom. All teachers, but especially teachers working in grades four or higher, want to teach the reading components in the context of classroom content, such as social studies and science. Most teachers will pose questions about the child's reading skills under one or more of the following four categories: word analysis, word recognition, oral reading, and comprehension. By completing an error analysis within one, all, or some combination of these four categories, the teacher can identify specific program needs resulting in additional instruction and appropriate accommodations in classroom.

Many reading tests have been designed to measure one specific skill. Other reading tests intersperse questions over the four component skill areas.

Word Analysis

Examples of word analysis test items are as follows:

Example 1:   What sounds do these letters make?
m a n d
ma an da co
ing spl tion ed

Example 2:   How do you break these words into syllables?
revolution
century
parliament

Example 3:   Read the following nonsense words to me:
nog
blip
pamsot
meldrup

Nonsense words are used to determine if a child understands the principles of how sounds work together. The ability to apply principles of sounds is particularly important when dealing with syllabication. Example 2 can give information about how children syllabicate meaningful terms, whereas example 3 provides the teacher with insights about the child's ability to apply syllabication to unknown terms. In order to decode previously unseen multisyllabic terms, a combination of word analysis skills plus reading from context is critical.

Continued work on word analysis skills is particularly beneficial when the teacher uses vocabulary from the classroom texts to practice and demonstrate syllabication rules. Working on skills in isolation has limited value for older children and may actually detract from building their general knowledge base about classroom content. Questions that focus on sounds or sound combinations almost always relate to a child's skills in word analysis.

Word Recognition

Tasks for oral reading and word recognition are similar. The major difference is that in some kinds of word recognition tasks, the child reads the word in isolation, usually from a word list, but in oral reading the child typically reads a cluster of words. The cluster might be a phrase, a sentence, or a short passage. Reading the words in isolation is much more difficult than reading a word or words in clusters. When the words are in isolation, the reader has no meaningful context clues. Words must be retrieved entirely from memory. Thus, when testing a child's ability to read words in isolation, the teacher is testing the child's memory for whole words.

When testing for words in isolation, time limits often are imposed. For example, Sydney had to read a word in five seconds or less for that word to be considered correct. The main reason for the time constraints is to discourage the use of phonic or word analysis skills to determine words. The ability to read a word without hesitation, to draw upon memory automatically, is one of the major measures of reading fluency. Care must be taken, however, to note which children take more time to process and retrieve words from memory than others. Sydney's 5-seconds-or-less rule makes sense for her because her processing skills are slower than those of many of her peers. Children with more normal processing and motor skills would be expected to produce a word correctly from memory within one second.

Oral Reading

Oral reading often is thought of as an extension of word recognition, but it is more likely the first step in word recognition. When children read aloud, they use their language skills to predict appropriate words. If I ask Tyson to read the word "place," he has no clues or helping word to give him hints. But if he gets the sentence, "McDonald's is your kind of place!", Tyson is more likely to read the word correctly. Tyson can use his culinary and TV-watching experiences plus his knowledge of how language usually works to guide him to read the word correctly. Examples of oral reading items are as follows:

Example 1:   New Deal reforms
                rights of people
                civil rights movement
                protection of resources

Example 2:   Most mountains are very old. Mountains have been here longer than people. Mountains seem to last forever, but some mountains will not last. Some mountains are volcanoes.

Oral reading is not so much a measure of word identification as a peek into how a child uses language to help predict meaning in reading. Good language skills or familiarity with language structure can disguise reading problems that otherwise would be identified with word recognition or word analysis measures. At this point some would say, "Bravo! Language competence can get around all those nasty word lists and sound–symbol activities." Reality paints a different picture, however. If language skills were all that was necessary for effective and efficient reading, the lists of children referred for special services in reading would be short. Unfortunately, as readers enter into more complex reading material, language skills alone are not enough to support meaning.

Comprehension

Comprehension questions also may focus on isolated sounds, words, or passages. For the most part, reading comprehension activities are accomplished through silent reading. Reading comprehension activities extend beyond the reading period and are integral to all content areas—social studies, health, science, even arithmetic. Skills in word identification strongly influence reading comprehension ability. Good readers even use sound in silent reading tasks. To be proficient at silent reading comprehension at any level of text difficulty, children must be accurate and automatic (without conscious decision of the sound or word) in word identification (Armbruster & Osborn, 2001).

Typically, comprehension items focus on main ideas and detail questions, but defining terms is also related to meaning. The ability to understand the difference in the meaning of words that change endings is also a comprehension task. Adding the –s at the end of most words has meaning (e.g., *the duck* vs. *the ducks*). As can easily be seen, reading comprehension and language comprehension are related. When analyzing a child's reading comprehension skills, written words have to be dealt with in some discernible fashion. Unless the child can read the words, at least in a short passage, reading comprehension from the printed word cannot be tested. Here are some examples of comprehension test items:

Example 1: Define the following words:
constitution _____
independence_____
authority _____
taxation _____

Example 2: Read the following:
Margaret has two dogs. One dog is black, and the other dog is black and white. The black dog's name is Pepper. The other dog's name is Max. Margaret likes her dogs.
What is this story about? _____
What color is Max?_____

Identifying comprehension level is important when working with children with poor word recognition or word analysis skills. But comprehension measures that require children with low reading skills to read provide only part of the diagnostic picture. True, these measures indicate the child's comprehension when forced to use materials that essentially are nonfunctional, but how this information is instructionally useful is questionable. Inclusion teachers realize that comprehension of content found in classroom material is not always accessible through reading the printed word. For students like Steve, who get lost in the tangle of letters and words, comprehension of classroom material can be measured through listening.

Listening comprehension for written material can be tested with nonreaders like Steve, children whose word analysis or word recognition skills are too low to access classroom material through print. To evaluate listening comprehension, Steve's teacher reads material to him and asks him to recall and relate orally all the information he can remember from the passage. If Steve recites information verbatim, then the teacher asks him to retell the story in his own words. If Steve cannot tell the story in his own words, then the teacher has another piece of information about Steve's comprehension ability. That is, students who cannot paraphrase what they have read typically do not comprehend what they have read or what has been read to them. In part, the reason they cannot paraphrase may have to do with language issues such as vocabulary development or processing of information. The teacher then can match the child's recall against the material. Important questions are as follows:

- Did the child recall the topic or main topics of the passage?
- Did the child recall subtopics? Which ones?
- Did the child sequence the story correctly?
- Was the child's recall accurate?
- Did the child add information from other sources not found in the passage?

Answers to these questions can give the teacher a better understanding of the child's listening comprehension and can lend instructional direction. Rather than leaving the child sitting in the corner with an undecipherable text or equally confusing audiotape, answers to the retell questions permit the teacher to design appropriate activities. Audiotapes are not the ultimate teaching tool for children who have not yet mastered reading. Listening is listening. Philip could recall only one idea from the listening retell, and that idea was incomplete. Instructionally, "tape listening" (and even verbal directions) is a yet-to-be-acquired skill for Philip. In contrast, Sheila, his table partner, recalled the main topic and several subtopics and sequenced the story as it was read to her. Sheila can benefit from listening to taped stores, text material, and class discussion.

The first step in measuring listening comprehension is to choose the testing material. This material should be age- and topic-appropriate. Reymundo is unlikely to be thrilled at hearing a story about Clifford, a big red dog. He might be more interested (and more attentive) in hearing about his parents' native country, Puerto Rico, or a newspaper article about Russ Ortiz, Reymundo's favorite baseball pitcher. The length of the passage to be read also varies. Though no set rules have been delineated, the teacher most likely can learn all that is necessary from a 2- to 3-minute reading.

Language issues and reading or listening comprehension cannot be separated. Many children in the United States come from families where English is not the first language. In order to develop appropriate reading programs based on instructional needs and to ensure that English language learners (ELL) can access content, the initial reading evaluation tool should be new to the student and written in the language that the student understands best. Even though the language of instruction and the textbooks are most likely to be presented in English, the teacher must separate those children whose comprehension issues are solely related to linguistic background from those students who, regardless of linguistic background, cannot comprehend print or orally presented information.

In Reymundo's case, his language is Spanish, not English. Since his teacher does not speak Spanish, she has to find someone who does. If no one is available, this evaluation component should be skipped for the time being. An invalid measure is just that—invalid, useless, and highly frustrating—for the child being evaluated. In addition, designing a program on invalid data can lead to misclassification and wasted instructional time.

Identification of Reading Problems

Having identified four basic areas of reading skills, the next step is to identify the level, and possibly the rate, at which the child is reading. Identification of level and rate leads easily to selection of appropriate material. The catch is how the rate and level vary for each reading component for a given child. Children who have problems in reading may not have problems in each of the four components. Whenever Cliff reads orally, he stumbles over words. He often confuses the middle of a word and substitutes one word for another. Cliff was asked to read the following passage (Liddle, 1970):

> An Indian put his ear to the ground. He heard many horses. They were coming his way. He ran to tell his people. Then he ran to tell the people of the next village. He was a runner. Using runners was one way Indians sent messages. (p. 74)

Cliff's version sounded more like this:

> The Indians put their ears on the grass. He heard many horses. They are coming to him. He ran to talk to some people. He ran to let the people of the next town know. He was running. Running was the way Indians sent messages.

Cliff received a little help now and again from his teacher. Few teachers would argue that Cliff has a reading problem. At best, his oral reading skills seem a bit shaky. The surprise is that he comprehends exceedingly well. When given questions regarding the main idea and specific details, Cliff did very well. How Cliff can comprehend with such restricted word recognition and word analysis skills is puzzling. Although the goal of all reading instruction is comprehension, Cliff still could use some reading instruction in word recognition and word analysis.

Selected Reading Tests

Normative Measures

Most achievement tests yield only a general notion of areas of difficulty for each child. If a child's overall reading score is low, an additional reading test may be needed. Many standardized diagnostic reading tests are available. Some of the more commonly used standardized diagnostic reading tests include the Diagnostic Reading Scales (Spache, 1972), the Durrell Analysis of Reading Difficulty (Durrell, 1955), and the Stanford Diagnostic Reading Test (Karlsen, Madden, & Gardner, 1976). These tests, and others like them, usually are administered individually. The tests have been designed for use with primary- or intermediate-grade children or with readers who have disabilities.

Diagnostic Measures

Diagnostic reading tests are divided into more than just the four areas of word recognition, word analysis, oral reading, and comprehension. They also may examine specific areas within a general reading area. The Brigance Diagnostic Inventory of Basic Skills (Brigance, 1983), for example, examines word analysis through multiple subtests.

Diagnostic tests may require a lot of time to administer. The thought of giving seven or eight of these tests to low functioning readers in a class may be less than welcome for an overwhelmed inclusion teacher.

Alternatives to Diagnostic Measures

Possible options should be considered. One option for obtaining diagnostic information is to get information from others. If some of the slow readers in the class also have disabilities, the teacher could ask the special education teacher to provide test information from a standardized diagnostic test. Other low-functioning readers might be referred to the remedial reading specialist or the school psychologist for reading evaluation.

Inclusion teachers can administer the tests themselves. Little in-depth training is necessary to administer, score, and interpret test results properly. Parents may assist, but more than likely the teacher should be the examiner. Also, results from the previous year's general achievement test could be examined.

Let's explore third-grader Kevin's test results. His total score for reading was low on a standardized survey reading measure. On closer inspection, Kevin's subtest scores varied considerably. Word knowledge was at the second-grade, second-month (2.2) level, comprehension at 3.3, and word analysis at 2.1. Both word knowledge and word analysis are low, but comprehension is about grade level. Roughly translating word knowledge to mean word recognition, we can see how word recognition and word analysis should be evaluated further.

If the child's folder contains test information, the teacher can begin to look for error patterns. A score reveals only a rough idea of what a child can do. In trying to identify error patterns, the teacher not only observes what a child can or cannot do but also may identify the procedures the child is using. In analyzing the child's response, the teacher may be able to determine specific areas for further testing. For example, if the problem is one of substitution in word endings, all areas of word analysis do not have to be tested. Only additional information on the child's reading technique as related to word endings is sought.

Informal Testing

At this juncture in evaluation decision making, one choice is to ignore the test results, place the child in the lowest reading group in the class, and hope to see progress by the winter break. A second choice is to forge ahead and continue testing with more specific standardized diagnostic tests in the areas of word recognition and word analysis.

A third choice is to initiate informal testing based on class materials related to word recognition and word analysis. The first choice obviously is undesirable. The second and third choices can provide information on which to base instruction.

The second choice directs the teacher to formal diagnostic tests. Based on an analysis of errors, a specific subtest focusing on the suspected problem may be chosen. Returning to Kevin and his apparent difficulty with word endings, the teacher might choose to administer the Consonant Blends and Digraphs subtest on the Brigance (Brigance, 1983). Having done so, the formal score can be translated into a grade equivalency. The only problem is that sometimes the grade equivalency, as measured by the test, does not match the grade level of the class materials. Thus, a formal diagnostic measure may support the teaching decision but may not help the teacher choose among the available classroom materials (Gillet & Temple, 1990).

Informal Reading Assessment Battery

Evaluation based on a combination of observation and use of classroom material is matched more closely with performance expectations than is possible using more formal measures. Materials actually used in the classroom become the evaluation tools. The first step in measuring word analysis skills, for example, is to have the child identify rhyming words with reading, social studies, or science terms, or any other words that are part of the curriculum. Other aspects of word analysis that can be evaluated by using class vocabulary are syllabication, initial, medial, and final consonant sounds, and blends. The value of using class material is twofold:

1. The material is at hand.
2. Class material is expected to be taught in one way or another.

Assignments that incorporate class material are called "twofers"—two activities are accomplished with one lesson preparation.

Formal and informal writing assignments also are important sources of evaluation for sound–symbol relationships. The student's approximations to conventional spelling can reveal phonemic awareness (Ball & Blachman, 1991).

Specific components of reading (e.g., word recognition, word analysis, and word meaning) can be measured in a number of ways by using class material as an evaluation tool. Oral reading, word recognition in context, and comprehension can be measured using an approach referred to as an informal reading inventory (IRI) or a more modern counterpart known as a running record. High student literacy and engagement in systematic classroom assessment procedures, especially running records, are consistently reported in studies of effective schools (Pressley et al., 2001; Taylor, Pearson, Clark, & Walpole, 2000; Wray, Medwell, Fox, & Poulson, 2000).

Many similarities exist between IRIs and the running record approach. Each uses classroom material, one-on-one interaction with oral reading, a system for marking mechanical reading errors, and a means of evaluating comprehension skills. The major difference is that an IRI is used to determine placement in texts and a running record is used to measure progress in reading material at least two or three times a week.

Formal descriptions of IRIs usually focus on using reading passages from basal readers. To be more efficient, the teacher may want to develop an IRI from a classroom social studies or science series. Typically, IRIs are created using the following steps (Betts, 1957; Haring, Lovitt, Eaton, & Hansen, 1978; Otto, McMenemy, & Smith, 1973).

Step 1:   Select a series for instruction.

Step 2:   Select a 100-word passage from each level. Some systems recommend three 100-word samples from each level.

Step 3:   Develop about six comprehension questions for each passage. Questions should focus on literal meaning, inferential meaning, and meaning of vocabulary. Questions also can be reduced to two recall, two sequence, and two interpretation.

Step 4:   Have the child read one of the passages. A good place to begin is a passage one grade level below his or her standardized score. If Bill's score is 4.5, he would begin reading a sample passage from the third-grade reader. Reasons for choosing one grade level below the standardized score are:

    1) Standardized scores usually represent the "frustration," or most difficult, level of reading.

    2) Sampling on a level slightly below grade gives the child a chance for immediate success in an evaluation session. Children with a history of reading failure often need to feel successful during an evaluation situation if the teacher is to get an accurate picture of their skills.

Step 5:   Once the initial passage has been selected, have the child read orally. As the child reads, note the errors. The simplest format for recording errors is a follow-along sheet. This is a duplicated sheet identical to the child's reading page that can be personalized. As the child reads, record the errors on the follow-along sheet. By recording what the child actually reads, you will be able to determine error patterns. If you are not interested in identifying patterns, simply note errors by crossing out words or by tallying the errors (/////). If the goal is to determine error patterns, the child's problems likely will fall under five major headings: omissions, substitutions, mispronunciations, insertions, or repetitions.

Interpreting Results

Omissions are words that are left out or words to which the child responds, "I don't know." A hesitation of 4 or more seconds usually is considered an omission. Upon careful analysis of omissions, the teacher may wish to adhere to the spirit of the rule rather than the letter (or in this case, the word) of the rule. Inadvertently skipped words probably are not the same kind of error as "I don't know" words. Sometimes children omit words in a passage. The occasion and number of times this problem occurs should influence teacher judgment as to whether the omission constitutes a significant problem.

If Eddie, for example, omits one or two words in a 100-word passage, he probably does not have a major problem. Nor would Eddie have a serious problem had he omitted 11 words in 100 if 6 of the 11 words were *the* and 5 were *a*.

Substitutions occur when a child reads (or misreads) one word for another. The two major types of substitution are confabulations (Otto et al., 1973), or obvious guesses, and the type that make sense contextually. An example of the latter is when Sandra reads the sentence "The flower is pretty" as "The flower is beautiful." Substitutions in context are not always cause for alarm. The occasions for and frequency of substitutions should influence teacher judgment, however.

Substitution error patterns are found in the beginning, middle, or ending of a word. Children often read the first letter of the word correctly but then substitute the second consonant sound. Examples are *bleak* for *break, plow* for *prow,* and *slop* for *stop.*

Medial substitutions usually involve vowel sounds. Examples are *dasy* for *daisy, cat* for *cot,* and *trap* for *trip.*

The short-*a* sound is a popular substitution choice, but sometimes the only discernible pattern is random substitution of vowels. This type of error is referred to as a hit-and-miss error. Another fairly common substitution error occurs when the child employs the "heads, it's one vowel; tails, it's another" strategy. The child usually has confused one or two vowels and is lucky or unlucky with a guess. If the child is consistently unlucky, the teacher should teach one or both vowels. Kelly always read short-*a* words correctly, but when doubting another vowel, he continued to substitute the short *a*. Kelly needed help not only with the vowels *e, i, o,* and *u,* but also in discriminating when not to use short *a*.

Substitution of word endings is another common error pattern. Dropping *–s*'s or *–ing* or *–ed* can reflect a reading problem. Caution must be taken when working with children whose native language is not English, for whom errors in word endings may reflect spoken language rather than a misreading.

Mispronunciations refer to errors in which no apparent rule has been applied. Miscalls or mispronunciations suggest that the child simply is unable to attack new words. Tienna's pattern (with the correct words in brackets) provides a good example of mispronunciations:

> Once out [upon] a time, a beautiful red saw [rose] grew in the house [garden]. The rose had some [many] water [friends]. Birds after [landed] on its vase [branches] and sang going [sweetly]. Bees buzzed now [happily] on the lovely red water [petals].

For the sake of illustration, Tienna's errors have been kept only to mispronunciations. More than likely, in a real sample of Tienna's work, she also would make omissions, substitutions, insertions, and repetitions. A child like Tienna, who mispronounces words, may have no concept of the relationship between sounds and symbols. This problem may be resolved in the general education classroom or, depending on the cause, may require extensive remedial assistance in a special setting. If Tienna has learned sounds in isolation, she may need help in realizing that these same sounds apply to words. Some children, especially those with mild learning problems, need assistance in making generalizations. Simply calling attention to the sound often can end the problem with mispronunciations. The remediation required for other children may have to be more extensive. If the remediation activity is beyond the scope of the classroom, either the reading specialist or the special education teacher can work with the child. Again, degree and kind of mispronunciation become the teacher's guideline for instruction.

Insertions, unlike omissions, occur when a child adds a word or words. Larry, for example, tends to make frequent insertion errors. He may read the sentence, "The man called the dog," like this: "The great big man called the little white dog." Similar to mispronunciations, Larry's problem may be resolved easily by calling attention to his errors.

In general, an insertion error pattern is not too serious. If the child is adding words, at least the teacher knows that he or she is actively involved in reading. Active involvement is a plus in the grade book of reading. The only serious problem that insertions can create is in the area of comprehension. The child may be reading much more than the author intended. As such, the child may not really understand the information communicated by the reading material.

Repetitions occur when an individual reads a word correctly but then rereads it. Repetition errors, like spontaneous self-corrections, are not always regarded as errors. Self-correction occurs when the child misreads a word and, without teacher intervention, rereads it correctly. For some children, however, repetition becomes a style of reading. If the repetition errors occur infrequently, no real concern is necessary. Manuel, for example, repeats each new vocabulary term before he proceeds to the next word in a passage. This technique helps him remember the new words, and because it does not interfere with his comprehension, he has no major problem.

Blanche, in contrast, repeats both old and new words. She seems to use repetitions to avoid reading further in the passage. Not only are Blanche's repetitions tedious to hear, they also slow down her reading rate. In turn, her slow rate may be responsible for her poor performance in comprehension.

Informal Reading Inventories and Time Management

Finding the time to conduct an informal inventory for an entire class can be overwhelming at first. To conduct IRIs in a general education classroom, time management skills must come into play. For most children an IRI takes 5–10 minutes. The teacher already has a general idea of how well the child is reading, and intuition likely will put the teacher close to the appropriate passages. Not all children need to read all levels of the IRI, nor will all children need the same amount of time to complete the IRI.

Meanwhile, while the IRI is being administered to an individual student, the other children are participating in some manner in the classroom. What can these children be doing while the teacher is working one on one with a student?

What to do with these children is related to the way the teacher has organized students' independent time. (Refer to suggestions in chapter 6.) If the children are working on material they can do independently, most of them will be on task. During the time the teacher is working individually with one child, others can be working alone, with a partner, or in small groups. The few who will not be on task can be moved closer to the teacher for better eye contact (and positive control).

A quick calculation suggests that at 10 minutes per IRI for 32 children, the teacher will spend approximately 320 minutes plus 40 minutes, give or take, for transitions and group interaction between tests. Roughly speaking, the teacher will be administering IRIs for six hours. What teacher can administer IRIs for six hours in a row? And what group of 32 children can work independently for six hours straight? Most groups can work independently for 30–60 minutes.

The plan for administering an IRI, then, is to give the tests over several days for no longer than 30–60 minutes per day. By administering the tests over a longer time, the teacher will be able to score a few IRIs each day rather than all at one time. The bonus is that the teacher will be making educational decisions about a few children each day rather than trying to do this for all the children at one time.

Running Records, unlike IRIs, are used to assess reading progress and can be used to improve or alter instructional programs to increase reading proficiency. A running record assesses literacy in a way that can be used to improve students' reading. The steps involved in using a running record are as follows:

1. The student sits or stands beside the teacher so that both can see the reading material.
2. As the child reads, the teacher codes each word as correct or incorrect.
3. The teacher codes

   - the percentage of words correctly read,
   - the self-correction ratio (errors plus self-corrections divided by the number of self-corrections, and
   - the categories of errors made (meaning, visual, or structure).

4. After reading the story, the child retells the story from memory and answers questions about the story content.

The student has successfully completed a running record when the retold story and accompanying questions are answered correctly and the passage has been read with about 90–94% accuracy. The difficulty level of the passage and the number and types of errors provide direction for immediate future reading instruction (Clay, 1993).

Effective teachers have used running records during individual reading conferences. In fact, frequent classroom assessment is one of the most important factors in monitoring progress and shaping instruction (Matsumara, Patthey-Chavez, Valdes, & Garnier, 2002). The advantage of the running record approach is that the assessment can occur in just a few minutes. As a result, the teacher can monitor student reading during class time while other students are working on small-group or individual literacy activities.

Error Analysis and Classroom Reading Tasks

By using classroom material in conjunction with error analysis, teachers can quickly determine not only the appropriateness of the classroom reading material, but also areas to target for specific reading instruction. Primary-grade teachers may find that some of their students cannot read any text at either the instructional or the independent level. Some upper- and intermediate-grade children with learning problems, uneven experiential backgrounds, or a past history of failure may be similar to the primary-grade children. They, too, may not be able to use their classroom texts for oral reading practice or comprehension activities. Even if the child cannot use the text for oral reading practice, the teacher can use the text to test for word recognition, word analysis, and comprehension.

WORD RECOGNITION   Word recognition, the immediate recall of a word's pronunciation and meaning, can be analyzed using a variety of classroom materials. Textbooks often identify key terms, usually listed at the beginning of the chapter, the end of the chapter, or in the teacher's manual. If these terms are not listed, they can sometimes be found in accompanying textbooks or highlighted in some ways in the body of the texts.

Another valuable source of determining key words are words the child frequently uses in writing assignments. Words that are important to students are often repeatedly found in their writing. These words can be included as part of the child's word recognition vocabulary. The decision of which words to include to build sight word vocabulary, regardless of source, is based on the teacher's experience with the English language, the frequency with which a word is used, and the relevance of the word to classroom content.

A word list is developed for each unit or story in the text and can be presented to the child as another measure of word recognition. How the list is formatted is a matter of personal taste. Most primary teachers prefer flashcards;

others like flipcharts. Upper-elementary teachers usually like to present the words in vertical or horizontal columns or rows.

The purpose of using word lists is to determine a starting point for instruction. In whatever format, word lists should have an accompanying follow-along sheet. This guide sheet provides a record of the day of testing—errors and level or source of words. Once a child misses approximately 8–10 words, these become identified as the words to be taught. When the initial set of words has been learned, testing can continue.

Two useful sources of information may be obtained from this type of testing. The first relates to the rate of student progress, the other relates to the type of progress the student is making.

Samples of Barbara's follow-along sheets are presented in Figure 7.2. Even before any formal instruction had begun, Barbara got more words correct per unit, as noted on the follow-along sheets between November 3 and November 25. Barbara's errors also began to change in character. In the first sample she refused to try some words by responding "don't know" (dk). In five of the new words, she either omitted or substituted word endings.

Nearly 2 weeks later, on November 14, Barbara had mastered the first set of words and was ready to be tested on the words for unit 2. The new test results indicated that Barbara attempted every word; "don't knows" were absent. She

---

Sample 1   Date: *November 3*

| *(dk)* | | | *(vege)* | | *(dk)* | *(exch)* |
| age | cage | wage | vegetable | huge | change | exchange |

| *(dk)* | *(dang)* | *(dang)* | | | *(bag)* |
| strange | danger | dangerous | large | orange | baggage |

Sample 2   Date: *November 14*

| *(cab)* | | *(vill)* | | | |
| cabbage | cottage | village | package | sausage | voyage |

| | | *(gent)* | | | |
| carriage | college | gentle | gentleman | general | giant |

Sample 3   Date: *November 25*

| | | | | | |
| gingerbread | giraffe | magic | magical | engine | engineer |

| *(pige)* | | | | | |
| pigeon | ache | toothache | school | schoolroom | character |

dk = don't know

Figure 7.2   Samples of Barbara's Follow-Along Sheets

still showed evidence of some difficulty with word endings, but not quite as much as on the first test. By the time Barbara had been tested over unit 3 material, her reading growth was even more evident. She read the majority of the words correctly and had word ending problems on only one word.

By inspecting Barbara's three tests, we can see that she not only was learning unit words at a rate of about one to two a week but that she also was mastering learning skills (word endings). Barbara's progress reflected her speed in learning new unit words as well as her progress in the general education class.

We find the opposite result with Brian. Samples of his sheets are presented in Figure 7.3. A quick glance at Brian's testing dates shows that he is taking longer and longer to master word lists. His learning rate is a signal that he has trouble achieving success in the general education classroom. Closer inspection of Brian's errors adds to his teacher's concerns. Unlike Barbara, Brian continues to make the same type of errors after 3 months of instruction. He either says "don't know" to a word or uses the first two letters of the word to form the basis of a substitution.

Apparently, Brian is not learning from experience. For whatever reason, he is not making much progress in the general education classroom and may need special help or some other form of instruction. Based on information on Brian's follow-along sheets, the teacher can request assistance from a reading or learning specialist. A basis clearly exists for questioning Brian's placement. Whether he

---

Sample 1   Date: *November 3*

			(dk)		*(chair)*	*(dk)*
age	cage	wage	vegetable	huge	change	exchange

(dk)	*(dark)*	*(dk)*			*(dk)*
strange	danger	dangerous	large	orange	baggage

Sample 2   Date: *November 30*

(dk)	*(color)*	*(dk)*		*(sam)*	*(dk)*
cabbage	cottage	village	package	sausage	voyage

(dk)			*(dk)*	*(gentle)*	
carriage	college	gentle	gentleman	general	giant

Sample 3   Date: *January 12*

(dk)			*(dk)*	*(enter)*	*(dk)*
gingerbread	giraffe	magic	magical	engine	engineer

(pick)	*(dk)*	*(dk)*			*(chair)*
pigeon	ache	toothache	school	schoolroom	character

dk = don't know

Figure 7.3   Samples of Brian's Follow-Along Sheets

remains in a general education classroom may depend on the type and degree of instruction that best fit his needs.

WORD ANALYSIS   Word analysis skills, the child's ability to use sounds and symbols to decode unknown words, can also be determined through an error analysis of the child's oral reading. The same passage or passages used to determine the child's independent (98–100% accuracy) or instructional reading level (95% accuracy) can be used to analyze errors in decoding. Because the teacher has already noted errors, reading patterns are likely to emerge. Some of the patterns show the student's strengths, while other patterns suggest areas for instruction. For example, Barbara was always able to provide information about the initial sounds and miscalled words. Her strength was the ability to use the initial sounds of new words; her errors occurred primarily with the endings of terms. Analysis of her errors suggests that Barbara might benefit from instruction in how to break words into syllables.

Word lists can also be used to examine word analysis skills. Identification of error patterns from word lists is the same as identification of error patterns from oral passages. The type of errors the child makes once again translates into the word analysis instructional target area.

COMPREHENSION   To test reading comprehension from print the child must be able to read the material; that is, the child must demonstrate word recognition skills of at least 98–100% accuracy for the passage, or in the case of emerging readers, a phrase or sentence. The first level of questioning can be a story retell. In the story retell, teachers can learn a lot about the child's overall understanding of the passage as well as main ideas, details, and sequence. After a story retell, the teacher can ask more specific questions to determine how well the child can read for information and for understanding.

Informational types of questions can be literal or factual in nature, inferential, or represent any type of organizational structure. The questions that elicit literal or factual concepts typically begin with *who, what, where, when*, and *why*. Inferences can be elicited by asking children for another name for a particular term or questions, such as, "What you think would happen if…?" Main-idea questions, such as, "What is the passage about?," can provide a child with the framework to recall important ideas that reflect true understanding. Three other questions that may be used to elicit the recall or comprehension level are:

1. What is the author trying to tell you?
2. Does the information in the passage make sense, in part or overall?
3. What is important to you about this passage?

The child's response to these questions will provide a lot of insight into how actively he or she is engaged in the reading. If the story is about the polar ice caps and the child responds with animated information related to baseball headwear, the odds are high the child does not comprehend the content, may not be interested in cold weather, does not have the experiential background to make sense of the printed words, or some combination of these factors. In any event, analysis of the student's responses can provide direction for creating appropriate instruction.

Questions using signal terms, like *however, first, second, third, why, because,* or *numerous,* can provide insight into how well the child comprehends comparison, sequence, causation, or classification concepts. Returning to the passage about polar ice caps, consider Gabriel's response to the question, "Why should anyone care if the ice caps melt?" Gabriel responds, "Caps are important because they keep the baseball players' heads warm." Gabriel's response, while inaccurate, suggests that he understands the concept of causation. His teacher most likely will not need to teach Gabriel about cause and effect but, instead, may need to focus on experience and vocabulary development.

Time Samples

Sometimes teachers want to know how quickly a student reads. In order to evaluate rate of reading, the teacher can collect what is called a *timed reading sample.* The amount of time the teacher chooses varies with the teacher's purpose and the complexity of the material. Most often, however, the timing is restricted to about 2 minutes. During the timing, the student reads orally, and the teacher records errors and notes how much the student can read in 2 minutes. Some children, especially children who have poor histories with reading, become terribly anxious when being timed. To alleviate such problems, one variation of the timed reading sample is to ask the child to read a passage or word list of a particular length adding no time constraints. When the child has finished reading the passage, the teacher notes how long the child took and divides the time by the number of words read to establish a reading rate.

To score, the teacher has to establish a reading rate and an error percentage. To determine the reading rate (correct words read per minute), all the words the student read correctly in the 2 minutes are counted, and the total is divided by 2. Ted read 350 words correctly in 2 minutes; 350 divided by 2 equals 175 words per minute. Next we determine Ted's error percentage. Ted missed 70 words. To find his error percentage, the number of errors is divided by the number of words in the sample. We can quickly determine that the passage Ted read contained 420 words: 350 words read correctly plus 70 words read incorrectly results in a total of 420 words. Then:

$$420\overline{)70.00}^{.17}$$

From this, .17 converts to a 17% error rate. With 17% errors, we have 83% reading accuracy. For students, frustration begins to set in at around the 90% accuracy rate (10% error rate). In other words, this text is too difficult for Ted.

Should the teacher throw out the text? The answer is yes and no. Yes, the book is far too difficult for oral reading practice, but it can still be used to establish word lists and provide direction for word analysis instruction.

The words chosen for the lists reflect the content of the material and the teacher's professional judgment. Usually, important words are isolated in the text in some fashion. They may be listed in the teacher's manual, at the front of the chapter or unit, or at the end of a chapter, unit, or text. Key words also may be found with the chapters of the text, perhaps italicized or printed in bold type. The reading evaluator presents these selected words just as any other word list. Errors are noted and patterns identified, pointing the way for word analysis instruction.

The teacher may question the value of teaching sight words contained in a book that the student is unable to read. In reality, however, this provides the strongest argument for using the content words. By teaching the student key words, at least the teacher can cover basic information from the text. The student's vocabulary—sight and comprehension—will grow and, through discussion, he or she may be able to keep pace with other students in the class.

Time samples can come from any source: a trade book, a textbook, or a basal reader. The only requirement for the testing material is that the student can read the words with approximately 98% accuracy. To time students over reading material that they cannot recognize is pointless and a waste of everyone's time and energy.

READING RATE AND DECODING SKILLS Development of phonological skills that allow readers automatic access to using letters to sound out words has become emphasized more strongly at the beginning of the 21st century. Readers not only need to know the sounds and how to apply them, they must also be able to use the sounds at a rate that allows them access to word meaning. Literacy accountability, otherwise known as ensuring that the reading program is creating skillful readers, is targeting primary-age children. Prevention of reading problems through close monitoring of progress for emerging readers is a major goal at the local, state, and federal levels. One of the most powerful evaluation systems that measure literacy in kindergarten through third grade is called the Dynamic Indicators of Basic Early Literacy Skills (DIBELS®) (Kaminski & Good, 1998).

DIBELS® are teacher-friendly, scientifically developed measurement tools used for kindergarten through third grade basic reading skills. They are repeatable 1-minute probes of word analysis measuring skills critical to the development of reading fluency. The skills represented in the DIBELS® system include reading readiness, beginning reading, and basic reading development. Based on validated fluency rates, 1-minute probes give teachers a vehicle for monitoring progress and moving children from one basic reading skill to the next, until basic reading has been developed. With minimal training, probes can be administered by the teacher, a paraprofessional, or a parent helper. Each student's level of fluency is assessed every week or two to adjust instruction to meet prescribed benchmarks. Children who are able to reach the benchmark goals designated for each grade level (i.e., kindergarten through third grade) have a high probability of accessing material from print for the rest of their lives (Kame'enui & Simmons, 2003).

As an evaluation system for primary-level skills in word analysis, DIBELS® produces information regarding how well instruction in reading is working. The system does not tell the teacher what to teach or how to teach, but rather provides a measure of the reader's progress through continuous and quick feedback (Langdon, 2004).

As with all evaluation systems, interpretation of DIBELS® results must take into account psychological and physiological development of the students. DIBELS®, like any other rate-based system, will need to be modified for children whose anxiety is raised when under the pressure of a timed system. Likewise children with motor issues involving sound production or their visual system will need accommodations or modifications to use DIBELS® effectively.

Establishing Evaluation Sequences

PURPOSE   The purpose of reading evaluation is to determine areas of instruction. Skill sequences that are used for reading instruction can come from a variety of sources. The skill sequences in currently existing classroom materials would be a logical first choice in evaluation/instruction. Evaluation procedures involve establishing or identifying existing hierarchies or skill sequences as presented in classroom materials. For reading, the skill sequences that are selected most often for evaluation and subsequent instruction include word analysis, word recognition, oral reading, and comprehension. The child's reading performance then is compared against the standards set for mastering a specific skill in the sequence.

PRETESTS BASED ON CLASS SEQUENCES   If a student is having problems in all areas of reading or is just beginning reading instruction, the evaluation should be based on a sequence of skills by unit. The actual order of the skills is unimportant in most cases. The systematic evaluation and subsequent instruction of the sequence are the critical aspects.

One of the most practical techniques for pretesting word analysis skills is to sequence the pretest to materials available in the classroom. Several sources of skill sequences are commonly found in the classroom. For example, phonics workbooks present sounds in a sequence, starting with the first sound on the first page and continuing with the sounds that follow on the succeeding pages.

Basal readers also provide a sequence of sounds. The sequence may have to be culled from the teacher's manual or reader. Generally, sounds will be introduced in some segment of a meaningful word. By careful analysis of word-order presentation, a sequence of sounds corresponding directly to the reader can be compiled. For example, students may be presented with the following sight words: *mother, mouse, come, summer.* The lesson in the basal has two objectives: to teach the four sight words and to teach the sound of the consonant *m.* The focus of the basal reader's next lesson may be on sight words *saw, lesson, sit, kiss.* The intent of this lesson is to teach four sight words and the sound of *s.* With this approach, we can see the emergence of a sequence of sounds. The first letter sound is *m,* and the second is *s.* A glance at ensuing lessons will reveal the remainder of the word analysis sequence for that specific basal reader. Ideally, the sequence of sounds for word analysis can be coordinated with the sequence of words presented in the text.

Reading Evaluation for Special Populations

Emotional and Psychological Considerations

Children with disabilities, whether in learning or emotional areas or a combination thereof, will need only minor modifications in the testing techniques described thus far. Teachers, as evaluators and trained observers of human behavior, recognize the emotional component associated with reading success or failure. Putting the student at ease may be the first step in accurately assessing a student's reading skills. Because of his past experiences with reading failure, Andrew has developed an ingenious set of avoidance behaviors, especially when he is expected to "show what you can do" in reading. What Andrew "cannot do" is to perceive himself as "failing." What Andrew "can do" is throw the teacher off task by asking an unending string of questions or gazing off into the distance when the task gets too threatening. His ultimate avoidance weapon is "I don't know," which enables him to avoid taking any chances. To identify Andrew's reading needs, his teacher must be able to determine the real "I-don't-knows" from the camouflage "I-don't-knows." Reducing the other avoidance behaviors also would be a positive step in evaluating his skills.

Enter the evaluation modifier, a white rabbit puppet. Andrew's teacher no longer requests that he complete the evaluations. Instead, she has Andrew become the puppet's teacher. The same tests that he found so threatening now have become an arena in which he can be in charge. An Andrew in charge is a safe Andrew. He no longer makes mistakes, because he is the teacher and—as we all know—teachers are almost always right!

The magic worked by the rabbit was the only modification made to assess Andrew's skills. For Andrew and all the other avoiders, the skills to be evaluated remain the same. The areas to be evaluated, regardless of the disability, continue to be word analysis, word recognition, oral reading, and comprehension. Only the means have been changed.

Testing Environment

As with any child who has experienced failure in testing or other school situations, the teacher will have to promote a positive testing environment. Smiling and maintaining a friendly posture are good first steps. During initial testing, the teacher also may wish to provide the child with surefire success activities. If, for example, the teacher knows that Bree is terrified of taking formal tests, that teacher may wish to adapt or disguise the test form. Instead of presenting Bree with a 20-word typed list, the teacher could print the words with colored pens and put them on individual cards.

Allan, on the other hand, has had enough of positive environments. He detests letters and sounds. Whenever the teacher shows him a set of cards with letter blends, Allan won't talk to the teacher for 45 minutes. The key to the Allans in a class is to capitalize on their anger. Allan's monster is isolated sounds, so he is given the opportunity to play "Monster Mash." His teacher glues a picture of a green-faced, befanged Frankenstein onto a popsicle stick. Allan can "mash" the letter combination by pouncing the monster on a card and saying its sound. Allan's aggression is expended, and his teacher gains insight into Allan's skills.

Two variables in the environment can lessen test-taking anxiety: classroom routine and the evaluator. First, the environment can be adjusted from a formal to a less formal one by including the evaluation activity as a routine part of daily class-work. Second, probes can be given routinely and valuable information gathered through whole-class activities. The teacher does not have to be the evaluator. With a little training, children can learn to time each other and record errors in many reading areas. Older students can be used as cross-age evaluators. As long as a sequence of skills and a standard of acceptable performance have been identified, the teacher can be flexible about who is directed to collect evaluation information.

Specific Suggestions

The following suggestions can help the teacher adapt evaluation materials.

- Put isolated words or sounds on individual 3" x 5" cards.
- Print words on regular tablet paper or on a "magic slate."
- Print words in colors other than the standard black.
- Use a flipchart.
- Put words on a word wheel.
- Play games such as Word Bingo™ or Boggle™.
- Duplicate passages from books instead of using an entire manual.

Presenting one word at a time is a lot less threatening to the child than presenting a whole page of typed words. Also, presenting words on a tablet or a magic slate makes the testing less formal. Children are used to teachers writing on tablet paper, so the activity itself might reduce a certain amount of test-taking anxiety. And who could equate reading words printed on a Mickey Mouse or Snoopy magic slate with the Dolch word list? The same is true for presenting words in different colors. Because the teacher is using the colored words for initial screening or posttesting only, the risk of having the child "read the color" is eliminated if the child doesn't receive corrective feedback (receive the correct response to a miscalled word or sound).

The informality of flipcharts and word wheels also can lessen test-taking anxiety. They are especially useful for word analysis evaluations. Both flipcharts and word wheels are easy to make and can be coded directly to classroom material. To make a flipchart, the only materials needed are a three-ring binder, a marking pen, and some 3" x 5" index cards. Consonant cards, one consonant per card, go on the first and third rings of the binder. Vowels, or vowel cards, are placed on the middle ring. The word wheel is made from heavy construction paper that can be laminated to preserve it.

Playing games with test items, another option, is a little more elaborate and time-consuming. Further, word games such as bingo, card games, and tic-tac-toe can be adapted to test sounds and words found in predesignated sequences. Constructing these games takes time, so this may not be practical. Nevertheless, the teacher can adapt any game simply by using a correct reading response to earn the right to move a player or take a turn.

Billy, who is terrified of formal tests, loves to play checkers, so he and his teacher play a weekly checkers game. The teacher has a stack of 3" x 5" cards with a word from Billy's word list on each. When it is Billy's turn to play, he picks up a card, identifies the word, and moves his checker. He does not have to get the word correct to move. Billy's teacher has a follow-along sheet. She records Billy's responses and notes deviations. Because this is an "evaluation-by-checkers" approach, Billy's responses are not corrected; they are simply noted. Based on Billy's answers, his teacher knows whether to proceed to the next set of words. The same approach can be used to evaluate sounds or sound combinations.

Finally, oral reading can be tested outside of a standardized test and even outside of a textbook. Instead of handing a child a book to read, the teacher can duplicate pages from the various texts in the classroom. For a child with reading problems, facing only one or two pages to read is a lot more inviting than an entire story from the not-so-user-friendly classroom text.

Duplicated pages also mask the source of the pages. This is advantageous because most children know which books are for the "smart" kids and which ones are for those who are "not-so-smart." Passages taken from each level of a series can be used for informal reading inventories. Rather than thumbing through an entire set of basals, selected passages can be extracted and placed in one handy spot.

Many ways exist to assess student progress in applying specific mechanical skills and comprehending printed material (Gifford, 2002). Evaluation does not need to be formal nor threatening but rather a means by which children's true reading ability can be determined. Establishing a child's PLEP can and should be a standard part of classroom routine. Evaluation tools should be aligned with instructional activities, including creating stories, writing songs, and playing games, to be analyzed for skill acquisition and appropriateness of the reading instruction program.

Sensory Disabilities

The areas of evaluation for children with sensory disabilities are the same as those for children without sensory disabilities: word analysis, word recognition, oral reading, and comprehension. However, reading evaluation of children with sensory disabilities must consider the special nature of the deficit. A child with a visual disability, for example, should not be tested on word recognition presented from a typed word list. Nor should a child with a hearing disability be tested for letter sounds—at least not in a way typically done in the general education classroom.

Two critical areas of consideration for evaluating reading of children who have sensory disabilities are format and mode of response. *Format* refers to the way that evaluation is administered. *Mode of response* refers to the way in which the child is expected to demonstrate knowledge.

Format Changes

Many formal tests have been developed for use with children who have sensory disabilities. Unfortunately, informal tests or tests coded to classroom materials often are most useful in a general education classroom. If teachers are not certain how to adapt testing to the sensory needs of children with disabilities, they should seek out the nearest specialist and request immediate assistance.

Vision specialists can transcribe most teacher-made and standardized tests for use with students who have visual disabilities. The transcribed tests can be made available in large print or Braille. Another tool to increase font size or intensity of hues is the standard word processing program found on most classroom personal computers. For the teacher whose district is a little more affluent and current, scanners can also be linked to the personal computer. For very little money, printed evaluation material can be scanned into the computer, and the size, color, and the amount of print for each page can be modified to fit the visual needs of most readers.

Format modifications can range from extending time limits to making major changes. For example, the teacher might allow a multiple-choice response rather than require verbal explanation (Bigge & O'Donnell, 1976). Modification in format also may consist of altering the material in some fashion, such as producing words in larger print for children with visual disabilities or presenting sounds to children with hearing disabilities through a headset to eliminate competing noises.

Testing materials for children with visual disabilities usually have large, clear type, nonglossy finish, and maximum contrast between background and printing. Testing materials for children with hearing disabilities should be presented in a noise-free environment, on glare-free paper, and with a good overall lighting system. Testing materials used with children who have physical disabilities should take into account the child's unique disability. For example, materials that require a child with arthritis to spend a great deal of time in one physical position may interfere with the child's ability to complete the task.

Test Characteristics

Modification of testing materials usually takes into account the properties of the materials. Some properties to consider are as follows:

Visual

- Size of print
- Clarity of print
- Contrast between print and background

- Number of items presented on a page
- Distracting features such as pictures or designs that draw attention away from the evaluation material
- Calming factors, such as pictures or designs that evoke positive feelings

Auditory

- Amplitude (loudness) of presentation
- Clarity or crispness of oral directions or items
- Contrast between item and competing background noise
- Rapidity with which items are presented
- Visual access to evaluator's lip movements

Mechanical

- Length of time required to complete the evaluation task
- Type of response required to complete the evaluation (e.g., vocal as in speech, or fine motor as in writing)
- Language requirements (type of syntax and grammar used when delivering directions)

Test Materials

With a little imagination, most teachers can alter their testing materials by considering their properties and the needs exhibited by children with sensory or physical disabilities.

CHILD DISABILITIES   Suppose you are teaching Leon, Steve, Ted, and Charles. You wish to evaluate their ability to identify a certain sequence of sounds: *i, n, c, l, u, s, i, o.* The evaluation question is: "When presented with a letter (visual symbol), can the child identify the corresponding sound?" Two questions immediately leap to mind.

1. Will any specific physical, sensory, or psychological characteristic need to be considered for any of these children?
2. Could any specific physical property of the test interfere with the results in determining if a child knows the sounds?

A checklist that will help evaluate the children is presented as Figure 7.4. A checkmark appears in the grid wherever an issue has to be addressed. The grid reveals that Leon needs assistance primarily in auditory areas. The teacher might assume that Leon has a hearing disability, but that would be incorrect. Leon does not have a sensory disability. He has a mild learning/behavior problem. Leon's attention is best while performing tasks that present some sort of auditory demand.

How about Steve? He does have a visual impairment. Therefore, he must have high-quality visual materials. Ted's accommodation needs seem a lot like Steve's, but he has no known visual impairment. Ted has cerebral palsy, which accounts for some weakness in the control of his neck muscles. Frequently,

Properties of Test	Leon	Steve	Ted	Charles
Visual				
Size of print		✓	✓	
Clarity of print		✓	✓	
Contrast between print and background				
Number of items on a page		✓	✓	
Distracting features		✓	✓	
Calming factors				
Auditory				
Loudness of presentation	✓			
Clarity of oral presentation	✓			
Background noise				
Rapidity of presentation	✓			
Visual access to examiner's lips	✓	✓		
Mechanical				
Time requirement				
Response requirement				✓
Language requirements				

Figure 7.4   Checklist Matching Child's Needs to Test Properties

though just momentarily, he loses sight of a page. Visually clear and clutter-free evaluation materials are easier for Ted because he can find his place more quickly than with visually disorganized or distracting materials.

Finally we come to Charles. His only major problem involves the response required to complete the task. Charles does not have enough fine-motor control to use a pen or a pencil.

PROPERTIES OF TEST MATERIALS   Returning to the original evaluation question: "When presented with a letter (visual symbol), can Leon, Steve, Ted, and Charles identify *i, n, c, l, u s, i, o*?" The question remains the same, but the means of answering it has changed. The answer is obtained by using basic classroom evaluation materials, especially the ever-popular 3" x 5" cards.

No change in evaluation material is necessary for Leon. The teacher simply has to determine whether he needs to hear the directions each time a card is presented. To check on his needs, the first card is presented with oral directions and then the next two or three cards are shown without oral directions. If Leon miscalls the sounds, the teacher knows that (a) he doesn't know the sounds, (b) he's not attending, or (c) he doesn't know the sounds and he is not attending. Because the objective is to evaluate Leon's knowledge of sounds, the "attending or not attending" question must be ruled out. To do so, the miscalled sounds are presented individually, and oral directions are provided each time the sound is shown. If Leon still is miscalling, the odds are high that he does not know the sounds. With no major adjustment, the teacher has answered the original question for Leon.

What about Steve and his visual impairment? If his disability does not permit him to use print, this may be a problem. Because the question has to do with actually looking at a letter and producing a sound, the inclusion teacher would not be able to test him. If Steve is a Braille reader, his special teacher has to evaluate him. If Steve has some vision, the inclusion teacher has to adjust the material to account for his vision level. A quick check with the special teacher should help with specific materials. In Steve's actual situation, a modification of print size was the only major adaptation required.

Ted needs no modification. His teacher alternates the 3" x 5" cards, which contain only one sound each. Even when Ted's lack of muscle control causes him to lose his place, he has no difficulty reestablishing visual focus.

Charles also needs no modification. His major problem involves impaired fine-motor skills. The classroom evaluation question does not demand fine-motor skills. His teacher can elicit the answer to the question for sounds Charles knows by using 3" x 5" cards. If the task were to demand that Charles make a fine-motor response, the mode of response would have to be examined.

Response Mode

How a person is required to respond to a test item mechanically is called the *response mode*. Response modes in most classrooms require fine-motor skills (the ability to complete a paper-and-pencil test) or demand speech (the ability to respond orally to an item or test question). If a child cannot speak well enough for the teacher to understand or cannot write (print) legibly, the teacher may have to alter the response mode of the evaluation instrument.

COMMUNICATION PROBLEMS   If a child cannot use speech to communicate, the following guidelines may be helpful.

Word analysis/word recognition

- Print, write, type the sound.
- Circle or underline the correct sound/word.
- Identify (match, circle, etc.) objects/pictures that contain the desired sound/word.
- Discriminate (match, touch, underline) the desired sound/word from a list.

If the child cannot use speech or fine-motor responses to communicate, the teacher might consider the following responses:

- The child signals yes/no responses when asked to identify specific sounds or words.
- The child signals yes/no responses to the examiner's verbal selection of specific sounds or words. The type of signal is important only insofar as the child has the skills to produce it. Head-nod signals, finger-raising signals, or computer-generated signals are equally valuable for communicating responses.

LEVEL OF RESPONSE DEMAND   Response modes can be thought of in terms of a sequence hierarchy or level of response demand. A response that requires the student's head to nod in agreement or disagreement with the examiner's response requires much less effort than a response that requires legible writing on designated lines. Ideally, no single response mode is mandatory for a child to answer a question. If changes become necessary, the teacher–evaluator should structure the modified response mode as close to the original mode as possible. The teacher is more interested in receiving an answer to the evaluation question than in knowing whether a child can respond—speak, point, nod, gesture—in a manner required by the evaluation tool. The response mode can be modified for a child with a disability in many simple ways:

1. The child agrees or disagrees with the teacher's selection or answers. For example, the teacher prints three letters on the chalkboard and says, "Tell me when I touch the letter that says *m*." Each time the teacher touches a letter, the child either agrees or disagrees with the *m* sound.
2. The child sorts pictures, objects, forms, or sounds according to categories corresponding to the teacher's models. Categories may be sounds, words, phrases, or passages. For example, the teacher provides a word list for the child to underline all the words that contain the short-*a* sound.
3. The child compares and selects or points to a picture, object, form, or letter that corresponds to the teacher's model. For example, the teacher shows a picture of a farm scene. She asks the child to read a card with the word *cow* and point to the corresponding animal.
4. The child selects one of a series that is different from the rest of the series. For example, the child reads a story about a pet show before the teacher asks for the animal that was not in the story. The teacher can elicit the response by presenting the material either orally or in the form of a written multiple-choice question such as the following:

   Animals *not* in the pet show:

   a. dogs
   b. kittens
   c. frogs
   d. rabbits

FACTORS INFLUENCING SKILL SCORES   Two other areas that could lead to false interpretation of a skill level include (a) amount of time required and (b) type of written response.

Time Demands   The amount of time within which the evaluation must be completed has to be considered for all children, especially learners with mild disabilities. For speed tests, the extra tine allowed for children with visual impairment will not influence the test's reliability or validity. A helpful rule allows two and one-half times the amount of testing time for Braille students and one and one-half times for readers of large print.

With the evaluation question always in mind, a teacher may wish to explore whether that question can be answered in more than one way. If, for example, the question tries to determine story comprehension, the teacher could ask the child either to write as much of the story as he or she remembers or to answer multiple-choice items about the story. If a child tires or becomes frustrated easily, the teacher probably would get a more accurate answer to the question by asking for a short multiple-choice response.

The time allowed between test items also can affect a child's performance. If change flusters the child, more time may have to be allowed between test items. For example, Willy can say isolated letter sounds, and he can blend consonant-vowel-consonant (CVC) words accurately. If he is asked to respond to a CVC item immediately after he has responded to a short vowel, however, he may have problems. It is almost as if Willy needs a little startup time to reorganize his thinking before he is ready for the next task. Why not give him a few extra seconds to process the task?

Then there is Ryan. In timed test situations, it is almost as if the second hand on the clock has blocked his ability to respond. Ryan needs to know that he is totally in charge of the time. When evaluating children like Ryan, timed reading probes do not make a great deal of sense. Yet two questions remain: "Can Ryan produce the correct sound or combination of sounds accurately?" and "How can Ryan's reading rate be determined?" First, the teacher should not time Ryan, and second, he or she should make an intelligent decision concerning when to increase his rate.

Type of Written Response   As mentioned earlier, written responses require fine-motor skills and expressive language. When evaluating reading, written response demands also must be kept in mind. If the evaluation response requires fine-motor skills, the student must have adequate fine-motor skills. If the response requires the student to have good expressive language, the student must have good expressive language. If the student lacks fine-motor skills or expressive language, the response demand must be altered.

Sanford can use a pencil, but his skill level can be likened to a cat barking. A concerted effort with the pencil produces some spiderlike, barely recognizable letters of the alphabet. A truer evaluation of Sanford's skills would involve questions that ask him to circle, underline, cross out, or mark the correct answer. For children who may have more serious disabilities in fine-motor skills, computers with special modifications have been developed. District specialists can assist teachers with evaluation materials.

Oral Language Skills

Oral language skills are sometimes overlooked when readers appear to have functional phonological skills; oral language skills are sometimes not seen and not heard when evaluating word recognition development. But oral language skills do have a significant influence on word recognition ability (Nation & Snowling, 2004).

Oral language is typically used when asking children to read from a text. These reading-aloud tests often do not take into account the influence of oral language development. Many children who fall into the categories deaf, language impaired, or ELL students have everyday language that functions well, but may not meet the speech production demands of the oral reading tests. Consequently, their scores are likely to be inaccurate (van Bon, Hoevenaars, & Jongeneelen, 2004).

In addition, due to the nature of the evaluation experience, most readings samples are given individually. For some classroom teachers, finding the time to evaluate using read aloud tests is cumbersome from a managerial perspective. An alternative procedure to the read-aloud tests, which appears to have good test-retest reliability and validity, to screen readers has been used successfully. The format for this alternative test asks readers to cross out as many pseudowords as possible in one minute, thus eliminating the need to produce words orally and be tested individually (Van Bon et al., 2004; Van Bon, Tooren, & van Eekelen, 2000). This alternative evaluation process provides accuracy and rate of performance measures, which can be used to judge the value of the instructional reading program relative to word recognition without confounding reading scores with oral language skills.

Summary

The purpose of reading evaluation is twofold: First the teacher must use evaluation to determine the reader's PLEP. Second, the teacher-evaluator must analyze the impact of the reading program on the reader's development. Accountability for reading instruction hinges on the validity and reliability of the evaluation tools employed. Many reading evaluation measures are available. Some tests are highly structured and formal while others are more informal and child friendly. Regardless of the test utilized, the information gained must be aligned with the classroom curriculum.

When evaluation the reading performance of any child, but especially children who qualify for special education services, the emotional, physical, and cognitive skills must be identified and taken into account when determining the most valid and reliable testing instrument. Task demands within any test must be considered in relation to the reader's cognitive, psychological, and physiological strengths and needs. Many commercial and teacher-made reading evaluation measures may need to be adapted in order to provide meaningful and accurate reading assessment for children in inclusion settings.

References

Adams, M. J. (1990). *Beginning to read: Thinking and learning about print.* Campaign: University of Illinois, Center for the Study of Reading.

Adams, M. J., & Collins, A. (1977). A *schema-theoretic view of reading* (Tech. Rep. 32). Urbana: University of Illinois, Center for the Study of Reading.

Armbruster, B. B., & Osborn, J. (2001). *Put reading first: The research building blocks for teaching children to read.* Washington, DC: National Institute for Literacy.

Ball, E. W., & Blachman, B. A. (1991). Does phoneme segmentation training in kindergarten make a difference in early word recognition and developmental spelling? *Reading Research Quarterly, 26,* 49–66.

Betts, E. A. (1957). *Foundations of reading instruction.* New York: American Book.

Bigge, J. L., & O'Donnell, P. A. (1976). *Teaching individuals with physical and multiple disabilities.* Columbus, OH: Charles E. Merrill.

Bowers, B. C. (1990). Meeting the needs of at-risk students. *Research Roundup, 7,* 1–4.

Brigance. (1983). *Brigance Diagnostic Inventory of Basic Skills.* North Billerica, MA: Curriculum Associates.

Chall, J. S. 1996. *Learning to Read: The Great Debate* (1967). New York: McGraw Hill.

Clay, M. M. (1976). Early childhood and cultural diversity in New Zealand. *Reading Teacher, 29,* 333–342.

Clay, M. M. (1993). *An observation survey of early literacy achievement.* Auckland, New Zealand: Heinemann.

Cunningham, J. W. (1993). Whole-to-part reading diagnosis. *Reading and Writing Quarterly: Overcoming Learning Difficulties, 9,* 31–49.

Durrell, D. D. (1955). *Durrell Analysis of Reading Difficulty.* New York: Harcourt Brace.

Frederiksen, C. H. (1979). *Semantic processing units in understanding text.* In R. O. Freedle (Ed.), Discourse production and comprehension (pp. 57–87). Norwood, NJ: Ablex.

Gifford, A. P. (2002). Is there only one way to evaluate students? *Reading Improvement, 39,* 25–31.

Gillet, J. W., & Temple, C. (1990). *Understanding reading problems: Assessment and instruction* (3rd ed.). Glenview, IL: Scott, Foresman.

Goodman, K. S., & Burke, C. L. (1973). *Theoretically based studies of patterns of miscues in oral reading performance* (U.S. Office of Education Project No. 9-0375). Washington, DC: U.S. Government Printing Office.

Goodman, K. S., & Goodman, Y. M. (1979). Learning to read is natural. In L. B. Resnick & P. A. Weaver (Eds.), *Theory and practice of early reading* (pp. 137–154). Hillsdale, NJ: Lawrence Erlbaum.

Guron, L. M., & Lundberg, I. (2003). Identifying multilingual students: Can phonological awareness be assessed in the majority language? *Journal of Research in Reading, 26,* 69–82.

Halliday, M. A. K. (1969). Relevant modes of language. *Education Review, 22,* 1–128.

Haring, N. R., Lovitt, T. C., Eaton, M. D., & Hansen, C. (1978). *The fourth R: Research in the classroom.* Columbus, OH: Charles E. Merrill.

Heymsfeld, C. R. (1992). The remedial child in the whole-language, cooperative classroom. *Reading & Writing Quarterly: Overcoming Learning Difficulties, 8*(3), 257–273.

Inman, D., Marlow, L., & Barron, B. (2004). Evaluation of a standards-based supplemental program in reading. *Reading Improvement, 41,* 179–187.

Kame'enui, E. J., & Simmons, D. C. (2003). *Early reading intervention.* New York: Pearson Education.

Kaminski, R. A., & Good, R. H., III. (1998). Assessing early literacy skills in a problem-solving model: Dynamic indicators of basic early literacy skills. In M. R. Shinn (Ed.), *Advanced applications of curriculum-based measurement* (pp. 113–142). New York: Guilford Press.

Karlsen, B., Madden, R., & Gardner, E. F. (1976). *Stanford Diagnostic Reading Test.* New York: Harcourt Brace Jovanovich.

Kauffman, J. M., & Hallahan, D. P. (2005). *Special education: What it is and why we need it.* Boston: Pearson.

Koriat, A., Greenberg, S. N., & Kreiner, H. (2002). The extraction of structure during reading: Evidence from reading prosody. *Memory and Cognition, 30,* 270–280.

Langdon, T. (2004). DIBELS: A teacher-friendly basic literacy accountability tool for the primary classroom. *Teaching Exceptional Children, 37,* 54–58.

Liberman, I. Y., & Liberman, A. M. (1990). Whole-language versus code emphasis: Underlying assumptions and their implications for reading instruction. *Annals of Dyslexia, 40,* 51–76.

Liberman, I. Y., & Shankweiler, D. P. (1985). Phonology and the problems of learning to read and write. *Remedial and Special Education, 6,* 8–17.

Liddle, W. (1970). *Reading for concepts—Book A.* New York: McGraw-Hill.

Marsh, D. (1999). *Preparing our schools for the 21st century: The ASCD yearbook—1999.* Alexandria, VA: ASCD.

Mason, J. M., & Au, K. H. (1990). *Reading instruction for today* (2nd ed.). New York: Harper-Collins.

Matsumara, L. C., Patthey-Chavez, G. G., Valdes, R., & Garnier, H. (2002). Teacher feedback, writing assignment quality, and third-grade students' revision in lower- and higher-achieving urban schools. *Elementary School Journal, 103,* 3–25.

Mindes, G. (2003). *Assessing young children* (2nd ed.). Upper Saddle, NJ: Pearson Education.

Moseley, D. (2004). The diagnostic assessment of word recognition and phonic skills in 5-year-olds. *Journal of Research in Reading, 27*(2), 132–140.

Murphy, J. C. (2004). Urban children and reading mastery: An examination of the language vocabulary acquisition approach to teaching reading. *Reading Improvement, 41,* 13–17.

Nation, K., & Snowling, M. J. (2004). Beyond phonological skills: Broader language skills contribute to the development of reading. *Journal of Research in Reading, 27*(4), 342–356.

National Institute of Child Health and Human Development. (2000). *Report of the National Reading Panel. Teaching children to read: an evidence-based assessment of the scientific research literature on reading and its implications for reading instruction.* Retrieved August 23, 2007, from http://www.nichd.nih.gov/publications/nrp/smallbook.htm

Naslund, J. C., & Samuels, S. J. (1992). Automatic access to word sounds and meaning in decoding written text. *Reading & Writing Quarterly: Overcoming Learning Difficulties, 8*(2), 135–156.

National Institute of Child Health and Human Development. (2000). *Report of the National Reading Panel. Teaching children to read: an evidence-based assessment of the scientific research literature on reading and its implications for reading instruction.* Retrieved August 23, 2007, from http://www.nichd.nih.gov/publications/nrp/smallbook.htm

Otto, W., McMenemy, R. A., & Smith, R. J. (1973). *Corrective and remedial reading* (2nd ed.). Boston: Houghton Mifflin.

Papalewis, R. (2004). Struggling middle school readers: Successful, accelerating intervention. *Reading Improvement, 41,* 24–37.

Perfetti, C. A. & Hogaboam, T. (1975). Relationship between single word decoding and reading comprehension skill. *Journal of Educational Psychology, 67,* 461–469.

Pressley, M., Wharton-McDonald, R., Allington, R., Block, C. C., Morrow, L., Tracey, D., et al. (2001). A study of effective first-grade literacy instruction. *Scientific Studies of Reading, 5,* 35–58.

Ross, J. (2004). Effects of running records assessment on early literacy achievement. *Journal of Educational Research, 97,* 186–198.

Rummelhart, D. E. (1989). The architecture of the mind; A connectionist approach. In M. I. Posner (Ed). *Foundations of Cognitive Science.* (pp. 133–160). Cambridge, MA: The MIT Press.

Sinatra, R. (1992). Mini-theme: Approaches to word recognition for at-risk readers. *Reading & Writing Quarterly: Overcoming Learning Difficulties, 8*(2), 131–134.

Smith, F. (1971). *Understanding reading: A psycholinguistic analysis of reading and learning to read.* New York: Holt, Rinehart and Winston.

Spache, G. D. (1972). *Diagnostic Reading Scales.* Monterey, CA: McGraw Hill.

Taylor, B. M., Pearson, P. D., Clark, K., & Walpole, S. (2000). Effective schools and accomplished teachers: Lessons about primary grade reading instruction in low-income schools. *Elementary School Journal, 101,* 121–166.

Topping, K. J., & Fisher, A. M. (2003). Computerised formative assessment of reading comprehension: Field trials in the UK. *Journal of Research in Reading, 26,* 267–279.

Turnbull, H. R., & Turnbull, A. (2007). *Free appropriate public education: The law & children with disabilities* (7th ed.). Denver, CO: Love.

Van Bon, W. H. J., Hoevenaars, L. T. M., & Jongeneelen, J. J. (2004). Using pencil-and-paper lexical–decision tests to assess word decoding skill: Aspects of validity and reliability. *Journal of Research in Reading, 27*(1), 58–68.

Van Bon, W. H. J., Tooren, P. H., & van Eekelen, M. C. J. D. (2000). Lexical decision and oral reading by poor and normal readers. *European Journal of Psychology of Education, 15,* 259–270.

Weaver, P. A., & Resnick, L. B. (1979). The theory and practice of early reading: An introduction. In L. B. Resnick & P. A. Weaver (Eds.), *Theory and practice of early reading* (pp. 1–7). Hillsdale, NJ: Lawrence Erlbaum.

Wray, D., Medwell, J., Fox, R., & Poulson, L. (2000). The teaching practices of effective teachers of literacy. *Educational Review, 52,* 75–84.

CHAPTER

8

Reading Methods
in Inclusion Settings

KEY TERMS

- accelerated reader (AR)
- anecdotal records
- basal reader
- classroom reading kits
- comprehension
- curriculum-based assessments
- English language learners (ELL)
- good readers
- Individuals with Disabilities Education Improvement Act of 2004 (IDEA)
- informal reading inventory (IRI)
- learning information systems (LIS)
- linguistic approach
- No Child Left Behind Act of 2001 (NCLB)
- oral language skills
- oral reading
- poor readers
- reading fluency
- running record
- story retell
- whole-language approach
- word analysis
- word recognition

Amy describes herself as reluctant to read in class. She says she doesn't like to read her books at school very much, but she does enjoy reading her own writing. Amy especially likes to read from her personal journal in the solitude and comfort of her bedroom. Amy says that she's like her friend Zoey. Zoey's parents told her that she has dyslexia and must try very hard to read. Amy says she's a little bit like Zoey, but she doesn't really have as much dyslexia as Zoey. Amy says that she can read all the words on the blackboard backwards and is very proud of this accomplishment. She thinks that there are many kinds of dyslexia, but she's not sure what type she has. She does know that she's not very good at reading. Amy takes a long time to read a book, and then she still forgets what she's read. Amy has a very hard time keeping focused and remembering where she is on a page. Even when Amy does remember where she is, she reads so slowly that she rarely finishes her work at school.

Amy can pronounce a lot of the little words but does not remember how to sound out the big words, so she just skips them. Amy says that her parents think that if she keeps reading she will get better, but she knows that she's trying as hard as she can and practicing is becoming tedious. Amy is getting frustrated by working on reading so much with her parents at home, her teacher in school, and her tutor on Saturdays and still not being able to read like the other kids at school. Amy has not ever read a whole book without stumbling and doesn't even remember the names of the characters. Amy believes that learning to read is extremely important. She knows that when she gets to high school she will have to read a lot more than she does now. Amy has been trying to think of what would help her learn to read better, but she has run out of ideas and is running out of time.

Extent of the Literacy Problem

Children and adults who use traditional, culturally agreed upon reading and writing behaviors are demonstrating conventional literacy (Kaderavek & Sulzby, 2000). Young or low-skilled children may be described as demonstrating *emergent literacy*, the range of activities and behaviors related to literacy found in creative play or social context (Burns, Griffin, & Snow, 1999). Violet and Klaus are excellent readers. They enjoy reading and learning from print. Despite being exposed to a sometimes fragmented reading program, both children are considered literate. Sunny, however, is still developing literacy. She has been through the same programs as Violet and Klaus, yet conventional use of print to access meaning in not yet in Sunny's world. Sunny is an emerging reader; she uses language to describe important events in her life. She interacts well with others and appears to have a very active imagination.

Literacy cuts across categorical definitions. Some children with Down syndrome, for example, have achieved reading competencies equivalent to fifth-grade levels and children as young as 3 and 4 years old, who lacked all the typical preskills to reading readiness, including alphabetic knowledge, have been reported to learn sight words (Buckley, 1996; Layton, 2000).

Students like Amy and Zoey with reading disabilities have a difficult time completing assignments in school, taking tests, and viewing themselves as bright and capable individuals. No one knows for sure why Amy and Zoey cannot read very well, but many theories have been proposed. Students like Amy desperately want to be good readers; they want to be smart like their peers who can sound out words they don't know and who can remember what they have read. Amy and Zoey are not demonstrating conventional literacy. They are demonstrating dyslexia.

Dyslexia

The term *dyslexia* has multiple meanings, which ultimately result in the circular definition that the individual cannot read very well. Dyslexia and reading disabilities are on the Mobius strip of the educational world. No matter which direction is traveled, the destination is the same; dyslexics and individuals with poor reading performance are not able to read very well.

Reading disabilities have been attributed to neurological problems that limit the capacity and ability to store and manipulate or process information, as well as the inability to recall speech-based sounds or hold visual-spatial information found in letters and words (Shaywitz & Fletcher 2005; Swanson, 2005). Reading disabilities have also been attributed to poor or inappropriate teaching practices (Smith, 1998; Wilson-Bridgman, 2003).

Determining causation for reading disabilities is challenging at best and frustrating at worst. If, however, specialized programs designed to account for reading problems are not successful, a reasonable assumption is that the problems are inherent in the way the students are processing the information needed to acquire reading literacy (Swanson & Seigel, 2001; Torgesen, 2000). The reading methods to which a learner has been exposed may be excellent, and the lack of reading success may not be due to poor teaching, but rather to a poor fit between the student's information processing skills and the reading approach. Reading Recovery, for example, is a reading program designed to raise the lowest achieving readers in first grade up to the average of their class within four months (Wilson-Bridgman, 2003). Jamal and Darren both participated in Reading Recovery. At the end of 16 weeks Jamal was reading on grade level; Darren had made no significant progress. Darren participated in an excellent reading program, but not a program that was excellent for his needs. Darren's reading difficulties are not due to either instructional or environmental factors.

Results of various reading studies are strongly suggesting that some reading deficits related to the verbal system are less changeable for children with inherent reading disabilities, like Darren, than for children who are either poor readers, like Jamal, or for skilled readers. One simple measure suggesting inherent processing reading difficulties includes listening to the sequence of events in a story while trying to understand what the story means (Swanson & Howard, 2005). Children with certain types of intrinsic processing problems have a difficult time keeping information in memory while dealing with incoming ideas. The practical implication for the inclusion teacher is that the typical processors may be identified from the atypical processors and reading approaches appropriate to their needs developed earlier in their academic careers.

Difficulty acquiring reading literacy skills is found among speakers of many languages (Smythe, Everatt, & Salter, 2003) and is a predominant characteristic of many individuals with disabilities (Manset-Williamson & Nelson, 2005). In the area of learning disabilities, for example, most of the approximately 2,887,217 school-aged children in the United States who are receiving services (U.S. Department of Education, 2002) have been identified because of poor reading ability (Lyon et al., 2001; Shaywitz, 2003). Problems acquiring reading literacy are not limited to students with high-incidence disabilities, however. Reading below proficiency levels cuts across students with and without disabilities, and the achievement differences in literacy skills is particularly noticeable in children from urban areas and among specific ethnic populations (National Assessment of Educational Progress [NAEP], 2000). Moreover, reading scores have not significantly improved over the last three decades and, disturbingly, the reading skills of students graduating from high school declined significantly in 2004 (Bryan, Owens, & Walker, 2004).

Need for Reading Literacy

Without belaboring the obvious, the ability to read or at least access print is a critical factor in successful school achievement. Not so surprisingly, a strong correlation exists between poor reading ability and school failure. Students who do not have access to information contained in textbooks and related printed class material are at a significant disadvantage for acquiring the school curriculum. The importance of providing appropriate instruction for all students cannot be overstated, and the search for techniques to raise literacy for students with high-incidence disabilities (i.e., behavior disorders, learning disabilities, mild mental retardation, and speech or language impairments), who constitute about 85% of the approximately 5 million school-aged youth classified with disabilities, is a high priority for educators (Schmidt, Rozendal, & Greenman, 2002).

An important goal for general and special educators is improving reading instruction at as early an age as possible. The "Matthew Effect" paints a grim picture of failure to thrive in school by pointing out that small problems in reading ability in the primary grades spiral to huge gaps by the elementary and upper grades, resulting in the placement of some children in special education classes

(Stanovich, 1998). Without becoming overly fatalistic, the impact of poor reading skills on students is magnified at every successive grade level, and, simultaneously, opportunities for intervention are reduced (Spadorcia, 2005).

In spite of many extensive and praiseworthy efforts to develop strategies to prevent reading problems, an overwhelming number of middle and high school students read significantly below grade-level expectations (Archer, Gleason, & Vachon, 2003). In support of the Matthew Effect, only 26% of students who display literacy disabilities in third grade continue on to become successful readers; 74% of the students with reading disabilities will continue to struggle to access print in ninth grade and beyond (Lyon, 1995).

Increasing Literacy Rates

Based in part on the Matthew Effect and the large number of students with poor reading skills, and even poorer prospects of a meaningful school career, the No Child Left Behind (NCLB) legislation of 2001 provided guidelines for educational reform and accountability for reading instruction with all students in the Reading First initiative, an ambitious attempt at ensuring that primary-age children receive effective reading instruction. Reading First is a national effort to enable all students to become successful readers by acquiring reading skills by third grade. Funds have been targeted to aid states and school districts to eliminate reading deficits by providing high-quality comprehensive reading instruction in kindergarten through third grade. One of the major reasons for targeting the primary grades was the startling 2001 statistic that found only approximately one third of fourth-graders were achieving at or above the proficient level in reading (Donahue, Finnegan, Lutkus, Allen, & Campbell, 2001).

Reading First legislation is an attempt to identify and provide interventions for struggling readers before they get caught up in the Matthew Effect and to reduce the number of children entering special education due to inappropriate or inadequate reading instruction. Yet, Reading First, however well-intentioned, is not likely to provide the type of reading instruction that can or will prevent reading difficulties for many children like Roger, who cannot learn to access print without extraordinary means. Children requiring extraordinary means to access print may be found in any special education category, although not all children eligible for services have special reading needs.

Roger, a bright and charming fifth-grader, is one of the children who has not learned to read beyond the first-grade level in spite of instruction using traditional and even exemplary reading strategies. Roger is considered a nonresponsive reader. He has a low performance level and an inadequate learning rate even though he has received reading instruction that is generally effective for most children. Even when given a lot of special support, nonreaders or poor readers like Roger make little or no progress in acquiring meaningful reading skills in whole-class, inclusion settings (Klinger, Vaughn, Hughes, Schumm, & Elbaum, 1998). In fact, even though the results of some reading intervention research are encouraging, not all children respond to even the best current methods of reading, including one-to-one tutoring (Dion, Morgan, Fuchs, & Fuchs, 2004).

Reading First proponents, at their most extreme, suggest that children like Roger who are not ready to read by third grade should be retained until proficiency is achieved. Acting on this philosophy would mean that Roger, a budding mathematician, might forever find himself with age-inappropriate peers and curricula. Literacy does not happen for all children at the same time and in the same way (Graves, 2002). Literacy goes beyond the capability of translating the printed word through sight. Literacy is the ability to grow in knowledge by interacting with and learning from a variety of sources; reading is just one of the paths to learn about the world, not the only road. Children like Roger may need an alternate route to the printed page on their journey to literacy.

Early literacy is a reasonable place to focus reading instruction. Many children entering kindergarten and first grade have developed physiologically and cognitively to the point that they are able to learn the relationships between abstract symbols and meaning. Hand–eye coordination increases quickly in these early years, and most 5- and 6-year-old children have developed sophisticated language concepts. Most young children are social beings and like to communicate with each other. Most have been exposed to print and are ready to learn to read affectively and cognitively.

Reading as Communication

Reading, writing, and thinking are interrelated processes that foster communication. Reading and writing are socially constructed communicative practices that grow in sophistication as the students' skills become more refined. Intervention at the beginning levels of reading and writing may increase the student's ability to create a sound foundation for more sophisticated literacy practices (Kaderavek & Rabidoux, 2004). Reading and writing are not an end product but rather an ongoing, lifelong developmental process. Just like most bent twigs can be staked and redirected into becoming straight, tall trees, with a little assistance from a sound intervention, many floundering readers can become models of literacy. Some children with atypical communication may flourish with early intervention, while others may not develop age-appropriate skills. Early intervention is to be praised, but interventions need not stop at grade 3.

In spite of the emphasis on early literacy, not all children learn to read in grades K–3. Although the skill levels of beginning readers and poor readers may look the same on an evaluation measure, a quick look at physical differences between a 5-year-old and an 11-year-old would suggest otherwise. Interventions for older children need to account for experiential interests as well as the impact of past instructional strategies. Unfortunately, interventions for middle and secondary school readers are often modeled on strategies used with much younger children.

Steve's situation is typical of many older children with reading difficulties. By sixth grade, Steve had made several failed attempts at better reading. He was not very receptive to beginning the reading process again, especially when most of the reading is the same material used by his second-grade sister, Susan. To make matters worse, while Steve fumbles through the low-level books, Susan's reading is much more fluent, a phenomenon not unnoticed by her big brother. Steve, like many nonresponsive readers over age 9, would rather not engage in reading activities that promise more of the same uninteresting and "little-kid" material with which he has already experienced failure over and over and over again (Guthrie, Alao, & Rinehart, 1997; Spadorcia, 2005).

Middle school students like Steve are given the almost impossible task of reading complex textbooks, which are built upon the premise that the targeted middle- and upper-grade readers possess vocabularies and comprehension skills suitable for accessing printed curricular content. However, not all students have highly developed language skills that are in tune with the language of the textbooks and related curricular material. Some children in both high- and low-incidence disabilities categories have language deficits. If the student's first language is English, the struggle for print literacy becomes almost overwhelming.

Despite reading interventions, Steve and his older classmates with reading deficits continue to drown in a sea of meaningless symbols and words that constitute textbooks—their primary source of information. Most students like Steve will continue to experience reading-based learning problems well into adolescence and beyond (McCray, Vaughn, & Neal, 2001). Reading disabilities do not end with high school graduation. Some students with dyslexia and other reading difficulties go on to college and even graduate school, but reading continues to take a lot of effort, time, and energy for them (Shaywitz, 2003). Many of the older readers with serious skill deficits are so delayed that they struggle with remembering words, sounding out new terms, and comprehending simple information (Fletcher, Morris, & Lyon, 2003).

The Reading Sum Is Greater Than Its Parts

Many definitions propose that reading is an active and interactive process between print and higher level thinking skills based on past and current experiences of the reader. In the language of the 21st century, the most popular reading definitions are based on some variation of a cognitive-constructivist model (Graves, Juel, & Graves, 2004). A cognitive-constructivist model is a sophisticated way of saying that the reading process is composed of many interrelated components, some of which are based on higher level thinking processes usually associated with comprehension, while others are grounded in lower level mechanical skills usually associated with word recognition and sound–symbol correspondence.

Reading could be considered *thinking guided by print* or *print guided by thinking*. Realistically, however, a person can engage in all kinds of comprehension activities but not be able to read print. In turn, an individual may sound out symbols and recall whole words but not be able to comprehend. Reading from print requires the ability to engage higher level skills with lower level skills, but in different degrees of interaction depending on the nature of the reading material and the developmental and experiential sophistication of the reader.

With many instructional reading approaches, first steps in acquiring reading ability typically focus on sounds and symbols and recognizing words. Yet, these mechanical components of reading are meaningful only when the emerging reader (i.e., a reader who is just learning how to use mechanical skills) can associate words or sounds and symbols with prior knowledge. Take 5-year-old Stan, as he carefully sounds out words as he reads. Stan is actively engaged in the act of reading. He has been organizing his personal body of knowledge, called *schemata,* since the day of his birth. Stored in his brain are personally meaningful memories, some of which he experienced directly and others vicariously. All the objects, situations, events, actions, and their respective sequences Stan has valued have been carefully stored and internalized in Stan's young mind, and now he is matching his schemata with the print in front of him. Stan has a schema for animals like dogs, for situations like being in kindergarten, for events like going to the movies, for smells like popcorn and chocolate, and for sequences of events like locating a friend or a skateboard.

Stan is making sense of what he is reading out of his experiences by making connections between the printed word and his schemata. When a match between the reading material and Stan's schemata is found, the printed information can be cataloged with similar experiences or concepts. When a match is not found, the information can be put into a new category to be matched with future experiences. The concepts in Stan's mind are organizing and networking with each other. Having rich and interconnected networks of schemata allows Stan to almost instantaneously access massive amounts of knowledge. Too many isolated categories negatively impact Stan's reading; in essence, a network-poor Stan would not be able to make matches rapidly or efficiently with print.

Stan is constructing meaning or interpreting the printed material based on his personal experiences. His best friend Gabriele, newly arrived from Italy, is also constructing meaning from print, but his life experiences are different from Stan's. Gabriele and Stan may read the same printed material but use different reference points in their schemata to arrive at the correct sound for short *a* or the meaning of the word *home.*

Effects of Disability

The type of disability is one factor that forms a child's experiences. It is therefore integral to the development of schemata. Children with disabilities, including many who have language and learning disabilities, often display expressive and receptive communication difficulties. Typically, children with language issues engage less in social interactions than students with more typical language skills. Accordingly, their experiences and resulting schemata are different from the norm and may be impoverished due to lack of social interaction—an important source for acquiring incidental knowledge. Incidental knowledge is gathered informally from life experiences in contrast to formal, classroom-based instruction. Incidental knowledge is a major contributor to developing schemata. Gaining meaning from reading for children with disabilities depends on the number and type of mental networks created. Children with various types of disabilities can learn to read, but they may need specialized techniques to access print.

The type of disability shapes the number, kind, and quality of mental networks developed. Children with visual impairments, for example, have different experiences with the sounds of letters and words than a child whose language deficits are distorted due to blocked access to hearing or saying letter sounds and words. Children who have limited or no access to sensory input develop schemata, but their references or networks are built upon somewhat different experiences than the schemata of children whose sensory and motor skills are more typical.

Due to an accident at age 3, Jared has minimal use of his legs; David has poor fine-motor skills, and he is blind. During recess Jared and David have fun with their friends on the playground equipment. Jared uses a special swing with straps; David uses the same swings as the other children. David cannot see the swings, but he knows the feel of the chains and rubberized seat. Jared has one kind of schemata for "swinging routines," and David has another. Therefore, when they read about "swinging," their schemata will provide them with different concepts. When Jared hears about Tarzan swinging through the trees, he may initially see a very buff fellow attached with a strap to a jungle vine. David's idea of Tarzan's vine might be linked pieces of sturdy metal similar to those found on the swings at school.

Furthermore, children who can be characterized as having particular challenges related to acquiring reading cannot be educated as if the skill deficits determine one instructional approach per category. For example, Marcy has severe visual restrictions; she is not blind, but she has low vision. Marcy and partially sighted children like her typically require special aids such as large type, magnifiers, and special lighting so they can complete work that requires detailed vision. Janine also has visual impairments, but her visual issues have a lot to do with ocular fine-motor control. As Janine's visual system fatigues, so does Janine. Janine uses a lot of energy to keep her ocular system focused, but after 5–10 minutes the letters on the page become blurry, melt into each other, and eventually disappear altogether. Janine and Marcy, both exhibiting visual problems and both experiencing fatigue from the reading act, need very different instructional approaches.

Reading Dissected

The goal of all reading instruction is to create readers who are efficient and effective in comprehending print as a means of communication. Keeping in mind that reading is an active and interactive process, strategies and techniques have been designed to help readers maximize integral components of this complex activity. Effective and efficient readers apply all areas of reading to obtain meaning; however, struggling readers often have difficulty in one or more subareas. Four broad areas commonly addressed in the reading instruction literature are phonics, word recognition, vocabulary development, and comprehension. Each area has specific subareas and accompanying instructional strategies. Lowered ability to use one or more reading components impacts the reading process as a whole.

Phonics

English is one of many written languages that use letters to represent sound. Phonics, often referred to as decoding, is a way of matching spoken sounds with letters. Phonics consists of visual letter–sound relationships and various approaches to teaching readers how to pronounce words they have never seen before. Applying phonics helps readers identify a large number of words with relatively small amounts of information and provides them with a certain degree of independence. Because Sharona, for example, understands how to rhyme and knows her letter sounds, she has a powerful set of tools for learning many new words. Sharona knows the sound for short *a* and all the consonants. She also understands that sounds move from left to right and that they blend together to form words. Sharona's reading vocabulary was dramatically increased when she learned the word *cat* by drawing a picture of MaeMae, her 4-year-old feline friend. Based on Sharona's knowledge of phonics she generalized to other words that looked and sounded like *cat* and arrived at eight new words—*bat, fat, mat, hat, pat, sat, rat,* and *vat*—entirely on her own. Sharona's phonics insights and her eight new words served to reinforce her notion that she is a very good reader and has encouraged her to pursue reading activities even more vigorously. A few representative subareas that fall under the umbrella of phonics are found in Table 8.1.

Alphabet recognition and phonemic awareness are two subcomponents of phonics that are highly predictive of success in beginning reading (Graves et al., 2004). Letter knowledge helps children understand the relationship between sounds and symbols. In fact, the emerging-reader crystal-ball predictions for which children are most likely to be very good at reading are usually based on analyzing skill level with letter knowledge (Blaiklock, 2004; Burgess & Lonigan, 1998). A lot of evidence indicates that phonological processing abilities are closely and probably causally related to success or failure in beginning reading. Without some sort of intervention, the most telling detail of reading disability even up through high school is difficulty with phonological awareness (Shaywitz

Table 8.1   Selected Examples of Phonics Subareas

- Phonemic insight: Awareness of the sequence of almost separable sounds in words
- Phonological awareness: Ability to separate sentences into words and words into syllables
- Rhyme awareness: Identifying, predicting, and producing rhyming words
- Application of letter sounds and patterns: Isolated sounds, blends, consonant clusters, vowel–letter patterns, etc.
- Prefixes and suffixes
- Alphabet recognition: Awareness that spoken sounds are represented by written letters
- Tracking print: The ability to keep the eyes moving correctly on the line being read
- Understanding vocabulary used when talking about print; for example, letter, word, space

& Fletcher, 2005). Awareness of the phonemic components of any written language, English included, is crucial for being successful in learning to read (Duncan, Seymour, & Hill, 2000; Hulme, 2002). Skill needs rather than disability category is the determining factor for how much or how little emphasis should be placed on instruction in phonemic areas of reading.

The potential for children with mental retardation to understand and generalize literacy skills has been overlooked by many educators and researchers. Historically, reading instruction for individuals with mild to moderate retardation has focused on teaching words by sight (Katims, 2000). Children with mental retardation have been found to be capable of grasping and generalizing phonetic analysis skills from one context to another context. Inclusion teachers of students with mental retardation need to consider incorporating explicit teaching of letter–sound relationships, as well as prerequisite skills such as phonemic awareness, in their literacy programs (Joseph & Seery, 2004).

Readers at Risk

Letter–sound knowledge and the ability to manipulate phonemes are important predictors for growth in reading for children at risk for reading disabilities (Savage & Carless, 2004). Many ways to develop phonological awareness exist. Some children expand their phonological awareness informally by becoming sensitized to sound-related events in their daily lives. Without formal instruction some children understand the relationship between sounds by experiencing nursery rhymes and songs, listening to stories read by relatives and teachers, and manipulating plastic letters on the front of the refrigerator. Programs like *Sesame Street* also heighten letter–sound correspondence.

Children at risk may also experience nursery rhymes and songs, listen to stories, and manipulate plastic letters, but unlike their counterparts, no matter how much or how often they watch programs like *Sesame Street,* they do not or cannot integrate and relate such phonemic information when attempting to read. Such children, especially those at risk for reading disabilities, become phonologically sensitive primarily through formal instructional approaches, of which a multitude exist. Development of phonological awareness cannot be left to chance for most children with disabilities because their disability puts them at risk for reading problems. These children need to be taught explicitly how to identify rhyming and nonrhyming word pairs, blend isolated sounds to form words, and segment spoken words into individual syllables (Lyon & Moates, 1997).

Explicit Instruction

For the last decade, many reading intervention specialists have concluded that some form of explicit and direct instruction in phonemic awareness/analysis and decoding is essential for students who are at risk for or those who already demonstrate reading difficulties (Torgesen, Rashotte, Alexander, & MacPhee, 2001). Children with disabilities in language, hearing, vision, and combinations of each usually fall into the category of students who are at risk for reading failure.

Techniques most often associated with explicit instruction incorporate elements of direct instruction, especially direct explanation, modeling, guided practice with continual monitoring and feedback, review, and mastery learning (Manset-Williamson & Nelson, 2005). Letter sounds and names, syllable identification, and common vowel rules are explained, modeled, and practiced under a variety of reading situations, checked and rechecked for understanding, and reviewed until the phonics skills are automatic and fluent.

Six-year-old Tyler could not distinguish rhyming from non-rhyming words. Tyler's parents, hoping an Ivy League university is in the future for their son, have been very conscientious about providing him with a reading-rich environment. They read stories to him after breakfast, lunch, dinner, and before bedtime, taught him nursery rhymes and children's songs, and engaged him in clever, age-appropriate reading material using the computer. But upon entering kindergarten, Tyler could still not rhyme *Mickey* with *sticky* or *mouse* with *house*. Tyler's kindergarten teacher was sure that he would pick up rhyming as the year progressed, but by mid-May Tyler still could not distinguish between words that rhymed and words that did not rhyme. Tyler was also having problems hearing individual syllables in multisyllabic words and did not know all the letter sounds.

The reading clock struck time for an intervention. In the summer between kindergarten and first grade, Tyler's parents hired a tutor who utilized a direct instruction approach. His tutor, Ms. Pitassi, approached teaching rhyming from many different instructional angles. She taught rhyming awareness by using Tyler's understanding of family as an analogy. She reminded Tyler how much he looks like his little sister because they were in the same family. They had the same color hair and eyes, but they were different, too. She went on to explain that words that looked alike usually belonged to the same word family.

Ms. Pitassi introduced him to the *-at* family. Together they created sentences and phrases using two or more members of the *-at* family. Together they practiced identifying words that looked and sounded like *-at* family words. Once Tyler had mastered identifying *-at* family words without assistance, he was ready to be introduced to the next family. Ms. Pitassi then introduced Tyler to the *-an* family. The next direct instructional piece of information was that words in the same family also sounded alike. The *-at* family words all sounded alike; the *-an* family words all sounded like each other, but did not sound the same as the members of the *-at* family. Ms. Pitassi continued to review the *-at* family while introducing the *-an* family. She did not wait for Tyler to come up with any generalizations or rules. She gave him explicit direction by modeling word families and by playing instructional games utilizing guided practice to help Tyler see and hear phonetic differences in his word families. Along the way to reading acquisition, Ms. Pitassi also taught Tyler the sounds for the consonants he did not already know and three of the short vowels. Through direct instruction Ms. Pitassi taught Tyler how to listen to sounds in words and in isolation. Ms. Pitassi did not wait for Tyler to get ready to read, nor did she make him figure out how letters and sounds worked together. Ms. Pitassi taught Tyler the rules for hearing and seeing the relationships between sounds and symbols in the context of meaningful information.

Fortunately for all concerned, especially Tyler's parents, who were unjustifiably feeling guilty for failing their child, once Tyler became sensitized to sounds and letters, he was able to generalize to other words and other word families. Tyler became one of the reading stars throughout the remainder of his primary years and was considered an expert reader for the rest of his life.

Tyler's story has a happy ending, as some researchers would say, because he received explicit and systematic instruction in phonics. In first grade he did not have to figure out the code on his own. His initial low level of phonemic awareness, which would have doomed him to reading failure, was thwarted because he was fortunate to receive strong code-based instruction (Compton, 2000), and because he was capable and receptive to the instruction provided. Reading First can provide tremendous assistance to students like Tyler, and success stories like his have served to create a renewed interest in legislating phonics instruction in the primary grades. Common sense and research findings, found in Table 8.2, suggest eight prudent procedures to use when teaching beginning readers how to decode written language.

Instruction from the phonological pot should be a major boost for acquiring reading proficiency, and for many at-risk readers such is the case, but then along comes a child like Joe. Joe had the same instructional opportunities as Tyler. Joe received explicit instruction in a phonics-rich reading environment. While Joe's reading story has the same plot as Tyler's, it has a very different ending. In spite of instruction that specified letter–sound relationships, practice in converting letters to sounds, and making words out of letters, Joe continued to show no gains

Table 8.2   Procedures for Teaching Beginning Readers How to Decode Written Language

From the first day of reading instruction:

1. Teach written letters and their sounds.
2. Teach spelling sound relations directly and systematically.
3. Assess spelling sound knowledge frequently until children acquire proficiency.
4. Encourage spelling and writing.
5. Teach sounding out.
6. Provide opportunities to practice reading words that are consistent with phonics instruction.
7. As short-word proficiency is reached, incorporate strategies for reading multisyllabic words.
8. As long as gains continue to occur, find ways to provide more instruction in decoding for struggling students.

Source: Adapted from "Early Identification and Intervention for Young Children With Reading/Learning Disabilities," (p. 131), by J. R. Jenkins and R. E. O'Connor, 2002, in R. Bradley, L. Danielson, and D. Hallahan (Eds.), *Identification of Learning Disabilities: Research to Practice.* Manwah, NJ: Erlbaum Associates, Inc. Adapted by permission of the publisher.

in reading. Joe is among the 30–50% of low-achieving children who, despite exemplary and explicit instruction, never acquire sufficient language and decoding skills to become fluent readers (Fuchs et al., 2001).

Unfortunately, neither common sense nor research findings have been able to find ways for Joe and others like him to access print fluently in the primary grades. For Joe and other nonresponsive primary-age readers, the reading picture is dismal. Techniques for improving reading and spelling skills for nonresponsive readers beyond the primary grades remain unclear. Nevertheless, repeatedly continuing phonics instruction and expecting significant change in reading performance for nonresponsive readers is an all too common exemplar of educational insanity. Herein lies the chicken-and-egg reading conundrum: Learners must be fluent readers before they can derive meaning from text, but Joe and others like him cannot develop enough fluency in applying what they have learned about letter–sound combinations to be able to derive meaning from the printed words (Hasselbring & Goin, 2004). Phonological processing problems have serious ramifications for acquiring basic word reading and developing reading comprehension.

Basic Word Reading

Word recognition, synonymous with *sight words*, is the ability to look at a word and immediately recognize how it is pronounced. A major goal of word recognition instruction is to help students develop a large bank of words that can be accessed without using phonics. Many factors influence the number and type of words that a reader can recognize. Some of these factors include the amount and kind of sounds in the word, the personal meaningfulness of the word, and the number of known to unknown words in reading materials (Hiebert, Martin, & Menon, 2005). Most children learn to identify written words in stories that are interesting and understandable to them. Very young or low-skilled readers initially need someone to read to them or with them, but eventually they recognize some words, which then become part of their word recognition vocabulary (Smith, 2003).

Words can be taught in isolation; however, children learn to read and remember new words more quickly when they can apply decoding skills and meaningful information drawn from their personal memories. New or unknown words are learned through interactions between sounds, experiences, and memory. Words that are firmly stored in memory no longer need sound or experiential cues for retrieval.

Ted, for example, has an easier time reading words than his friend Billy. When Ted sees a new word, he can use his phonics skills and personal background to give him some insights. When he comes across the word again, he no longer needs to rely on his phonics skills to recall the term. Ted is building a large sight word vocabulary. Billy, on the other hand, has a very difficult time using the sounds he knows when he encounters a new term. He can summon up sounds, but he recalls them very, very slowly. For Billy, reading words is a laborious task. Worst of all, he usually does not remember the new word he has so carefully decoded. As a result, no matter how many times Billy has seen a word, the word must be approached as if he had never seen it before. Billy is not developing a large sight word vocabulary.

Capacity for remembering words is also a factor in predicting who will be a good reader and who may need extraordinary means to access meaning from print. Even the best readers probably have an upper limit to the number of new words they can read and remember (Hiebert et al., 2005). When asking children to read words in short, predictable books in a period of 3 weeks, the highest or best readers remembered 30 new words, the middle readers, 15, and the lowest readers, 6 (Johnston, 2000). Children whose disabilities include memory issues are likely to fall into the category of nonresponsive readers.

Experiences also play a large role in determining vocabulary growth. Long before children come to school, they have developed word identification strategies. They use *environmental cues*; that is, they associate meaning with print in their everyday world. Very young children often link significant persons, places, or objects in their environment. A few examples include Ronald McDonald, Disneyland, and ice cream. Very young children also use *picture cues* to infer meaning. Illustrations can be found in multiple sources in the environment: in storybooks, posters, packaging for toys, clothing, foods, billboards, and advertisements on TV. Another word recognition strategy often developed by children prior to school is reading by *configuration*. Configuration consists of the word's shape, length, or even significant letters such as the first letter of a child's name. Mary, for example, can read the words *Mom* and *Dad* even though she has never been to school. She recognizes the shape of the word *Mom* and knows that it begins with the same letter as her name. *Dad* looks different and does not begin with the same letter as Mary's name.

For children who are experiencing physical, cognitive, or emotional challenges or whose surroundings are print-poor, access to environmental, picture, and configuration cues may be limited or distorted. Many children with disabilities are disadvantaged relative to their peers in acquiring words through these cue strategies. Visual, auditory, motoric, affective, or cognitive challenges in their everyday world may limit contact with the environment. Martin, for example, has normal intelligence, cerebral palsy, and cystic fibrosis. Consequently, he has been in and out of hospitals for most of his young life. Due to complications with breathing, focusing his eyes, and speaking, Martin is easily fatigued. He often has difficulty concentrating on the storybooks being read to him. Martin is susceptible to infections, so he does not get out much. He has never been to a fast-food restaurant, amusement park, or the zoo. Martin's life experiences are more limited than those of most of his peers. Even before Martin attends school, he is at risk for developing an impoverished sight vocabulary.

Fluency

Fluency, speed, and accuracy in reading are the most significant characteristics of reading words. Speed and accuracy are developed as readers start to internalize letter–sound correspondences, word patterns, and the relation of a word's pronunciation to its spelling. Repeated reading of words is usually the final step that anchors words in the reader's memory and speeds sight word recognition during reading. The more quickly the reader can recognize a word, the more quickly he can gather communication from print. An appropriate level of fluency provides the reader with more cognitive space for processing the meaning of the word or text (Deno, Fuchs, Marston, & Shin, 2001; Reynolds, 2000).

As beginning readers, who of necessity rely heavily on phonics to learn new terms, commit words to memory, they experience a kind of attentional emancipation. Mental resources that would have been focused on sounding out letters can now be redirected to tap into the reader's fertile schemata, a veritable rain forest of interconnected and multiple networks of meaning. Once again, the roles of schemata, phonics awareness, and word recognition cannot be separated, but play different parts at different developmental levels.

During the reading process, Sierra constructs meaning from the text. Her oral reading fluency helps her become comfortable with reading. The more comfortable Sierra becomes with sight word recognition, the more her word recognition rate and understanding are strengthened, which in turn positively impacts her ease of reading and continues to enhance her word recognition fluency. Sierra's positive, upward reading cycle is the aim for all students. Sierra, a very good reader, is an example of a reading-rich reader becoming ever more affluent in the world of reading fluency. The converse is also true. Trevor, a nonresponsive fourth-grader, is uncomfortable with reading. The more he is exposed to words, the greater his dislike of reading and all associated print material, specifically books. Trevor avoids reading whenever possible and has often vehemently proclaimed that reading is not important in his life. Trevor is not developing word recognition fluency.

Readers like Trevor, who do not construct meaning from the text, will not develop oral or silent reading fluency. Beginning readers and less skilled older readers typically read aloud slowly, haltingly, and with little or no expressions. Undoubtedly, their silent reading, if such students ever open a book, is not much more fluent. Development of text comprehension and reading affect is significantly damaged.

A variety of fluency levels have been established for word recognition. Systems based on broad guiding principles for minimum oral reading fluency rates, like the one below (Guzak, 1985), also include grade levels:

1. 60 words per minute for grade 1
2. 70 words per minute for grade 2
3. 90 words per minute for grade 3
4. 120 words per minute for grades 4 and 5
5. 150 words per minute for grades 6 and 7

As with any generalization, exceptions will be the rule, especially for children who have disabilities. Many children with disabilities will meet the normative expectations, but others bring into question the fluency guidelines. The fluency rate for children whose speech and language skills are affected by motoric issues, or who have cognitive challenges, or who have visual or auditory processing difficulties may not match the norm. For children who see very little or none of the page, the suggested reading rates are not likely to be a good fit. Since the goal of word recognition is to establish communication through print between the reader and the author, teachers must monitor word recognition development by assessing the reader's ability to comprehend text. Rate will play a factor, but rate is not sacrosanct. Forcing readers to meet an expected norm can be damaging or even lethal to word recognition literacy.

Techniques for Increasing Sight Word Vocabulary

A multitude of techniques and strategies are used to help children develop large sight vocabularies. One of the best predictors of reading progress is the amount of reading students do. At least that holds true for the majority of readers, as long as the appropriate reading material is used. Since most struggling readers read more slowly than typical readers, they are exposed to fewer words when reading independently. Not surprisingly, struggling readers read less during class time (Allington, 2001). They also rank toward the bottom of the motivation scale for recreational reading, an oxymoron for most nonresponsive readers. Decisions for how to get stressed readers to read are based in large part on curricular philosophy.

Philosophical Approaches to Teaching Word Recognition

For well over a quarter of a century, reading specialists, classroom teachers, and special educators have been exposed to what appears to be countless approaches to word recognition reading instruction. The type of reading strategy chosen depends on a large array of interconnected reasons, some of which are based on belief systems, others on financial considerations, and still others on research findings. All methods, or most of them, claim to teach reading with improved achievement for all (Bryan et al., 2004).

Belief systems, fueled by publishing houses and impractical research approaches, typically reduce to variations of reading instruction associated with two, sometimes adversarial and often competing, factions: skill-building theory versus comprehension theory. These two camps have been given a variety of names: bottom-up versus top-down, text-based versus reader-based, and phonics versus whole-word instruction. Most instructional reading approaches are composed of variations of these two philosophical camps. True believers claiming to be purists strictly adhere to one camp only, often to the detriment of struggling readers. Most reasonable thinkers integrate aspects of the two positions to fit the needs of the learner.

Text-Based Models

Many philosophical and financial battles have been fought in the tug-of-war world of text-based versus reader-based models. Text-based advocates claim that literacy is developed from the bottom up; the child learns to read by first learning to read aloud, by learning sound–spelling correspondences. The reading process is made clear through explicit and direct instruction with words and word components, practice, and correction. Text-based models place instructional focus on processing skills in a sequential and systematic manner.

In variations of text-based models, readers might first learn letters and build upon them and then gradually and systematically move into more complex aspects of reading. As children become more proficient with letter sounds, they can use those letters to develop words, which in turn form phrases, and ultimately sentences. The text construction model of instruction drives the reading child's word recognition experiences. Most text-driven approaches focus on various aspects of phonics. Actual textbooks contain words that are typically phonetically regular, following the phonics rules for sounding out.

Critics trample the text approach by reminding the reading world that every letter and sound of English can be represented by more than one sound or letter (or silence) (Smith, 2003). Letters and sounds in English are not reliable, providing too many alternatives and exceptions, detractors say. Case in point, when Freddy is trying to figure out the word *cat* from his reading book, how will he know *cat* from *kat*? On the printed page, Freddy is not given the choice. *Cat* is printed as *cat*, not *kat*. If Freddy is spelling *cat* from memory, both versions are phonetically correct, but with explicit instruction, the conventional spelling will be shown. Critics of the text-based approach have very little faith in Freddy's ability to create meaningful schema for sounds and related words, nor do they give Freddy credit for memory skills.

Reader-Based Models

Proponents of reader-based models generally believe that reading begins with the reader making a hypothesis about the author's intentions. Readers read to verify or refute their hypothesis and do so by selecting words or passages to validate their thoughts. In these models, readers only use the lower units of reading (e.g., letters to a limited extent). Reader-based instructional models often use literature or trade books. According to the supporters of reader-based models, literature and trade books provide a more natural language flow, even with the lowest level material.

The emphasis of reader-based models of instruction is on developing communication between students and author through text discussion. Typical instructional formats include shared or guided reading, reading circles, and literature circles. All of these techniques require students to use their language to comprehend text. Teachers only teach skills, especially those related to phonics, if such skills make the text more understandable (Krashen, 2002). Children who have difficulty understanding spoken language and are limited in their ability to express themselves are likely to be at a disadvantage in a reading world that emphasizes conversation and discussion. The reader-based models, while intrinsically enticing with their attractive illustrations and beautifully worded stories, might not be so appealing to children whose understanding of language is literal at best, or to students who cannot process auditory information at the same rate as their peers during the literature circle.

Differentiating Instruction

Most teachers recognize that aspects of text-based and aspects of reader-based models are necessary in order to learn to read words fluently and ultimately comprehend large bodies of print. Instructional models in each camp potentially have much to offer, but belief systems die hard. Colleagues who are normally rational and respected seem to lose perspective when placed in charge of recommending or selecting reading approaches. Textbook representatives seem to emit a "Pick me! Pick me!" message, regardless of learner needs.

All teachers agree that students are unique, and that generalization extends to literacy levels. Students like Kyle excel, some like Mandy develop along more typical developmental rates, and others like Hannah put a great effort into trying to read and write, but experience little to no success.

In an attempt to meet the different needs of children, some teachers have tried to create a balanced literacy environment, where children receive word recognition instruction utilizing components from both philosophical orientations (i.e., aspects of phonics as well as reading literature-based material). The key to providing a balanced reading program resides in the term *balanced*. Balancing does not mean providing all students the same amount of instruction, regardless of their individual talents and needs. Balance refers to providing students with differentiated instruction according to their level of achievement and their cognitive, affective, and sensory abilities.

A fundamental source of differentiation in a balanced, comprehensive, and equitable reading program is time. For some students the balance will tilt toward more time spent on acquiring phonics skills; for others the balance can lean more into whole-word acquisition. Greater instructional attention and time spent with students in their areas of reading deficit are characteristic of a balanced literacy program (Rasinski & Padak, 2004).

Students will need to sample from both instructional plates until the effort put into the instructional technique is not producing sufficient reading benefits. If Betty has been given instruction in phonics and 4 years later still cannot process the sounds fluently, the effort she takes to try to use a sounding system is not worth her time. If Carlos, after 3 years in special education has a sight vocabulary of about 1,000 words, most of which are similar to the words he had in first grade, instruction designed to develop word banks is probably pointless and even demeaning.

Blending Models

Programs that utilize components from both instructional orientations require careful thought in designing and implementing. Highly fragmented instructional programs, regardless of their instructional orientation, have the potential for confusing students about the nature and process of reading. Material that teaches sounds in one sequence and requires children to read words with sounds not yet mastered is as fragmented as programs that require children to discuss literature that they cannot read. In order to establish cognitive clarity, teachers must develop reading programs that incorporate a differentiated approach in which text-based and reader-based lessons are complementary and fit the instructional needs of the student.

As students become more proficient with lower level strategies like sounding out, most move to a higher stage of word recognition and meaning (Wilson-Bridgman, 2003). Most students, when given the opportunity, will move back and forth between higher and lower level reading strategies, blending techniques provided through text-based and reader-based models. Thus, most beginning readers simultaneously will be at multiple higher and lower stages of word recognition fluency for particular sounds and words.

Paloma, for example, has a very sophisticated understanding of language. She also has a fluent sight vocabulary based on words she has written in her stories. As Paloma continues to write and begins to use more sophisticated and unfamiliar terms, she cannot recall some of her multisyllabic terms. Paloma is struggling with reading her own stories; she needs to become fluent with her new words. Drill can help Paloma memorize her new words. Memorization is a lower level strategy. Drill, repeated exposure to and practice with information, can serve as an important strategy for children who lack prerequisite skills or must first master basic information well before performing higher level tasks (Burns, 2004).

In a differentiated and balanced program, Paloma will receive only as much drill as she needs for mastery, and time spent in drills will be shared with meaningful literacy activities such as literature circles (Routman, 2003). An overemphasis on or exclusion of either skill drills or literature discussions would not be meeting Paloma's needs. Once Paloma has mastered her new terms, she can generalize them to new settings, thus engaging in higher level strategies. On the other hand, Paloma may not be very conversant with vowel-sound–letter relationships. She may be at a lower level for letter–sound correspondence than for acquiring and generalizing sophisticated word strategies. The variation in Paloma's reading skills is typical of emerging readers and readers who are in need of remediation. In both cases, differentiation of instruction and instructional styles are based on the learner's needs. Aspects of the curriculum that can be differentiated include philosophy, instructional materials, instructional methods, student activities, reading strategies, reading goals, and time on task.

Connected Text and Fluent Vocabulary Development

A primary source of reading material is the classroom text, followed closely by literature or trade books. Books are connected texts; they contain a lot of related information presented in a context that communicates ideas by one or more authors. As has been established by even the most philosophically divided reading specialists, readers must engage in reading to become proficient (Mesmer, 2005a). From within the lofty ivory towers housing the most analytical minds to the midafternoon talk shows spreading simplistic information to the masses rings the same revered belief that simply letting children read is one of the best ways of opening the door of literacy for struggling readers. With billions of dollars spent on texts and trade books in the schools, all the children in the land ought to be fluent readers. Yet this happy ending does not appear to be the case. A closer look at the kind of connected texts students are asked to read may unlock some of the barriers to acquiring reading vocabulary through reading. The key to the reading-begets-reading intervention for struggling readers may be found in the way connected text is connected.

Instructional Level

Almost half a century has passed since the concept of instructional level, or appropriate level of challenge, was first proposed (Betts, 1946), but almost 25 years passed before research could adequately define the concept. Appropriate reading material is related to comfort zone. When a student has sufficient prior knowledge and skill to successfully interact with the task, a comfort zone is created that enables the learner to access new information (Gravois & Gickling 2002). Research has consistently shown what observant teachers have always known: that all children, with and without disabilities, increase their learning when presented with material at their individual instructional level (Burns, 2002). Thus, students, with and without learning disabilities, show better task completion, task comprehension, and on-task behavior when using reading material written at their comfort zone (Gickling & Armstrong, 1978). Material used for reading practice must be matched with the student's achievement level. Reading practice is the heterogeneous, multifaceted activity affecting the quality and effectiveness of student learning. All students are appropriately challenged by exposure to new vocabulary and concepts written within their comfort zone. Most students will increase their vocabulary when they use materials that minimize failure and frustration and that are written at levels neither too high nor too low for effective fluency to take place.

The difficulty of the text has important implications for reading instruction. If students are to learn and gain knowledge from connected text, they must use material that they can access. Since not all students are in the same comfort zone relative to print, differentiated instruction must extend to all printed classroom material, especially textbooks and trade books.

A rough, but relatively objective, means of estimating the instructional level of a text uses a variety of readability formulas, running the gamut from simple to highly complex (Mesmer, 2005a). Readability formulas define the level of text difficulty based on word difficulty and syntactic complexity. Other, more subjective measures of text difficulty consider factors based on psychological and linguistic research such as familiarity and interest level, sentence complexity, length and vocabulary, and organization of the text (Graves & Graves, 2003).

Possibly the simplest and most direct measure for busy inclusion teachers, when identifying the appropriateness of text levels, is obtained by having each student orally read a sample from the text in question. If Gary reads fluently and can paraphrase the reading content, the probability is high that the text is at an appropriate level for him to learn new information. The converse is also true. If Gary's reading is slow and labored, the text is probably too difficult. Likewise, even if Gary's reading is fluent, if he cannot paraphrase the content, the text is most likely not within an appropriate comfort zone for him.

Gary's interest level may be a spoiler. He may be able to gain meaning from text that would normally be considered too difficult for him if he were passionate about the topic. In addition, when students are asked to read to themselves, in programs like Sustained Silent Reading (SSR) or simply classroom reading time, they develop significant positive attitudes toward reading if they can choose their own texts (Yoon, 2002).

Influence of Text Format

The source of one important, and sometimes overlooked, means of differentiating instruction in word recognition and, ultimately, comprehension is text construction. Just as alternative instructional methods are based on student strengths and needs, alternative formats in texts can be matched to student processing abilities. Text construction affects cognitive load. Cognitive load has to do with the amount of new linguistic information beginning readers can handle while comprehending the text's message (LaBerge & Samuels, 1974). No one really knows how many new words can be introduced in a text at a time, how many repetitions of words are needed before fluency is reached, or how linguistic content influences the rate of word acquisition and fluency (Hiebert et al., 2005). Generalizations can be made, but the ultimate answer is dependent on many factors directly related to the reader's affective, cognitive, and sensory strengths and challenges.

The nature and type of disability, not categories like learning disabilities, emotional disorders, or any of the other classifications, can be directly related to the amount of linguistic information a student can process in order to develop literacy. Students with poor visual memory, auditory processing problems, and or restricted schemata are at risk for reading disabilities. Typically, they cannot access enough information to acquire the same level of reading fluency as their peers. The organizational nature of the textbook can hinder, ignore, or provide assistance for students with automatic information processing and cognitive load issues.

Careful text selection is always important, but may be even more significant for struggling emerging primary readers and middle school readers. Emerging readers typically focus on developing sound–symbol correspondence and basic sight vocabulary. For middle school and older students, emphasis on vocabulary development shifts to specific content areas. Acquiring basic reading skills is downplayed. Because many struggling readers cannot read content textbooks in their comfort zone, teachers sometimes oversimplify important text content and in some cases abandon the use of textbooks altogether. Such practices can result in reduced text coherence and structure.

Tampering with the textbook can create a situation that makes the material more difficult to understand (Boyle et al., 2003; Fulcher, 1997). Ms. Landers, for example, found that by giving students reading materials that were too easy or watered-down, Nancy, a student with a hearing impairment, was not being exposed to higher level ideas and therefore was unable to develop metacognitive skills appropriate to her intelligence level. Many deaf children and others with auditory processing issues need complex reading material to develop metacognitive skills in thinking about and getting meaning from connected print (Strassman, 1997).

Finally, educators must acknowledge that not all students are going to be able to use textbooks without major modifications. Fortunately, assistive technology offers an affordable means of using the text for those students who are not able to access print in a meaningful manner. By honestly addressing the learners' persistent performance deficits, compensatory approaches involving technology can be provided that may reduce or eliminate the effect of the disability and allow meaningful use of textbooks as information sources for struggling readers (Edyburn, 2003).

Three technology areas that have the capacity to allow access to texts are (a) text-to-speech capability, (b) varying text size, and (c) reference data, such as online dictionaries. These features are found in electronic books (e-books), online publications, and digital libraries (Boone & Higgins, 2003).

E-books have the advantage of presenting the class text without any simplification of the content. By using e-books, struggling print readers can avoid unpleasant and frustrating battles with words in print and direct their energy toward developing literacy with the same content as their peers. E-books can be created by scanning the class text and creating a document on the computer. This document can then be saved to a CD-ROM.

The advantage of the CD-ROM over earlier technologies like books on tape is that students and teachers can immediately select any track in the material without having to fast-forward, rewind, or repeatedly stop and start. Thus, CD-ROMs are particularly helpful for students who have organization and attention problems (Boyle et al., 2003). Print that is provided digitally is a valuable format for developing supportive or cooperative learning experiences (Higgins, Boone, & Lovitt, 2002). Digital libraries open the floodgates of knowledge for students previously trapped in a nonmeaningful world of print.

The World Wide Web

Another major source of connected print for inclusion classes is the World Wide Web. According to the National Center for Educational Statistics (NCES), about 90% of kindergarten through high school use computers, and almost 31 million of these students use the Internet (Wirt et al., 2001). Unfortunately, the NCES also has determined that 5- to 17-year-olds with a disability were significantly less likely to use the computer and the Internet as a social or academic source of knowledge.

Until the last decade, the rich network for accessing facts, figures, and friends on the Internet was too cost ineffective either in accommodation development or money for many children with disabilities. In addition, many educators were unaware of the significant possibilities for using the Net as a connected print source for students with disabilities. Without access to the Internet, opportunities for employment, advancement, education, and even leisure activities for many individuals were limited (Gerber, 2003). Students with mild disabilities can profit from using the Internet as a reading source. Tips for using the Web with students with mild disabilities are found in Table 8.3.

Student Skills and Task Demands

Just like any reading resource, access depends on an appropriate fit between the demands of the task and the skills of the learner. Accessing the world via the Net, therefore, also requires accommodations for some children with disabilities. Language and communication ability impact technology use in several ways. Some students with intellectual disabilities will be limited to the degree that they can use telecommunication technology (Wehmeyer, Smith, Palmer, & Davies, 2004). Students with articulation problems will need a way to input information that involves speech-input systems. Sadly, students with disabilities, especially those with cognitive impairments, who most need access to the larger world of the Internet, have had the least access.

Language and communication skills must be assessed in order to ensure a student will profit from technology. Intellectual ability, fine-motor skills, and visual strengths are areas that must be considered when designing or providing technological assistance that involves accessing the Internet. Luckily for students with disabilities, significant advances in computer applications have occurred in the last 20 years.

Complex verbal instructions, such as those found in past applications of voice mail systems, have become much simpler to understand through the use of pictures, buttons, and programs that route the user with the press of one finger. Pictures, more formally called graphical user interfaces (GUI) (Shneiderman, 2003), have greatly improved the convenience of computer use for sighted people of all cognitive levels.

Table 8.3   Tips for Use of the Web

Learning can become more meaningful to students with mild disabilities when the teacher imposes an external structure over a collection of Web sites and takes responsibility for the following:

1. Select only those sites that are directly relevant to the learning objectives.

2. Inform the student of the learning activities for each site.

3. Sequence how students should access the sites (e.g., establish the order in which students should ideally view sites for the first time).

Source: From "Enhancing Thematic Units Using the World Wide Web: Tools and Strategies for Students with Mild Disabilities (p. 28), by J. E. Gardner and C. A. Wissick, 2002, *Journal of Special Education Technology, 17*. Reprinted by permission of the publisher.

Access and Visual Impairment

Individuals with visual impairment used to be at a disadvantage because they typically could not use pictures, icons, and other graphics commonly associated with the Internet (Alty & Rigas, 1998; Donaker, Klante, & Gorny, 2002). They did not have access to semantic data conveyed through visual elements like font size, style, typeface, or background and foreground colors (Asakawa, Takagi, Ino, & Ifukube, 2002). Now, recently developed techniques transform GUIs into non-speech sounds such as tapping to represent edit buttons and abstract sounds called *earcons* (e.g., different rhythms, pitches, intensity) to represent operations or objects (Rantanasit & Moore, 2005). Along with other assistive devices, such as screen magnifiers and Braille displays, software and hardware advances provide access to computer-based resources, including the Internet (Jones, Farris, Elgin, Anders, & Johnson, 2005). The earcons are also helpful in alerting individuals who are cognitively delayed and highly distractible by cuing sounds with meaning (e.g., a melody coupled with Web links to remind the student where he or she can find more information).

Access for One and for All

Technological advances are among the most powerful tools for inclusion for struggling readers. Technological accommodations are not limited by category. They are designed to fit specific needs for specific individuals. Thus, systems developed primarily for the needs of a particular category of disability can and must be applied to any learner whose needs match the technology. The following situation is a good example of the importance of generalizing an application designed for one population to meet the needs of another.

Ms. Baton was reading a journal in the teacher's lounge and came across a story about a student named Mary. Mary, as a result of an automobile accident, was classified as legally blind. Mary's situation was described in the journal as follows:

> Mary had a detached retina in her right eye as the result of an automobile accident. She was able to detect visual information, but had lost all peripheral vision in her right eye and had double vision, frequent perceptions of flashing light, and problems with extraocular muscles. She said that her left eye usually felt fatigued. Mary reported that looking at a monitor for longer than 20 minutes was painful and therefore she wanted to learn how to use a purely auditory interface. (Jones et al., 2005, p. 43)

Ms. Baton thought about Mary's situation. While she did not have any students in her class who were identified as visually impaired, she did have Wandajune, a student who complained a lot about letters and words disappearing after reading a page or two. Wandajune seemed to tire easily when reading and was beginning to avoid printed material. Wandajune explained that she hated reading, but she liked the computer, especially computer games. Wandajune had also picked up a large speaking vocabulary and could recall and contribute meaningful information during class discussion. Thinking of Mary and her need for auditory access to print, Ms. Baton contacted her district's computer support technician, who was more than willing to research the type of programming accommodations that would provide Wandajune with auditory access to the Internet. In conjunction with assistance from the local visual technology specialist, a program to meet Wandajune's needs was soon established.

Now Wandajune's fear and loathing of connected print had been replaced with joyous exploration of the newly discovered and hugely popular Word Wide Web. Among other skills acquired by using the Net, Wandajune has become a "blogger's blogger." By using a little imagination, Ms. Baton had found a way to adapt technology designed for one student to meet the needs of another. Wandajune now has more opportunity to improve her education and participation in an inclusion setting. LOL, Ms. Baton.

Embedded Cues and Scaffolds

Form Constancy

In spite of the fact that many students can recognize thousands of different objects by sight, the same students cannot necessarily recognize thousands of words. Many reasons exist for this seeming contradiction. Perhaps the simplest explanation for a child's ability to remember persons, places, and things has to do with form constancy and cues. *Form constancy* is a term that refers to the phenomenon that a *puppy* is a *puppy* is a *puppy*, but a *p* can be a *d* can be a *b,* and depending on the font, can even be a *q* or a *g!* Form constancy means that an upside-down puppy is still the same puppy curled up in a little ball or galloping down the street. In spite of position or directionality, a puppy is always a puppy. The same cannot be said for letters, however. Changing the orientation of the letter may create an entirely new letter, such as *b* and *d,* or *u* and *n,* or *w* and *m.* Form constancy of words, especially for emerging readers, can create similar recognition problems, for example, *was* and *saw.*

Cues

Cues are signals that assist learners in perceiving the nature of a person, place, or object. Cues, in conjunction with form constancy, are like directors guiding their actors to perform or respond in a particular manner. Most objects, including people, are surrounded by cues that help reduce cognitive load or activate schemata. Isabella, who only sees a little light, always recognizes the difference between her mother and her grandmother. Isabella's mother smells like roses, whereas the aroma of chocolate chip cookies precedes her grandmother's entrance. Scent is one of the cues that Isabella uses to recognize people in her world. Unfortunately, words and letters have no such olfactory merits.

Scaffolds

If students are to learn thousands of words on sight, then words need to be surrounded by various cues in the book environment. Textbook cues are called *scaffolds.* Scaffolds are means by which words, sentences, and books are manipulated to assist struggling and nonstruggling readers alike in developing sight word vocabulary and reading comprehension. Some types of cues include adjustments that limit the number of words or letter sounds, provide sets of high-frequency words, and repeat words across and within texts. Other types of scaffolds focus on manipulating sentences by restricting the number of words per sentence, the number of sentences per page, and the predictability and richness of sentences and level of decodability. Physical cues that provide scaffolding in texts also include teachers who match the content, font size and style, amount of content per page, interest level, and size and shape of books (Mesmer, 2005a).

The type of cue or scaffold must be aligned with the student's needs. For children who often lose their place, the internal cue of uncluttered pages coupled with using a place marker like an index card or bookmark under each line while reading may be an adequate scaffold. On the other hand, if these scaffolds are insufficient, teachers must go to the next level of cueing, for example, bolding the first word of each line in addition to using uncluttered pages and a place marker. No magical book exists that provides the exact recipe for measuring how much or what kind of scaffold is sufficient relative to reading need. Determining the type and amount of scaffolding is based, in part, upon materials readily available, the reading objective, student skills, and teacher imagination. Student interest is also a significant scaffold, supporting instruction by accessing schemata (Spadorcia, 2005). Rate of achievement must be the basis for the types of scaffolding that are most successful for a particular student at a particular time. Initially, teachers can try out materials provided by the district. If the child's rate of acquisition is appropriate, then the materials are a good fit. On the other hand, if the materials are not working well with the child's development, using experience, gut-level intuition, and a roll of the dice, the teacher must try to document the results of other approaches on the child's reading growth.

The roll-of-the-dice approach can be tempered by using *successive approximations* to reach an instructional reading goal. Take the example of Katie. Katie has sustained injury to her central nervous system, which has impacted her ability to remember sight words. The reading objective for Katie is to acquire at least 50 new sight words by the end of the 9-week grading period. Up to this time, Katie had been making very little progress using the district-adopted text series. Finding the textbook series inappropriate for Katie, her teacher decided to go another route.

Katie's inclusion teacher, Ms. Mariotti, decided to build upon Katie's language base to develop reading skills with words. On the first day of the lesson, Katie drew a picture of her favorite food, popcorn, and dictated the sentence "I like popcorn." Ms. Mariotti, on a separate page, wrote Katie's dictation. Together they created a writing book. The illustration and ideas were Katie's, thus drawing upon Katie's schemata. Ms. Mariotti facilitated the budding author's work by limiting the number of sentences Katie could dictate. Even though Katie would happily have dictated 10 more sentences, Ms. Mariotti recognized Katie's limitations in remembering whole words. Ms. Mariotti only wrote the amount of information that she felt Katie would be able to retrieve at the next reading. She and Katie did spend some time talking about popcorn but only wrote one sentence.

From the basis of Katie's favorite food word, Ms. Mariotti began to build phonetic awareness of word families and sight word vocabulary. Ms. Mariotti also wrote the word *popcorn* on the front of a 3" x 5" card. The card was placed in Katie's designer word bank, a 3" x 5" file box decorated with as many rhinestones, stickers, and glitter as Katie could fit on the container. When Ms. Mariotti and Katie met the next time, Ms. Mariotti showed Katie the card. At first Katie could not remember the word, so she and Ms. Mariotti went to her writing book and matched the card with the word in the story. Then Katie read her story, "I like popcorn," and was able to match the word on the card with the word in the story. Katie and Ms. Mariotti repeated this procedure until Katie immediately was able to recognize the word *popcorn* without looking in her writing book. Katie practiced recognizing this word in the context of her story until she became fluent with the term. Katie had one word down and 49 to go.

Ms. Mariotti then took the word *popcorn* and broke it into two parts: *pop* and *corn*. Ms. Mariotti was now able to use Katie's sounding skills to generate many new words. *Pop* became the progenitor for: *bop, cop, hop, mop,* and *top; corn* begot *born, horn, torn,* and *worn.* Out of one word came nine, and when suffixes and prefixes were added, it jumped to 25. In the meantime, once Katie had mastered *popcorn,* Ms. Mariotti determined that she was ready to write another story. This time Katie wrote a one-sentence story about her dog, Mike. Ms. Mariotti, thanks to Katie, had another word for generating new words as well as one to add to Katie's word bank. Not all words lend themselves to word families (e.g., Katie's favorite place, Disneyland), but in the meantime, Katie was beginning to recall more words and as time passed could dictate longer and more sentences. Whole-word recognition through connected text was developing.

Ms. Mariotti used small steps to help Katie make long reading strides. Sensitive to Katie's short-term memory issues, she used Katie's new words as a scaffold upon which to build additional sight vocabulary. Katie increased in sight vocabulary by using connected text based on her own language and interests. One of the key components to the success of Katie's word recognition development was the limited number of words to which she was exposed. Other reading programs, placing emphasis on high-frequency sight words, also restrict the number of words the student reads.

High-Frequency Words as Cues

Some reading instructional programs place importance on students learning often-used sight words. The purpose of such sight word–based program is to increase the number of words a student can recognize instantaneously without having to sound them out. High-frequency cues, as the term would imply, are those repeated often within the text. The most common high-frequency cues or scaffolds include using high-frequency words and predictable features.

High-frequency words are based on their occurrence rather than consistency with letter–sound correspondences. Initially children are presented with very few different words, but these words are seen over and over again. High-frequency words were first associated with the infamous *Dick and Jane* basal readers. Over 60 years ago *Dick and Jane,* the prototype of most basal readers, controlled the number and rate of words presented as well as the number of words seen on the page. *Dick and Jane* also provided illustrations that cued the reader. The *Dick and Jane* series and basals to follow used tightly controlled vocabulary and short sentences, which sometimes resulted in stilted and unnatural sentence structure.

In spite of linguistic limitations, many basal readers have provided some children with a great sense of reading accomplishment. Many a reading light bulb went on when children found that they could master print, however dim in meaning. Ironically, *Dick and Jane* have taken the hit for all that is wrong with basal reading series, but even today children who grew up with *Dick and Jane* often can recite entire passages and have maintained a great affection for Dick and Jane's dog, Spot.

Variations of the basal or sight word approach have made additional contributions to helping children access words in connected text. The updated versions of *Dick and Jane* often include predictable features such as rhyming, alliteration, repeated sentence stems, and rhythm (Brown, 2000). Basals with these features can be useful for some children, but not all. Scaffolding within the text must meet the reading needs of the student, otherwise, the cues are meaningless and so is the textbook.

Decodability

Some basals use decodability as the basis for instruction in word recognition. Decodable reading series or texts theoretically are characterized by instructional consistency between the letter–sound relationships in the reading material and the letter–sound relationships the reader has been taught (Hoffman, 2001). In some systems, word families are at first restricted and gradually expanded to include additional families. The word families conform to basic phonics or sound–letter conventions. Exceptions to the word families include *glue words,* affectionately known as blue-collar working words, because they hold what semantic sense is available when using phonically restricted connected text (Heilman, 2002). Some examples of glue words are *about, an, for,* and *of.* Glue words are meaningless in isolation, which can make them difficult for children to learn, but they add essential meaning to text. The word *cat* has meaning, the glue word *about* does not have meaning in itself, but the sentence, *It is about the cat,* gives readers information related to the cat. In other highly decodable systems, specific words may not be repeated more often, but certain universal word parts, such as rimes, bigrams, and specific patterns, are recurring (Mesmer, 2005).

Highly decodable texts are often used as the primary source of connected text for struggling readers, including those receiving special education services for reading (Wilson, 1996). Depending on the philosophical point of view of the textbook adoption committee, highly decodable texts may be seen as debasing the world of literature (Allington, 2001; Hicks & Villaume, 2001) or as allowing emerging readers to soar (Groff, 1999; Moats & Hall, 1999). Detractors contend that the beauty of language is distorted in sentences such as *The man can fan Dan*. Supporters adamantly insist that phonetic regularity provides readers predictability and consistency with the sound–symbol system found in English. As with most arguments, kernels of truth may be found in both positions. Aside from using hypotheses and a limited amount of research, the only legitimate reason for using or not using highly decodable texts is based upon the readers' ability to access and develop fluency in reading skills. For some readers highly decodable texts are dead meat, for others they are the filet mignon of connected print.

A third way through these diametrically opposed extremes considers the utility of the decodability as another form of text scaffold offered to readers (Brown, 2000; Hoffman, 2001). Decodability, like other text scaffolds, represents a deliberate manipulation of reading material in an effort to help students acquire literacy. For many children, sound–symbol relationships presented in the context of words, however stilted, provide cues to using letter–sound strategies in word identification (Stahl, Duffy-Hester, & Stahl, 1998). The phonetic regularity and lesson-to-text match in highly decodable texts help some children pay more attention to letter–sound information and application.

Lucretia, and others like her, use the initial sound of a word as a reading strategy, but lately Lucretia has been coming across a lot of words that begin with the same sound. Her strategy is not working. Her teacher, Mr. Maher, has been teaching rules for sounding out, but Lucretia did not seem to be making much progress with her reading book. As Lucretia learned how to apply sounding-out rules, she became frustrated with her texts, and for good reason; the books did not match the rules she was learning.

Lucretia and her teacher got lucky when their enlightened school district adopted multiple basal reading series. One of the series allowed phonic regularity and coordination with phonics instruction. Since no one sequence of sounds and rule introduction is better than another, Mr. Maher recognized that opportunity for consistency was the true sequence for introducing sounds. He quickly adapted his phonics lessons to reflect the order of sounds and rules introduced in the text. Lucretia's text matched her classroom lessons. Lucretia could apply what she learned in her lessons to the materials she was reading. The texts provided the decodability scaffold that Lucretia and some of her peers desperately needed. Lucretia could now concentrate on new words and had a higher probability of success, which in turn begot more success. Children like Lucretia, who have difficulty decoding, benefit from very consistent teaching to generalize reading behaviors (Mesmer, 2005b). Lucretia needed and benefited from using the type of scaffolding found in highly decodable texts. Not all children have the same reading needs; so not all children need the type of scaffolding provided through highly decodable texts to develop literacy.

Technological Cues and Scaffolds

Many scaffolding strategies can be implemented using e-books and electronic readers. Best practices for using digital format as cues and scaffolds are described in Figure 8.1 and can be beneficial for both struggling and nonstruggling readers in inclusion settings. These same practices may be used with connected print found in traditional textbooks.

Interventions to Increase Word Recognition Vocabulary

A large and easily retrievable sight vocabulary is a characteristic of fluent readers and leads to higher level comprehension ability. Many approaches have been developed to help increase word recognition. Strategies that have been tried and proven successful for many less skilled readers include promotion of reader engagement, incidental word study, positive interactions between skilled and less skilled readers, explicit vocabulary instruction, extended practice, concrete evidence of progress, and reader voice in selection of interesting materials. Most of these strategies overlap instructionally and serve as scaffolds for learning new words and concepts. All of these interventions can be used to enhance access to the general education curriculum in any content area in inclusion settings.

Promotion of Reader Engagement

Reader engagement means commitment on the part of the learner to be involved with the reading act. One of the most involving reading activities teachers can provide is to read to their students.

- **Digitized text to speech**: Text can be translated into a computer-generated voice by almost any computer system currently available.

- **Pictures, recordings, or video**: These types of media are well established on the Web and are easily incorporated into HTML, PDF, and other file formats for electronic books.

- **Abridged material**: This can be done by including chapter outlines, summaries, graphic organizers, or study guides. This can include alternate media as well as text rewritten at different reading levels.

- **Key vocabulary**: Different text styles can indicate new vocabulary and at the same time provide a hypertext link to reference materials or text-to-speech pronunciation of the word.

- **Content organization and modification of space:** Font size and pagination can organize content into more readable units.

- **Study skills**: Electronic note taking, underlining, and bookmarking can provide students with options and encourage using the functions for studying.

Source: From "Reading, Writing, and Publishing Digital Text," (pp. 135–136), by R. Boone and K. Higgins, 2003, *Remedial and Special Education, 24*(3). Reprinted by permission of the publisher.

Figure 8.1   Best practices for using digital format as cues and scaffolds.

Read-alouds engage students by reading from texts that are intrinsically interesting to them. Fine literature taps into basic life themes or experiences of the listeners and is rich with imagery; these are *hooks* designed to catch even the most reluctant readers.

Read-alouds are more than an activity to calm children down after lunch. Read-alouds provide at least three important facets of reading development. First, by listening to the sound of good reading, children hear how printed language is connected to spoken language. Second, through listening to good reading, children can begin to develop strategies for organizing and remembering large bodies of connected text. Third, children can begin to develop vocabulary from context of words in connected print. Reading research and expert opinion agree on the value of interactive read-alouds to demonstrate the variety of purposes and types of texts to be read, the recreational and functional value of reading, and how to read for different purposes (Reutzel & Smith, 2004). As long as the teacher is reading the good stuff, listeners will be enriching their language-based schemata and building the foundation for reading printed material.

A variation of the read-alouds is *choral reading.* Choral reading is exactly what the term suggests—reading aloud simultaneously within a group. Choral reading can occur between two or more readers; the teacher can also be part of the reading chorus. Everyone is reading the same content at the same time. Just like singing in a choir is comforting through the support of the group's musical skills, choral reading takes the pressure off the solo reading act. The safety-in-numbers choral reading technique also sets up the connection between print and reading. The readers see the words as they read together, creating a means of focusing attention as well as hearing and participating in fluent reading.

Incidental word study, as opposed to formal word study, is nonintentional learning of vocabulary intentionally arranged by the teacher. Engaging readers in a wide variety of texts that include high-frequency words often typify incidental word study scenarios, content-specific specialized vocabulary, and repeated general knowledge. The incidental word study process begins with the text being read aloud in a shared reading experience. As a result of the shared reading experience, the learners see and hear words simultaneously. Word knowledge schemata strengthens with repeated exposures to the text content. The incidental word study can be elaborated through more specific word recognition activities, such as developing word or concept walls, creating a word for the day, or using graphic organizers or templates.

Ms. Cohen uses a combination of all these techniques to develop sight vocabulary with her students. Before the students read about a topic in their science text, Ms. Cohen assigns a variety of books to different members or pairs of students in the class. Book assignment is based on comfort level and interest. As a result, before ever opening the text the students have already developed prior knowledge about the topic. Thus, when the topic in the text is introduced, the children can use their prior knowledge to make stronger learning connections in terms of word recognition and word meaning. After the students have finished reading about a particular topic, discussions are held, and concept walls are created.

Critical concepts typically reflect concept-specific specialized vocabulary. The students brainstorm to identify critical concepts and, ultimately, categorize and arrange them using a graphic organizer. Ms. Cohen and her students put the specialized vocabulary on the science wall using the graphic organizer they have created. Next, students individually or in small groups create cues for five concepts of their choice from the graphic organizer. Cues can include illustrations, poems, definitions, or any type of mnemonic that is helpful in recalling the term. The children share their techniques for remembering the science concepts on the concept wall. Each day one student picks a concept for the day. The concept is framed in red, and the child leads the class in a discussion about it.

Ms. Cohen's approach provides many repeated systematic opportunities for her students to develop content specific vocabulary. Ms. Cohen has provided her students with multiple exposures to words across time. She has enriched their knowledge base prior to reading the text through early and individualized reading experiences. And through discussion she has reinforced the text content. Brainstorming results in more contact with concepts as well as organizational strategies developed through the graphic organizer. Ms. Cohen has accounted for learning styles by permitting her students to create their own cues, and she has empowered her students to become teachers themselves through the concept-of-the-day activity. In short, Ms. Cohen, a highly successful inclusion teacher, has set up the children to be reading winners.

Positive Interactions Between Skilled and Less Skilled Readers

Children typically like to work together when learning new words. Because children come with diverse experiential backgrounds, their knowledge bases can be complementary. Discussion can supplement and provide opportunities to expand knowledge about the words used in life and in school, which in turn can influence contextual reading ability. Many readers who are less skilled seem to be able to profit from class discussion (Krashen, 1999). Discussion can take place with the whole class, in small group settings, or between partners.

Reading between partners can be a good arena for discussion as well as reading practice with new words. Reading between partners is a form of one-to-one instruction. One-to-one instruction for students has typically been limited due to financial considerations (Nes, 2003), but depending on the personalities and ego needs of the partners, this type of intervention can be beneficial. Partner reading, sometimes called *paired reading* or *peer tutoring,* typically matches a skilled reader with a not-so-skilled reader. Instead of working in isolation, children can work together on special reading projects. Most children are capable of completing their work if they get some help from one of their peers. Some authorities have even suggested that children learn more from their peers than from adults. Peer tutoring provides for immediate and regular feedback.

In the spirit of inclusion, both the tutor and the tutored must benefit from the one-on-one experiences. Beneficial experiences are not born by chance but made by teacher design. Selection of partners must be based on a variety of factors, not the least of which are the desire to be partnered, the partners' desires to be with each other, and the academic and interpersonal abilities of the partners. Not all children wish to have a partner or would profit from working with a peer.

Setting up an effective paired reading program in the inclusion classroom can be very informal and simple for most children, but may require extensive attention to detail for some children. Factors such as amount of tutor training, degree of supervision, and spatial and material resources can contribute to the success or failure of a paired reading program.

The most effortless approach to designing a paired reading program places the decision to be or not to be tutored as well as the choice of partners in the hands of the students. The next level of involvement might include a system for rotating partners. Random rotations can be a great source of drama and accomplished by pulling names out of a hat. More sophisticated rotations can involve matching skills levels, but by now the teacher is entering a more complicated peer tutoring scenario.

Cost–benefit analysis relative to time devoted to training the pairs, creating schedules, and record keeping, weighed against the instructional benefit to the child to be tutored are the decision-making factors for some inclusion teachers. Marcus and Natalie could both benefit from one-to-one instruction. Given workload and budget constraints, Ms. Oppenheimer, their inclusion teacher, considered paired tutoring as an instructional strategy. Raymond is the class clown. Everybody loves Raymond. Unfortunately, Raymond has been reinforced so often from his peers for his funny behavior that no one, except his teacher, can keep him on task. Ms. Oppenheimer decided paired reading with any member of the class would not be beneficial for Raymond or his partner. Instead, the tutoring partner for Raymond became his personal computer, which did not find him particularly entertaining in any way. Ms. Oppenheimer spent very little time and no money at all in providing Raymond paired reading instruction.

Natalie, on the other hand, is a quiet, shy child. Natalie has learned to camouflage her reading problem in group settings, by being very accommodating, always letting her peers take the lead when reading was involved. Ms. Oppenheimer knew that Natalie could not be paired with a student whose reading skills were better than hers. Natalie would need to be paired with a student who needed her help. The solution Ms. Oppenheimer devised was to create a cross-age tutoring system. At a casual conversation at lunch, Ms. Oppenheimer solicited names of children who could potentially benefit from Natalie's assistance. Determining factors included reading level, personality, and scheduling convenience. With very little effort, a team was created.

In this paired partner system, Natalie, a fifth-grader reading at the third-grade level, became the tutor for second-grade Olivia. Natalie's interaction with Olivia promoted a rapid turnaround in reading fluency proficiency for both of them. Their levels of accuracy became higher and more stable, and as their word recognition increased so did their ability to comprehend reading material.

Explicit Vocabulary Instruction

Sometimes students can learn vocabulary from explicit and direct instruction. Many approaches are available, and the utility of the instruction can only be determined by the effectiveness of student performance. If the student is remembering many words and is fluent in recall, then the method used, regardless of research findings and philosophical orientations, is appropriate for that learner. If the student rarely proceeds to mastery, is disfluent, and is repeatedly relearning new words, the approach, regardless of research findings and philosophical orientations, is not appropriate for that learner.

Rereading a passage is one explicit technique for increasing sight vocabulary and fluency in context. The basic format is to have the student first orally read a passage independently. Then the student reads the same passage orally again, but faster, with the instructor, and finally reads the passage orally alone, again as fluently as possible. This simple technique has proven to significantly increase the fluency of students with reading disabilities (Wong, Harris, Graham, & Butler, 2003).

Word Memorization

Memorization of word lists has been an established practice since the first school door opened in this country. Typical word lists include Dolch and Fry, allegedly representing the most frequent words students will use during their primary grades. With the advent of trade books and the modernization of basal readings texts, the formerly frequent words are found less and less often. In addition, memorization of words without reference to the schematic net has not proven to be very successful for long-term retention. Many children receiving special services for reading have been subjected to the same words on the same word lists year after year. Results suggest that children who are not retaining words are neither increasing sight word vocabulary nor becoming fluent readers. If words are so important that they must be retained, then the terms must be anchored to meaningful information or activities.

Interactive Approaches

Learning new words together either as a class, small-group, or partner activity can be enjoyable and effective in developing sight vocabulary. In contrast to memorizing meaningless word lists, children often enjoy mediated and explicit instruction with new words. Interactive approaches such as mnemonics or other memory aids, graphic depictions like semantic maps, grids, and illustrations, when paired with direct instruction, show potential for promoting word recognition and meaning and, ultimately, reading comprehension for larger passages. In content classes like science and social studies, as well as basic classes in English and mathematics, children can tie word lists to dictionary definitions, writing sentences, and texts (Allen, 2003). The more actively students are involved in learning new words, the more likely they will capture the words in their mental networks.

Dictionary Work

Looking up words and definitions in dictionaries is another common practice that works well for developing sight vocabulary for some children. However, research has disclosed that it is insufficient for students with learning disabilities (Bryant, Goodwin, Bryant, & Higgins, 2003). Writing definitions can be deadly and boring or exciting and entertaining. Deadly boring does not need to be reexamined, but exciting and entertaining seems like an oxymoron, and definitely calls for a little creativity on the part of the inclusion teacher.

Ms. Spinelli, a veteran inclusion teacher, has several students with reading needs. Ms. Spinelli knows that Marta, Noah, and Opal need vocabulary development related to word recognition, fluency, and meaning. Pilar and Ricardo have similar needs and, except for recognition of initial and final consonants in words, application of sound generalizations with vowels and syllabication also has eluded them. Ms. Spinelli is fully aware that these students and all the others in her sixth-grade class need an entrée to the words found in their texts if they are to profit from the classroom curriculum.

Before moving to dictionary definitions, Ms. Spinelli writes the words critical to accessing the text on the board. She then underlines the decodable chunks or morphographs (often prefixes, suffixes, and root words). Next, she says one word aloud and then has the children engage in choral response for the term, chunks and all. This process continues until Ms. Spinelli is certain that everyone has at least heard how the key words sound. Leaping over the sounding-out hurdle gives Opal and Ricardo a running chance at moving into word meaning and sight vocabulary. Preteaching the pronunciation of words critical to accessing text meaning not only increases students' accuracy and fluency, but when repeated over time, may even build competency in independently sounding out multisyllabic terms (Archer et al., 2003).

Meanwhile, back to the dictionary and definitions, Ms. Spinelli pulls out all the instructional stops using brain-based research and active learning and has even created a Dictionary Club. The purpose of the Dictionary Club is to increase sight vocabulary and associated word meaning through a variation of the define-and-grind traditional dictionary approach.

Depending on the composition of the class and Ms. Spinelli's time, students have access to several formal sources for word meaning: glossaries in the texts, page numbers in the class dictionary, words and definitions provided by Ms. Spinelli, and dictionaries on the computer. Ms. Spinelli does not accept verbatim or even paraphrased definitions. Instead she expects her students to produce dictionaries, unlike those produced by Mr. Webster, that become alive with illustrations, rhyming couplets, and living drama. Students opt for membership in one of the three groups: the Artists, Rappers, or Actors Dictionary Club. Each group is given no more than five terms a day to produce an illustration, generate a two-line rhyme, or create a dramatic tableau. The class has 15 minutes to complete the representation of the five words. At the end of 15 minutes, five members are chosen across the class. Now each of these members shows an illustration, rap piece, or tableau of their word of choice. The entire daily dictionary activity takes 20 minutes.

By the fourth day of the week, each group has rotated through 20 words. The class now has 20 illustrations, 20 couplets, and 20 dramatic renditions of the significant class vocabulary. On the fifth day, the groups share and compare performances in a gamelike atmosphere for randomly selected terms. Ms. Spinelli incorporates these terms into classroom teaching to the maximum extent possible. Ms. Spinelli's Dictionary Clubs represent some of the effective teaching practices designed to increase sight vocabulary and associated word meaning:

- Multiple exposure to words
- Contextual exposure
- Small-group active learning tasks
- Small number of words to master

Computer-Assisted Instruction

For teachers who are becoming overwhelmed with the amount of individualization needed for some of their inclusion students, technology may be able to provide some respite. For students who need additional practice over and above what the teacher can reasonably give, computer-assisted instruction (CAI) is an excellent option. The good news is that initial research suggests that vocabulary instruction helps students with learning disabilities develop vocabulary. Even better news is that preliminary results indicate that it also helps typically achieving students. Best news of all—instructional time spent on vocabulary development via CAI can be worthwhile for all students in content classes (Bryant et al., 2003).

Reading Comprehension

The jewel in the crown of reading is comprehension. Comprehension is the link that establishes communication between the reader and the author. All the effort that goes into learning the alphabetic system, developing sight vocabulary, and becoming fluent with letters, words, and connected print is intended to result in reading comprehension. Comprehension, however, has many facets. Typically, comprehension is associated with eliciting meaning from passages, but comprehension also occurs at the word and sentence levels (Manset-Williamson & Nelson, 2005).

In order to comprehend, readers must be conversant with sound–letter systems, whole-word recognition, and the nuances of the language of the written material. Students with limited language have difficulty comprehending material regardless of ability to decode or memorize whole words. Mastering the rules of reading is one very important part of literacy, but it must be complemented with the ability to read for understanding and the desire to read for pleasure (Bryan et al., 2004). Effective readers use cognitive strategies and metacognition to select, monitor, and control reading comprehension. Cognitive strategies and metacognition are executive functions of the brain that allow the reader to monitor personal behavior, plan how to learn, and self-regulate by keeping on task and not becoming distracted (Kirk, Gallagher, Anastasiow, & Colemen, 2006).

A lot of research has been conducted in the area of reading, but for the most part it focuses on the development of the alphabetic principle and phonological awareness. Research findings on reading comprehension, especially for students with learning disabilities and other exceptionalities, is more sparse (Boulineau, Fore III, Hagan-Burke, & Burke, 2004). Results from at least one reading comprehension study suggest that upper-middle-grade students with reading disabilities, when provided with a balanced and strategic intervention, can make comprehension gains over a relatively short time (growth of a half year when given only 20 sessions over 5 weeks) (Manset-Williamson & Nelson, 2005).

Three pieces of news, two good and one not-so-good, may be gleaned from this study. First the good news: (a) Older students with reading disabilities can make reading progress, and (b) The time frame for instructional intervention is realistic. Now for the not-so-good news: Little evidence exists that instruction in an inclusive classroom or even a traditional resource room that does not use an intensive tutorial system will produce reading gains for students with reading disabilities. Although the gains represented only about 6 months' worth of growth, the results provide preliminary support for delivering individualized, intensive reading instruction as an indispensable complement to an inclusion education.

No delivery system is an island; inclusion settings must be linked with intensive tutorials if middle school and higher level students with reading disabilities are to raise their level of reading comprehension. Previous research, along with the results of the study cited above, suggests that many middle school students who have reading problems also have phonological awareness deficits. The doggedness of reading problems beyond the primary grades strongly suggests that many students are not getting the intensive intervention they need, either in or out of the inclusion setting (Bhat, Griffin, & Sindelar, 2003).

Strategies for Developing Comprehension

Need for Comprehension Strategies

Whether or not intensive tutorials can be accomplished in the context of an inclusion setting has yet to be determined. What has been cited through research clearly and repeatedly is that students with high-incidence disabilities need strategies to help them comprehend texts (Swanson, 2001; Vaughn, Levy, Coleman, & Bos, 2002).

A reading comprehension strategy is a deliberate and flexible plan that readers can apply to a multiplicity of narrative and expository texts. In essence, comprehension strategies provide scaffolds for assimilating text information while simultaneously tapping into the learner's mental network of knowledge. Strategies most often used to increase reading comprehension for students with reading disabilities include an assortment of techniques for organizing routines, paraphrasing, and linking new knowledge with prior knowledge. Strategy instruction can also be incorporated within the inclusion setting with the primary purpose of teaching students how to learn.

Comprehension cognitive strategies that are either ineffective or of no use whatsoever characterize the tools of many students within the high-incidence disability categories. Students with poor reading comprehension often are not aware that strategies for reading comprehension exist. Others, who are conscious of strategies, are unable to use them spontaneously or flexibly (Torgesen, 1977, 2000; Williams, 2000; Wong, 1996).

Comprehension cognitive strategies that more typical readers develop independently usually must be directly taught to students with reading comprehension problems. Students with high-incidence disabilities who have difficulty using texts to identify relevant information or organize content in some way to facilitate memory can learn to use cognitive strategies (Butler, 2003). General guidelines for teaching cognitive strategies are found in Figure 8.2.

To be beneficial, cognitive strategy instruction must provide students with models, guided practice, and independent application of the strategies that are intended to enable them to comprehend reading material. *Beneficial* can only be determined through constant and systematic monitoring. When comprehension improves at an appropriate rate, the strategy is beneficial. Little to no improvement in comprehension suggests a strong need for program change.

- Teach a few strategies at a time, intensively and extensively, as part of the ongoing curriculum.

- Model and explain new strategies.

- Model again and re-explain strategies in ways that are sensitive to aspects of strategy use that are not well understood.

- Explain to students where and when to use strategies.

- Provide plenty of practice, using strategies for as many appropriate tasks as possible.

- Encourage students to monitor how they are doing when they are using strategies.

- Encourage continued use of and generalization of strategies.

- Increase students' motivation to use strategies by enlightening students' awareness that they are acquiring valuable skills that are at the heart of competent function.

- Emphasize reflective processing rather than speedy processing; do all possible to eliminate high anxiety in students; encourage students to shield themselves from distraction so they can attend to academic tasks.

Source: From Cognitive Strategy Instruction That Really Improves Children's Academic Performance (p. 18), by M. Pressley et al., 1995. Cambridge, MA: Brookline Books. Reprinted by permission of the publisher.

Figure 8.2   General Guidelines for Teaching Cognitive Strategies

Characteristics of Comprehension Strategies

Many cognitive strategies can be used across a wide variety of ages, abilities, and reading material. *Summarization,* for example, is a widely used strategy. Ms. Cunningham has taught all her students the basic steps for summarization. The class is currently working on concepts related to outer space. Selina, Tasha, and Ursula, three of Ms. Cunningham's students, apply summarization skills to widely divergent texts. Selina, an avid reader and budding astronaut, summarizes major tenets of space taken from expository texts and ideas found via the Internet. Tasha summarizes the major ideas in her science text and ideas found in grade-level narratives. Finally, Ursula summarizes picture books that pertain to the cosmos.

Instruction with particular types of comprehension strategies also may vary from student to student. Factors that influence the type of strategies presented to students for teaching comprehension include students' cognitive skill, affective level, sensory abilities, as well as type of reading material. Victor, for example, has difficulty recalling information. He is somewhat disorganized in thinking and has difficulty separating main ideas from details. To get a sense of the author's organization and to identify major and minor concepts, Victor surveys a two- to three-page assigned section. He then copies the major and minor headings from the text in the order presented in the book. Now Victor has a reasonably organized framework for comprehending the social studies material. He can use this outline to take notes, which can later be used to study for tests.

Victor's classmate Walter also has comprehension issues. He does not need to outline his social studies text because he has different comprehension needs. Walter has difficulty remembering ideas from the text because he does not seem to make the social studies information a part of his schemata. Walter needs a more personal level of interaction with the text. Walter is at a disadvantage because he can neither use nor store the social studies information for use at a later time for projects, class discussion, or tests.

The strategy Ms. Cunningham chose for Walter is a variation of the K-W-L (what I **k**now; what I **w**ant to know; what I **l**earned), an active learning approach that builds upon the reader's background knowledge. Ms. Cunningham places emphasis on drawing out and focusing Walter's attention on the knowledge he already possesses. The K-W-L procedure (Ogle, 1986), one of many different types of strategies associated with developing comprehension, helps Walter organize information and engages him on a personal level with the text. Using K-W-L Walter strengthens his reading schemata. Walter essentially writes the topic of the social studies section in the top middle of a blank page. Walter is going to brainstorm, develop questions to establish the author's purpose, and finally answer his own questions. An example of Walter's partially completed K-W-L for *Endangered Species* is found in Figure 8.3. Ms. Cunningham also encourages Walter to work with other students either before, during, or after establishing the questions and responses to the K-W-L.

Endangered Species		
What do I know about Endangered Species?	What do I want to Find Out?	What have I learned?
Many animals are Disappearing	How fast are animals becoming extinct	
Wolves	What other animals	
People are killing Animals	Where have most disappeared	

Figure 8.3   Example of Walter's K-W-L Comprehension Strategy Sheet

Mnemonic Strategies as Memory Aids

Mnemonics can be very effective in recalling difficult-to-remember facts or routines (Kavale & Forness, 2000). But while some students with memory and organizational problems may benefit highly from strategies aligned with catchy strings of letters, other students may have difficulty remembering either the term or the meaning behind the letters.

Inclusion teachers have a couple of options for facilitating the use of mnemonic-based comprehension strategies:

- Personalize the mnemonic.
- Provide a visual prompt:
  1) To use the strategy
  2) To remember what the letters are telling them to do
- Be selective with mnemonics.
- Develop self-monitoring techniques.

Personalizing Mnemonics

Many clever mnemonics have been created by highly intelligent and knowledgeable educators. For some students, predesigned mnemonics are the perfect cues for facilitating comprehension. For others, especially students with attention, memory, and language issues, the predesigned mnemonic may be just one more piece of frustrating nonsensical information added to the already exasperating world of reading comprehension. The mnemonic RAP (Schumaker, Denton, & Deshler, 1984), for example, can create more confusion than direction for children who cannot distinguish between main ideas and details or who, due to language difficulties, are literal and have not learned how to paraphrase.

R—Read a paragraph.
A—Ask yourself "What are the main ideas and details in this paragraph?"
P—Put the main idea and details into your own words.

For some learners, actively participating in the development of a personal mnemonic may lead to a higher probability of student implementation. Student-designed mnemonics are helpful for the same reasons that learners remember personally meaningful terms and concepts—personally developed mnemonics carry personal significance. When students create their own mnemonic, they can tap into individual reserves, thereby making the information relevant to their lives. Equally important is the fact that children are using language that makes sense relative to their language skills. Xavier, Yolanda, and Zack all have language issues. Xavier is an ELL student, Yolanda has a very limited vocabulary, and Zack has difficulty with syntax. These children need a mnemonic that supports their language skills; they do not need to be learning the language of the mnemonic as well as attempting to use the strategy to gain access to text construction. In order to use the comprehension strategy, each of these children needs to use a mnemonic that matches his or her particular language needs.

Visual Prompts

Some children have verbal memory deficits. They may not remember how to apply or, in some cases, even to use, a mnemonic strategy. Regardless of the number of colorful posters plastered on the walls and the bulletin board, the rule of classroom physics is that the more distance between the prompt and the student, the less likely it is that the information will be used. For children with memory issues, a visual prompt (e.g., a picture, a cartoon, or any other object taped to the learners' desks) can serve as visual prompts to use a particular mnemonic. The taped visual can be elaborated to jog students' memories about what the steps in the mnemonic are, helping them to complete the sequence of the mnemonic.

Mnemonic Selectivity

Just as with cheap perfume, less is better when pouring on the mnemonic options. More mnemonics are not better—on the contrary, they can become confusing to many children. Learners who are highly distractible, low functioning, have language, memory, or attention issues, or any combination of these, are not likely to benefit from exposure to a huge array of mnemonic strategies. The brain can become overloaded when presented with excessive information. If a mnemonic is in the instructional cupboard, pick the one that works the best—the one that is most likely to be understood. A general rule to follow when picking a comprehension mnemonic is KISS, "Keep It Simple, Sweetheart." *Simple* refers to the match between the student's skills and the demands of the mnemonic. *Sweetheart* refers to either the teacher or the learner, depending on the implementer's perspective.

Self-Monitoring

One of the primary goals of using a mnemonic strategy is to develop a sense of empowerment in the reader. To become an independent learner, the student ultimately must be able to follow the mnemonic steps without a lot of teacher direction. Initially, most students with organizational issues will not be able to self-monitor without some kind of prompt. Self-monitoring skills can be developed by utilizing a very simple system to indicate when each step in the mnemonic has been followed (e.g., a checksheet on which each step in the mnemonic is either checked off, highlighted, or underlined). For example, each reading assignment can be accompanied by a checksheet to be completed as each step in the strategy has been completed.

Until a routine has been established, most children with comprehension challenges will need a reminder to use the mnemonic checksheet. By now, however, the top of the student's desk may be a little crowded with visual prompts. One of the prompts could be to indicate to be sure to use the cognitive strategy checksheet.

Metacognitive Strategies

Metacognition refers to a personal awareness of how much a reader understands during the reading act and how to make mental changes to increase understanding while reading. Metacognition is a kind of out-of-mind experience in which readers observe their personal level of understanding. Metacognition facilitates the ability to make corrections midword to self-regulate thoughts, strategies, and reading behaviors to enhance comprehension. Metacognition allows learners insights into how well they are or are not using cognitive strategies. Metacognition permits intentional and thoughtful interaction between readers and connected print.

Michael, for example, has excellent metacognitive skills. When reading a text, Michael recognizes what he does not know and uses strategies to figure out what he needs to learn. When he comes across a word he does not know, he reads ahead a little to see if he can get the meaning from context. He also rereads material when the meaning is not clear, and he slows down his reading when encountering difficulty with syntax. Michael also knows how to pick and choose a strategy for a particular situation. In fact, he creates new strategies when encountering unfamiliar situations.

In contrast, Connie is a less proficient reader. Readers like Connie typically are more concerned with getting through the material as fast as possible than making sense of text meaning. Readers with poor comprehension do not appear to be self-regulating or to monitor reading for meaning (Moore & Brantingham, 2003; Wilde, 2000). Errors in sounds as well as errors in meaning do not strike any metacognitive warning bells for many readers struggling with comprehension. Without appropriate instruction, Connie and other less skilled metacognitive readers are likely on a vicious reading treadmill—always moving through texts but never mentally going anywhere. Repeated failures with strategies that supposedly should be helpful can open the perfidious door of self-doubt that persists throughout the child's school career (Strickland & Walker, 2004).

Fortunately for Connie and her inclusion teachers, metacognitive strategy training using collaborative instruction approaches has proven to be very powerful (Crowe, 2005). Connie can be taught to become aware of the sense and the nonsense of the material she comes across while reading complex material.

Literature Discussions

One of the most common and popular collaborative approaches to understanding complex material is classroom conversation, more formally labeled *literature discussion*. Conversation, especially reciprocal discussion, emphasizes student participation and interaction with each other, the teacher, and the text. In reciprocal literature discussions, students are expected to engage in higher thought processes (e.g., make inferences, recognize text genres, apply themes, describe personal responses to text, and provide evidence to support an interpretation or finding) (Morocco, Cobb, & Hindin, 2002; Morocco, Hindin, Mata-Aguilar, & Clark-Chiarelli, 2001). Conversation can also be used to promote higher level thinking collaboratively through the give-and-take of multiple points of views in which students theoretically engage in actively thinking about what their peers are saying and drawing upon prior knowledge to participate in the dialogue. Acquisition of higher order thought and mental processes as well as the development of conversational skills may all be developed through reciprocal book discussions (Raphael, Pardo, Highfield, & McMahon, 1997). In essence, the structure of the conversation becomes an additional comprehension scaffold.

A hidden task requirement lurks in the apparently simple and gentle conversational technique associated with literary discussions. The devil residing in the literary discussion details is the ability to be proficient in expressive and receptive language. Students must be able to express their ideas as well as to process the ideas sent by others. Children like Ruth and Carol Sue, who have language and learning disabilities, often display expressive and receptive communication difficulties. In addition, such children are less likely to engage in social interactions or conversation and seem to have a lot of difficultly understanding the pragmatics (i.e., social nuances) of conversation. Just to add conversational insult to injury, children like Ruth and Carol Sue are expected to use language skills in which they have deficits to assist them in developing higher level comprehension skills associated with complex printed material. Implementing literary discussions involving conversation and competence in addition to meaningful depth of response to literature for children with language and learning disabilities is demanding, complicated, and potentially discouraging (Berry & Englert, 2005).

Another detail that must be considered when using literary discussion as a means of developing comprehension skills is the individual variation in cognitive, neurological, sensory, or physical potential, and experiences of the conversationalist. Children who are deaf and hard of hearing, like Ronnie and Levi, vary in their abilities to converse (Truax, Foo, & Whitesell, 2004). Ronnie and Levi face major difficulties in the acquisition of reading. Ronnie has overcome these difficulties to become a proficient reader, but Levi is not very skilled for his age. Ronnie's metacognitive strategies are similar to those of skilled hearing readers, but Levi's metacognitive strategies are more like those of much younger children (Strassman, 1997). Levi could easily be lost in the art of the conversation.

Before demonizing literary discussion, remember that two of the reasons for inclusion classes are to provide (a) models and (b) opportunities for students with disabilities to interact with more typical peers. Literary discussions can present reading behaviors that show not only what printed codes mean, but also how a literate person processes information before, during, and after reading (Morrow, 2001). For students with auditory issues, or language or learning disabilities, adaptations will have to be made to the literary discussion approach. With proper accommodations, however, book discussions can offer students opportunities to participate in conversations and become active thinkers and participants in classroom texts.

Reciprocal Teaching

One metacognitive approach that has been demonstrated to improve reading comprehension through discussion is called *reciprocal teaching*. Reciprocal teaching (Palincsar & Brown, 1984) requires students to use four comprehension development activities:

- Self-questioning
- Summarizing
- Clarifying
- Predicting

In reciprocal teaching, the teacher and the students take turns leading a dialogue. As students learn to conduct conversations, the responsibility for leading the discussion shifts to the students. Procedures for conducting a reciprocal teaching lesson are found in Figure 8.4.

In the collaborative reciprocal teaching approach, initial discussion, prior to reading, is designed to activate prior knowledge, increasing students' receptivity to new information. Based on the students' current schemata, they can use their knowledge to predict the content to be read. For some students, instruction with the four strategies (self-questioning, summarizing, clarifying, and predicting) may need to be expanded in supplementary lessons. A supplementary lesson, for example, could include teaching the student how to use the SQ3R approach when forming questions or reviewing information. The procedure for SQ3R is as follows:

- Survey—Visually check the print for highlights, italicized terms, pictures, and headings.
- Question—Create questions around what these highlights, italicized terms, pictures, or headings might mean.
- Read—Read the passage with the purpose of answering your questions.
- Recite—Tell yourself the answers you find in the text.
- Review—Review or check the match between your guesses to your questions and the answers in the text.

The student does not necessarily need to learn the acronym; it is far more important to use the organizing strategy to focus on forming questions and predictions. By learning how to find information through a more explicit strategy, the

1. Initially, the teacher explains and models the key activities of
   - self-questioning (related to the main idea),
   - summarizing,
   - clarifying, and
   - predicting (identifying and clarifying difficult sections of the text).

2. The dialogue leader usually begins by discussing the topic to be read.

3. The students divide into small groups, and then the text is read in segments silently, orally by students, or orally by the teacher depending on the decoding ability of the students.

4. Following each segment of the text, the dialogue leader (teacher or student) within the group begins the discussion by asking questions about the content.

5. The dialogue leader acts as a guide while the students question, summarize, predict, or clarify the topic thought to be related to the chapter to be read.

6. Gradually, the teacher's role as dialogue leader decreases, and the students assume more responsibility for being self-regulated in their use of prediction, summarization, and clarification strategies.

Source: Adapted from Teaching Students With Mild and High-Incidence Disabilities at the secondary Level (2nd ed., p. 139) by E. J. Sabornie and L. U. deBettencourt, 2004. Upper Saddle River, NJ: Pearson. Adapted by permission of the publisher.

Figure 8.4   Procedures for Conducting a Reciprocal Teaching Lesson

student will be more capable of participating in the discussion surrounding reciprocal teaching lessons.

Collaborative reciprocal teaching lessons need not stand alone. Integration with other complementary metacognitive strategies strengthens opportunities to create mental networks necessary for comprehension. Some children have difficulty following and recalling oral language. Because language is so fluid, children with memory or receptive problems are likely to profit from some type of fixed organizational structure.

Graphic Organizers

Graphic organizers are visuospatial metacognitive strategies that can be used to promote reading comprehension. Three of the most respected graphic organizers that can assist students by providing a more permanent organizational structure for reading comprehension are *semantic mapping, semantic webbing,* or *semantic feature analysis,* and various teacher-designed support tools for specific texts. Representative examples are presented in Figures 8.5, 8.6, and 8.7, respectively. Story mapping, in particular, has been shown to increase the reading comprehension skills of many students with and without learning disabilities (Boulineau et al., 2004).

Graphic organizers use some form of diagram to help students create a visual to develop and connect a key concept to their prior knowledge and understanding

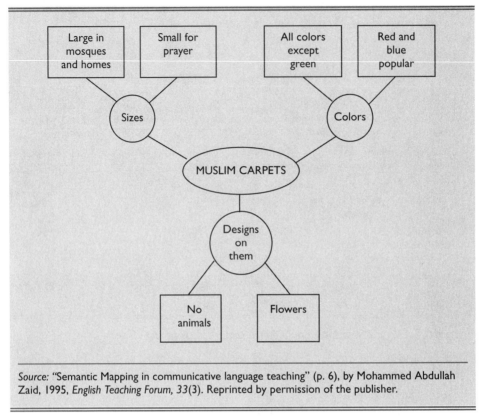

Source: "Semantic Mapping in communicative language teaching" (p. 6), by Mohammed Abdullah Zaid, 1995, *English Teaching Forum, 33*(3). Reprinted by permission of the publisher.

Figure 8.5   Example of Semantic Map/Web for Reading about Muslim Carpets

of a subject. Graphic representations enable students to literally see relationships among main ideas and details for major concepts and vocabulary found in the passage or text. Specific steps for creating semantic maps and semantic feature analysis are presented in Appendix A. Graphic organizers may be designed by teachers for particular purposes or groups of students. Figure 8.8 was designed to help students get a visual picture of how to read a difficult text.

Graphic organizers link new information in a meaningful way to preexisting concepts. Graphic organizers can be used before, during, or after a text has been read and serve as complements to or are integrated with reciprocal teaching. During the process of constructing a semantic map, Ms. Fleener, an inclusion teacher, can identify what is in and what is outside of her learners' current knowledge about core ideas and supporting details. Through careful analysis of student responses, Ms. Fleener also obtains important diagnostic information that can help her determine cognitive strengths and weaknesses of specific students as well as the awareness level of the class as a whole.

Below is a completed grid that might be used if students were going to be reading a text that focused on the last eight presidents of the United States.

	Democrat	Republican	Former Governor	Former Vice-President	2 Full Terms in Office	Still Living
L. B. Johnson	✔	—	—	✔	—	—
Nixon	—	✔	—	✔	—	—
Ford	—	✔	—	✔	—	—
Carter	✔	—	✔	—	—	✔
Reagan	—	✔	✔	—	✔	—
Bush (Sr.)	—	✔	—	✔	—	✔
Clinton	✔	—	✔	—	✔	✔
Bush (Jr.)	—	✔	✔	—	—	✔

Source: From URL: http://www.indiana.edu/~l517/semantic.htm, by Jennifer M. Conner, 2004. Reprinted by permission of the author.

Figure 8.6   Semantic Feature Analysis: An Example

Color coding content can also provide models to help students see how much they have learned. When graphic organizers are generated prior to the reading or discussion, the entries may be in blue. After reading or discussion, new information may be added in red. Seeing is believing, and with color coding the learners can believe they have truly grown in knowledge. Overall, graphic organizers can provide a bridge for creating a forum for discussion. Graphic organizers set the stage for children who otherwise might not participate in class discussion, to become actively engaged in a discussion about a topic or reading text.

Graphic organizers in combination with reciprocal teaching, though time consuming in the short run, may be time saving in the long run. Since language is the basis for most learning, especially that found in school, any metacognitive approach that expands word meaning and relationships between concepts builds language. Graphic organizers like semantic mapping and semantic feature analysis can be especially helpful for students who are having difficulty developing language or seeing relationships between words and concepts.

Chapter Title: _____

Key Words   Headings   Subheadings

_____ _____ _____ _____

_____ _____ _____ _____

_____ _____ _____ _____

_____ _____ _____ _____

Picture Walk: What predictions can you make about the contents based on visuals?

Caption: Caption: Caption:

_____ _____ _____

Connections & Questions

_____

_____

_____

_____

Source: From *On the Same Page: Shared Reading Beyond the Primary Grades* (p. 283), by Janet Allen, 2002, Portland, ME: Stenhouse. Reprinted by permission of the publisher.

Figure 8.7   Content Brainstorming

Graphic organizers are also a kind of visual scaffold for words and concepts. Children with memory, auditory processing, or attention issues can find an anchor in the visual representation found in many graphic organizers. They can use this anchor to participate more meaningfully in book discussions, literary circles, and reciprocal teaching situations. Caitlyn, for example, was hesitant to participate in discussion, in part because she did not know how to interact, in part due to a limited knowledge base. When shown how to use a graphic organizer as a placeholder for knowledge, Caitlyn's passivity gradually gave way to confidence in sharing her thoughts. Caitlyn decreased her dependence on the teacher and her classmates and began to make contributions that showed she was capable of supplying evidence and explanations to hold up arguments, ask for clarification from other speakers, and make personal connections with the material. Children with reading, language, or various other types of learning disabilities need opportunities to learn how to acquire the skills required for conversation-based activities. Additionally, an important aspect of demonstrating reading skills through discussion is the opportunity to show off, to be one of the smart kids.

Reading and Social Identity

Educators and psychologists of the late 20th and early 21st centuries have begun to acknowledge that reading and writing must be considered more than acquiring academic or intellectual skills. Reading and the other two Rs are more than academic skills; they are also important social, cultural practices (Landis, 2003). The ability to read, in particular, is often a defining characteristic of who the student is and who the student will become. Social hierarchy in classes is subtly and sometimes not-so-subtly established by a variety of parameters, but most often with academic reading success as the primary determiner of who will be the class leader, who is accepted in social cliques, and who will ultimately become the movers and shakers in the world of adults. Academic prowess, especially in skilled reading, is a significant factor in determining a student's social position and identity in the classroom and in the world at large.

Hierarchy

For children like Sarup and Martha, learning to read in school is fun and affirming on at least two levels. Success with classroom reading lessons, especially those involving the Internet, content texts, and trade books, affirms that they are readers. Their reading expertise also affirms that they are better readers than the other students, like Michelle, Rob, and Lynette who are working on lower level reading material. For students like Michelle, Rob, and Lynette, reading activities verify that they are not good at reading. Perhaps more or equally disturbing is the perception, real or imagined, that they are on the lower status ring of the classroom hierarchy.

In inclusion settings, the difficulty associated with varying levels of achievement is not simply a matter of providing more reading skills. When students stumble on words, fail to gather meaning, and compare themselves to the academic reading stars, classwork can become a constant reminder of all the concerns related to lower social status. Classroom status, self-worth, and learning to read are without a doubt linked to social identity and inextricably intertwined for most children (Christian & Bloome, 2004).

In inclusion settings, not only must mastery of academics be a focus, development of reading must be viewed within the context of self-worth and a positive self-concept. Proponents of inclusive settings must face head-on the challenges to developing positive social identity in a classroom world that contains learners with wildly diverging reading skills and potential. Preventing or at least diminishing the role of the academic pecking order as a primary measure of self-identity is a serious and challenging issue in inclusion settings.

Resistance to Instruction

Struggling students have a heightened vigilance for potential failure. They develop all kinds of resistance to attempts to raise their reading level. Struggling readers, who either already are or are becoming alienated, often reflect a significant concept found in chaos theory. Chaos theory supports the concept of sensitive dependence on initial conditions. Roughly translated, this means that "tiny differences in input can quickly become overwhelming differences in output" (Gleick, 1988, p. 8). No matter how gentle or kind the teacher, the fight-or-flight instincts are ready to go the moment the student suspects that the slightest failure is imminent. Like sharks sniffing for blood, the struggling alienated reader is distinctly aware of every nuance of any lesson involving reading (Ostermann, 2000). At the first hint of failure, real or perceived, the struggling reader becomes overwhelmed and resorts to inappropriate and dysfunctional behaviors. Michelle becomes argumentative; Rob attempts to manipulate the situation; and Lynette closes down and refuses to even attempt the task.

Changing social identity and associated perceptions, real or unreal, for alienated, struggling students, their teachers, and parents is perhaps the most taxing task faced in inclusion settings. All the new methods and all the new materials and reforms cannot put the shattered self-identity of a child together again. Overcoming beliefs that inhibit learning takes more than wishful thinking (Hensen & Gilles, 2003).

Developing Positive Self-Identity

Developing a positive social identity for struggling readers is paramount in teaching reading and reflecting true inclusion. Inclusion teachers must make a thorough analysis of the skills of each student, provide maximum opportunity for each student to demonstrate competence in academic tasks, and constantly monitor that students find themselves in an academically welcoming setting. The task is to raise the struggling student's self-identity as a learner. Past inclusion practices have suggested that children with disabilities need opportunities to demonstrate value as class members. Tasks within their skills were assigned and praise given when the task was completed. Most of these tasks did not focus on academics, but rather alternatives to academics (e.g., erasing the blackboard, distributing papers, leading the lunch line). Notwithstanding the value of these activities, the celebration of diversity must go beyond the-leader-of-the-line mentality to encompass observable and multiple instances of intellectual proficiency associated particularly with reading tasks.

To make headway in our reading-based world, struggling readers need access to print in a way that preserves their dignity and empowers them. When working with a struggling reader, the inclusion teacher must step into that student's world and identify the student's comfort zone. One way to enter the comfort zone is to form a "cultural circle," which permits recognition of *generative words,* words that are a reflection of the learner's worldview. Generative words can be used to build reading skills and improve literacy (Freire, 1968).

Ms. Cocchiarella used her knowledge of reading as a reflection of social identity and generative words to begin instruction with Sam, a very reluctant and low skilled reader. Sam felt valued by his clique, the lowest functioning students in the class. These peers formed Sam's social group, or as other might say, his gang. Ms. Cocchiarella began creating a cultural circle by exploring the names of Sam's homies. She also asked Sam to tell her names of the people he would like to have included in his group. Since Sam was acquainted with many people in the school and his neighborhood, the list grew. He could write some of the names, and Ms. Cocchiarella wrote the names of the others. Together they made a list of names of people who could be in Sam's gang. Now, Ms. Cocchiarella and Sam could compare the list of names. They found similarities, like names that began with *A* (e.g., Alonzo and Alfredo) and names that ended in *o,* like Alonzo, Manuelo, and Rudolfo.

They talked about the people on the lists, told stories, and in general had fun with the gang names. The names were the generative words that connected the safety of friends to the threatening world of words (Hensen & Gilles, 2003). Ms. Cocchiarella and Sam developed literacy around Sam's interests. Using the generative words, Sam created rap songs and wrote short stories. The songs and stories provided opportunities for adding more words to Sam's growing sight vocabulary. From the generative words, Ms. Cocchiarella also derived a set of friendly terms that could be used to teach Sam the most significant or critical sounding-out applications. Even more important, the word chaos in Sam's reading world was coming under control. He had a system that he felt comfortable using. As Sam's comfort with words grew, so did his comfort with reading in general.

Ms. Cocchiarella had set Sam up to be a reading winner and to raise his level on the social identity hierarchy. By building from Sam's cultural circle, Ms. Cocchiarella could praise his reading on a wide variety of dimensions (e.g., the number of words he was learning, his cleverness for finding similarities and differences in word structures), so the possibilities for praise were often and many. Clever Ms. Cocchiarella also could publicly acknowledge the value of Sam's reading work, not only through verbal praise, but by putting his rap work in a place of honor on the class bulletin board labeled Superstars!

When Sam, like most learners, finds something painfully difficult and sees others around him succeeding and progressing, he often makes excuses and avoids that which would help him, thus impeding any further improvement. Sam got lucky because his inclusion teacher understood human nature and the need to spend time doing what is enjoyable, which in turn continues to add to skills in that area. Ms. Cocchiarella's goal, and the goal of inclusion teachers everywhere, is to assist learners in spending their literacy wealth to enrich their lives and the lives of others (Kaderavek & Rabidoux, 2004).

Literacy and Inclusion

Can all students develop reading literacy in the general education setting? The answer is a resounding ... *maybe*. Maybe students with disabilities can become literate when provided with instruction that:

- individualizes to meet their special processing needs,
- reflects the most effective practices in reading,
- provides more time in intensive reading instruction,
- reduces excessive wait time,
- increases time allocated to actual reading of connected print in the students' comfort zone,
- utilizes appropriate assistive technology,
- builds on student interest, and/or
- provides positive affect.

Reading does not occur by skill development alone. Personal interests, values, and a positive attitude are necessary requirements for skilled reading. Students can be given the most beautifully written and best-practice-based texts, but they cannot be made to read them. The degree to which learners are successful with reading and how much they truly engage in the reading process is solidly related to how they feel about reading (NAEP, 2000) and themselves as readers. The affective component of reading significantly impacts a student's ability to read for enjoyment and information (Calkins, 2001; Stanovich, 2000).

The affective component of reading, especially for struggling readers, should be targeted and systematically monitored by inclusion teachers. Many suggestions for increasing students' positive attitudes are available (Garrett, 2002). General suggestions for developing positive attitudes toward reading include the following:

- Asking the students what interests them through informal interest inventories and then providing reading material and alternate forms of content access such as videos and DVDs when available
- Designing literacy tasks that set up the children for success
- Rewarding children with acts of public and private praise for their accomplishments in reading
- Identifying and discussing from the children's perspectives the usefulness or logic of the reading task
- Providing direct and indirect experiences to expand knowledge base (e.g., field trips and shared storybook reading)
- Comparing children only to their personal growth, avoiding comparing children with each other
- Engaging children in class discussions at their personal comfort level

The Perfect Literacy Model

The perfect literacy model is one that fits the needs of the student. Since not all students' requirements are the same, not one but many perfect models exist. No room exists in inclusion settings for the "one-size-fits all" literacy program. Not all transformations from emerging literacy to literacy will be based in connected print. For some students the cost is too expensive for the emotional debt accrued. Strengths and weaknesses in broader language skills are also important in determining the ease with which children learn to read (Nation & Snowling, 2004). Each program of instruction must meet the needs of each learner. Analysis of each school of thought relative to an individual student's needs is necessary to determine appropriateness of fit into a quality program. Meeting learners' needs is an ethical and intelligent approach of thinking about the curriculum.

Literacy for those whose memory, visual, and language systems confound the traditional reading act can be achieved through total or partial use of technology to access printed content. Rather than emphasizing one traditional model of instruction, inclusion teachers can determine what fits into the learner's repertoire of skills by analyzing curricular strengths and weakness. Regardless of philosophical orientation, the proof of literacy progress is documented accelerated reading growth. Harmony between a child's learning profile and instruction should provide the inspirational melody that creates literacy in inclusion settings. Children optimally can achieve literacy when material and methods are based on their curricular achievement rather than emphasizing one traditional plan of teaching (Ediger, 2004).

Summary

Literacy for all children is a goal for all inclusion teachers. Many learners, especially those who are eligible for special education services, are struggling readers. Readers who do not make reading progress even with excellent programs may need extraordinary means to access print. Accessing print is the key to literacy, and technology may provide the way into text content for some children who were previously locked out from meaningful use of print.

Differences in philosophical orientations, based on selected psychological schools of thought, are found in differentiated programs of instruction. Inclusion teachers must base program development on the needs of the student. Progress children make in learning to read is, among other factors, strongly related to individual differences in language, phonological skills, listening comprehension, and vocabulary knowledge. A child's disability may or may not affect his or her reading progress, but reading task demands must be analyzed relative to the child's strengths and weaknesses. To provide effective programs, inclusion teachers must address the type of reading errors and development of fluency and comprehension against the child's intellectual, emotional, and sensory repertoire.

Finally, the overarching theme of reading instruction resides in the mind of the learner. Each child is actively constructing new meaning based on comparisons with prior knowledge. Children as constructivists need the support and guidance of inclusion teachers who eliminate learning barriers and who build on the child's ability to read semantically, syntactically, and linguistically meaningful content.

Appendix A: Specific Steps for Creating Selected Graphic Organizers

These graphic organizers may be varied in many ways according to the content, level of student performance, and instructional purpose.

Semantic Mapping/Webbing

Step 1: Select a word or topic central to the reading lesson.

Step 2: Write that word on the chalkboard, overhead, or large sheet of butcher paper.

Step 3: Ask the students to think of as many words or ideas as they can that are related to the targeted concept, and write their words on paper either collectively or as partners.

Step 4: Have students relate the words they have written. As the words are spoken, create categories on the board.

Step 5: Number the categories and create an "arm" that connects each category to the word or topic central to the lesson.

Semantic Feature Analysis

This strategy is used to develop vocabulary and to help students understand shared meaning relationships among words.

Step 1: Construct a grid that has a main topic.

   - List the components that make up that topic vertically on the left side.
   - List horizontally across the top of the grid characteristics that describe various components listed vertically.

Step 2: Hand out a grid to each student and have them decide individually which components match which characteristics.

   - If there is a relationship, the student puts a plus (+) sign in the corresponding space.
   - If there is not a relationship, the student puts a minus (–) sign.

Step 3: After students complete a grid, they may share their responses with a group or with a class. They may also add more components or characteristics.

Connecticut State Department of Education. (n.d.) Learning unit three: instructional design and implementation. Retrieved May 1, 2007, from http://www.sde.ct.gov/sde/cwp/view.asp?a=2609&q=319244&pp=12&n=1

References

Allen, J. (2002). *On the same page: Reading beyond the primary grades*. Portland, ME: Stenhouse Publishers.

Allen, J. (2003). But they still can't (or won't) read! Helping children overcome roadblocks to reading. *Language Arts, 80,* 268–274.

Allington, R. (2001). *What really matters for struggling readers*. New York: Addison Wesley Logman.

Alty, J. L., & Rigas, D. I. (1998). Communicating graphical information to blind users using music: The role of context. In *CHI '98: Conference on human factors in computing systems* (pp. 574–581). New York: ACM Press.

Archer, A. L., Gleason, M. M., & Vachon, V. L. (2003). Decoding and fluency: Foundation skills for struggling older readers. *Learning Disability Quarterly, 26,* 89–101.

Asakawa, C., Takagi, H., Ino, S., & Ifukube, T. (2002). Auditory and tactile interfaces for representing visual effects on the Web. In *Proceedings of the fifth International ACM Conference on Assistive Technologies* (pp. 65–72). New York: ACM Press.

Berry, R. A., & Englert, C. S. (2005). Designing conversation: Book discussions in a primary inclusion classroom. *Learning Disability Quarterly, 28,* 35–58.

Betts, E. A. (1946). *Foundations of reading instruction*. New York: American Book.

Bhat, P., Griffin, C. G., & Sindelar, P. T. (2003). Phonological awareness instruction for middle school students with learning disabilities. *Learning Disability Quarterly, 26,* 73–87.

Blaiklock, K. E. (2004). The importance of letter knowledge in the relationship between phonological awareness and reading. *Journal of Research in Reading, 27,* 36–57.

Boone, R., & Higgins, K. (2003). Reading, writing, and publishing digital text. *Remedial and Special Education, 24,* 132–140.

Boulineau, T., Fore III, C., Hagan-Burke, S., & Burke, M. D. (2004). Use of story-mapping to increase the story-grammar text comprehension of elementary students with learning disabilities. *Learning Disability Quarterly, 26,* 203–214.

Boyle, E., Rosenberg, M. S., Connelly, V. J., Washburn, S. G., Brinckerhoff, L. C., & Banerjee, M. (2003). Effects of audio texts on the acquisition of secondary-level content by students with mild disabilities. *Learning Disability Quarterly, 26,* 203–214.

Brown, K. (2000). What kind of text—for whom and when? Textual scaffolding for beginning readers. *The Reading Teacher, 53,* 292–307.

Bryan, L., Owens, D., & Walker, L. (2004). Y-RAP (Young readers art project): A pragmatic solution for reluctant readers. *Reading Improvement, 41,* 235–240.

Bryant, D. P., Goodwin, M., Bryant, B. R., & Higgins, K. (2003). Vocabulary instruction for students with learning disabilities: A review of the research. *Learning Disability Quarterly, 26,* 117–128.

Buckley, S. J. (1996). *Reading before talking: Learning about mental abilities from children with Down syndrome* (University of Portsmouth Inaugural Lectures). Hartford, CT: Down Syndrome Congress, Inc.

Burgess, S. R., & Lonigan, C. J. (1998). Bidirectional relations of phonological sensitivity and prereading abilities: Evidence from a preschool sample. *Journal of Experimental Child Psychology, 70,* 117–141.

Burns, M. K. (2002). Comprehensive system of assessment to intervention using curriculum-based assessments. *Intervention in School and Clinic, 38,* 8–13.

Burns, M. K. (2004). Empirical analysis of drill ration research. *Remedial and Special Education, 23,* 167–173.

Burns, M. S., Griffin, P., & Snow, C. E. (1999). *Starting out right: A guide to promoting children's reading success*. Washington, DC: National Academy Press.

Butler, D. L. (2003). Structuring instruction to promote self-regulated learning by adolescents and adults with learning disabilities. *Exceptionality, 11,* 39–60.

Calkins, L. M. (2001). *The art of teaching reading.* New York: Longman.

Christian, B., & Bloome, D. (2004). Learning to read is who you are. *Reading & Writing Quarterly, 20,* 365–384.

Compton, D. L. (2000). Modeling the response of normally achieving and at risk first-grade children to word reading instruction. *Annals of Dyslexia, 50,* 53–84.

Connecticut State Department of Education. (n.d.) Learning unit three: instructional design and implementation. Retrieved May 1, 2007, from http://www.sde.ct.gov/sde/cwp/view.asp?a=2609&q=319244&pp=12&n=1

Crowe, L. K. (2005). Comparison of two oral reading feedback strategies in improving reading comprehension of school-age children with low reading ability. *Remedial and Special Education, 26,* 32–42.

Deno, S. L., Fuchs, L. S., Marston, D., & Shin, J. (2001). Using curriculum-based measurement to establish growth standards for students with learning disabilities. *School Psychology Review, 30,* 507–524.

Dion, E., Morgan, P. L., Fuchs, D., & Fuchs, L. (2004). The promise and limitations of reading instruction in the mainstream: The need for a multilevel approach. *Exceptionality, 12,* 163–173.

Donahue, P. L., Finnegan, R. J., Lutkus, A. D., Allen, N. L., & Campbell, J. R. (2001). *The nation's report card: Fourth-grade reading 2000* (Report No. NCES 2001–499). Washington, DC: U.S. Department of Education, Office of Educational Research and Improvement, National Center for Education Statistics.

Donaker, H., Klante, P., & Gorny, P. (2002). The design of auditory user interfaces for blind users. In *Proceedings of the second Nordic conference on human-computer interaction* (pp. 149–155). New York: ACM Press.

Duncan, L. G., Seymour, P. H. K., & Hill, S. (2000). A small to large unit progression in metaphonological awareness and reading? *The Quarterly Journal of Experimental Psychology, 53,* 1081–1104.

Ediger, M. (2004). The psychology of reading instruction. *Reading Improvement, 41,* 157–164.

Edyburn, D. L. (2003). Reading difficulties in the general education classroom: A taxonomy of text modification strategies. *Closing the Gap, 21*(16), 1, 10–13, 30–31.

Fletcher, J. M., Morris, R. D., & Lyon, G. R. (2003). Classification and definition of learning disabilities: An integrative perspective. In H. L. Swanson, K. R. Harris, & S. Graham (Eds.), *Handbook of learning disabilities* (pp. 30–56). New York: Guilford.

Freire, P. (1968). *Pedagogy of the oppressed.* New York: Seabury.

Fuchs, D., Fuchs, L. S., Thompson, A., Al Otaiba, S., Yen, L., Yang, N., Braun, M., & O'Connor, R. E. (2001). Is reading important in reading-readiness programs? A randomized field trial. *Journal of Educational Psychology, 93,* 251–267.

Fulcher, G. (1997). Text difficulty and accessibility: Reading formulae and expert judgement. *System, 25,* 497–513.

Gardner, J. E., & Wissick, C. A. (2002). Enhancing thematic units using the World Wide Web: Tools and strategies for students with mild disabilities. *Journal of Special Education Technology, 17,* 27–38.

Garrett, J. E. (2002). Enhancing the attitudes of children toward reading: Implications for teachers and principals. *Reading Improvement, 39,* 21–24.

Gerber, E. (2003). The benefits of and barriers to computer use for individuals who are visually impaired. *Journal of Visual Impairment & Blindness, 97,* 536–550.

Gickling, E. E., & Armstrong, D. L. (1978). Levels of instructional difficulty as related to on-task behavior, task completion, and comprehension. *Journal of Learning Disabilities, 11,* 559–566.

Gleick, J. (1988). *Chaos.* New York: Viking.

Graves, D. H. (2002). The energy to teach. *Voices from the Middle, 10*(1), 8–10.

Graves, D. H., & Graves, B. B. (2003). *Scaffolding reading experiences: Designs for student success* (2nd ed.). Norwood, MA: Christopher-Gordon.

Graves, M. F., Juel, C., & Graves, B. B. (2004). *Teaching reading in the 21st century* (3rd ed.). Boston: Pearson Education, Inc.

Gravois, T. A., & Gickling, E. E. (2002). Best practices in curriculum-based assessment. In A. Thomas & J. Grimes (Eds.), *Best practices in school psychology* (4th ed., pp. 885–898). Bethesda, MD: National Association of School Psychologists.

Groff, P. (1999). *Decodable words in reading textbooks: Why they are imperative.* The National Right to Read Foundation. Retrieved October 20, 2004, from http://www.nrrf.org/27_decode_txtbooks.htm

Guthrie, J. T., Alao, S., & Rinehart, J. M. (1997). Engagement in reading for young adolescents. *Journal of Adolescent and Adult Literacy, 40,* 438–446.

Guzak, F. J. (1985). *Diagnostic reading instruction in the elementary school.* New York: Harper and Row.

Hasselbring, T. S., & Goin, L. I. (2004). Literacy instruction for older struggling readers: What is the role of technology? *Reading & Writing Quarterly, 20,* 123–144.

Heilman, A. W. (2002). *Phonics in proper perspective* (9th ed.) Upper Saddle River, NJ: Merrill Prentice-Hall.

Hensen, J., & Gilles, C. (2003). Al's story: Overcoming beliefs that inhibit learning. *Language Arts, 80,* 259–261.

Hicks, C. P., & Villaume, S. K. (2001). Finding our own way: Critical reflections on the literacy development of two Reading Recovery children. *The Reading Teacher, 54,* 398–412.

Hiebert, E. H., Martin, L. A., & Menon, S. (2005). Are there alternatives in reading textbooks? An examination of three beginning reading programs. *Reading & Writing Quarterly, 21,* 7–32.

Higgins, K., Boone, R., & Lovitt, T. C. (2002). Adapting challenging textbooks to improve content area learning. In G. Stoner, M. R. Shinn, & H. Walker (Eds.), *Interventions for academic and behavior problems* (2nd ed., pp. 755–790). Silver Springs, MD: National Association of School Psychologists.

Hoffman, J. V. (2001). Decodable texts for beginning reading instruction: Leadership or politics in California and Texas? *The California Reader, 34,* 2–8.

Harding, B., & Tanner, M. W. (2001). English language literacy development in deaf individuals: The role of environmental factors. *JADARA, 35,* 1–25.

Hulme, C. (2002). Phonemes, rimes, and the mechanisms of early reading development. *Journal of Experimental Child Psychology, 82,* 58–64.

Jenkins, J., & O'Connor, R. E. (2002). Early identification and intervention for young children with reading/learning disabilities. In R. Bradley, L. Danielson, & D. Hallahan (Eds.), *Identification of learning disabilities: Research to practice* (pp. 99–138). Mahwah, NJ: Erlbaum Associates, Inc.

Johnston, F. R. (2000). Word learning in predictable text. *Journal of Educational Psychology, 92,* 248–255.

Jones, K. S., Farris, J. S., Elgin, P. D., Anders, B. A., & Johnson, B. R. (2005). A report on a novice user's interaction with the Internet through a self-voicing application. *Journal of Visual Impairment & Blindness, 99,* 40–54.

Joseph, L. M., & Seery, M. E. (2004). Where is the phonics? A review of the literature on the use of phonetic analysis with students with mental retardation. *Remedial and Special Education, 25,* 88–94.

Kaderavek, L. M., & Rabidoux, J. (2004). Interactive to independent literacy: A model for designing literacy goals for children with atypical communication. *Reading & Writing Quarterly, 20,* 237–260.

Kaderavek, L. M., & Sulzby, E. (2000). Issues in emergent literacy for children with specific language impairments: Language production during storybook reading, toy play and oral narratives. In L. R. Watson, T. L. Layton, & E. R. Crais (Eds.), *Handbook of early language impairment in children, Volume II: Assessment and treatment* (pp. 199–244). New York: Delmar.

Katims, D. S. (2000). Literacy instruction for people with mental retardation: Historical highlights and contemporary analysis. *Education and Training in Mental Retardation and Developmental Disabilities, 35,* 3–15.

Kavale, K., & Forness, S. (2000). Policy decisions in special education. In R. Gersten, E. Schiller, & S. Vaughn (Eds.), *Contemporary special education research* (pp. 281–326). Mahwah, NJ: Erlbaum.

Kirk, S. A., Gallagher, J. J., Anastasiow, N. J., & Coleman, M. R. (2006). *Educating exceptional children* (11th ed.). Boston: Houghton Mifflin Company.

Klinger, J. K., Vaughn, S., Hughes, M. T., Schumm, J. S., & Elbaum, B. E. (1998). Outcomes for students with and without learning disabilities in inclusive classrooms. *Learning Disabilities Research & Practice, 13,* 153–161.

Krashen, S. (2002). Defending whole language: The limits of phonics instruction and the efficacy of whole language instruction. *Reading Improvement, 39,* 32–42.

Krashen, S. D. (1999). *Three arguments against whole language and why they are wrong.* Portsmouth, NH: Heinemann.

LaBerge, D., & Samuels, S. (1974). Toward a theory of automatic information processing in reading. *Cognitive Psychology, 6,* 293–323.

Landis, D. (2003). Reading and writing as social, cultural practices: Implications for literacy education. *Reading & Writing Quarterly, 19,* 281–308.

Layton, T. (2000). Young children with Down syndrome. In T. Layton, E. Crais, & L. Watson (Eds.), *Handbook of early language impairment in children: Nature* (pp. 193–232). Albany, NY: Delmar Publishers.

Lyon, G. R. (1995). Research initiatives in learning disabilities: Contributions from scientists supported by the National Institute of Child Health and Human Development. *Journal of Child Neurology, 10,* 120–126.

Lyon, G. R., & Moates, L. (1997). Critical conceptually methodological considerations in reading intervention research. *Journal of Learning Disabilities, 30,* 578–588.

Lyon, G. R., Fletcher, J. M., Shaywitz, S., Shaywitz, B., Torgeson, J. K., Wood, F., et al. (2001). Rethinking learning disabilities. In C. Finn, A. Rotherha, & C. Hokanson (Eds.), *Rethinking special education for a new century* (pp. 259–287). Washington, DC: Thomas B. Fordham Foundation.

Manset-Williamson, G., & Nelson, J. M. (2005). Balanced, strategic reading instruction for upper-elementary and middle school students with reading disabilities: A comparative study of two approaches. *Learning Disabilities Quarterly, 28,* 59–74.

McCray, A. D., Vaughn, S., & Neal, L. I. (2001). Not all students learn to read by third grade: Middle school students speak out about their reading disabilities. *The Journal of Special Education, 35,* 17–30.

Mesmer, H. A. E. (2005a). Introduction: Text accessibility and the struggling reader. *Reading & Writing Quarterly, 21,* 1–6.

Mesmer, H. A. E. (2005b). Text decodability and the first grade reader. *Reading & Writing Quarterly, 21,* 61–86.

Moats, L., & Hall, S. J. (1999). *Straight talk about reading: How parents can make a difference during the early years.* Chicago: Contemporary Books.

Moore, R., & Brantingham, K. (2003). Nathan: A case study in retrospective miscue analysis. *Reading Teacher, 56,* 466–474.

Morocco, C., Cobb, C., & Hindin, A. (2002). The role of conversation in a thematic understanding of literature. *Learning Disabilities Research & Practice, 17,* 144–159.

Morocco, C., Hindin, A., Mata-Aguilar, C., & Clark-Chiarelli, N. (2001). Building a deep understanding of literature with middle grade students with learning disabilities. *Learning Disability Quarterly, 24,* 381–335.

Morrow, L. (2001). *Literacy development in the early years: Helping children read and write* (4th ed.) Boston: Allyn & Bacon.

National Assessment of Educational Progress (NAEP). (2000). *The nation's report card on reading—2000.* Washington, DC: National Center for Education Statistics.

Nation, K., & Snowling, M. J. (2004). Beyond phonological skills: Broader language skills contribute to the development of reading. *Journal of Research in Reading, 27,* 342–356.

Nes, S. (2003). Using Paired Reading to Enhance the Fluency Skills of Less-Skilled Readers. *Reading Improvement, 40,* 179–92.

Ogle, D. (1986). K-W-L: A teaching model that develops active learning of expository text. *Reading Teacher, 39,* 564–570.

Osterman, K. (2000). Students' need for belonging in the school community. *Review of Educational Research, 70,* 323–368.

Palincsar, A. S., & Brown, A. L. (1984). Reciprocal teaching of comprehension-fostering and comprehension-monitoring activities. *Cognition and Instruction, 1,* 117–175.

Pressley, M. et al. (1995). *Cognitive strategy instruction that really improves children's academic performance.* Cambridge, MA: Brookline Books.

Raphael, T., Pardo, L., Highfield, K., & McMahon, S. (1997). *Book club: A literature-based curriculum.* Littleton, MA: Small Planet Communications.

Rasinski, T., & Padak, N. (2004). Beyond consensus—Beyond balance: Toward a comprehensive literacy curriculum. *Reading & Writing Quarterly, 20,* 91–102.

Ratanasit, D., & Moore, M. M. (2005). Representing graphical user interfaces with sound: A review of approaches. *Journal of Visual Impairment and Blindness, 99,* 69–84.

Reutzel, D. R., & Smith, J. A. (2004). Accelerating struggling readers' progress: A comparative analysis of expert opinion and current research recommendations. *Reading and Writing Quarterly, 20,* 63–90.

Reynolds, R. E. (2000). Attentional resource emancipation: Toward understanding the interaction of word identification and comprehension processes in reading. *Scientific Studies in Reading, 4,* 169–195.

Routman, R. (2003). *Reading essentials.* Portsmouth, NH: Heinemann.

Sabornie, E. J., & deBettencourt, L. U. (2004). *Teaching students with mild and high-incidence disabilities at the secondary level* (2nd ed.). Upper Saddle River, NJ: Pearson.

Savage, R., & Carless, S. (2004). Predicting growth of nonword reading and letter-sound knowledge following rime- and phoneme-based teaching. *Journal of Research in Reading, 27,* 195–211.

Schmidt, R. J., Rozendal, M. S., & Greenman, G. G. (2002). Reading instruction in the inclusion classroom: Research based practices. *Remedial and Special Education, 23,* 130–140.

Schumaker, J. B., Denton, P. H., & Deshler, D. D. (1984). *Learning strategies curriculum: The paraphrasing strategy.* Lawrence: University of Kansas.

Shaywitz, S. E. (2003). *Overcoming dyslexia: A new and complete science-based program for reading problems at any level.* New York: Knopf.

Shaywitz, S., & Fletcher, J. (2005). Persistence of dyslexia: The Connecticut longitudinal study at adolescence. *Pediatrics, 104,* 1351–1360.

Shaywitz, S. E., Fletcher, J. M., Holahan, J. M., Shneider, A. E., Marchione, K. E., Stuebing, K. K., et al. (1999). Persistence of dyslexia: The Connecticut longitudinal study at adolescence. *Pediatrics, 104,* 1351–1359.

Shneiderman, B. (2003). *Designing the user interface* (3rd ed.) Reading, MA: Addison-Wesley.

Smith, C. R. (1998). *The interaction of learner, task, and setting: Learning disabilities* (4th ed.). Boston: Allyn and Bacon.

Smith, F. (2003). The just so story—Obvious but false. *Language Arts, 80,* 256–258.

Smythe, I., Everatt, J., & Salter, R. (Eds.). (2003). *The international book of dyslexia, Parts 1 and 2*. London: Wiley.

Spadorcia, S. A. (2005). Examining the text demands of high-interest, low-level books. *Reading & Writing Quarterly, 21*, 33–60.

Stahl, S., Duffy-Hester, A., & Stahl, K. A. D. (1998). Everything you wanted to know about phonics (but were afraid to ask). *Reading Research Quarterly, 33*, 338–336.

Stanovich, K. E. (1998). Twenty-five years of research on the reading process: The grand synthesis and what it means for our field. In T. Shanahan & F. V. Rodriquez-Brown (Eds.), *National reading conference yearbook 47* (pp. 44–58). Chicago: National Reading Conference.

Strassman, B. (1997). Metacognition and reading in children who are deaf: A review of the research. *Journal of Deaf Studies and Deaf Education, 2*, 140–149.

Strickland, K., & Walker, A. (2004). "Revaluing" reading: Assessing attitude and providing appropriate reading support. *Reading & Writing Quarterly: Overcoming Learning Difficulties, 20*, 401–417.

Swanson, H. L. (2001). Searching for the best model for instruction for students with learning disabilities. *Focus on Exceptional Children, 34*, 1–16.

Swanson, L. (2005). Learning disabilities as a working memory deficit. *Issues in Education, 7*, 1–48.

Swanson, H. L., & Howard, C. B. (2005). Children with reading disabilities: Does dynamic assessment help in the classification? *Learning Disability Quarterly, 28*, 17–34.

Swanson, H. L., & Seigel, L. (2001). Learning disabilities as a working memory deficit. *Issues in Education: Contributions from Educational Psychology, 7*, 1–48.

Torgesen, J. K. (1977). The role of nonspecific factors in the task performance of learning disabled students. *Journal of Learning Disabilities, 10*, 23–40.

Torgesen, J. K. (2000). Empirical and theoretical support for direct diagnosis of learning disabilities by assessment of intrinsic processing weaknesses. In R. Bradley, L. Danielson, & D. Hallahan (Eds.), *Identification of learning disabilities: Research to practice* (pp. 565–603). Mahwah, NJ: Erlbaum.

Torgesen, J. K., Rashotte, C., Alexander, A., & MacPhee, K. (2002). Progress toward understanding the conditions that are required to remediate reading difficulties in older children. In R. Papalewis (2004), Struggling middle school readers: Successful, accelerating intervention. *Reading Improvement, 41*, 24–37.

Truax, R. R., Foo, S. F., & Whitesell, K. (2004). Literacy learning: Meeting the needs of children who are deaf or hard of hearing with additional special needs. *The Volta Review, 104*, 307–326.

U.S. Department of Education. (2002). *Twenty-fourth annual report on the implementation of the Individuals with Disabilities Act*. Retrieved October 22, 2004, from http://www.ed.gov/about/reports/annual/osep/2002/execsumm.html

Vaughn, S., Levy, S., Coleman, M., & Bos, C. S. (2002). Reading instruction for students with LD and EBD: A synthesis of observation studies. *The Journal of Special Education, 36*, 2–13.

Wehmeyer, M. L., Smith, S. J., Palmer, S. B., & Davies, D. K. (2004). Technology use by students with intellectual disabilities: An overview. *Journal of Special Education Technology, 19*, 7–21.

Wilde, S. (2000). *Miscue analysis made easy: Building on students' strengths*. Portsmouth, NH: Heinemann.

Williams, J. P. (2000). *Strategic processing of text: Improving reading comprehension of students with learning disabilities*. Washington, DC: Special Education Programs. (ERIC Document Reproduction Service No. ED449596)

Wilson, B. A. (1996). *The Wilson Reading System*. Millbury, MA: Wilson Language Training Corp.

Wilson-Bridgman, J. (2003). Curricular congruence at conceptual level: Does curricular congruence exist between two programs that constitute one district's early literacy project (the classroom language arts program and the reading recovery program)? *Reading Improvement, 40,* 153–163.

Wirt, J., Choy, S., Gerald, D., Provasnik, S., Rooney, P., Watanabe, S., et al. (2001). *The Condition of Education.* Retrieved from NCES on October 12, 2004 from http://www.nces.ed.gov/pubsearch/pubsinfo.asp?pubid=2001072

Wong, B. Y. L. (1996). *The ABCs of learning disabilities.* San Diego, CA: Academic Press.

Wong, B. Y. L., Harris, K. R., Graham, S., & Butler, D. L. (2003). Cognitive strategy instruction research in learning disabilities. In H. L. Swanson, K. R. Harris, & S. Graham (Eds.), *Handbook of learning disabilities* (pp. 383–402). New York: Guilford.

Yoon, J. (2002). Three decades of Sustained Silent Reading: A meta-analytic review of the effects of SSR on attitude toward reading. *Reading Improvement, 39,* 186–196.

Zaid, M. A. (1995). Semantic mapping in communicative language teaching. *English Teaching Forum, 33,* 6.

CHAPTER

9

Literacy in the
Language Arts

KEY TERMS

- articulation
- D'Nealian writing
- fluency
- invented spelling
- journal writing
- modeling
- receptive language
- syntax

Eleven-year-old Kyle is a devotee of computer games. His best friends can be found on Nintendo, PlayStation, and Game Boy. Ask Kyle any question about the Silver Wizard or the Dragon Slayer, and he will go into details that make Shakespeare pale by comparison. Kyle's fantasy life is active, alive, and healthy. He draws characters with vigor and gusto, detailing heroes and villains from the tops of their multicolored toes to the tips of their chain-mailed tails. Kyle weaves characters throughout his stories like the master storyteller that he is. Except that at school, Kyle is faced with his nemesis—the dreaded pencil-and-paper duo. When asked to write about his fantasy creatures, Kyle is impaled by the pen, which refuses to put his ideas in print, spell words correctly, or add the appropriate punctuation marks.

Children like Kyle almost always have difficulty with writing literacy. These children may or may not have a reading problem, but they typically have difficulty spelling, writing a simple sentence, or using correct syntax when speaking and writing. They often draw ideas from the television and video or computer games, but they rarely read outside of school (Higgins, 2002).

Kyle is among the growing numbers of middle and high school students performing at or below the basic levels in reading and writing. At the middle school level, 66% of the students are reading at or below the basic level in reading and 73% at or below the basic level in writing. The numbers at the secondary level are not much more encouraging, with a resounding 53% struggling in reading and 78% falling at or below the basic skill level in writing (Slater & Horstman, 2002).

Practice in reading will not automatically lead to improvement in writing. Some students learn to read and comprehend written material well, but their problems with written expression and literacy skills, such as spelling, are masked or ignored until requirements for written language assignments increase, and by then intervention may be very difficult to implement (Berninger et al., 2000).

Nevertheless, a written literacy problem is often a signal to the inclusion teacher that a student may have other language-based academic problems. A student's poor handwriting or inability to speak or write a good sentence is frequently what prompts a referral to special education. Similarly, children with learning problems who are integrated into general education classes for science or social studies may do quite well in discussions but have a hard time with projects, reports, or tests that require written responses.

The inclusion teacher may work with a speech–language specialist or a special education teacher in planning and implementing a language arts program for students with special needs. Or resource help may not be readily available. In either case, knowing about language problems will help as the teacher takes responsibility for some, if not all, of the students' literacy instruction.

Oral Language: Listening and Speaking

Many educators believe language is the single most important tool a child can have. It is an important social skill, the means by which a child can communicate—and thereby build relationships—with other children. It also is crucial to extended thought, the means by which we store and recall information and manipulate abstract concepts. As parallels between language and other areas of cognition are revealed, there is greater reason to believe that any language skill children acquire is only one aspect of more general cognitive abilities (Moskowitz, 1982).

For the most part, teachers have the opportunity to teach only the subtle refinements of language. The greater part of the language acquisition process has been completed by age 5 (Gleason, 2001). Unfortunately, this small proportion of subtle details is what distinguishes an articulate student from one who has trouble speaking.

Reasons for Language Delays

Possible indications of a hearing loss are shown by the following:

- A child who is easily irritated or frustrated when directions are given
- A child who acts "lazy" and begins an assignment only after everyone else has begun
- Any child with a speech problem
- A child who is "too attentive" and strains to "see" what is being said
- A child who cannot sit still during an activity that requires listening
- A child who frequently asks for instructions to be repeated

If any of these behaviors occurs, the teacher should not hesitate to refer a student for a hearing test.

Language problems also can occur in children who have adequate hearing but who are raised in households where not much language is exchanged. Some children do not get enough language stimulation or may not be encouraged to talk. Bilingual children, learning different syntactic rules for each language, may also have problems.

Identifying Language Problems

Occasionally all of us express ourselves awkwardly or become confused while speaking. However, a real language problem occurs when the quality or quantity of a person's speech is so low that it interferes consistently with communication and maintenance of normal relationships with peers. Students may have problems understanding language coming to them (language-in) or problems expressing themselves to others (language-out), or both. These are termed *receptive* and *expressive* language difficulties, respectively.

Receptive Problems

A few ways to identify students who have receptive language problems are as follows:

1. Look for the student who is easily confused by a two- or three-step direction.
2. Notice the student who does not understand common idioms, such as "Get a life," or "Time to get the lead out," or takes them literally.
3. Test relational concepts with riddles, such as "Dan stood in back of Beth. Who was in front?" or "What is the day after tomorrow?"
4. Say something absurd, and see if the child reacts to the absurdity.

Expressive Problems

A few ways to spot expressive language problems include the following:

1. Listen for confusion or inconsistency in the use of verb tense, such as "John hit me, but I don't hit him back."
2. Listen for telegraphic speech, the omission of articles and words such as *is*.
3. Notice the child who often starts to give an answer but interrupts it with "you know" or "I don't know."
4. Notice the student who confuses pronouns, such as *he* instead of *she,* or utters sentences such as, "Her washed her hair."
5. Listen for words in mixed-up order within a sentence, such as "The teacher took away it."
6. Take note of children who speak in a monotone or with a broken, irregular rhythm.
7. Don't overlook the student who is shy in school but seems to talk a lot to parents or one special friend.

Articulation Differences

Everyone makes mistakes in pronouncing words now and then. Nevertheless, if a child seems to exhibit the same problem consistently and to the degree that it diminishes his or her social acceptance and academic success, language should be a primary concern.

Language problems and articulation problems should be differentiated. *Articulation problems* are difficulties only in producing the correct speech sound. Many children in the primary grades lisp or substitute *w* for *r*. In most cases, as the child matures, the problem disappears. Articulation problems usually are not serious, and seldom are detrimental to the child's school success, as language problems are.

Should teachers correct every language mistake they hear? No, leave some problems to time to change. Sentences such as "Her washed her hair" are not unusual for a 2- or 3-year-old but definitely should be a concern when the child is 6 or 7. Also, teachers should proceed cautiously with bilingual children. Opportunities to practice English and exposure to good language models will result in better speech eventually.

From the linguist's perspective, black English is another dialect, no better or worse than standard English. It has its own grammatical rules and is just as effective in conveying the speaker's message as any other dialect. From another perspective, however, it is often reported that African American parents believe that black English has no place in school and prefer that their children be taught standard English (Cazden, 1972; Spears, 1992). Standard English is the dialect that carries prestige and is used by those with power and influence in our society.

Promoting Oral and Written Literacy

In most school districts, speech–language clinicians are spread thin over several schools and many children. Some therapists see their clients as little as 15 or 20 minutes a week. Even if a child receives speech services for two or three times that length of time, it may have little effect on changing patterns that the child has used habitually for many years. In addition, speech–language clinicians often find unsatisfactory carry-over from the therapy session to the classroom. Although the child learns to say a sentence correctly in a one-to-one session with the clinician, he or she may forget to do so when caught up in classroom activities or playing with friends after school.

The ideal program is one in which the inclusion teacher can listen for and reinforce the same things the clinician is teaching. The teacher may want to ask the clinician for recommendations to give the parents, too. Consistency across all settings will improve a child's speech and language skills much faster than spending just a few minutes per week in a room with a clinician.

Techniques for Nurturing Expressive Language

A teacher can help by establishing a classroom environment in which language expression is nurtured and by directly teaching important language skills. Teachers who encourage their students to actively participate in oral and written expression rather than passively receive information are more successful in developing literacy skills. Techniques that promote active learning are called *cognitive strategies*. Cognitive strategies guide students to become more aware, involved, and responsible for their own learning, and help them organize both oral and written language. Cognitive strategies can be as simple as conversing informally with students. Questioning, clarifying issues, summarizing, and predicting events provide important scaffolding for writers (Slater & Horstman, 2002).

INTERACTIVE ENVIRONMENT   Teachers should talk a lot with their students. They should describe and discuss everything they do as a class as they are doing it. Language is interactive, so "talking a lot" means the children get at least as many opportunities to speak as does the teacher. To encourage children to speak and listen, the environment must be warm and nurturing. In most inclusive classrooms more than one language will be present. Preschool and elementary programs for children whose first language is English as well as for English language learners should build on the premise that children's native languages are valuable positive features to be encouraged. A fostering environment contributes significantly to developing children's social and emotional development and promotes a safe environment in which language can be developed without fear of embarrassment.

Drama is one means of presenting a relaxed, warm atmosphere in the classroom. One simple technique for improving expressive vocabulary is to write a list of vocabulary words connected with a piece of literature. Students can learn the meaning of the word and use it in context by creating a skit from the story in which they must use the selected vocabulary words. Teams of children act out the skit. After each skit, the rest of the students discuss the selected vocabulary words and how they were used in the context of the story.

Charades are also valuable instructional tools to help develop expressive language. Children can have fun acting out the charades, and the charades, in turn, provide a vehicle for questioning, clarifying, and conversing informally about words, metaphors, and other literary conventions (Foil & Alber, 2002).

READING TO STUDENTS   Literature is an important part of a child's linguistic environment (Corden, 2000). One of the foremost avenues for expanding vocabulary and the general knowledge it represents is reading itself. Children who cannot or do not read are often limited in their ability to understand or express what they experience in their immediate environment due to impoverished vocabulary (Foil & Alber, 2002). By reading and discussing information found in trade books and textbooks, children's vocabularies can grow.

Shared book reading is an opportunity to gain knowledge about the conventions of print. Equally important is the fact that shared reading also provides the chance to engage in extended talk stimulated by the material being read. Children can be encouraged to verbally participate in discussions about the contents of their texts and trade books (Haden, Reese, & Fivush, 1996; Senechal, 1997). In order for children to understand what they read, they must be familiar with the language in which the stories and textbooks are written. Reading can be a particularly potent form of language stimulation.

CONVERSING WITH STUDENTS   Conversations should be warm and enthusiastic. Teachers are an external source of stimulation and reinforcement for the child who is learning personal expression. Enjoying the conversation will make the child more likely to want to speak to the teacher again; this motivation is essential. Children should be allowed plenty of time to answer questions and be praised for their contributions to discussions.

SENSITIVITY AND DISCRETION   A teacher should not correct a child's speech in front of other students, as this will make the child more self-conscious about speaking. Further, practice activities should not put the spotlight on the child's weaknesses, and students should not be pressured into activities they may not have the confidence to attempt.

Language Dimensions

Language consists of many interrelated components having to do with sound, grammar, meaning, and vocabulary. In addition, it is important to know the right way to say something on a particular occasion in order to achieve a specific purpose (Gleason, 2001). Form, content, and usage are three ways to describe these language functions. *Form* is saying the correct sounds, attaching the proper inflectional endings to words, and putting the words in the appropriate order to make an acceptable sentence. *Content* is the meaning conveyed as we listen or speak, and *usage* is the practical, day-to-day function of language.

FORM   Learning the form of language does not mean learning rules of textbook grammar. No evidence indicates that knowing parts of speech or diagramming sentences makes any difference in verbal performance, oral or written (Straw, 1981). Trying to differentiate adjectives and adverbs probably will only add to students' frustrations with language, and they will not be better speakers because of it.

One good way to teach correct form is to expand and elaborate whatever the child expresses, carefully modeling correct word endings and word order while speaking.

Teacher:	So what happened at recess?
Student:	Well, Billy ... he jump on the board and fall off.
Teacher:	Billy jumped on the board? What board?
Student:	The board the men leave ... by dirt pile.
Teacher:	Do you mean the construction men who've been constructing our new play equipment?
Student:	Yeah—the construct men.
Teacher:	Where is this board?
Student:	The board by dirt pile ... by the fence—the other fence.
Teacher:	It was on a dirt pile by the fence. Tell me what happened to Billy.

Another technique for teaching form is modeling for imitation. A child's ability to imitate is related strongly to other measures of language ability (Mittler, Jeffree, Wheldall, & Berry, 1977). Because imitation seems to play a minor role in a child's acquisition of language, many educators doubt its usefulness as a remedial technique. However, several behavioral language programs, such as DISTAR and Monterey Language, incorporate patterned modeling in combination with reinforcement for correct responses. The success of these techniques with children who have disabilities demonstrates their value.

One way to make an imitation activity more fun is to use silly sentences, such as "My goldfish is eating my clothes." The child imitates short, simple sentences after the teacher says them. The sentences should contain grammatical structures that are a special problem for the student. For example, if Manuel says "I seen" instead of "I saw," the sentences might be:

> I saw a purple dog.
> Mary saw the sky fall down.

As Manuel learns to repeat simple sentences correctly, the teacher should gradually make them longer and more complex:

> I saw a dog.
> I saw a purple dog.
> I saw a purple dog in the sink.
> I saw a purple dog riding a bicycle in the sink.

The activity should be brief—light and success-oriented.

CONTENT   As part of effective receptive abilities, the child must understand the meanings of words and phrases other people use. At the beginning of a science or social studies lesson, for example, the teacher introduces a new word and looks for opportunities to use it throughout the day. Words can be chosen from current events as reported on the radio or in the newspaper: *economy, ballot, veteran, environment, promotion, demonstration, toxic.* Learning new meanings of words that have multiple definitions also is valuable.

The teacher should point out the ways in which words and the ideas they represent are related to each other. For example, words are related to different words that mean approximately the same thing (synonyms) and to words that mean the opposite (antonyms). Words represent objects or ideas that are part of a larger class. When reading a story about penguins, for example, the teacher might stop and talk about penguins belonging to a larger class of animals—birds. In what ways are penguins like other birds? In what ways are they different? What does a penguin have that makes us think of it as a bird? Objects and ideas also are composed of smaller parts. For example, a discussion about a bicycle can lead to a discussion of its components and the introduction of still more vocabulary.

There are several ways to teach students to listen for the content in what they hear. Riddles do just that and are a lot of fun.

> If an airplane crashes on the U.S.–Canada border, where would the survivors be buried?

In a social studies lesson, the teacher could deliver a brief monologue and have students guess the name of the historical character by what the teacher said. On the basis of an oral description, the students can draw the character or the scene described.

An activity that requires students to follow directions is a good way to teach them to listen for content. Arts and crafts projects require listening for content so students are able to produce the desired product. Direction games also are fun. In the shopping list game, Caroline is sent around the room to get Sally's pencil ... get John's shoelace ... get Philip's science book ... and put the items in a large shopping bag. When Caroline returns to the teacher, she must try to name everything before unpacking it. As discussed previously, reading to students is important. Appreciating the sentiment in stories or poems requires listening for content.

Children with hearing impairments have a particular problem understanding the figurative uses of language (Rittenhouse & Steams, 1982). To many students who are deaf, something is either literal or absurd and, therefore, insignificant. This contributes to poor reading comprehension. Rittenhouse and Steams reported extensive use of idiomatic expressions and similes throughout children's fiction and basal readers, mostly related to key ideas. The authors demonstrated that even 10-year-old deaf children could begin to understand metaphors if they understood clearly what was expected of them through careful teaching. Children in the study were asked to read a short, one-paragraph story and then select the metaphor that most closely expressed the idea of the story.

1. After reading the story, the teacher showed the accompanying picture and asked the child to explain it.
2. The teacher reinforced the idea that the picture was related to the story.
3. The teacher explained that only one of the sentence metaphors below the story was related to it.
4. The child chose a metaphor and gave an explanation for the answer.
5. The teacher gave the correct answer and explained the analogy.

Children with hearing impairments and language disorders may have trouble understanding meaning in sentences in which the syntax, or order and arrangement of words, does not follow the usual simple sequential rules (van der Lely, 1990). Passive constructions are an example of this problem:

The angry boy was scolded by the old woman.

Some children tend to treat all sentences as straight subject-verb-object constructions. Consider the sentence just cited and the subsequent exchange:

Teacher: Who was scolded?
Student: The old woman.
Teacher: Who scolded her?
Student: The boy.
Teacher: Tell me what happened.
Student: The boy scolded the old woman.

Similar problems occur with postmodified nouns.

The chicken in the box is red.

The adjective usually is assumed to refer to the noun closest to it.

    Teacher: What is red?
    Student: The box is red.

Dealing with problems like these requires the same approach as in teaching metaphors: careful explanation, corrective feedback, and practice from time to time. There are no magic remedies.

Teachers also can enhance a child's expression of meaning. In a science lesson, the students can describe the attributes of something observed. Students also should be able to describe something in terms of its function. The teacher might bring to class an unusual tool and ask the students to invent as many possible uses for it as they can imagine. One popular game is to have a child reach into a grab bag, select an object, and describe it in as much detail as possible without the other children being able to see it. From the description, the others try to guess what the object is.

Pictures from magazine ads, especially humorous ones, provide an excellent stimulus for children to describe events. After the student has described the situation in the picture, he or she could be asked to tell what happened just before the picture was taken or what happened immediately after. Children also can invent stories after listening to tapes with assorted sequences of sound effects.

The ability to report events in sequence is important. A good way to provide opportunities for the student to do this is through *how* questions.

    Tell me how ...
        you tie your shoes.
        you come to school.
        your father washes his car.

To point out cause–effect relationships, ask *why* questions.

    Tell me why ...
        you tie your shoes.
        you come to school.
        your father washes his car.

This should not be grilling inquisition. Questions should be asked to stimulate conversation and create an interactive environment.

USAGE   Teaching function means stressing the uses of language in day-to-day events: giving and following directions, making phone calls, chatting with friends, asking for information. To use language functionally, the child must learn to act as both a sender and a receiver of information. The best way to teach this is through simulated practice and role playing. A few ideas for simulation games are as follows:

1. Make phone calls in response to an ad.
2. Take a message when answering the phone.

3. Act as a seller of pens and pencils (or other "products" found in the class-room).

4. Act as a person at home trying politely to get rid of the pencil seller at the door.

5. Give directions to help another student find hidden treasure in the room.

6. Find hidden treasure by following another's directions.

7. Be a TV talk-show host (learn how to maintain a conversation through questioning).

8. Make introductions at a class "party."

9. Play the hidden treasure game by using only hints and indirect statements. ("Have you thought of looking in other cupboards?" versus "Open the cupboard door below the sink.")

10. Build conversations by expanding and elaborating on the statement of the previous speaker.

Acting out these activities with a tape recorder may be more motivating and less threatening for some students than doing them before other students.

Written Language

Development of Written Expression

Written expression develops in much the same way as oral language, but it is much more complex and does not develop as soon or as fast. According to Vygotsky (1962), there is a lag of as much as 6 to 8 years between a child's linguistic age in speaking and in writing. Writing requires a solid base of receptive and expressive language. In addition, it requires good visual abilities integrated with the fine-motor skills necessary for the physical task of writing.

The difference between speaking and writing lies not just in its mechanical aspects. Written expression is a separate linguistic function that is different in both its structure and its style. Vygotsky (1962) pointed out several unique aspects of writing:

- Writing is more abstract because it lacks the intonation and body language components of spoken language.
- The writer must disengage from the immediate sensory aspects of speaking and replace words with graphic images of words.
- The writer does not have an interlocutor (or immediate responsive recipient); the recipient is either absent or imaginary.
- Writing does not carry the same motivation as speech, which is more immediately useful.
- Writing is detached in time and space from the real event it seeks to recreate; the writer must create the situation in his or her own mind.
- Writing is deliberate and analytical; speech is spontaneous.

Writing also can be thought of as the tension between the two competing roles of the writer: the author and the secretary (Smith, 1982). The author thinks about the message, the organization of ideas, the language in which to express those ideas, and the effect the writing will have on the intended audience. The secretary, on the other hand, worries about the mechanical concerns: margins, spelling, punctuation, and handwriting. Students with learning problems usually have difficulties with both the author and the secretary roles. Thus, they often have difficulty organizing ideas and keeping the reader's needs in mind as they compose (Englert, Raphael, Fear, & Anderson, 1988). They also make more spelling, capitalization, punctuation, and handwriting errors (Deno, Marston, & Mirkin, 1982; Graham, Boyer-Schick, & Tippets, 1989).

Assessment of Written Language

Written expression include five basic components that combine to make a good composition: fluency, content, conventions, syntactic maturity, and vocabulary.

Fluency

Fluency is the student's ability to generate written language from his or her own inner language and to write compositions of gradually increasing length. To evaluate fluency, the teacher looks at quantity (the number of words the student can write).

Here is an example of how a child's paragraph may be analyzed according to fluency. Billy wrote this paragraph about his favorite TV show:

> After dinner me and my brother like to watch *Mathew Star.* My favrite show. Mathew comes from outer space. He does magic things. He makes things fly across the room. He saves people.

If the objective were simply to get Billy to write more and practice putting his thoughts on paper, the teacher would look only at fluency. Counting the words—33—the teacher might gently encourage Billy to make his compositions longer, and eventually he might write stories of 50 or 60 words.

When teaching a beginning or reluctant writer, fluency is the first goal. The teacher should give positive, enthusiastic feedback on the student's first attempts at writing, responding to the ideas expressed and not the correctness of word choice, punctuation, or spelling. If the student already can write compositions of 50 words or more, the teacher should focus on a different objective, such as content.

Content

Content is the most difficult aspect of a composition to evaluate objectively. The primary question the evaluator asks is: Did the student express creatively and clearly what she intended to say? A checklist probably is the best way to look for the important content components. Cooper (1977) suggested six general qualities to be assessed.

1. *Author's role:* keeping the correct role of either the participant or the observer throughout.

2. *Style or voice:* stating what the writer really thinks in a personal, interesting way.
3. *Central figure:* describing the character in such detail as to seem real.
4. *Background:* describing the setting, giving the events a real place in which to happen.
5. *Sequence:* making clear the order of events.
6. *Theme:* holding it all together by choosing incidents and details that relate to the subject matter or purpose.

Cooper's six attributes apply best to narrative compositions. In descriptive or expository writing, attention must also be given to elements of accuracy, relevance, and clarity.

Let's use Cooper's checklist to evaluate the content of Billy's paragraph.

Author's role:	Billy begins as the participant but soon changes to an observer.
Style or voice:	The first two sentences share personal feelings, but the last four are written without much feeling or interest.
Central figure:	Billy does not describe Mathew's appearance or personality.
Background:	The background seems adequate in proportion to the size and scope of the paragraph.
Sequence:	This, too, is adequate, considering that the paragraph is *descriptive* rather than *narrative*.
Theme:	Incidents are presented rather randomly. No central event or attribute acts as a focus for the detail.

Billy's content is restricted somewhat by his limited fluency and vocabulary, which are more appropriate objectives to work on.

Conventions

The conventions of a composition consist of the mechanical aspects of writing: correct grammar, punctuation, spelling, and so forth. They reflect how well a student can recognize his or her own errors and rely a great deal on reading, spelling, and oral language skills. Though these are the polishing touches to written expression, they receive a disproportionate amount of critical attention from teachers. When the other facets of writing have developed and conventions become the main objective, they can be evaluated by a checklist such as the one shown in Figure 9.1.

Syntactic Maturity

Syntactic maturity refers to the type and complexity of the sentences the student writes. Beginners write simple subject-verb-object sentences. Mature writers create more complex, interesting sentences. For example, a 7-year-old may write these sentences:

> She saw the dog.
> The dog was running to the gate.

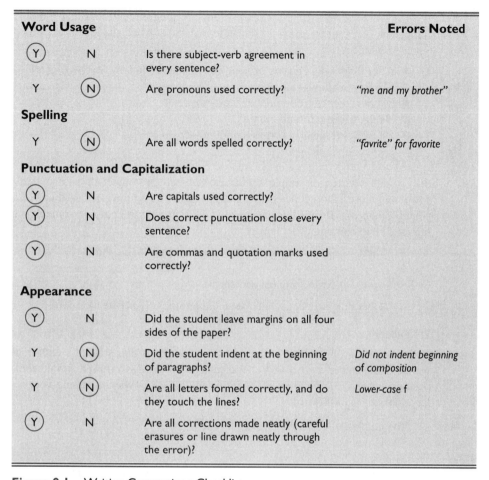

Word Usage			Errors Noted
(Y)	N	Is there subject-verb agreement in every sentence?	
Y	(N)	Are pronouns used correctly?	*"me and my brother"*
Spelling			
Y	(N)	Are all words spelled correctly?	*"favrite" for favorite*
Punctuation and Capitalization			
(Y)	N	Are capitals used correctly?	
(Y)	N	Does correct punctuation close every sentence?	
(Y)	N	Are commas and quotation marks used correctly?	
Appearance			
(Y)	N	Did the student leave margins on all four sides of the paper?	
Y	(N)	Did the student indent at the beginning of paragraphs?	*Did not indent beginning of composition*
Y	(N)	Are all letters formed correctly, and do they touch the lines?	*Lower-case f*
(Y)	N	Are all corrections made neatly (careful erasures or line drawn neatly through the error)?	

Figure 9.1   Writing Conventions Checklist

An 11-year-old usually combines these two sentences into one more like this:

> She saw the dog running toward the gate.

A simple way to evaluate syntactic maturity is to count the number of sentences that fall within the following categories to see which type is most predominant in the composition:

- incomplete sentences
- simple sentences
- compound sentences
- complex sentences

Let's assume that Billy's compositions are long enough and that the next component we want to assess is syntactic maturity. Of his six sentences, which type is prominent?

- After dinner me and my brother like to watch Mathew Star—*complex*
- My favrite show—*incomplete*
- Mathew comes from outer space—*simple*
- He does magic things—*simple*
- He makes things fly across the room—*complex*
- He saves people—*simple*

Billy usually writes in simple sentences (subject-verb-object or subject-verb-adverbial phrase), though he can use more complex structures. (He used no compound sentences.) Billy's teacher could show him how to combine some of his sentences into compound sentences:

Matthew comes from outer space, and he does magic things.

Or he could try to write complex sentences:

He does magic things, such as making things fly across the room.

Vocabulary

Vocabulary is evaluated by looking at the diversity in the student's choice of words. Some students are able to write sentences fluently to form a simple composition but tend to overuse certain words and phrases. When assessing vocabulary, look for the following:

1. The number of repeated words.
2. The number of unusual or new words.

Notice whether the student incorporates new vocabulary introduced in the science or social studies lessons. Compare other key words used with grade-level word lists.

Evaluating Billy's vocabulary begins with counting the number of repeated words.

After dinner me and my brother like to watch Mathew Star. <u>My</u> favrite show. <u>Mathew</u> comes from outer space. He does magic things. <u>He</u> makes <u>things</u> fly across the room. <u>He</u> saves people.

Not many words are repeated. Using more complex sentences would eliminate several repetitions of *he*, for example. As Billy's vocabulary increases, he could substitute several words for *things*.

Increasing Written Language Skills

Deciding what to teach depends on which component of written expression presents the greatest difficulty. Billy, for example, needs to expand his fluency before his teacher can evaluate the content of his work fairly. Basal language arts texts are not always helpful in this regard. Most deal with a wide range of language and study skills and give the student relatively little opportunity to engage in actual composition. Let's look at one component at a time in the same order they were evaluated.

Increasing Fluency

Children do not have to be proficient readers before they begin to write. Some children write words and short messages in their own invented spellings for up to a year before they begin to read (Chomsky, 1969). Writing with invented spelling is a more concrete, accessible skill than reading. Children already know the words and messages they communicate. The need to identify a message written by someone else is a significant extra step. Maria Montessori (1964) said, "Experience has taught me to distinguish clearly between writing and reading and has shown me that the two acts are not absolutely contemporaneous. Contrary to the usually accepted idea, writing precedes reading" (p. 296). First a child must learn the function of language in communication: What is read has been written by someone, and what is written will be read by someone.

Here are some activities that will reinforce this idea of language's function for young beginning writers:

1. Have the children color a picture and label its various parts: "house," "tree," "Mom," and so on. Spell the words for them only if they ask for help. If not, accept invented spellings.
2. Have the children make a little book or diary in which to draw pictures and write a few words every day. (One day Joey asked his teacher how to spell *baby* and *sister;* his mother had just given birth to a baby girl. All Joey wrote in his book that day was "baby sister baby sister baby sister baby sister ..." but those were two words he never forgot.)
3. Attach a message pocket to the student's desk and one to your own. Leave simple messages for the student: "I'm glad you're here today," "You did a good job on your math." More important, encourage the child to leave messages for you.

The barriers to fluency that students with learning problems face reflect both the author and secretary roles of the writer. As the author, many students have trouble deciding on a topic and generating ideas. The secretary aspects of writing—mechanical concerns of spelling, handwriting, and punctuation—also interfere with fluency. Methods for increasing a student's fluency, therefore, should take both areas into account.

Here are a few ideas for helping the author generate ideas for writing:

1. Polloway and Smith (1982) suggested journal writing as a way to increase expression and ideation, claiming that journals or diaries can significantly increase interest and competency in writing, especially when tied to reinforcement for length and improved quality. Teachers should make it clear that these are not

confidential diaries but, instead, interactive journals that the teacher will read and respond to with written comments. Encourage expression and do not correct for spelling, grammar, or punctuation.

2. The Matrix of Three is a discussion game that prepares the student to write a story (Marcus, 1977). Introduce the activity by saying something like: "On your way to school today, you saw many things. Tell me what you saw as I make a design out of it." As the student describes things, write them in a 3 x 3 matrix.

cat	bird	tree
lost shoe	police officer	lady
car	dog	bus

Have the student choose a line of three items, horizontally, vertically, or diagonally (like Tic-Tac-Toe). Then set up the situation: "Can you think of a situation in which we could find a lost shoe, a police officer, and a lady?" Establish a setting, set up a problem, and have the student find a solution to the problem.

3. Gleason and Isaacson (1991) taught a group-brainstorming technique using a picture stimulus. After the students looked at the picture, the teacher asked each student to say one thing about it. Next, the teacher asked students to take turns saying one word they could use in their story or description. The teacher wrote the words on the chalkboard or overhead projector until 10–12 words were listed. Some teachers take this a step further by having students list *naming* words, *action* words, and *describing* words. Generating words often helps students also generate ideas.

The mechanical aspects of writing also present obstacles to fluency for students with learning problems. If students worry about how to spell a word or how to make a cursive *Y*, they may be distracted from and possibly forget their topic ideas. Mechanical concerns also affect the readability and legibility of the written message. The teacher, therefore, should consider ways to help students overcome the mechanical obstacles to writing. A few ideas, largely from Gleason and Isaacson (1991), follow.

COLLABORATION   The teacher and the student can collaborate in writing a composition. In the author's role, the student generates ideas and composes sentences as the teacher, in the secretary's role, takes responsibility for the production. During the planning stage of the writing process, they may brainstorm together, and the teacher may suggest ways of organizing their ideas. During the drafting stage, the teacher can rehearse the sentences with the student and assist the student with spelling and punctuation. If the student has great difficulty in writing, the teacher may even write the sentences as the student dictates. During the rewriting stage, the teacher prompts evaluation of the composition as they read it together. After changes and corrections have been made, the student copies the final draft. While helpful in certain areas, collaboration has a major limitation: It may create a "false paradise" that shelters the student from the aspects of writing that are the most difficult but also the most important to learn.

TOPIC WORD LIST   Using a brainstorming strategy such as Gleason and Isaacson's (1991), the teacher can precue the spelling of important content words by listing topic words on the chalkboard or overhead and leaving them for students to refer to as they write. Because topic words carry much of the meaning in a composition, the correct spelling of such words can improve the readability of the message considerably.

PERSONAL WORD BOOKS   Many teachers have students develop a personal word book that lists the spelling of frequently used words alphabetically. Gleason and Isaacson (1991) found this to be a successful strategy for some students with learning problems but a risky one for others. Specifically, students who wrote fewer than 50 words in the personal word book became more fluent, perhaps because the word book gave these reluctant writers a little more confidence in overcoming the secretarial aspects of the task. However, the fluency of students who began writing more words in the personal word book decreased. It seemed to focus their thoughts on spelling concerns and distract them from generating ideas.

INVENTED SPELLING   Some teachers promote writing fluency by instructing students not to worry about punctuation and letter formation and to use *invented spelling*. Teachers should make it clear that this is not standard English spelling but that spelling inventions are okay for writing first drafts. Teachers should also model a strategy for inventing spellings. For example, the teacher may begin to write this sentence on the board, "He tossed it in the washing machine." Coming to the end of the sentence, the teacher could say, "*Machine.* I'm not sure how to spell this word, so I'll use invented spelling. What is one letter that might be in *machine*? Yes, *M*. I think I hear a */sh/* sound, so I'll write *S-H*. What other letters do we hear? Okay, *E* and *N*. I'll want to check that later, but right now I keep writing." The strategy for students is twofold: to (a) write as many letters as they can, and (b) keep writing.

Invented spelling does increase students' fluency in first-draft writing (Gleason & Isaacson, 1991). However, it does not improve spelling accuracy. Therefore, a writing program that incorporates invented spelling must be supplemented with a strong spelling program to teach students the words they will not learn incidentally by writing them.

Enhancing Content

As students begin writing compositions of gradually increasing length, the next instructional target is to give shape and cohesion to their compositions. Good compositions should have a beginning, a body in which information is presented in a logical, orderly fashion, and an ending.

Enhancing the organization and quality of content begins in the planning stage of the writing process. Long before a student puts pencil to page or fingers to keyboard, discussion about the topic must occur. These discussions are shaping experiences that convince the child he or she has an ample stock of ideas and experiences related to the topic. Before writing, the teacher also can teach an explicit strategy for steering students through the writing process and model text structures that guide organization of the composition.

ORIENTING STRATEGIES   Writing is a means of communication. Authors not only must activate their own knowledge of a topic but must also keep in mind what the intended reader does or doesn't know about the topic. Most prewriting processes include the following basic elements:

- Why am I writing this?
- What am I writing about?
- What do I want to say about my subject?
- What kind of voice or style do I want to use?
- Who do I want to tell my story to?

Students should also have opportunities to share their writing with others. Students learn to be aware of audience needs by having an audience that can respond to the writing. It is crucial to note that student audiences must be trained to give the kind of feedback that promotes this awareness in the writer and to prevent unkind feedback that will discourage the beginning writer.

PROCESS STRATEGIES   Models of the composing process vary according to the number of stages or steps, ranging from two steps (Elbow, 1991) to eight (Frank, 1979). Englert, Raphael, and Anderson (1992) recommended a five-step process using the acronym POWER: *planning, organizing, writing, editing,* and *revising.* Other educators add *sharing* or *publishing* as the final step.

Another process strategy used in narrative story writing is the W-W-W,W-2, How-2. Who (is the main character)? When (does it take place)? Where (does it take place)? What (does the main character wanted to)? What (happens when he or she does it)? How (does it end)? How (does the character feel)? (Graham & Harris, 1992).

When teaching a process strategy, the teacher should not only explain the process but also model it (Marchian & Alber, 2001). When modeling, the teacher demonstrates the process by writing a short composition, highlighting each step, and thinking aloud while moving from the planning stage on through to the final editing stage.

TEXT STRUCTURES   Recent approaches to improving the quality of compositions of children with learning problems have focused on teaching the explicit text structures. A text structure represents the way authors organize their thoughts according to common elements found in writing of the same genre by other authors. The use of writing strategies that incorporate text structures has significantly improved the quality of written expression among students with learning problems (Englert et al., 1992; Graham, Harris, MacArthur, & Schwartz, 1991).

Different text structures correspond to different purposes for writing: to relate events, to inform, to persuade, to analyze, or to compare. Instruction often begins with story structures because they represent the genre that is most familiar to children. Story structures vary from simple to complex. A basic story has at least four elements: a *character*, a problem that the character faces or a *goal* to be achieved, *actions* the character takes to achieve the goal, and a *result*. Other story structures include setting and the character's emotional reactions.

As students become more sophisticated with language, they are required to produce ideas in a variety of writing formats. They are expected to write many different types of essays. The most common types of essays include opinion, compare-and-contrast, and persuasive essays.

Students can be taught to write opinion essays by placing them in dyads. Each partner takes the opposite side of an issue; for example, middle school students should not be required to follow a dress code. The students next generate two or three arguments to support their opinions and put their ideas on plan sheets. They discuss their arguments with their partners and finally produce an essay (Wong, Butler, Ficzere, & Kuperis, 1996).

Students are often asked to write compare-and-contrast essays. A technique that has proven useful with students with learning problems is to have the students work in pairs to select the topic, for example, concerts. They next generate two categories of the topic for comparison purposes—for example, rock concerts vs. school concerts. They then brainstorm features of the topic, such as, goals, content, interest, and behavior. For each feature selected, the students list details and identify each detail as either being similar or different for the topic. The students then use their compare-and-contrast plan to write their essays (Wong, Butler, Ficzere, & Kuperis, 1997).

Using the concept of text structure, Graham and Harris (1989) devised a three-step strategy for writing short persuasive essays:

1. *Think,* who will read this, and why am I writing this?
2. *Plan* what to say using the mnemonic TREE (**T**opic sentence, **R**easons, **E**xamine reasons, and **E**nding).
3. *Write* and say more.

Effective authors also use keywords that signal to the reader the text structure the author is using. For example, "similarly," "on the other hand," and "in contrast to" suggest to the reader that the author is using a compare-and-contrast structure. Similarly, words such as *first, then, next,* and *finally* (as in Figure 9.2) guide the reader through a sequential narrative.

Figure 9.2   Using Sequence Words

Increasing Correct Use of Conventions

Basal language arts texts are full of exercises for teaching the formal or mechanical components of composition. Learning to capitalize, substitute pronouns, or identify incomplete sentences, however, may be putting the cart before the horse if the student cannot yet write more than a labored sentence. When the student begins to write a fairly good paragraph and is ready to tackle indentation, punctuation, and the finer points of grammar, two tips will help teach conventions.

1. Employ a verbal mediation strategy by teaching students a simple rhyme or rule to remember as they write, such as the following:

   "Name, date,
   Skip a line, title,
   Skip a line, work."
   Make up your own strategy for teaching other skills, such as capitalization:
   "Names of people, names of pets,
   Titles such as Mrs.,
   Special places, months, and days
   First word in a sentence."
   (No, it doesn't rhyme, but the rhythm is catchy.)

2. Always have the students edit and correct their own work. Because there are many things to look for, a simple checklist will help the student remember what to check. Some teachers attach a small self-check slip of paper to each page of work; the student can then mark each item as it is checked (see Figure 9.3).

The world of symbols affects the learner. Poor skills with symbols makes students susceptible to misunderstanding and errors. In contrast, students with strong skill are empowered to enter the universe of print. As a writer, the student must learn and use the symbol system shared by other writers and readers to ensure readers understand the message. Teaching authoring functions does not mean the student will necessarily learn the secretary skills. No evidence is available to show that students with learning problems master spelling, punctuation, and handwriting through incidental learning. Experiences in the process of writing, therefore, must be accompanied by a strong instructional program in spelling, punctuation, and other writing conventions.

Developing Syntactic Maturity

As the student masters the spelling of many frequently used words and writes original compositions with gradually longer sentences, the goal becomes expanded, more complex sentences. In the past 15 to 20 years, several researchers have discovered the dramatic effects of sentence-combining practice on increasing the complexity of sentences written in compositions. Sentence

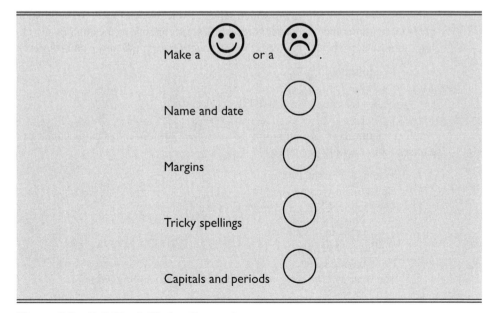

Figure 9.3   Self-Check Slip for Conventions

combining is the process by which complex sentences can be made from simple kernel sentences.

Sentences can be combined in several ways. The easiest is by *conjoining,* the union of two sentences by a conjunction:

> The man is in the kitchen.
> He is baking cakes.
> The man is in the kitchen, *and* he is baking cakes.

Combining also can be done by *coordination* of either two subjects or two predicates, deleting the redundant words.

> Sally will wash the car.
> *Sally will* drive it home.
> Sally will wash the car and drive it home.

> The boy liked to eat ice cream.
> His dog *liked to eat ice cream.*
> The boy and his dog liked to eat ice cream.

Sentences can be combined by *connecting,* using a semicolon and connecting words such as *however, nevertheless, therefore,* and *moreover.*

> I didn't go to school.
> I saw John after school.
> I didn't go to school; however, I saw John after school.

Subordinating is another way in which sentences can be combined. Subordination gives more importance to one message and less importance to the other by attaching subordinators such as *if, unless, because, until, when, whenever,* and *wherever.*

> I go to school.
> I will see Jill.
> If I go to school, I will see Jill.

Another mature type of combining is to embed kernel sentences as phrases or clauses within another sentence.

> The man is in the kitchen.
> He likes ice cream.
> The man *who likes ice cream* is in the kitchen.

> The man is in the kitchen.
> He likes ice cream.
> He is baking cakes.
> The man who likes ice cream is in the kitchen *baking cakes.*

> The man is in the kitchen.
> He likes ice cream.

He is baking cakes.
He is large.
The *large* man who likes ice cream is in the kitchen baking cakes.
(embedded as a prenominal adjective)

Sentence combining can begin with just two sentences in each problem:

The girl is smiling.
She is winning the game.

When several such pairs of sentences are combined, they form a complete paragraph. Again, several ways of combining the kernel sentences are acceptable.

The girl is smiling and winning the game.
The girl is smiling while winning the game.
The girl who is smiling is winning the game.
The smiling girl is winning the game.
The girl smiling is winning the game.

If the child favors one combination almost exclusively, encourage other types of transformations. Transformations allow the student alternate means of conveying information. By teaching children how to transform very simple structures into more complex ones, they can begin to build more sophisticate language schema.

Model: 1. The boy eats hamburgers.
           2. The boy is at McDonald's.
              The boy at McDonald's eats hamburgers.

Exercise: 1. The little girl laughed.
           2. The little girl is on her skateboard.

Combining sentence structures can become even more complex. A curriculum can consist of a series of short sentences to be combined in a certain way, signaled by both indentation and symbols.

Elizabeth wondered SOMETHING.
   Patrick would come home from swim practice sometime. (WHEN)
Elizabeth wondered when Patrick would come home from swim practice.

Syntactic maturity is not the only benefit to be gained from sentence-combining practice. Hughes (1978) reported several studies (including his own) that also showed significant gains in reading comprehension as a result. This should not be surprising because both concern the structure of meaning.

Increasing Vocabulary

Written vocabulary may be developed in many of the same ways as oral vocabulary. The following strategies that pertain to written expression in particular may supplement oral vocabulary strategies.

VERBAL LABELS   Supplying verbal labels is a useful and possibly important vocabulary skill. From their review of the research, Torgesen and Kail (1980) suggested that the slow naming speed of poor readers interferes with their ability to process information efficiently. Supplying word labels is a language process that is important to composition, too. Exercises can take the form of supplying one-word or phrase descriptions of novel line patterns or pictures depicting scenes of various kinds. Writing titles is a form of verbal labeling, requiring the naming of complex, abstract information.

IDEAS FOR DEVELOPING VOCABULARY   Some other ideas for providing practice in vocabulary skills are as follows:

1. Set up a writing center in a corner of the classroom and supply it with pencils and lined paper. In the writing center also have charts for synonyms, antonyms, and frequently misspelled words. At the top of one chart, write *said,* a word that is repeated frequently and excessively in children's writing. Under the word *said,* list several words that can be used in its place (e.g., *asked, declared, exclaimed, reported*). A similar chart can be made for other frequently overused words, such as *nice.*

2. Give the student a short passage in which several words are underlined. Have the student substitute for the underlined words more colorful or interesting ones that fit the context of the passage.

3. Play Facts in Five on a large 5 x 5 grid (see Figure 9.4). Ask the student to draw five category cards and place them to the left of the grid, one card per row. Then have the student draw one letter card for each of the five columns. Set a timer for 3 minutes, during which time the student tries to fill in as many squares as possible, finding words that match the appropriate category and that begin with the letter at the top of the column. If the child is a slow writer or a poor speller, the game may be played orally, putting markers in the squares (Bailey, 1975).

4. Use classroom discussions about recent news events to introduce new vocabulary. Words such as *economy, toxic, ethnic, embargo, proponents,* and *trade deficit* appear frequently on the pages of newspapers and magazines. Begin teaching vocabulary by discussing the context in which the new word is found. Then give a synonym or simple definition followed by one or two examples. Often nonexamples are helpful if they focus attention on the critical features of the concept. A nonexample of the category "food" might be *shoes* or *balloons.* Finally, give students an opportunity to practice using the word.

5. Use word banks as another way to assist students to clearly communicate their ideas. Various types of word banks can be provided. Action verb word banks may be used to make student writing more expressive. Adjective word banks can also help students create more interesting works. Adjective word banks can be also arranged by category—for example, colors, sad words, happy words, and so forth. Students may continuously develop individualized banks of frequently used words that either they or the teacher selects (Marchian & Alber, 2001).

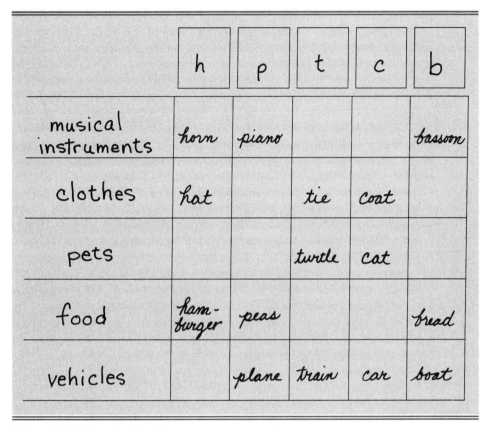

	h	p	t	c	b
musical instruments	horn	piano			bassoon
clothes	hat		tie	coat	
pets			turtle	cat	
food	hamburger	peas			bread
vehicles		plane	train	car	boat

Figure 9.4   Facts-in-Five Game

Effective Practices

TIME ON TASK   There is no guarantee that additional time spent on a task will produce better education. The key to spending more time on a task is to identify the appropriate task given the needs of the student. Labels affixed to children are not indicators of how much time they will spend on a task. For example, extreme variability has been found in the amount of time children who are labeled as having learning disabilities, emotional disorders, and mental retardation spend in writing activities or in receiving written language instruction (Christenson, Thurlow, & Ysseldyke, 1989). Continuous adult direction has been found to increase writing productivity through increased time on task (Morton, 1986); however, with ever-increasing class sizes, continuous adult direction may not be a viable option.

FEEDBACK   The type of feedback given to a student learning to write is a sensitive and important part of teaching. To a child who is painfully aware of a literacy problem, insensitive correction can be perceived as criticism and can detrimentally affect the child's attitude toward writing. Polloway and Smith (1982) recommend a technique of selective checking, whereby the teacher avoids excessive correction by selecting just one skill to reinforce and one to correct. Skills should relate directly to the teacher's evaluation of the student's abilities in each of the five basic components, as described earlier.

Teachers' responses to students' first drafts of written assignments should provide positive and constructive feedback, suggesting ways in which the students can rethink and rewrite. Dialogue feedback, student conferencing, and reader reaction summary are three relatively easily implemented approaches that provide useful feedback on written compositions (Valcourt, 1989).

Let's take the example of dialogue feedback with Eldon. Eldon and his teacher dialogue through his daily journal. Both he and the teacher make comments to each other; in other words, they maintain a running conversation through writing. Eldon's teacher writes questions that encourage Eldon to think more broadly about his topic.

Eldon is writing a report about frogs, one of his favorite topics. Each day the teacher has a short conference with him to discuss his progress in planning, drafting, and revising his frog report. Eldon has more than one source of feedback. He can also engage in a reader reaction summary activity with his classmates. When it's Eldon's turn to share his first draft of the frog report with the rest of the class, the class discusses the main ideas presented and what they liked best, and they ask him questions that might stimulate him to add information to make his report clearer or more interesting. The teacher might also ask the kids to write a short reaction summary to Eldon's report.

Kitagawa (1982) described beautifully the way in which Japanese elementary teachers use positive comments on a child's paper to teach the elements of good writing. *Sei katsu tsuzuri kata* is a philosophy of writing education that uses teacher–pupil dialogue to promote a child's own style in expressive writing. The teacher joins the child in the spectator's role and reinforces keen multisensory perception with remarks such as the following:

> You are recalling the cat's behavior very well here.
> Here you are remembering just what went through your mind.
> You are recalling subtle details clearly.
> Strong feeling, directly expressed.
> You use the present tense for a feeling of now.
> Your writing really makes us see the cat's behavior.

In addition, word processing can be a useful technique for providing students with feedback on written compositions. Research is continuously finding that students who use personal computers rate higher on a variety of dimensions of holistic/analytic writing. Students using computers continuously revise at all stages of writing, although most revisions were microstructural rather than macrostructural (Owston, Murphy, & Wideman, 1992). That means that kids are more inclined to fix the spelling or change the capitalization of a letter than to add or rearrange sentences to improve the clarity of meaning. However, with computer-assisted instruction the teacher can more easily see the work in progress and more readily give feedback to the student. Both peers and teacher can suggest content changes as the composition is being drafted. In this way feedback becomes continuous and timely.

Integrating Reading and Writing

Functional writing and reading systems both use low-level and high-level processes. The degree to which low-level processes become automatic and are coordinated with high-level processes affects the overall efficiency and quality of writing products (Berninger, 1994). Instructional practices that overemphasize meaning, process, or form in writing instruction are likely to interfere with the child's ability to become a competent writer.

Instructional practices clearly influence how well a child learns ideation, handwriting, and spelling. Current educational practice minimizes direct instruction and practice of handwriting and spelling skills. The natural approach to learning suggests that skills can be "caught" by immersing children in a literacy-rich environment where they have plenty of opportunities to write for meaningful reasons. The belief behind a natural approach to learning is that the child will acquire most of the spelling and writing skills they need through writing and reading.

Even though the concept of acquiring reading, writing, and spelling skills naturally is not new, little evidence exists showing the effectiveness of this approach with children who have learning problems (Graham, 1999). Without direct instruction and practice in handwriting and spelling, children who start out at the low end of the continuum of spelling or handwriting are put at risk for developing significant problems in written expression later in school (Berninger, 1999). An integrated reading and writing approach can result in enhanced comprehension and writing if it increases readers' involvement with the text, heightens their awareness of text structures, and is complemented by lessons that provide instruction systematically as well as sequentially in spelling and handwriting.

Using literature as an inspiration, children can also write original compositions. They can borrow ideas and plots from literature and, with assistance from the teacher, begin to learn about the more subtle stylistic elements authors use. By examining the literary devices used by adult authors, children can begin to develop their own writing skills and become more reflective writers. Teachers can begin to develop children's awareness about how texts are constructed by providing models, demonstrating, and drawing attention to the features of narrative texts, and through focused group discussion (Corden, 2000).

Recommendations for integration range from simple to large-scale modifications of instructional programs. For example, Shanahan (1988) and Gleason (1995) have recommended using writing activities to replace or supplement activities from reading workbooks. Bartley (1993) suggested that, before beginning to read a selection, students write to make predictions. While reading they can take notes, develop or respond to questions, fill in charts, or comment on the text; after reading they may summarize or paraphrase what they have read.

Some methods incorporate highly defined text structures. Teachers begin by preparing an outline or frame consisting of the important text elements. Students fill in important material as they read. These frames or outlines can then be used to study the information or to organize one's own written response.

Knowledge of discourse structure assists thinking because readers can predict and understand the texts they are reading, while writers are obligated to observe conventions of style to make their messages comprehensible. Identifying important elements is a strategic skill that underlies both reading comprehension and written summarization and must be taught before students can learn the higher order strategies (Gleason, 1995).

The teacher begins by explaining the common elements of a familiar genre, such as a story, and modeling how to look for those elements in a story. Predicting and finding story elements is emphasized by recording text information on a text map or story frame, as in Figure 9.5. Students are provided both prompted and independent practice in finding and recording information from stories they read. The teacher then models how to use story notes from the text map or story frame to compose a summary of the story. When students are able to write their own story summaries, they are taught how to plan and write original stories using a story map.

Shanahan (1988) suggested several guidelines for integrating reading and writing, among which are the following:

1. Teach both reading and writing. They are not as similar as once widely believed. Studies show only low to moderate correlations between single measures of reading and writing. Sometimes good readers are poor writers, and good writers are not always the best readers.
2. Reflect the developmental nature of the reading–writing relationship, which changes across developmental levels. For beginning readers and writers, an integrated approach might emphasize sound–symbol correspondence and spelling patterns. Higher level ways of relating reading and writing are through organizational style, syntax, and word knowledge.
3. Make the reading–writing connection explicit. Encourage students to recognize the similarities.
4. Emphasize communications. Critical reading requires consideration of the author's intentions and evaluation of quality of text. Similarly, a good writer considers the needs of the audience, taking the reader's perspective.
5. Teach reading and writing in meaningful contexts. Emphasize the purposes for which adults use literacy.

Gleason and Issacson (2001) believe the word *connected* may represent the desired goal better than the word *integrated* does. Not every literacy-building activity requires reading and writing simultaneously. Instead, "side-by-side" instruction reveals the sameness of language structures, and in connecting reading and writing, literacy skills can build upon each other.

Story		
Character	Who is the story about? Describe the character.	
Setting	Where does the story take place?	When does the story take place?
Goal	What is the problem that has to be solved?	
Actions	What happens? What does the character do to achieve his or her goal? First, Next, Then,	
Result	How does the story end? How does the character feel?	

Figure 9.5 An Organizational Frame Using a Story Text Structure

Spelling

Spelling is part of the conventions component of writing. Most children with learning problems have difficulties with spelling. Some cannot even demonstrate basic sound–symbol correspondence as they write two- and three-letter words. Others may practice for hours at home with their parents, only to forget almost all the words a week after the Friday test.

Basal Spellers

Content

When using a basal spelling text with a student who has learning problems, a few things must be kept in mind. Many of the activities in a spelling text are not really spelling. Copying or alphabetizing words, doing crossword puzzles, or looking up definitions may have value for certain study skills, but these activities are not spelling. Strictly speaking, spelling is defined as writing a word after hearing it (in your head or when spoken by some else) without a visual cue. This is the skill that must be taught and practiced.

Sequence of Skills

Not all basal texts are sequenced well. For example, children who are just learning to spell can be easily confused by having to sort out whether to use *ir, er,* or *ur* when they hear these sounds all presented together. Being able to discriminate which one to use is important to a good speller, but discrimination should come later. When words are first introduced, any possible confusion should be avoided.

Amount of Review

Insufficient review is another common problem in basal texts. The authors of many basal texts make the class wait 6 or 7 weeks before providing review units. A child who could barely remember 15 words long enough to spell them correctly on Friday will be hopeless at keeping them in long-term memory for 6 weeks without any practice.

Assessing Spelling Problems

Error Analysis

The first step in helping students with a spelling problem is to look at the type of mistake they make most frequently. Do spelling errors occur most frequently at the beginning, the middle, or the end of the word? Is the problem usually with vowels, consonants, or those funny vowel–consonant clusters such as *igh, alk,* and *ough*? Often the problem lies in not knowing an important rule, such as doubling the final consonant before adding the suffix, or dropping the silent *e* before adding *-ing*.

Let's use Millie as an example. Although Millie did fairly well the first 2 or 3 weeks of school, she began doing badly on spelling tests, even with help from her parents in the evenings. It soon became clear to her teacher that Millie could not keep up with the rest of her class. The teacher was prepared to put Millie on an individualized spelling program but did not know exactly where to start her. The teacher decided to test Millie informally, selecting one or two representative words from each lesson, going back to the beginning of the book. She made an answer sheet for Millie like the one shown in Figure 9.6. Then she gave Millie 10 to 15 words each day until she thought she had a good enough sample to place her appropriately in an individualized program.

From this informal assessment, Millie's teacher identified five spelling objectives to work on: (a) words with the vowel combination *oa,* (b) words beginning with the digraph *wh-,* (c) words with the *igh* cluster, (d) two or three irregular words such as *enough,* and (e) the spelling rule about changing *y* to *i* before adding the *-es* suffix. Finding words for each objective in the basal text was easy. The teacher decided to look quickly through a lower level spelling book as well, to find a few more words that would fit the objectives for Millie.

Spelling Test

	Vowel	Consonant	Cluster	Irregular Word	Rule
c 1. said					
✓2. bot (boat)	oa				
✓3. site (sight)			igh		
✓4. enof				enough	
✓5. babys					y→i
✓6. wich (which)		wh			
7.					
8.					
9.					
10.					

Figure 9.6 Informal Spelling Assessment for Millie

Individualized Spelling

Spelling words may be given to students in two ways:

1. A fixed list, which is a group of related words that a student must learn in its entirety before going on to the next group.
2. A flow list, to which new words are added one at a time and other words are dropped one at a time as they are mastered. A flow list changes every day as words are dropped and added.

FIXED LIST   Each week's word list can be chosen from the problems identified through the informal assessment. They may be grouped according to a common phonic element (e.g., *oa* or *wh*), or they may be simply a list of various misspelled words in the order they were given on the test. If the student had trouble mastering 15 to 20 words per week, the contract should start with only 5 to 8 words per week. If the student spells all 8 correctly, he or she then can tackle 10 words per week, then perhaps 12, and so forth. In addition to the words the teacher chooses, the student may want to choose some words—vocabulary from a reading or social studies lesson. The teacher also may want to add one or two words misspelled in the student's written composition. Figure 9.7 is an example of a weekly fixed-list contract from which the student can choose a variety of practice activities.

From the figure it is clear that the students are tested on the words every day; every day they must spell the words. The practice activities are useful reinforcement of spelling skills, but they are not intended as a substitute for the actual exercise of hearing the word and writing it without a visual cue. Words can be dictated by another student as well as by the teacher. After the test the students correct their own words. The teacher—or tutor—can either spell the words aloud, write the words on the chalkboard, or both, as the children follow along, comparing the teacher's spelling to their own. Finally, review words are added to every group of words. Each word learned should pop up periodically and frequently as a review word, keeping it in the students' minds, rather than appearing only in a review test 6 or 7 weeks later.

FLOW LIST   Words also can be presented on a flow list, a list that changes every day as the student masters each word. An example of a flow list is shown in Figure 9.8. The teacher circles the number of each new word assigned to the student. A correctly spelled word is marked with a C and an incorrect one with a checkmark. Words that are learned are crossed out. Millie's teacher decided that Millie should be able to spell each word correctly for 3 days in a row before it could be crossed off the list.

Even when a word is crossed off the list, it is not forgotten. Beginning the second week, Millie's teacher quizzed her every day on two review words from previous weeks, as Millie had a tendency to forget them. Overlearning (spelling each word 3 days in a row) and periodic review are two teaching strategies that increase retention.

Spelling Contract

Name _____ Week of _____

Tricky Words	Reading Book	Review Words
_____	Choose _____ Words	_____

_____   _____   _____

_____   _____   _____

_____

_____

Every day:

Test

Correct

Practice

Practice Activities:

☐ Write your words on the chalkboard using your very best writing. Erase them, and write them again without looking at your contract.

☐ Do a spelling worksheet.

☐ Do Copy-Cover-Compare.

☐ Spell all your words on the computer.

☐ Write each word in a sentence.

☐ Spell each word to a friend.

☐ Use the tape recorder. Say the word. Look and spell. Turn your contract over and spell it without looking. Play it back to check.

Figure 9.7   Fixed-List Spelling Contract

Teaching Concepts

A considerable amount of research has been done on methods of teaching spelling. Incidental instruction during "teachable moments," weekly spelling tests, and use of personal dictionaries alone are unlikely to provide appropriate instruction for poor spellers. According to Berninger and colleagues (2000), the most effective programs for children who have difficulty spelling consist of the following (p. 133):

1. A systematic spelling curriculum used at all grade levels with students placed at their instructional (not grade) level each year
2. Daily writing from dictation, child-generated composing

Spelling list: __6__ words   Name __Millie__

Word	M	T	W	Th	F	M	T	W	Th	F	M	T	W	Th	F
(1) coat	c	c	c			c									
(2) boat	c	c	c				c								
(3) soap	c	c	c												
(4) soapy	✓	c	c	c		c									
(5) road	c	c	c				c								
(6) fight	✓	✓	c	c	c										
(7) fighter				c	✓	c	c	c							
(8) fighting					✓	c	✓	c	c						
(9) sight						c	c	c							
(10) night						c	c	c							
(11) tonight						c	✓	c	c						
(12) midnight							✓	c	✓						
(13) mighty							c	c							
(14) mighty							c	c							
(15) light															
(16) lighter															
(17) babies															
(18) pennies															
(19) families															
(20) stories															

(Review — bracket grouping words 1–6)

Figure 9.8   Example of a Flow List

3. Explicit instruction and feedback at multiple levels, especially for letter sounds, whole word, onset-rime, and syllable structure types

A few tips follow.

Study Strategy

Teaching students with learning problems a metacognitive strategy has been shown to be effective in increasing their ability to learn and remember the spelling of words. Copy-Cover-Compare (in Figure 9.7) is a simple study strategy. Others require more involvement from the student. The steps in this strategy are as follows:

1. Read the word and spell it aloud.
2. Close your eyes and try to remember how the word looks.
3. Copy the word.
4. Trace the word with your pencil and spell it.
5. Cover the word and write it.
6. Check your spelling and fix if necessary.
7. Repeat steps 5 and 6 two more times.

Guided Self-Correction

Have the students correct their own spelling. Spell the word aloud as the students point to each letter on the paper. Immediately correct misspelled words and praise generously for words spelled correctly. Guided self-correction (under the teacher's direction) is the single most important factor in learning to spell (Christine & Hollingsworth, 1966).

Peer Tutoring

Students improve their spelling skills when given time and opportunities to practice. The Classwide Peer Tutoring (CWPT) (Delquadri, Greenwood, Whorton, Carta, & Hall, 1986) approach is a strategy students can use to receive immediate feedback and continual error correction. The approach takes about 20 minutes a day for at least three days a week. The basic strategy for the CWPT is to have students work in pairs with the teacher providing feedback. Pairing can either be random or based on personality or ability.

On the first day of instruction, the spelling words are selected. The words can come from any source, including a basal, word banks, or student self-selection. Each student creates a set of flashcards; each card has one spelling word written on it. During the next two, three, or four days the students practice spelling words together. During CWPT one student is the tutor and the other is the tutee for 10 minutes; then they switch roles.

Cooperative Practice

Another approach that uses peer interaction is called *cooperative practice*. With this spelling strategy, pairs of students study together. The tutor dictates each spelling word while the tutee simultaneously writes and spells the dictated term. When the word is spelled correctly, the speller earns 2 points. If the word is spelled incorrectly, the tutor spells the word correctly aloud, and the tutee writes the word correctly three times before being awarded 1 point. Bonus points are awarded by the teacher for good tutoring behavior (Graham, 1999).

Cooperative practice may be built around any kind of game format—for example, basketball or football. For the nonsports enthusiast, points can be earned that correspond to the number of moves a child can make on any standard game, such as, checkers or Chutes and Ladders.

Spell-Checkers

As technology becomes more sophisticated, less expensive, and easier to use, the use of spell-check programs to assist with spelling has become increasingly popular. Careful analysis of the students' skills is necessary to determine what type of spell-checker would be most useful. In order to spell, students must be able to name letters and produce letters with a pencil or word processor without too much fine-motor difficulty. In addition, spelling requires the students to have knowledge of spelling rules, such as capitalization, punctuation, and specific irregular sound–symbol relationships, for example, /ph/, *qu* (Maki, Vauras, & Vainio, 2002).

Spell-checkers are able to provide corrections for misspelled words using keyboarding and spelling-rule probabilities. In other words, spell-checkers make the best guess based on typical types of spelling errors. Unfortunately, students with severe spelling issues do not make typical kinds of spelling errors (Montgomery, Karlan, & Coutinho, 2001). To be effective with students with severe spelling issues, therefore, spell-checkers must have a voice-recognition or speech-recognition component.

Handwriting

Research Findings

Handwriting legibility is important not only as a means of communication, but also as a factor influencing perceptions about how well a person thinks or presents ideas. When adults are asked to rate several versions of a child's paper that differ only in handwriting legibility, neatly written papers are always assigned higher marks for overall quality than are papers of poorer penmanship (Graham, 1999).

Rate of production is also an important factor when discussing handwriting. Students whose handwriting rate is very slow or much slower than the class average can lose valuable information when attempting to take notes or complete essays in class assignments or on tests. For example, students with learning disabilities have been found to require 50 minutes to complete a task that would take most students just 30 minutes to finish (Graham, 1999).

Existing speech-to-text voice- or speech-recognition programs such as Dragon NaturallySpeaking from Dragon Systems, Inc. are now able to transcribe continuous speech or dictated speech with relatively high accuracy approximately 46 times faster than adults typically write. Such programs have the potential to revolutionize writing instruction or, at a minimum, to compensate for slow rates of writing production (De La Paz, 2000).

Patterns in Young Children

In his study of very young children, Simner (1981) uncovered a "grammar of action," tacit rules that guide the way children construct geometric figures. Typically, children begin at the topmost, leftmost point and proceed downward and around. For example, the expected stroke for *b* is shown in Figure 9.9. This stroke pattern occurred in 85% of the letters and numerals tested. When strokes from the top-left point did not fit the figure to be copied, children selected strokes that minimized the complexity of the copying task. Formal printing instruction does instill new stroke patterns in many children, but Simner found second-graders who still used the predicted pattern.

Cursive Writing

The challenge of learning new stroke patterns is complicated further when children learn cursive writing. Several cursive strokes run opposite to manuscript stroke patterns. Using *b* again as an example, the manuscript pattern that is taught begins with a downward vertical stroke followed by a clockwise circular stroke. The proper cursive *b,* however, begins with an upward vertical stroke, comes back down to the base line, and then makes a counterclockwise movement toward the midline, closer to the very young child's natural inclination. The beginning writer has to overcome natural inclinations to learn the prescribed form and then break those movement patterns to learn yet another set of movements.

Hand–Paper Positions

Most teachers insist on one hand-and-paper position. Wellman (1983) claimed that this is contrary to the child's natural orientation. Children often go through a range of positions that change as part of a developmental process. Wellman concluded, "It follows logically that children should be allowed to use whatever hand position is natural for them" (p. 56).

Teaching Implications

What are the implications of these findings for teaching? First, legibility, not aesthetically pleasing form, should be the major objective in handwriting. Cursive styles that involve ornate loops or varying letter heights are unnecessarily difficult for students who lack fine-motor skills.

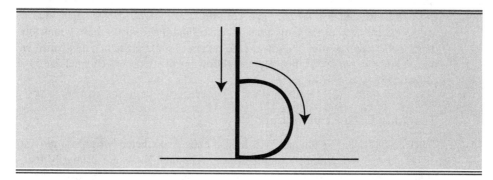

Figure 9.9   Expected Stroke for *b*

Further, primary students should not be taught letter strokes that later will have to be broken and relearned an entirely different way. Many districts are adopting italic or continuous flow scripts as a way of avoiding this problem. D'Nealian writing (Scott, Foresman, 1981) is an example of continuous flow style in which the connected and unconnected forms of writing use both the same slant and letter strokes. Children with learning problems, especially, should have a program in which writing patterns are consistent as practiced throughout their school careers.

A teacher should not meddle with a student's letter formation, slant, or hand-and-paper position unless these behaviors interfere with legibility or fluency. Obviously, when the letters a student makes cannot be deciphered, the teacher will have to teach the correct way to write them. Similarly, when a student's writing is legible but painstakingly slow because of hand position or the way the pencil is held, the student might be better off being taught a different way. If, however, a student writes as fluently as most students with a style that can be read easily, even if it is not pretty, the teacher should leave well enough alone and concentrate on spelling, reading, or other more important goals.

Assessing Handwriting

Assessing the effectiveness of a student's handwriting is a simple two-step process. First, fluency of handwriting can be measured informally by watching the student as the class copies a poem or a language-experience story from the chalkboard or overhead projector. The student's fluency is adequate if he or she finishes at about the same time as the other students.

The second measure is legibility—the speed and ease with which the student's writing can be read compared to other students' writing. A stopwatch may be useful here. If the writing sample is as easy to read as that of the other students, it is adequately legible. If a student's writing takes longer to produce or longer to read, the teacher should look more closely at specific behaviors, including position of the hand, how the pencil is held, spacing, or certain problematic letters or strokes.

Some letters are more difficult to create than others. In a study involving 300 children, Graham, Berninger, and Weintraub (1999) identified letters that were especially difficult for primary-age children. Six letters, *q, j, z, u, n,* and *k,* accounted for 48% of the omissions, miscues, and illegibilities these young students made when writing the lower-case letters of the alphabet. When considering illegible responses exclusively, the following five letters accounted for 54% of the miscues: *q, z, u, a,* and *j.*

Teaching Letter Formation

Three instructional techniques will help a child learn better writing: a moving model, verbalized prompts, and feedback. Although these are primarily techniques for use with students who have learning disabilities, they are effective with all children.

Moving Models

Models of letter formation depicting motion (the moving model) are more effective than still models (Wright & Wright, 1980). In individual or group instruction, the teacher starts by demonstrating the formation of the letter from beginning to end while pointing out the critical features of the letter. Most often the teacher models the letter more than once before asking the student to write it. The teacher also may demonstrate writing the letter again as part of a correction procedure if the student has difficulty forming it.

Verbalized Prompts

More effective than moving models alone are verbalized prompts, that is, auditory processes to reinforce visualization of letters. Verbal descriptions of the stroke sequence draw attention to previously unnoticed features and help the student remember the sequence. In addition, Hayes (1982) found that children who were taught to verbalize the stroke sequence themselves did better at reproducing letters than those who only listened to the teacher's verbal prompts. Providing children with visual and verbal demonstrations of letter motion, while directing them to say the sequence as they form the letters themselves, is the most effective strategy in teaching handwriting.

In the following example, the lowercase cursive *h* can be taught using the following verbal prompt:

> Up to the top,
> Loop down,
> Over the hump,
> Swing.

Some teachers ask students to visualize a human head, using ears, top of the head, nose, and chin as guide points. For example, *c* (either uppercase or lowercase) can be taught as follows (see Figure 9.10):

> Start at the ear,
> Over the top,
> Around,
> And under the chin.

Figure 9.10   Images for Verbalizing Stroke Sequences

A tricky letter such as *s* can be taught as follows:

> Start at the ear,
> Over the top,
> Across the nose,
> Under the chin.

Feedback

Teachers should always monitor children's first attempts to form letters and disallow unsupervised practice. Several researchers have demonstrated the effectiveness of immediate corrective feedback and positive reinforcement in improving students' handwriting. Hansen (1978), for example, found that having students evaluate their own writing produced positive changes in both rate and form. Teachers also have been successful in using reinforcement strategies ranging from giving stickers for carefully completed assignments (Idol-Maestas, 1983) to short free-activity periods for those whose writing has improved (Polloway & Smith, 1982).

Reversals

The best approach to letter reversals is immediate corrective feedback followed by massed practice of the problem letter. In addition, Graham and Miller (1980) have suggested the following strategies:

1. Have the student say the letter name while tracing and writing it simultaneously.
2. Associate the problem letter with another that does not cause confusion (e.g., *c* within *d*).
3. Give a verbal cue the child can use for writing the letter correctly.

Summary

Many children with learning problems have language problems. Language problems can also occur in children with hearing impairments, children who come from language-impoverished environments, or sometimes bilingual children who confuse the syntax of one language for another. Inclusion teachers are called upon to augment the limited time the speech clinician can spend with the student and also to expand the settings and situations in which new language skills can be applied and practiced.

Problems with language can be receptive, expressive, or both. An inclusion teacher can encourage language development by describing and discussing everything that happens in the classroom, reading to students, keeping conversations warm and reinforcing, and being sensitive to students who are self-conscious about their speech.

Written expression requires a solid base of language abilities, but it is a separate linguistic function, requiring additional cognitive and visual–motor processes. The five components of written expression are fluency, syntax, vocabulary, content, and conventions.

Spelling is an important aspect of written language. Allowing students to correct their own spelling is the single most effective way of improving spelling performance. Spelling contracts are useful in individualizing a spelling program for students who need special help.

The two most important criteria for acceptable handwriting are fluency and legibility. The most effective methods of teaching handwriting utilize a moving model and verbalized prompts. As in every other language skill, plenty of practice, careful feedback, and reinforcement are valuable in teaching handwriting.

References

Bailey, E. J. (1975). *Academic activities for adolescents with learning disabilities.* Denver, CO: Learning Pathways.

Bartley, N. (1993). Literature-based integrated language instruction and the language-deficient student. *Reading Research and Instruction, 32*(2), 31–37.

Berninger, V. (1999). Coordinating transcription and text generation in working memory during composing: Automatic and constructive processes. *Learning Disability Quarterly, 22*(2), 99–111.

Berninger, V. (1994). *Reading and writing acquisition: A developmental neuropsychological perspective.* Madison, WI: WCB Brown & Benchmark. Reprinted 1996, Westview Press, Boulder, CO.

Berninger, V., Vaughan, K., Abbott, R., Brooks, A., Begay, K., Curtin, G., et al. (2000). Language-based spelling instruction: Teaching children to make multiple connections between spoken and written words. *Learning Disability Quarterly, 23*(2), 117–135.

Cazden, C. B. (1972). *Child language and education.* New York: Holt, Rinehart & Winston.

Chomsky, C. (1969). *The acquisition of syntax in children from 5 to 10.* Cambridge, MA: MIT Press.

Christenson, S. L., Thurlow, M. L., & Ysseldyke, J. (1989). Written language instruction for students with mild handicaps: Is there enough quantity to ensure quality? *Learning Disability Quarterly, 12*(3), 219–229.

Christine, R. O., & Hollingsworth, P. M. (1966). An experiment in spelling. *Education, 86,* 565–567.

Cooper, C. R. (1977). Holistic evaluation of writing. In C. R. Cooper & L. Odell (Eds.), *Evaluating writing: Describing, measuring, judging* (pp. 3–31). Buffalo, NY: National Council of Teachers of English.

Corden, R. (2000). Reading-writing connections: The importance of interactive discourse. *English in Education, 34*(2), 35–44.

De La Paz, S. (2000). Composing via dictation and speech recognition systems: Compensatory technology for students with learning disabilities. *Learning Disability Quarterly, 22*(3), 173–182.

Delquadri, J., Greenwood, C. R., Whorton, D., Carta, J. J., & Hall, R. V. (1986). Classwide peer tutoring. *Exceptional Children, 52*(6), 535–542.

Deno, S., Marston, D., & Mirkin, P. (1982). Valid measurement procedures for continuous evaluation of written expression. *Exceptional Children, 48,* 368–371.

Elbow, P. (1991). *Writing with power: Techniques for mastering the writing process.* New York: Oxford University Press.

Englert, C. S., Raphael, T. E., & Anderson, L. M. (1992). Socially mediated instruction: Improving students' knowledge and talk about writing. *Elementary School Journal, 92*(4), 411–449.

Englert, C. S., Raphael, T., Fear, K., & Anderson, H. (1988). Students' metacognitive knowledge about how to write informational texts. *Learning Disability Quarterly, 11,* 18–46.

Foil, C. R., & Alber, S. R. (2002). Fun and effective ways to build your students' vocabulary. *Intervention in School and Clinic, 37*(3), 131–139.

Frank, M. (1979). *If you're trying to teach kids how to write, you've gotta have this book!* Nashville, TN: Incentive Publications.

Gleason, J. B. (2001). *The development of language* (5th ed.). Boston: Allyn & Bacon.

Gleason, M. M. (1995). Using direct instruction to integrate reading and writing for students with learning disabilities. *Reading & Writing Quarterly: Overcoming Learning Difficulties, 11*(1), 91–108.

Gleason, M., & Isaacson, S. (1991). The effects of four types of teacher spelling assistance on the written expression of mildly handicapped students. *Oregon Conference Monograph 1991* (pp. 107–111). Eugene: University of Oregon, Division of Teacher Education and Division of Special Education & Rehabilitation.

Gleason, M. M., & Issacson, S. (2001). Using the new basals to teach the writing process: Modifications for students with learning problems. *Reading and Writing Quarterly, 17,* 75–92 (18).

Graham, S. (1999). Handwriting and spelling instruction for students with learning disabilities: A review. *Learning Disability Quarterly, 22*(2), 78–94.

Graham, S., Berninger, V., & Weintraub, N. (1999). *What letters are difficult for young children?* Unpublished manuscript.

Graham, S., Boyer-Schick, K., & Tippets, E. (1989). The validity of the handwriting scale from the Test of Written Language. *Journal of Education Research, 82,* 166–171.

Graham, S., & Harris, K. R. (1989). Improving learning disabled students' skills at composing essays: Self-instructional strategy training. *Exceptional Children, 56,* 201–214.

Graham, S., & Harris, K. R. (1992). Cognitive strategy instruction in written language for learning disabled students. In S. Vogel (Ed.), *Educational alternatives for teaching students with learning disabilities* (pp. 95–115). New York: Springer Verlag.

Graham, S., Harris, K. R., MacArthur, C. A., & Schwartz, S. (1991). Writing and writing instruction for students with learning disabilities: Review of a research program. *Learning Disability Quarterly, 14,* 89–114.

Graham, S., & Miller, L. (1980). Handwriting research and practice: A unified approach. *Focus on Exceptional Children, 13*(2), 1–16.

Haden, C. A., Reese, E., & Fivush, R. (1996). Mothers' extra textual comments during storybook reading: Stylistic differences over time and across texts. *Discourse Processes, 21,* 135–169.

Hansen, C. L. (1978). Writing skills. In N. G. Haring, T. C. Lovitt, M. D. Eaton, & C. L. Hansen (Eds.), *The fourth R: Research in the classroom* (pp. 93–126). Columbus, OH: Charles E. Merrill.

Hayes, D. (1982). Handwriting practice: The effects of perceptual prompts. *Journal of Educational Research, 75,* 169–172.

Higgins, C. (2002). Using film text to support reluctant writers. *English in Education, 36*(1), 31–37.

Hughes, T. (1978). *What the British tell the U.S. about writing and reading.* Paper presented at Great Lakes Regional Conference of International Reading Association, Cincinnati. (ERIC Document Reproduction Service No. ED 175 020)

Idol-Maestas, L. (1983). *Special educator's consultation handbook.* Rockville, MD: Aspen.

Kitagawa, M. M. (1982). Expressive writing in Japanese elementary schools. *Language Arts, 59,* 18–22.

Maki, H. S., Vauras, M. M. S., & Vainio, S. (2002). Reflective spelling strategies for elementary school students with severe writing difficulties: A case study. *Learning Disability Quarterly, 25*(3), 189–207.

Marchian, M. L., & Alber, S. R. (2001). The write way: Tips for teaching the writing process to resistant writers. *Intervention in School and Clinic, 30*(3), 154–162.

Marcus, M. (1977). *Diagnostic teaching of the language arts.* New York: Wiley.

Mittler, P., Jeffree, D., Wheldall, K., & Berry, P. (1977). Assessment and remediation of language comprehension and production in severely subnormal children. *Collected Original Resources in Education, 1*(2), 2572–2799.

Montessori, M. (1964). *The Montessori method* (A. E. George, Trans.). New York: Schocken Books.

Montgomery, D. J., Karlan, G. R., & Coutinho, M. (2001). The effectiveness of word processor spell checker programs to produce target words for misspellings generated by students with learning disabilities. *Journal of Special Education Technology, 16*(2), 27–41.

Morton, L. L. (1986). A single subject study of the effects of time on task and time of day on productivity and achievement in a dysgraphic student. *Canadian Journal for Exceptional Children, 3*(1), 23–28.

Moskowitz, B. A. (1982). The acquisition of language. In H. B. Allen & M. D. Linn (Eds.), *Readings in applied English linguistics* (pp. 164–180). New York: Knopf.

Owston, R. D., Murphy, S., & Wideman, H. H. (1992). The effects of word processing on students' writing quality and revision strategies. *Research in the Teaching of English, 26*(3), 249–276.

Polloway, E. A., & Smith, J. E., Jr. (1982). *Teaching language skills to exceptional learners.* Denver, CO: Love.

Rittenhouse, R. K., & Steams, K. (1982). Teaching metaphor to deaf children. *American Annals of the Deaf, 127,* 12–17.

Scott, Foresman and Co. (1981). *D'Nealian handwriting.* Glenview, IL: Author.

Senechal, M. (1997). The differential effect of storybook reading on preschoolers' acquisition of expressive and receptive vocabulary. *Journal of Child Language, 24,* 123–138.

Shanahan, T. (1988). The reading-writing relationship: Seven instructional principles. *Reading Teacher, 41,* 636–647.

Simner, M. L. (1981). The grammar of action and children's printing. *Developmental Psychology, 17,* 866–871.

Slater, W. H., & Horstman, F. R. (2002). Teaching reading and writing to struggling middle school and high school students: The case for reciprocal teaching. *Preventing School Failure, 45*(4), 163–166.

Smith, F. (1982). *Writing and the writer.* New York: Holt, Rinehart & Winston.

Spears, A. K. (1992). Reassessing the status of Black English. *Language in Society, 21*(4), 675–682.

Straw, S. B. (1981). Grammar and the teaching of writing: Analysis versus synthesis. In V. Froese & S. B. Straw (Eds.), *Research in the language arts: Language and schooling* (pp. 147–161). Baltimore: University Park Press.

Torgesen, J., & Kail, R. V. (1980). Memory processes in exceptional children. In B. Keogh (Ed.), *Advances in special education* (pp. 55–99). Greenwich, CT: JAI Press.

Valcourt, G. (1989). Inviting rewriting: How to respond to a first draft. *Canadian Journal of English Language Arts, 12*(1-2), 29–36.

van der Lely, H. K. J. (1990). Comprehension of reversible sentences in specifically language-impaired children. *Journal of Speech and Hearing Disorders, 55*(1), 101–117.

Vygotsky, L. S. (1962). *Thought and language.* Cambridge, MA: MIT Press.

Wellman, M. A (1983). Teaching handwriting: Implications of neuropsychological research. *Reading Improvement, 20,* 54–57.

Wong, Y. L., Butler, D. L., Ficzere, S. A., & Kuperis, S. (1996). Teaching low achievers and students with learning disabilities to plan, write, and revise opinion essays. *Journal of Learning Disabilities, 29,* 197–212.

Wong, Y. L., Butler, D. L., Ficzere, S. A., & Kuperis, S. (1997). Teaching adolescents with learning disabilities and low achievers to plan, write, and revise compare-and-contrast essays. *Learning Disabilities Research and Practice, 12,* 2–15.

Wright, C. D., & Wright, J. P. (1980). Handwriting: The effectiveness of copying from moving versus still models. *Journal of Educational Research, 74,* 95–98.

Mathematics Evaluation in Inclusion Settings

Kathleen McCoy and Rebecca Gehrke

KEY TERMS

- ◆ algorithms
- ◆ conceptual learning
- ◆ error analysis
- ◆ Piagetian theory
- ◆ problem solving
- ◆ procedural learning

Today is the day for the district math test. Ms. Hermansen takes a deep breath and looks at the expectant faces of her fourth-grade students. What they are expecting varies with each expression. Matt looks worried. He is in a white-knuckled hand grip. Steven is tapping his leg up and down to the tune of a very anxious drummer. Yvonne, in contrast, appears to have zoned out, alerting Ms. Hermansen that this student has already given up hope for success even before seeing the test material. Ms. Hermansen can relate to Yvonne because once upon a time she too felt at a loss when looking at numbers. Ms. Hermansen thanks her fourth-, fifth- and sixth-grade teachers for helping her unlock the mysteries surrounding missing variables and trains that meet somewhere along an imaginary track. Now the time has arrived for Ms. Hermansen to spring into action. Time to reduce the negatives and exaggerate the positives of the experience … hmm, sounds like a math solution, thinks Ms. Hermansen with an internal chuckle.

Children who have problems with mathematics fall everywhere along the intelligence continuum. Very bright children, as well as children with known *organic disorders* (i.e., disorders found in physical or neurological, usually brain, injury or damage), can all have difficulty learning math. Once children have gone beyond learning the rote skills involved in arithmetic and are asked to solve problems, the number of learners who have trouble with mathematics increases considerably. This increase is also apparent in children who have disabilities.

Just as in the general population of children, not all children with disabilities have problems learning mathematics, but a great many do. Materials and techniques designed to compensate for sensory deficits, such as visual or auditory impairments, may be the only accommodations necessary for some of these children. The teacher will have to manipulate the teaching–learning situation for other children in ways that best fit their mathematical learning needs, as well as attend to cognitive and affective factors that influence mathematics learning.

Factors Affecting Math Learning

Whether students are identified as having a learning disability in mathematics or not, several factors can affect students' successful acquisition of math skills. These factors, which are related to both teacher and student attitudes and abilities, include such variables as math anxiety, math self-concept, learned helplessness, individual learning style, teacher attitude, and teacher content knowledge. The task of the mathematics teacher is to consider the effect of these factors on the students' ability or inability to learn mathematical content and processes.

Math Anxiety

The negative response to mathematics learning has reached such a grand proportion as to merit its own label: math anxiety. Math anxiety is among the fairest of the equal-opportunity phobias, crossing boundaries of sex, race, age, and intelligence. Research shows that more than two thirds of Americans have had negative experiences with mathematics from kindergarten through college (Jackson & Leffingwell, 1999). These negative experiences include teachers exhibiting hostile and impatient behaviors with students who do not immediately grasp a concept and instructors perpetuating gender bias in teaching mathematics. Math anxiety also may be caused by a mismatch between instruction and student ability. Indeed, the National Council of Teachers of Mathematics (NCTM, 2000) recognizes the severity of the problem when they identify equity as their first principle for mathematics. This principle states that mathematics education requires high expectations and strong support for all students and that all students have the right to learn math and feel confident in their math abilities.

Teachers may employ many strategies to help students overcome math anxiety. They can change attitudes by using useful instructional techniques, by focusing on what each individual student can do, and by being sensitive to past histories of frustration and failure (Furner & Duffy, 2002). Since the likelihood of mathematics anxiety increases as students progress through the grades, early detection and remediation are imperative (Furner & Duffy, 2002; Renga & Dalla, 1993). When teachers employ best practices for teaching mathematics and differentiate their instruction to accommodate the abilities and learning styles of students with a range of abilities, anxiety is lessened.

Math Self-Concept

Math anxiety is both a product of and an influence on one's self-concept of ability. Many math-anxious children view themselves poorly and think they have low ability. Students who constantly receive messages about their low ability come to expect negative feedback about their performance; conversely, students who have a well-established positive self-concept about their capabilities do well (Furner & Berman, 2003; Renga & Dalla, 1993).

Self-concept with respect to mathematics is well established in the early school years. As early as fourth grade, fatalism toward math achievement begins to set in, and that fatalism grows steadily with each succeeding grade. Studies that relate math self-concept or self-confidence to achievement show a positive significant correlation between achievement and confidence. The more confident students are in their ability to calculate and problem solve, the higher their tests scores are likely to be (Senturk, Whipple, Ho, Zimmer, Chiu, & Wang, 2000).

Learned Helplessness

The need to relieve the tension surrounding math learning is closely related to the psychological term *learned helplessness*. In learned helplessness the critical factor is not the aversive event or situation (in this case, math learning) but, rather, the perception or feeling surrounding the relationship between the learner's behavior and the occurrence of math instruction. If learners interpret failure in one or many math problems as inevitable, they can easily begin to feel that learning mathematics is beyond or out of their control. Students see no sense in trying to solve the problem because the chances for success are not within their control. Learners must come to believe that success in mathematics is possible. This feeling can be brought about through class management of the mathematics material itself.

Renga and Dalla (1993) along with Furner and Duffy (2002) recommend the following teacher behaviors as ways to ease anxieties about math and prevent the development of learned helplessness related to math:

- Provide an environment in which children experience success.
- Help children emphasize the positive attributes of effort and persistence, while assisting them in tolerating frustration.
- Give feedback on both correct and incorrect work. For incorrect work, point out patterns of errors and suggest strategies for improvement.
- Be alert to behaviors such as delaying tactics or handing in poor-quality work that may signal a problem.
- Relate past learning to concepts currently being taught.

Providing successful experiences for students involves paying close attention to the level of difficulty of the tasks and providing students with strategies for dealing with difficult tasks so they are able to feel a sense of control over the outcome.

Learning Style

Failure to learn mathematics can also be attributed to the type and amount of instruction the student receives. Teachers in inclusive settings bear the responsibility for creating materials and learning environments that are conducive to the mathematics learning style of all students. Recognizing different learning styles and subsequently adapting teaching strategies accordingly can facilitate student learning. Teachers can identify learner styles by asking screening questions and then use this information to direct successful instruction for all learners.

Strong, Thomas, Perini, and Silver (2004) reported that student differences in learning mathematics tend to cluster into four mathematical learning styles:

- The mastery style, in which people tend to work step by step
- The understanding style, where learners search for categories and patterns
- The interpersonal style, where students learn through conversation and personal association
- The self-expressive style, characterized by a student's visualizing and creating images

Students favoring the *mastery style* learn most easily from repetitive practice and instruction that emphasizes step-by-step demonstration. Jody prefers to work step by step. She feels a certain degree of comfort and security when she knows exactly what she is supposed to do and what sequence to follow. Teachers who work with students like Jody can compile check sheets and attach them to assignments. This allows students to check off the steps as they complete the task.

James, on the other hand, searches for categories and patterns when learning math. As a result, he falls into the second category—the *understanding style*. He benefits most from approaches that emphasize the concepts and the reasoning behind mathematical operations. Teachers of students like James need to encourage and then praise their students when they discover patterns. Initially, the teacher will need to make the patterns very obvious and then gradually increase the complexity.

Blaine is a social creature. Left alone he wilts and dies mathematically speaking, but when he is with his peers he loves to talk about and apply mathematical concepts. Students favoring the *interpersonal style* learn best with cooperative learning techniques, as well as real-life contexts that connect learning to everyday life.

Arnis is a free spirit when approaching mathematics. He has a *self-expressive style* of learning. He despises routine drill and practice, struggling with memorization for the sake of memorization. Arnis and other learners like him learn best when allowed to explore and visualize nonroutine approaches to problem solving (Strong et al., 2004).

By incorporating a variety of activities, materials, and techniques into mathematics instruction, the teacher is able to address the needs of an array of learning styles and strengths. Mathematics instruction cannot happen without considering the role of the child's learning problems and styles. Identifying learner styles by asking screening questions can direct how instruction is to take place. Whether the child does or does not have disabilities, the teacher must be sensitive to the extent to which learning styles influence math lessons. Learning style inventories, whether teacher-made or commercially produced, should be included in math evaluation.

Teacher Attitude

The classroom math environment affects the learner's math performance and interest. The teacher is by far one of the most significant people influencing the learner's willingness to approach mathematics. To truly understand mathematics education, the effects of the teacher's attitudes must be considered (D'Emidio-Caston, 1993; Furner & Berman, 2003; Jackson & Leffingwell, 1999). Even though the teacher may enjoy mathematics, this enjoyment may not transfer to the students. The joyful mathematics teacher, however, can at least model through body language and verbal expressions how interesting, fun, and exciting math can be. The enthusiastic math teacher is also most likely to bring in real world examples that engage the students.

In contrast, a greater number of teachers fall into the category of having a negative attitude toward math themselves. Their anxiety is evident in research with preservice teachers as well (Wodlodko, Willson, & Johnson, 2004). Teachers who are afraid of math can pass on math anxiety to their students by modeling their own discomfort with the subject (Furner & Berman, 2003). Students tend to internalize their instructors' interest in and enthusiasm for teaching mathematics (Jackson & Leffingwell, 1999). Jackson and Leffingwell (1999) recommended the following behaviors for teachers to create a positive environment for learning mathematics:

- Disclosing that they may have overcome math anxiety as a student
- Making a conscious effort to project their interest in and enjoyment of mathematics
- Offering positive reinforcement and time to students suffering from math anxiety
- Making mutual respect a rule in order to ensure that the classroom environment is psychologically safe—this, more specifically, involves eliminating any hostile instructor behavior in terms of embarrassing students who are having difficulty and not assuming gender differences in mathematical interest and ability.

By manipulating the environment as well as the material and by presenting high probabilities of success systematically, confidence and subsequent higher expectation levels can be built in the math-fearful child. Success is the most powerful tool the teacher of mathematics can use when working with math-anxious students.

A supportive teacher is vital to a healthy instructional atmosphere. Anxiety can be reduced by manipulating the social climate within the classroom. Teachers who show a positive attitude toward math and avoid the negative experiences that increase anxiety in students can reduce math anxiety (Reys, Lindquist, Smith, & Suydam, 2004). Openness to learning mathematics is the first step toward high-level skill acquisition.

Teacher expectations are especially critical when instructing math-anxious students. Teachers who believe their students will achieve usually find ways to make their beliefs come true. The reverse is also true. By attributing success or failure in mathematics to disability labels and associated characteristics in ability, teachers may inadvertently create an environment of failure. A teacher's image of the child's low ability is likely to result in an unwillingness to interact with or even help the child because of a belief that the child cannot learn. On the other hand, if the teacher holds the belief that "all children can learn," he or she can assess those factors in the environment that may be causing anxiety or a fear of failure in students and adjust materials and instruction accordingly.

Mathematics Evaluation

Evaluation of math performance should include an accounting of the child's physiological and psychological makeup as well as an examination of the teacher's behavior in relation to fostering positive attitudes toward mathematics. With children who typically experience failure in mathematics, these areas of evaluation may be as important to math success as the actual content of math itself.

Attitudes and physiology aside, the entire area of mathematics content should be evaluated. In 1989 the NCTM published its *Curriculum and Evaluation Standards for School Mathematics*, which comprehensively outlined the content for K–12 curricula. In 2000, the NTCM published an update of the standards in *Principles and Standards for School Mathematics,* which stated the essential components of a high-quality school mathematics program. Both documents emphasized the shift of evaluation and instruction from strictly computing skills toward the acquisition and application of math content. Detailed descriptions of the subdivisions of content and process standards can be found in mathematics texts or at the NTCM website: www.ntcm.org. For practical reasons, if not necessarily mathematically precise ones, math content may be reviewed from three general skill areas: *fundamental* or *basic concepts, algorithms*, and *problem solving*. We will look briefly at evaluation in these three areas.

Evaluating Fundamental and Basic Concepts

Definitions

Basic concepts consist of the most rudimentary but fundamental ideas upon which all further arithmetic or mathematics instruction is based. They include topics in number, spatial, or data categories, in some combination. The content that usually receives the most instructional attention is number facts. Basic facts for addition and multiplication are defined as combinations in which both addends or factors are single digits (Van de Walle, 1994). Subtraction and division facts are related to a corresponding addition or multiplication fact. Thus, 13 - 4 = 9 is a basic subtraction fact because both "parts" or addends are single digits (4 and 9). But 13 - 2 = 11 is not a basic fact, as 11 is not a single digit. The commutative law (a + b = b + a) helps children organize math facts into manageable chunks (e.g., 3 + 2 = 5, 2 + 3 = 5, 5 – 3 = 2, 5 – 2 = 3). If students have not developed an understanding of commutativity, they perceive 390 separate facts (100 addition; 100 subtraction; 100 multiplication; 90 division, as division by 0 is undefined), which they must master individually. These number facts and their various combinations sometimes are referred to as addition, subtraction, multiplication, and division tables.

Even with widely available technology such as hand-held calculators, solving basic facts ultimately requires automatic stimulus–response performance. Automaticity is achieved through appropriately designed drill activities (Usnick, 1991). Knowledge of basic facts in arithmetic is similar to word recognition skills in reading. The stimulus in word recognition is the written word; in basic facts the stimulus is the number combination (e.g., 1 + 1 =). The goal is automatic recognition that lets the learner advance to more complex activities. In reading, these activities culminate in comprehension. In mathematics, they culminate in problem solving.

Example 1: Look at these flash cards and tell me the answers:

$3 \times 3 =$ _____ $7 \times 6 =$ _____ $5 \times 9 =$ _____

Example 2: Write the answers to these problems as quickly and accurately as you can:

6	4	3	1	9
+2	+3	+1	+1	+6

Evaluation of basic facts can be written or verbal. It also can include the notion of rate (e.g., "as quickly as you can," "in your fastest time").

Evaluation Components

Each additional evaluation component (e.g., written or oral, timed or untimed) gives the teacher more information about the child's flexibility in using or reading the basic concepts tested. The evaluative catch is to be sure that the additional information is valuable instructionally. If, for example, the teacher is interested in determining if a child can identify circles, squares, and triangles, he or she probably will design items that require the child to identify those shapes.

Identification tasks usually require activities such as marking, selecting, and pointing out, any of which can be done either orally or in writing. Unfortunately, because these concepts are so rudimentary, teachers tend to complicate the child's action (e.g., "draw" a circle, square, or triangle). By changing the word *mark* to *draw,* they have asked a fundamentally different question. A *mark* question requires a simple discrimination task. A *draw* question requires the child to create some desired product. A production task is not appropriate if the teacher's interest is in the child's ability to identify an item.

Task Demands for Children With Disabilities

Attention must be paid to the task demands relative to the child's skills. Some children, with and without disabilities, show delays in the fine-motor skills of writing; others (e.g., some children with cerebral palsy) cannot write at all. Production tasks or tasks that require manual dexterity may place unrealistic demands on these children. Therefore, results from tasks that are not sensitive to the child's skill levels most likely will result in a misleading interpretation of actual task knowledge. Knowledge of task demands, children's skills relative to task response, and specific information to be evaluated apply equally to the basic skills, algorithms, and problem-solving areas of mathematics.

Evaluating Skill in Using Algorithms

Definitions

Algorithms are the natural extension of basic number–fact computations. Whereas number facts require simple associations, algorithms are the series of separate steps required in more complex calculations such as long division and addition of fractions with unlike denominators. An algorithm consists of a precise, systematic method for solving a class of problem and includes the ability to take the input information, follow a set of rules, perform the definitive number of steps, and arrive at an accurate, conclusive answer (Mauer, 1998).

Doing problems or computations that require algorithms is somewhat similar to using phonics skills to determine a new word. Just as the individual sounds are learned previously in phonics, the number facts are readily within the learner's grasp. With phonics, a reader uses systematic rules for applying sounds both in terms of the isolated sound and in an acceptable sequence for blending. The ultimate conclusion is production of the appropriate word. So, too, with the application of algorithms.

Using isolated number facts, a child also must follow a prescribed step-by-step sequence to arrive at the correct solution of a complex computation.

Example 1: Solve the following problems:

$$14 \qquad 36 \qquad 930$$
$$\underline{+\ 14} \qquad \underline{+\ 6} \qquad \underline{-\ 127} \qquad 52\ \overline{)\ 3895}$$

Example 2: Compute the following:

$$\frac{5}{6} = \frac{\ }{12} \qquad \frac{1}{3} = \frac{\ }{9} \qquad \frac{3}{7} = \frac{\ }{14}$$

Example 3: Calculate the following:

$$80\% \times 50 =$$
$$160\% \times 10 =$$
$$25\% \times 73 =$$
$$9\% \times 100 =$$

Algorithms permit the user to perform calculations that require more than memorizing a single idea or association. A lot of time is spent teaching algorithms in elementary school. Generally, the teacher shows the learners a standard algorithm (e.g., regrouping in addition or subtraction*). The child is expected to memorize the sequence and then apply the algorithm in various problems. A more developmentally appropriate approach to algorithms is to encourage students to construct their own. Students often "discover" algorithms that are historically older than those commonly taught in American schools. Students have been known to generate algorithms that mathematicians used more than 500 years ago. Unfortunately, many students are told that their way is incorrect simply because it is not the way the teacher or the parent solves the problem.

---

* Historically, regrouping in addition has been called *carrying* and in subtraction *borrowing*. Mathematicians are now referring to regrouping in addition as *trading* or *exchanging*. Regrouping in subtraction is now called *decomposition*. For the sake of nonmathematicians, *carrying* and *borrowing* will be used in this text.

Conceptual Versus Procedural Learning

The debate concerning the relative importance of conceptual versus procedural knowledge spanned much of the 20th century. Many educators have tried to differentiate students' skill at using algorithms from their understanding of the concepts involved in the algorithm. Some believe that teaching an understanding of the algorithm is essential for correct usage; others do not. Those who espouse conceptual understanding often stress that the abstract nature of the math relationship must be presented more concretely. Those who place themselves exclusively in one or the other camp are wrong, as procedural knowledge and conceptual knowledge are both important. Discussion should focus on how these two types of knowledge are related and how they support each other rather than on the superiority of one or the other.

MANIPULATIVES In the belief that manipulatives help develop conceptual knowledge, many mathematics educators advocate using hands-on materials such as sticks and blocks to represent the arithmetic concepts. The use of manipulatives provides an additional means of enhancing learning by connecting abstract concepts with concrete materials. To be effective, manipulatives must support the lesson's objectives and involve the active participation of each student (Reys et al., 2004). Focus should always remain on students' understanding of the concepts they are constructing while completing concrete, real-life activities related to the abstract symbols of mathematics. The length of time and the number of repetitions of activities using manipulatives are not necessarily as important in evaluating students' learning of math concepts as is allowing students the opportunity to discuss and reflect on their findings (Dougherty & Scott, 1993).

Children may calculate accurately but understand little of the "why" in the process of the algorithms. Understanding, then, must not be equated with the ability to follow a predesignated sequence leading to the solution of a given problem. The ability to manipulate an arithmetic algorithm correctly, with or without specified concrete objects, can develop with or without understanding. Many children routinely complete rote steps for working with algorithms. For example, Ricky always gets 100 on his math sheets, but he has no idea why the numbers are moved the way they are; he simply follows the directions and uses the appropriate sequence. For some children like Ricky, understanding the concepts behind the steps is developmentally too complex. At a later date, these children may begin to understand "the why of the what" they were doing. Although procedural understanding may help a child understand an algorithm, conceptual understanding of the algorithm may come later. When students encounter a problem that differs from problems for which they have learned an algorithmic procedure, conceptual knowledge enables them to see similarities between problems so they can adapt their procedural knowledge to the new situation or problem (Zemelman, Daniels, & Hyde, 1998).

EDUCATIONAL IMPLICATIONS The educational and evaluation implications are clear. For some children conceptual knowledge of the algorithm may not occur with initial teaching—or perhaps ever. Yet, many of these children can be expected to use the algorithm in a functionally positive way. After all, how many times do you think of the concept of place value (other than the decimal point as you balance your checkbook)? To wait for conceptual understanding of any given algorithm may prevent the child from using that and more complex algorithms in advanced arithmetic. However, though conceptual understanding is not necessary for algorithmic proficiency, it becomes important when students engage in problem-solving activities, especially those where no algorithmic (procedural) solution is obvious.

Evaluating Problem Solving

Definitions

Children use both conceptual and procedural knowledge in problem solving. When they use only a procedural approach, they miss out on developing a conceptual understanding and are subsequently unable to transfer math skills to new situations (Jonassen, Howland, Moore, & Marra, 2003). Although the term *problem solving* has many definitions, historically it has meant *word problems* or *story problems*. Students begin solving word problems early on in elementary school and continue on through high school mathematics. Story problems require students to do the following:

- Comprehend text information
- Visualize the data
- Recognize the structure of the problem
- Sequence and execute the solution activities
- Evaluate procedure and calculations (Lucangeli, Tresoldi, & Cendron, 1998)

The more able students are to relate story problems to their own environments, the greater their chances of success. The more firmly basic facts and computation procedures are established, the better able students are to concentrate on the problem-solving process.

Renewed Instructional Emphasis

Instruction in problem solving as being more than just word problems has gained considerable stature. Support for instruction in problem solving came in 1989 when the NCTM identified "mathematics as problem solving" in its standards. This emphasis stemmed from a number of sources, not the least of which was the National Assessment of Education Progress (NAEP) (National Assessment Governing Board, 2005). NAEP presented strong evidence suggesting that students were unable to choose correct operations in problem solving. The 2000 NCTM standards include problem solving among process standards. NCTM clearly supports the idea that solving problems is *the* major means of learning mathematics. Much current research and literature in the area of problem solving attempts to assist classroom teachers in moving mathematics instruction from strictly drill and practice towards teaching math through problem solving (Buschman, 2004).

IDENTIFYING CRITICAL SKILLS   The skills to be evaluated in problem solving are complex. Learning to solve problems and learning to memorize information require different ways of thinking and responding (Buschman, 2004). Jonassen (2003) recommended evaluating students' problem-solving skills using the following three kinds of assessment:

1. *Problem-solving transfer.* In order to determine if the students are able to apply problem-solving ability to new or different contexts, present the same kind of problems in a different context from that of the learning environment. Rate, time, or task can be transformed in new problems. Complexity of new problems can be increased in order to determine if students grasp the conceptual and procedural processes of the type of word problem you are presenting.
2. *Problem classification test.* Present students with a story problem and ask them to classify the problems rather than solve it. This is important in determining students' models and schema for different types of problems.
3. *Conceptual knowledge test.* Remember that students may not have learned the conceptual factors related to a type of story problem and are, instead, relying on a direct translation approach (i.e., they search for key words and numbers and translate them into an algorithm and do not understand relationships or underlying concepts). Students can be presented with word problems and asked to identify a statement that accurately states the relationships in the problem.

By focusing the evaluation on students' reasoning processes, the teacher is able to determine if students are grasping the underlying concepts and will be able to apply their learning to real-world situations.

INSTRUCTIONAL IMPLICATIONS   Problem solving, then, consists of more than simple memorization. Problem solving demands the use of various strategies, the ability to choose appropriate operations, and the ability to transfer problem-solving skills to other contexts (Fuchs & Fuchs, 2005). The increased emphasis on teaching and evaluating problem solving has implications for all inclusion teachers at all grade levels.

First, problem-solving strategies can be specifically taught. Teachers should systematically evaluate students' procedural and conceptual understanding in order to determine if students are using an effective strategy. Second, no one strategy is best for every type of problem or for every type of student. Supplying students with multiple tools from which to test their problem-solving abilities is essential. Some types of strategies used for problem solving are presented in chapter 11 on mathematics instruction. Last, students should be encouraged to verbalize as well as write about their problem-solving reasoning. An informal diagnostic math interview can be held between the teacher and an individual student to determine if the student is using any deficient or faulty cognitive routines to solve problems. Reflective and collaborative work in math helps both the teacher and the student determine the student's thinking processes (Kersaint & Chappel, 2004; Zemelman, 2003).

Diagnostic Mathematics Tools

Conceptual Analysis

To determine the teaching needs of a child, the teacher must perform a diagnostic evaluation of math content. True math diagnosis tells *why* something went wrong. Most evaluations, sadly, focus on the *what,* not the *why.* Commercial and teacher-made evaluations alike usually account for the correctness of a response only. Although production of an accurate response is a fundamental goal of math instruction, the logic of the child's thinking is equally important. Don't reject an answer without examining the work produced by students, as they may have used an alternative process that indicates either that they grasp the concept or that they have gaps in their prerequisite learning (Kersaint & Chappel, 2004). Analysis of the reasoning used to solve arithmetic computation or problems allows the teacher to determine not only the child's ability to complete math assignments but also the extent to which the child has grasped the concept behind the solution.

Take the example of Cal and Alexandra. Both students worked the problem 17 + 26. They arrived at different answers, each of which was wrong. Cal determined that 17 + 26 = 313. Alexandra computed 17 + 26 to be 88. An analysis of their logic shows different problems. Cal had no regard for place value. He added 7 + 6 to get 13 and then added 1 + 2 to get 3. Ergo:

$$
\begin{array}{r}
17 \\
+\ 26 \\
\hline
13 \\
\\
3 \\
\hline
313
\end{array}
$$

Alexandra was playing with a different deck of cards. She did not even understand the first phase of the algorithm, vertical computation. She could calculate only horizontally, regardless of a problem's format. For Alexandra, 2 + 6 = 8 and 1 + 7 = 8, ergo 88. To be effective, instruction for Cal and Alexandra must take into account each child's logic.

Invented Procedures

The creative computation procedures that Cal and Alexandra used were noticed only because they arrived at incorrect responses. Common standard algorithms are just one of the methods children use to calculate. Many times students calculate and problem-solve using methods they have invented themselves. A current body of research is exploring the idea that students' creating mathematical procedures can lead to improved conceptual understanding as students develop strategies related to their existing knowledge within a context that is familiar to them (Baek, 1998; Carroll & Porter, 1997).

USE OF PREVIOUS MATH KNOWLEDGE   Invented procedures, characterized by the application of previous math knowledge, allow the learner to assimilate past knowledge in current problem-solving or computation strategies. Awareness of a child's invented strategies can provide a successful transition to future or new math knowledge. By building upon what the child knows, the teacher can begin to show the child the relational nature of math. The teacher can also refine strategies that work well at a fairly unsophisticated level but may interfere with learning at more advanced levels. For instance, addition by counting is fine for beginning computations but can be cumbersome for multistep algorithms such as two- and three-digit multiplication problems.

NEW MATH LEARNING   Children gain most new mathematical knowledge by constructing for themselves new organizations of concepts and new procedures for doing mathematical operations. New information takes on significance and is likely to be retained only to the degree that it can be incorporated into the learner's organized and connected systems of knowledge (Baek, 1998; Van de Walle, 1994). By watching children work and asking from time to time how they arrived at a solution, the teacher can get the kind of diagnostic information that is so crucial for math concept building.

Error Analysis

PROCEDURAL TYPES OF ERRORS   Error analysis is an effective instructional diagnostic tool for all types of math learning, calculation as well as problem solving. Errors in basic facts and algorithms often reflect the child's math conceptual strategies. No one sets out to teach children incorrect algorithms; yet students having difficulty with arithmetic often turn out to be using systematic routines that yield incorrect responses. If teachers want to truly understand patterns of performance, they must determine whether errors are a systematic misunderstanding of math procedures or concepts (Fleischer & Manheimer, 1997). Analysis of errors from several examples of a student's work helps determine if errors are the result of the following:

- *Inadequate mastery of facts.* The student is able to perform operations correctly and applies the correct strategy; errors are the result of a weakness in the automatic recall of the basic facts of addition, subtraction, or multiplication.
- *Incorrect operations.* The student is proficient with basic facts but performs the incorrect operation. For instance, adds instead of subtracts.
- *Ineffective strategy.* The student is able to perform operations accurately and has proficiency with basic facts, but makes procedural errors, usually in terms of algorithms (Fleischer & Manheimer, 1997).

Math errors in calculation may be systematic, long term (unless corrected), descriptive, and usually related causally to some aspect of math instruction. Armed with this information, math teaching can focus on error patterns on the optimistic note that proper instruction can remediate even long-term problems.

PROBLEM-SOLVING ERRORS   The teacher's knowledge of what students are thinking as they problem-solve is important to fully determine students' understanding of math (Breyfogle & Herbel-Eisenmen, 2004). Analysis of student's errors in word problems begins with conducting a reading miscue analysis as students read problems silently then aloud (Parmar, 2003). Such analysis helps determine how reading miscues affect problem solving in relationship to any possible difficulties with calculation. Next, when analyzing both correct and incorrect student responses for word problems, teachers should (a) allow ample time and opportunities for students to verbally "think out loud" and without interruption as they explain their reasoning processes in problem solving, (b) ask comprehension questions that enable students to give greater detail about their thinking, and (c) perhaps even ask students to teach to others their steps taken during problem solving (Breyfogle & Herbel-Eisenmen, 2004; Bryant & Rivera, 1997).

DIAGNOSTIC TECHNIQUES   For word problem and computation error analysis, current research recommends a systematic approach that includes the following steps (Taylor, 2000):

1. Obtain a sufficient number of samples of the students' work.
2. Interview students to determine their thought processes. Have them "talk their way" through the problems completed.
3. Analyze errors and identify patterns.
4. If a pattern is found, show it to the student.
5. Demonstrate the correct procedure.
6. Implement instructional strategies that use the correct procedure.
7. Allow the student sufficient practice in the correct procedure.
8. Constantly evaluate student progress.

Error analysis is a powerful tool for evaluating student learning and subsequently determining appropriate instruction for all students. Standardized tests alone do not diagnose individual student procedural or conceptual difficulties in mathematics. Even if students arrive at a correct answer, their processes may be faulty. The current NCTM (2000) standards emphasize that communicating reasoning ability both verbally and in writing leads to better mathematical thinkers. Careful analysis of students' mathematical calculating and problem solving, along with including students in evaluating their daily work, results in more effective teaching and learning.

A WORD OF CAUTION   Oral expression is not a particularly strong point for some children. Children who have difficulty expressing themselves or who have English as a second language may not be able to provide a clear picture of their math processing, but every bit of information can be of diagnostic help. Even if the verbal picture is not clear, the teacher can couple the description with information derived from written work to form at least a tentative hypothesis. The hypothesis then can be judged against teaching goals, objectives, and student performance. The greater the child's language problem, the less information the teacher will receive from self-reporting. Consequently, the teacher must pay even greater attention to errors as they emerge over time in the child's written material.

Types of Evaluation Tools

Math evaluation is an ongoing process that enables teachers to monitor and improve an instructional program while it is in process. Evaluation data routinely allow teachers to make decisions and form opinions about student growth. Many kinds and levels of evaluation materials are available—readiness tests, achievement tests, and inspection of daily classroom activities, to name a few. The tools themselves may be categorized into (a) general or survey, and (b) specific, individual, or group.

The key to using evaluation data effectively is to be certain that the tools measure what teachers need to know and that they can do something educationally about what they find out (Van de Walle, 1994). More than likely, the more directly teachers ask the evaluation question, the greater the chances are of discovering the answer. Furthermore, the more simplified the data-collection process, the more likely that useful answers will be derived.

Readiness Tests

Specific Meaning in Mathematics

Young children enter school with a natural curiosity about quantitative concepts as well as some informal problem-solving skills. The role of formal education is to determine when and how to enhance children's learning of mathematics (Carroll & Porter, 1997; Ginsburg & Baron, 1993). Because of the logical nature of arithmetic, all tests should be broadly considered readiness tests for the next concept. Yet, we have special uses for the term *readiness*. In arithmetic instruction, readiness has come to focus on two somewhat different aspects of learning:

1. The content of arithmetic itself (e.g., the ability to count, recognize number quantities)
2. Cognitive development, usually à la Piaget (e.g., the child's ability to perform certain tasks associated with cognitive developmental milestones such as conservation and operational thought)

Skill Mastery Versus Cognitive Development

Skills associated with the arithmetic notion of readiness often are taught in preschool, kindergarten, and even first grade. Some consider these skills precursors of arithmetic performance. Items that test readiness skills often are found in the first part of basic achievement tests. For example, the Wide Range Achievement Test–Revision 3 (WRAT3) (Wilkinson, 1993) includes a small readiness component that can be given prior to evaluating basic facts and algorithmic skills. A fairly broad list of readiness areas is as follows:

> Counting
> Number recognition
> Identification of number groups
> One-to-one correspondence
> Matching number symbols to objects
> Recognition of number symbols
> Sorting and classifying
> More-or-less relationships

Readiness tests accompany most preschool and first-grade basal math texts. Teacher-made readiness tests also can focus on the content of kindergarten through first-grade texts.

TIMELINE FOR SKILL DEVELOPMENT   That the child must be skilled in readiness areas is not debatable. What is debatable is *when* the child must possess these skills. How long should the child with counting skills from 1 through 20 wait to add 1 + 1? The answer may be found by analyzing the minimum skills the child needs before proceeding to the next task in the sequence. A child does not need to be able to count to 20 to be able to conceptually comprehend that 1 + 1 = 2. However, the child does need to know counting from 1 to 2, number recognition of 1 and 2, and numerical correspondence for 1 and 2. With these readiness concepts firmly in place, the child now is prepared to learn +, =, and 1 + 1 = 2. Perhaps the most important point to be made about evaluating arithmetic readiness is simply to use test results as a means for determining the next teaching concept. Don't wait for readiness. As soon as the child's performance indicates mastery of one concept, it is time to teach a new one. The child is ready for teaching.

PIAGETIAN THEORY   Readiness à la Piaget presents a different sort of problem. Piagetian theory as applied to math readiness is developmental. The theory emphasizes the interaction between intellectual activity and the kind of mental organization that characterizes children at various levels of development. The ways by which children organize their experiences develop sequentially and in progressively more sophisticated and well-defined stages. During the traditional school years (K–12) children should evolve through three stages: preoperational, concrete operations, and formal operational levels. Each of these stages is associated with the child's ability to learn. Different levels allow for different types of learning. Theoretically, the more advanced the child is in the three stages, the more sophisticated the learning can be.

Piagetian readiness applies to all levels and focuses especially on the type of thought (preoperational, operational, or formal) the mathematics problem demands. Readiness in this sense is not limited to pre-arithmetic skills, but encompasses all mathematics skills. Formal evaluation measures for the three stages are fairly complicated and not found in typical math achievement tests. If further evaluative information is desired, a conversation with a school psychologist or Piagetian scholar is a good starting point.

RESEARCH FINDINGS   Some Piagetian scholars believe that identification of thinking levels has important instructional implications; others are not so sure. Informal mathematical abilities develop similarly across individuals from different cultures, races, and classes. This statement is not based on evidence showing identical mathematical thinking but on evidence showing that children are able to construct their own understanding of more formal mathematics earlier than would be expected (Carroll & Porter, 1997; Ginsburg & Baron, 1993).

Readiness may depend primarily on the teacher's ability to assess children's general level of informal mathematic thinking and to take advantage of opportunities to relate existing knowledge to more formal mathematics instruction, no matter what the "expected" developmental stage of the child. Math readiness and instructional practices are not necessarily based on one unified theory, but rather on relating many theories to practice. Good practice includes the teacher listening to students' explanations of their thinking processes, recognizing the number and complexity of processes required for a procedure, and providing experiences for students to construct and relate new knowledge to what they already know (Davis, 1996). As more and more state curriculum developers and test publishers align themselves with the NCTM's emphasis on problem solving and conceptual knowledge, Piagetian developmental levels and their relationship to learning may have to be revisited, as waiting for Piagetian readiness may not be the best use of a child's instructional time.

Formal/Commercial Tests

Normative Measures

Formal tests are instruments designed to measure the child's performance against some prespecified criterion or standard. Most formal tests used to evaluate mathematics in the classroom are normative; they compare the child's performance to the performance of a typical group of children who are of the same general age, experience, and cultural background. The most common type of normative test is the achievement test.

ACHIEVEMENT TESTS   Achievement tests can be given individually but are primarily designed to be given to large groups. The most commonly given ones are the Iowa Tests of Basic Skills (Hoover, Hieronymous, Friskie, & Dunbar, 1996), Metropolitan Achievement Tests—Eighth Edition (Harcourt Educational Measurement, 2001), Comprehensive Tests of Basic Skills (CTB-McGraw Hill, 1990), and the Stanford Achievement Test—Ninth Edition (Harcourt Brace Educational Measurement, 1997). Achievement tests typically result in grade-equivalence scores, percentiles, standard scores, and, occasionally, mental-age-equivalency scores. Although most achievement tests emphasize arithmetic and give lip service to geometry and data sense, they usually provide a good classroom screening of students' procedural knowledge. A very high or low score is an immediate flag for additional testing.

MINI-ERROR ANALYSIS   Another equally valuable use of the achievement test is for the purpose of analyzing individual items missed by certain children. In essence, a mini-error analysis can be completed on each child's test. Error patterns on achievement tests, though not complete, can point the teacher in the direction of additional testing within a specific area. Figure 10.1 shows the responses of a child on the WRAT3 (Wilkinson, 1993). An analysis of this protocol shows that the test, like most achievement tests, samples only a small amount of the content covered at various grade levels. However, even from this small sample, the teacher can begin to get a better idea of this student's math needs. In the example in Figure 10.1, the teacher can draw the following conclusions.

The student needs additional testing in the following:

1. Multiplication of single-digit numbers: $4 \times 2 = 6$; $23 \times 3 = 26$
2. Regrouping in both addition and subtraction:

28	75	452
− 19	+ 8	137
		+ 245

3. Basic multiplication and division facts:

$4 \times 2 = 6$

$$\begin{array}{r} 23 \\ \times\ 3 \\ \hline 26 \end{array}$$

Unless otherwise noted, the student needs no testing in:

1. Basic addition and subtraction facts:

$1 + 1 = 2, 4 - 1 = 3$

$$\begin{array}{r} 6 \\ +2 \\ \hline 8 \end{array} \qquad \begin{array}{r} 5 \\ -3 \\ \hline 2 \end{array}$$

2. Addition without grouping:

$$\begin{array}{r} 32 \\ 24 \\ +40 \\ \hline 96 \end{array}$$

The teacher should postpone testing in all other advanced areas until the student has mastered the areas indicated for testing.

REDUCE ALL ANSWERS TO LOWEST TERMS

2 + 1 = _____	6 + 2	5 − 3	4 − 1 = _____	8 − 6
1	2	3	4	5
51 + 27	497 − 176	4 × 2 = _____	6 × 3	417 + 534
6	7	8	9	10
5) 15	452 137 + 245	512 × 3	46 − 29	34 × 21
11	12	13	14	15

Figure 10.1　Sample Math Protocol

In the areas indicated for further testing, the teacher can expand upon both the number and type of items given in the original tests. In the example in Figure 10.1, only three items required grouping:

$$\begin{array}{ccc}
28 & 75 & 452 \\
-19 & +\ 8 & 137 \\
& & +245
\end{array}$$

The teacher can broaden the type and number of examples of regrouping problems by difficulty level. Items such as

$$\begin{array}{r}
51 \\
+27
\end{array}$$

(double digit + double digit) can be expanded to include:

triple digit + single digit

$$\begin{array}{r}
396 \\
+\ \ 7
\end{array}$$

triple digit + double digit

$$\begin{array}{r}
895 \\
+\ 28
\end{array}$$

triple digit with zero + double digit

$$\begin{array}{r}
706 \\
+\ 27
\end{array}$$

Relating Scores to Curricula

The degree to which the original items are expanded is related somewhat to the child's expected grade level. A second-grader, for instance, may not be expected to regroup triple-digit numbers with zero, whereas a third-grader would be expected to do the more sophisticated regrouping problems. Nor would one expect a child who cannot complete double digit + double digit regrouping to proceed to more advanced problems. Evaluation is, after all, information seeking, not a test of courage under overwhelming, impossible odds.

Although no magic number of items is preferable, a good choice might be three items of each type. If one item is missed, perhaps a combination error is at fault, but at least a warning note is sounded. Two or three items missed is a fairly clear direction for additional instruction.

Individually Administered Achievement Tests

Another form of achievement test has been designed primarily for use with individual students. Such tests are associated most commonly with special education classes but may be used in general education classes as well, as the content does not differ significantly from the content of instruction in the general education class. The distinctive difference between tests designed for individual administration and those designed for group administration is the number and variety of items asked. Because individually administered tests are longer, they typically take more time to administer. Fortunately, many of the individually administered tests come with test-scoring programs.

Commonly used tests in special education that are applicable to general education classroom math settings include the Woodcock-Johnson III (Woodcock, McGrew, & Mather, 2001), the KeyMath—Revised/NU (American Guidance Service, 2004), the Wechsler Individual Achievement Test—Second Edition Abbreviated (The Psychological Corporation, 2001), and the Kaufman Test of Educational Achievement—II, comprehensive form as well as brief form (American Guidance Service, 2004). All of these tests lend themselves to a mini-error analysis.

KEYMATH—REVISED/NU   The KeyMath—Revised/Normative Update includes another feature—all the test items are coded to specific, well-stated math objectives. This commercial test consists of 13 specific subtests grouped by three broad catagories: basic concepts, operations, and applications. These categories are roughly analogous to basic facts, algorithms, and problem solving. Table 10.1 lists the 13 KeyMath—Revised/NU subtests. Each of the subtests can be given individually and interpreted against the child's current grade level. Subtests of the KeyMath—Revised/NU can be especially useful when group achievement tests omit particularly relevant areas such as time or money.

OTHER DIAGNOSTIC MEASURES   Other tests that provide a criterion system in addition to or in place of normative information are the math subtest of the Brigance Diagnostic Comprehensive Inventory of Basic Skills Revised (Brigance & Glascoe, 1999) and the Stanford Diagnostic Mathematics Test (SDMT) (Harcourt Brace

Table 10.1   Thirteen KeyMath—Revised Tests and Subtests

Tests	Subtests
Basic Concepts	Numeration Rational Numbers Geometry
Operations	Addition Subtraction Multiplication Division Mental Computation
Applications	Measurement Time and Money Estimation Interpreting Data Problem Solving

Source: From *KeyMath—Revised/Normative Update* by American Guidance Service, 2004. Circle Pines, MN: Author.

Educational Measurement, 1996). These tests assess skill development strengths and weaknesses in mathematics for the individual child. Because the individual's needs are identified, the teacher has a clearer understanding of the student's instructional needs. Reliance on these tests alone, however, can be somewhat misleading. The best use of these tests is in conjunction with teacher observation and, in some cases, expanded area evaluations of problems completed incorrectly.

With the exception of the SDMT, which also can be given to a large group, the individually administered diagnostic math tests are best used with children having problems in math or performing at a math level much more advanced than most of the students in the class. Tests of this sort are designed as a part of a system used to develop individualized math programs.

Informal Measures

Informal measures usually provide the teacher with comparisons of the child's work to prespecified goals or objectives. Informal math measures stem from three basic sources: daily classwork, informal survey tests, and informal specific tests. All of these data sources lend themselves to error analysis. The basic difference between the three measures is the type of information given.

Daily Classwork

Analysis of daily work reveals how the child works over time and in a less supervised or time-structured situation. Problems tangential, but nonetheless relevant, to math instruction can be found and remedied by an analysis of daily work.

TANGENTIAL PROBLEMS   Take the example of Kari Dee. Day after day she did not complete her math classwork. She took her work home every night, completed it perfectly, and continued to chatter away her math time with her desk partner. Even when moved to a desk without a partner, Kari's math pattern continued as before. On math achievement tests she had scored well into the average and above-average range. Lest one be suspicious of Kari's ownership of her math work, a conversation with her mother testified to Kari's honesty.

However, the conversation also revealed the math-related problem. As her mom explained, when doing homework, Kari would do a single problem, then ask her mother if the problem was correct, which it typically was. Kari then would say that she couldn't do the next problem. Her mother would tell her that she could. Given this reassurance from Mom, Kari would complete one more problem. This pattern continued until the whole assignment was completed. Kari Dee did all the work tensely and was seemingly paralyzed without continuous positive feedback from her mother. (She could complete tasks on the achievement test because the tests were highly time structured and could not be taken home to be finished.)

Mother and teacher both appreciated that Kari had math skills. They also recognized that her skills were not functional. The Kari–Mom math team was not a viable option for the real world. With some cooperative planning between teacher and parent, Kari was systematically allowed to bring less and less work home, and Mom systematically reduced the amount of feedback given. Instead of responding to one problem at a time, Mom would wait for two to be completed, then three, then a row, and finally the whole practice page. Within about 3 weeks, Kari Dee began to find that math problems could be finished in school, which brought her teacher praise and self-satisfaction.

RATE OF WORK   A more obvious use of daily classwork derives from the direct relationship between the number of problems completed and the way they are completed. The number of problems completed in a given time is the rate of work. Assuming no other competing social intruders (garrulous neighbors or talkative phone callers) or academic problems (algorithms or basic fact knowledge), a measure of rate can add valuable teaching information. In Kari Dee's case, rate seemed to be the problem, but it was not. For other children, rate is the problem but not an obvious one. Labels such as *lazy* and *disinterested* and all sorts of special education tags often are quickly attached to the child who does not complete classwork in the allotted time.

The most common cause (barring the academic and social ones mentioned above) for slow rate is unfamiliarity with the task at hand. The child understands what needs to be done but has not worked enough problems to be proficient. Two solutions follow:

1. Allow the child more time in the math activity during the day.
2. Increase the number of days on which the child can practice the same activity.

Although both solutions involve use of more rather than less time, the sequential nature of mathematics, especially at the elementary level, demands a well-established foundation. This strong foundation allows for better problem-solving rates later.

Another fairly common cause for slow rate is well-developed familiarity with the task at hand. The child thinks, "Why do I have to do 35 problems when I already know how to do them?" One solution is to allow the child to choose only five problems but to extend the assignment beyond purely computation. The child may be asked to explain how the problems were solved, draw pictures of how manipulatives could model the exercise, or write story problems that would be solved by the computation.

Timings

Daily or weekly timings on certain key facts or algorithms also can be a way to measure as well as increase rate. Timings most often are taken on number facts and one- or two-step algorithms. For ease of measurement and consideration of the children, timings (especially those involving number facts) are usually restricted to 1 minute each. For more complex algorithms, timings can be extended to 5 or 10 minutes.

RECORD KEEPING   For ease of record keeping, children can keep copies of their work in a special folder, with the work on one side and a graph on the other. The dated chart can allow the teacher, the child, and the parents to analyze daily or weekly progress on the timed skill.

CRITERION   How many problems answered correctly are enough to move to the next set or concept? Three common guidelines for basic facts are 1 second per fact, 3 seconds per fact, and 5 seconds per fact. Application of these rules would mean 58 to 60, 18 to 20, or 10 to 12 correct responses in 1 minute, respectively. The rule would vary depending upon the child's response mode. A child who has a motor disability or one who is very young may not have the fine-motor skills necessary to complete an appropriate number of items per minute. In such cases, an oral response might be faster, and more facts could be completed.

To determine the most appropriate rate for a class, time the entire class on a concept. Eliminate the five highest and the five lowest scores, and average the remaining ones. The average is the best-guess rate for that particular class. This rate may be used for all timings of material in the same class of materials. For example, if the original best-guess rate was on simple addition facts, this rate also can be used safely in other fact areas but not in simple algorithm areas. Figure 10.2 shows how to find a best-guess rate for number facts in a typical 28-member classroom.

FEAR OF TIMINGS   Care must be taken when conducting daily or weekly timings. For children who are averse to timings, it might be best to assess rate in a fundamentally different format or perhaps not at all. The teacher can ascertain the rate surreptitiously by noting how long a child takes to complete a task rather than by giving a specific amount of time in which to work. If, for example, Dewey begins a 10-problem paper at 9:05 and completes it at 9:30, he has taken 25 minutes. Dewey has taken about 2½ minutes per problem. If the best-guess rate were

	Student	Score
Procedure	Corde	58
*1. Eliminate the 5 lowest scores.	Melinda	46
*2. Eliminate the 5 highest scores.	Gigi	44
3. Add the remaining scores.	Antone	48
4. Divide the sum by the number of scores left (18).	Valerie	55
5. Arrive at a best-guess rate for the class.	Allie	56
	Scott	49
	Victoria	60
	Donna	56
	Cornelia	59
	Grady	48
	Dewey	65
	Mason	61
	Rickie	57
	Lucas	59
	Lydia	48
	Alfie	49
	Max	+ 60
		978

*Steps I and 2 are not illustrated.   Best-Guess Rate = $18\overline{)978}$ = 54.3

Figure 10.2   Finding Best-Guess Rate for Classroom Data

54 problems in 1 minute, Dewey would be expected to complete approximately 1,350 problems in 25 minutes (54:1 minute = 1,350:25 minutes). By these standards, Dewey is very, very slow. Naturally, if he were this slow, the teacher would not even bother to time him, but the principle for finding rate is still the same.

1. Find the total amount of time the child needs to complete the assignment.
2. Divide the time by the number of problems to get an average time per problem.
3. If a best-guess rate or standard has been determined, compare the standard number of problems and the rate of time to an expected standard and the time it took the child to complete the task (e.g., 54:1 minute = x:25 minutes).

The purpose for taking rate data is to determine whether the child is at an appropriate instructional point. Once a rate signaling proficiency has been reached, the natural decision is to move to the next concept. However, if children have had a history of "poor" learning or "memory problems," it may be preferable to have them reach the best-guess rate 2 or 3 days in a row before moving on to the next concept.

A word of caution is in order regarding the use of timed testing of basic facts. Many teachers hold the mistaken belief that timed tests help children memorize the facts. Time tests help children become faster at whatever method they are using to arrive at the fact's solution. If children are finger counters or pencil tappers, timed tests will help them become faster finger counters or pencil tappers. Timed tests involving all 100 addition facts (or all of any other operation) should not be used until children have committed both the stimulus *and* response of all the facts to memory. If teachers are concerned that students use inefficient methods (such as finger counting), they should create test sheets that involve only those facts the children already have committed to memory. Timed tests (drills) should be used to maintain automaticity, not develop it.

Error Analysis With Daily Work

How a child completes tasks may also be found by examining daily work. Error analysis of daily work can reveal quickly what should be reviewed or even retaught on the following days. It is identical in form to an error analysis completed on any specific evaluation measure. An error analysis checksheet kept with the child's folders is a convenient and quick method of record keeping. Figure 10.3 gives an example of an error analysis record-keeping sheet.

RECORD KEEPING SHEETS   Because arithmetic skills can be categorized so easily, an all-purpose error analysis checksheet can be used for record keeping with

ERROR ANALYSIS CHECKSHEET

Name: *Wayne*   Teacher: *Mr. Bellow*

Content: *Multiplication*   Date: *Spring 1994*

	DATE		
Error in fact			
Carried wrong number			
Error in addition			
Forgot to regroup			
Error in writing product			
Used the wrong process			
Error in algorithm			
Multiplied out of sequence	2/17	2/18	
Forgot to add a regrouped number			
Skipped a number			
Improper placement of columns			
Problems with zero			
As a multiplier			2/20
As a multiplicant			
No errors			2/19

Figure 10.3   Error Analysis Checksheet for Multiplication

most children. The purpose of dating the checsheet is to provide once again an objective and clearly defined record of each child's progress. Types of errors that can be noted in addition, subtraction, and division are presented in Table 10.2.

CHECKLISTS   Checklists for most areas typically can be found in arithmetic methods texts or even some basal arithmetic series. They also can be developed around the basal text used in the classroom. If, for example, the unit is covering fractions, a checklist can be developed quickly around the objectives associated with that particular unit and the text content for the class. A fractions checklist developed from a third-grade text would be very different from one developed from a sixth-grade text. Some areas (e.g., errors in basic number facts) would overlap. Yet, the sixth-grade fractions checksheet would be more inclusive and contain much more sophisticated material. Daily or weekly checklists, however unsophisticated, provide a source of informal evaluation that can be compared to class progress and other formal or informal evaluations.

Informal Tests

CODING TO BASAL TEXT   Informal survey or specific math tests are those that provide a sample of problems but are not coded formally to norms or grade levels. Often, informal tests measure specific skill areas or areas associated with texts or kits.

Figure 10.4 shows an informal survey test coded directly to the math basal text. In fact, the items have been taken from the text itself. Questions 1 through 3, for example, deal with 2 as a factor, and are taken from pages 281, 282, and 284, respectively. The informal survey specifies a particular unit in the text: multiplication of 2 and 5. The items have been coded to topics (2 and 5 as factors, number line, commutative property, and name product or factor). The +/- column is a code to indicate correct (+) or incorrect (-). By examining the coded responses, the teacher can get a quick notion of when to enter the student in the chapter or remediate if necessary.

The figure provides an example of a coded pre/posttest on Ellis's work. Ellis was in and out of various schools for the first 2 years of his rather spotty academic career. His knowledge of mathematics reflected all this instability. Ellis had learned many concepts in isolation, but he never really had the chance to complete any sequence systematically. He was adept at what he had learned, but he had not been exposed to many concepts. To put Ellis on page 281 of chapter 10 would have been unfair and also might have incited a behavior problem where none had existed before. (Perhaps boredom rather than necessity is the true mother of invention—if not the inventor of certain categories of special education classes.) What Ellis needed instructionally was to learn the commutation property. This need was reflected in his informal survey.

What the informal survey can demonstrate so clearly is the relationship between the child's knowledge and the material at hand. In using an informal survey coded to class materials, the teacher can move directly into instructional activities without having to search out teaching material initially. (Eventually, the text may have to be supplemented, but that discovery occurs during instruction.)

Table 10.2   Types of Errors

Addition
Errors in facts

Errors in regrouping
- "Lost" regrouped number
- Forgot to add regrouped number
- Regrouped wrong number
- Wrote regrouped number in columns
- Added the regrouped number twice

Problems with zero
- Regrouping zero
- Adding numbers to zero

Problems with columns
- Lost place
- Ignored place value
- Failure to follow algorithm
- Wrote same digit in two columns

Subtraction
Errors in facts

Errors in regrouping
- Failed to regroup
- Subtracted the top number from the bottom
- Skipped over columns
- Didn't subtract from regrouped number
- Misplaced alignment

Problems with zero
- Zero at the unit place
- Zero at the tens place
- Zero at the hundreds place
- Zero between two numbers

Problems with columns
- Lost place
- Ignored column
- Failure to follow algorithm
- Misplaced alignment

Division
Errors in facts

Errors in regrouping
- Multiplicative
- Subtractive

Problems with zero
- In the divisor
- In the dividend
- In regrouping

Problems with columns

Misplaced alignment

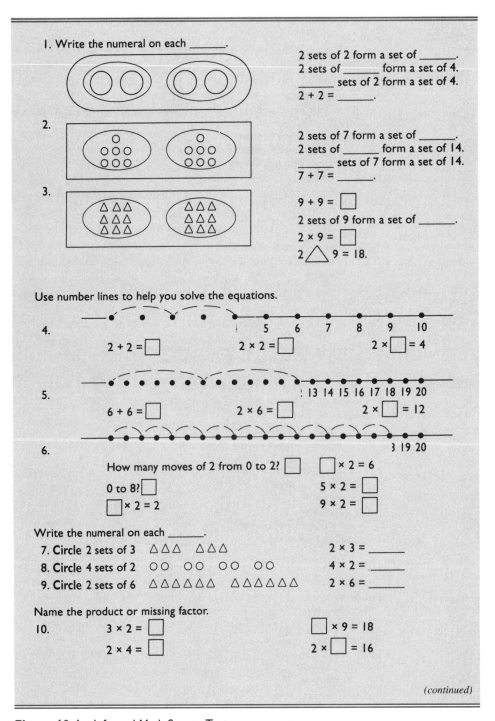

1. Write the numeral on each _____.

2 sets of 2 form a set of _____.
2 sets of _____ form a set of 4.
_____ sets of 2 form a set of 4.
2 + 2 = _____.

2.

2 sets of 7 form a set of _____.
2 sets of _____ form a set of 14.
_____ sets of 7 form a set of 14.
7 + 7 = _____.

3.

9 + 9 = ☐
2 sets of 9 form a set of _____.
2 × 9 = ☐
2 △ 9 = 18.

Use number lines to help you solve the equations.

4.
2 + 2 = ☐   2 × 2 = ☐   2 × ☐ = 4

5.
6 + 6 = ☐   2 × 6 = ☐   2 × ☐ = 12

6.
How many moves of 2 from 0 to 2? ☐   ☐ × 2 = 6
0 to 8? ☐   5 × 2 = ☐
☐ × 2 = 2   9 × 2 = ☐

Write the numeral on each _____.
7. Circle 2 sets of 3   △△△ △△△   2 × 3 = _____
8. Circle 4 sets of 2   ○○ ○○ ○○ ○○   4 × 2 = _____
9. Circle 2 sets of 6   △△△△△△ △△△△△△   2 × 6 = _____

Name the product or missing factor.
10.   3 × 2 = ☐   ☐ × 9 = 18
           2 × 4 = ☐   2 × ☐ = 16

(continued)

Figure 10.4   Informal Math Survey Test

11.
　　　　2　　　　　　　8　　　　　　1
　　　　×2　　　　　　×2　　　　　×2

12.
　　　　2　　　　　　7　　　　　　2
　　×☐　　　　×☐　　　　×☐

TOTAL_____

Book: Modern School Mathematics   Date _____
　　　　Level 2
　　　　Chapter 10; Multiplication 2 and 5   Name *Ellis* _____
　　　　Teacher's Copy

Code:	Question	Unit	Page	+/−
	1	2 and 5 as factors	281	+
	2		282	+
	3		284	+
	4	Number line	285	+
	5		286	+
	6		287	+
	7	Commutative property	288	−
	8		288	−
	9		288	−
	10	Name product or factor	289	+
	11		290	−
	12		290	+

Student's Form

Name: _____   Score: _____

Date: _____   Unit: _____

Figure 10.4   Informal Math Survey Test (continued)

COMPARISON WITH RESULTS OF FORMAL MEASURES   Informal surveys also can be compared to more formal achievement tests. The results of the formal and informal tests, combined with teacher evaluation of daily work, can provide a powerful and objective source of information about the child's mathematics needs. The degree to which the comparisons agree may provide the basis for choosing the most appropriate service or combination of services for the child in question. Robert, for example, scored well on the KeyMath and on an informal classroom survey, but his daily work was poor. Robert needed motivation in mathematics. This assistance could take place in the general education classroom. Dewey, in contrast, scored poorly on all three evaluative measures. His perform- ance was so consistently low that special services outside of the classroom became necessary. Finally, Alec scored low on the Iowa Math Achievement Subtest, yet his daily classroom performance and informal test results were among the best in the class. Thus, in spite of his formal test results, Alec belonged in the general education classroom. The moral of these three stories is to never make judgments based on one data source alone.

Evaluation and Special Children

Evaluation in mathematics is essentially the same for children with disabilities as it is for all children. The content of arithmetic is constant regardless of the eccentricities or unique characteristics of the learner. The sum of 2 and 2 should equal 4 whether the child being evaluated has a visual impairment or is gifted. The major concern in evaluation is to be certain that the content is what is being evaluated, not some problem unique to the child.

Children with a sensory or physical impairment may need their own testing format. Children with learning or social problems, too, may need a format change addressing length of evaluation and psychological factors such as stress from fatigue or fear. When evaluating math skills, language problems also can be a confounding factor. Directions, both written and verbal, must be clear and sensitive when evaluating all children, but especially when dealing with those who have disabilities.

Most formal math tests have not been designed for special populations. As a consequence, the inclusion teacher and the specialist should carefully monitor both the classroom setting and the format of the test before administering any of these measures. Results of the formal test gain credibility only when the test is delivered with regard for the child's specific needs and is compared against teacher observation, informal tests, and daily classwork.

Summary

In evaluating mathematics, psychological attitudes as well as cognitive knowledge must be considered. Math anxiety in all its varied forms runs rampant and is especially troublesome in children who already have a low self-concept. For many children the mathematics problem resides in fear of failure rather than in an actual inability to learn math.

With respect to cognitive mathematics assessment, no single test can be used as the sole criterion for determining the appropriateness of a mathematics program. Teachers can use formal tests, informal tests, and daily records. Error analysis is the basis for comparison for all three measures. The major purpose of assessment in mathematics is to give the child an appropriate math program. Though the format may vary, the content of the math program remains constant and does not recognize disabilities. The answer to the problem 2 + 2 always must be 4, regardless of whether the child signs, points, speaks, or writes the response.

References

American Guidance Service. (2004). *Kaufman Test of Educational Achievement—II*. Circle Pines, MN: Author.

American Guidance Service. (2004). *KeyMath—Revised/Normative Update*. Circle Pines, MN: Author.

Baek, J. M. (1998). Children's invented algorithms for multidigit multiplication problems. In L. J. Morrow (Ed.), *The teaching and learning of algorithms in school mathematics* (pp. 151–160). Reston, VA: NTCM.

Breyfogle, M. L., & Herbel-Eisenmann, B. A. (2004). Focusing on students' mathematical thinking. *Mathematics Teacher, 97,* 244–247.

Brigance, A. H., & Glascoe, F. P. (1999). *Brigance™ Diagnostic Comprehensive Inventory of Basic Skills—Revised*. North Billerica, MA: Curriculum Associates, Inc.

Bryant, B. R., & Rivera, D. P. (1997). Educational assessment of mathematics skills and abilities. *Journal of Learning Disabilities, 30,* 57–68.

Buschman, L. (2004). Teaching problem solving in mathematics. *Teaching Children Mathematics, 10,* 302–309.

Carroll, W. M., & Porter, D. (1997). Invented strategies can develop meaningful mathematical procedures. *Teaching Children Mathematics, 3,* 370–374.

CTB-McGraw-Hill. (1990). *Comprehensive Tests of Basic Skills: Fourth edition*. Monterey, CA: CTB-McGraw-Hill.

Davis, R. B. (1996). Classrooms and cognition. *Journal of Education, 178,* 3–12.

D'Emidio-Caston, M. (1993, April). *Ambition, distraction, uglification and derision: The case for confluent education in math procedures*. Paper presented at annual meeting of American Educational Research Association, Atlanta.

Dougherty, B. J., & Scott, L. (1993). Curriculum: A vision for early childhood mathematics. In R. Jensen (Ed.), *Research ideas for the classroom: Early childhood mathematics* (pp. 294–310). New York: Macmillan Publishing Company.

Fleischer, J. E., & Manheimer, M. A. (1997). Math intervention for students with learning disabilities: Myths and realities. *The School Psychology Review, 26,* 397–413.

Fuchs, L. S., & Fuchs, D. (2005). Enhancing mathematical problem solving for students with disabilities. *Journal of Special Education, 39,* 45–57.

Furner, J. M., & Berman, B. T. (2003). Math anxiety: Overcoming a major obstacle to the improvement of student math performance. *Childhood Education, 79,* 170–174.

Furner, J. M., & Duffy, M. L. (2002). Equity for all students in the new millennium: Disabling math anxiety. *Intervention in School and Clinic, 38,* 67–74.

Ginsburg, H. P., & Baron, J. (1993). Cognition: Young children's construction of mathematics. In R. Jensen (Ed.), *Research ideas for the classroom: Early childhood mathematics* (pp. 3–21). New York: Macmillan Publishing Company.

Harcourt Brace Educational Measurement. (1996). *Stanford Diagnostic Mathematics Test*. San Antonio, TX: Author.

Harcourt Brace Educational Measurement. (1997). *Stanford Achievement Test: Ninth edition*. San Antonio, TX: Author.

Harcourt Educational Measurement. (2001). *Metropolitan Achievement Tests: Eighth edition*. San Antonio, TX: Author.

Hoover, H., Hieronymous, A., Friskie, D., & Dunbar, S. (1996). *Iowa Tests of Basic Skills*. Chicago: Riverside Publishing Company.

Jackson, C. D., & Leffingwell, R. J. (1999). The role of instruction in creating math anxiety in students from kindergarten through college. *Mathematics Teacher, 97,* 583–586.

Jonassen, D. H. (2003). Designing research-based instruction for story problems. *Educational Psychology Review, 15* (3), 267–296.

Jonassen D. H., Howland, J., Moore, J., & Marra, R. M. (2003). *Learning to solve problems with technology: A constructivist perspective* (2nd ed.). Columbus, OH: Merrill/Prentice-Hall.

Kersaint, G., & Chappel, M. F. (2004). What do you see? A case for examining students' work. *Mathematics Teacher, 97,* 102–105.

Lucangeli, D., Tresoldi, P. E., & Cendron, M. (1998). Cognitive and metacognitive abilities involved in the solution of mathematical word problems: Validation of a comprehensive model. *Contemporary Educational Psychology, 23,* 257–275.

Mauer, S. B. (1998). What is an algorithm? What is an answer? In L. J. Morrow (Ed.), *The teaching and learning of algorithms in school mathematics* (pp. 21–31). Reston, VA: NTCM.

National Assessment Governing Board (2005). *National Assessment of Educational Progress.* Retrieved August 29, 2007 from http://nces.ed.gov

National Council of Teachers of Mathematics. (1989). *Curriculum and evaluation standards for school mathematics.* Reston, VA: Author.

National Council of Teachers of Mathematics. (2000). *Principles and standards for school mathematics.* Reston, VA: Author.

Parmar, R.S. (2003). Understanding the concept of "Division": Assessment considerations. *Exceptionality, 11,* 177–189.

The Psychological Corporation. (2001). *Wechsler Individual Achievement Test—Second Edition Abbreviated.* San Antonio, TX: Author.

Renga, S., & Dalla, L. (1993). Affect: A critical component of mathematical learning in early childhood. In R. Jensen (Ed.), *Research ideas for the classroom: Early childhood mathematics* (pp. 22–37). New York: Macmillan Publishing Company.

Reys, R. E., Lindquist, M. M., Smith, N. L., & Suydam, M. N. (2004). *Helping children learn about mathematics.* Hoboken, NJ: John Wiley & Sons, Inc.

Senturk, D., Whipple, A., Ho, H., Zimmer, J., Chiu, S., & Wang, C. (2000). A cross-national study: Children's math self-concept and its relationship with mathematics achievement. In S. George (Ed.), *The academic achievement of minority students: Perspectives, practices, and prescriptions* (pp. 65–91). Lanham, MD: University Press of America, Inc.

Spinelli, C. G. (2002). *Classroom assessment for students with special needs in inclusive settings.* Upper Saddle River, NJ: Pearson Education, Inc.

Strong, R., Thomas, E., Perini, M., & Silver, H. (2004). Creating a differentiated mathematics classroom. *Educational Leadership, 61,* 73–78.

Taylor, R. L. (2000). *Assessment of exceptional students: Educational and psychological procedures.* Boston: Allyn and Bacon.

Usnick, V. (1991). It's not drill *and* practice; it's drill *or* practice. *School Science & Mathematics, 91,* 344–347.

Van de Walle, J. A., & Thompson, C. S. (1981). Fitting problem solving into every classroom. *School Science & Mathematics, 81,* 289–297.

Wilkinson, G. S. (1993). *Wide Range Achievement Test—Revision 3.* Wilmington, DE: Jastak Associates.

Wolodko, B. L., Willson, K. J., & Johnson, R. E. (2004). Metaphors as a vehicle for exploring preservice teachers' perceptions of mathematics. *Teaching Children Mathematics, 10,* 224–229.

Woodcock, R., McGrew, K., & Mather, N. (2001). *Woodcock Johnson III—Tests of Achievement.* Salisbury, MA: Riverside.

Zemelman, D. H. (1998*). Best Practice: New Standards for Teaching and Learning in America's Schools.* Portsmouth, NH: Heineman.

Zemelman, S., Daniels, H., & Hyde, A. (1998). *Best practice: New standards for teaching and learning in America's schools.* Portsmouth, NH: Heinemann.

Mathematics Instruction
in Inclusion Settings

Kathleen McCoy and Rebecca Gehrke

Virginia Usnick cowrote this chapter for the second edition. Although the chapter has been significantly changed for the third edition, Dr. Usnick's contributions to the second edition are still very much appreciated.

KEY TERMS

◆ array
◆ Cartesian cross-product
◆ decomposition
◆ diagnostic teaching
◆ estimation
◆ regrouping
◆ rubrics
◆ standard algorithms

Six pairs of eyes dart furtively toward the classroom wall clock. Suddenly a siren reverberates throughout the school, announcing a fire drill. The six pairs of eyes light up, undergoing an amazing metamorphosis. For one more day the group will be able to postpone the task of learning the long-division algorithm. This "saved by the bell" mentality is all too common in math instruction.

Assuming that the children's mathematical skill needs have been assessed thoroughly, mathematics classes must involve instruction. Motivation may be less than high for teacher and students alike, as was discovered in the previous chapter. Students with remedial needs may feel as though they are faced with a repetitive, no-win learning situation when they are confronted with a classroom textbook. An overreliance on any textbook may not result in adequate development of problem-solving strategies (Deshler, Ellis, & Lenz, 1996). However, the National Council of Teachers of Mathematics (NCTM, 1989, 2000) has shifted the emphasis of mathematics teaching and learning from addressing strictly computing skills toward the acquiring and applying of math content. In addition to this current emphasis on problem solving over basic-skills learning (NCTM, 2000), technology advances and the inclusion of special education students in general education classes demand that both general and special education teachers employ a variety of instructional methods and materials in order for all students to experience success in mathematics.

For children who have problems learning mathematics, the need for appropriate instruction is critical. Mathematical learning is a process that requires years of development and depends upon specific individual characteristics as well as on influences of the learning environment (Reys, Lindquist, Lambdin, Smith, & Sudyam, 2004). The following chapter addresses (a) factors that teachers are able to manipulate in attempting to provide effective instruction, (b) the content of instruction, and (c) the unique needs of special learners. The importance of both basic skills and problem-solving instruction is addressed, as is the use of instructional strategies for teaching children to "learn how to learn" mathematics.

Factors Teachers Can Manipulate

Teachers have a great deal of latitude in presenting math classes. This allows them to manipulate various instructional factors that affect student learning. Four of the most easily manipulated factors within the instructor's command are time, size of group, reinforcement, and materials. The ways in which the teacher uses these four factors can significantly increase or decrease the amount of math learning that takes place.

Time

The more time that is spent working on a task, the more likely the task is to be mastered. This statement is somewhat simplistic, as factors other than time on task contribute to learning. Nonetheless, time on task is critical, as are the decisions as to what strands of math content receive the most instructional and practice time in the classroom. Time constraints may impact what and how a student learns.

Time on Task

Students experience feelings of success when allowed sufficient time to persevere until problems are solved correctly. Effective teaching and practicing of problem solving takes time. Students need to be allowed sufficient time to work on problems before giving up, as it takes them more time to solve problems that they do not know how to do than those they do (Reys et al., 2004). Therefore, Reys and colleagues (2004) recommend that students be allowed time to (a) understand the task, (b) explore various methods of solution, and (c) think about and evaluate their solution as to its appropriateness. Many times, students in special education are shortchanged when it comes to time spent on mathematics instruction due to other academic or behavioral needs (Woodward & Montague, 2002). For instance, issues relating to math anxiety, a history of failure in math, or an attention deficit may require that the teacher spend an inordinate amount of time on just building confidence and promoting a positive attitude toward daily math activities. If a student has reading or vocabulary difficulties, sufficient time for practice and error analysis should be allowed in order to determine if the student understands what is being required of him or her.

Procedural Versus Conceptual Emphasis

Researchers continue to conduct international comparative studies of mathematical achievement in response to concerns over the United States' lagging achievement scores in comparison with other developed countries. Some data from the Third International Mathematics and Science Study (TIMSS) (Gonzales et al., 2004) indicated that students in higher performing countries spent more time on problem solving or conceptual aspects of content rather than on calculation procedures (Maccini & Gagnon, 2000; Stigler & Hiebert, 2004). In the TIMSS study, U.S. eighth-graders rarely spent time engaged in the study of concepts, but focused on practicing procedures. The current NTCM (1989, 2000) emphasis on problem solving and conceptual understanding grew, in part, from this and similar research. For students with learning difficulties, endless drill without an understanding of underlying concepts may lead to frustration and negative feelings toward math (Karp & Howell, 2004). On the other hand, there are critics who recommend that instructional time spent on problem solving not be at the expense of failing to master the basic skills of computation that are necessary to advancing in math (Loveless & Coughlan, 2004). Expecting students with special learning needs to continue in the mathematics curriculum means maintaining rigorous standards and providing challenging, broad, and well-balanced instruction (Maccini & Gagnon, 2000; Thornton, Langrall, & Jones, 1997). This has not always been the case in special education, where the emphasis has traditionally been placed on rote mastery of basic facts and algorithms and on finding the key words in solving written problems.

For students with learning disabilities, a strictly procedural approach to the teaching of mathematics may not be the most efficient use of time, as it can take two to three months for low-achieving students to master a procedure (Woodward, Baxter, & Robinson, 1999). Earlier research by Woodward and Baxter (1997) compared various approaches to mathematics instruction with the resulting achievements of at-risk students and students with learning disabilities in inclusive settings. They found that students exposed to innovative curriculum (i.e., settings where students discussed multiple solutions to problems) were able to defend their problem-solving solutions, used an array of tools to find solutions and answers, and scored better on standardized tests.

Other research findings support the premise that students with difficulties in mathematics procedures also need to understand the conceptual background or, in other words, the big picture of the concepts underlying basic calculations, in order to experience success (Jarrett, 1999; Woodward et al., 1999). Researchers are continually developing approaches to mathematics that focus on both the knowing and the doing aspects of teaching and learning mathematics (ERIC Clearinghouse on Disabilities, ERIC/OSEP Special Project, 2002; Sherman, Richardson, & Yard, 2005). A greater understanding of numbers, their relationships, and the underlying concepts of basic facts and algorithms leads to greater flexibility in problem solving and the ability to move on to higher levels of math thinking and achievement.

Providing Time for Math Learning

To increase the level of proficiency of student learning in math, a teacher should increase the amount of time spent working in math and balance instruction between conceptual and procedural learning. Time is one easily manipulated instructional factor. Increased time can be achieved either by extending the time allotted to a mathematics lesson or by integrating mathematics with other content subjects. The newest NCTM (2000) process standards include connecting mathematical topics to contexts that relate mathematics to other subjects and to students' experiences and interests. One of the reasons why Johnny cannot learn math may be that he has never been given enough time to learn or enough opportunities to practice what he has learned in other settings. In order for skills to generalize, students must have opportunities to practice in life and to integrate mathematics into other subject areas (Deshler et al., 1996; Gelzheiser, Griesemer, & Pruzek, 2000; Zambo, 2005).

Size of Group

Like instruction in any other content area, math instruction can be delivered in a variety of settings. Math can be taught in large groups, small groups, or one-to-one settings. The advantages and disadvantages of each setting have been detailed elsewhere in this book. A quick review reminds us that large-group instruction in which all children are receiving the same information at the same pace is not particularly successful in a classroom that includes children with various levels of skills.

Uses of Large-Group Instruction

Large-group settings may be useful for brainstorming and aspects of problems solving that are tied more directly to logical deductions than to applications of specific algorithms. For example, problem-solving questions such as "How many showers can you take with a bar of soap?" lend themselves equally to children with low and high technical arithmetic skills. In addition, questions of this nature expand a child's ability to think through a problem without the fear of making a skill error. (Some of the answers are: Depends on the size of the soap. Depends on the type of soap being used. Depends on the length of the shower.)

Heterogeneous classroom grouping of students does not necessarily undermine the achievement levels of high-performing students, and often results in more better achieving students, given a rigorous curriculum (Burris, Heubert, & Levin, 2004). Within a large-group setting, teachers can employ methods such as differentiated instruction, cooperative learning, or peer-assisted learning strategies in order to effectively meet the academic needs of a wide range of students (Fuchs & Fuchs, 1998; Strong, Thomas, Perini, & Silver, 2004; Xin, 1999). In addition, large-group instruction is useful for introducing a new procedure or concept to all students at the same point in time (Reys et al., 2004). Most important, a classroom environment in which all students feel "safe" to participate in discussions and explain their thinking is essential for development of self-confidence and communication skills (Furner & Duffy, 2002; Renga & Dalla, 1993; Senturk et al., 2000).

Small-Group Instruction

PERSONAL ATTENTION   Small-group instruction can be especially useful when grouping children of comparable skill levels. In the small-group setting, children can get more personal attention and benefit simultaneously from collaborative work with other members of the group. Discussion is limited to group members, but the group still can support discussion. As long as the members are at approximately the same skill level, small-group instruction may be the preferred method of instructional grouping. Burris et al. (2004), though, cautioned against the use of less rigorous standards in any grouping of students by skill level. In the current era of standards-based reform (NCTM, 2000), excellence in math performance requires high expectations and strong support for all students. Therefore, an approach that includes flexible grouping is in order (Strong et al., 2004). Change group members, activities, and strategies to avoid students getting "stuck" at a skill level and to improve students' procedural and conceptual understanding of mathematics.

RATE VARIABILITY   Small-group instruction allows children who are ready to go on in the curriculum to continue and those who are not or who need more time for mastery to continue at their own rate. In a class of 30-plus students, the teacher could develop six to eight small learning groups.

TYPES OF GROUPINGS   Teachers make judgments on what is needed to improve a student's self-image and what diagnostic procedures should be used to determine the material or activity that will best improve student progress. When grouping students, the teacher is responsible for structuring the purpose of the group and the level of direction and interaction of the members. Students' anxiety is lessened in a small-group setting if the teacher has done an appropriate job of matching student interests and abilities. Types of groups may include either skill level or cooperative grouping.

Small-group instruction based upon skill level often is referred to as *diagnostic teaching*. Because a child's skills fluctuate from topic to topic, a diagnostic grouping is often temporary, as children move from group to group based upon skill need. Flexibility and assessment are the cornerstones of diagnostic skill grouping.

Another kind of small-group structure is called *cooperative grouping*. Groups of this sort are formed more along the notion of peer tutoring than diagnosed math skill needs. In cooperative math groups, the children teach each other. As a result, the learning activity is enhanced by social factors such as friendship and common interests. Cooperative grouping promotes (a) students with and without disabilities working together, (b) students helping and supporting each other in order to accomplish academic tasks, (c) students learning to accept different views from each other, and (d) students building communication skills (Reys et al., 2004; Xin, 1999).

Individualized Instruction

Individualized instruction in mathematics has a valuable place in the classroom. The question sparked by the term *individualization* is, "How can a teacher provide individualized instruction to a class of 30-plus children in the course of a 45- to 60-minute math period?" If the answer is that individualized instruction means diagnosing the optimum learning experience for a child and providing an environment in which the child can learn, individualization is not so formidable.

Individualization of instruction does not mean that one student sits in a classroom all day and interacts with only a teacher or a math worksheet. Individualization requires that the teacher take a child or a group of children and set up experiences that enhance each child's opportunities to learn math. These opportunities include rate or pace of instruction as well as extra practice materials that reflect skill level.

Karp and Howell (2004) aptly summarized individualization as: (a) removing any barriers specific to each student, such as visual, auditory, or language processing difficulties; (b) structuring an environment conducive to learning and teaching; (c) incorporating sufficient time and practice into each lesson; and (d) providing clarity. In contrast, use of individual instruction is appropriate if students are able to follow a sequence or conduct an activity on their own or if the focus is on practice for individual mastery of a procedure (Reys et al., 2004).

A Continuum of Methods

When it comes to selecting effective teaching practices, most teachers combine large-group, small-group, and individual instruction into their classroom structure. Expecting students to problem solve on a conceptual level and communicate their learning, as per the standards and principles of NCTM (1989, 2000), means the teacher must employ flexibility in lesson design. No longer should teachers rely on a traditional large-group presentation followed by individual seatwork as the sole means of mathematics instruction. A more developmental approach, which takes into account diverse student needs, includes a combination of individual instruction, cooperative learning, cross-disciplinary/real-life applications, math stations, and flexible grouping (Gelzheiser et al., 2000; Zemelman, Daniels, & Hyde, 1998). For students with learning disabilities in any setting, researchers continue to find that effective teaching at all grade levels includes modeling the task, providing guided and independent practice, reviewing frequently, and offering positive corrective feedback (Gagnon & Maccini, 2001).

Reinforcement

Mathematics instruction requires reinforcement that yields positive feelings. Students can be reinforced for completing various components of a math problem. The "right answer" is just one of the components of the math problem. Simply initiating the work involved with a problem is worthy of reinforcement for some students. Following directions, completing the work, and being neat and orderly also are praiseworthy accomplishments.

Process and Product

To emphasize mathematics as a process rather than a product, teachers must reinforce the student's approach to problems and solutions just as much as the correct answer. By approaching mathematics as an activity for finding solutions to problems, the teacher can isolate many factors, not just the correct solution, that can be reinforced. Rubrics, scoring systems focusing on the solution process as well as the answer, can be used to reinforce students' problem-solving processes. The more positive reinforcements or strokes a child receives, the greater is the chance that the child can develop positive feelings and attitudes.

Nate always has been afraid of mathematics. His fear seemed to begin early in the second grade when his teacher remarked casually that math did not seem to be Nate's best subject. The next few times that Nate got low marks on his math papers lent more credibility to his teacher's remark. By the time he reached fifth grade, he was a full-blown math-anxious student. He stalled and avoided doing math work in class whenever possible. Nate's teacher, recognizing his avoidance behavior and sympathizing with his dilemma, began to slowly improve Nate's skills in math by first working on his attitude. The teacher praised all the students in class for their neatness on worksheets. Even though Nate did not have much done, what he did have done was as neat as a CPA's ledger, earning his first bit of praise involving a math activity. Even though his skills did not improve, he seemed less reluctant to begin his math assignments. Now that Nate has begun to do his work, his teacher can identify skill deficits in order to provide materials and activities to improve his math abilities.

Desensitizing Materials

If children have had bad experiences in math and developed poor attitudes as a result, the teacher can introduce materials that they do not associate with math failure. For example, the teacher can teach math skills directly through concrete manipulative materials or indirectly by using real-world applications involving math skills or embedding mathematical skills in other content areas.

Manipulatives

When teaching double-digit multiplication, instead of pulling out a paper and pencil, the teacher might bring out blocks, an abacus, chips, or any other concrete material to illustrate the concept. The teacher guides the student through a problem, allowing the student to work with the manipulative while the teacher records on the symbolic level. So the teacher writes

$$\begin{array}{r} 53 \\ \times\ 21 \\ \hline \end{array}$$

on the board. Using chips with colors representing place values of tens and ones, the student would arrange 21 rows of 53, where 53 is represented by 5 blue chips (tens) and 3 yellow chips (ones). While the student manipulates the chips, the teacher records the student's actions through numerical symbols. When the student has had considerable success with the manipulatives, the teacher presents more problems, allowing the student to work these problems with manipulatives and writing down the answers. Next, the student uses the manipulatives to solve numerical problems and records all his or her actions, such as using a "carried" number to indicate that some ones were traded for tens. Finally, the student works the problem using numbers only.

Technology

Technology may also be used with children who have had bad experiences with mathematics, most often in terms of use of a calculator. However, there does exist the potential for unwise use or abuse of calculators and computers, especially in the area of drill and practice in basic math facts and algorithms (Campbell & Stewart, 1993; Usiskin, 1998; Woodward & Montague, 2002). Technology should not be a substitute for the conceptual understanding of math procedures (NCTM, 1999; Woodward & Montague, 2002). On the other hand, for students who struggle with problem solving due to lack of proficiency with basic facts, introducing the use of a calculator may eliminate the frustrations created by poor computational skills and enable them to concentrate on the conceptual nature of the problem. The NCTM's current emphasis is on a balanced use of technology, paper and pencil, and mental tools (Cavanagh, 2005).

Games

One last option for providing math instruction in a varied format is the use of games. Board or dice games and activities can be hands-on, motivational tools with which students can practice and apply math skills (Shaftel, Pass, & Schnabel, 2005). If not overused, mathematical games afford students opportunities to reinforce existing knowledge and practice problem-solving strategies outside of the context of paper-and-pencil tasks. An array of games are commercially produced (or can be produced by students) that allow players to apply budgeting and problem solving to real-life scenarios.

Other Content Areas

Not all classrooms have access to manipulatives, nor do all teachers feel comfortable using them. In situations like these, the teacher can approach instruction in another manner. Math can be slipped in under the guise of social studies or science—even art and music. Continuing with the example of 53×21, the teacher can present a story problem involving these numbers and allow students to find the answer in nontraditional ways, such as acting the problem out or drawing pictures. For example, if relating this problem to a music class, the teacher might say that she has 53 pieces of music and needs arrangements of each piece for all 21 band members. One student might draw 53 squares to represent the music and repeat this arrangement 21 times. Another student might write 53 in a column 21 times and add the numbers. Through class discussion, the teacher and students can analyze the different ways in which the problem was solved and relate each way to the traditional math approach. A variation of traditional story problems is to personalize them by using a child's own name or interests. If the problem is personalized, the student is likely to be more interested and more attentive to instruction.

No matter what approach the teacher uses, the main point is that the materials engage the child in active learning. Students with a history of math failure tend to be unwilling to participate in activities associated with their previous failures. By providing new kinds of materials or activities, the teacher lets the students pursue mathematics learning in a nonpunitive fashion.

Instructional Content

In 1989, the NCTM published its *Curriculum and Evaluation Standards for School Mathematics* and in 2000, they published *Principles and Standards for School Mathematics*. Together these documents describe in broad terms the content, principles, and standards that NCTM advocates as appropriate for children in kindergarten through 12th grade. The goals that the NCTM delineates for *all* students are as follows:

1. Students become better problem solvers.
2. Students learn to reason mathematically.
3. Students learn to value mathematics.
4. Students become more confident in their mathematical abilities.
5. Students learn to communicate mathematically.

Implicit in these goals, and explicitly stated within the content standard entitled "Number and Operations," is the belief that all students can and should develop reasonable proficiency with basic mathematical facts. The NCTM (2000) process standards include students being able to (a) problem solve, (b) provide reasoning and proof, (c) communicate their thinking, (d) connect mathematics to real life, and (e) create representations across all content standards.

Meaningful understanding and reasonable proficiency with basic facts is critical for competency in arithmetic. Students must develop an awareness of the conceptual relationships between quantities and numerical symbols. In learning to do so, computation becomes more than just learning basic facts (Griffin, 2004) and is easily applied to more complex algorithms and problem solving. Basic fact knowledge is also necessary to advance in mathematics (Loveless, 2004). In the current era of No Child Left Behind, it is essential to provide all children with effective instruction in the fundamentals of mathematics so that everyone has the opportunity to succeed in the math curriculum (Loveless & Coughlan, 2004).

Major Goals

Historically, a major goal of elementary mathematics education has been for children to recall facts rapidly ("know them by heart"). With the accessibility of technology such as hand-held calculators, many mathematics educators now question the large percentage of classroom time spent on memorizing basic facts. Even with the new emphasis on conceptual learning in mathematics (NCTM, 1989, 2000), successful math education involves both the mastery of basic skills and the efficient use of higher order processes (Isaacs & Carroll, 1999). For all students, and especially for those with learning disabilities, grasping the concepts related to basic facts (i.e., number sense, more/less than, part and whole) is a prerequisite for beginning instruction in basic facts (Gersten & Chard, 1999; Van De Walle, 1998). For efficiency's sake, "knowing" the basic facts often involves automatic recall, much of which can be accomplished through a combination of drill, proper sequencing of instruction, and teaching alternate strategies to memorization. In essence, mastery of concepts and automaticity as related to the basic facts of addition, subtraction, multiplication, and division is as necessary for computing algorithms and problem solving as phonemic awareness is for reading fluency and comprehension (Gersten & Chard, 1999).

Principles for Enhancing Recall of Basic Facts

Drilling is the process of fixing something in the mind through repetition. When providing drill, the following principles apply:

1. Children should have a reasonable understanding of the material they are attempting to memorize (Griffin, 2004). They should know the numbers by both their names and the quantities they represent (e.g., in addition facts, recognizing that the + sign is the symbol for addition and that equality can be represented with the = sign or the line under the last number in a vertical problem).

2. Children should enter drill activities with the intention of memorizing the facts or material. The teacher's responsibility is to alert the students that this is a drill and that they should try to become quick or proficient with the facts to make other mathematical calculations easier.

3. Drill sessions should be short, varied, and daily (until achieving mastery). Drill activities can occur in the spare minutes that arise naturally during the school day (e.g., the 5 minutes spent lining up at the door for lunch or the last 3 or 4 minutes before dismissal). Drill activities need not be restricted to the traditional and ubiquitous flash cards. Problems can be generated through dice rolls, spinners, playing cards, and so forth (Reys et al., 2004). The format can be paper and pencil, board games, or oral responses to problems on the overhead projector.

4. During initial drill activities, students should be provided with both the stimulus and the response (e.g., $3 + 4 = 7$ rather than just $3 + 4 =$). This form of presentation allows students to build the association between stimulus and response without the intervening pause often used to finger count. Associations such as these build speed and accuracy but not necessarily understanding of the facts.

5. Students need to feel confident in their ability to memorize the facts. The teacher should encourage the students, praise them for their good efforts, and keep visual records of each student's progress so the student can see growth. These records could include bar graphs and cumulative charts or other creative ways of depicting progress, such as the example in Figure 11.1.

6. Each drill session should incorporate only two or three new facts and constantly review previously memorized facts. By memorizing only a few new facts at a time, students will not be overwhelmed by the seemingly monumental task of memorizing all facts for a given operation.

Strategies for Basic Fact Instruction

After applying these six principles and following the sequence of instruction provided in the classroom text, the hope is that all the students have become masters of the basic facts. This is not always the case, however. What then? Many current math educators recommend assisting students in developing efficient strategies that are easy for them to access and are based on using the facts that they already know (Isaacs & Carroll, 1999; Leutzinger, 1999; Van De

Figure 11.1   Cumulative Graph Showing Progress in Math Facts

Walle, 1998). An effective sequence for teaching these strategies might be the following:

1. Facts with zero. For example, 3 + 0 and 0 + 3. Note that students must have a firm concept of the commutative property of addition.
2. One more than or two more than. When adding 1 or 2, students should be taught the strategy of *counting on* from the larger addend. For instance, whether the problem is 2 + 9 or 9 + 2, students say to themselves: "9, 10, 11."
3. The "doubles." For some reason, children seem to learn these basic facts automatically. If students are automatic with the doubles, they are able to employ strategies that make other basic facts easier to recall.
4. Near-doubles. For example, if the student knows the double 4 + 4 = 8, that knowledge can be applied to the fact 4 + 5. Recall that 5 is one more than 4, so if 4 + 4 = 8, then 4 + 5 must equal 9 because 9 is one more than 8.
5. Complements of 10. Students can practice and learn the strategy of looking for basic facts that equal 10. For example, 9 + 1, 8 + 2, 6 + 4, 7 + 3. If students are able to identify facts that equal 10, they may be able to use that information to solve 8 + 7 more easily. Strategizing may go something like this: If 8 + 2 = 10, then 10 + 5 = 15. Note: the students must have firmly in their conceptual understanding the relationship between parts and whole

(i.e., that both addends can be broken into parts). Practicing with manipulatives as well as requiring students to talk through their reasoning allows the teacher to ensure underlying concepts are grasped.

For some students, especially those with short- or long-term memory problems, memorizing basic facts is difficult. Many mathematics educators advocate teaching strategies such as counting on and making 10. Even though these strategies may not provide students with quick recall, they do help students to conquer the basic facts by making reasoning tools available that enable them to derive answers for facts they do not know from those facts that they do know (Isaacs & Carroll, 1999).

Strategies for Subtraction Facts Instruction

Addition and subtraction are generally not taught as separate entities. Indeed, the sequencing of mathematics basic facts instruction may group facts by strategy rather than by sum (Isaacs & Carroll, 1999). For instance, after going through the +0, +1, +2, doubles, and complements of 10 for addition, the teacher may introduce the basic concepts of subtraction before tackling the most difficult addition facts. Teachers must show students how addition and subtraction are related. If children understand the relationship between addition and subtraction facts, they can use the known addition facts to find the unknown subtraction facts.

Sally knows all of her addition tables, but she has problems with the – 4 subtraction tables. Sally knows that 5 + 4 = 9. She does not know that 9 – 4 = 5. Her problem may be a lack of awareness that addition and subtraction are related. To teach Sally the relationship between the two problems, the teacher can first use partitioning activities (Isaacs & Carroll, 1999; Leutzinger, 1999). These involve separating a group of objects or pictures into two smaller groups; for example, giving Sally 9 chips and having her form one group of 5 chips and one of 4 chips. The same 9 chips also could be separated into sets of 3 and 6 or 7 and 2. Sally is to make as many combinations from the 9 chips as she can. After she has demonstrated partitioning skills, she progresses to recording activities.

While Sally is forming the groups, the teacher should talk with her about ways to keep track of the groups she has made. She might have Sally use a chart titled "9" and write down the numbers associated with each of her groups. This can lead to "the way mathematicians record" the groups—addition and subtraction facts. By writing both addition and subtraction facts for each partition, Sally should begin to see that addition and subtraction are related. She then is ready for the next type of activity, which involves working with missing addends, in other words, "thinking addition" (Van De Walle, 1998).

After giving Sally 5 markers, the teacher asks her how many more she needs to make a group of 9. Sally can count from 5 on (that is, begin counting at 6 and keep track of how many numbers it takes to get to 9), or she can make another group of 9, match her 5 with 5 from the new group, and count how many are unmatched. The teacher shows Sally that these problems can be written as addition facts in the form 5 + __ = 9 or as subtraction facts in the form 9 – 5 = __. Here again the teacher should point out that addition and subtraction are related and that knowing the addition facts helps solve the subtraction problems. Up to this point, the symbolic level (9 – 5 = __) is used as a way to record Sally's discoveries. This approach helps Sally develop confidence in her mathematical power.

The final step in this sequence is to apply the known addition facts directly to solve subtraction problems. Sally's teacher presents her with a written addition fact and has Sally write the subtraction facts that go with it. For example, Sally sees 9 + 5 = 14 and writes "14 – 9 = 5" and "14 – 5 = 9." Given subtraction facts (14 – 9 = 5), she provides the related addition facts (5 + 9 = 14 and 9 + 5 = 14). These activities should help Sally realize that because addition and subtraction are related, she can "think addition" when working subtraction problems. When shown 15 – 8 = __, Sally can rely on her addition facts and think "8 plus what equals 15?"

Developing efficient thinking strategies that are easy to access allows students without automatic recall of basic facts to have an alternative route to drill and practice (Leutzinger, 1999). The sequencing and strategies applicable to the basic facts of addition also work for subtraction (Isaacs & Carroll, 1999; Van De Walle, 1998), as illustrated in the following:

1. Basic concepts of subtraction with sums to 10. Modeling and practice with the concept of missing addend.
2. Subtraction of zero.
3. Easy subtraction facts, 1 less or 2 less. An effective strategy for these facts is instruction in "counting back" from the larger numeral.
4. Calculating differences based on the marker 10. For example, 11 – 4 = __. What number plus 4 equals 11? If 4 + 6 = 10, then 4 + 7 = 11. The missing addend is 7.
5. Facts derived from the doubles. Students are easily able to recall these facts if doubles in addition are known and if they have grasped the concept of the relationship of addition to subtraction.
6. Near doubles. 13 – 6 = __. If 6 + 6 = 12, then 12 – 6 = 6, so 13 – 6 must be one more, or 7.
7. For more difficult facts, such as 15 – 8 = __, counting up from the number being subtracted may be an effective strategy to teach the student until the facts become more and more familiar.

If basic facts of subtraction and addition are not at the proficiency level desired, the teacher can structure lessons and activities to help children develop an understanding of the operations as well as provide practice in strategies that may help them recall facts more efficiently.

Alternatives for Teaching Multiplication and Division

Just as addition and subtraction facts are related, so are multiplication and division facts. Van De Walle (1998) suggested an alternative sequence when the classroom textbook sequence does not work. The first step is to begin with the 0 and 1 facts. These account for 36 of the 100 basic multiplication facts. Next, even as early on as grades 1 and 2, students develop the skills of counting by 2s and by 5s (Reys et al., 2004). That knowledge provides a basis for understanding the patterns that occur in the multiplication table for the 2s and 5s. Learning the 2s and 5s adds 28 more combinations to the students' repertoire. Remember that for multiplication, just as for addition, a thorough understanding and application of the commutative property is essential. The 9s are then introduced. Multiplication tables for nines are fairly easy because we carry them around on our fingers. (Samples of finger tables are presented in Figure 11.2.) An additional strategy, more complicated but effective, for the 9s that may work for some students is the following: When given the fact $9 \times 7 = ?$, the student knows that the first digit in the correct answer will be one less than the factor being multiplied by 9 (in this case, a 6) and the second digit in the answer will be whatever remains to sum the two digits to 9 (i.e., 6 + 3 = 9). Therefore, the correct answer to 9×7 is 63. The next set of facts to learn is the squares (e.g., 6×6, 7×7, 4×4). These four sets—0s and 1s, 2s and 5s, the

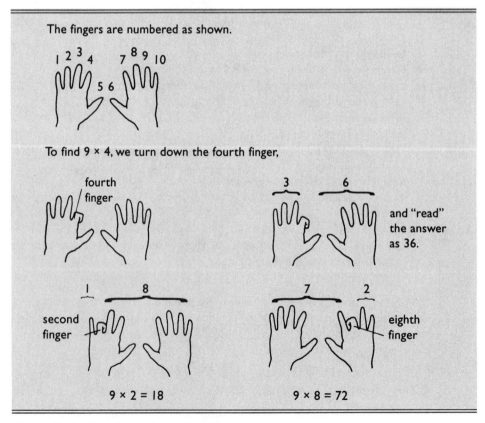

Figure 11.2   Samples of Finger Tables

9s, and the doubles—have covered 80 of the original 100 facts. Only 20 facts left to go! The last 20 are cut to 10 if the students know the commutative property. Students with remedial needs generally appreciate this sequence as they need to "remember" relatively few concepts to master the facts.

Another way of learning the basic multiplication facts is to learn all the facts whose product is less than 10. Next, the student learns all those combinations whose product is less than 20, and so forth. An example of this sequence is presented in Table 11.1.

Just as subtraction facts can be taught by relating them to addition facts, division facts can be taught by relating them to multiplication facts. The basic strategies and sequence presented to Sally for relating addition and subtraction can be adapted to multiplication and division. Using partitioning activities, followed by the teacher helping the student record, and finally the student recording alone, is a useful technique for teaching division. For instance, when giving Sally those same 9 chips, she can group them into 3 piles with 3 chips in each pile. When given 12 chips, she can make 6 piles of 2 chips each, 1 pile of 12 chips, 2 piles of 6 chips, 3 piles of 4 chips, and so on, just as long as there are no "remainders."

Many mathematics instructors today believe that drill and practice and rote memorization of basic facts should be tied to conceptual understanding of operations. Effective learning may not occur with mere drill and practice. Taking that into consideration, Van De Walle (1998) suggested the following steps to effective mastery of the basic facts for all operations:

1. Help children develop a strong understanding of each operation as well as the relationships among numbers.
2. Develop efficient strategies for the retrieval of basic facts.
3. Provide practice in the use and selection of these strategies.

Rote memorization should be tied to conceptual understanding when children are learning the basic facts of addition, subtraction, multiplication, and division (NCTM, 1999). From elementary school to middle school, the emphasis should be on thinking. As children acquire conceptual understanding of operations, they develop a sound basis for higher level thinking in mathematics (NCTM, 1999).

Meaning of Basic Operations

Each basic operation has more than one interpretation. Students must learn to recognize the type of interpretation the math situation or question requires.

Addition

Addition has two situations/meanings.

1. *Joining of sets.* For example: "Two gremlins are on the kitchen counter, and four more gremlins join them. How many gremlins are on the counter?" This

Table 11.1 Multiplication Facts Classified by Products

	0–10	10–20	20–30	30–40	40–50	50–60	60–70	70–80	80–90
									Intervals
Facts	0 × 0	2 × 6 6 × 2	3 × 7 7 × 3	5 × 7 7 × 5	5 × 9 9 × 5	6 × 9 9 × 6	7 × 9 9 × 7	9 × 8 8 × 9	9 × 9
	0 × 1 1 × 0	2 × 7 7 × 2	3 × 8 8 × 3	5 × 8 8 × 5	6 × 7 7 × 6	7 × 8 8 × 7	8 × 8		
	0 × 2 2 × 0	2 × 8 8 × 2	3 × 9 9 × 3	6 × 6	6 × 8 8 × 6				
	0 × 3 3 × 0	2 × 9 9 × 2	4 × 6 6 × 4	4 × 8 8 × 4	7 × 7				
	0 × 4 4 × 0	3 × 4 4 × 3	4 × 7 7 × 4	4 × 9 9 × 4					
	0 × 5 5 × 0	3 × 5 5 × 3	5 × 5						
	0 × 6 6 × 0	3 × 6 6 × 3	5 × 6 6 × 5						
	0 × 7 7 × 0	4 × 4							
	0 × 8 8 × 0	4 × 5 5 × 4							
	0 × 9 9 × 0								
	1 × 1								
	1 × 2 2 × 1								
	1 × 3 3 × 1								
	1 × 4 4 × 1								
	1 × 5 5 × 1								
	1 × 6 6 × 1								
	1 × 7 7 × 1								
	1 × 8 8 × 1								
	1 × 9 9 × 1								
	2 × 2								
	2 × 3 3 × 2								
	2 × 4 4 × 2								
	2 × 5 5 × 2								
	3 × 3								
Number	44	17	13	9	7	4	3	2	1

Source: From "The Monsters in Multiplication" by E. J. Bolduc, Jr., 1980. *Arithmetic Teacher, 28*(3), pp. 24–26.

is a dynamic situation in that students can visualize the motion of the four gremlins joining the two resting on the kitchen counter. This is the most commonly taught of the two.

2. *Part-part whole.* In this situation no movement is visualized. The two gremlins are still resting on the kitchen counter. The student is now told about four other gremlins that are resting on the bathroom counter. The question is, "How many gremlins are sitting on counters?" No action has occurred. The gremlins do not leave their respective counters. This kind of problem, less often presented, is static.

Teachers should provide students with numerous examples of both kinds of addition situations.

Subtraction

Subtraction has three meaningful situations.

1. *Take away.* Take away is the most easily understood, which is not surprising, as it is typically the only situation presented. An example of a take-away problem is: "Peter had eight pies. He ate three of them. How many does he still have?"

2. *Comparison.* This is exemplified by, "Peter had eight pies, and Simon had three pies. How many more pies does Peter have than Simon?" This is a truly simple comparison because nothing is taken away. The two sets (Peter's pies and Simon's pies) are compared directly.

3. *Missing addend.* This type of subtraction is probably the most difficult for students to understand, as it can be used to explain two different situations. Relating subtraction to addition, however, may avoid many difficulties. In both missing addend situations, the whole and one of the parts is known and the size of the other part has to be found. An example of one type of missing addend, where the unknown part is present, is: "I have five dolls. Three of them are Barbie dolls. How many are not Barbies?"

   In the other type of missing addend the other part is completely missing. For example: "My cake recipe calls for five cups of flour. I have only three cups. How many more do I need?" Both situations involve finding the size of the missing addend. The former is more likely to be solved by counting on (an addition process), whereas the latter probably will be solved by partitioning the whole into its two component subsets. Figure 11.3 shows pictorial models for subtraction.

Multiplication

Multiplication has two meaningful situations, both of which are commonly used.

1. *Repeated addition.* Repeated addition typically is used to teach the basic facts (e.g., "Conan captured six wizards. Each wizard had four magic stones. How many magic stones did Conan get?"). Figure 11.4 shows Conan's repeated addition approach to multiplication. If the six groups of stones were

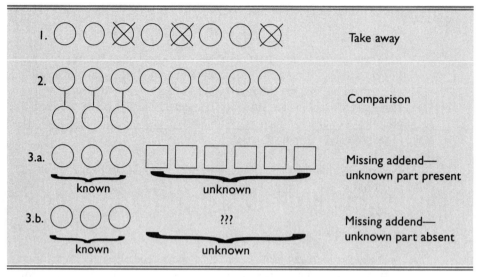

Figure 11.3   Pictoral Models for Subtraction Situations

arranged in an organized group—almost military fashion—with six rows of four stones each, the arrangement would be called an array. Figure 11.4 depicts Conan's magic stones in an array.

2. *Cartesian cross product.* Cartesian cross product, which also can be modeled as an array, involves identifying combinations. For example: "Conan has collected six wizard capes and four magic hats. How many different cape/hat combinations can Conan wear without repeating himself?" Because each of the 6 capes can be matched with each of the 4 hats, 24 combinations are possible. Figure 11.5 provides a graphic presentation of the Conan's apparel.

Division

Division also has two distinct meanings: *partition* and *measurement*. The main differences in these two meanings of division is the way in which the divisor is interpreted and the meaning of the answer.

1. *Partition.* In partition the total is known, and the divisor indicates how many equal-sized groups are to be made from the total. The problem is to determine how many there are in each group. For example: "Michelle has 15 dolls. If she shares them equally among her three friends, how many will each friend get?" Students must understand that each group (in this case, group of dolls) must be the same size.

2. *Measurement.* In measurement situations we already know the size of each group. For example: "Michelle has 15 dolls. If she puts 3 dolls on each shelf, how many shelves will she need?"

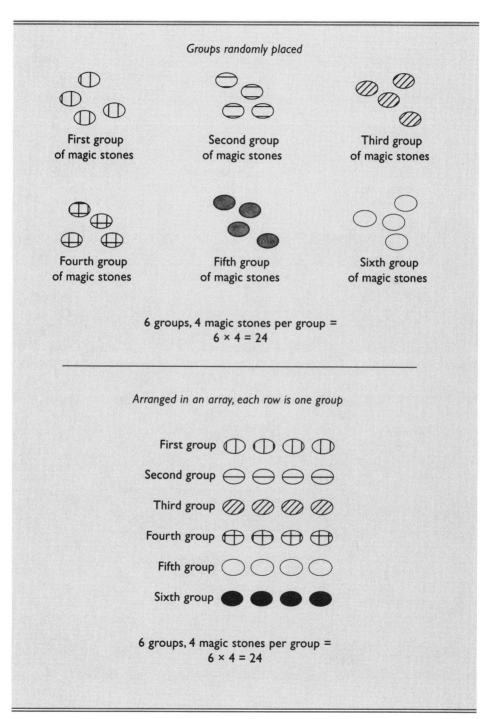

Figure 11.4   Multiplication as Repeated Addition

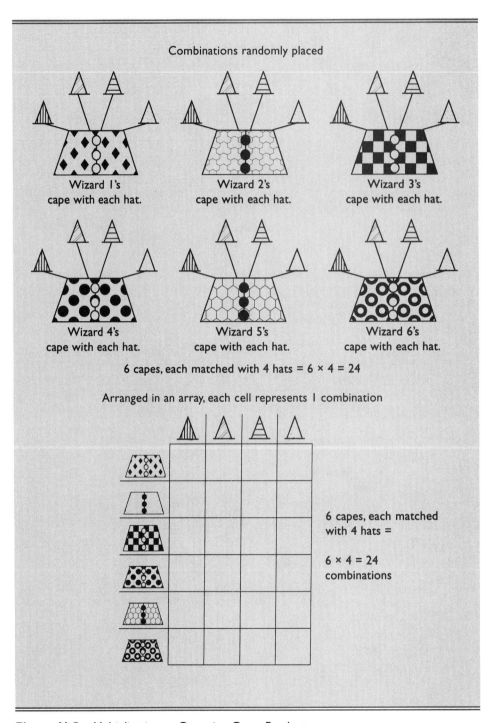

Combinations randomly placed

Wizard 1's
cape with each hat.

Wizard 2's
cape with each hat.

Wizard 3's
cape with each hat.

Wizard 4's
cape with each hat.

Wizard 5's
cape with each hat.

Wizard 6's
cape with each hat.

6 capes, each matched with 4 hats = 6 × 4 = 24

Arranged in an array, each cell represents 1 combination

6 capes, each matched
with 4 hats =

6 × 4 = 24
combinations

Figure 11.5   Multiplication as Cartesian Cross Product

Both of these problems can be solved by the division fact 15 ÷ 3, but the visualization and meaning of the answers (5) are totally different. In the partition problem the answer meant five dolls, and in the measurement problem the answer meant five shelves. Figure 11.6 shows partition, and Figure 11.7 shows measurement. Possibly students have difficulty with division because teachers do not spend enough time helping them interpret the answer.

Figure 11.6   Partition Approach to Division

Figure 11.7   Measurement Approach to Division

Algorithms

Historically, a major goal of elementary education has been to make children proficient in arithmetic computation. Thus, a significant portion of children's elementary mathematics training is devoted to mastering computational algorithms. To recap, an algorithm is a rule or procedure for solving a problem (Mauer, 1998; Van de Walle, 1998).Within this definition, technology such as hand-held calculators also may be considered an algorithm. Algorithms are tools, not educational goals. To be used effectively, therefore, they must be understood and mastered.

Common Algorithms

Although the four basic operations of addition, subtraction, multiplication, and division have many algorithms, some are more common than others. Historically, addition with regrouping has been called *carrying,* even though nothing gets carried. Subtraction with regrouping has been known as *borrowing,* even though the action was more like stealing. Combinations of addition and subtraction regroupings are involved in multiplication and division.

Because algorithms are basically steps or rules to follow in computing an arithmetic problem, they can be likened to the mechanics of composition. A person can complete an operation by following the rules (algorithms) without knowing the meaning of these rules. For example, a person can determine the cost of four new tires ($4 \times \$56.00$) without understanding why the decimal point must stay after the ones column, or why the 20 of the 4×6 must be regrouped with the other tens column.

Syntax

The mechanics or algorithms used in arithmetic have become known as the *syntax* of the operation. Although syntax can stand by itself, the ability to use it is enhanced greatly by understanding the meaning associated with it. Meaning in both language and arithmetic is called *semantics.* Together, syntax and semantics provide the learner with the broadest possible knowledge of arithmetic operations.

Prior to the inception of new math, arithmetic instruction was almost always syntactical. The rules were learned with little regard for why they worked. After World War II, mathematicians and math educators were concerned that students could compute but did not understand why the rules worked. This lack of semantic knowledge limited students' ability to solve problems. All corners of the country demanded reform of curriculum and methodology.

Semantics

During the ensuing new math era and continuing through the latest NCTM standards and principles statements, instructional emphasis has been placed on learning or discovering the meaning behind mathematics. The belief for many educators was that knowledge a person discovers, as opposed to being taught directly, is better understood and retained longer (De Corte, Greer, & Verschaffel, 1996).

Currently, the term *constructivism* in education refers to this approach (Thornton et al., 1997; Woodward & Montague, 2002). If the process for finding an answer is forgotten, it can be regenerated with a little meaningful reflection. As a result of this instructional approach, some students began to understand the structure of mathematics and why algorithms work (semantics). Unfortunately, these same students could not compute quickly, if at all. As would be expected, many educators became concerned that understanding did not mean skill and skill did not mean understanding. Mathematically stated, semantics does not imply syntax, and vice versa. The question then is: "What approach should teachers take?"

Educational Implications

The educational implications are clear. Some children will not attain conceptual knowledge of the algorithm with initial teaching, or perhaps ever. Yet, most of them can be expected to use the algorithm in a functionally positive manner. Stated another way, many children may learn the syntactic (rules) constraints of a given algorithm without connecting them to the semantic (meaning) information that underlies the algorithm. The lack of a bridge between the syntax and the semantics of the algorithm may lead to some serious errors in performance.

The traditional method of drill and practice has not always enabled students to see the connection between the mechanics of algorithms and the conceptual basis for the sequence of steps required in mathematical operations. Neither has it resulted in effectively helping students to learn how to become problem solvers (Buschman, 2004). Gagnon and Maccini (2001) recommended the following best practices for how to prepare students with disabilities for higher level math and reasoning skills while integrating the standards and principles outlined by the NCTM (2000):

- Teach prerequisite skills, definitions, and strategies. Use quizzes and reviews to determine if the student has difficulties with basic facts or algorithm processes.
- Provide direct instruction in problem representation and problem solutions. Because many students with learning disabilities have difficulty visualizing a problem situation, they may need direct instruction in creating a representation of the problem and in how to apply the correct procedure for solving it.
- Provide direct instruction in self-monitoring procedures. Thinking aloud and checking off steps in a procedure help students work independently.
- Teach students to use organizers. Graphic organizers and structured worksheets help all students analyze and solve problems.
- Incorporate manipulatives into instruction.
- Teach conceptual knowledge. Always demand explanations from students as they calculate and problem solve.
- Provide effective teaching. Model the task, provide guided and independent practice, review frequently, and provide corrective, immediate, and positive feedback.

Activities With Basic Algorithms

As we have been seeing, considerable emphasis is currently being placed on understanding the relationship between the meaning of algorithms and their respective mechanics. Each of the basic operations has several algorithms. Some algorithms are used more commonly than others and are generally accepted as being quicker. These usually are referred to as standard algorithms. Even though standard algorithms are considered quick, they become that way only after development and practice. Students with learning disabilities or students at risk for failure often do not use efficient strategies in their approaches to solving problems (Woodward & Montague, 2002). In such cases, they may need to be provided with a variety of strategies from which to proceed with their calculations.

Addition Algorithms

CARRYING   Although several algorithms can be used for addition of multidigit numbers, the most commonly used algorithm in the United States is the one typically called *carrying,* but more appropriately called *regrouping*. In this algorithm students begin in the ones place, add the digits, regroup (form groups of 10) if necessary, and indicate that regrouping has taken place by writing above the tens place the digit that indicates how many regroupings were done.

$$
\begin{array}{r}
{}^{1}37 \\
+\ 26 \\
\hline
63
\end{array}
$$

The process then is applied to the tens place, and so on. For students who do not attach meaning to the algorithm or have the concept of place value, this algorithm may be difficult. When students have difficulty with this standard form, alternative methods can be taught. Two common alternatives are *expanded notation* and *partial sums*.

EXPANDED NOTATION   Expanded notation, which is often used when first teaching multidigit addition, requires that students know some place-value concepts. For example, 43 has tens and ones—to be specific, 4 tens and 3 ones. When adding two multidigit numbers, students can use the expanded forms, shown in Figure 11.8.

Even though this algorithm is developmental (taught before the standard algorithm), it is useful when reteaching the concept.

PARTIAL SUMS   Partial sums, also a developmental algorithm, show the sum of the ones and the sum of the tens, as in Figure 11.9.

These approaches might trigger mental overload for some students, as they must think of more parts than before, causing even more frustration. Yet, the novelty of these approaches might be just what other students need. An advantage to the partial-sum method in both addition and multiplication algorithms is that it includes the opportunity to work from right to left or from left to right for students who may have difficulty with directionality (Randolf & Sherman, 2001).

48 = 4 tens and 8 ones
+ 37 = 3 tens and 7 ones

Step 1: Add the ones and tens.
Step 2: Regroup the ones, if necessary.
Step 3: Put the tens together.
Step 4: Write the tens in a simpler way.
Step 5: Write the answer in number form.

48 = 4 tens and 8 ones
+ 37 = 3 tens and 7 ones

(Step 1): 7 tens and 15 ones
(Step 2): 7 tens and (1 ten and 5 ones)
(Step 3): (7 tens and 1 ten) and 5 ones
(Step 4): 8 tens and 5 ones
(Step 5): 85

Figure 11.8 Expanded Notation

48
+ 37
15 (sum of the ones)
70 (sum of the tens)
85

Figure 11.9 Partial Sums

HUTCHINGS' LOW-STRESS ALGORITHM   An approach developed specifically for students with learning disabilities is Hutchings' low-stress algorithm, also referred to as the *scratch method* (Randolf & Sherman, 2001). In this method students are not required to keep a running total in their heads but write down an answer whenever the sum is greater than 9. The power of this algorithm is that students need to know only the basic facts. A step-by-step description of Hutchings' algorithm for finding a sum is given in Figure 11.10.

Several other algorithms for addition are also available. They may be found in a good math methods text.

Subtraction Algorithms

DECOMPOSITION   Just as in addition, subtraction has several algorithms. The standard one is decomposition, commonly but inappropriately called *borrowing*, since it suggests that something needs to be returned (Ross & Pratt-Cotter, 2000). Vocabulary in most current mathematics texts refers more often to this process as *regrouping*. The decomposition method remains the most popular today. It was developed in 1937, when William Brownell first conducted research in which

---

Problem: 57 + 68 + 76 + 87 + 99 + 58

57	
68	(1) Student adds 7 + 8 and records 15, putting the "1" above the tens.
76	(2) Student adds 5 + 6 and records 11, putting the "1" above the tens.
87	(3) Student adds 1 + 7 and records 8, no tens to regroup.
99	(4) Student adds 8 + 9 and records 17, putting the "1" above the tens.
_58_	(5) Student adds 7 + 8 and records 15, putting the "1" above the tens.
445	Student proceeds to the tens column and continues in the same manner.

Figure 11.10   Modified Hutchings' Low-Stress Addition Algorithm

students were able to use the "crutch" of marking through numerals to keep track of the steps in the algorithm (Ross & Pratt-Cotter, 2000).

The most common error with the decomposition algorithm is to reverse digits within a column. That is, students take the smaller from the larger, regardless of placement in the column. For example, when working 73 – 29, students often think of "9 minus 3" rather than "3 minus 9," which will produce an answer of 56 instead of the correct answer of 44.

TECHNIQUES FOR STUDENTS WITH LEARNING DISABILITIES   One approach developed for students with learning disabilities involves doing all the borrowings first. Teachers must caution the students to regroup only when necessary. For example, when solving 3,241 – 1,736, students have to regroup from the tens to the ones and the thousands to the hundreds, but not from the hundreds to the tens. When using this approach, care must be taken to ensure that students do not overgeneralize the "do all the regrouping first" rule to "regroup in every place." Figure 11.11 shows how this problem should be worked.

Many other subtraction algorithms are available. Most of these require math skills beyond the entry level, however.

Multiplication Algorithms

PARTIAL PRODUCTS   When students have problems learning the standard multiplication procedure, the partial products algorithm can be used. This approach is similar to the partial-sums approach in addition. Subproducts in the multiplication

---

3,247	3,247	3,247	3,247	3,247
−1,736	47	247	2,247	2,247
	−1,736	−1,736	−1,736	−1,736
				1,511

Figure 11.11   Hutchings' Low-Stress Subtraction Algorithm

problem are found and then totaled, just as subsums in the addition problem are found and then totaled.

ARRAYS   Again, students have to be familiar with arrays for finding answers to basic multiplication facts. This concept can be expanded to multiplication of multidigit numbers. Using graph paper to outline the arrays works well. For example, the outline for the problem 12 × 23, is a rectangle 23 squares long and 12 squares tall, as shown in Figure 11.12. The individual squares within the rectangle may be counted to find the total, or the concept of repeated addition may be applied to shorten the counting process.

The partial-products algorithm may be used to further shorten the counting process. However, students must understand and be able to write numbers in expanded notation. They must know that 23 can be rewritten as 20 + 3 and 12 as 10 + 2. The multiplication problem now becomes

$$\begin{array}{r} 20 + 3 \\ \times\ 10 + 2 \\ \hline \end{array}$$

This form highlights the partial products, which can also be found within the 12 × 23 array:

    2 × 3 = 6 (see A in Figure 11.12)
    2 × 20 = 40 (see B in Figure 11.12)
    10 × 3 = 30 (see C in Figure 11.12)
    10 × 20 = 200 (see D in Figure 11.12)

Division Algorithms

DEMYSTIFYING DIVISION   Division is often taught last and with much dread in an instructional sequence because it is complex and requires so many prerequisite skills (Bryant, Hartman, & Kim, 2003; Reys et al., 2004). However, just as with

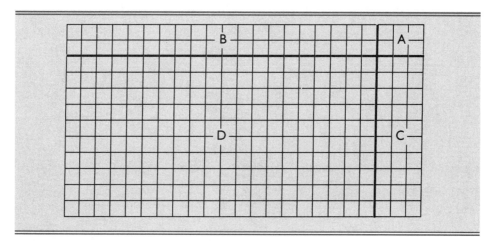

Figure 11.12   Using Arrays in Multiplication

all other algorithms, an essential first step is to develop a strong conceptual basis for division before teaching the long-division algorithm. Yet, students may have the prerequisite skills and understand the concept, but lack skill and practice in performing the steps required for the division algorithm.

Brett's long-division problems are incorrect because he does not know how to do long division, not because he does not know the multiplication or subtraction facts. In all probability, the most effective technique to use with Brett is the traditional long-division approach but in a modified form. This form, presented in Figure 11.13, allows Brett to clearly attend to the meaning of the process of long division. In solving the problem 64 ÷ 3, Brett can be taught to realize that the 3 means three groups that must be exactly equal in quantity. He has 6 tens. He can

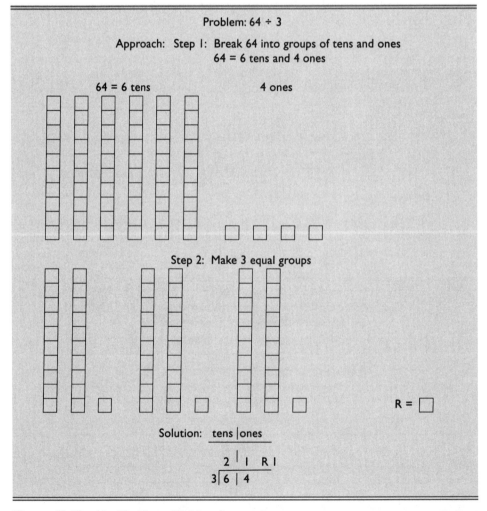

Figure 11.13   Modified Long Division Approach

distribute 2 tens to each of the 3 groups. No tens are left over, so he moves to the ones. He has 4 ones and can distribute 1 to each group with 1 left over—a number that does not fit into the three groups. All distributions have been made, and each group is the same size, 21. The answer is recorded as 21 with a remainder of 1.

Division problems that require regrouping can be solved in much the same manner. For example, in the problem $54 \div 4$, the divisor indicates there are to be four groups, each of which must be the same quantity. The 5 tens are distributed one to each group, leaving 1 ten. The leftover 10 is regrouped, or broken into 10 ones. These 10 ones are combined with the original 4 ones. Now there are 14 ones. (This combining process is the reason why students "bring down" numbers in the standard long-division procedure.) The 14 ones are distributed evenly to the 4 groups, 3 to each group, leaving 2 ones. The answer is 13 with a remainder of 2. Figure 11.14 provides a diagram of this process.

DEVELOPMENTAL ALGORITHMS   The two most commonly taught developmental algorithms in long division are *scaffolding* and *pyramid*. Examples of problems worked with these two algorithms are presented in Figures 11.15 and 11.16. Unfortunately, these two algorithms may confuse the students rather than assisting them. One source of confusion lies in the task demand of estimating two-, three-, and sometimes four-digit quotients. This skill in estimation may be too sophisticated for most upper-elementary-level students. Another source of confusion lies in attempting to transfer from an algorithm based upon measurement (scaffolding or pyramid) to one based upon partitions (standard algorithm).

Principles of Instruction

For any algorithm, certain principles of instruction apply.

1. *Identify prerequisite skills.* Three prerequisite skills for any algorithm include mastery of the basic facts, understanding of the meaning of the problem (e.g., addition is joining of sets or part-part-whole), and place value.
2. *Provide students with prerequisite skills or skill substitutes such as number tables* (fact charts found in the back of most folders). Prerequisite skills should be taught before teaching the algorithms (Isaacs & Carroll, 1999).
3. *Provide a strategy for applying preskills.* Teaching preskills alone does not ensure that students, especially those with learning problems, will complete the algorithm correctly (Isaacs & Carroll, 1999; Van De Walle, 1998).
4. *Make a judgment call as to the relative amount of time spent on developing meaning and time spent in drill.* Even though meaning is the major goal of mathematics instruction, some students may never understand the underlying concepts and may need to learn the mechanics by rote to survive in the academic and real worlds.
5. *Give the students drill and practice and also relate algorithms to real life.* Drill and practice is an integral part of the math program and it is critical that students be allowed to master procedures and concepts before moving on (De Corte et al., 1996; Gagnon & Maccini, 2001; Maccini & Gagnon, 2000).

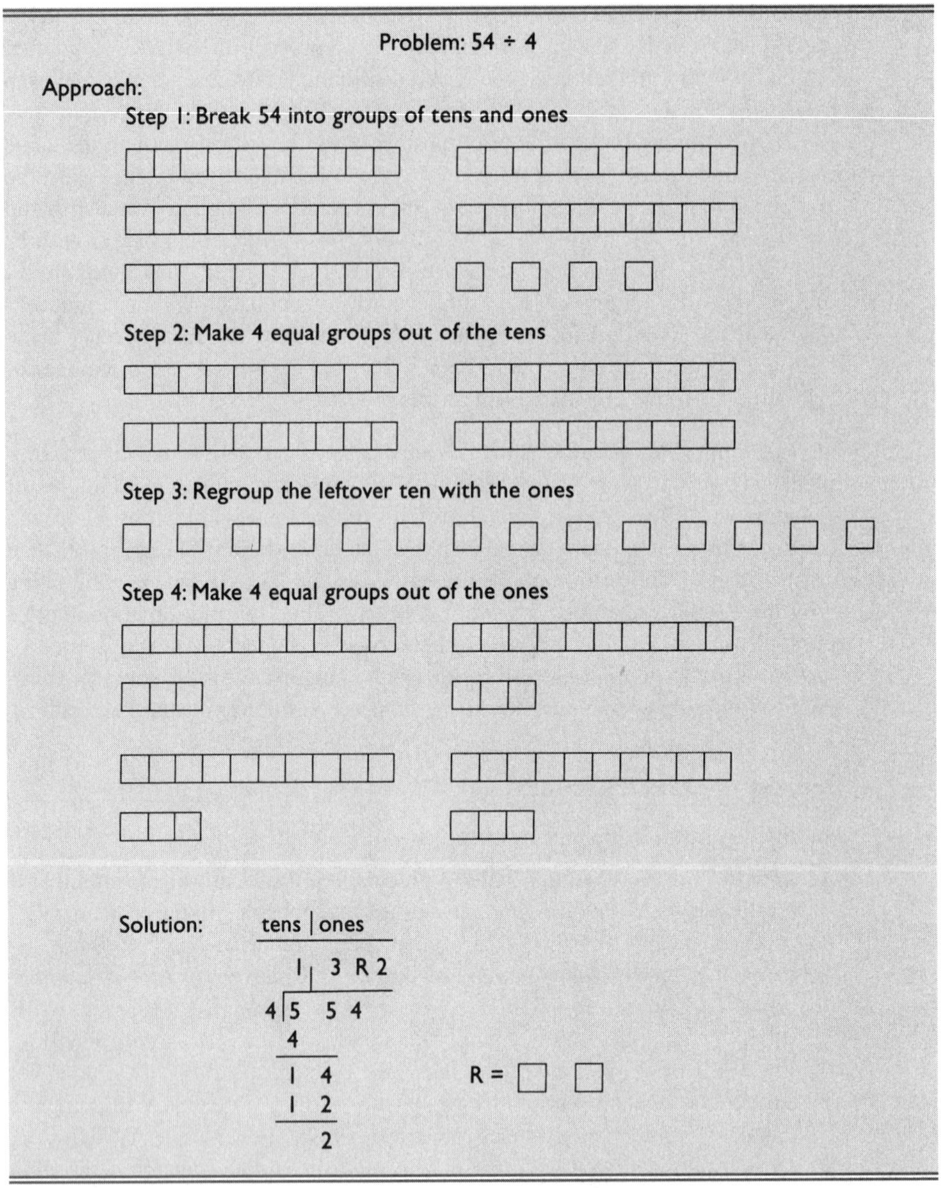

Problem: 54 ÷ 4

Approach:

Step 1: Break 54 into groups of tens and ones

Step 2: Make 4 equal groups out of the tens

Step 3: Regroup the leftover ten with the ones

Step 4: Make 4 equal groups out of the ones

Solution: tens | ones

```
        1 | 3 R 2
      4|5   5  4
        4
        1   4        R = ☐ ☐
        1   2
            2
```

Figure 11.14   Modified Long Division Approach With Regrouping

Problem Solving

The end goal of mathematics education is problem solving. All of the energy spent in learning facts and algorithms will be reaped with the student's ability to apply them in problem-solving situations. This is not automatic, though. Students

Scaffolding

$$5\overline{)177}$$

100	20
77	
50	10
27	
25	5
2	35

Solution

Step 1: Determine the number of times 5 occurs at the **hundreds** level and subtract from 177.

$5\overline{)177}$	
−100	20
77	

Step 2: Determine the number of times 5 occurs at the **tens** level and subtract from 77.

$5\overline{)177}$	
−100	20
77	
−50	10
27	

Step 3: Determine the number of times 5 occurs at the **ones** level and subtract from 27.

$5\overline{)177}$	
−100	20
77	
−50	10
27	
−25	5
2	

Step 4: Add the hundreds, tens, and ones and note the remainder.

$5\overline{)177}$	
−100	20
77	
−50	10
27	
−25	+5
r 2	35 r 2

Figure 11.15   Long Division Problem Worked With Scaffolding Algorithm

must be given numerous opportunities to learn, through either direct instruction or discovery, how to apply facts and algorithms.

Pyramid

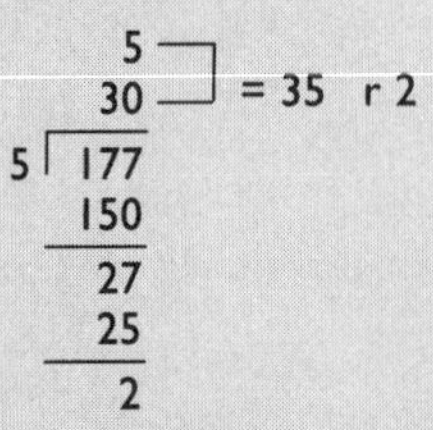

$$
\begin{array}{r}
5 \\
30
\end{array} \Bigg]= 35 \ r \ 2
$$

$$
\begin{array}{r}
5\,\overline{)\,177} \\
150 \\
\hline
27 \\
25 \\
\hline
2
\end{array}
$$

Solution:

Step 1: Estimate the number of times 5 occurs in 177 and subtract from 177.

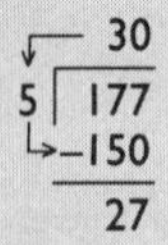

$$
\begin{array}{r}
30 \\
5\,\overline{)\,177} \\
{-150} \\
\hline
27
\end{array}
$$

Step 2: Determine the number of times 5 occurs in 27 and subtract from 27.

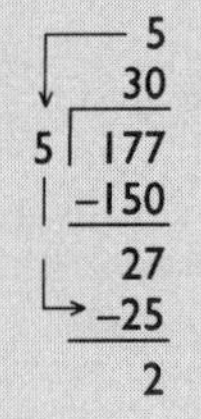

$$
\begin{array}{r}
5 \\
30 \\
5\,\overline{)\,177} \\
{-150} \\
\hline
27 \\
{-25} \\
\hline
2
\end{array}
$$

Step 3: Add 30 + 5 and note the remainder 2.

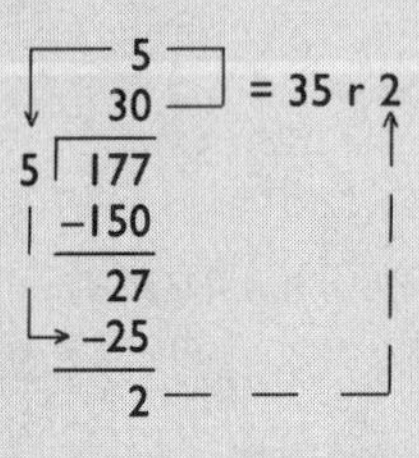

$$
\begin{array}{r}
5 \\
30
\end{array} \Bigg]= 35 \ r \ 2
$$

$$
\begin{array}{r}
5\,\overline{)\,177} \\
{-150} \\
\hline
27 \\
{-25} \\
\hline
2
\end{array}
$$

Figure 11.16   Long Division Problem Worked With Pyramid Algorithm

Story Problems

Problem solving is often confined to verbal or story problems, typically found at the end of the chapter in the math book. This is the portion of the chapter on which many students do poorly, and the part of the chapter that the teacher is most likely to skip. Children often dislike working on word problems because they don't have the strategies to solve them. Sometimes they don't know which operation to perform. An indication of this type of difficulty can be heard in the familiar "Just tell me if I need to add, subtract, multiply, or divide!"

NECESSARY SKILLS   According to the Office of Special Education Programs' 2002 report on effective mathematics instruction for students with disabilities, the skills and cognitive processes that are critical to problem solving in math require that the students be able to do the following:

1. Read the problem. Students must be able to comprehend linguistic and numerical information in the problem.
2. Paraphrase. Students transform that information into their own words and are able to convey the meaning of them.
3. Visualize, either mentally or on paper, the relationships among elements of the problem (e.g., draw a picture that represents the situation).
4. Hypothesize about problem solutions and formulate a plan to solve the problem.
5. Estimate the answer or predict the outcome.
6. Compute the answer by recalling the correct algorithms and procedures.
7. Check the answer. Detect and correct errors during the problem solution.

Strategies for Solving Word Problems

Problem solving encompasses more than story problems. It is the process used when a solution to a situation is sought but is not apparent immediately. This is the part of mathematics that does not rely so much on numbers as on reasoning ability. Problem solving is a skill, and, like any other skill, can be taught. Students with learning disabilities often need direct instruction in applying strategies that address the specific skills involved in choosing and applying an appropriate problem-solving strategy (ERIC/OSEP, 2002; Jarrett, 1999). The NCTM (1989, 1999, 2000) has recommended more emphasis on the study of problem-solving strategies and less emphasis on the use of "clue words." To enhance students' problem-solving skills, the teacher must teach strategies that can help students understand the problem, organize information, and use the information to find a solution. Strategies (each will be discussed in further detail) include the following:

1. Looking for patterns
2. Drawing a diagram or picture
3. Using manipulatives
4. Constructing a table or graph
5. Acting it out
6. Working an easier problem of the same type/Reducing and simplifying
7. Breaking set/Taking a new point of view

LOOKING FOR PATTERNS   Problems involving patterns typically ask, "What is the next entry in the series?" and then provide sequences with missing elements, as in 1, 3, 5, __, or 0, 1, 3, 6, 10, __ . Once students have found the next entry, they should be encouraged to verbalize the pattern. In the first example, they would state "7" because the series is odd numbers. In the second example, they would say "15" because the series added 1, then 2, then 3, then 4, and now is supposed to add 5. Having students verbalize their reasoning may bring to light different explanations for the same pattern. For example, given the sequence 5,

10, 25, __, a student may explain that the blank should be 50 because the sequence is values of U.S. coins. Another student may decide that the blank represents 105 because the difference between the first two is 5 and between the second two is 20 (4 × previous difference of 5). The difference between the third and fourth then should be 80 (4 × previous difference of 20), making the blank worth 105 (25 + 80). When students hear other students' answers and reasoning, they begin to understand that "real" problems, unlike traditional story problems, may have more than one right answer.

DRAWING A DIAGRAM OR PICTURE   This strategy is included in Dunlap's approach to solving word problems. For example, while driving along the freeway, a driver notices a road sign that reads, "Barlow 38 miles, Fremont 105 miles." How far apart are Barlow and Freemont? A diagram would help the child see the relationships within the problem and could suggest the operation needed to solve it. Figure 11.17 depicts this problem.

USING MANIPULATIVES   Manipulatives would be of great help in solving the following problem: "Last Saturday I saw seven cyclists pass my house. I counted 17 wheels. Some riders were on bikes, and the rest were on trikes. How many bikers and trikers did I see?" Students could use 17 markers and begin arranging them in groups of 2 (to represent bikes) and groups of 3 (to represent trikes) until they had used all 17 markers, keeping in mind that they could have only 7 groups altogether. They should discover that there were 4 bikers and 3 trikers.

MAKING A TABLE OR GRAPH   This strategy helps students organize any information given in the problem and generate new information to help find a solution. For example: "Carmen is knitting a sweater. Every 7 rows make 1 inch of sweater. How many rows will she have to knit to make the sweater 15 inches long?" Figure 11.18 shows how to use a table to organize this information.

ACTING IT OUT   By becoming actively involved in a problem situation, students may gain a better understanding of the information in the problem and the relationship between the pieces of information presented. A problem that can be acted out is: "A farmer is taking a goose, a fox, and a sack of grain to the market. On the way, he must cross a river. The farmer, who is the only one who can row,

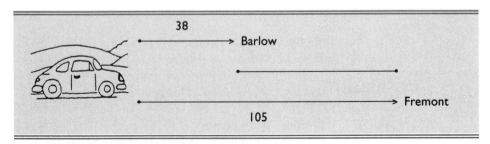

Figure 11.17 Using Diagrams to Solve Problems

Rows	Inches
7	1
14	2
21	3
...	...
70	10
...	...
105	15

Figure 11.18   Using a Table to Organize Information

finds a boat, but he can take only one commodity at a time with him. If he leaves the fox with the goose, the goose will be eaten. If he leaves the goose with the grain, the grain will be eaten. How does he get all three commodities across the river?"

To solve the problem, four students can act out the parts of the farmer, goose, fox, and sack of grain. By trying different actions and discussing what they have done, they finally will decide that the farmer should take the goose across first. He then rows back alone and gets the grain. When he gets the grain across the river, he picks up the goose and brings it back to the original side. He then takes the fox across and comes back alone to get the goose.

Another potential solution that was presented by a group of elementary students is to allow the goose to eat the grain and then swim across while the farmer rows the fox. They defended their answer by claiming the problem did not indicate all three commodities *had* to reach market or that the goose must remain dry!

WORKING AN EASIER PROBLEM   The stumbling block in problem solving frequently is the virtual size of the numbers used in a problem. When smaller numbers are substituted, students often are able to decide what to do and then reinsert the original numbers. Another use of this strategy is with problems involving fractions. If students substitute whole numbers, the situations often are easier for them to solve. For example, in the problem "What number divided by $\frac{1}{5}$ equals $\frac{1}{5}$" (see Figure 11.19), the student could use whole numbers for the $\frac{1}{5}$s. The problem then becomes "What number divided by 2 equals 2?" or "What number divided by 7 equals 7?" The pattern often is more evident with the whole numbers than with the fractions: Multiply the two given numbers, as we are looking for a missing product. The original problem can be solved by $\frac{1}{5} \times \frac{1}{5}$, and the solution ($\frac{1}{25}$) found.

$$? \div 1/5 = 1/5$$
$$? \div 2 = 2$$
$$? \div 7 = 7$$

Figure 11.19   Using Substitution to Work Difficult Problems

BREAKING SET/TAKING A NEW POINT OF VIEW   This strategy is useful for nontraditional problems and often involves brain teasers. It probably is one of the most useful strategies because real-life problems do not always follow text-book formats. Teachers must choose brain teasers carefully to provide enough success experiences so that students will continue to participate in problem-solving activities. Students also should be encouraged to use any other known strategies to help them solve these problems. An example of a brain teaser is: "A farmer plants 10 trees in 5 straight lines, 4 trees to a line. How does she do this?" Unless students are taught that some problems cannot be solved with their pre-conceived ideas, they can become frustrated by brain teasers and nontraditional problems. In the example given, many students attempt to order the trees in ver-tical or horizontal lines and ignore other possibilities, such as diagonal or criss-crossing lines. Figure 11.20 shows one solution.

Employing Strategies

Students need to know that each strategy can be used to solve many types of prob-lems and that any one problem can be solved by several strategies. Teachers must distinguish between lessons for teaching a strategy and lessons for teaching prob-lem solving. A strategy is similar to a prerequisite skill in that students need to know it before they can be expected to apply it in a problem-solving situation. Once students know the strategies, teachers must demonstrate how and when to use them. This can be done in problem-solving lessons in which everyone, includ-ing the teacher, is involved in using learned strategies to solve problems.

Reading and Problem Solving

Competent problem solvers have to engage in activities that allow them to gain meaning from written material. They have behaviors common to any competent reader. A few of the behaviors associated with competent readers are as follows:

1. They constantly monitor understanding by using certain strategies—reread-ing, skimming, or looking for some easier but related example of the prob-lem, underlining key words, rewording in their own language, or going to another person for a discussion of the topic.
2. They stop reading when the information doesn't make sense.

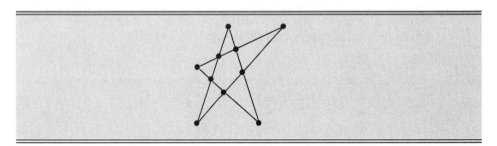

Figure 11.20   Solution to Tree-Planting Problem

3. They find help when clarification is needed.
4. They isolate the key elements and eliminate unnecessary detail.
5. They relate information to previously learned concepts.
6. They predict what's going to happen next and then confirm or deny the information.

Strategies for teaching readers to be competent can be taught best through a process developed by Ann Brown called *reciprocal reading instruction* (1980). Although reciprocal reading was not designed specifically for teaching problem solving in mathematics, the strategies and teaching techniques can be used successfully in math. The four strategies associated with this approach are as follows:

1. Summarizing
2. Developing questions (pointing out what is important)
3. Analyzing reader problems (difficulties the reader might be having, such as "I don't understand what this sentence says" or "How am I going to find out this word?")
4. Predicting the outcome

These strategies are coupled with a three-step teaching technique:

Step 1:   Teacher models.
Step 2:   Teacher requests student to summarize.
Step 3:   Teacher works with student response.

Students must understand that teachers and other adults go through a thinking process to solve problems—the answers do not appear magically in the adult's mind. Teachers can demonstrate these thinking processes by talking aloud as they model the process of solving a problem. Teacher modeling is more than writing the equation and searching for an answer. To model for students effectively, teachers must summarize the information from the problem orally, verbalize questions that ordinarily would be internalized, state the parts that require clarification, and present students with their predictions (Isaacs & Carroll, 1999; Montague, 2003; Reys et al., 2004). Inexpert problem solvers become extremely frustrated when they are presented with a problem and then have an adult show them a nice, clean solution without any evidence of struggle. Students develop the idea that unless they can solve problems quickly, neatly, and precisely, they are mathematics losers.

In trying to solve the problem of the farmer with 10 trees planted in 5 lines, 4 trees to a line, the teacher reads the problem aloud and, using her own words, tells the class what she thinks the problem means. She might say that she knows she can work with 10 trees, 4 in a line, and 5 lines. Some questions she might ask of herself are whether the lines cross, whether they all go in the same direction, and whether she can figure out which strategy (such as drawing pictures or using manipulatives) would be best to use. An item that might need clarification could be whether the lines are straight or curved or whether this makes any difference. She then makes some guesses such as, "I wonder if it's going to be a rectangle."

After trying that shape and seeing that it doesn't work, she makes a new prediction and tests it. This last step might have to be done several times before a solution is located.

The next step is for the teacher and the student to go through the four-strategy process together. Finally, the student assumes the part of the teacher and models the process. The student's first attempts at modeling might not be fully developed or give complete answers; some parts even may be blatantly wrong. The teacher must salvage what is correct and elaborate wherever necessary.

This three-step process of teacher modeling, student–teacher cooperation, and student modeling is carried out over a series of lessons and several different problems. Students do not model problems the teacher has solved already. They should have new problems at their level of difficulty.

Suggestions for Problem Solving

1. Practice translating words from English into mathematical symbols ("seven more than" would be "+ 7"; "twice as many as" would be "2 × ").
2. See if relaxation exercises prior to math or problem-solving instruction calm students down and relieve frustration.
3. If students come up with the wrong solution, help them find the question they answered and compare that to the question that actually was asked.
4. Provide students with an equation and solution and have them create a problem that could be solved with it.
5. Provide students with ample opportunities to verbalize ("think aloud"), ask questions, and explain their results (Reys et al., 2004).
6. Help the students make the idea their own. First *reread the problem*, then write the problem in your own words, then teach how to do the problem. Show students how to make the problem fit in with their own perspectives and experiences (Simonson & Gouvea, nd).
7. Never, ever say, "Now, wasn't that easy?"

Estimation and Mental Computation

Although paper-and-pencil computation constitutes a major portion of elementary mathematics instruction, children should develop reasonable estimation and mental computation skills (Reys et al., 2004). The two topics are closely related, and both skills allow students to learn various ways of looking at and working with numbers (ERIC/OSEP, 2002). The thinking strategies introduced in the discussion of basic facts acquisition are an example of mental computation skills and can be extended to more complex computations. Consider the following example of mental computation for 6×700. The student may think, "I know that 6×6 is 36. So, 6×7 is 6 more, or 42. I'm multiplying with 7 in the hundreds place, though, so I add two zeros and the answer is 4,200." Proficiency with mental computation also contributes to an increased skill with estimation (Reys et al., 2004). When students see the problem 734×6, they are able to automatically predict that the answer will be slightly more than 4,200.

Such techniques may or may not be included in the formal curriculum, but can be directly taught, while keeping in mind the following:

1. Examples for practice should be realistic and related to real-world situations.
2. The language of estimation is used. Vocabulary related to estimation includes such terms as *about, near, almost, just over*, or *nearly*. The words *approximate* and *reasonable* are appropriate for older students.
3. Estimation and mental computation build on the related skills and concepts that students already possess.
4. A group of students will arrive at more than one "right" estimate. A range of estimates is always acceptable (Reys et al., 2004; Van De Walle, 1998).

Students need to be taught that estimation means making an educated guess and, therefore, should be done before the paper-and-pencil computation, not afterward by simple rounding off the number.

Techniques

Three common estimation techniques are *front-end estimation, rounding off,* and *stating the range.* Front-end estimation considers only the digits in the left-most column of the problem and operates with them (i.e., adds, subtracts, multiplies, or divides them). (See Figure 11.21.) Rounding off is slightly more precise than the front-end technique in that each number in the problem is rounded off and operated on. In front-end estimation the estimates might end up being tens, hundreds, or thousands too low because the left-most column might not always be filled. Rounding off can be done to the nearest tens, hundreds, thousands, and so forth, and provides a more accurate estimate. Figure 11.22 shows the rounding-off technique using the same numbers from the front-end approach.

2,398	2,000
846	---
3,265	3,000
+1,423	+1,000
	6,000

Figure 11.21   Front-End Estimation

2,398	2,000
846	1,000
3,265	3,000
+1,423	+1,000
	7,000

Figure 11.22   Rounding to Nearest Thousand

Stating the range involves a bit of rounding off. Numbers are rounded down to the nearest ten, hundred, and so on, and an estimate is found. Then they are rounded up to the nearest ten, hundred, and so on, and a second estimate is found. This gives two values between which the actual answer usually falls. (See Figure 11.23.)

Special Considerations for Special Children

Perceptual Considerations

Perceptual and cognitive aspects of approaching mathematics are different. *Cognitive aspects* refer to processes such as solving problems—problems that are verbally expressed and require logical thinking. *Perceptual aspects* refer to factors such as working from up to down or right to left (Randolf & Sherman, 2001). Some children with learning difficulties have problems with directionality. Unless assisted, they can have serious trouble with any kind of columnar work, such as regrouping in addition or subtraction. Using color codes to indicate place value and aids such as graph paper can help a student keep the ones in the ones place and the tens in the tens place. Some students may also have problems with visual perception. They may misperceive a mathematical sign by rotating it (e.g., confusing "×" for "+."). Turnbull, Turnbull, Shank, and Smith (2004) identified a number of problem areas related to perceptual difficulties that can affect mathematics performance:

- *Visual perception:* The ability to differentiate numbers or signs may be impaired. Visual–motor integration difficulties may result in the inability to copy numbers and shapes accurately. Calculators with large print or color printouts may be helpful to students with visual processing problems (Montague, 2003).
- *Memory:* Students may experience difficulty recalling math facts, performing calculation procedures, or recalling strategies due to either short- or long-term memory problems or both. Repeated practice, teaching mnemonic strategies, and constant review are all effective means of strengthening skills in this area.

	Lower Limit	Upper Limit
2,398	2,300	2,400
846	800	900
3,265	3,200	3,300
+1,423	+1,400	1,500
	7,700	8,100

Figure 11.23   Range Estimates, Rounding to 100s

■ *Auditory processing/language:* Difficulty with auditory perception or with relating mathematics terms to meaning or to vocabulary may be a cause of underperformance in mathematics.

These kinds of perceptual problems can be found across a wide variety of disabling conditions, but not all children with disabilities exhibit visual, auditory, or memory problems.

Language Concerns

Difficulties in understanding mathematics have been attributed at times to the difficulty of the vocabulary. Both the strangeness of the symbols used in mathematics and the vocabulary related specifically to mathematics can contribute to misunderstandings for students with learning disabilities. We cannot assume that a student will simply "pick up" the symbolic material associated with math. In addition, students need to know the meaning of mathematical vocabulary in order to succeed in problem solving. Eliminating language-processing barriers for students with learning disabilities as well as for those with limited English proficiency is critical (Adams, Thangata, & King, 2005).

Because of the high occurrence of unfamiliar vocabulary in mathematics, teaching unknown words becomes necessary and is especially important for students with any type of language or auditory-processing difficulties. According to Monroe and Orme (2002), students experience problems because many terms have meanings for mathematics that differ from their everyday use and because many terms are abstract. They suggest a combination of two approaches for the effective learning of math vocabulary:

1. *Meaningful context:* Students construct meaning by observing, discussing, reading, writing, and listening to math vocabulary within the context of its use rather than "definition only" instruction.

2. *Direct teaching:* Once students have had some experiences with the concept or vocabulary being taught, direct teaching tools, like a graphic organizer, may help students organize and access the new information (Monroe & Orme, 2002).

Our previous discussions on the syntax and semantics of mathematics, as well as on the relationship of reading and problem solving, remind us that the best practices relating to teaching reading comprehension are just as applicable to understanding mathematical concepts and vocabulary. In addition, the use of cues, manipulatives, cooperative learning groups, relating mathematics to real-life experiences, and requiring students to verbalize their processes and thinking improves mathematical comprehension for any student with language difficulties (Lee & Sikjung, 2004; Torres-Velasquez & Lobo, 2004/2005).

Summary

The difficulties of teaching math to children who have special instructional needs are compounded when teachers think they must cover the text page by page. Certain strategies designed to teach children how to learn mathematics have been useful with children who have problems in learning basic facts, algorithms, and problem solving.

Teachers can manipulate instructional factors that impact a student's learning. Four of the most easily manipulated factors within the teacher's command are time, size of instructional groups, reinforcement, and materials. The way teachers use these four factors can significantly increase or decrease the amount of math learning that takes place.

Although most teaching recommendations are similar for any child experiencing math learning difficulties, special considerations may have to be made in light of certain disabling conditions. For example, children who have perceptual difficulties (e.g., left-to-right confusion) may need special adaptations in materials. Children with language problems may need syntax simplification before math problem solving. Any child with a sensory difficulty, such as a visual or an auditory impairment, will need materials and techniques that account for these deficits. Instructional emphasis, regardless of accommodations, always should focus on identifying skills acquired by students and skills still needed for a successful mathematics experience.

References

Adams, T. L., Thangata, F., & King, C. (2005). "Weigh" to go! Exploring mathematical language. *Mathematics Teaching in the Middle School, 10,* 444–448.

Bolduc, E. J., Jr. (1980). The monsters in multiplication. *Arithmetic Teacher, 28*(3), 24–26.

Bryant, D., Hartman, P., & Kim, S. (2003). Using explicit and strategic instruction to teach division skills to students with disabilities. *Exceptionality, 11,* 151–164.

Burris, C., Heubert, J., & Levin, H. (2004). Math acceleration for all. *Educational Leadership, 61,* 68–71.

Buschman, L. (2004). Teaching problem solving in mathematics. *Teaching Children Mathematics, 10,* 302–309.

Campbell, P., & Stewart, E. (1993). Calculators and computers. In R. Jensen (Ed.), *Research ideas for the classroom: Early childhood mathematics* (pp. 251–268). New York: Macmillan.

Cavanagh, S. (2005). NCTM to revise position on calculator use. *Education Week, 24,* 10.

De Corte, E., Greer, B., & Verschaffel, L. (1996). Mathematics teaching and learning. In D. Berliner & R. Calfee (Eds.), *Handbook of educational psychology* (pp. 491–594). New York: Simon & Schuster Macmillan.

Deshler, D., Ellis, E., & Lenz, B. (1996). *Teaching adolescents with learning disabilities: Strategies and methods.* Denver, CO: Love Publishing.

ERIC Clearinghouse on Disabilities, ERIC/OSEP Special Project. (2002). Strengthening the third "r": Helping students with disabilities achieve in mathematics. *Research Connections in Special Education, 11,* 1–10.

Fuchs, L., & Fuchs, D. (1998). General educators' instructional adaptation for students with learning disabilities. *Learning Disability Quarterly, 21,* 23–33.

Furner, J. M., & Duffy, M. L. (2002). Equity for all students in the new millennium: Disabling math anxiety. *Intervention in School and Clinic, 38,* 67–74.

Gagnon, J., & Maccini, P. (2001). Preparing students with disabilities for algebra. *Council for Exceptional Children, 34,* 8–15.

Gelzheiser, L., Griesemer, B., & Pruzek, R. (2000). How are developmentally appropriate or traditional teaching practices related to the mathematics achievement of general and special education students? *Early Education and Development, 11,* 217–238.

Gersten, R., & Chard, D. (1999). Number sense: Rethinking arithmetic instruction for students with mathematical disabilities. *The Journal of Special Education, 33,* 18–38.

Griffin, S. (2004). Teaching number sense. *Educational Leadership, 61,* 39–42.

Jarrett, D. (1999). *The inclusive classroom: Mathematics and science instruction for students with learning disabilities. It's just good teaching.* Portland, OR: Northwest Regional Educational Laboratory.

Karp, K., & Howell, P. (2004). Building responsibility for learning in students with special needs. *Teaching Children Mathematics, 11,* 118–125.

Isaacs, A., & Carroll, W. (1999). Strategies for basic math instruction. *Teaching Children Mathematics, 5,* 508–515.

Lee, H., & Sikjung, W. (2004). Limited-English-proficient students: Mathematical understanding. *Mathematics Teaching in the Middle School, 9,* 269–272.

Leutzinger, L. (1999). Developing thinking strategies for addition facts. *Teaching Children Mathematics, 6,* 14–18.

Loveless, T. (2004). *Trends in math achievement: The importance of basic skills.* Presentation of the Secretary's Summit on Mathematics, Washington, DC. Available at www.ed.gov/print/rschstat/research/progs/mathscience/loveless.html

Loveless, T., & Coughlan, J. (2004). The arithmetic gap. *Educational Leadership, 61,* 55–59.

Maccini, P., & Gagnon, J. (2000). Best practices for teaching mathematics to secondary students with special needs. *Focus on Exceptional Children, 32,* 1–22.

Maccini, P., & Gagnon, J. (2002). Perceptions and application of NCTM standards by special and general education teachers. *Exceptional Children, 68,* 325–344.

Mauer, S. B. (1998). What is an algorithm? What is an answer? In L. J. Morrow (Ed.), *The teaching and learning of algorithms in school mathematics* (pp. 21–31). Reston, VA: NCTM.

Monroe, E., & Orme, M. (2002). Developing math vocabulary. *Preventing School Failure, 46,* 139–142.

Montague, M. (2003). Teaching division to students with learning disabilities: A constructivist approach. *Exceptionality, 11,* 165–174.

National Council of Teachers of Mathematics. (1989). *Curriculum and evaluation standards for school mathematics.* Reston, VA: Author.

National Council of Teachers of Mathematics. (1999). *Back to the basics or forward to the basics—Which philosophy should we embrace?* Reston, VA: Author.

National Council of Teachers of Mathematics. (2000). *Principles and standards for school mathematics.* Reston, VA: Author.

Randolf, T., & Sherman, H. (2001). Alternative algorithms: Increasing options, reducing errors. *Teaching Children Mathematics, 7,* 480–484.

Renga, S., & Dalla, L. (1993). Affect: A critical component of mathematical learning in early childhood. In R. Jensen (Ed.), *Research ideas for the classroom: Early childhood mathematics* (pp. 22–37). New York: Macmillan.

Reys, R. E., Lindquist, M. M., Lambdin, D. V., Smith, N. L., & Suydam, M. N. (2004). *Helping children learn about mathematics.* Hoboken, NJ: John Wiley & Sons, Inc.

Ross, S., & Pratt-Cotter, M. (2000). From the archives … Subtraction in the United States: An historical perspective. *Mathematics Educator, 10,* 49–56.

Senturk, D., Whipple, A., Ho, H., Zimmer, J., Chiu, S., & Wang, C. (2000). A cross-national study: Children's math self-concept and its relationship with mathematics achievement. In S. George (Ed.), *The academic achievement of minority students: Perspectives, practices, and prescriptions* (pp. 65–91). Lanham, MD: University Press of America.

Shaftel, J., Pass, L., & Schnabel, S. (2005). Math games for adolescents. *Teaching Exceptional Children, 37,* 25–30.

Sherman, H., Richardson, L., & Yard, G. (2005). *Teaching children who struggle with mathematics.* Upper Saddle River, NJ: Pearson Education.

Simonson, S., & Gouvea, F. (nd). How to Read Mathematics. Retrieved October 7, 2007 from http://www.stonehill.edu/compsci/History_Math/math-read.htm

Stigler, J., & Hiebert, J. (2004). Improving mathematics teaching. *Educational Leadership, 61,* 12–17.

Strong, R., Thomas, E., Perini, M., & Silver, H. (2004). Creating a differentiated mathematics classroom. *Educational Leadership, 61,* 73–78.

Thornton, C., Langrall, C., & Jones, G. A. (1997). Mathematics instruction for elementary students with learning disabilities. *Journal of Learning Disabilities, 30,* 142–150.

Torres-Velasquez, D., & Lobo, G. (2004/2005). Culturally responsive mathematics teaching and English language learners. *Teaching Children Mathematics, 11,* 249–255.

Turnbull, R., Turnbull, A., Shank, M., & Smith, S. (2004). *Exceptional lives: Special education in today's schools.* Upper Saddle River, NJ: Pearson Education.

Usiskin, Z. (1998). Paper-and-pencil algorithms in a calculator-and-computer age. In L. Morrow & M. Kenney (Eds.), *The teaching and learning of algorithms in school mathematics* (pp. 7–20). Reston, VA: NCTM.

Van De Walle, J. (1998). *Elementary and middle school mathematics: Teaching developmentally.* New York: Addison Wesley Longman.

Woodward, J., & Baxter, J. (1997). The effects of an innovative approach to mathematics on academically low-achieving students in inclusive settings. *Exceptional Children, 63,* 373–388.

Woodward, J., & Montague, M. (2002). Meeting the challenge of mathematics reform for students with LD. *The Journal of Special Education, 36,* 89–101.

Woodward, J., Baxter, J., & Robinson, R. (1999). Rules and reasons: Decimal instruction for academically low-achieving students. *Learning Disabilities Research and Practice, 14,* 15–24.

Xin, J. (1999). Computer-assisted cooperative learning in integrated classrooms for students with and without disabilities. *Information Technology in Childhood Education, 1999*(1), 61–78.

Zambo, R. (2005). The power of two: Linking mathematics and literature. *Mathematics in the Middle School, 10,* 394–399.

Zemelman, S., Daniels, H., & Hyde, A. (1998). *Best practice: New standards for teaching and learning in America's schools.* Portsmouth, NH: Heinemann.

CHAPTER

12

Social Aspects
of Inclusion:
Preparing Students
for Life

Kathleen McCoy and Kathleen Danielson

KEY TERMS

- categorical dispositions
- climate
- constructivism
- conversational language
- culture
- discipline
- entry/exit tips
- four principles of conversation
- help signals
- intent
- intonation patterns
- pragmatics
- predictable routines
- principles of shaping
- schemata
- self-determination
- signal system
- social–emotional issues
- socioemotional expression
- sociometric techniques
- structure
- student-led IEPs
- teacher-controlled transition time
- transition time

Understanding the Social Aspects of Inclusion

Paradigm Shift

As students with disabilities increasingly receive educational services in inclusion classrooms, educators have had to undergo a profound paradigm shift. Many students with high- and low-incidence disabilities obtain educational services in the general education setting within the general education curriculum. Nearly all of these students will spend no part of their lives segregated from the general population and will live and function, to a greater or lesser degree, in the larger society. Possessing appropriate social competence is an important and requisite goal for access to all levels of society (Elksnin & Elksnin, 2006).

Social aspects of integration for children with disabilities take a slightly different turn than academic integration. Development of social skills must involve interactions with others, especially peers. Inclusion teachers, therefore, must both teach appropriate social interaction skills to students with disabilities who need such teaching and instruct other students in how to interact with persons with limited social skills. Children who share classroom experiences with individuals who have poor social skills need to be taught to think in new ways to see the inherent value and worth in children who may not know how to communicate appropriately or have poor socioemotional control.

Children with disabilities, like all individuals, need to develop a positive societal self-image. As socially competent individuals, they must understand the effect of their behaviors on the feelings of others as well as be able to interpret the messages other members of society are sending. The position that children with disabilities have the same rights and responsibilities as their nondisabled peers is one that needs continual monitoring.

Cultural lags often exist between perceptions and feelings emanating from the law, the heart, and the mind. Attitudes about the societal competencies expected of individuals with disabilities, as well as attitudes and expectations of members of the society toward individuals with disabilities, need constant examination and vigilance to develop or maintain appropriate social integration. Children with disabilities should no longer be thought of as children with anomalies or as "broken" people who need to be "fixed" (Fitch, 2002), but rather as individuals with strengths and value. Their educational experiences need to prepare them to live in and contribute to a democratic society and to realize their own individual potential. Inclusion, therefore, "support[s] the broader goal of societal integration" (Heir, 2003, p. 36), not merely school integration.

Constructivism

Social integration and school integration practices can be based on a social constructivist perspective, which emphasizes how individuals create their realities through language, beliefs, and social interactions with others. Constructivism suggests that learning involves creating, inventing, and developing our own knowledge and sense of self (Gagnon & Collay, 2001). Attitudes are shaped by interactions. Positive attitudes create positive behaviors and negative attitudes create negative behaviors. To develop reality-based attitudes and related behaviors, interaction between those labeled disabled and those labeled typical is necessary. Sense of self and place in the community is developed through interactions with others.

Sense of self for many students with disabilities, unfortunately, is based on a deficit model. For most of these students, a three stage process occurs in which (a) mismatches between students' learning or social abilities and academic demands are interpreted as within-the-student deficits, (b) students are labeled and categorized based on deficit, and (c) students must deal with the consequences of the label in a variety of social contexts (Luna, 2003). Developing a positive social self and an affirmative identity becomes a tricky and upward struggle for many students with disabilities. Even though many educators have decried the use of labels and downplayed disability categories, the stigma related to such labels is prevalent and insidious. Many times unthinking adults use terms, quickly adopted by children, like *retarded* or *spastic* when referring to some unpleasant person, place, or action. "Riding the short bus" is not considered an honor. Until the deficit model is replaced, individuals with disabilities and people who love and care for them will face social integration issues.

Social Schemata

Interactions with others shape children's beliefs about themselves as social beings. Children develop schemata, that is, mental networks that allow them to learn new ideas based on prior knowledge. The mental schemata for becoming included in society and role definition are shaped by interactions with others in the home, classroom, school, and community. When Tisha makes a mistake in number facts and the other students laugh, Tisha is categorizing two major ideas: (a) she is not very smart in math, and (b) the other children think she is less able than they are. As a result, Tisha may demean her worth based on what she perceives her peers think about her. The number, level, and type of responses children like Tisha receive in the society of the classroom will shape their feelings about themselves not only as learners, but as members of society. The students who are laughing at Tisha are also forming a mental network about their feelings toward her and other children who demonstrate similar behavior.

Social Constructivism

One of the educational theorists most often linked with social constructivism is Lev Vygotsky. More than 30 years ago, Vygotsky, a Russian psychologist, originated the phrase *zone of proximal development* in which he identified various stages of development (Vygotsky, 1978). Of particular interest to inclusion teachers is Vygotsky's belief that patterns and levels of thinking are developed and shaped by the activities practiced in the social institutions of the culture (Lee & Smagorinsky, 2000; Morris, 1998). School is one of the primary social institutions experienced by children beginning as early as preschool and continuing for an additional 10 or more years. In essence, concept development occurs through the mediation of others (Moll, 2004). Thus, the mediation of the other students, teachers, staff, and administration helps create students' concept of self as members of society.

Vygotsky's ideas about the learning potential of students and the formative role of others have particular implications for students with disabilities. Vygotsky's concepts can be applied to attempts to understand the social organization of classroom interactions as affecting development of self as a learner and self as a social being. Children who are ridiculed openly or secretly will develop a role in social settings that is very different from that of students who are publicly praised and valued.

Acknowledgment of value in the school society includes the kind of grades students receive, the ability to do classroom assignments, and contributions to the class as a whole. Without intervention, children who have difficulty reading, writing, computing, and understanding language are usually at a disadvantage. Many of these children, who are often also found in disability categories, may not receive sufficient opportunities for positive acknowledgment as members of the classroom. True inclusion settings benefit all children. But inclusion provides experiences for children with disabilities that empower them to live in a society where they can reject the within-the-person deficit and celebrate their unique strengths. Inclusion classrooms, therefore, must be designed to provide maximum opportunity for positive recognition of self and self as a member of society with all rights, duties, and responsibilities.

Social integration in inclusion classes can be difficult, yet it is not impossible. It does require systematic analysis of the players and the social system in which the social development game is played. Analysis begins with the relationship between results of social assessment and behavioral influences of a child's disability. The impact of the disability on conversational interaction is the first consideration when attempting to provide social communication. Communication, social and emotional skills, and physical presence are three key factors in promoting socialization.

Social Communication and Social Interaction

Social Communication

Language skills, especially those involved in conversation, need to be considered when designing appropriate socialization activities in an inclusion setting. Children's ability to receive and express information is directly proportional to their ability to communicate and establish social ties with other class members. Children whose speech is unintelligible or difficult to understand may need assistive technology to help make their needs clear. Other children may have language issues related to the ability to receive, express, and process ideas. An inclusion teacher must take into account language skills when promoting social interactions like class discussion, peer tutoring, or academic tasks like oral reports.

Some children with disabilities have challenges communicating with others in their environment. For example, children with cerebral palsy may have motor limitations affecting speech production. Children with low cognitive functioning or disabilities involving processing sounds may have problems using and/or understanding various aspects of language. Communication aids can be used to facilitate speech and language interactions. These aids can be low tech (e.g., pointing to pictures to indicate ideation) or high tech (e.g. hearing aids or computers with voice output) (McDonnell, Hardman, & McDonnell, 2003). Although assistive devices are powerful aids for some children with certain types of language disabilities, inclusion teachers must also instruct their students in etiquette and conventions of language as social and interactive communication.

Language for socialization purposes is multifaceted. Inclusion teachers, like Ms. McDonnell, engage in systematic analysis of their students' level of skill with each of the four principles of conversation (Twachtman-Cullen, 2000):

- Quantity: Be informative without being verbose.
- Quality: Be truthful.
- Relevance: Contribute only information that is pertinent to the topic and situation.
- Clarity: Convey information in a manner that is clear and understandable to the listener.

Ms. McDonnell uses anecdotal observations to get a general sense of the language interactions between her students. Once she has identified children who are having significant discussion or conversation issues, she begins more methodical record keeping. Tally marks, specific situations, and specific issues are detailed for the children who are most likely to become socially isolated due to poor conversation and discussion skills. Ms. McDonnell typically only needs about 3 to 4 days to identify the language issue. Determining the intervention is a lot more challenging.

Ms. McDonnell is used to working with children who exhibit issues related to the four principles of conversation. Her student John, for example, speaks "nonstop"; he is oblivious to the social distress signals being sent by Michael, who is tapping his foot to an unknown beat, and Andrea, whose looks should have imploded John's ebullient discourse about 5 minutes into the topic. Regardless of whether John is aware of his communication style, his garrulousness may be a significant social barrier to winning friends. Ms. McDonnell will need to provide a means by which John can monitor his output.

Donovan is another student with language issues. All the students in the class, as well as Ms. McDonnell, love to listen to Donovan's stories. The problem is that no one is sure where the truth ends and his stories begin. In fact, one day

Donovan came to school explaining that he was going to have emergency open-heart surgery. Ms. McDonnell was so concerned that she contacted Donovan's mother to see if she could be of any assistance. As it turned out, only a visit to the doctor was in store. In his mind, Donovan had exaggerated his annual sports physical to become a much more medically dramatic event. No amount of explanation could convince Donovan that he was not scheduled for surgery. Most of Donovan's peers now find his words suspect. Ms. McDonnell needs to intervene before Donovan's confabulations cause him to lose all social credibility and his status is reduced to class clown or worse.

Two of Ms. McDonnell's students, Richard and Paul, have problems sticking to the topic. During class discussion, Richard and Paul appear anxious to share information. Unfortunately, both boys seem to focus on one or two words in the topic. They then contribute information relative to the word, but not to the topic. For example, the class was discussing desert flora and fauna. The hot topic was the size of the desert animals' ears. Foxes, jackrabbits, and mule deer all have very large ears as a survival mechanism for staying cool. Richard's contribution was that Rudolph the red-nosed reindeer had a very shiny nose. The class laughed, but Richard was confused about why his peers were making fun of his statement.

In last year's class, Ms. McDonnell had a student named Laurie who often sent incredibly unclear messages to her classmates. When Laurie was trying to explain an idea to someone, she never gave enough background for the person to grasp what she was intending to say. Laurie seemed to be starting a conversation in the middle of a thought. If the listeners did not know Laurie very well, they would have no idea what she was talking about. Clarity in communication was not one of Laurie's strong points, but she was lucky because her best friend often explained what Laurie was trying to say. Laurie did get a little resentful of her friend's "interference," but Ms. McDonnell intervened and the friendship was saved.

Teacher Intervention

Ms. McDonnell is an inclusion teacher with very little educational background in language and language development. However, she has lots of experience discussing and conversing with others. She has also been observing the interactions of students for many years. Ms. McDonnell may not have a certificate that describes her as a language expert, but her proficiency in social interactions cannot be denied. When Ms. McDonnell consults with language experts face to face or vicariously through books, journals, or the World Wide Web, she continues to add a level of sophistication to her language intervention expertise.

Intervention for Each of the Four Conversational Issues

Quantity, quality, relevance, and clarity must also take into account the particular characteristics of the children involved, both the specific child and the class as a whole. Ms. McDonnell's first level of intervention is to address specific issues with the entire class. In this way she is using the least intrusive accommodation for the students with serious language issues and the class as a whole.

Ms. McDonnell teaches the entire class about what is appropriate and respectful behavior, with an emphasis on taking turns and sharing time, backing up statements with real or hypothetical examples, how to stick to a topic, and how to make ideas clear to the listeners. Appropriate communication behaviors are taught through a variety of active learning techniques such as brainstorming, multiple-intelligence activities, or role playing. Ms. McDonnell has learned that the more her students are able to discuss and converse with each other, the more academic learning and positive social interactions can occur.

General Interventions for Discussion

Discussion and conversation constitute a significant amount of instructional time in inclusion settings. Stop and start times or transitions between speakers are important aspects of conversation and discussion that can be controlled by either the teacher or the students. In teacher-controlled transition time, the teacher provides direct input into the transition. When students control transitions, the teacher provides indirect input or control. An important aspect of interventions designed to increase or decrease quantity of input must focus on intention.

Intention means the speakers have a definite idea of why they are speaking and what they plan to say. The difference between truth and fantasy, significance of the contribution to the discussion, and techniques for expressing information in a clear and understandable manner are all related to intention. Intention, like any behavior, can be taught. The principles of instruction are similar to a teach, model, lead, and test paradigm. Ms. McDonnell typically follows and tweaks this paradigm to fit the social needs and academic content of her classes. However, like all inclusion teachers, she has limited instructional time. Rather than isolate lessons for content and lessons for learning appropriate discussion principles, she creates a twofer, a lesson combining principles of discussion with particular subject matter.

On a day when Ms. McDonnell wants the children to participate in a literature circle, she uses a student-centered approach to focus on clarity. Accordingly, she teaches students by having them brainstorm ideas about how to make themselves clearer in a discussion of their literature. Next, one or more students model examples and nonexamples of clearly expressed ideas from their literature. Then, Ms. McDonnell sensitively assists children in expressing themselves clearly by offering encouraging and content-laden cues and prompts when necessary. Finally, she reduces her role in assisting with the clarity aspect of the literature circle, noting instances of success and cases that need more practice in a later discussion.

Allowing children to continue to violate any or all of the four principles of conversation puts them at risk for social isolation and can stunt their social growth and development. Some children may need more practice in intention than is available in whole-class activity. Other children may need additional prompts or cues to help remember the expected intentional behavior. For children who require more than a teach, model, lead, test paradigm embedded in a whole-class setting, at least two additional instructional approaches may be tried: (a) a signaling system and (b) sources of feedback other than the teacher.

SIGNALING SYSTEM   Because discussion and conversation are fluid, children need to know as quickly as possible when a breach has occurred or is occurring. Take the example of John, a filibusterer's poster child, who cannot seem to figure out when his talk time is sufficient. Rather than singling John out, Ms. McDonnell has set a time limit for discussion for all the students. She uses a model of a traffic signal to remind students to share the discussion highway. Green means go, yellow means prepare to stop, and red (accompanied by the tinkle of a crystal bell) means stop talking.

SOURCES OF FEEDBACK OTHER THAN THE TEACHER   Ms. McDonnell does not always use the traffic signal, but John always needs feedback. Ms. McDonnell has privately arranged for John and his best friend Edward to be signal partners. When either John or Edward is on a talking roll, the other plays monitor. They have arranged a secret signal, to which even Ms. McDonnell is not privy, that keeps them both on the time track.

Reinforcement

Like all other learned behaviors, reinforcement has a profound effect on how many times children continue to apply principles or use signal systems in discussions or conversations. The way children use the signal system depends almost entirely upon how the teacher responds to their behaviors. Initially, the teacher needs to respond every time appropriate principles of discussion or conversation occur—with or without signals. Gradually, however, the teacher must systematically decrease the positive corroboration to a more irregular rate of support. If children expect to be praised every time they demonstrate appropriate discussion behavior, they may become dependent on the teacher's signal and fail to generalize to other times and settings. Inclusion teachers need to encourage independent use of appropriate behaviors and discourage inappropriate dependencies.

Shaping Discussion and Conversational Behaviors

Even with a signal system, some children need a lot of help learning and practicing appropriate discussion and conversational behaviors. Inclusion teachers have the same responsibility to teach discussion and conversation skills as they have to teach academics. Shaping appropriate discussion and conversation behaviors follows the same rules as shaping behaviors for reading and writing. To get students like John, Donovan, Richard, Paul, and Laurie, who have a variety of conversational and discussion language issues, teachers must first identify any language behavior that is on the right track and mold this behavior one tiny step at a time. Because John's language problem relates to quantity (i.e., how much time he spends talking), his language issue is much easier to shape. Donovan's problem is much more difficult to manage. For example, he cannot be expected to distinguish between fact and fiction every time he opens his mouth. He does not make that distinction himself. On those occasions when reality does break through Donovan's world, he can be praised with the sincere hope that praise will encourage him to attend more to the world he shares with his peers and other members of his community.

For the educator, intellectual brilliance and multiple degrees can be helpful in teaching children appropriate classroom discussion and conversation skills, but the lynchpin to success or failure most likely resides in persistence. A teacher's persistence, in conjunction with the principles of shaping, may increase the rate at which a child develops a positive self-image and social acceptance in the inclusion setting. Principles of shaping are the guidelines that help teachers decide when to change expectations, how to speed up expectations, what to do when expectations are not being met, and when to start over. Principles of shaping can apply to any instructional area, including discussion and conversational expertise. Seven guidelines for shaping behavior are as follows:

- Raise expectations in small enough steps so that success, and subsequent reinforcement, is attainable.
- Shape only one behavior at a time.
- Once a transitional expectation has been reached, reinforce irregularly before establishing the next expectation.
- Plan the shaping program from start to finish.
- Change the shaping procedure if it is not working.
- Step back to previous criteria and reinforce if the current behavior deteriorates.
- Praise the students at the end of the day or class session for successes achieved.

Principles of shaping may be applied to any behavior that can be measured or in which progress can be documented.

Social Acceptance and Language Skills

Social acceptance, more often than not, is based on informal language skills. Conversational language, for example, even more than language of classroom discussion, includes the ability to understand and produce appropriate sociocultural words, intonation patterns, and nonverbal aspects of informal conversation or communication. Many aspects of peer-to-peer interactions are not directly taught. Children need to be able to understand the vocabulary, the intonation patterns, and the nonverbal aspects of formal and informal conversation to gain meaningful communication and develop acceptance into the society of their peers. Likewise, children need to be able to express their ideas. Intention, again, is demonstrated through vocabulary, intonation patterns, and nonverbal aspects of formal and informal conversation. Acceptance into a social group often hinges on the ability to use language in an age- and norm-appropriate way.

Vocabulary

The kind of vocabulary needed for communication between peers, parents, teachers, and community members in general is very different from the word knowledge needed for specific academic content. Conversational vocabulary is developed through incidental learning—that is, learned through unplanned and spontaneous experiences through the context of interactions with others in social settings. The phrase "my dog sometimes spelled my dawg" may refer to Germaine's yellow Labrador or may refer to his best friend. Social context and experience set the meaning. Children develop shared vocabulary, intonation patterns, and nonverbal aspects of language through mutual experiences, real or vicarious.

Intonation Patterns

Intonation patterns are the melodies of speech. They carry meaning. If, for example, the sentence is, "Yes, I really like the school uniform," intention can be inferred by the speaker's voice pattern. Edward, who really likes the uniforms, uses a pleasant and upbeat tone. Tom, on the other hand, who would rather be wearing anything else, would have a heavily sarcastic quality in his voice.

Nonverbal Aspects

Nonverbal aspects of communication are often classified as *pragmatics*. Pragmatics involves a kind of information processing between the communicating parties. Pragmatics is a term for social communication monitoring; it is a kind of language street smarts that facilitates judgment of appropriateness between communicators. As such, pragmatics guides communicators to adjust for meaning or intention based on knowing how much information to provide, sensitivity to social judgment, listener needs, and context. Knowing words and phrases is only one aspect of language. To be socially integrated, children must express themselves in a situationally appropriate manner (Cohen & Ishihara, 2004); that is, they must process

- what can be said,
- where it can be said,
- when it can be said, and
- how to say it most effectively.

Not all children can express themselves in a traditional, situationally appropriate manner, regardless of intervention. Yet, they need to make their intentions clear. In such cases, the inclusion teacher, with a lot of help from the students in the class, must develop a nontraditional language code. A nontraditional language code is based on the way the student with pragmatics deficits expresses intention or requests. When LaToya, for example, wants to join in a class discussion, she rocks back and forth making high-pitched sounds. Based on her tone, the children in LaToya's class can translate her intentions. A higher pitch means "no," and a slightly lower pitch means she wants to add some information. LaToya uses a special computerized program to voice her thoughts.

Academic Intelligence and Pragmatics

Academic intelligence is not necessarily related to skills in pragmatics. Anthony is a bright academically achieving student who does not know how to express himself in an appropriate manner. Anthony wants to make friends and has discovered that he can attract sympathetic peers by talking about how miserable his life has become. True, many classmates steer clear of him, but usually one or two will try to help Anthony solve his never-ending problems.

At school, Anthony has found that the threat of suicide increases his social contacts appreciably. Anthony has passed the boundaries of what can be said, where it can be said, when it can be said, and how to say it most effectively. Threats, real or feigned, of suicide require immediate intervention. Anthony must be taken seriously, but unfortunately, like Peter, Anthony has cried "suicidal wolf" once too often and is suspected of soliciting attention rather than intervention. In addition to immediate intervention for the threatened suicide, Anthony is slated for psychological evaluation and speech and language assessment. Anthony is an honor student, but he just doesn't understand the ramifications of the kinds of statements he makes.

Socioemotional Expression

Pragmatics also includes socioemotional expression; that is, body language such as posture and facial expressions. The ability to interpret meaning from body language, tone of speech, and facial expression develops very early in life. For example, little preschoolers know the difference in meaning between a gentle tone and a strident comment or a rigid stance in comparison to a welcoming posture. Pragmatics covers almost any aspect of society that involves meaning in language.

As children proceed through school, their social circles typically widen, resulting in greater demands on their language ability. Competent language users learn the rules of pragmatics, such as how to initiate and maintain conversation or what kind of speech is appropriate for which kind of person, almost without any formal instruction (Piper, 2003). Breaking conversational rules can contribute to more severe communicative and social breakdowns than can poor reading, writing, or arithmetic skills.

A higher percentage of children with disabilities have issues related to pragmatics than their more typical peers. Issues with pragmatics may be found in any disability category but most often are noticed in children with Asperger's syndrome, nonverbal learning disabilities, and language impairments. Pragmatics skills can also be impacted by damage to certain language areas of the brain. Regardless of the cause or category, interventions are necessary for individuals with pragmatics problems if they are to become fully accepted into their social setting.

Interventions are often initiated for children with obvious and severe pragmatics issues, while many times students with milder pragmatics issues are overlooked or misjudged. Tony, for example, received all of his education in the general education setting. Tony had some serious reading and writing issues, but he was beloved because he always had a beatific smile on his face. However, his belovedness score plummeted considerably the day that he got into a fight on the playground. As he was pummeling another boy, he smiled. When he was reprimanded by the playground monitor, he smiled. When he was sent to the principal's office, he smiled. Soon the term *sociopath* cropped up. Fortunately for Tony, his inclusion teacher testified that he appeared to know right from wrong. What Tony didn't know was more than one facial expression. Tony has all the necessary skills in phonology, morphology, syntax, and semantics, yet he has difficulty communicating with others. Tony needed intervention to teach him how to use situationally appropriate facial expressions and body language.

Tony's inclusion teacher, Ms. Piper, never pretended to be a speech and language expert. In fact, she had never heard the term pragmatics. However, she did know that Tony needed to learn how to use appropriate facial expressions to avoid getting into serious trouble with his peers and the school faculty and staff. Ms. Piper put in an immediate call for a reassessment of Tony's IEP goals and, even before the meeting was convened, developed an instructional intervention for him. Following the seven guidelines for shaping behavior, Ms. Piper created the following intervention for Tony.

Ms. Piper initially decided to work on identifying only two facial expressions: happiness and sadness. Using a direct instruction approach, Ms. Piper and Tony looked at pictures of faces that showed one of these two emotions. Building on Tony's home and school experiences, they talked about when someone would have a happy face and when someone would have a sad face. This step was small enough and easy enough that Ms. Piper could reinforce Tony for his successes. Once Tony had mastered distinguishing a happy face from a sad face, she introduced faces with other expressions as nonexemplars. Now, Tony was ready to transition to real faces, not just pictures. Images shot with the school videorecorder helped bridge the gap between examples of static and fluid facial expressions. Ms. Piper and Tony were at this transition point when the new IEP meeting was called. During that meeting, based on results of specific assessments given by the language specialist, the facial expression program initiated by Tony's inclusion teacher was planned from start to finish. The team built upon Ms. Piper's humble but timely initial pragmatics program, which would ultimately lead to better social integration for Tony.

Commercial Interventions

Commercial programs for developing pragmatics are available and easily found on the World Wide Web. School, playground, home, church, parks, and recreation programs are just a few of the social environments most children experience. Commercial programs must be examined in light of the appropriateness of fit between the student and the targeted communities in which the student lives. Some programs are generic, and most programs, for better or worse, are targeted to address conventions found in middle class Anglo society. No commercial program will fit the needs of all children. Just like academic programs need to be modified to match student skills, so do programs designed to enhance pragmatics.

Splinter Skills

Because skill in pragmatics is so closely linked to thought, not all children develop the kind of language processing necessary to make seamless social adjustments and judgments. Some children can learn particular pragmatics skills but not others. Knowing a part of the picture is a splinter skill because only a portion of the larger overriding ability is mastered.

Consider pragmatics as a language-based dot-to-dot picture. A lot of dots are needed to create the whole image. Even if all the skills related to each dot can be taught, the connections may not be made. The question for most inclusion teachers, then, must focus on which dots are most critical for the social success of their students. While identification of the single most important pragmatics skill for a particular student in a particular inclusion class may be highly subjective, it is also most likely to be the most appropriate.

Social and Emotional Skills

Problems fitting in socially in inclusion settings are sometimes referred to as *social–emotional issues*. Not all children with disabilities have difficulty fitting into social situations, but a significant number remain socially segregated. Some students with disabilities have experienced difficulties in social acceptance when placed in inclusive classrooms. Others actively redirect social rejection at their nondisabled peers (Sabornie & deBettencourt, 2004). Social–emotional skills are impacted by the ability to focus attention, control impulsivity, or manage stress (Elksnin & Elksnin, 2006).

Temperament also influences how children, with and without disabilities, react to and in social situations. At least five basic categorical dispositions for students with high needs may be found in isolation or in combination: passive, aggressive, attention problems, perfectionist, and socially inept. Definitions and characteristics of these dispositions, as well as suggestions for how to deal with them in the classroom are found in Table 12.1.

Not all children with disabilities have temperament issues that negatively affect social integration. Intervention is needed when temperament issues are interfering with a child's ability to learn how to make and keep friends, demonstrate age-appropriate or acceptable social behaviors across a variety of settings, or access to academics. Even though one temperament may seem dominant, aspects of other dysfunctional categories are likely to coexist depending on the situation, the student's level of fatigue, and mitigating factors such as illness, reaction to medication, and family circumstances. Exhibiting inappropriate behaviors too frequently can lead to psychological, emotional, and even physical exclusion.

In addition, an often overlooked aspect of inclusion is the lack of age-appropriate social skills development among some children with high- and low-incidence disabilities. One representative study designed to investigate the social competence and social status of sixth-grade children diagnosed as having learning disabilities and placed in inclusive classrooms found that students

Table 12.1   Five Basic Categories of Students With High Needs

Category	Definitions & Source	Characteristics	Suggestions
Passive	Behavior that avoids the domination of others or the pain of negative experiences. The child attempts to protect self from criticism, ridicule, or rejection. Can have a biological basis, such as anxiety.	**Fear of relationships**: Avoids connections with others, is shy, doesn't initiate conversations, and attempts to be invisible. **Fear of failure:** Gives up easily, is convinced success is not possible, is easily frustrated, uses negative self-talk.	Provide safe adult and peer interactions and protection from aggressive people. Provide assertiveness and positive self-talk training. Reward small successes quickly. Withhold criticism.
Aggressive	Behavior that overpowers, dominates, harms, or controls others without regard for their well-being. The child often takes aggressive people as role models. Has had minimal or ineffective limits set on behavior. Condition may have a biochemical basis, such as depression.	**Hostile**: Rages, threatens, or intimi-dates others. Can be verbally or physically abusive to people, animals, or objects. **Oppositional:** Does opposite of what is asked. Demands that others agree or give in. Resists verbally or nonverbally. **Covert**: Appears to agree but then does the opposite of what is asked. Often acts innocent while setting up problems for others.	Describe the student's behavior clearly. Contract with the student to reward corrected behavior and set up consequences for uncorrected behavior. Be consistent and provide immediate rewards and consequences. Encourage and acknowledge extracurricular activities in and out of school. Give student responsibilities to help teacher or other students to foster successful experiences.

(continued)

Table 12.1   Continued

Category	Definitions & Source	Characteristics	Suggestions
Attention Problems	Behavior that demonstrates either motor or attentional difficulties resulting from a neurological disorder. The child's symptoms may be exacerbated by family or social stressors or biochemical conditions, such as anxiety, depression, or bipolar disorders.	**Hyperactive**: Has difficulty with motor control, both physically and verbally. Fidgets, leaves seat frequently, interrupts, talks excessively. **Inattentive:** Has difficulty staying focused and following through on projects. Has difficulty with listening, remembering, and organizing.	Contract with the student to manage behaviors. Teach basic concentration, study, and thinking skills. Separate student in a quiet work area. Help the student list each step of a task. Reward successes; assign a peer tutor.
Perfectionist	Behavior that is geared toward avoiding the embarrassment and assumed shame of making mistakes. The child fears what will happen if errors are discovered. Has an unrealistically high expectation of self. Has possibly received criticism or lack of acceptance while making mistakes during the process of learning.	Tends to focus too much on the small details of projects. Will avoid projects if unsure of outcome. Focuses on results and not relationships. Is self-critical.	Ask the students to make mistakes on purpose, then show acceptance. Have the student tutor other students.
Socially Inept	Behavior that is based on the misinterpretation of nonverbal signals of others. The child misunderstands facial expressions and body language. Hasn't received adequate training in these areas.	Attempts to make friends but is inept and unsuccessful. Is forced to be alone. Is often teased for unusual behavior, appearance, or lack of social skills.	Teach the student to keep the appropriate physical distance from others. Teach the meaning of facial expressions, such as anger and hurt. Make suggestions regarding hygiene, dress, mannerisms, and posture.

Source: Adapted from "What Works in Schools: Translating Research into Action" by R. J. Marzano, 2003, *Educational Leadership,* pp. 104–106. Alexandria, VA: ASCD. Adapted by permission of the publisher.

with disabilities frequently have developmental social delays that "mirror their academic delays" (Pavri & Luftig, 2000). In addition, "in 1987, the Interagency Committee on Learning Disabilities proposed modification of the definition of learning disabilities to include social skill deficits as a primary learning disability" (quoted in Pavri & Luftig, p. 1). Children will seek to interact with others who have the same level of social skill savvy.

If students are to find success at school and prepare for future success, development of their social skills needs must be addressed. Social skills can be developed through building a sense of community within the school and classroom, through more comprehensive and systematic classroom management, and through actively teaching social skills in the schools.

Building a Sense of Classroom Community

When children are ignored or rejected by their peers, they begin to believe that they are incapable of making and keeping friends (Pavri & Luftig, 2000). Feelings of isolation and low self-worth are terribly difficult perceptions to challenge and change. Some students with disabilities have developmental social delays that are similar to their academic delays. These problems can include the following (Pavri & Luftig, 2000):

- Unable to initiate or sustain positive relationships
- Fail to interpret social cues
- Tend to be aggressive
- Fall on the extreme ends of a continuum between withdrawal on one side and aggression/disruption on the other
- Have fewer friends
- Are more likely to be rejected by peers

For children with special needs to be fully accepted within the inclusion classroom, teachers and other educational personnel must consider the impact of the three Cs: climate, culture, and community. The three Cs begin in the minds and the hearts of the educators, but are developed and implemented upon sound research findings and teacher experience.

Climate

Climate refers to the emotional tone of the classroom. Teachers set the tone. Thus, when teachers tease, ignore, or reject a child with a disability—even if the rejection is subtle—students are likely also to tease, ignore, or reject the child (Erwin & Guintini, 2000; Pavri & Luftig, 2000). A climate of mutual acceptance, respect, and trust must exist for learning to take place. As Pariser noted: "How easy is it for us to learn in an environment we perceive as hostile, or inattentive? How readily can any of us assimilate information from someone we do not trust?" (2002, p. 2). A similar climate of trust needs to exist among the professionals working with the child in order to achieve the integrated services that are the hallmark of true social inclusion (Slater, 2004). In an inclusive classroom, the overall philosophy of acceptance, trust, respect, and responsibility must be reflected in the system of management philosophy adopted by the inclusion teacher and all other school personnel.

In a comparative study of five different behavior-management philosophies designed to ascertain which were the most successful in terms of student behavior and classroom climate, five philosophies emerged (Traynor, 2002):

1. *Coercive,* marked by intimidation, anger, sarcasm, yelling, threatening, and demeaning on the part of the teacher as a means of controlling student behavior.
2. *Laissez-faire,* marked by a high degree of tolerance on the part of the teacher for disruptive student behavior. Although the atmosphere in such classrooms was friendly, the teacher acted more like a peer than an authority figure.
3. *Task-oriented,* marked by the students doing a lot of busywork, such as individual work packets, segmented material, short-answer material, fill-in-the-blanks, and so forth. There was far less teacher–student interaction in these classrooms than in the other styles of management studied.
4. *Authoritative,* marked by a teacher who presents and enforces clear, specific, and reasonable rules. Consequences for behavior, both positive and negative, are clearly communicated at the beginning of the school year and consistently reinforced throughout, so the students always know what to expect as a result of their choices. The consequences are never harmful to the students, either physically or emotionally. Such teachers are often described by their students as firm, fair, and consistent. These teachers tend to correct negative behavior privately rather than publicly. They give reminders, redirect negative behaviors, are nonconfrontative, and employ positive strategies that make the classroom atmosphere one of safety and trust.
5. *Intrinsic,* marked by well-planned efforts to increase students' control over their own behavior. Rewards given for positive behavior include praise and other social reinforcers; tangible rewards such as stars, tokens, and food; and privileges.

The findings suggested the following (Traynor, 2002):

- Authoritative and intrinsic styles were the most effective. Both styles created a positive atmosphere in the classroom, minimized disruptive behaviors, and encouraged academic progress.
- The task-oriented style kept the students busy, but it was not an effective technique for either instruction or management. One of the major drawbacks was that the instructional material was often chosen for busywork value rather than for academic worth within the curriculum.
- The laissez-faire style of management was likewise ineffective. While the friendliness of the teacher helped create an atmosphere that did not provoke misbehavior on the part of the students, it did not produce or encourage positive behavior either. Far less time on task was noted because the atmosphere in the classroom was often chaotic and not conducive to learning.

■ While the coercive style of management gave the appearance of control in the short term, coercive management was unsuccessful long term and had "a devastating effect on children" (Traynor, 2002, p. 494). No value was found in this toxic classroom climate for children with special needs.

Culture

As the school year progresses, each classroom within the school begins to develop a unique culture. *Culture* refers to a cumulative set of shared experiences, customs, and traditions that occur over the course of the school year. If all students participate in a positive manner in those shared experiences, the classroom will develop a cooperative and collaborative culture that can result in improved behavior and high levels of time on task and academic achievement. If, on the other hand, the culture is one of competition and coercion, the opposite can result. Coercion and high levels of competition can create an unhealthy situation, which can have a negative impact on learning (Slater, 2004). The culture of the classroom needs to move away from focusing on the negative—what students cannot do—toward focusing on the positive—identifying and supporting what the students *can* do (Hester, 2002; Krajewski & Krajewski, 2000).

Community

Just as each classroom develops its own culture, each classroom is its own small community. The classroom, in turn, is part of the larger community of the school, which is part of the even larger community of the neighborhood, district, town, or city. Since schools are preparing students to live in and contribute to a democratic society, schools and classrooms should reflect those values. Democratic schools need to challenge behaviors that exclude rather than include, such as bullying, teasing, and putdowns. According to Sapon-Shevin (2003), "When one student is not a full participant in his or her school community, then we are all at risk" (p. 27).

Teachers who create positive classroom communities model respect, compassion, kindness, and other supportive behaviors; they provide the necessary accommodations for all children without unduly drawing negative attention to any child's weaknesses or disability (Erwin & Guintini, 2000). Teachers who have a vision of what an inclusive classroom can be and who are able to share that vision with its associated values teach both by precept and example. Shared vision and shared values should be an accepted part of the culture of the classroom. They should be taught through daily routines, procedures, and curriculum. Erwin and Guintini (2000) go on to say:

> The ability to make friends is perhaps one of the most meaningful skills a child can learn. . . . Like friendship, the process of becoming a member of the classroom [community] can lay an essential cornerstone for a young child's later social experiences and self-esteem. A sense of belonging, acceptance, and a positive relationship to the larger social network are all images associated with belonging. Becoming a member of the classroom community has been identified as an essential value for general education. (p. 238)

Specific community-building activities include morning routines, such as calendar; team-building group activities, such as favorite songs, poems, games, and stories; structured sharing times; and classroom meetings. All can increase the cohesiveness of the group and create a sense of belonging for each student (Kriete, 2003).

Developing community within an inclusion classroom is too important to be left to chance. Inclusion teachers must be proactive in arranging instructional events that can double for developing social interaction skills. Community building can be created by using various types of cooperative learning approaches, either with small groups or partners.

Sociograms

To determine group and partner composition as part of creating positive working relationships, teachers can use various sociometric techniques. One of the most common and simple techniques is the sociogram (Borgatti & Molina, 2003; Newcomb, Bukowski, & Pattee, 1993). A sociogram approach requires children to respond to teacher-designed questions, such as, "List the three people with whom you would most like to do your social studies work," and "Who are the two people you would like to sit next to in class?"

Sociograms give teachers insight about how students are interacting with each other. As such, they provide students' perspective on the interrelationships within the classroom or any other social setting, such as the soccer team or drama club. Student responses are graphically plotted to identify social isolates, popular students, disliked youngsters, and changes in interaction patterns over time. By charting the students' replies, a basic network of social patterns emerges. Analysis of the network enables inclusion teachers to better understand the group and develop a strong match between group management, curriculum development, and students with class-perceived problematic interaction issues.

Enthusiasm can be raised when students are allowed to work with a self-selected peer. Identification of social isolates (children not selected by anyone in the class) can lead to designing specific social interaction activities. Korey, for example, was an invisible student on Ms. Simpson's sociogram. Helen, on the other hand, seemed to be at the top of the chart. Ms. Simpson understood why Helen was so popular. She was funny, smart, and very accepting. Ms. Simpson arranged for Korey and Helen to be in several group activities together and to be study partners on two projects. Over the course of several weeks, Ms. Simpson began to notice a change in Korey—she seemed to blossom as a result of her time spent with Helen. She appeared more self-confident and assured. Like bees attracted to honey, other children began to view the new Korey in a more positive manner. The social interaction network in Ms. Simpson's class now included Korey.

Aaron, on the other hand, was very difficult to be around. He was bossy, overpowering, and generally annoying. His spot on the sociogram fell into the negative zone. For example, in response to the question "Who would you not want to play with during recess?" Aaron was the winner, thumbs down. Ms. Simpson decided the intervention with Aaron would be to place him in the position of being the center of attention. Aaron became team captain for the geography bee and director for the class play. Ms. Simpson also featured some of Aaron's art-work on the class bulletin brag board. She supplemented attention derived from class leadership roles with educational social skills activities.

Information from sociograms can also be used to develop IEP goals and pro-gram planning. Sociograms are one source that can be used to evaluate the effec-tiveness of either teacher-made or commercially produced social skill interventions.

Socioemotional Behaviors and Classroom Management

Classroom management is as vital a component of increasing student achieve-ment as is building a positive school climate, culture, and community. Management of student behaviors is a must for teaching academics (Marzano & Marzano, 2003). Out-of-control classrooms rarely provide a healthy atmosphere for either learning or social inclusion.

School climate plays an important role in the philosophical underpinnings of the teacher's classroom management. A teacher who looks for, recognizes, and encourages positive behaviors will have fewer discipline problems than a teacher who focuses on seeking out and dealing with inappropriate behaviors (Hester, 2002). Most important, classroom management must be a comprehensive system of compatible philosophy and practice and not merely a cookbook of assorted techniques. A comprehensive system of classroom management consists of three components: discipline, instruction, and motivation (Jones, Jones, & Jones, 2000). Like a tripod, all three "legs" must be firmly and equally planted for a classroom management system to be successful.

Discipline is a subcategory of management. The word *discipline* comes from the same root as the word *disciple*. Discipline implies that students are learning and moving toward the ultimate achievement of self-discipline. A constructive discipline program includes clear consequences for unacceptable behavior and clear recognition of appropriate behavior, as well as a daily routine that is consis-tent and predictable (Hester, 2002).

Inclusion teachers' ability to develop and implement successful discipline reduces time spent in dealing with inappropriate classroom behaviors and increases instructional time, thus creating positive community in an academic environment. Inability to create or deliver a successful discipline program, on the other hand, can cause valuable instructional time to be lost due to misbehavior and disruption. Inclusion teachers must be aware of everything that is going on in their classrooms at any given time, a sort of multitasking, sixth-sense ability that Kounin (1970) called *with-it-ness*. Successful inclusion teachers are the ones with the eyes in the backs of their heads. They mysteriously have the capacity to mon-itor all the classroom action even while working with a student away from the center of the class. Effective inclusion teachers apparently can attend to everyone and everything in the classroom at all times. Beyond a doubt, *with-it-ness* adds to successful classroom management, low levels of disturbance, and keeping stu-dents on task and achieving (Sabornie & deBettencourt, 2004).

One of the most powerful tools at a teacher's disposal is modeling. Inclusion teachers can model many social problem-solving skills by talking aloud as they work through daily challenges. When teachers make a mistake, they should talk about how they will deal with and correct the mistake, and make an apology if appropriate. Teachers also can observe during the day and nip inappropriate behaviors in the proverbial bud before they have time to escalate. By paying careful attention to the specific behaviors they are seeing, teachers also can identify many of the social skills lessons their students need (Hester, 2002). These skills can then be addressed through structured social-skills lessons/curriculum.

Effective inclusion teachers design classroom management systems that anticipate students' social and behavioral needs. They reduce or eliminate inappropriate behaviors by designing settings that minimize interruptions by controlling transition times, provide opportunities for teaching classroom etiquette, promote student independence, and establish classroom routines. In other words, an inclusion classroom is structured but allows for flexibility within the structure based on individual as well as whole-class needs.

Structure

Structure includes environmental organization, which incorporates teacher use of space in the classroom, availability of materials, and clear expectations as to their use (Coleman, 2003). Room size, number of children, material and equipment, and amount of shelf space are a few of the structural variables that contribute to classroom management and discipline. The physical arrangement of the classroom dictates the type of instructional groupings that can occur. Structure includes many of those common-sense things that teachers have done for years, such as arranging the classroom so that the teacher can move close to any student in the room in the shortest amount of time or is able to engage in eye contact with all students in the class.

Structure also includes the following:

- Teaching rules, routines, and procedures beginning the first day of school (Hester, 2002)
- Focusing on the expectation that learning begins at the door (Kriete, 2003)
- Assigning regular "bell work" so that students are productive while the teacher takes care of morning procedures
- Establishing high standards for behavior and clearly communicating those standards to students and parents
- Organizing classroom chores in such a way that the teacher does not do anything for the students that they can do for themselves (Jones et al., 2000)

Transition Times: Holding Starts and Stops to a Minimum

In the general education classroom, "stops" occur when the class completes an activity or class period, and "starts" occur when the class initiates an activity. The time in between is called *transition time*. As mentioned, transition time can be controlled on a number of levels by either the teacher or the students. In teacher-controlled transition time, the teacher provides direct input into the transition. When students control transitions, the teacher provides indirect input or control. The most obvious transition times are between subjects (e.g., between reading and math periods). In transitions between subjects, children generally put away one set of materials and bring out another or wait for further instructions. What occurs during that "wait" time can make the difference between a pleasant, well-run day and a potentially unpleasant environment bordering on chaos.

Starts and stops between subjects take time. Whenever large-group behavior is synchronized, time is spent in repeating directions, waiting for everyone to find the proper materials, and bringing the entire group to attention. The more between-subject transitions there are, the less time there is for teaching. Reducing large-scale or whole-class transitions can result in increased teaching time in most cases. To guide transition times, the teacher can institute a few ground rules, including a clearly perceived message of intent and a predictable routine.

Clearly Perceived Message of Intent

Intent means teachers have a definite idea of why they are stopping and what they plan to do next. Once teachers have established their intentions for themselves, they must make sure that the students understand them.

Take the example of Ms. Esch. Ms. Esch has decided to finish the spelling lesson and move into the natural science lesson. She closes her spelling book and pulls out the science materials. Meanwhile the students are hard at work with their spelling exercise. She gives them a signal that the spelling lesson is over. This signal is a combination of verbal and nonverbal communication. Ms. Esch goes to the front of the room, stands tall, and says in a calm but authoritative voice, "Please put away your spelling books and clear off your desks." The children do so. After the desks are cleared, she proceeds to say, "Today in science we are going to learn about the plants that grow in our state."

Ms. Esch has provided a clear set of directions for conveying her intention. She has (a) provided a stopping time ("Please put away your spelling books"), (b) allowed for a settling-down period ("Clean off your desks"), and (c) set the stage for the next subject ("Today in science we ..."). For most children, Ms. Esch has done a more than adequate job of controlling the transition between two subject areas. For a few, especially children with sensory disabilities, she may need to go a little further. The child with a hearing disability may need a more obvious clue to realize that a transition is occurring. If, for example, the child is looking down at his desk during the spelling period, he may not be able to hear his teacher's verbal signal. If a child with a visual disability is listening to audiotapes or working with a Braille writer during the spelling time, she may not see the teacher move to the center of the room or hear the verbal signal. A child who is inattentive may need a slight tap on the shoulder or some similar physical signal to realize that a transition is taking place.

Some children with mild behavior problems may find that transition times between subjects give them a chance to get attention; they may refuse to comply, through either active or passive means. Another type of child who may need special consideration during transition time are those whose language skills are somewhat low. Such children may need directions repeated or may need to have the directions accompanied by some sort of visual aid. Rather than putting away materials before making the transition, the inclusion teacher can put her materials away as the children are putting theirs away. Ms. Esch could come to the center of the room and hold up her spelling text, point to the text, and say, "Please put away your spelling workbooks." After she has made that statement, she could put her own spelling text on her desk. In this way, she is modeling the desired behavior for her students.

Promoting Independence

Transitions During Independent Activities

Transition times, including stops and starts, also can be child directed. Cases in which children determine when to begin and end a task usually occur during independent work time. During independent work time children are given directions on what to do if they have problems or need help during the work time. The children are also provided with directions on what to do after completing the task.

For children with learning problems in social or academic tasks, many small tasks during an independent work time may be appropriate. Working for 30–45 minutes on one task may be too demanding. Concentrated effort may be difficult for some children with sensory or health impairments. Also they may tire more easily when doing an extended independent activity.

Stops and Starts

Stops and starts for mini-lessons can allow a child to take acceptable breaks from assigned tasks. One caution is to structure the start and stop times carefully. Suppose a child has three mini-assignments to complete during a 30-minute period. Some children will have no problems, but others may have a difficult time deciding the order in which to do the work. The teacher may have to number the pages and have them complete the work in numerical order. For other children, use of time may be a problem. These children might spend the full 30 minutes on one task without even beginning the others. For children who have trouble judging time, the teacher may want to indicate, at the top of the worksheet, the amount of time to spend on the assignment (e.g., 10 minutes). If a child cannot tell time, the teacher can provide a kitchen timer and show how to use it, or draw a picture of a clock face on each assignment.

Help Signals

Children also need to know appropriate means for getting help. Suppose a child has difficulty understanding how to complete an independent assignment. The child has begun the work but gets bogged down toward the middle of the task. Teachers have several options. They can:

1. Allow the child to interrupt them while they are working with other students
2. Ignore their teaching group and rush to the child's side
3. Set up a signaling system
4. Provide sources of explanation other than themselves

Allowing the child to interrupt as the teacher works with others probably is not a good choice. Not only does the teacher have less time to respond appropriately, but interrupting also teaches the child to seek immediate self-gratification regardless of others' needs.

In smaller special classes, the teacher or aide can respond quickly, and some children will have learned to expect immediate feedback. As a result, the inclusion teacher may have to teach some mainstreamed children that class expectancies in a group of 30 are somewhat different than those in a class of 15.

Option 2 is not a good choice either. A teacher may have taught one child not to rush up and interrupt but still have set up the child to expect that the teacher will rush over to him. Option 2 has the same drawbacks as option 1.

Appropriate signaling systems include visual signs, activities to engage in while waiting for help, and understanding that there will be time delays between the appearance of a signal and teacher attention. Visual signals can be a raised hand, a help sign on the student's desk, or the student's name written on the chalkboard. Signals for use with children with disabilities are not much different from signals students who do not have disabilities use. Common sense will guide the choice of such signals.

If, for example, a class includes several students who are highly distractible or overly active, the teacher does not want a signaling system that requires a lot of movement. Getting up and writing his or her name on the board may add to the child's activity level and provide an opportunity for additional peer interaction— a chat with a neighbor, a friendly punch on a good pal's arm. If the signal is some sort of desk object (e.g., a small flag or a picture of an unhappy face), the teacher must be sure that all the children are physically able to manipulate the device. The child with physical involvement in the arms or shoulders may need some modifications. Likewise, children with language difficulties may need to be instructed through a modeling technique—actually demonstrating to that child how and when to set up a signal.

Appropriate Waiting Behavior

Children need to know what behaviors are appropriate while waiting for help. Just sitting and waiting will not do. If the children have more than one assignment, they might be directed to take out a reading book or to practice on some related task. In any event, the children have to be constructively occupied.

Choices confuse some children. Children who have difficulty making decisions should be allowed only one prespecified waiting-time activity—one the child can perform independently.

Children need to know approximately how long they will have to wait until they receive help. Knowledge of delay time may influence the type of request they make. If the child knows the delay is likely to be 5–10 minutes, he or she is more likely to settle into the alternative activity fairly quickly. If, on the other hand, the child anticipates a delay of less than a minute or so, the likelihood of initiating an alternative activity is lessened, and the child is more likely to wait patiently. Knowledge of delay time allows for clarification of expected student behavior and reduction of uncertainty, which brings us to another point: Children also must be able to have some consistency in the teacher's response time. Signals must be honored consistently if they are to be used effectively. Children need to be able to trust the system; otherwise the system will not work.

Like all other forms of reinforcement, response to signals (option 3) has a profound effect on how many times the child will continue to use the system. The way the child uses the system depends almost entirely upon how the teacher responds to the signals. If, in the past, the teacher appeared immediately each time the child signaled (continuous reinforcement), the child will expect that behavior to continue. If the teacher does not appear immediately, the child will quit using the signal to elicit attention. If, in contrast, the system varies the amount of time (intermittent reinforcement) between the child's signal and the teacher's response, the child learns to be more persistent in waiting for attention.

Some children, like Juan, need help learning how to use the signal system. Ideally, his teacher would reinforce Juan for his current correct behavior so it will occur more often. Unfortunately, Juan does not provide many opportunities to praise his correct behavior. His teacher has told him all the rules, and he can verbally describe them. The reality, however, does not match expectations or Juan's explanation of how the system works. Juan needs help to master the system. He can be successful if taught in small steps how to use it.

Just as teachers would not expect children to read *Crime and Punishment* simply because they have taught them the alphabet, a teacher cannot expect all children, especially children with learning and social problems, to utilize even the most perfectly crafted classroom management system. The mental leap between the teacher's response and some children's ability to use signals, for example, is too large. To give children like Juan a chance at success, teachers may have to use shaping techniques.

Teachers have the same responsibility to teach attending, listening, or rule-following behavior as they have to teach academics. Shaping behaviors such as attention or following rules are just like shaping behaviors for reading and writing skills. To get Juan to use the signal system effectively, his teacher first must identify any behavior that is on the right track and mold it one tiny step at a time. Juan's tolerance for waiting for teacher response is only about 20 seconds. Realistically, to function in a class of 30 students, Juan (or any other child) has to assume a delay of 10 minutes before his teacher can respond to signals. The ultimate goal for Juan is to have him be able to wait up to 10 minutes in an acceptable manner for attention.

Juan cannot immediately change his ⅓-minute wait time to a 10-minute wait time; the difference is too great. For Juan to reach that goal, his teacher need to establish a series of intermediate goals. First, Juan is reinforced every time he waits 60 seconds. Having reached this goal, Juan can wait consistently for 1 minute for attention. Now his teacher is ready to raise the criterion and sets a new goal of 2 minutes. As Juan gradually learns to delay, the teacher can raise criteria gradually until reaching the goal of 10 minutes.

Juan's success or failure lies not in his teacher's pedagogical or intellectual capability but, rather, in his persistence. Persistence, in conjunction with the principles of shaping, can shorten the time needed to reach the final goal. Principles of shaping are the guidelines that help teachers decide when to change criteria, how to speed up criteria, what to do when criteria are not being met, and when to start over.

The final alternative for providing assistance (option 4) is to have someone other than the teacher help the struggling student. This assumes that someone else is as qualified to convey the same information the teacher would. The best source of "others" is students. The odds are high that of 32 children at least 22 or 23 will have a fairly clear idea of how to complete assignments independently. All the teacher has to do is decide how the children are to assist each other. Two basic systems may be used. In one, a child functions as a designated teacher helper. In the other, children simply work together as they deem necessary.

TEACHER HELPERS   A signaling system may be a good idea in a teacher-helper system. In effect, the teacher helper follows the signaling system just like the teacher would. If several children need assistance throughout an independent activity, two or three children might function simultaneously as teacher helpers. Weekly or monthly rotation of teacher helpers is advisable to prevent the teacher helpers from being labeled "teacher's pets." All of the students should get a chance to be helpers, even children who are functioning at a lower level than most. The assistance the latter children provide could be less instructional and more logistical. Children who know content or directions can provide actual instruction, whereas a child with limited academic skills could distribute or collect assignments—in some cases even help correct assignments.

WORK GROUPS   In an informal system, children simply help each other. Children form more or less permanent work groups or group as needed. As in all the systems mentioned so far, the students must understand the teacher's expectations clearly. In most classroom settings these expectations will probably center on the degree of assistance and noise level tolerated. In some classrooms, assistance may consist of two or three explanatory sentences. In still other classrooms, children may be encouraged to complete joint assignments. Noise level will vary as a function of teacher tolerance and the needs of the classroom. If children are highly distractible or have hearing impairments, their needs are a critical determinant of a noise-level ceiling. In most settings, a library-level whisper is likely to be appropriate.

Daily Routines

Predictable Routines

Developing a predictable routine for teaching events can maximize teaching time during transitions as well as enhance students' understanding of class logistics. Children, with disabilities or otherwise, gain a sense of stability when events in their lives are fairly predictable. Some children, especially those with mild behavior or learning problems, need routine even more than typical children do. Evidence has shown that children with learning problems often are viewed as impulsive (Mather & Goldstein, 1993). Generally, impulsive behavior that is reflected in a tendency to respond with a high rate of error in uncertain situations (Mezzacappa Kindlon, Saul, & Earls, 1998) is restricted to academic tasks. However, if all learning is basically founded on the same principles, this finding can extend to other situations. If impulsive children are uncertain about the organization of the day's events, they can be expected to have an incomplete notion of class requirements or at least to feel uncertain of expected behaviors.

Varying Activities Within a Schedule

All routine and no variety can make Jack a dull boy and his classroom a dull experience. The overall schedule can remain the same, but activities within the schedule can vary. For example, health education can occur every day at 11:30 a.m., but on Monday the health activity may be a movie and on Tuesday it may be a small-group activity.

A daily schedule can be provided for children who have difficulty remembering even the overall structure. The format will depend on the child's level of understanding or sensory need (e.g., a child who cannot read print will need a different format than one who can). In a general education classroom, the teacher most likely would provide a schedule for the morning or basic skill activities. Morning activities usually require the most independent work.

Scheduling time either across activities (such as reading, math, or science time) or within activities (such as independent study and teacher-directed instruction during the spelling period) becomes fairly easy once teachers decide what they want to teach. The trick, of course, is in deciding what they want taught, to whom, and how. What to teach should flow from a list of observable (and some not quite so observable) objectives and should be based on the needs of students. With children identified as having disabilities, the decision of what to teach is a joint effort between the inclusion and the special teachers.

Complementary Scheduling

Choosing the manner in which the "what" is taught to "whom" becomes tricky when dealing with children who have disabilities. Although many of these children are in a general education classroom for part or most of the day, some also spend time with the special teacher. Therefore, the special teacher time must be considered in setting up the classroom routine. Both the inclusion and the special teachers' schedules will influence how the student is taught the "what."

Basically, the two teaching options are (a) teacher-directed and (b) student-initiated activities. If the child with a disability needs a concentrated amount of work that is teacher-directed, some, but not all, of the student's teacher-directed time may need to be scheduled with the special teacher. The advantage of working with the special teacher is that the inclusion teacher still has time to work with the other 31 children in the classroom without feeling guilty about the special ones.

Time spent in teacher-directed activities can be maximized by using peer or cross-age tutors. This assumes that the students, too, are on a predictable schedule and that their schedule is compatible with the inclusion teacher's.

Master Schedule Grid

With so many schedules, a master chart can be helpful. Using a step-by-step procedure, the puzzle of schedules can begin to fit together in a fairly simple fashion. The first step is to draw a grid, as shown in Figure 12.1. This grid blocks out time for each day. The grid is filled in with general entries, such as math and reading. A similar grid is completed for special teachers and tutors, as shown in Figure 12.2. In the "other teachers' schedules" (see Figure 12.3) the names of the children who leave the room are listed next to the special teacher's name. The time and number of tutors also is filled in.

Having established the general teaching schedule, the next step is to proceed to a more specific or daily schedule. The daily schedule should be consistent for the day of the week (e.g., every Monday geography is presented between 2:30 and 3:00). However, it need not be the same every day (e.g., 2:30 to 3:00 can be geography on Mondays, Wednesdays, and Fridays and music on Tuesdays and Thursdays). Schedules can repeat once a week, once every other week, or any way that is convenient to meet the needs of the teacher and students in a specific classroom.

Week	Monday	Tuesday	Wednesday	Thursday	Friday
8:30–9:00	Opening	Opening	Opening	Opening	Opening
9:00–10:00	Reading	Reading	Reading	Reading	Reading
10:00–10:15	Recess	Recess	Recess	Recess	Recess
10:15–11:00	Math	Math	Math	Math	Math
11:00–11:30	Lang. Arts	Lang. Arts	Lang. Arts	Lang. Arts	Lang. Arts
11:30–12:30	Lunch	Lunch	Lunch	Lunch	Lunch
12:30–12:45	Story	Story	Story	Story	Story
12:45–1:30	Science	Science	Science	Science	Science
1:30–2:30	P.E.	Library	P.E.	P.E.	Art
2:30–3:00	Geography	Music	Geography	Music	Geography
3:00–3:10	Dismissal	Dismissal	Dismissal	Dismissal	Dismissal

Figure 12.1   Grid for Weekly Schedule

Week_____	Monday	Tuesday	Wednesday	Thursday	Friday
8:30–9:00					
9:00–10:00	LD-R	LD-R	LD-R	LD-R	LD-R
9:00–9:15					
9:15–9:30	15		5		5
9:30–10:00	Cross-Age Tutors		Cross-Age Tutors		Cross-Age Tutors
10:00–10:15					
10:15–11:00	LD-R	LD-R	LD-R	LD-R	LD-R
	3 Cross-Age Tutors	3 Cross-Age Tutors	3 Cross-Age Tutors	3 Cross-Age Tutors	3 Cross-Age Tutors
11:00–11:30		Speech Therapist		Speech Therapist	
11:30–12:30	Lunch	Lunch	Lunch	Lunch	Lunch
12:30–12:45					
12:45–1:30					
1:30–2:30	P.E. Teacher	Librarian	P.E. Teacher	P.E. Teacher	
2:30–3:00		Music Teacher		Music Teacher	
3:00–3:10	Dismissal	Dismissal	Dismissal	Dismissal	Dismissal

Figure 12.2   Grid for Special Teachers and Tutors

The next step requires the inclusion teacher to mesh his or her schedule with that of other teachers. Let's take Monday as an example. Figure 12.3 shows that Steve, CeCe, Trudie, Jim, and Ron will be out of the reading period for half an hour. Ideally, Mrs. Bickley could work with these children on reading tasks. Sometimes the ideal does not work out. Mrs. Bickley may be working on math or some other area. In this case, the inclusion teacher will have to work with this small group of children from 9:30–10:00. Direct teacher instruction, whether from the inclusion teacher or tutors, can occur from 9:30–10:00. If the inclusion teacher wants to use tutors, they will also need to be scheduled for the reading activities.

In the last step, the teacher refines his or her own schedule once more, taking each subject and breaking down the activities for that time. Figure 12.4 shows this more detailed schedule.

Student schedules can vary as class periods do. The teacher need not work with the same children or groups every day. For example, the inclusion teacher can hear Suzanna's oral reading three times a week and Morgan's only once. Suzanna needs more oral reading instruction than Morgan does, and Suzanna needs direct input much more than Morgan does. Morgan is merely refining or practicing a learned skill. How often the teacher schedules direct instruction time with students is a function of student need.

Teacher	Student	Time	Subject
9:00 - 10:00			
LD-R (Mrs. Bickley)	Steve	9:00 - 9:30	Reading
	CeCe		
	Trudie		
	Jim		
	Ron		
Cross-Age Tutors		9:00 - 9:30	Reading
Shannon	Thomas		
Tang	Robert		
Phillip	Felicity		
Eric	Drew		
Mikhail	Eliza		
		9:30 - 10:00	Reading
Shannon	Thomas		
Tang	Charles		
Phillip	Holly		
Eric	Steve		
Mikhail	Kerry		
10:15 - 11:00			
LD-R (Mrs. Bickley)	Jeff	10:15 - 11:00	Math
	Steve		
	Jim		
Cross-Age Tutors		10:15 - 11:00	
Daisy - Small group working on 2 x's tables			
Drew - Floater			
Ken - 1-minute timings with individuals *according to schedule*			
11:00 - 11:30			Language development
Speech (Mr. B.)	Meiko		
1:30 - 2:30			
P.E. (M/W/Th)	Whole class		
Library (T)	Whole Class		
2:30 - 3:00			
Music (T/Th)	Whole class		

Figure 12.3 Other Teachers' Schedules

Time	Monday

9:00-9:15 Group A (10 kids) works in small group with teacher on decoding
Group B (15 kids) works on an independent reading activity
Group C (5 kids) goes to Ms. C.'s room

9:15-9:30 Group A (10 kids) works independently
Group B (15 kids) works with teacher on word recognition
Group C (5 kids) still in Ms. C.'s room

9:30-10:00 Group A works independently
Group B works independently
Group C works with tutors on a one-to-one
Members of A, B, C work on a one-to-one with teacher in oral reading

Figure 12.4   Student Schedules

Although the steps in scheduling may seem superfluous at first, when working with 30 children, a master chart is a necessity to keep track of who is teaching what to whom and when. With so many curious minds at stake, the planning schedule can prove invaluable.

Flexibility in Scheduling

The initial schedule often is found in need of adjustment as time passes. Some schedule bending, poking, and shaping is the rule, not the exception. The schedule will change as the teacher's needs, the team's needs (special education and cross-age tutors), and the children's needs demand. Teaching is a dynamic process, and as such, instruction, events, and plans are directed toward growth. Flexibility in scheduling is not only to be desired but is to be expected.

ENTRY/EXIT TIPS   Many children with disabilities will be in and out of the classroom during the day. Special classes in reading or language often require children to go to the special teacher's room for one or two periods and then return to the general education setting. Each time that child enters or leaves the general education setting, two kinds of disruptions occur. The first affects the child who is moving. When the child reenters the classroom, he or she must reorient to the ongoing classroom activity—an activity for which the student has probably not been formally prepared. Take the example of Viola. Viola leaves the classroom Mondays, Wednesdays, and Fridays to go to a special reading class. She knows that the rest of her class is working on language arts while she is out of the room. After Viola finishes her reading, she knows she is expected to work on a language arts activity, too. However, she is not quite sure what the language arts activity is. She has a general idea, but because she was out of the room when the directions were given, she doesn't know what she's expected to complete.

Meanwhile, Viola's teacher is in the middle of teaching. Here is where the second disruption comes in. Viola's teacher, no matter how patient or understanding, is also disrupted, as she must stop her group activity to help Viola. In the process she runs the risk of being exasperated, and Viola runs the risk of feeling guilty for some unknown reason or feeling bewildered by the reentry.

POSSIBLE SOLUTIONS   The most desirable solution is to set up the classroom in such a way that the special teacher can work with Viola in the general education room. That way, Viola doesn't have to leave. Her special teacher comes to Viola's room, and when they are done working together, she helps her reorient to classroom activities. When the special teacher cannot work in the general education setting, the next best choice is to have a peer orient the reentering child.

The teacher has to remember that the reentering child often is confused—even if only momentarily. Depending on the ease with which the child readjusts, the point of reentry can be a delicate time for the inclusion teacher, Viola, and all the other students in the room.

Productive and Counterproductive Social Behaviors

Once upon a time, most students learned social behaviors and developed self-control at home, but times have shifted more responsibility for teaching socioemotional behaviors to teachers. Teachers are now recognized as major contributors in developing students' social skills, sense of responsibility, and self-control (Howard, Nash, & Jagers, 2005). Internet research will yield a plethora of commercial curricula for teaching social skills; however, many successful noncommercial techniques have been used by effective teachers for years. A few such practices suggested by Hester (2002) include the following:

1. Support the child's communication skills by asking open-ended rather than closed questions
2. Listen reflectively to both content and feelings
3. Use positive body language and tone of voice
4. Build new behaviors on existing behaviors, a process Hester calls *scaffolding*
5. Help children meet needs in a healthy manner by teaching positive behaviors that can replace current inappropriate behaviors
6. Affirm the child for his/her strengths, skills, and abilities in the social milieu as well as the academic

Personalization of Interventions

Not all children learn at the same pace or with the same approach. Some children need more instruction than others in how to behave in school and society in general. Inclusion teachers strive to replace inappropriate and dysfunctional behaviors with appropriate and useful responses that are matched with the child's temperament, as well as cognitive and linguistic levels.

Most children learn very early in life that their behavior is either acceptable or not. They also learn which behaviors will get them what they want (e.g., a piece of chocolate, a kiss from grandma, or permission to play with a friend). Some children have learned that certain inappropriate behaviors will get them what they feel like having. Others continue doing behaviors that once got them what they wanted when they were younger but are no longer effective. These children have no age-appropriate replacement behaviors.

Many inclusion teachers are faced with teaching children that their behaviors have good and not-so-good consequences. To change behaviors, teachers need to know what incentives are valued by their students. Incentives, or reinforcers, are activities or objects that students desire. Incentives can be tangibles like food, stickers, or grades; they can also be social–emotional intangibles, like praise, smiles, or free time. Many students need incentives in order to replace one set of behaviors with another. Inclusion teachers often must use incentives to replace inappropriate socioemotional behaviors with more positive and functional conduct.

Merely ignoring inappropriate behavior is counterproductive. Ignoring such behavior does not extinguish it because the teacher does not control all of the reinforcement. Attention from the peer group, positive or negative, is often enough to reinforce the inappropriate behavior, as is the self-reinforcement of wasting time and not doing work (Jones et al., 2000).

In an inclusion setting, the use of activities that students enjoy and value as incentives is a particularly powerful instructional approach for developing appropriate socioemotional skills. One example of using social activities as an incentive is called Preferred Activity Time (PAT) (Jones et al., 2000). Students can earn time toward a fun activity by acts of cooperation. For example, if the students usually take 5 minutes for a lesson transition (the national average) and they do it in 2 minutes, they can earn 3 minutes toward the preferred activity. If all students are in their seats on time, with books and pencils ready, the class can earn a hurry-up bonus of an additional minute or two. The teacher keeps track of the minutes in a corner of the board and at regular intervals (depending on the age/maturity of the students) gives the students their PAT (Jones et al., 2000).

The flip side of PAT is that students can also lose time for fooling around, talking to neighbors, taking more time than necessary to complete a task, and the like. In order for children to learn to manage time, the teacher must first give the students some time. Without time to protect, the students have no incentive toward which to work. For young children, children with low cognitive skills or severe emotional disabilities, initial starting time may be only 5–10 minutes several times a day. With older students or more cognitively sophisticated children, initial time can be longer or can be distributed once or more throughout the week.

The elegance of PAT is ease of implementation and low cost in terms of money and effort. PAT can be linked to the curriculum through a wide variety of learning games. The biggest challenge to teachers is to keep accurate records of time earned and to plan high-interest PATs. Research has shown that simply giving the students "free time" does not work well over time, so it is important that the PAT involve some sort of well-organized learning game or activity (Jones et al., 2000).

Inclusion teachers need to teach their students that positive consequences will occur when they are using appropriate social behaviors. For some children with disabilities, distinguishing between positive and negative behaviors or understanding consequation needs to be added to their emotional, social, and cognitive schema. Students with good socioemotional skills are made, not born.

Teacher Depersonalization

Procedures to remediate chronic behavior problems are inextricably intertwined with the teacher's temperament, sense of self, and knowledge base related to social–emotional development. Some teachers have a greater tolerance for inappropriate social behavior than others. Most teachers have some area of social behavior to which they are particularly sensitive (e.g., being called a four-letter word or lying and cheating). Many children with poor socioemotional skills have an almost gifted perception of how to push those teachers' emotional buttons.

At one time or another, all inclusion teachers will meet students who violate their peers' or teachers' personal space by using foul language, standing too close or touching, or demonstrating inappropriate gestures or expressions. Teachers will be in classrooms with children who use verbally annoying or even abusive words, phrases, and argument to avoid on-task behavior, as well as children who challenge their authority through defiance and stubborn refusal to follow classroom rules and requests. In extreme instances, some children with significant socioemotional disabilities may physically threaten or assault their peers or teachers. Since many of these inappropriate behaviors are either directly or indirectly leveled at the teacher, depersonalization of the situation is sometimes difficult.

Maintaining a sunny outlook may require some serious teacher self-talk. Ineffective inclusion teachers cannot separate their feelings about the deviant behavior from the socioemotional needs of the student. They fall into the blaming-the-victim trap when dealing with students who chronically exhibit demanding social–emotional issues. Overworked and frustrated teachers may assume the student is:

- not trying to make correct social responses,
- deliberately engaging in inappropriate social behaviors, and/or
- refusing to cooperate.

Focus on Problem Solving

The best practice for diminishing hurt feelings and replacing chronic behavior problems with suitable social performance is to find a nonsubjective measure for determining the degree and frequency of the behavior. To develop appropriate social–emotional behaviors in children, inclusion teachers need to separate their emotional responses to the child's behavior and focus on problem solving.

Procedures for remediating chronic behavior patterns are similar to steps used to remediate chronic academic errors. A comparison of steps to remediate chronic behavior and academic problems, taken from an unknown and very wise source, is presented in Table 12.2.

Table 12.2 Comparison of Steps to Remediate Chronic Behavior and Academic Problems.

Steps	Chronic Academic Problem	Chronic Behavior Problem
1	Identify the error pattern, misrule, or misunderstanding	Identify functional relationships between behavior & environment
2	Identify the rule (i.e., rubric, heuristic, etc.)	Identify expected or acceptable behaviors
3	Modify examples and presentation to provide clearer focus on rule and provide less opportunity for practice of misrule	Modify environment to allow practice of expected behaviors and remove stimuli that are likely to occasion the inappropriate behavior
4	Provide differential feedback so that more accurate responses are more strongly reinforced	Provide differential reinforcement so that direction of correct responding is reinforced
5	Shape context ■ Toward target context ■ Provide review ■ Integrate skill with other skills or content	Move toward least restrictive environment program for generalization and maintenance

Ms. Carter is an expert in using the five steps when designing and implementing interventions for students in her inclusion setting. One time, for example, Ms. Carter asked the class to begin working on the questions at the end of the math text. Chris raised his hand and said, "Do we have to do all the questions?" Without missing a beat, Maggie chimed in with, "Why do we have to do this dumb stuff?" Ms. Carter, carefully and briefly, responded, "Yes, you have to answer all the questions. We are doing all the questions to practice becoming used to the topics. These problems will be on the next test. Please begin now." Chris persisted, "There are too many. Can't we just do the odd ones?" When given a class assignment, Chris was oppositional and enjoyed confronting his teacher's requests.

Ms. Carter had already used several low-profile techniques, such as answering briefly to ensure understanding, providing a reason, and signaling the starting time for the task. These were insufficient for Chris, and Ms. Carter launched into the five-step process for remediating chronic behavior problems.

Step 1: Ms. Carter identified Chris's unwarranted verbal stalling as an avoidance behavior for beginning new assignments. Most of the time, when a new independent activity in any area except art was given, Chris would find all kinds of reasons for not beginning the task.

Step 2: Chris is expected to begin the task without undue and unnecessary criticism. Clarification questions were acceptable.

Step 3: Ms. Carter could not very well eliminate assigning classwork, but she could modify the environment. She chose one academic area as the first place to begin increasing appropriate social behavior when beginning a new task. In order to replace or at least decrease Chris's inappropriate behavior, she opted to provide vicarious reinforcement to the first three students who began the math task appropriately. In addition she intermittently gave a piece of sugarless hard candy to the entire class when all students started the math task without complaints. In so doing, Ms. Carter did not draw undue attention to Chris, but she provided him with a model and a means for acquiring verbal and tangible reinforcement for appropriate task initiation.

Step 4: Ms. Carter was on the lookout to provide Chris with reinforcement. The more quickly he and the class began the math task, the more praise she bestowed.

Step 5: Once Chris began demonstrating appropriate verbal responses when given math assignments, Ms. Carter gradually and simultaneously extended reinforcements for all classroom areas. She also leveled her rate of intervention across all academic areas so that reinforcement during math time was consistent with that in other subjects.

Rather than getting upset, nagging, insulting, or sending Chris from the room, Ms. Carter problem solved. Due to her excellent insights and application of behavioral principles, Chris, the class, and Ms. Carter were able to learn in a positive classroom environment. Most important, such techniques assisted the students and teacher in maintaining and developing positive relationships with each other and other members of the class.

Beyond the Classroom Community

Community Within the School

Practicing inclusion also means that both inclusion teachers and specialists need to redefine their roles to include true social integration. Progress is beginning to be made in academic inclusion, but true social inclusion is still paid little more than lip service. Thus, inclusion teachers may have to meet the challenge of educating children in social–emotional skills with very little education or prior experience in how to do so. Specialists find themselves working as coaches, consultants, and coteachers (Vella & Thousand, 2003). Both specialists and generalists have need of far more pre- and inservice education than they have customarily received in the delivery of services to children with physical, cognitive, social, and behavioral problems (Stevenson, Linfoot, & Martin, 2000).

Creating a positive climate, a caring culture, and a community built on democratic values is just as important in the total school as it is in the individual classroom. For true social and academic inclusion to work, collaboration among all the stakeholders must be productive. Many inclusion teachers feel inadequate to handle the academic and behavioral challenges of children with special needs. For their part, specialists may have a hard time adjusting to their new roles in an inclusive environment, including what Eisenberger, Bertrando, and Conti-D'Antonio (2000) called "job-imbedded staff development" for the inclusion teachers with whom they team.

Just as children must feel supported, accepted, and respected in the class-room, inclusion teachers must feel supported, accepted, and respected within the larger school community. On-site professional training opportunities, such as team-building activities for everybody involved in the educational process (including, when appropriate, the parents), technical assistance, and shared deci-sion making are techniques that build positive social interactions (Krajewski & Krajewski, 2000; Oremland, Flynn, & Keiff, 2002; Stevenson et al., 2000). Creating a positive climate, culture, and community, whether in the classroom or the entire school, is an unending process leading to an ideal product. All individ-uals responsible for the product should take part in the process. All faculty and staff, ranging from the principal to the school cafeteria workers, have a stake in developing community in inclusion settings.

Playground Community

The playground is one important source for creating a positive climate, culture, and community. Play and recreation are widely accepted as fundamental to the health, well-being, and social and physical development of children. Time spent in play can teach and reinforce many important life skills, such as teamwork, cooperation, leadership, motivation, confidence, perseverance, citizenship, tol-erance, and an ability to set goals and achieve them (Coakley & Donnelly, 2003).

One of the challenges inherent in making what happens on the playground part of the school's community-building effort is the fact that recess is often supervised by untrained personnel. Some do an excellent job of carrying forth schoolwide goals and providing a safe environment for play. All too often, how-ever, such personnel are not part of the overall school planning and have neither the training nor the support to do the job. Negative experiences in the schoolyard can undo many of the positive experiences within the classroom.

In true inclusion schools, playground supervisors, with other classroom teachers, aides, or volunteers, must, at a minimum, be informed of the effects of a child's disability on social interactions and, ideally, participate in strategies that foster social interaction. Playground supervisors need to understand the ramifica-tions of a student's disability. Phillip, for example, is physically challenged with spinal muscular atrophy (SMA), a congenital and degenerative condition. The playground supervisor needs to know what physical abilities Phillip has, what activities he should and should not do on the playground, and his current level of functioning.

When included as part of the IEP team, playground supervisors can help organize and monitor a wide variety of activities during recesses, taking into account the abilities and interests of students with and without disabilities. They can also ensure that playground activities do not exacerbate a student's disability.

Community Outside the School Day

Children with disabilities live in more places than the classroom. Just like their nondisabled peers, students with high- and low-incidence disabilities should engage in a wide variety of social interactions. Many students with disabilities are in after school programs. Some after school programs exist solely as childcare, providing supervision of young people during the time between the end of the school day and parents returning from work. Other programs provide vital social- and life-skills development for children, including the opportunity to develop new interests, to try out new skills, to socialize with other students—usually in a multi-age setting—and to work with interested adults in roles that are supportive, yet different from those of teachers or parents (Granger & Kane, 2004). Interest in the importance of quality after school programming as part of the larger educational process has been growing in the past few years.

For social integration to occur, school personnel should seek out opportunities to give and obtain input from other adults who instruct or supervise social settings that include children with disabilities. The value of after school programming for the development of life skills for children with disabilities has yet to be documented (Perkins-Gough, 2003), but the mere fact that students interact in a social environment in these settings begs for appropriate social integration strategies and techniques.

After school programs, sports events, church activities, camps, clubs, and other leisure opportunities are part of the world of children. Most of these social opportunities are staffed by personnel not directly related to schools—even individuals running programs that meet at the school site may not have any direct contact with school personnel.

School personnel can create opportunities to interact, inform, and be informed with other "teachers" who are part of the child's social world. When social integration goals are part of the IEP for a student, persons who instruct or conduct social events for that child can be invited to participate in planning. At a minimum, single-page introductory letters can be created and sent to the child's outside-of-school teachers. The letter can include a brief description of the child's needs and the types of interventions that have been helpful in social settings.

Self-Determination and Social Integration

Among other purposes, school is designed to prepare students for a life far greater than that bounded by four classroom walls. Self-determination is one of the stepping stools that helps scale those boundaries. Self-determination is a major social characteristic that contributes to positive social integration. Definitions of self-determination can best be summarized in the following description:

> Self-determination is a combination of skills, knowledge and beliefs that enable a person to engage in goal-directed, self-regulated, autonomous behavior. An understanding of one's strengths and

limitation together with a belief in oneself as capable and effective are essential to self-determination. When acting on the basis of these skills and attitudes, individual have greater ability to take control of their lives and assume the role of successful adults in our society. (Field, Martin, Miller, Ward, & Wehmeyer, 1998, p. 2)

Encouraging development of self-determination requires teaching students with disabilities the knowledge, skills, and attitudes needed to take more control and responsibility for their lives.

Inclusion teachers must facilitate the growth of self-determination. Characteristics of environments that support the development of self-determination include individuals who are models of self-determination, self-determination skill instruction, opportunities to make choices, positive communication patterns, and relationships and availability of supports (Field, Sarver, & Shaw, 2003). Effective inclusion classrooms encourage the development of self-determination for all students, but make sure that opportunities to learn and practice self-determination activities are systematic and targeted particularly for students with disabilities.

A review of the self-determination literature (Malian & Nevin, 2002) suggests the following:

- Self-determination is a developmental phenomenon (i.e., a process that involves continuous development across emotional, social, communication, and behavioral actions).
- Self-determination is a constructivist phenomenon shaped by interactions between the individual and others.
- Self-determination is a valuable skill that can be measured and correlated with success in adult lives.
- Self-determination is situational, characterized by self-regulation and adaptability.

Most of the literature on self-determination addresses the instructional needs of secondary and postsecondary students. Yet, since self-determination is developmental, taking into account mental as well as chronological ages, various instructional activities can be promoted at different grade levels. Grade-appropriate activities addressing many of these components are found in Table 12.3.

Best practices for teaching self-determination have been developed by teachers, advocates, and parents, as well as students with disabilities themselves. When inclusion teachers become coadvocates with students with disabilities, best practices smooth the progress of the development of self- determination knowledge, skills, and practices, which will ultimately assist integration into adult society.

Personal Control

Most individuals with disabilities desire control over their own lives, preferring to make decisions for and about themselves (Ward, 1996). Self-determination skills like goal setting, problem solving, and decision making enable individuals

---

Table 12.3 Grade-Appropriate Activities for Developing Self-Determination

Early Elementary

- Provide opportunities for students to make choices, teaching them that they can exert control and that most choices have limited options from which to select.
- Promote early problem-solving skills by encouraging students to think aloud as they address simple problems. Teachers should model their own problem-solving processes.
- Provide feedback regarding the outcomes of their choices to begin to teach students to link choices and consequences.
- Teach students to evaluate their work in comparison to a standard ("Does your paper look like this?") to lay the foundation for later self-management skills.

Late Elementary and Middle School

- Teach students to systematically analyze potential options with related benefits and disadvantages in order to participate in simple decisions, and to examine past decisions to determine if the consequences were anticipated or desired.
- Coach them in setting and committing to personal and academic goals, including identifying steps to achieve goals and obtaining support to monitor progress.
- Encourage them to evaluate task performance and reflect on ways to improve and enhance performance.

Junior High and High School

- Encourage students to make decisions that affect their day-to-day activities, including academic goals, post-school outcomes, schedules, and others.
- Use a problem-solving process to identify a problem, gather information, list and consider options, consider advantages and disadvantages, choose and implement a solution, and evaluate the effectiveness of the solution.
- Use a decision-making process to identify a situation that requires a decision, gather information, identify options, predict consequences, and take action to implement a decision (Texas Education Agency, 1997).

Source: From "Promoting the Development and Acquisition of Self-Determined Behavior" by E. Doll, D. Sands, M. L. Wehmeyer, and S. Palmer, 1996, in D. J. Sands and M. L. Wehmeyer (Eds.), *Self-Determination Across the Life Span: Independence and Choice for People With Disabilities* (pp. 65–90). Baltimore: Paul H. Brookes. Reprinted by permission of the publisher.

---

to assume greater responsibility and self-control (Wehmeyer, Agran, & Hughes, 1998). To assume control over their lives, individuals with disabilities must be given opportunities to learn about their disability and how it affects them academically, emotionally, and functionally.

Understanding how they learn or interact with others gives individuals with disabilities a chance to identify what they need to do in order to access knowledge and become a part of the community. More than anyone, most persons with disabilities are aware of the accommodations they need to be successful participants in the community. Finally, in order to ensure that their needs are being met, individuals with disabilities need to understand, to the greatest extent possible, the basic laws addressing their rights.

Student-Led IEPs

One particular right for students who have not yet graduated from high school is the right to participate in IEP development. For some children with disabilities, in-person contributions to an IEP meeting is a good way to take responsibility for planning and decision-making related to their school careers. Some students enjoy assuming the leadership role in conducting the IEP meeting, along with providing their personal views and insights. In the IEP meeting, students with disabilities can change or influence the views of others toward their educational needs and wants.

Practicing and developing self-determination via IEP input is not a new idea. Legally, students of any age must be invited to join their IEP meetings if the purpose of the meeting is targeted on transition services (services focused to assist students with disabilities to make positive postsecondary achievement). According to IDEA, transition planning must begin for students with disabilities by age 14 or younger if the IEP team concludes that inclusion of the student at the transition meeting is appropriate.

However, not all children are prepared to go into a meeting surrounded by adult authority figures. Many students need instructional assistance and training to know how to conduct themselves and how to conduct an IEP meeting. Many commercial guides are available that can help students develop their IEPs. One excellent resource is found in the *Technical Assistance Guide* developed by the National Dissemination Center for Children with Disabilities (2002). Some students have a lot they want to say about their education. They know their strengths and weaknesses, their interests, and what they would like to do in the future.

The true story told by Deborah Leuchovius (2002), Freddy's mother, puts into perspective how her son developed self-determination and learned how to provide input to his IEP meeting. Freddy's story:

> For years I asked teachers to implement curriculum that would help my son prepare for a more meaningful role in his Individualized Education Program (IEP) meetings. For years, his teachers agreed, but could never quite manage to squeeze one extra thing into the school day. Two years ago we postponed Freddy's IEP meeting until he could talk with key members of the team to develop and write IEP goals in his own words. The transformation resulting from this simple approach was dramatic. For years Freddy attended IEP meetings, but he was barely able to sit through an entire session. When Freddy was prepared for the meeting, however, he was more comfortable talking about his disability and was better able to express his needs and goals. Technology played a key role in helping Freddy prepare for his IEP meeting. By writing out his goals in advance, and replaying them at the meeting, he became a confident and active member on his IEP team who made sure everyone else had an opportunity to contribute at the meeting. Based on Freddy's experience, as well as a growing body of research on the importance of developing self-determination skills, I believe that all students with disabilities should have the opportunities they need to develop self-determination skills while they are still in school.

Even with preparation, not all children are as self-determined as Freddy, nor as prepared to participate in a student-led IEP meeting. Some children, however well prepared, simply do not want to attend IEP meetings. Others are not able to. In such cases, school personnel have the responsibility to ensure that the student's preferences are considered. Inclusion teachers can help students by asking them a simple question: "What can your teachers do to make learning easier for you?" Many teachers are surprised at the insights that students have into their own learning needs. Children usually know what kind of accommodations work for them. What they often are lacking and need are self-advocacy skills and a forum for expressing their needs.

Facilitating growth leading to self-determination need not be a special part of the school day, but can be embedded into the normal classroom climate and culture. One of the ethical responsibilities of inclusion teachers is to create environments that support the development of self-determination by providing models of self-determination, opportunities for making choices, examples of constructive communication, and promoting healthy and positive interpersonal relationships, not just for students with disabilities, but for all members of the classroom society.

Inclusion Conclusion

After reading about the many challenges surrounding the social aspects of inclusion, you may be tempted to ask: "Is inclusion worth the effort?" According to the most recent position statement from the National Association of School Psychologists (2004), the answer is "yes" and for the following reasons:

1. Nondisabled peers can serve as models for students with disabilities.
2. Students with disabilities are not clustered in one segregated location.
3. Social interaction and friendships can develop at school and carry over into the home community because the children will be attending school with children in their own neighborhood.
4. All students can learn new skills—social as well as academic—in a more natural setting.
5. All students may gain a greater respect for and appreciation of human differences/diversity.

As students with disabilities grow and mature, they will be required to enter a much larger and more inclusive society today than was the case in the past. In the words of Aefsky (1995), "The educational needs of children need to be addressed as societal issues in today's world, not as separate molecules of non-related matter" (p. 130). According to Krajewski and Krajewski (2000), "The less special needs students interact with regular students, the more skewed their sense of normalcy becomes . . . they remain childlike" (p. 49). Inclusion teaches vital life skills—academic, behavioral, and social. These skills help make students—particularly those with disabilities—more independent today and tomorrow (Oremland et al., 2002).

Summary

Social inclusion is a manifestation of the broader ambition of social integration, not only school integration. Social integration requires more than idealistic words reflecting a Pollyanna world. Social integration of persons with disabilities is hard work, but well worth the effort in terms of the benefits to the individuals involved as well as society at large. Social integration requires interaction with other members of society. Since most children spend a majority of their time with other children in school or leisure activities, the impact of their disability on their communication and social–emotional behavior must be assessed in terms of effect on interactions with others. Pragmatics and temperament are characteristics that significantly impact social interaction.

Children's sense of self in society is shaped by their contacts with others, and in turn they shape the ideas and thoughts of the persons with whom they interact. Children with and without disabilities need to be taught how to interact in a productive and respectful way with each other. Children are not square pegs, and society is not a round hole. The puzzle pieces that comprise true social integration are varied in shape, size, and color and, in the case of children, distinctive strengths and weakness without which the picture could never be complete. Not all children with disabilities will fit the model of the typical child, nor should they be expected to change to an unrealistic ideal. Instead, true social integration requires respect and willingness to change on the part of the typical toward their atypical peers.

The notion of the helpless person with disabilities is outdated, outmoded, and outlandish. Many individuals with disabilities want control over their lives. They want to be independent and self-sufficient. Teaching self-reliance is a natural part of the classroom climate in inclusion settings.

References

Aefsky, F. (1995). *Inclusion confusion: A guide to educating students with exceptional needs.* Thousand Oaks, CA: Corwin Press.

Borgatti, S. P., & Molina, J. L. (2003). Ethical and strategic issues in organizational network analysis. *Journal of Applied Behavioral Science, 39*(3), 337–349.

Coakley, J. & Donnelly, P. (2003). *The role of recreation in promoting social inclusion* (Monograph in the Working Paper Series on Social Inclusion). Toronto: Laidlaw Foundation.

Coleman, M. R. (2003). Four variables for success. *Gifted Child Today, 26,* 22–24.

Cohen, A. D., & Ishihara, N. (2004). *A web-based approach to strategic learning of speech acts.* Report to the Center for Advanced Research on Language Acquisition (CARLA). Available online at http://www.carla.umn.edu/speechacts/Speech_Act_Project_Rept.pdf

Doll, E., Sands, D., Wehmeyer, M. L., & Palmer, S. (1996). Promoting the development and acquisition of self-determined behavior. In D. J. Sands & M. L. Wehmeyer (Eds.), *Self-determination across the life span: Independence and choice for people with disabilities* (pp. 65–90). Baltimore: Paul H. Brookes.

Eisenberger, J., Bertrando, R., & Conti-D'Antonio, M. (2000). Block scheduling and inclusion: Meeting the challenge. *High School Magazine, 7,* 32–37.

Elksnin, L. K., & Elksnin, N. (2006). *Teaching social–emotional skills at school and home.* Denver, CO: Love.

Erwin, E. J., & Guintini, M. (2000). Inclusion and classroom membership in early childhood. *International Journal of Disability, Development, and Education, 47,* 237–257.

Field, S., Martin, J., Miller, R., Ward, M., & Wehmeyer, M. (1998). *A practical guide to teaching self-determination.* Reston, VA: Council for Exceptional Children.

Field, S., Sarver, M. D., & Shaw, S. F. (2003). Self-determination in postsecondary education for students with learning disabilities. *Remedial and Special Education, 24,* 339–349.

Fitch, E. F. (2002). Disability and inclusion: From labeling deviance to social valuing. *Education Theory, 52,* 463–377.

Gagnon G., & Collay, M. (2001). *Designing for learning: Six elements in constructivist classrooms.* Thousand Oaks, CA: Corwin Press.

Granger, R. C., & Kane, T. J. (2004). Improving the quality of after-school programs. Commentary submitted to *Education Week,* January 16, 2004. Retrieved September 14, 2004, from http://www.wtgrantfoundation.org

Heir, T. (2003). Beyond inclusion. *The School Administrator, 60,* 36–39.

Hester, P. (2002). What teachers can do to prevent behavior problems in schools. *Preventing School Failure, 47,* 33–38.

Howard, T., Nash, L., & Jagers, R. J. (2005, December). *Relationships among teacher rated social behaviors and child self-reports of social reasoning and skills.* Paper presented at American Public Health Association 133rd Annual Meeting & Exposition, Philadelphia, PA. Retrieved October 7, 2007 from http://apha.confex.com/apha/133am/techprogram/paper_112547.htm

Jones, F. H., Jones, P., & Jones, J. J. (2000). *Tools for teaching.* Santa Cruz, CA: Frederic H. Jones & Associates.

Krajewski, B., & Krajewski, L. (2000). Inclusion planning strategies: Equalizing opportunities for cognitively disabled students. *NASSO Bulletin, 84*(613), 48–53.

Kriete, R. (2003). Start the day with community. *Educational Leadership, 61,* 68–70.

Kounin, J. (1970). *Discipline and group management in classrooms.* New York: Holt, Rinehart, & Winston.

Leuchovius, D. (2003). Student directed IEPs. Adapted from *PACESETTER, 26*(1). Retrieved June 18, 2005, from http://www.pacer.org/tatra/self.htm

Lee, C. D., & Smagorinsky, P. (2000). Constructing meaning through collaborative inquiry. In C. D. Lee & P. Smagorinsky (Eds.), *Vygotskian perspectives on literacy research: Constructing meaning through collaborative inquiry* (pp 1–15). Cambridge, UK: Cambridge University Press.

Luna, C. (2003). (RE)writing the discourses of schooling and of "learning disabilities": The development of critical literacy in a students' action group. *Reading and Writing Quarterly, 19,* 254–280.

Malian, I., & Nevin, A. (2002). A review of self-determination literature: Implications for practioners. *Remedial and Special Education, 23,* 68–74.

Marzano, R. J. (2003). What works in schools: Translating research into action. *Educational Leadership, 61,* 104–105.

Marzano, R. J., & Marzano, J. S. (2003). The key to classroom management. *Educational Leadership, 61,* 6–12.

Mather, N., & Goldstein, S. (2001). *Learning disabilities and challenging behaviors.* Baltimore: Brookes.

McDonnell, J. J., Hardman, M. I., & McDonnell, A. P. (2003). *An introduction to persons with moderate and severe disabilities.* Boston: Pearson.

Mezzacappa, E., Kindlon, D., Saul, J. P., & Earls, F. (1998). Executive and motivational control of performance task behavior, and autonomic heart-rate regulation in children: physiologic validation of two-factor solution inhibitory control. *The Journal of Child Psychology and Psychiatry and Allied Disciplines, 39,* 525–531.

Moll, L. C. (2004). Through the mediation of others: Vygotskian research on teaching. In V. Richardson (Ed.), *Handbook on teaching* (4th ed., pp. 111–132). Washington, DC: AERA.

Morris, C. (1998). Lev Semyonovich Vygotsky's zone of proximal development. University of Ottawa Chapter 0195, *Phi Delta Kappa News Newsletter.*

National Dissemination Center for Children with Disabilities. (2002). Helping students develop their IEPs. In L. Kupper (Ed.), *Technical assistance guide 2 (TA2B)* (2nd ed.). Washington, DC: NICHCY. Retrieved September 14, 2004 from http://edres.org/eric/ED477659.htm

National Association of School Psychologists. (2002). *Position statement on inclusive programs for students with disabilities.* Retrieved September 14, 2004, from http://www.naspon line.org/ information/pospaper_ipsd.html

Newcomb, A. F., Bukowski, W. M., & Pattee, L. (1993). Children's peer relations: A meta-analytic review of popular, rejected, neglected, controversial, and average sociometric status. *Psychological Bulletin, 113,* 99–128.

Oremland, J., Flynn, L., & Kieff, J. E. (2002). Merry-go-round: Using interpersonal influence to keep inclusion spinning smoothly. *Childhood Education, 78,* 153–159.

Pariser, E. (2002). *A steadiness from within: Building a sense of community at the community school.* Retrieved September 14, 2004, from http://www.thecommunityschool.org/steadi ness.php3

Pavri, S., & Luftig, R. (2000). The social face of inclusive education: Are students with learning disabilities really included in the classroom? [electronic version]. *Preventing School Failure.*

Perkins-Gough, D. (2003). Special report: Do after-school programs help students succeed? [electronic version] *Educational Leadership, 61.* Retrieved September 14, 2004, from http://www.ascd.org/publicatons/ed_lead/2003-9/perkinsgough.html

Piper, T. (2003). *Language and learning: The home and school years* (3rd ed.). Upper Saddle River, NJ: Merrill/Prentice Hall.

Sabornie, E. J., & deBettencourt, L. U. (2004). *Teaching students with mild and high-incidence disabilities at the secondary level* (2nd ed.). Upper Saddle River, NJ: Pearson.

Sapon-Shevin, M. (2003). Inclusion: A matter of social justice. *Educational Leadership, 61,* 25–28.

Slater, L. (2004). Relationship-driven teaching cultivates collaboration and inclusion. *Kappa Delta Pi Record, 40,* 58–59.

Stevenson, J., Linfoot, K., & Martin, A. (2000). Behaviors of concern to teachers in the early years of school. *International Journal of Disability, Development, and Education, 47,* 225–235.

Traynor, P. L. (2002). A scientific evaluation of five different strategies teachers use to maintain order. *Education, 122,* 493–510.

Twachtman-Cullen, D. (2000). There's a lot more to communication than talking! In A. M. Wetherby & B. M. Prizant. *Autism spectrum disorders: A transactional developmental perspective* (p. 240). Baltimore: Brookes Publishing. (Original work published Summer 1996)

Vella, R. A., & Thousand, J. S. (2003). Making inclusive education work. *Educational Leadership, 61,* 19–24.

Vygotsky, L. S. (1978). *Mind in society.* Cambridge, MA: Harvard University Press.

Ward, M. J. (1996). Coming of age in the age of self-determination: A historical and personal perspective. In D. J. Sands & M. L. Wehmeyer (Eds.), *Self-determination across the life span: Independence and choice for people with disabilities* (pp. 1–16). Baltimore: Paul H. Brookes.

Wehmeyer, M. L., Agran, M., & Hughes, C. (1998). *Teaching self-determination to students with disabilities: Basic skills for successful transition.* Baltimore: Paul H. Brookes.

APPENDIX

General Characteristics

Normative tests are used to compare a student's score to the distribution of scores earned by a child in a norm group. The norm group is supposed to represent all children of a given age and background. Hence the term *norm* or *normal.* For all norm-referenced tests the distribution of scores obtained by the norm group is assumed to be a bell-shaped *normal curve,* as shown in Figure A.1. This curve represents the frequency with which each possible score was earned by the children in the norm group. In constructing a norm-referenced test, test questions are given to a sample of children representing the norm group. Based on scores of children in the sample, test items are manipulated to create a test such that the frequency of scores obtained matches the normal distribution—so that a certain percentage of children score within prescribed intervals.

Means and Standard Deviations

A basic understanding of means and standard deviations is necessary to understand the meaning of norm-referenced test scores. In Figure A.1 the mean and standard deviation of the normal curve are labeled. The 0 represents the *mean*

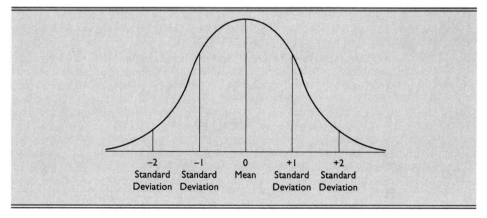

Figure A.1   Normal Curve

score, the arithmetic average of all the scores. The mean is obtained by adding all the scores obtained by people in the norm group and then dividing this sum by the number of people in the norm group. A score other than the mean score represents variability. Some people in the norm group earn scores that are higher than the mean, and other people earn scores that are lower than the mean. The difference between individual scores and the mean is calculated and is called the *standard deviation*. Thus, the standard deviation is a measure of the variability of scores.

If a score does not differ from the mean, the score is 0 distance from the mean. Thus, if the score for Carlos is 50 and 50 is the mean score for the norm group, his score is 0 distance from the mean. Usually, when the mean and standard deviation for a test have been calculated, three reference points are considered on each side of the mean. Reference points occur at +1 and –1 standard deviations, at +2 and –2 standard deviations, and at +3 and –3 standard deviations. Because the zero or mean score is at the middle of the normal curve and the curve is symmetrical, the distance (or number of points, if you are looking at a test) between 0 and +1 standard deviation is the same as the difference between 0 and –1 standard deviation. The score earned is different, though.

Recall that Carlos received a score of 50, which is 0 distance from the mean. If the value of the standard deviation is 15 points and his friend Tim obtained a score that was one standard deviation above the mean, Tim would have a score of the mean (50) plus one standard deviation (15). As shown in Figure A.2, Tim's score would be 65. Mary Lou, whose score was one standard deviation below the mean, would have a score of 50 minus 15, which is 35.

In constructing a norm-referenced test so the distribution of scores can be represented by a normal curve, a test constructor manipulates items to create a test on which approximately 68% of the normative group earn scores in the inter-

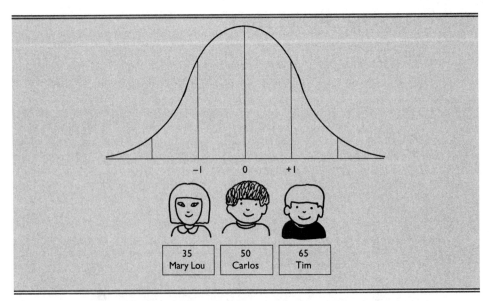

Figure A.2   Scores of Children Representing –1 Standard Deviation, the Mean, and +1 Standard Deviation on a Normal Distribution Curve

val between +1 and –1 standard deviations from the mean. That is, about 34% of the normative group earn scores between 0 and +1. Thus, the majority (68%) of the scores of the normative group are between –1 and +1 standard deviation. Moving away from the mean, about 14% of the scores earned by the normative group must fall between –2 and –1 standard deviations. Finally, only about 2% of the people in the normative group score between –3 and –2 standard deviations, and about 2% score between +2 and +3 standard deviations. The relationship of percentages and standard deviations is shown in Figure A.3.

Test Error

Besides determining where a student's test score falls under the normal curve, test error must be considered. Tests and their respective scores always have some margin of error. This margin of error is called *test error,* standard error, or error of measurement. The standard error for a test can be computed using a statistical formula. For most published tests, however, the standard error of measurement has been calculated by the test constructor and is reported in the test manual.

Basically, the standard error of measurement accounts for chance variations in a student's earned score. Sometimes conditions such as fatigue, improper lighting, or classroom distractions contribute to the variability of a test score. Thus, a student may receive a score slightly higher or slightly lower than the "true" score because of circumstances unrelated to the test. Although no one can know precisely what the student's true score would be if chance variations were eliminated, a test constructor can use statistical analysis to calculate an interval within which the true score is likely to fall.

For example, if the standard error of measurement for a given test has been calculated to be 6 and a student earns a score of 85, the true score (if chance variation did not exist) is likely to fall in the interval between 79 and 91. This range was determined by subtracting 6 from 85 (85 – 6 = 79) and adding 6 to 85 (85 +

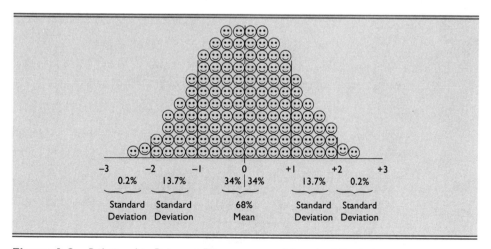

Figure A.3   Relationship Between Percentages and Standard Deviations as Seen in a Normal Distribution

6 = 91). The educator can be more confident in predicting that the student's true score falls within this interval than in predicting that the true score is exactly 85.

Every normative test has a calculated standard error of measurement. The error of measurement is different for each test. For some tests the error may be as small as ±10; for other tests the error may be as great as ±30. In general, the smaller the error, the more confidence can be placed in the test score.

Comparison Between Percentile Equivalents and Normal Curve

As can be seen in Figure A.4, a percentile equivalent anywhere between 15 and 85 is within the range of scores that fall between one standard deviation below the mean and one standard deviation above the mean. That is, percentile equivalents of 16 to 84 represent a range including scores of approximately 68% of a given standardization or norm group. Anyone whose percentile rank is 15 or lower or 85 or higher is not as typical. These atypical students must be watched carefully for the possibility of program modification.

Although the distribution of scores must follow a normal curve for all normative tests, the scale used to represent scores is arbitrary. For example, not all normative tests are based on a scale of 0 to 100 like the percentile equivalents. Some scores, such as the College Entrance Examination Board scores, are based on a scale of 200 to 800. Others, such as *stanines,* are scaled from 1 to 9. Still others, such as the WISC-III (an intelligence test; Wechsler, 1991), are scaled from 40 to 160. A test constructor may use any scale as long as the conventions prescribed by a normal distribution are followed.

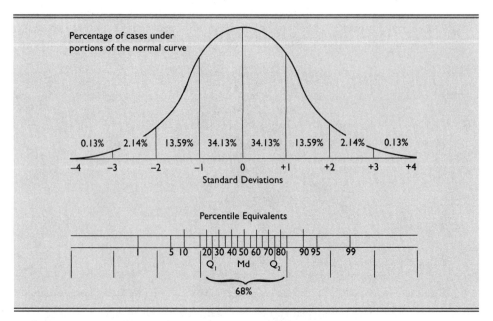

Figure A.4   Comparison Between Percentile Equivalents and the Normal Curve

NAME INDEX

A

Abrami, P. C., 268
Adams, M. J., 280, 281
Adams, T. L., 507
Adelman, H. S., 25
Aefsky, F., 553
Agran, M., 91, 92 , 93, 551
Alao, S., 328
Alber, S. R., 391, 404, 410
Alberto, P. A., 77
Albrecht, S. F., 166, 167
Alexander, A., 332
Alexander, P. A., 71
Alfassi, M., 54
Algozzine, B., 14
Allen, J., 356, 370
Allen, N. L., 326
Allen, T. E., 124
Allington, R., 338, 350
Allsop, J., 106
Alper, S., 91, 92
Alty, J. L., 346
Alwell, M., 93
Anastasiow, N. J., 359
Anders, B. A., 346
Anderson, H., 397
Anderson, L. M., 404, 405
Anderson, R. M., 106
Anzalone, M., 122
Archer, A. L., 326, 357
Arends, R. I., 201
Arman, J. F., 42
Armbruster, B. B., 292
Armstrong, D. L., 342
Arnold, M., 255
Arora, T., 15
Asakawa, C., 346
Ashcroft, S. C., 114
Asmus, J. M., 165
Astleitner, H., 243
Atkinson, L., 56
Au, K. H., 281
Auerbach, S., 92
Axelrod, M. I., 8

B

Baek, J. M., 445
Baggett, W. B., 255
Bagnato, S., 212
Bailey, E. J., 410
Baird, S. M., 118
Baker, J. M., 90
Baker, P., 118
Ball, E. W., 297
Balthazar, E. E., 37
Bank-Mikkelsen, N. E., 12
Barber, B., 152
Barnes-Holmes, D., 56
Barnes-Holmes, Y., 56
Baron, J., 447, 449

Barrie, W., 186
Barron, B., 277
Bartley, N., 413
Bashinski, S., 93
Baxter, J., 469
Beers, K., 43
Berk, L. E., 10, 68
Berliner, D., 252
Berman, B. T., 434, 436, 437
Berninger, V., 387, 413, 419, 424
Berry, P., 392
Berry, R. A., 365
Bertrando, R., 548
Bess, F., 137
Bess, F. H., 123
Best, S. J., 111
Betts, E. A., 297, 342
Bhat, P., 359
Bigby, L., 178
Bigge, J. L., 111, 311
Billingsley, F., 91
Billington, E., 67
Blachman, B. A., 297
Blackhurst, A. E., 176
Blaiklock, K. E., 331
Blair, M., 86
Bloome, D., 371
Boardman, A. G., 15
Boekaerts, M., 66
Bol, L., 152
Bolduc, E. J., Jr., 482
Bollard, P., 138
Boone, R., 344, 352
Borgatti, S. P., 530
Borgioli, J. A., 111
Borrero, J. C., 165
Bos, C. S., 359
Bosman, A.M.T., 116
Boulineau, T., 359
Bowers, B. C., 282
Box, J. A., 251, 252
Boyer-Schick, K., 397
Boyle, E., 343, 344
Bradely, D. F., 4–5
Bradley, R., 334
Bradley-Johnson, S., 118
Brandon, D. P., 252
Brantingham, K., 364
Branwell, G., 252
Brazelton, T. B., 215
Breyfogle, M. L., 446
Brigance, 295, 296
Brigance, A. H., 452
Brigham, F. J., 8
Broer, S. M., 91
Brothen, T., 62
Browder, D. M., 89
Brown, A. L., 366
Brown, K., 350, 351
Brown, L., 86

Brownell, K., 8
Browning, C., 44
Bryan, L., 325, 338, 358
Bryant, B., 110
Bryant, B. R., 446
Bryant, D., 110, 493
Bryant, D. P. 358
Bryant, D. P., 357
Buchele-Ash, A., 4
Buckley, S. J., 324
Buhrow, M. M., 118
Bukowski, W. M., 530
Bulgren, J. A., 14
Burden, P. R., 255
Burgess, S. R., 331
Burke, C. L., 280
Burke, M. D., 359
Burns, M. K., 341, 342
Burns, M. S., 323
Burris, C., 470
Bursuck, W. D., 11, 17
Butler, D. L., 356, 360, 405
Butler, R., 12
Byrd, D. M., 255

C

Calkins, L. M., 374
Cambra, C., 135
Cameron, J., 54
Campbell, J. R., 326
Campbell, P., 473
Carless, S., 332
Carroll, W. M., 445, 447, 449, 475, 476, 478, 479, 495, 503
Carta, J. J., 14, 421
Casanova, U., 252
Cashwell, C. S., 61
Castagnera, E., 93
Caudle, A., 57
Caughey, E., 13
Cavanagh, S., 474
Cazden, C. B., 390
Cendron, M., 442
Chambers, J. G., 16
Chappel, M. F., 444
Chard, D., 475
Chen, D., 113
Chi, M.T.H., 254
Chien, D. H., 43
Chiu, S., 434
Choate, J. S., 67
Chomsky, C., 401
Chomsky, N., 71
Christenson, S. L., 411
Christian, B., 371
Christine, R. O., 421
Chung, S., 9
Chute, P. M., 138
Clark, K., 297

Clark, S., 148
Clark-Chiarelli, N., 365
Clay, M. M., 280, 301
Cleary, M., 139
Cloninger, C. J., 97
Coakley, J., 548
Cobb, C., 365
Cobb, S. E., 57
Cohen, A. D., 521
Cohen, P., 15
Cohen, R., 44
Coie, J. D., 97
Coleman, M., 359
Coleman, M. R., 359, 532
Collay, M., 514
Collins, A., 281
Compton, D. L., 334
Conner, J. M., 369
Conroy, M. A., 165
Conti-D'Antonio, M., 548
Cook, B. G., 9
Cook, L., 8, 9
Cooper, C. R., 397
Cooper-Duffy, K., 89
Copeland, S. R., 93
Corden, R., 391, 413
Coughlan, J., 469, 475
Coutinho, M., 422
Cox, P. R., 97, 113
Craig, K. E., 57
Crandell, C. C., 138, 139
Craven, R., 12
Crowe, L. K., 364
CTB-McGraw Hill, 449
Culatta, R., 181
Cushing, S., 14, 15

D

Dalla, L., 434, 435, 470
Daniels, H., 441, 472
Danielson, L., 334
d'Apollonia, S., 268
Das Gupta, P., 66
Daugherty, D., 27
Davenport, S. V., 255
Davies, D. K., 345
Davis, J. C., 15
Davis, R. B., 449
Day, J. N., 175, 176
deBettencourt, L. U., 10, 11, 153, 367 , 524, 531
Debus, R., 12
Deci, E. L., 54
De Corte, E., 488, 495
De La Paz, S., 422
de la Ronde, M., 14
Delquadri, J., 421
Dembo, M., 55, 62
Demchak, M. A., 122
D'Emidio-Caston, M., 436
Deno, S., 397

SUBJECT INDEX